# TEACHERS AND THE LEARNING PROCESS

**ROBERT D. STROM**

*Professor of Education*
*Arizona State University*

PRENTICE-HALL, INC., Englewood Cliffs, New Jersey

*Also by Robert D. Strom*
PSYCHOLOGY FOR THE CLASSROOM
EXPERIENCES IN EDUCATIONAL PSYCHOLOGY
THE INNER-CITY CLASSROOM: TEACHER BEHAVIORS
MENTAL HEALTH AND ACHIEVEMENT
*(with E. Paul Torrance)*
TEACHING IN THE SLUM SCHOOL
THE TRAGIC MIGRATION
DROPOUT STUDIES: DESIGN AND CONDUCT
*(with D. Schreiber and B. Kaplan)*

370
S+R

P: 13–891002–2
C: 13–891010–3

Library of Congress Catalog Card No. 70–126830

Printed in the United States of America

Current printing (last digit)

10   9   8   7   6   5   4   3   2   1

PRENTICE-HALL INTERNATIONAL, INC., *London*
PRENTICE-HALL OF AUSTRALIA, PTY. LTD., *Sydney*
PRENTICE-HALL OF CANADA, LTD., *Toronto*
PRENTICE-HALL OF INDIA PRIVATE LIMITED, *New Delhi*
PRENTICE-HALL OF JAPAN, INC., *Tokyo*

12/73

# CONTENTS

Chapter 3

## RELATING AS A PROFESSIONAL

Chapter 4

## LEARNING THEORY, A RESOURCE FOR METHOD

Chapter 5

## EDUCATING FOR CREATIVE BEHAVIOR

Chapter 6

## EVALUATION IN THE CLASSROOM

**Chapter 7**

## MENTAL HEALTH AND PERSONALITY DEVELOPMENT

# PREFACE

We are witness to the passing of a time when students are referred to as the learners and teachers as the learned. This is not to suggest today's educators know less than scholars before them or that they are undeserving of respect. On the contrary, their level of leadership is without parallel in its beneficial effect. Basing the new leadership is an awareness that, given the increase in potential sources of knowledge, more persons than school faculty ought be perceived as teachers. Accordingly, rather than continue to persuade parents they can best help the school by encouraging children, it seems appropriate to invite their instructional talent as an adjunct influence. With the advent of large numbers of parents as aides, we may be seeing the days of one-teacher classrooms drawing to a close.

Similarly, there is occurring a revision in the way educators perceive students. Unlike the past when they were seen only as an audience, the young now are also being viewed as sources of knowledge with whom interaction can enable mutual learning. This willingness to abandon presumption in favor of respect makes it possible to understand *Teachers and the Learning Process.*

While *Teachers and the Learning Process* was planned as a companion to *Psychology for the Classroom,* it would have equal utility with any educational psychology text. In order to enlarge the perspective offered in that basic text, I have assembled here forty-nine articles divided equally into seven major chapters, each of which parallel in title and content issue the chapters of *Psychology for the Classroom.* Along with relevance, readability also served as a criterion for article selection. In my judgment, the papers presented are more readable for the undergraduate than is usually the case among books of readings in educational psychology and human development. Together the volumes are expected to achieve the following purposes: (1) to present ways by which teachers can maintain pupil respect without recourse to coercion and punitive techniques; (2) to enable a better understanding of the student view regarding school life, its problems and their resolution; (3) to define the ethic and its proper teacher response in relating to pupils, parents, and colleagues; (4) to describe certain prominent theories of learning as well as the consequent methods of teaching; (5) to urge the recognition, acceptance, and encouragement of creative behavior in the classroom; (6) to indicate the importance and process of evaluation as a part of teaching; and (7) to suggest an orientation for ensuring student mental health and personality development.

Friends always enter a constructive influence upon my work. For their suggestions and encouragement, I wish to thank Dr. E. Paul Torrance, Chairman and Professor of Educational Psychology, University of Georgia; Dr. Sidney L. Pressey, Emeritus Professor of Psychology, The Ohio State University; and Dr. Don E. Hamachek, Professor of Educational Psychology, Michigan State University. I am also grateful to Shirley, my wife and valued partner in this and every other important endeavor.

ROBERT D. STROM

# CONTRIBUTORS

Gordon W. Allport, Late Professor of Psychology, Department of Social Relations, Harvard University

Louise Bates Ames, Director and Professor of Research, Gesell Institute of Child Development, Yale University

Bernard Asbell, Free Lance Writer, New York City

Orville G. Brim, Jr., President, Russell Sage Foundation, New York City

Jerome S. Bruner, Professor of Psychology, Harvard University

Robert Bush, Professor of Education and Co-Director, Center for Research and Development in Teaching, Stanford University

Bettye M. Caldwell, Director, Children's Center, Department of Pediatrics, Upstate Medical Center, University of New York, Syracuse, and Professor of Child Development and Education, Syracuse University

Dorwin Cartwright, Professor of Psychology and Coordinator of the Research Center for Group Dynamics, University of Michigan

Arthur W. Combs, Professor of Education, University of Florida

Donald R. Cruickshank, Chairman and Professor, Faculty of Early and Middle Childhood, College of Education, The Ohio State University

Robert L. Ebel, Professor of Education and Psychology, Michigan State University

Elliot W. Eisner, Professor of Education, University of Chicago

Richard E. Farson, Director, Western Behavioral Services Institute, LaJolla, California

John C. Flanagan, Board Chairman, American Institute for Research, Palo Alto, California

Ned A. Flanders, Professor of Education, University of Michigan

Thomas J. Fleming, Free Lance Writer, New York City

Jack R. Frymier, Chairman and Professor, Curriculum Faculty, College of Education, The Ohio State University

N. L. Gage, Professor of Education and Psychology, Stanford University

Charles Galloway, Associate Professor, Curriculum Faculty, College of Education, The Ohio State University

Ira J. Gordon, Professor of Education, University of Florida

J. P. Guilford, Emeritus Professor of Psychology and Director of the Aptitudes Research Project, University of Southern California

Seymour L. Halleck, Professor of Psychiatry, University of Wisconsin

Don E. Hamachek, Associate Professor of Educational Psychology, Michigan State University

HELEN HEFFERNAN, Former Chief, Bureau of Elementary Education, California State Department of Education

ERNEST R. HILGARD, Professor of Psychology, Stanford University

FRANCES L. ILG, Director and Professor, Gesell Institute of Child Development, Yale University

PHILIP W. JACKSON, Professor of Education and Human Development, University of Chicago

R. D. KITCHEN, Professor of External Studies, University of Queensland, Australia

NATHAN KOGAN, Chairman, Personality Research Group, Center for Psychological Studies of the Educational Testing Service, Princeton, New Jersey

WILLIAM C. KVARACEUS, Professor of Education and Youth Studies, Lincoln Filene Center for Citizenship and Public Affairs, Tufts University

JOHN KORD LAGEMANN, Free Lance Writer, New York City

MARGARET MEAD, Adjunct Professor of Anthropology, Columbia University

RAPHAEL O. NYSTRAND, Associate Professor, Faculty of Educational Administration, College of Education, The Ohio State University

A. HARRY PASSOW, Professor of Education, Teachers College, Columbia University

SIDNEY L. PRESSEY, Emeritus Professor of Psychology, The Ohio State University

JAMES H. RICKS, Associate Director of the Test Division, The Psychological Corporation, New York City

CARL R. ROGERS, Resident Fellow, Western Behavioral Science Institute, LaJolla, California

ROBERT ROSENTHAL, Professor of Social Psychology, Department of Social Relations, Harvard University

JOHN L. SCHIMEL, Psychiatrist, New York City

JOAN E. SIEBER, Professor of Education, Stanford University

JEROME L. SINGER, Professor of Psychology, Columbia University

B. F. SKINNER, Edgar Pierce Professor of Psychology, Harvard University

FRED L. STRODTBECK, Associate Professor of Psychology and Director of the Social Psychology Laboratory, University of Chicago

ROBERT L. THORNDIKE, Chairman and Professor, Department of Psychological Foundations and Services, Teachers College, Columbia University

E. PAUL TORRANCE, Chairman and Professor, Department of Educational Psychology, University of Georgia

MICHAEL A. WALLACH, Professor of Psychology, Duke University

KAORU YAMAMOTO, Professor, Department of Educational Services, College of Education, The Pennsylvania State University

# CHAPTER 1

# RESPECTING

# DIFFERENCES

# AMONG PUPILS

SEYMOUR L. HALLECK

# 1. WHY THEY'D RATHER DO THEIR OWN THING

On either side of today's generation gap, the young and the old often see each other as guided by opposite values. Each group insists that his own value system is the right one. Students insist that their parents' values are misguided and out of date. Their parents fear that youth either lack values or are adopting new ones that are unwholesome.

How much do student values differ from their parents'?

The most striking change in student value systems is in the direction of values which lead to immediate gratification. Students today have little reverence for the past and little hope for the future. They are trying to live in the present.

The most important reason for this is the ever-increasing rate of change which characterizes our society. When no one can predict what the world will be like in 20, 10 or even 5 years, man must alter his psychological perspectives. The lessons of the past become less relevant; planning for the future appears futile. One is driven to gear his value systems toward enjoyment of the present.

Financial success and competitive striving for success have a revered place in the American values system—the person who devotes himself to the long-term struggle for acquisition of status and goods will be rewarded in the future. Where the future is unpredictable, however, such values lose meaning. Youth who are in process of preparing themselves for adult roles are more likely to appreciate the uncertainty of the future than their parents. Consider, for example, the different perspectives of a mother and son in discussing the boy's prospects as a physician. The mother sees a doctor as a scientist and helper, one who does good works within the community and is rewarded with prestige and money. The son, however, is aware that by the time he spends 12 years training to become a medical specialist the nature of medical practice will hardly resemble what it is today. If he has hopes of

---

Reprinted by permission from THINK Magazine (September-October, 1968), pp. 3-7, published by IBM, copyright 1968 by International Business Machines Corporation.

using medicine as a vehicle for satisfying his needs for personal interaction with people, he may become uncomfortable at the thought that medicine of the future may be highly scientific and impersonal. Medicine may not, of course, go in such directions, but no one can really tell him in which direction it will go. One can consider almost any profession in a similar manner.

## "YOU GOT ME, DAD"

The differences in perspectives of the generations is beautifully illustrated in *The Graduate*, a film in which the main character is "a little worried about his future." When he is angrily asked by his father, "What did I send you to college for?" the graduate replies, "You got me, Dad." I am told when this scene is viewed by student audiences they break out into wild cheers. When I saw the movie with a much older audience, the reaction was one of dismay. The graduate's remarks poignantly reflect the differing perspectives of the generations. Youth are no lazier, no more hedonistic or passive than their parents. Rather, conditions do not favor future-oriented values, and youth are being forced into the role of the "now" generation.

This, perhaps, is one reason why college students tend to downgrade the acquisition of property, why they are unimpressed and sometimes even contemptuous of it. Recruiters for industrial firms on our campuses are learning that some of the best students are not interested in business careers. Few young people can view a life that is dedicated to trade and the acquisition of wealth as meaningful. Some conservative adults fear that this new devaluation of capitalistic enterprise represents a shift to communistic or socialistic philosophies. This fear seems exaggerated. Acquisition of capital is a rational enterprise only when there is some reason to believe that it will have the same usefulness in the future as it does in the present. When this is not true the amount of self-expenditure involved in obtaining capital seems wasted.

The rejection of material values may account for certain kinds of selective stealing on the part of college students. It is probably true that more students than ever engage in shoplifting. This behavior is usually rationalized by the argument that big companies are too impersonal to be affected by minor pilfering and that since property is not very important anyway, there is no harm done in taking some of it away from those who have too much. Surprisingly, no large organization, even those created by students themselves, is immune: at the University of Wisconsin a new student cooperative is in danger of going out of business because of shoplifting.

As reverence for property has diminished, youth have come to value the intrinsic worth of human relationships. There is an emphasis on being rather than doing. Youth are preoccupied with the need for being good people who can form good relationships. Whether they are more capable than their parents of finding such relationships is debatable, but their commitment to the search for intimacy is indisputable. A "beautiful" person, in the vernacular of today's youth, is not one who is physically attractive or one who has the personal qualities that guarantee success. He is an individual who has the capacity to relate openly and warmly with others.

In focusing upon one another's personal worth, youth have emphasized the development of their innate potentialities. Unwilling to evaluate themselves by the measure of what they can produce or sustain, they focus on the process of creativity and its appreciation. The attractiveness of psychedelic drugs may be related to this new emphasis. By altering the state of their own consciousness many students hope to find new truth and power—creativity—by looking inward. But in using such drugs they also demonstrate their lack of conviction that they can shape the world and are searching for a strength and constancy within an unreal inner world.

### INCREASING SKEPTICISM

Not only creative activities but also intellectual pursuits are increasingly valued as ends rather than means. This change has important ramifications for our educational system. Adults are accustomed to thinking of education as a means to success and progress. Since these values do not have the same meaning to youth, they are skeptical of the practical benefits of learning. They tend to see education as an end in itself, something to be enjoyed, even worshiped as a noble activity of man. There is much emphasis on doing away with the competitive aspects of education, with the regimentation and emphasis on grading that has served to produce citizens who would easily fit into an industrial society. Nothing enrages students more than the feeling that they are being processed to take their place in a competitive society rather than being educated to become better people.

It can be argued that youth's rejection of some of the values of the Protestant ethic or of capitalism is a result of newfound affluence and leisure. It is probably true that those who have been raised in an affluent world do not find it easy to appreciate the value of sacrifice and hard work. Yet, while affluence seems to play some role in reinforcing an emphasis on "nowness" it is also true that all classes of youth, even those who have been raised in poverty, show similar characteristics. Poor and oppressed youth may still be committed to finding a place in this capitalistic system, but even among them the rumblings of discontent with our society seem to be related to more than their inability to share in our affluence. They, too, seem to be showing an increasing skepticism toward hope and planning.

The rate of change in our society also seems to make youth more aware of the problems of commitment and fidelity. Earlier generations resolved this ambivalence by institutionalizing their commitments. Only 20 years ago the young college man's obligations to his family, his career and his community were clearly defined. Today, young people talk about the need for fidelity and at the same time emphasize the philosophy of "doing your own thing and being responsible to no one but oneself." The problem here is that while an orientation toward life in the present is more likely to increase concern with human values, it also puts a premium on flexibility. It is not easy to be flexible and committed at the same time. When the future is uncertain, one must travel lightly, must be wary of how he invests his emotional energy and must be ready to move on when there is change. Where "coolness" and intimacy are valued concurrently there exists a situation of conflict which produces a variety of unpleasant emotional reactions.

Social change influences other values, including society's attitude toward change itself. Throughout history youth have always been more open to change than their elders. There are natural reasons for this. As one grows older, his commitments to others encourage him to hold onto his position in life by supporting the status quo.

Youth today, as in the past, seem to revere change but they are also peculiarly wary of it. They are highly indignant of injustices perpetrated by the status quo. Nevertheless, in their uncertainties as to the future they have difficulty in coming up with the long-term plans for change. The New Left can propose few alternatives to our present society and can only speak of tearing it down.

A second major shift in the value systems of today's youth is also related to changes in society, particularly to the impact of new communications media. The rearing of children requires a certain degree of protectiveness and even deception; if children were prematurely exposed to information about the harsh realities of life they simply could not tolerate it. But the new media deluge today's youth with information. Children learn the cynical truths of life at a very young age. They can sense when parents and other authority figures are mildly deceptive and know when those in authority are outright deceitful or hypocritical. No institution—family, church, the university or even the law—can any longer hide behind dogma or tradition.

One of the things that is happening in every society exposed to new technology and new media, is that young people are vigorously questioning whatever arbitrary structure is imposed upon them. When students begin to perceive what is so often a weak intellectual base for behavioral demands made upon them, they become angry and rebellious. Simple answers such as, "We should do it this way because it is right," or "because we have always done it this way," will no longer satisfy them. It is futile to demand that young people bring more order into their lives unless the merits of such order can be persuasively described.

## EXCESSIVE FREEDOM, EMOTIONAL CHAOS

At the moment, youth's capacity to decipher the inconsistencies and hypocrisies of the older generation has led them to adopt some rather extreme value positions with regard to the issue of freedom. Young people place increasing emphasis on the virtues of a structureless world and many seem convinced that total freedom from the dictates of authority would be an ideal existence.

This new emphasis on freedom is not without emotional consequences. Even the most rebellious student is still dominated by certain dependency needs which create an almost automatic drive toward obedience. Furthermore, as I shall attempt to elaborate later, structure and the need to rely on the wisdom or strength of others seems to be an innate human need. There comes a point when too much freedom, particularly freedom to choose from an almost unlimited set of alternatives, becomes incapacitating and paralyzing. In the struggle for autonomy some youths seem to achieve a premature or pseudomature autonomy which does not satisfy their needs, and tends to breed emotional chaos.

Another aspect of value change related to the impact of media has to do with the issue of self-revelation. In a world where deception can be easily exposed and where youth have seen so many of their faithful beliefs ruthlessly destroyed, there is a tendency to value openness in interpersonal relationships. Many of today's youth are quite willing to reveal themselves. They will talk openly of things that would have shamed their elders.

## TOLERANCE AND MORALITY

A final aspect of value change related to the impact of media has to do with the issue of power. Youth are keenly aware of the capacity of the establishment to oppress others. They are also sensitive to what is often an irrational basis by which established power justifies its tenure. Students are learning they can diminish certain oppressions in their own life by attacking what often turns out to be a highly vulnerable and surprisingly defenseless authority.

Sometimes value differences between generations cannot be phrased in terms of direct conflict. Both adults and students, for example, advocate racial and ethnic tolerance. Yet, youth are probably more capable of adhering to this value than their parents. An adult would be more likely to limit his advocacy of tolerance when that value began to interfere with other values such as stability, status or wealth. In other situations, what appears to be a value conflict between generations is in reality an argument over which generation is more honest in its pursuit of values.

In emphasizing personal values and good relationships youth tend to maintain that they are more concerned with the needs of mankind and more compassionate than their parents. It is probably true that young people raised in a world which has been perceptually shrunk by the new media do have a great awareness of the plight of their oppressed fellows. Yet, it is rare to see this awareness translated into calls for action. The percentage of young people who are prepared to sacrifice comforts in order to help their fellowman is not overwhelming. I doubt that compassion either as a value or as an actuality is an exclusive possession of any generation. In this regard we must be aware of the existence of contradictory value systems among youth. While some are talking about the brotherhood of man, others are talking about the need for individual values and the importance of putting individual needs ahead of society's.

If we consider the values of adhering to principle versus willingness to compromise, we again find little change but much criticism between generations. Both parents and students at times accuse one another of being unwilling to adhere to principle. Both accuse one another of being unable to compromise. Students accuse parents of "selling out" for personal gain. Adults accuse students of being unwilling to compromise their idealism in the face of the realities of existence. Students accuse adults of blind adherence to irrational causes, an accusation particularly relevant to the war in Vietnam; most students see it as a conflict perpetuated by an adult generation unwilling to compromise ill-founded and destructive principles.

Is there a value crisis in American life today? In my opinion we are moving toward a crisis related to the manner in which values are generated and maintained in a changing world. As old values are attacked we are not creating new ones to replace them. There is a real danger that values of any kind may be losing their power, that young people in particular may find themselves existing in a valueless world. There may be an inherent rightness in doing away with traditional values that seem irrational and cannot be justified. Yet, if such values are indiscriminately destroyed before they are replaced by more rational values, our society will experience an unprecedented degree of chaos.

Those who are entrusted with the teaching of values in our society—educators, theologians, law enforcement officers and parents—seem totally unprepared to move from dogmatic to rational presentation of value systems. As their authority is threatened, some resort to preaching and exhortation rather than to reflection. Our youth respond by despair and violence.

Our society has an obvious need for a value system based on rational efforts to enhance the well-being of man. Such a system must recognize man's biological needs. It must be practical enough to provide answers as to how men can live together in peace and stability. Finally, it must recognize that certain values at times have to be institutionalized if for no other reason than to provide stability during periods of intensive change.

## SOME VALUES TO LIVE BY

It is presumptuous for anyone, including a psychiatrist, to attempt to tell other people how they should live. Yet I am convinced if one is concerned with other people's health and happiness he can find only so many guidelines by emphasizing adjustment or adaptation to what is. I do not believe that man can go on adjusting to changing conditions of our world and still be man. If there is to be a healthy society of the future we must search for positive values which transcend the nature of the immediate environment. No one can present a value system that is relevant to all men in all ages. I believe, however, that we know enough to at least try to describe certain basic guidelines.

1. There is ample scientific evidence that without some capacity to share strong feelings of affection with another person it is not possible to lead a happy or useful life. Most varieties of mental illness and many physical ailments may be traced directly to feelings that one is not receiving enough affection. This condition arises when man lacks the capacity to relate himself intimately to others. Any society then must come to value intimacy or love. Closely related to this is the value of compassion. Man is a unique animal insofar as he is able to identify with the feelings of others. He needs to feel a sense of community, to identify himself as a member of a society in which he is not a bystander.

2. A second value is openness to experience. I use this expression in a broad sense to include the ability to seek and evaluate without prejudice the wide variety of experience possible within the limits of one's commitment to others. Openness to experience means openness to change and personal growth. This includes the capacity to be aware of oneself. A person cannot be fully aware of the world unless he has some capacity to understand the manner in which he perceives that world. Self-understanding also implies being at ease with one's past. The healthy man cannot live wholly in the present nor can be base his existence on future rewards.

3. A third value is the ability to find an optimum amount of freedom. Although man needs to love others and rely on others if he is to survive, he must also be able to experience his distinctiveness. When man sacrifices autonomy or freedom he finds a certain amount of comfort, but this is always at the expense of adopting the role of the lesser being, someone not quite as good as others.

4. Because man is the only animal who is physically and psychologically helpless for a large part of his young life, he learns to rely on structure and authority as a prerequisite to comfort. Whatever tendency he might have to outgrow this need is thwarted by his appreciation of the imminence of his own death. Man is the only animal who comprehends his own mortality and he cannot live with this knowledge without belief in some power that transcends his own. For some individuals belief in a supreme being suffices. Others sustain themselves through belief in the perfectibility of man. In either case, man must have an ideology that he can value.

5. Man also has an innate need to interact with his environment and alter it in a manner which provides him with a sense of mastery. It is not crucial how he gains mastery. He may find it in daily work, in organized play or in efforts to create new art, music or literature. What is important is that

man must to some extent be active and must experience his activity as either having an impact on other people or as having the capacity to alter his physical surroundings.

6. On a pragmatic basis it would seem obvious that we must come to value order. Man can tolerate only so much change without experiencing his existence as chaotic. I am not speaking of change which relieves oppression and injustice. Such change is obviously useful. Changes brought about by scientific and technological progress, however, need to be rigorously scrutinized and controlled. A reverence for progress (except for that progress which directly contributes toward making man a better human being as opposed to making him a more comfortable human being) must be replaced by a valuation of stability.

7. Another value which is probably more correctly based on pragmatism than biology is the capacity to assume responsibility for one's own behavior. Adherence to this value provides dignity for the individual and stability for the group. It is the belief in this capacity to lead a responsible life which allows a man to experience himself as a unique animal who has some choice in his own destiny. He who denies responsibility for his actions or thoughts cannot be free since he must live as though he were governed by uncontrollable forces.

8. Another pragmatic value is honesty, the willingness to avoid deceiving oneself or others and the willingness to search for truth. Men could lead dishonest lives and survive with comfort. Yet almost any philosophy concerned with the betterment of man advocates the honest life. While there is much disagreement as to the content of the truth, few individuals—young or old—would argue with the contention that he who deceives himself or others is leading an inadequate life.

9. The events of the past months have convincingly demonstrated our society's urgent need to find a way of inculcating the value of nonviolence in our people. Because man is an aggressive animal it will no doubt be necessary to resort to institutionalized, even programmed methods of forcing real acceptance of this value. It seems to me we have no other choice.

10. Finally, every society must find the means of revering their elderly members. When aging means being less respected, less powerful and less relevant to this society, there can never be any joyous anticipation of the future. The question of how we can find some means of evaluating older members of our community may ultimately be the most illuminating issue in our quest to understand student values in a changing world.

### THE PRICE OF WISDOM

The calamity of modern existence is that the world changes so fast that there is little likelihood that the old will continue to remain very much wiser than the young. In this regard it is distressing to note how few young Americans can identify one older American whom they deeply admire.

As the old become relatively less wise, their influence is maintained primarily by the acquisition of political and economic power. The values which they pass onto the young are then more likely to be shaped by institution and custom than by their understanding of actual human needs. I have previously described how youth are increasingly capable of recognizing the arbitrary nature of power and values which are imposed upon them by their elders. It is likely that they will continue to use their new knowledge militantly to search for more rational values and for more pragmatic divisions of power. But even as they attack the adult world they become trapped in destroying themselves. For if they make their parents irrelevant they, will surely make themselves irrelevant.

In drifting into a youth-oriented culture we have ignored the teachings of philosophers who have since the time of Plato emphasized the need to revere maturity. We are often told that our youth are our future. Yet, unless we can create a world which offers the possibility of aging with grace, honor and meaningfulness, no one can look forward to the future.

BERNARD ASBELL

# 2.  THE CASE OF THE WANDERING IQs

Thirty years ago in an Iowa orphanage a young psychologist, Dr. Harold M. Skeels, and his assistant, Dr. Marie Skodak, tested two infants, each a little more than a year old.

"They were miserable pieces of humanity," Dr. Skodak recalls. "They were scrawny little girls. They couldn't sit up, or make a sound except to whine or cry. If you tried to play with them or talk to them, all you got was a feeble 'Waaa.' Nothing! In simple tests of responding to words, locating the direction of sounds, picking up small objects, these babies functioned at the age level of three to seven months."

The children scored as hopeless imbeciles. They had IQs of 46 and 35.

The scores were hardly surprising. Both babies had been born to mentally deficient mothers, fathers unknown. On an IQ test one mother had been found to be feebleminded; the other had been declared a "psychotic with mental retardation." It seemed to the young psychologists that these family histories clearly explained and corroborated their findings; the children were mental cripples. The psychologists did what seemed logical, necessary and routine. They recommended that the babies be committed to a home for the mentally retarded.

For thousands of babies before and since, similar decisions have marked the end of their sad stories. For these two infants, however, as well as for the two psychologists, that examination was a strange beginning.

The young professionals had no idea that they were soon to challenge two scientific beliefs which were then unquestioned. The first was that mental retardation (when not caused by brain damage or other specific conditions) is inherited. The companion belief was that a child born an imbecile is fated to live and die an imbecile.

The challenge of these beliefs by Dr. Skeels and his young assistant was at first greeted by uproarious controversy among their colleagues, a controversy followed by rejection and then, after 30 years, by a dramatic vindication. This recent vindication—and the remarkable scientific detective story that led up to it—now throws wide-open some fundamental questions of what intelligence is, how it is nurtured and how it may sometimes be destroyed.

The evidence that first fell into the hands of Dr. Skeels and Dr. Skodak three decades ago in Iowa was not the result of purposeful research. It was produced by pure accident—the fact that Iowa's institutions for retarded children were filled to overflowing when the doctors examined the two mentally deficient babies. So they were sent from the orphange to an adult institution, the Woodward State School and Hospital for the Mentally Handicapped.

As it also happened, Dr. Skeels and his assistant occasionally had to visit Woodward. On one such visit he and Dr. Skodak were making their rounds, giving tests in the women's wards, when they saw two jolly, pink-cheeked children about two years old at play. The two children looked strangely familiar, and the psychologists soon discovered that these were the two babies they had examined about eight months earlier.

"We could hardly believe it," Dr. Skodak recalls. "Here they were, bright, pretty, done up in hair ribbons, running around, playing, having a happy time with all kinds of toys. They just didn't look like the same children.

"We tested them again. A normal child of two can be expected to have a speaking vocabulary of at least a dozen words and to be beginning to put words together. He should understand simple commands like 'Bring me the shoe' and be able to draw something that can be taken for a circle. He should be able to thread large beads on a string, put a spoon in a cup and stir it—simple manual actions like that. On tests like these, the two little girls came out with IQs of seventy-seven and eighty-seven. This was about in the range of what we call 'dull normal', a remarkable leap from the imbecile level at which they had tested before."

"I was unable to account for it," Dr. Skeels says now. "The change might have indicated some accident in the earlier testing if it had happened to only one child but here were two. It was possible, of course, that the tests we'd just done were misleading; perhaps the improvement wouldn't last. We decided to leave the children just as they were and see what happened."

A year later the children were tested again—and the psychologists were astonished. The child who had first had an IQ of 35, then of 87, now showed an IQ of 88, only two points below the range of "average or normal." The other child, who had tested at 46, then 77, now scored around 100, precisely the norm for American children her age. Clearly these children no longer belonged in a home for the feeble-minded; at least one of them was decidedly eligible for adoption. The immediate impulse of the psychologists was to transfer the children to an orphanage at once. But they decided first to find out what had happened to the two babies in the year and a half since the first tests had been made.

They learned that the infants had been placed in separate wards with women ranging in age from 18 to 50 years, women whose mentalities approximated those of five-to-nine-year-olds. Each baby had been "adopted" by one of the inmates, who became a kind of mother. Others in the wards, less actively attached to the children, became adoring "aunts." Since the adults themselves had the mentality of children, each ward had a dollhouse; and as the children joined in the women's play they were spoken to a great deal: "See? This goes here. See the chair? Pretty chair."

Some of the inmates had been mothers and were quite competent in such motherly duties as bathing, feeding and diaper-changing; others enjoyed cuddling and singing to the children. The ward attendants, meanwhile, supervised the babies' diets and saw to it that they lived by a healthy routine.

Some of the inmates had spending money; they would give it to hospital employees for the purchase of small toys, pretty dresses and hair ribbons for the girls. Sometimes attendants on their days off would "borrow" the two children, give them automobile and bus rides or take them into stores to buy picture books that would then become the property of the ward. Most of the waking hours of all the people in the wards had begun to revolve around the two little girls.

"Here was a 'home' setting," points out Dr. Skeels, "abundant in affection, rich in wholesome and interesting experiences and geared to a preschool level of development."

A dilemma now confronted Dr. Skeels. Should he leave the three-year-olds among these feeble-minded women to whom they apparently owed their mental and emotional growth but where they certainly no longer belonged? Or should he transfer them to the state orphanage, which was crowded and understaffed and where they would receive only a minimum of attention? Dr. Skeels had seen many children of normal intelligence slide inexorably downhill in such institutions.

Unhappy with these alternatives, Dr. Skeels hit upon a third course, unusual but promising. He persuaded the orphanage staff to take special steps to find adoptive parents for the two little girls, even though most adoptions take place when babies are only a few weeks old.

"When adoptive parents were found," says Dr. Skeels, "I had a nice little explanation all prepared for them. I said, 'This is a fine youngster, but don't push her too far.' I still wasn't too confident of just what the potentials of these kids were. In case things didn't work out well, I had another lecture ready: 'Look, we made a ghastly mistake. This child wasn't supposed to be adopted. She's feeble-minded. Please let us take her from you and place her in an institution. We'll give you another fine, healthy child so you can start all over.' I'm happy to say, we never had to use the second explanation."

Dr. Skeels soon made an appointment with the chairman of the Iowa State Board of Control, which had charge of orphanages and homes for the retarded. Briefly he sketched for the board chairman the story of the two little girls and then put before him a bizarre idea. "I said to him, 'I would like permission to take eleven more feeble-minded babies less than a year old and put them in adult wards in institutions for the retarded, because I think that the babies will become normal.' As you can imagine, he looked at me queerly. He was not a professional, but an Iowa farmer who held his job by political appointment. He said, 'It sounds crazy to me, but tell me more.' "

Dr. Skeels then listed the depressing conditions for infant development in orphanages and other children's institutions at that time. Babies were kept in cribs surrounded by protective white sheeting, which shut out anything stimulating to look at. No toys dangled around them. The only adults they saw were preoccupied nurses who appeared for changes of diapers and bedding, for rapid bathing and medication, or to prop bottles into the babies' mouths with the use of efficient, impersonal holders. At six months of age the babies were moved into small dormitories, where for the first time they had a few playthings but if a ball rolled away, there was no friendly adult to retrieve it. When they were two years old the children were graduated to cottages housing 30 to 35 youngsters of the same sex in the charge of one matron and three or four untrained, often reluctant teen-aged girls, themselves reared in the deadening environment of the orphanage. In homes for feeble-minded children, Dr. Skeels pointed out, life was, if possible, even more stultifying.

Continuing further with his unusual suggestion, Dr. Skeels hastened to explain that in placing the babies in wards for feeble-minded adults he would not be playing lightly with the fates of the children. Since their mentalities were already low and, as he and his colleagues had noticed, the IQs of children in orphanages and other children's institutions tended to go down, not up, what harm could come to them through a few months of affection from the feeble-minded women? On the other hand, he said, look what had happened to the first two little girls. If that were to happen to even one of the additional 11 children, the effort would be more than worthwhile.

But there was one hitch, Dr. Skeels added. After spending a year or two in a grownups' ward, the children would be two or three years old, an age that would make it hard to place them for adoption. If, in addition, their records showed that they had been in an institution for the feeble-minded, adoption would be impossible, if not illegal. So Dr. Skeels proposed listing the children as "house guests" at the institution, an informal designation that would require no marking on their records.

It seemed to be a gamble with only winning possibilities—no child could lose, but the lives of one or more of them might be improved—and at first Dr. Skeels had no other idea in mind. Then he realized that there might be another benefit. "Here was a gold mine for formal research—a situation that could not have been set up by choice. You can't play with human lives—especially with babies' lives—moving them from one environment to another just for the sake of research. But here, quite by accident, life itself had set up the proper conditions for us, and the results so far seemed to justify trying again on a more formal basis."

But to make the experiment valuable as research, Dr. Skeels would have to show that any benefits that might befall the additional 11 children would not have happened if these children had not been placed in wards with the feeble-minded women. He therefore proposed that 12 babies remaining at the orphanage be chosen as a "contrast group." Again, the children would not be harmed for the sake of the research; their lives would continue at the orphanage as if no research were being done. No one but Dr. Skeels and his assistants would know that their records of development were being observed in a special way, except for Harold B. Dye, M.D., superintendent of a state institution for retarded children, who helped Dr. Skeels develop his plan.

The 12 "contrast" children would resemble the "house guest" children as closely as possible in health records and family background. They would differ in only one respect. Their IQs would be higher than those of the "house guests." This was to test Dr. Skeels's earlier observations. Would their near-normal IQs decline at the orphanage in the way that Dr. Skeels had observed the IQs of others decline? If at the same time the IQs of the retarded "house guests" rose, how would the IQs of the two groups compare after, say, a year?

Dr. Skeels won permission to make his experiment.

The IQs of the 11 babies sent to the adult institution ranged from 36, or seriously retarded, to 89, or dull normal. Of the "contrast" babies remaining at the orphanage, the one with the lowest IQ scored 50, the one with the highest scored 103, or normal. Although nine of the contrast group were in the intelligence range considered adoptable, they were ineligible because of poor family histories or legal restrictions.

What had happened to the first two babies at Woodward now happened to nearly all the experimental 11. In almost every ward one inmate became a baby's "mother" and others became "aunts." Each day, supervised by their "mothers" and "aunts," all the children frolicked together in a playground, riding tricycles and using the swings and slides. In the large living room of each ward there was plenty of space for indoor play. As soon as they could talk, the "house guest" children attended kindergarten and short daily chapel exercises that included group singing. When adults had dances and movies, the children went too. On the Fourth of July the residents put on a baby show. Each ward made a float upon which its baby rode, dressed in costume. Prizes were awarded for the nicest baby, most attractive costume and best float. Above all, there was the daily doting over the children by the "mothers" and "aunts."

The mental growth of the children was spectacular. The IQ of one child, originally 36, leaped to 81. Generally the greatest gains were made by those who had started lowest. Five of the 11 children attained IQs of 100 or higher. One boy astonished the psychologists by reaching 113. Every child gained, and the group's average rose from 64 to 92.

One child who leaped from 73 to 100 did so in only eight months. All the others, except one, made their gains in two years or less. The one exception, the girl who progressed from 36 to 81, took more than four years to do so. The doctors noted with interest that this child and one other originally had been placed in a ward with inmates whose average mental age was the lowest among the adults involved in the experiment. When these two children failed to show progress after many months, they were placed singly in other wards with brighter residents. After making new attachments with more active, attentive "mothers" and "aunts," they, like the other children, began to show marked gains in intelligence. Despite their later start, it wasn't too late to save them.

Of the 11 children, nine were placed in adoptive homes, just as the two girls who first went to Woodward had been. The remaining two, however, were returned to the orphanage. One of these, a child born to a 14-year-old mother, had been a guest in one of the brighter wards and had become the "daughter" of an inmate who was not only attentive but extremely possessive. The child's IQ had advanced from 57 to 94 in nine months. Her nursery teacher, however, felt the child was overdependent, and transferred her to a less stimulating group of inmates. Here she received hardly more special attention than the grown inmates of the ward. Her IQ receded to 84, and soon afterward to 77.

The other "failure," born prematurely with congenital syphilis that was soon cured, had experienced a rise in IQ from 61 to 80 between her second and third birthdays. At this point a newly employed administrator sent her back to the orphanage, feeling the child no longer belonged in an institution for the retarded. The psychologists felt it impolitic at the time to fight the case. Before long the child's IQ declined to 63.

About two and a half years after the "house guest" children were adopted, Dr. Skeels visited them in their new homes for follow-up tests. He could hardly believe what he found. No child had an IQ of less than 90, and the average of all of the children was a normal 96.

Meanwhile the 12 "contrast group" children in the orphanage had sadly deteriorated over these three or four years. Having started at a near-normal average of 87, their group average had sagged to 66. The child who had started as the brightest, with an IQ of 103, had plummeted 54 points.

Thus while the retarded children sent to the home for the feeble-minded had now become normal, the near-normal children left in the orphanage had now become slow or feeble-minded.

Today it is hard to imagine with what shock these findings were regarded by the psychologists of nearly 30 years ago. But studies of human intelligence then were dominated by two assumptions: that intelligence, like the color of one's eyes, is built into the genes and remains forever fixed; and that the way in which a child lives is not a major factor in fixing his intelligence.

Yet it was precisely because their evidence to the contrary was so extraordinary that Dr. Skeels and his band of eager young helpers assumed it would be received with excited attention by their scientific colleagues.

On May 6, 1939, before the annual convention of the American Association on Mental Deficiency, in Chicago, Dr. Skeels read a report on his experiment. The report, coauthored by Dr. Dye, was greeted with stony silence—a silence to be followed by scathing criticism soon after the convention closed. One authority on intelligence, B. R. Simpson, mocked Skeels and Dye in print as inventors of a "wandering IQ." An even more eminent authority, Florence Goodenough, a designer of intelligence tests, denounced the Skeels-Dye study later the same year from no less distinguished a platform than that of the American Association for the Advancement of Science. Skeels and his associates were charged with distorting their facts, perhaps even falsifying them to attract attention. The facts couldn't be true because they violated what all psychologists *knew* to be true—that intelligence cannot be changed. Marie Skodak particularly recalls the AAAS meeting, in Columbus, Ohio, where Florence Goodenough read her attack.

"I happened to be the only one of our group there," recalls Dr. Skodak, who is now Director of Psychological Services for the public schools of Dearborn, Michigan. "I rose in the audience with all my youth and all my inexperience for that kind of debate among important professionals. I don't know all the things I said, but I remember that it was a long, long speech I gave. To this day, some people still remember me for that speech. But the criticism only got louder and worse. Pretty soon almost everyone in the field heard of 'that Iowa study' and that it was wrong. No one could say exactly *what* was wrong, but it was wrong."

The Skeels group, while wounded, remained unshaken. They were developing far more evidence than that derived from their study of a mere handful of children in an asylum. They were putting together a whole jigsaw puzzle of studies, all contributing to a single subject: the impact of environment on intelligence.

With Eva A. Fillmore, one of his assistants, Dr. Skeels studied families in which parents seemed to give their children inadequate affection and attention. Older children of such parents most often grew up with borderline intelligence or were mentally retarded. Their younger brothers and sisters, however, were generally of normal ability. This seemed to suggest that a younger child, even though lacking attention from a parent, benefited by the stimulation of an older playmate in the house, even though not an intelligent one. Whatever the reason, this finding challenged the existing notion that the IQ score is fixed by heredity.

Meanwhile, Dr. Skeels worked on a broad-scale study to amplify his findings regarding the dozen children in the Skeels-Dye contrast group. This study showed that most children who remain for long periods of time in institutions supposedly for children of normal minds slowly but inevitably become retarded. The most revealing piece of the jigsaw puzzle was contained in still another study that Dr. Skodak coauthored with Dr. Skeels. When infants were placed for adoption, social workers, in matching children with adoptive or foster families, attempted to predict the mental level of the child. Because one can hardly test the mentality of an infant two or three weeks old, say, these predictions were based on the intelligence of their natural parents, which was usually low, and on the achievements of their older brothers and sisters. The Skodak-Skeels study, involving 100 children, found that a couple of years after adoption these children almost always surpassed the predictions of the orphanage social workers.

In all these studies, one thing seemed to account for a child's improvement. "The consistent element," wrote Dr. Skeels, "seemed to be the existence of a one-to-one relationship with an adult who gave generously of love and affection, together with an abundance of attention and experimental stimulation from many sources. Those children who had little of these did not show progress. Those who had a great deal did show progress."

If any psychologist was inclined to share the Skeels heresy by further testing his findings, his plans were upset by the coming of World War II, which directed almost all professional skills into channels of national survival. Dr. Skeels himself was conscripted into an Air Force desk job.

When the war ended, Dr. Skeels discovered that the Iowa records section had discarded the detailed notes of his studies. As though to emphasize his disgrace, it was explained to him that the notes had taken up too much file space. All that was left were some rough data that his assistants had squirreled away on their own. Discouraged and apparently defeated, Dr. Skeels took a job as a clinical psychologist in a Veterans Administration hospital in Denver and eventually joined the United States Public Health Service. His work on children's intelligence seemed to be finished.

Yet the story was not ended. Shortly after the war, a graduate student at Northwestern University made a study of backward children in Chicago public schools and came up with evidence that IQs can be raised as a result of stimulating experiences. A few years later, however, a University of Illinois professor of education, Samuel A. Kirk, refuted the study by revealing some major errors in its methods. But in the course of preparing this refutation, Dr. Kirk restudied the published papers of Dr. Skeels and began his own large-scale research on mentally handicapped children. In 1958 he published a book, *Early Education of the Mentally Retarded,* advancing results almost identical with those of Skeels and Dye. The documentation put forth by Dr. Kirk, plus his eminence in the field, forced the professional establishment to sit up and take notice.

About five years later, in four classrooms of a Harlem public school, Dr. Martin Deutsch, supported by a grant from the Ford Foundation, produced remarkable rises in the scoring IQ of four-and five-year-old slum children by exposing them to highly charged stimulation in preschool classes. This accomplishment was duplicated in the public schools of Baltimore, also with financial help from the Ford Foundation. These experiments, widely publicized, rapidly led to the multimillion-dollar Federal effort known as Project Head Start. Soon research was launched in the malleability of intelligence in children under nursery school age. Almost overnight the "wandering IQ" of young children became a subject of high fashion in educational and psychological research, although few of the professionals engaged in it had ever heard of Dr. Skeels.

One who had, however, was Dr. Robert J. Havighurst, of the University of Chicago. In 1961, attending a meeting one day at the National Institute for Mental Health, near Washington, he learned by chance that Dr. Skeels, now an administrator for the National Institute, had an office down the hall. Fired by an idea, Dr. Havighurst went to Dr. Skeels and introduced himself. Although Havighurst had never taken a position on the controversial work of Skeels, he realized that the early date of the study—more than a quarter century had gone by—presented a marvelous opportunity. These former imbeciles and dullards—the "house guests" and contrast group alike—were now adults. What had happened to them? Had the "house guests" who turned smart become dull again? Had those who began by being smart and then turned dull in the orphanage found their "natural level" and turned smart again? Did any of them have children? And if so, what were *they* like? It was urgent that a follow-up study be made, he told Dr. Skeels.

Dr. Skeels' first reaction was one of resistance—but somehow hopeful resistance. How would he get away from his job? Who would pay the enormous cost of tracking down the children of the experiment? Who would assist him? But regardless of the difficulties, the job was not to go undone. He took the matter up with authorities at the Institute. He found them—to his surprise—interested, and also willing to pay the cost. The Institute would provide funds to find not only the 25 children in the Skeels-Dye experimental and contrast groups, but also the 100 children of the Skodak-Skeels study who had been placed in adoptive homes. Dr. Skeels called Dr. Skodak at her job in Dearborn.

As the two long-time colleagues began to plan, they realized the immense difficulties of their undertaking. After a quarter of a century, in modern, mobile America, how do you track down children who have grown into adults?

For instance, of the 25 children in the Skeels-Dye study (the 13 "house guests," including the first two girls, and the 12 in the contrast group), 14 were girls. If they had married, their names were changed. How could they be located? There were further problems. Adoption agencies do not keep long-range records of children they place. One or both of the adoptive parents—or even the child himself—might be dead.

The new study now became a detective story. The psychologists began their sleuthing by searching old telephone books, city directories and files of local credit bureaus in Iowa. Some of these directories were found in, of all places, the Des Moines office of the Animal Disease Eradication Division of the U.S. Department of Agriculture, which maintained old lists of people living on farms. Musty directories eventually turned up two thirds of the former orphanage children.

To find the rest, Drs. Skeels and Skodak visited small-town postmasters, bankers, old-time storekeepers, and elderly ladies with long memories. In calling upon these people, the psychologists could not save the project money by driving government cars. Those whom they hoped would be their informants about families long since moved away might jump to the conclusion that the inquisitive visitors were from the Federal Bureau of Investigation—or, even worse, from the Bureau of Internal Revenue. So, each in a rented car, Dr. Skeels and Dr. Skodak went their separate ways, driving from one town to another, from one house to another, each introducing himself as a friend of the family that was being sought.

Six of the "house guest" children were found to be still living in Iowa. The other seven were finally tracked down great distances away: two in Minnesota and one each in Wisconsin, Kansas, Nebraska, Arizona and California. Of the contrast group, nine of the 12 had remained in Iowa. One was located in Nebraska; another was traced to Florida, then to Montana and finally to California. One, Dr. Skeels learned, had died. Remarkably, not only all 25 children in the Skeels-Dye experiment but every one of the 100 children in the Skodak-Skeels study was located.

Now the two psychologists faced the problem of approaching the people they had traced.

"You can't write them form letters, or even call them on the long-distance telephone," Dr. Skeels points out. "After all those years, you just don't open that way. Only Marie Skodak or I could do it. At one time we were considered part of these families. We had had an understanding with the adoptive parents that we could come back periodically and give tests as the children became older, which we had done. Either of us could appear as an interested old friend and resume our relationship."

The search had taken 16 months. Now that they had been found, 95 per cent of the adopted children—now adults—were glad to cooperate. Cooperation meant hardly more than easy, informal conversation. Early in their planning, Drs. Skeels and Skodak had decided that there was little point in giving intelligence tests. What seemed far more appropriate was to get information on the real, demonstrated abilities of these adults: educational achievement, occupations and an estimate of their general social competence. Where it seemed appropriate, a suggestion would be made for giving IQ tests to their children.

If ability to hold a good job is a measure of a successful life, the 13 children who once were "house guests" in an institution for the mentally retarded had turned out astoundingly well. All had become self-supporting. One of the three boys in the group was a staff sergeant in the armed forces, another was a sales manager and the third was a vocational counselor on his way toward earning a master's degree.

The staff sergeant had been born to a 16-year-old mother whose IQ was 69. His father was unknown. With an IQ score of 113 after his period as a "house guest," he was adopted by a mechanic and his wife, both of them high school graduates. As a teen-ager the boy dropped out of high school in his senior year, and after an act of vandalism spent a short time in a correctional school. He soon straightened out, joined the armed forces and later married a hospital technician, a high-school graduate. The couple have three small children whose IQs range from a bright 113 to a superior 125.

The sales manager was born to a houseworker who had quit school in the ninth grade; his father was believed to be a theater manager in a small town. After almost two years as a "house guest" he had an unimpressive IQ of 79, but was permitted to be adopted by a storekeeper and his wife. His childhood was marred by severe allergies. Recovering, he attended college for more than two years. He married. The IQs of the couple's three children range from 96 to 118.

The vocational counselor turned out to be one of the most remarkable of the "house guests." He had been a sickly baby. He was delivered by cesarean section to a woman whose IQ was 66; his father was unknown. At two years of age, with an IQ of 75, he spent hours incessantly rocking back and forth. He was one of the pair who had spent one and a half fruitless years among extremely dull inmates and then had been transferred to brighter "mothers" and "aunts." After attaining an IQ of 92, he was adopted by a college-graduate technician and his wife. The boy suffered severe asthma attacks as a small child, but these were brought under control. He completed high school and college, went on to postgraduate work at a good university and married a college-graduate commercial artist. They have no children.

Of the ten girls who were "house guests," eight married. One was subsequently divorced, but the others appeared to be enjoying stable, satisfying family lives. Of those who had been employed, one taught elementary school. Others in the group had become a registered nurse, a pratical nurse, a licensed beautician and an office clerk. Two married without taking jobs. The two girls who had never been placed in adoptive homes wound up in the lowest-status jobs, as domestic workers.

The prize among the girls was one whose IQ during her "house guest" period had jumped from 65 to 104. She was adopted by an accountant and his wife, both college graduates. The girl, who grew to be unusually attractive and vivacious, completed high school and began training to be an airline stewardess. She left this training, however, to marry a meteorologist. The above-average IQs of their three children are 107, 110 and 114.

The "house guests" who married had a combined total of 28 children. The IQs of these children averaged 104. Lowest among them was 85; highest, 125. When one considers the early dullness of mind of their parents and the miserable mentalities of their known grandparents, these cold numbers appear to demolish old notions about the unchangeability of intelligence.

The success in adult life of the "house guests" was the shiny face of a two-sided coin. On the other side of the coin was the sad picture—with one startling exception—of the contrast group, the children who had remained in the orphanage.

Of 11 surviving members of this group—one died at 15 in an institution for the mentally retarded—none was adopted. Only two married; one of these subsequently was divorced. Four were still residents of state institutions and unable to hold paying jobs. The most promising of these had intermittently been paroled to his grandmother and hired himself out to mow lawns and shovel snow, but he could not function as an independent citizen. A fifth is employed as a gardener's helper in the institution in which he spent much of his life as an inmate. An attempt was made to get him an outside job, but he failed at it. He has no interest beyond his simple work, no known friends among either inmates or fellow employees. Of the six living on their own, three work as dishwashers. One folds napkins in a cafeteria and another, a male, is classed as a "floater."

This leaves one self-supporting member of the contrast group—known as Case 19. He was to be the ultimate surprise of the search conducted by Dr. Skeels. Dr. Skeels found him working as a skilled linotyper for a newspaper in a sizable Midwestern city. His earnings are greater than that of the rest of the contrast group combined. He is the only one with a stable marriage, a family and a home of his own.

Oddly, his good fortune can be traced directly to an affliction he had suffered since early childhood. As an infant, Case 19 underwent a mastoid operation that resulted in a moderate hearing loss. Between the ages of 15 months and four years, which he spent at the orphanage, his affliction brought him more sympathetic attention from adults than other children enjoyed. Still his IQ descended from 87 to 67. When he was five, old enough for kindergarten, he was sent by the orphanage to a resident school for deaf children. His schoolmates, of course, were not "institutional" children as those at the orphanage were. They came from a normally wide range of homes and warm, concerned parents who kept close contact with their children. And like those in the "house guest" group, he informally acquired a "mother." The matron of his cottage took a special fancy to him partly because he had no family. She often took him home with her for family meals, and so did her daughter and son-in-law.

"There was something unusually charming about him as a little boy," Dr. Skodak recalls. "He was the kind of child who responded to people— and to whom people responded. He openly sought affection and got it. During summer holidays he returned to the orphanage. Because he'd been away, he wasn't a real member of the group. So he'd hang around the orphanage office or parking lot. Staff members, seeing him there alone, often would take him along on trips to the post office or to do other chores. Sometimes they would buy him ice cream on the way back. The fact that he was deaf led him to more experiences of this kind than the other orphanage children had."

By another happy accident, during his year in kindergarten he was chosen for a special study in mental growth that was being conducted by a researcher from a state university. This placed him in an intensified program of individualized instruction and frequent trips. About two years after the Skeels-Dye experiment ended, when other "contrast" children at the orphanage almost all had deteriorated, according to the scores of their follow-up tests, Case 19 showed a leap upward of 22 points.

At the school for the deaf, Case 19 was graduated from high school and went on to learn his trade as linotyper. Today he is an active leader in community organizations. His four children have IQs of 103, 107, 117 and 119.

His surprising history as one of the "contrast" children—but resembling that of the more fortunate "house guest" children—indeed appears to be the exception that proves the rule.

May, 1966, was the 27th anniversary of Dr. Skeels' embarrassing appearance before the American Association on Mental Deficiency. Although irony was not intended, on that anniversary Drs. Skeels and Skodak appeared before the same association—in the same city, Chicago, and at the same hotel—to report on the unique 30-year aftermath of what is now recognized as a brilliant pioneering study in child development. The report this time was widely acknowledged in the professional press and applauded by the scientific world.

One importance of the recent follow-up search, Dr. Skodak points out, is verification that the early changes in the children who were placed with the retarded adults were not merely a scientific "fluke." The gains in intelligence made by the "house guests" held fast; those children grew up to be bright, contributing members of society. The "contrast" children, after early years of neglect, deprived of stimulating experience, grew to be not only of little worth to themselves but of great cost to society.

The cost in dollars was not left unexamined by Drs. Skeels and Skodak. They calculated that the 12 children in the unfortunate contrast group had spent an aggregate of 273 years in institutions at a cost of $138,000 in public funds. They are still young; the cost to the public of these dozen souls may yet more than double. On the other hand, the "house guest" children during one year alone—1963—paid Federal income tax bills ranging from $38 to $848.

Another important point was made by the study, and in particular by the case of the "house guest" child who was transferred back to the orphanage by a new administrator and in consequence suffered a drastic decline in IQ. That point was also recently made when a study of Project Head Start showed that gains made by children in Head Start nurseries tend to be lost by those children who go on to inadequate schools.

"It's quite evident," Dr. Skodak points out, "that we can *create* people with severe mental handicaps, and, in fact, we do. The majority of mentally handicapped children don't come from orphanages, but grow up in disadvantaged homes and are educated in inadequate schools. Maybe society has more of a responsibility for the lives of these children than we have been willing to admit."

"Our little study made its point with only twenty-five children in an orphanage a long time ago," says Dr. Skeels, who is now retired and living in a seacoast town in southern California. "But there are hundreds of thousands of biologically normal babies born to cultural deprivation, social emptiness, maternal rejection or a combination of all of these. They grow up with the makings of juvenile delinquents, patients, in mental hospitals, inmates of institutions for the mentally retarded or just unproductive, unhappy people. If we can bring them the Head Start kind of experience early enough, widely enough and with adequate follow-through to make sure it sticks, we'll find that most of these children can become successful high-school and college graduates instead."

RICHARD E. FARSON

# 3. PRAISE REAPPRAISED

I am beginning to question the cherished idea that people enjoy being praised. I realize that I am in unfriendly territory because praise is perhaps the most widely used and thoroughly endorsed of all human relations techniques. Parents, businessmen, psychologists, teachers—everyone seems to believe in its value as a motivational tool, a reward, a way to establish good relationships.

But I wonder if praise accomplishes just what we think it does. Not that it does not have valuable functions (of which we are largely unaware), but I will bet our beliefs about its *value* are erroneous.

With considerable trepidation let me tentatively suggest:

Praise is not only of limited and questionable value as a motivator, but may in fact be experienced as threatening.
Rather than functioning as a bridge between people, it may actually serve to establish distance between them.
Instead of reassuring a person as to his worth, praise may be an unconscious means of establishing the superiority of the praiser.
Praise may constrict creativity rather than free it.
Rather than opening the way to further contact, praise may be a means of terminating it.

Although we may be fooling ourselves as to what praise accomplishes, some of its functions—such as maintaining distance, terminating contacts, establishing status or superiority—are in fact quite necessary and socially useful, even though we may prefer not to acknowledge these hidden benefits.

---

## DEFINITION

What is praise? We are all quick to distinguish praise from flattery, which has connotations of insincerity and expediency. For my purpose here, praise is any statement that makes a *positive* evaluation of an object, person, act, or event, and that contains very little supplementary information—for instance:

> "Nice work, you've done a fine job."
> "You're a good boy."
> "That painting of yours is excellent."

These are examples of praise—positive evaluations with little additional meaning.

On the other hand, a positive evaluation *plus* other information is not essentially, or merely, praise. A statement such as "The reason I think you've done such a good job ..." or "How did you get that beautiful effect with ink alone?" invites a response and extends the encounter. Obviously such statements are more than praise and have different qualities and perhaps different results.

A simple definition or a simple analysis of praise is, of course, not possible. One must take into account the situation in which praise occurs, the history of the relationship one has with the other person, the attitudes that underlie the act of praise, and the motivations for it. Also, specific acts and techniques can never overcome the effects of one's basic attitudes toward others. Good relationships are dependent on good fundamental attitudes. And a good relationship can withstand many difficulties—even such difficulties as are brought on by praise.

## NEGATIVE ASPECTS

What are the problems with praise?

First of all, the findings of scientific experiments on praise do not clearly demonstrate its value. Most of the studies done on this subject have compared praise with reproof or blame as motivational techniques. The results of these studies are mixed: in some cases praise was slightly more effective than reproof; in others, reproof was more effective than praise. In essence, all that can really be concluded from most research is that *some* response motivates people better than no response at all.

It has been demonstrated in psychological laboratories that we can shape human behavior by the use of rewards—symbols such as lights and bells which indicate that the subject is making correct responses or is gaining the approval of judges. But in the extremely complex situations of real life, does praise work the same way? Does praise reward? After considerable observation I have come to the conclusion that it usually does not.

Watch people responding to praise. Don't they usually seem to be reacting with discomfort, uneasiness, and defensiveness? I have noticed that a very common response is a vague denial or derogation:

"I really can't take the credit for it."
"You're just saying that."
"Well, *we* like it."
"It was just luck."
"I like yours, too."
"Well, I do the best I can."

The one element these statements have in common is that they are all defensive reactions—efforts to cope with a difficult situation. Praise a house or garden and its owner hastens to point out its defects; praise an employee for a project and he is quick to play down his role in it. Under the stress of praise, some people often become uncomfortable, almost to the point of imitating the toe-digging reactions of small children. Apparently praise is something to be coped with, to be handled.

### REASONS FOR DEFENSIVENESS

Why do people react to praise with defensiveness? Part of the reason may be that in praise there *is* threat—something one must defend against. After all, praise is an evaluation, and to be evaluated usually makes us uncomfortable. If we are weighed, we *may* be found wanting.

Most of us feel uncomfortable when we are negatively evaluated, so we tend to believe that positive evaluations should have the opposite effect, that they should be enhancing. Really, though, praise has many of the same basic problems and characteristics as do negative evaluations. Research indicates that *any* evaluation is likely to make people uncomfortable, defensive. Perhaps this is because, when you evaluate a person, you are often in some way trying to motivate him, to move him in a certain direction, to *change* him. Now while he himself may want to change, and while he may not like the person that he *is,* at the same time he is that person; his identity is very important, indeed essential, because it makes possible an answer to the question "Who am I?" Bad or good he must hold onto his identity. For this reason, the threat of change is one of the most fundamental and disquieting of psychological threats. So even though praise may only imply that one should change a bit in the direction one is already going, it *does* imply change, and therefore it may be almost as threatening as a negative evaluation.

Another reason why positive evaluation is discomforting lies in the fact that when a person praises us, it is clear that he is sitting in judgment. We become uneasy when we know someone is not only trying to change us but is continually judging us, grading us. In this situation, the absence of praise is especially threatening because we know that we are still being evaluated.

Often the change which praise asks one to make is not necessarily beneficial to the person being praised but will redound to the convenience, pleasure, or profit of the praiser. When we praise Tommy for making it to the bathroom in time, we are probably not so much delighted on Tommy's behalf as on our own; the change that complicated Tommy's life will make our own more convenient and pleasant. Much the same is true when we praise a salesman for neat call reports. Understandably, people feel threatened when they are being manipulated for another's benefit.

Our enthusiastic belief that praise is pleasing to people has resulted in its becoming a piece of psychological candy. We sugarcoat blame with praise, or use the "sandwich technique" whereby praise is followed by reproof, then again by praise. "I'm very pleased with your work, Fred," says the boss, "you're really getting the work out, *but* ..." Fred then gets the unhappy part of the story, the reprimand. The boss finishes up with "Keep up the fine work," and Fred is shuttled out without quite knowing what hit him. This is also a favorite technique of parents and teachers. In fact, we have become so conditioned by its use from early childhood that when we are praised, we automatically get ready for the shock, the reproof.

Undoubtedly, the most threatening aspect of praise is the obligation it puts on us to be praiseworthy people. If we accept praise, if we really believe the best about ourselves, then we are under an obligation to behave accordingly. This is deeply frightening to us. For if we really believe it when we are told that we are competent, or intelligent, or beautiful, then we are continually on the spot to be competent, or intelligent, or beautiful, not only in the eyes of the person who praised us but, even worse, in our own eyes. The responsibility to be continually at our best, to live up to our talents and abilities, is perhaps our most difficult problem in living—and we naturally defend against it.

## ISSUE OF CREDIBILITY

It may be that there simply is no effective response to praise given in a face-to-face situation. Even saying "thank you" is not entirely satisfactory— although it may be the least defensive way of coping with the behavioral impasse which praise uniformly produces. Perhaps this is one reason why written praise may be somewhat easier to accept. We can savor it without having to invent a modest response.

Of course, part of the problem hinges on the issue of credibility. Can we really believe what the praiser seems to want us to believe? Written praise may be more credible and therefore more rewarding to us. It most certainly is when we discover a praising remark about us written in a letter not intended for us to see. But part of credibility comes from within us. Are we psychologically prepared to accept the validity of comments which indicate our value? If you tell a person who strongly believes himself to be inadequate that he is in your opinion entirely adequate, then your statement is likely to be met with some resistance. The credibility of the praising remark has been determined by the person's internal needs to see himself in consistent ways.

### POSITIVE FUNCTIONS

If praise is threatening to people for so many reasons, then why do we use it so often? Surely we do not want to retain in our repertoire responses that do not serve us in some functional way. What are the functions of praise? Why is it a conversational staple?

For one thing, people expect praise. We fish for compliments, subtly or openly. Why do we do this, if we don't really like praise? Probably because it is so important for each of us to feel valued by others. We hope that praise will make us feel that way. Sometimes it does. But because praise means so many things and exists in such complicated motivational contexts, its ability to reward us and indicate our value is questionable. Still, we invite it at the same time that we resist it. Perhaps in our other-directed society we have become so dependent on the approval of others that we must continually check just to make sure that we are not being devaluated.

For another thing, giving praise is easy to do. It makes conversation, and most of us have not enough energy, interest, or imagination to offer witty retorts, penetrating criticism, brilliant insights, or sensitive responses. We really do not want the burden of conversation to be that heavy anyway. Gross evaluations, like praise, are simpler and less demanding.

Then, too, praise, as we have seen, is a way of gaining status over another by establishing the fact that one is capable of sitting in judgment. Status is important to all of us, and though the person being evaluated may feel that the praise is threatening or diminishing, the praiser himself has increased his psychological size or, if he praises an inferior, has claimed or reinforced his status. It is interesting to note here that when the work of a high-status person is praised by a low-status person, this is often seen as presumptuous or even insulting. If a layman should tell Picasso, "You're a very good painter," he is not likely to be particularly well received. In order to be acceptable, he must give the praise in a way that respects the status difference.

Praise is also useful in maintaining the inter-personal distance. We talk a good deal about wanting to be close to people, but when you come right down to it, there really are very few people whom we want to be close to, or whom we admit to closeness with us. It is necessary to be able to maintain distance from people, to keep a little free space around ourselves—psychological elbowroom—especially in a society which fills our daily lives with so many contacts. In the search for techniques to establish distance between ourselves and others we find that praise is one of the most effective, simply because, when we evaluate people, we are not likely to gain emotional proximity to them. Compare the effects of praise with other behaviors—for instance, listening to another or revealing your feelings to another, and see for yourself if praise doesn't tend to hold off, to separate, while the other behaviors tend to include, to embrace.

## CONTROL OF RELATIONSHIPS

Praise also helps to keep relatively stable patterns of relationship between people. If organizations are to function smoothly, it is probably quite important that certain hierarchies or structures be maintained.

How does praise work toward this end? Let's take as an example a problem-solving committee meeting that includes the executive vice president at one end of the hierarchy and a new junior assistant at the other:

If the assistant comes up with the brightest and most useful idea, some way must be found to accept it without lowering the status of the vice president in the eyes of the group, thereby disturbing the group's stability. Intuitively, the vice president may say to the young assistant, "That's a very good idea, young man." This not-so-simple act of praise has greased the whole situation. Status has been maintained (because as we remember, praise is a way of claiming status); the young man has been reminded of his place in the hierarchy; and the group is restored to comfortable equilibrium. Now the group can use the young man's idea without upsetting its psychological structure.

I am amazed to note how frequently we use praise as a sign that a conversation or interview is over. Listen and discover for yourself how many interpersonal transactions are ended with a positive evaluation. "It's good to talk with you" means "I've finished talking with you." And "You're doing fine; keep up the good work" communicates as well as any exit cue we have. For the busy parents to say to a child who has just offered her latest artistic creation, "Yes, Janie, that's a beautiful painting" may not better the relationship, but it will probably end the conversation. It is often tantamount to saying, "Go away; I'm busy right now." But of course we must have ways of doing just this, and praise is a very effective method.

So we see that by enabling us to terminate an encounter, by enabling us to keep a certain amount of psychological space between ourselves and others, by enabling us to maintain status—in short, to control our relationships—praise functions as one of the most important means by which we maintain consistent structure and equilibrium in any organization.

## A HELPFUL ALTERNATIVE

It is when we want to develop initiative, creativity, judgment, and problem-solving ability in people that praise fails us most. To liberate these qualities in people we need to rely on internal motivation. We need to make people feel that they are free of our control. We *may* need to establish a more equalitarian atmosphere, and sometimes we need to create a closeness with superiors. But if praise produces status differences, not equality; if it creates distance, not closeness; if it is felt as a threat, not as a reassurance; then how do you establish a free, accepting, yet close relationship that will encourage independent judgment, effective decisions, and creative actions?

There is much that is unknown about this, but from a variety of settings including psychotherapy, education, and business we are learning that perhaps the most important aspects of a helpful relationship are a person's ability to be *honest* and to *listen*. This sounds simple enough, but these behaviors are very seldom displayed in our relations with others.

### BEING HONEST

This does not mean being brutally frank; it means showing some of yourself to another person, transparently exhibiting some of your own feelings and attitudes. This is not easy because from early childhood we have learned to play roles which mask our feelings, as if being honest about them would only hurt others and destroy relationships. Actually, it is the other way around; we mask our feelings so that we will not have too many close—and possibly burdensome—relationships. The inevitable consequence of exposing and sharing feelings is emotional closeness. But closeness, as rewarding as it sometimes can be, is often uncomfortable, unpredictable. Masking our feelings may result in some alienation and anxiety but also in a lot of superficial psychological comfort.

Hiding our feelings and playing roles help to make situations predictable. We want to know what we and other people are going to do and say. We want behavior to be patterned and familiar, not continually spontaneous and varied. Maybe this is necessary in order to have a society at all. Perhaps there is a limit to the amount of spontaneity, emotionality, honesty, and variation that can be tolerated by any social system.

Curiously, we are no more honest about the positive, loving feelings we have than about our feelings of annoyance, mistrust, resentment, or boredom. As a matter of fact, negative feelings usually are less difficult to express honestly than are positive feelings. For some reason it is easier for most people to be honest about their feelings of anger than it is for them to be honest about their feelings of caring and love. In either case, the times when one can risk vulnerability are perhaps life's richest moments—but are not often psychologically comfortable moments.

### EMPATHIC LISTENING

The other response which we find helpful in creating close relationships is to listen. This does not merely mean to wait for a person to finish talking, but to try to see how the world looks to this person and to communicate this understanding to him. This empathic non-evaluative listening responds to the person's feelings as well as to his words; that is, to the total meaning of what he is trying to say. It implies no evaluation, no judgment, no agreement (or disagreement). It simply conveys an understanding of what the person is feeling and attempting to communicate; and his feelings and ideas are accepted as being valid for him, if not for the listener.

One reason we do not listen more, of course, is because it is too difficult. To see how difficult it is, try establishing in any group discussion the ground rule that no one may present his own view until he has first satisfied the person who has just spoken that he fully comprehends what this person meant to communicate. That is, he must restate in his own words the total meaning of the message and obtain the person's agreement that this was indeed his message—that accurate listening did take place. In doing this we will find out that—

> ... it is extremely difficult to get one person to agree that he meant what another thought he meant;
> ... we usually fail in our attempts to understand;
> ... we typically spend our listening time preparing what we are going to say;
> ... when we do listen intently, we have a hard time remembering what it was that we were going to say, and when we do remember, we discover that it is a little off the subject;
> ... most argument and emotionality goes out of such a discussion;
> ... after a few minutes of this sort of "complete communication" we become rather weary.

It is also difficult to listen because if we allow ourselves to see the world through another's eyes and to fully understand his point of view, then we run the risk of changing ourselves, our own point of view. And, as previously indicated, change is something we try to avoid.

But at times when we *do* want to develop creativity and self-confidence in others, when we *do* want to establish a close relationship in which the other person feels free "to be himself," then expressing our own feelings honestly and listening sensitively may be far more helpful than offering praise.

## TRY AN EXPERIMENT

If you doubt the effects of praise outlined here, you might experiment a bit with it. Check for yourself. The next time you praise someone, see what sort of reaction you get:

> Does he open up or does he become defensive, diffident, or uncomfortable?
> Does he appear to want to continue talking or to terminate the talk?
> Does he seem to be more motivated to work or does he seem less motivated?
> Then check yourself too:
> How do *you* feel when you receive praise?
> What do *you* do and say in response to it?
> How do *you* feel when you give praise?
> What are *you* trying to accomplish by it?

Another experiment, perhaps even more telling, is to accept the praise offered to you just as it seems to be intended. That is, the next time some praise comes your way indicating that the praiser wants you to believe that you are competent, or good, or smart, or attractive, show him that you accept this evaluation of you by saying something like, "I guess you think I'm very competent" or "You must think I'm a pretty good salesman." His reactions to this may indicate to you that his praise was intended to do much more than just convey that simple idea.

Let me sum up this way: It is questionable that praise is a fuel which motivates and stimulates people. On the other hand, praise is very useful indeed as a lubricant that keeps the wheels going around smoothly and predictably; we must have techniques like praise to keep our human relations in equilibrium.

Perhaps someday we will be able to look inward for evaluation rather than outward, to tolerate less order and equilibrium in our social organizations, and to enjoy increasing emotional closeness with greater numbers of people. But until that day praise will probably continue to serve us well in ways we seldom recognize.

ROBERT ROSENTHAL

# 4. TEACHER EXPECTATION AND PUPIL LEARNING

The primary purpose of the present paper is to consider the proposition that a teacher's expectation about her pupils' performance can come to serve as a significant determinant of that performance. Later in this paper we shall examine the evidence for and some implications of this proposition but first we shall want to provide an appropriate historical and conceptual per-

This previously unpublished paper appears by permission of the author.

Preparation of this chapter and much of the research summarized here was supported by research grants (G-17685, G-24826, GS-177, GS-714, and GS-1741) from the Division of Social Sciences of the National Science Foundation. Much of the research summarized here has also been summarized elsewhere but in the context of a more technical exposition (Rosenthal, 1969). Readers interested in the more technical details of the experiments summarized only briefly in the present chapter will want to refer to the more extensive bibliography of that paper.

spective. The goal of this perspective is to show that there is in fact, nothing very special about the "effects of teacher expectations." These effects may be seen to be only a specific instance of the operation of a far more general principle, a principle that holds that often in the course of interpersonal relationships, one person's expectation for the behavior of another person can come to be a significant determinant of that other person's behavior.

Most of the systematic evidence to support the idea of what we may call interpersonal self-fulfilling prophecies comes from experiments conducted not with teachers but with psychological experimenters. Simply to extend the generality of the principle of interpersonal self-fulfilling prophecies, any other group of persons might have served equally well. But the social situation which comes into being when a behavioral scientist encounters his research subject is a situation of both general and unique importance to the field of education and to the other behavioral sciences. Its general importance derives from the fact that the interaction of experimenter and subject, like other hierarchically ordered two-person interactions, may be investigated empirically with a view to teaching us more about such dyadic interaction in general. Its unique importance derives from the fact that the interaction of experimenter and subject, unlike other dyadic interactions, is a major source of our knowledge in the field of education and in the other behavioral sciences.

## EXPERIMENTER EXPECTATIONS

The particular expectation a scientist has of how his experiment will turn out is variable, depending on the experiment being conducted, but the presence of some expectation is virtually a constant in science. The variables selected for study by the scientist are not chosen by means of a table of random numbers. They are selected because the scientist expects a certain relationship to appear among them. Even in those less carefully planned examinations of relationships called "fishing expeditions" or more formally, "exploratory analyses," the expectation of the scientist is reflected in the selection of the entire set of variables chosen for examination. Exploratory analyses of data, like real fishing ventures, do not take place in randomly selected pools.

These expectations of the scientist are likely to affect the choice of the experimental design and procedure in such a way as to increase the likelihood that his expectation or hypothesis will be supported. That is as it should be. No scientist would select intentionally a procedure likely to show his hypothesis in error. If he could too easily think of procedures that would show this, he would be likely to revise his hypothesis. If the selection of a research design or procedure is regarded by another scientist as too "biased" to be a fair test of the hypothesis, he can test the hypothesis employing oppositely biased procedures or less biased procedures by which to demonstrate the greater value of his hypothesis. The designs and procedures employed are, to a great extent, public knowledge, and it is this public character that permits relevant replications to serve the required corrective function.

The major concern of this section will be with the effects of the experimenter's expectation on the responses he obtains from his subjects. The consequences of such an expectancy bias can be quite serious. Expectancy effects on subjects' responses are not public matters. It is not only that other scientists cannot know whether such effects occurred in the experimenter's interaction with his subjects, the investigator himself may not know whether these effects have occurred. Moreover, there is the likelihood that the experimenter has not even considered the possibility of such unintended effects on his subjects' response. That is not so different from the situations wherein the subject's response is affected by any attribute of the experimenter. Later, the problem will be discussed in more detail. For now it is enough to note that while other attributes of the experimenter may affect the subject's response, they do not necessarily affect these responses differentially as a function of the subject's treatment condition. Expectancy effects, on the other hand, always do. The sex of the experimenter does not change as a function of the subject's treatment condition in an experiment. The experimenter's expectancy of how the subject will respond does change as a function of the subject's experimental treatment condition.

That one person's expectation about another person's behavior may contribute to a determination of what that behavior will actually be has been suggested by various theorists. Merton (1948) elaborated the very useful concept of "self-fulfilling prophecy." One prophesies an event and the expectation of the event then changes the behavior of the prophet in such a way as to make the prophesied event more likely. The late Gordon Allport (1950) applied the concept of interpersonal expectancies to an analysis of the causes of war. Nations expecting to go to war affect the behavior of their opponents-to-be by the behavior which reflects their expectations of armed conflict. Nations who expect to remain out of wars, at least sometimes manage to avoid entering into them.

Drawn from the general literature, and the literatures of the healing professions, survey research, and laboratory psychology, there is considerable suggestive evidence for the operation of interpersonal self-fulfilling prophecies. The literatures referred to have been reviewed elsewhere (Rosenthal, 1964ab, 1965, 1966; Rosenthal and Jacobson, 1968) but it may be of interest here to give one illustration from the literature of experimental psychology. The case is one known generally to psychologists as a case study of an artifact in animal research. It is less well known, however, as a case study of the effect of experimenter expectancy. While the subject sample was small, the experimenter sample was very large indeed. The case, of course, is that of Clever Hans (Pfungst, 1911). Hans, it will be remembered, was the horse of Mr. von Osten, a German mathematics teacher. By means of tapping his foot, Hans was able to add, subtract, multiply, and divide. Hans could spell, read, and solve problems of musical harmony. To be sure, there were other clever animals at the time, and Pfungst tells about them. There was "Rosa," the mare of Berlin, who performed similar feats in vaudeville, and there was the dog of Utrecht, and the reading pig of Virginia. All these other clever animals were highly trained performers who were, of course, intentionally cued by their trainers.

Mr. von Osten, however, did not profit from his animal's talent, nor did it seem at all likely that he was attempting to perpetrate a fraud. He swore he did not cue the animal, and he permitted other people to question and test the horse even without his being present. Pfungst and his famous colleague, Stumpf, undertook a program of systematic research to discover the secret of Hans' talents. Among the first discoveries made was that if the horse could not see the questioner, Hans was not clever at all. Similarly, if the questioner did not himself know the answer to the question, Hans could not answer it either. Still, Hans was able to answer Pfungst's questions as long as the investigator was present and visible. Pfungst reasoned that the questioner might in some way be signaling to Hans when to begin and when to stop tapping his foot. A forward inclination of the head of the questioner would start Hans tapping, Pfungst observed. He tried then to incline his head forward without asking a question and discovered that this was sufficient to start Hans' tapping. As the experimenter straightened up, Hans would stop tapping. Pfungst then tried to get Hans to stop tapping by using very slight upward motions of the head. He found that even the raising of his eyebrows was sufficient. Even the dilation of the questioner's nostrils was a cue for Hans to stop tapping.

When the questioner bent forward more, the horse would tap faster. This added to the reputation of Hans as brilliant. That is, when a large number of taps was the correct response, Hans would tap very, very rapidly until he approached the region of correctness, and then he began to slow down. It was found that questioners typically bent forward more when the answer was a long one, gradually straightening up as Hans got closer to the correct number.

For some experiments, Pfungst discovered that auditory cues functioned additively with visual cues. When the experimenter was silent, Hans was able to respond correctly 31 percent of the time in picking one of many placards with different words written on it, or cloths of different colors. When auditory cues were added, Hans responded correctly 56 percent of the time.

Pfungst himself then played the part of Hans, tapping out responses to questions with his hand. Of 25 questioners, 23 unwittingly cued Pfungst as to when to stop tapping in order to give a correct response. None of the questioners (males and females of all ages and occupations) knew the intent of the experiment. When errors occurred, they were usually only a single tap from being correct. The subjects of this study, including an experienced psychologist, were unable to discover that they were unintentionally emitting cues.

Hans' amazing talents, talents rapidly acquired too by Pfungst, serve to illustrate the power of the self-fulfilling prophecy. Hans' questioners, even skeptical ones, expected Hans to give the correct answers to their queries. Their expectation was reflected in their unwitting signal to Hans that the time had come for him to stop his tapping. The signal cued Hans to stop, and the questioner's expectation became the reason for Hans' being, once again, correct.

Not all of Hans' questioners were equally good at fulfilling their prophecies. Even when the subject is a horse, apparently, the attributes of the experimenter make a considerable difference in determining the response of a subject. On the basis of his studies, Pfungst was able to summarize the characteristics of those of Hans' questioners who were more successful in their covert and unwitting communication with the horse. Among the characteristics of the more successful unintentional influencers were those of tact, an air of dominance, attention to the business at hand, and a facility for motor discharge. Pfungst's observations of 60 years ago seem not to have suffered excessively for the lack of more modern methods of scaling observations. To anticipate some of the research findings turned up much later, it must be said that Pfungst's description seems also to fit those experimenters who are more likely to affect their human subject's responses by virtue of their experimental hypothesis.

In summarizing his difficulties in learning the nature of Clever Hans' talents, Pfungst felt that he had been too long off the track by "looking for in the horse, what should have been sought in the man." Perhaps, too, when we conduct research in the behavioral sciences we are sometimes caught looking at our subjects when we ought to be looking at ourselves. It was to this possibility that much of the research to be summarized here was addressed.

### ANIMAL LEARNING

A good beginning might have been to replicate Pfungst's research, but with horses hard to come by, rats were made to do (Rosenthal and Fode, 1963a).

A class in experimental psychology had been performing experiments with human subjects for most of a semester. Now they were asked to perform one more experiment, the last in the course, and the first employing animal subjects. The experimenters were told of studies that had shown that maze-brightness and maze-dullness could be developed in strains of rats by successive inbreeding of the well- and the poorly performing maze-runners. Sixty laboratory rats were equitably divided among the 12 experimenters.

Half the experimenters were told that their rats were maze-bright while the other half were told their rats were maze-dull. The animal's task was to learn to run to the darker of two arms of an elevated T-maze. The two arms of the maze, one white and one gray, were interchangeable; and the "correct" or rewarded arm was equally often on the right as on the left. Whenever an animal ran to the correct side he obtained a food reward. Each rat was given 10 trials each day for five days to learn that the darker side of the maze was the one which led to the food.

Beginning with the first day and continuing on through the experiment, animals believed to be better performers became better performers. Animals believed to be brighter showed a daily improvement in their performance while those believed to be dull improved only to the third day and then showed a worsening of performance. Sometimes an animal refused to budge from his starting position. This happened 11% of the time among the allegedly bright rats; but among allegedly dull rats it happened 29% of the time. When animals did respond and correctly so, those believed to be brighter ran faster to the rewarded side of the maze than did even the correctly responding rats believed to be dull.

When the experiment was over, all experimenters made ratings of their rats and of their own attitudes and behavior vis-à-vis their animals. Those experimenters who had been led to expect better performance viewed their animals as brighter, more pleasant, and more likeable. These same experimenters felt more relaxed in their contacts with the animals and described their behavior toward them as more pleasant, friendly, enthusiastic, and less talkative. They also stated that they handled their rats more and also more gently than did the experimenters expecting poor performance.

So far we have given only one example of the results of studies of expectancy effect and the subjects were animals. Most of the research available, however, is based on human subjects and it is those results we now consider. In this set of experiments at least 20 different specific tasks have been employed but some of these tasks seemed sufficiently related to one another that they could reasonably be regarded as a family of tasks or a research area. These areas include human abilities, psychophysical judgments, reaction time, inkblot tests, structured laboratory interviews, and person perception. We have space, however, only to consider some examples.

## HUMAN ABILITIES

Especially instructive for its unusual within-subject experimental manipulation was an experiment by Larrabee and Kleinsasser (1967). They employed five experimenters to administer the Wechsler Intelligence Scale for Children (WISC) to 12 sixth-graders of average intelligence. Each subject was tested by two different experimenters; one administering the even-numbered items and the other administering the odd-numbered items. For each subject, one of the experimenters was told the child was of above average intelligence while the other experimenter was told the child was of below average intelligence. When the child's experimenter expected superior performance the total IQ earned was over 7 points higher on the average than when the child's experimenter expected inferior performance. When only the performance subtests of the WISC were considered, the advantage to the children of having been expected to do well was less than three IQ points and could easily have occurred by chance. When only the verbal subtests of the WISC were considered, the advantage of having been expected to do well, however, exceeded 10 IQ points. The particular subtest most affected by experimenters' expectancies was Information. The results of this study are especially striking in view of the very small sample size (12) of subjects employed.

The other experiment to be mentioned in this section is of special importance because of the elimination of plausible alternatives to the hypothesis that it is the subject's response that is affected by the experimenter's expectancy. In his experiment, Johnson (1967) employed the Stevenson marble-dropping task. Each of the 20 experimenters was led to believe that marble-dropping rate was related to intelligence. More intelligent subjects were alleged to show a greater increase in rate of marble-dropping over the course of six trials. Each experimenter then contacted eight subjects half of whom were alleged to be brighter than the remaining subjects.

The recording of the subject's response was by means of an electric counter and the counter was read by the investigator who was blind to the subject's expectancy condition. The results of this study, one of the best controlled in this area, were the most dramatic. Experimenters expecting a greater increase in marble-dropping rate obtained a much greater increase than they did when expecting a lesser increase.

### INKBLOT TESTS

In one of the most recent of the inkblot experiments, Marwit (1968) employed 20 graduate students in clinical psychology as his experimenters and 40 undergraduate students of introductory psychology as his subjects. Half the experimenters were led to expect some of their subjects to give many Rorschach responses and especially, a lot of animal responses. Half the experimenters were led to expect some of their subjects to give few Rorschach responses but proportionately a lot of human responses. Results showed that subjects who were expected to give more responses gave more responses and that subjects who were expected to give a greater number of animal relative to human responses did so. Marwit also found trends for the first few responses to have been already affected by the experimenter's expectancy and for later-contacted subjects to show greater effects of experimenter expectancy than earlier-contacted subjects.

## STRUCTURED LABORATORY
## INTERVIEWS

A number of experiments have been conducted in which the experimenters conducted a structured interview with their research subjects. One of these, an experiment by Raffetto (1968) was addressed to the question of whether the experimenter's expectation for greater reports of hallucinatory behavior might be a significant determinant of such reports.

Raffetto employed 96 paid, female students from a variety of less advanced undergraduate courses to participate in an experiment on sensory restriction. Subjects were asked to spend one hour in a small room that was relatively quite free from light and sound. Eight more advanced students of psychology served as the experimenters, with each one interviewing 12 of the subjects before and after the sensory restriction experience. The preexperimental interview consisted of factual questions such as age, college major, and college grades. The postexperimental interview was relatively well-structured including questions to be answered by "yes" or "no" as well as more open-ended questions e.g. "Did you notice any particular sensations or feelings?" Postexperimental interviews were tape recorded.

Half the experimenters were led to expect high reports of hallucinatory experiences and half were led to expect low reports of hallucinatory experiences. Obtained scores of hallucinatory experiences ranged from zero to 32 with a grand mean of 5.4. Of the subjects contacted by experimenters expecting more hallucinatory experiences, 48% were scored above the mean on these experiences. Of the subjects contacted by experimenters expecting fewer hallucinatory experiences, only 6% were scored above the mean.

### PERSON PERCEPTION

Although a good many experiments on the effects of experimenter expectancy have been conducted in the area of person perception, the basic paradigm of these investigations has been sufficiently uniform that we need only an illustration (Rosenthal and Fode, 1963b).

Ten advanced undergraduates and graduate students of psychology served as the experimenters. All were enrolled in an advanced course in experimental psychology and were already involved in conducting research. Each student-experimenter was assigned as his subjects a group of about 20 students of introductory psychology. The experimental procedure was for the experimenter to show a series of ten photographs of people's faces to each of his subjects individually. The subject was to rate the degree of success or failure shown in the face of each person pictured in the photos.

Each face could be rated as any value from −10 to +10 with −10 meaning extreme failure and +10 meaning extreme success. The 10 photos had been selected so that, on the average, they would be seen as neither successful nor unsuccessful, but quite neutral, with an average numerical score of zero.

All 10 experimenters were given identical instructions on how to administer the task to their subjects and were given identical instructions to read to their subjects. They were cautioned not to deviate from these instructions. The purpose of their participation, it was explained to all experimenters, was to see how well they could duplicate experimental results which were already well-established. Half the experimenters were told that the "well-established" finding was such that their subjects should rate the photos as of successful people (ratings of +5) and half the experimenters were told that their subjects should rate the photos as being of unsuccessful people (ratings of −5). Results showed that experimenters expecting higher photo ratings obtained higher photo ratings than did experimenters expecting lower photo ratings.

Subsequent experiments in the program of research launched with the experiment just described were designed not so much to demonstrate the effects of the investigator's expectancy as to learn something about the conditions which increase, decrease or otherwise modify these effects. It was learned, for example, that the subject's expectations about what would constitute behavior appropriate to the role of "experimental subject" could alter the extent to which they were influenced by the effects of the experimenter's hypothesis.

Through the employment of accomplices, serving as the first few subjects, it was learned that when the responses of the first few subjects confirmed the experimenter's hypothesis, his behavior toward his subsequent subjects was affected in such a way that these subjects tended to confirm further the experimenter's hypothesis. When accomplices, serving as the first few subjects, intentionally disconfirmed the expectation of the experimenter, the real subjects subsequently contacted were affected by a change in the experimenter's behavior so as also to disconfirm his experimental hypothesis. It seems possible, then, that the results of behavioral research can, by virtue of the early data returns, be determined by the performance of just the first few subjects.

In some of the experiments conducted, it was found that when experimenters were offered a too large and a too obvious incentive to affect the results of their research, the effects of expectancy tended to diminish. It speaks well for the integrity of our student-experimenters that when they felt bribed to get the data we led them to expect, they seemed actively to oppose us. There was a tendency for those experimenters to "bend over backward" to avoid the biasing effects of their expectation, but with the bending so far backward that the results of their experiments tended to be significantly opposite to the results they had been led to expect.

Individual differences among experimenters in the degree to which they obtain results consistent with their hypothesis have been discovered. The evidence comes both from additional experiments and from the analysis of sound motion pictures of experimenters interacting with their experimental subjects. Those experimenters who show greater expectancy effects tend to be of higher status in the eyes of their subjects and they seem to conduct their experiments in a more professional, more competent manner. They are judged more likable and more relaxed, particularly in their movement patterns, while avoiding an overly personal tone of voice that might interfere with the business at hand. It is interesting to note that, although the influence of an experimenter's expectancy is quite unintentional, the characteristics of the more successful influencer are very much the same ones associated with more effective influencers when the influence is intentional. The more successful agent of social influence may be the same person whether the influence be as overt and intentional as in the case of outright persuasion attempts, or as covert and unintentional as in the case of the experimenter's subtly communicating his expectancy to his research subject.

## EXPERIMENTER EXPECTATIONS: A SUMMARY

There have been 103 experiments testing the effects on subjects' responses of their experimenter's expectations and these studies can be classified into seven different research domains. Table 1 shows the number of studies conducted in each of these seven areas and the percentage of the studies in each area obtaining results with an associated probability of 10% or less. Table 1 also shows the number of principal investigators that conducted one or more studies in each of the seven areas and the percentage of these investigators in each area who obtained results with an associated $p$ of 10% or less. By chance we expect only about 10% of the experiments or the investigators to obtain results "significant" at the 10% level. In fact, we find about five times that number of experiments or investigators obtaining results at that level. The probability of this many positive results occurring by chance is infinitely small.

Because so much of the business of the behavioral sciences is transacted at a number of particular levels of probability, an additional summary is provided. Table 2 shows for 103 experiments, for 52 investigators, and for 33 laboratories (see Appendix A), the percentage obtaining results at five different levels of $p$.

Tables 1 and 2 tell us that the effects of experimenters' expectancies are "real" but they do not tell us whether they are large in magnitude in a given experiment. On the basis of analyses reported elsewhere (Rosenthal, 1969)

Table 1    EXPERIMENTER EXPECTANCY EFFECTS
IN SEVEN RESEARCH AREAS

| Research Area | By Experiments | | By Investigators | |
|---|---|---|---|---|
| | *Number of Studies* | *Percentage of Studies at $p \leq .10$[d]* | *Number of Investigators* | *Percentage of Studies at $p \leq .10$[d]* |
| Animal Learning | 6 | 100% | 5 | 100% |
| Human Abilities[a] | 10 | 40% | 9 | 44% |
| Psychophysics[a] | 9 | 33% | 6 | 33% |
| Reaction Time | 3 | 67% | 3 | 67% |
| Inkblot Tests | 5 | 80% | 4 | 75% |
| Laboratory Interviews[b] | 6 | 83% | 6 | 83% |
| Person Perception[a, b] | 64 | 36% | 22 | 27% |
| Total[c] | 103 | 48% | 52 | 50% |

[a] Indicates a single experiment or investigator represented in each of three areas by the same subject sample.

[b] Indicates another experiment or investigator represented in two areas by the same subject sample.

[c] Three entries were non-independent with respect to their subject samples and the mean standard normal deviate across areas was computed to obtain the independent *p* level entries.

[d] One-tail.

it can be estimated that about two out of three research subjects and about two out of three experimenters will give or obtain responses in the direction of the experimenter's expectancy.

Though we have been able to arrive at some estimate, however crude, of the magnitude of expectancy effects, we will not know quite how to assess this magnitude until we have comparative estimates from other areas of behavioral research. Such estimates are not easy to come by, but it seems worthwhile for us to try to obtain such estimates in the future. Although in individual studies, investigators occasionally give the proportion of variance accounted for by their experimental variable, it is more rare that systematic reviews of bodies of research literature give estimates of the overall magnitude of effects of the variable under consideration. It does not seem an unreasonable guess, however, to suggest that in the bulk of the experimental literature of the behavioral sciences, the effects of the experimental variable are not impressively "larger," either in the sense of magnitude of obtained *p*s or in the sense of proportion of subjects affected, than the effects of experimenter expectancy. The best support for such an assertion would come from experiments in which the effects of experimenter expectancy are compared directly, in the same experiment, with the effects of some other experimental variable believed to be a significant determinant of behavior. Fortunately, there are two such experiments to shed light on the question.

The first of these was conducted by Burnham (1966). He had 23 experi-

Table 2  EXPERIMENTER EXPECTANCY EFFECTS
OBTAINED AT VARIOUS *P* LEVELS

| *p* (One-tail) | I<br>*Experiments* | II<br>*Investigators*[a] | III<br>*Laboratories* |
|---|---|---|---|
| < .10 | 48% | 50% | 58% |
| < .05 | 34% | 37% | 48% |
| < .01 | 17% | 27% | 36% |
| < .001 | 12% | 19% | 27% |
| < .0001 | 5% | 10% | 18% |
| *N* | 103 | 52 | 33 |
| Grand Sum *z* | +100.86 | +69.75 | +57.86 |
| √Number of units | 103 | 52 | 33 |
| Combined *z*[b] | + 9.94 | + 9.67 | +10.08 |
| Null Replicates[c] | 3,656 | 1,746 | 1,204 |

[a] Principal investigators may be represented in more than one research area. Entries in Column III, however, are entirely independent with type of research area disregarded.

[b] Standard normal deviate associated with overall *p* for experiments, investigators, and laboratories.

[c] Number of additional experiments, investigators, and laboratories obtaining perfectly null results ($z = 0.00$, exactly) required to bring overall combined *p* to .05.

menters each run one rat in a T-maze discrimination problem. About half the rats had been lesioned by removal of portions of the brain, and the remaining animals had received only sham surgery which involved cutting through the skull but no damage to brain tissue. The purpose of the study was explained to the experimenters as an attempt to learn the effects of lesions on discrimination learning. Expectancies were manipulated by labeling each rat as lesioned or nonlesioned. Some of the really lesioned rats were labeled accurately as lesioned but some were falsely labeled as unlesioned. Some of the really unlesioned rats were labeled accurately as unlesioned but some were falsely labeled as lesioned. The results showed that animals that had been lesioned did not perform as well as those that had not been lesioned and animals that were believed to be lesioned did not perform as well as those that were believed to be unlesioned. What makes this experiment of special interest is that the effects of experimenter expectancy were actually greater than the effects of the removal of brain tissue.

The first of the experiments to compare directly the effects of experimenter expectancy with some other experimental variable, employed animal subjects. The next such experiment to be described employed human subjects. Cooper, Eisenberg, Robert, and Dohrenwend (1967) wanted to compare the effects of experimenter expectancy with the effects of effortful preparation for an examination on the degree of belief that the examination would actually take place.

Each of ten experimenters contacted ten subjects; half of the subjects were required to memorize a list of 16 symbols and definitions that were claimed to be essential to the taking of a test that had a 50-50 chance of being given, while the remaining subjects, the "low effort" group, were asked only to look over the list of symbols. Half of the experimenters were led to expect that "high effort" subjects would be more certain of actually having to take the test, while half of the experimenters were led to expect that "low effort" subjects would be more certain of actually having to take the test.

Results showed that there was a very slight tendency for subjects who had exerted greater effort to believe more strongly that they would be taking the test. Surprising in its magnitude was the finding that experimenters expecting to obtain responses of greater certainty obtained such responses to a much greater degree than did experimenters expecting responses of lesser certainty. The effects of the experimenters' expectancies were more than 10 times greater than the effects of preparatory effort.

### EXPERIMENTER EXPECTATIONS:
### MEDIATING PROCESSES

How are we to account for the results of the experiments described? What are the processes by which an experimenter unintentionally informs his subject just what response is expected of him?

We know that the process whereby the experimenter communicates his expectancy to his subject is a subtle one. We know that it is subtle because for six years we have tried to find in sound films the unintended cues the experimenter gives the subject—and for six years we have failed, at least partly. But there are some things about the unintentional communication of expectancies that have been learned.

We know that if a screen is placed between experimenter and subject that there will be a reduction of the expectancy effect so that visual cues from the experimenter are probably important (Rosenthal and Fode, 1963; Zoble, 1968). But the interposed screen does not eliminate expectancy effects completely so that auditory cues also seem to be important. Just how important auditory cues may be has been dramatically demonstrated by the work of Adair and Epstein (1968). They first conducted a study which was essentially a replication of the basic experiment on the self-fulfilling effects of experimenters' prophecies. Results showed that, just as in the original studies, experimenters who prophesied the perception of success by their subjects fulfilled their prophecies as did the experimenters who had prophesied the perception of failure by their subjects.

During the conduct of this replication experiment, Adair and Epstein tape-recorded the experimenters' instructions to their subjects. The second experiment was then conducted not by experimenters at all, but by tape recordings of experimenters' voices reading standard instructions to their subjects. When the tape-recorded instructions had originally been read by experimenters expecting success perception by their subjects, the tape recordings evoked greater success perceptions from their subjects. When the tape-recorded instructions had originally been read by experimenters expecting failure perception by their subjects, the tape recordings evoked greater failure perceptions from their subjects. Self-fulfilling prophecies, it seems, can come about as a result of the prophet's voice alone. Since, in the experiment described, all prophets read standard instructions, self-fulfillment of prophecies may be brought about by the tone in which the prophet prophesies.

Early in the history of the research program on self-fulfilling prophecies in the behavioral sciences it had been thought that a process of operant conditioning might be responsible for their operation (Rosenthal, 1966). It was thought that perhaps every time the subject gave a response consistent with the experimenter's expectancy, the experimenter might look more pleasant, or smile, or glance at the subject approvingly, even without the experimenter's being aware of his own reinforcing responses. The experimenter, in other words, might unwittingly have taught the subject what responses were the desired ones. Several experiments were analyzed to see whether this hypothesis of operant conditioning might apply. If it did apply, we would expect that the subjects' responses gradually would become more like those prophesied by the experimenter—that there would be a learning curve for subjects, but no learning curve was found. On the contrary, it turned out that the subjects' very first responses were about as much affected by their experimenters' expectancies as were their very last responses. Since the very first response, by definition, cannot follow any unwitting reinforcement by the experimenter, the mechanism of operant conditioning can be ruled out as necessary to the communication of experimenters' expectancies.

True, there was no learning curve for subjects, but there seemed to be a learning curve for experimenters. Several studies showed that expected results became more likely as more subjects were contacted by each experimenter (Rosenthal, 1966; 1969). In fact, there was very little expectancy effect in evidence for just the very first-seen subjects. If the experimenter was indeed learning to increase the unintended influence of his prophecy, who would be the teacher? Probably the subject. It seems reasonable to think of a subject's responding in the direction of the experimenter's hypothesis as a reinforcing event. Therefore, whatever the covert communicative behavior of the experimenter that preceded the subject's reinforcement, it will be more likely to recur. Subjects, then, may quite unintentionally shape the experimenter's unintended communicative behavior. Not only does the experimenter influence his subjects to respond in the expected manner, but his subjects may well evoke just that unintended behavior that will lead them to respond increasingly as prophesied. Probably neither subject nor experimenter "knows" just exactly what the unintended communication behavior is—and neither do we.

### EXPERIMENTER EXPECTATIONS: METHODOLOGICAL IMPLICATIONS

The implications of the research on the effects of the experimenter's expectancy on the results of his research are of two general kinds; those that are primarily methodological and those that are more substantive. Our focus in this paper is more on some of the substantive implications but brief mention may be made of some implications for how we conduct research in the behavioral sciences.

To the extent that the results of behavioral research are affected by the expectation of the experimenter, we can only place a lessened confidence in these results. But to say that our confidence is weakened in the results of many experiments as they are actually conducted is not to say that our confidence is weakened in the basic logic of the experimental method. We must simply take those, only sometimes inconvenient, extra precautions required to prevent or reduce expectancy effects or those procedures designed to permit us to assess whether they have or have not affected the results of our research.

It is possible for research investigators to employ, as data collectors, research assistants who have not been told the purpose of the research. As long as the investigator's expectation can be kept from these data collectors, there should be no effects attributable to the investigator's expectation. There are some experiments in which the experimenter need have no direct contact with the subjects and, in such studies, automated data collection systems should be employed to reduce any possibility of the unintended influence of the experimenter's expectation. When a human data collector is required and that is often the case, at least the amount of contact between experimenter and subject can be reduced in order to minimize any opportunity for unintended communication.

Not only because of the danger of expectancy effects but also because of the general nature of other experimenter effects, it would be desirable to employ larger numbers of experimenters for each study than are now routinely employed. That would permit the assessment of the extent to which different experimenters obtained different results and, in any area of psychological research, that is a fact worth knowing.

Only one final technique for the control of expectancy effects can be mentioned here and that is the employment of special control groups known as "expectancy controls." In any experiment employing an experimental (treatment) and a control (no treatment) condition, two extra groups are added. In one of these added groups, the data collector is led to believe that no treatment has been administered when, in fact, it has. In the other added group, the data collector is led to believe that the treatment has been administered when, in fact, it has not. Such a research design permits the assessment of the effects in which the investigator is primarily interested as well as the assessment of the magnitude or complicating effect of the experimenter's expectancy (Rosenthal, 1966). It may be noted that the important studies by Burnham (1966) and by Cooper et al. (1967), both described earlier, were the first to employ this basic research paradigm.

## TEACHER EXPECTATIONS

Most of what has been said so far may seem to be not very directly related to the title of this chapter and of this section. Yet what has been said is a necessary introduction to this section, an introduction designed to emphasize that there is nothing very special about the idea that a teacher's expectation about her pupils' performance can come to serve as a partial determinant of those pupils' performance. If rats can become brighter when expected to by their experimenter, it can hardly be thought to be farfetched to suppose that children could also become brighter when expected to by their teacher. Kenneth Clark (1963), in any case, has presented the view for some time that culturally disadvantaged children are the unfortunate victims of teachers' educational self-fulfilling prophecies. The following experiment, then, was simply an extension of the earlier work on interpersonal expectations (Rosenthal and Jacobson, 1968).

All of the children in an elementary school serving a lower socioeconomic status neighborhood were administered a nonverbal test of intelligence. The test was disguised as one that would predict intellectual "blooming." There were 18 classrooms in the school, three at each of the six grade levels. Within each grade level the three classrooms were composed of children with above average ability, average ability, and below average ability, respectively. Within each of the 18 classrooms approximately 20% of the children were chosen at random to form the experimental group. Each teacher was given the names of the children from her class who were in the experimental condition. The teacher was told that these children had scored on the "test for intellectual blooming" such that they would show remarkable gains in intellectual competence during the next eight months of school. The difference between the experimental group and the control group children, then, was in the mind of the teacher.

At the end of the school year, eight months later, all the children were retested with the same IQ test. This intelligence test, while relatively nonverbal in the sense of requiring no speaking, reading or writing, was not entirely nonverbal. Actually there were two subtests, one requiring a greater comprehension of English—a kind of picture vocabulary test. The other subtest required less ability to understand any spoken language but more ability to reason abstractly. For shorthand purposes we refer to the former as a "verbal" subtest and to the latter as a "reasoning" subtest. The pretest correlation between these subtests was +.42.

For the school as a whole, the children of the experimental group showed only a slightly greater gain in verbal IQ (2 points) than did the control group children. However, in total IQ (4 points) and especially in reasoning IQ (7 points), the experimental group children gained appreciably more than did the control group children.

When educational theorists have discussed the possible effects of teachers' expectations, they have usually referred to the children at lower levels of scholastic achievement. It was interesting, therefore, to find that in the present study, children of the highest level of achievement showed as great a benefit as did the children of the lowest level of achievement of having their teachers expect intellectual gains.

At the end of the school year of this study, all teachers were asked to describe the classroom behavior of their pupils. Those children from whom intellectual growth was expected were described as having a significantly better chance of becoming successful in the future, as significantly more interesting, curious, and happy. There was a tendency, too, for these children to be seen as more appealing, adjusted, and affectionate and as lower in the need for social approval. In short, the children from whom intellectual growth was expected became more intellectually alive and autonomous or at least were so perceived by their teachers.

We have already seen that the children of the experimental group gained more intellectually so that perhaps it was the fact of such gaining that accounted for the more favorable ratings of these childrens' behavior and aptitude. But a great many of the control group children also gained in IQ during the course of the year. We might expect that those who gained more intellectually among these undesignated children would also be rated more favorably by their teachers. Such was not the case. The more the control group children gained in IQ the more they were regarded as less well-adjusted, as less interesting, and as less affectionate. From these results it would seem that when children who are expected to grow intellectually do so, they are considerably benefited in other ways as well. When children who are not especially expected to develop intellectually do so, they seem either to show accompanying undesirable behavior or at least are perceived by their teachers as showing such undesirable behavior. If a child is to show intellectual gain it seems to be better for his real or perceived intellectual vitality and for his real or perceived mental health if his teacher has been expecting him to grow intellectually. It appears worthwhile to investigate further the proposition that there may be hazards to unpredicted intellectual growth.

A closer analysis of these data, broken down by whether the children were in the high, medium, or low ability tracks or groups showed that these effects of unpredicted intellectual growth were due primarily to the children of the low ability group. When these slow track children were in the control group so that no intellectual gains were expected of them, they were rated more unfavorably by their teachers if they did show gains in IQ. The greater their IQ gains, the more unfavorably were they rated, both as to mental health and as to intellectual vitality. Even when the slow track children were in the experimental group, so that IQ gains were expected of them, they were not rated as favorably relative to their control group peers as were the children of the high or medium track, despite the fact that they gained as much in IQ relative to the control group children as did the experimental group children of the high group. It may be difficult for a slow track child, even one whose IQ is rising, to be seen by his teacher as a well-adjusted child, and as a potentially successful child, intellectually.

The effects of teacher expectations had been most dramatic when measured in terms of pupils' gains in reasoning IQ. These effects on reasoning IQ, however, were not uniform for boys and girls. Although all the children of this lower socioeconomic status school gained dramatically in IQ, it was only among the girls that greater gains were shown by those who were expected to bloom compared to the children of the control group. Among the boys, those who were expected to bloom gained less than did the children of the control group.

In part to check this finding, the experiment originally conducted on the West Coast was repeated in a small Midwestern town (Rosenthal and Evans, 1968). This time the children were from substantial middle-class backgrounds, and this time the results were completely and significantly reversed. Now it was the boys who showed the benefits of favorable teacher expectations. Among the girls, those who were expected to bloom intellectually gained less in reasoning IQ than did the girls of the control group. Just as in the West Coast experiment, however, all the children showed substantial gains in IQ. These results, while they suggest the potentially powerful effects of teacher expectations, also indicate the probable complexity of these effects as a function of pupils' sex, social class, and, as time will no doubt show, other variables as well.

In both the experiments described, IQ gains were assessed after a full academic year had elapsed. However, the results of another experiment suggest that teacher expectations can significantly affect students' intellectual performance in a period as short as two months (Anderson and Rosenthal, 1968). In this small experiment, the 25 children were mentally retarded boys with an average pretest IQ of 46. Expectancy effects were significant only for reasoning IQ and only in interaction with membership in a group receiving special remedial reading instruction in addition to participating in the school's summer day camp program. Among these specially tutored boys those who were expected to bloom showed an expectancy disadvantage of nearly 12 IQ points; among the untutored boys who were participating only in the school's summer day camp program, those who were expected to bloom showed an expectancy advantage of just over three IQ points. (For verbal IQ, in contrast, the expectancy disadvantage of the tutored boys was less than one IQ point, while the expectancy advantage for the untutored boys was over two points).

The results described were based on post-testing only two months after the initiation of the experiment. Follow-up testing was undertaken seven months after the end of the basic experiment. In reasoning IQ, the boys who had been both tutored and expected to bloom intellectually made up the expectancy disadvantage they had shown after just two months. Now, their performance change was just like that of the control group children, both groups showing an IQ loss of four points over the nine month period. Compared to these boys who had been given both or neither of the two experimental treatments, the boys who had been given either tutoring or the benefit of favorable expectations showed significantly greater gains in reasoning IQ scores. Relative to the control group children, those who were tutored showed a 10 point advantage while those who were expected to bloom showed a 12 point advantage. While both tutoring and a favorable teacher expectation were effective in raising relative IQ scores, it appeared that when these two treatments were applied simultaneously, they were ineffective in producing IQ gains over the period from the beginning of the experiment to the nine month follow-up. One possible explanation of this finding is that the presence of both treatments simultaneously, led the boys to perceive too much pressure. The same pattern of results reported for reasoning IQ was also obtained when verbal IQ and total IQ were considered, though the interaction was significant only in the case of total IQ.

In the experiment under discussion, a number of other measures of the boys' behavior were available as were observations of the day camp counselors' behavior toward the boys. Preliminary analysis suggests that boys who had been expected to bloom intellectually were given less attention by the counselors and developed a greater degree of independence compared to the boys of the control group.

Another study, this time conducted in an East Coast school with upper middle-class pupils, again showed the largest effect of teachers' expectancies to occur when the measure was of reasoning IQ (Conn, Edwards, Rosenthal, and Crowne, 1968). In this study, both the boys and girls who were expected to bloom intellectually showed greater gains in reasoning IQ than did the boys and girls of the control group and the magnitude of the expectancy effect favored the girls very slightly. Also in this study, we had available a measure of the children's accuracy in judging the vocal expressions of emotion of adult speakers. It was of considerable theoretical interest to find that greater benefits of favorable teacher expectations accrued to those children who were more accurate in judging the emotional tone expressed in an adult female's voice. These findings, taken together with the research of Adair and Epstein (1968) and others (Rosenthal, 1969) described earlier, give a strong suggestion that vocal cues may be important in the covert communication of interpersonal expectations in both teachers and psychological experimenters.

In all the experiments described so far, the same IQ measure was employed, the Flanagan (1960) Tests of General Ability. Also employing the same instrument, Claiborn (1968) found among first graders a tendency for children he designated as potential bloomers to gain less in IQ than the children of the control group (two-tail $p < .15$). A similar tendency was obtained by Rosenthal and Anderson (1969) employing somewhat older children (two-tail, $p < .17$).

With fifth grade boys as his subjects and males as teachers, Pitt (1956) found no effect on achievement scores of arbitrarily adding or subtracting 10 IQ points to the children's records. In her study, Heiserman (1967) found no effect of teacher expectations on her 7th graders' stated levels of occupational aspiration.

There have been two studies in which teachers' expectations were varied not for specific children within a classroom but rather for classrooms as a whole (Biegen, 1968; Flowers, 1966). In both cases the performance gains were greater for those classrooms expected by their teachers to show the better performance.

A radically different type of performance measure was employed in the research by Burnham (1968); not intelligence or scholastic achievement this time but swimming ability. His subjects were boys and girls aged 7–14 attending a summer camp for the disadvantaged. None of the children could swim at the beginning of the two week experimental period. Half the children were alleged to the camp staff to have shown unusual potential for learning to swim as judged from a battery of psychological tests. Children were, of course, assigned to the "high potential" group at random. At the end of the two week period of the experiment all the children were retested on the standard Red Cross Beginner Swimmer Test. Those children who had been expected to show greater improvement in swimming ability showed greater improvement than did the children of the control group.

In their experiment, Meichenbaum, Bowers, and Ross (1968) also employed a very different type of criterion variable: appropriateness of classroom behavior. The choice of this variable was itself particularly appropriate in view of the fact that these workers employed as their research population a sample of institutionalized adolescent female offenders. Two weeks before the beginning of this experiment, classroom observers, who knew nothing of the experimental manipulations to come, began to record the behavior of both the girls and their teachers. These observations continued through the entire experiment, which remarkably enough, lasted only two weeks. Within two weeks after teachers were given the names of the "potential bloomers", the designated children already showed a significantly greater improvement in classroom behavior than did the children of the control group. This experiment was particularly important in suggesting that the benefits of favorable teacher expectations were associated with an increase in the teachers' positively toned attention to the designated children.

We may conclude now with the brief description of just one more experiment, this one conducted by W. Victor Beez (1968) who kindly made his data available for the analyses to follow. This time the pupils were 60 preschoolers from a summer Headstart program. Each child was taught the meaning of a series of symbols by one teacher. Half the 60 teachers had been led to expect good symbol-learning and half had been led to expect poor symbol-learning. Most (77%) of the children alleged to have better intellectual prospects learned five or more symbols but only 13% of the children alleged to have poorer intellectual prospects learned five or more symbols. In this study the children's actual performance was assessed by an experimenter who did not know what the child's teacher had been told about the child's intellectual prospects. Teachers who had been given favorable expectations about their pupil tried to teach more symbols to their pupil than did the teachers given unfavorable expectations about their pupil. The difference in teaching effort was dramatic. Eight or more symbols were taught by 87% of the teachers expecting better performance, but only 13% of the teachers expecting poorer performance tried to teach that many symbols to their pupil.

These results suggest that a teacher's expectation about a pupil's performance may sometimes be translated not into subtle vocal nuances or general increases in positively toned attention but rather into overt and even dramatic alterations in teaching style. The magnitude of the effect of teacher expectations found by Beez is also worthy of comment. In all the earlier studies described, one group of children had been singled out for favorable expectations while nothing was said of the remaining children of the control group. In Beez's short-term experiment it seemed more justified to give negative as well as positive expectations about some of the children. Perhaps the very large effects of teacher expectancy obtained by Beez were due to the creation of strong equal but opposite expectations in the minds of the different teachers. Since strong negative expectations doubtless exist in the real world of classrooms, Beez's procedure may give the better estimate of the effects of teacher expectations as they occur in everyday life.

In the experiment by Beez it seems clear that the dramatic differences in teaching style accounted at least in part for the dramatic differences in pupil learning. However, not all of the obtained differences in learners' learning was due to the differences in teachers' teaching. Within each condition of teacher expectation, for example, there was no relationship between number of symbols taught and number of symbols learned. In addition, it was also possible to compare the performances of just those children of the two conditions who had been given an exactly equal amount of teaching benefit. Even holding teaching benefits constant, the difference favored significantly the children believed to be superior though the magnitude of the effect was now diminished by nearly half.

We have now seen at least a brief description of 13 studies of the effects of interpersonal expectancies in natural learning situations. That is too many to hold easily in mind and Table 3 provides a convenient summary. (For each experiment the directional standard normal deviate ($z$) associated with each $p$ level is given as well as a brief identification of the dependent variables employed. As was the custom in an earlier paper (Rosenthal, 1969), a standard normal deviate greater than $-1.28$ and smaller than $+1.28$ has

Table 3   TEACHER EXPECTANCY EFFECTS IN
13 EXPERIMENTS

| *Study* | *Results* | | *Criterion* |
|---|---|---|---|
| | $p$ | $z$ | |
| 1. Anderson & Rosenthal, 1968 | — | 0.00[a] | Total IQ |
| 2. Beez, 1968 | .000002 | $+4.67$ | Symbol learning |
| 3. Biegen, 1968 | .002 | $+2.89$[b] | Achievement |
| 4. Burnham, 1968; Burnham & Hartsough, 1968 | .005 | $+2.61$[a] | Swimming score |
| 5. Claiborn, 1968           $(-)$ | .08 | $-1.45$[a] | Total IQ |
| 6. Conn, Edwards, Rosenthal, & Crowne, 1968 | — | 0.00[a] | Total IQ |
| 7. Flowers, 1966 | .06 | $+1.60$ | Achievement + IQ |
| 8. Heiserman, 1967 | — | 0.00 | Aspiration |
| 9. Meichenbaum, Bowers, & Ross, 1968 | .02 | $+2.02$[b] | Classroom behavior |
| 10. Pitt, 1956 | — | 0.00 | Achievement |
| 11. Rosenthal & Anderson,     $(-)$ 1969 | .08 | $-1.40$[b] | Total IQ |
| 12. Rosenthal & Evans, 1968 | — | 0.00[a, b] | Total IQ |
| 13. Rosenthal & Jacobson, 1968 | .02 | $+2.11$[a] | Total IQ |
| Overall | .0002 | $+3.61$ | |

[a] Indicates the interaction of teacher expectancy and some other variable.
[b] Preliminary data.

been recorded as zero.) Of the five experiments tabulated as showing no main effect of teacher expectation, it should be noted that at least three of them showed significant interactions of teacher expectation with some other primary variable such as special tutoring (study 1), accuracy of emotion perception (6), and sex of pupil (12). The combined one-tail $p$ of the main effects of teacher expectancy in the studies shown in Table 3 is less than 1 in 5,000. It would take an additional 50 studies of a mean associated $z$ value of 0.00 to bring the overall combined $p$ to above .05.

Shall we view this set of experiments in natural learning situations in isolation or would it be wiser to see them simply as more of the same type of experiment that has been discussed throughout this paper? Since the type of experimental manipulation involved in the laboratory studies is essentially the same as that employed in the studies beyond the laboratory, it seems more parsimonious to view all the studies as members of the same set. If, in addition to the communality of experimental procedures, we find it plausible to conclude a communality of outcome patterns between the laboratory and field experiments, perhaps we can have the greater convenience and power of speaking of just one type of effect of interpersonal expectancy. Table 4

Table 4 PERCENTAGE OF STUDIES OF EXPECTANCY EFFECT OBTAINING RESULTS AT VARIOUS *P* LEVELS AMONG EXPERIMENTERS AND TEACHERS

| *p (one-tail)* | *Experimenters* | *Teachers* | *Total* |
|---|---|---|---|
| $< .10$ | 48% | 46% | 47% |
| $< .05$ | 34% | 38% | 34% |
| $< .01$ | 17% | 23% | 17% |
| $< .001$ | 12% | 8% | 11% |
| $< .0001$ | 5% | 8% | 5% |
| Grand sum $z$ | + 100.86 | + 13.05 | + 113.91 |
| $\sqrt{}$ Number of Experiments | $\sqrt{103}$ | $\sqrt{13}$ | $\sqrt{116}$ |
| Combined $z$ | + 9.94 | + 3.61 | + 10.58 |

allows each reader to make his own judgment or test for "goodness of fit." At each level of $p$ we find the proportion of laboratory and educational studies reaching that or a lower level of $p$. The agreement between the two types of studies appears to be remarkably close.

If there were a systematic difference in sample size between studies conducted in laboratories and those involving teachers, then we might expect to find that for similar $z$s or $p$s the average effects would be smaller in magnitude for the set comprised of larger sample sizes. For this reason it seems necessary also to compare magnitudes of expectancy effect for studies involving experimenters and teachers. Table 5 shows this comparison. For

Table 5 PERCENTAGE OF EXPERIMENTERS AND TEACHERS SHOWING EXPECTANCY EFFECTS

| | *Experimenters* | *Teachers* | *Total* |
|---|---|---|---|
| Number of Studies Included | 59 | 7 | 66 |
| Percentage of These Studies with $p < .10$ (One-tail) | 49% | 43% | 48% |
| Number of Experimenters or Teachers | 548 | 140 | 688 |
| Mean Number per Study | 9 | 20 | 10 |
| Percentage of Biased Experimenters or Teachers | 70% | 67% | 70% |

59 studies of experimenters and for seven studies of teachers it was possible to calculate the proportion of each that was affected in the predicted direction by their expectancy. Again the agreement is very good. About 7 out of

10 experimenters or teachers can be expected to show the effects of their expectation on the performance of their subjects or pupils.

This paper began its discussion of interpersonal expectancy effects by suggesting that the expectancy of the behavioral researcher might function as a self-fulfilling prophecy. This unintended effect of the research hypothesis itself must be regarded as a potentially damaging artifact. But interpersonal self-fulfilling prophecies do not operate only in laboratories and while, when there, they may act as artifacts, they are more than that. Interpersonal expectancy effects occur also among teachers and there seems no reason to doubt it, among others as well. What started life as an artifact continues as an interpersonal variable of theoretical and practical importance.

## SOME IMPLICATIONS

The implications of the research described in this paper are of several kinds. There are methodological implications for the conduct of educational research, and these have been discussed elsewhere in detail (Rosenthal, 1966; Rosenthal and Jacobson, 1968). There are implications for the further investigation of unintentional influence processes, especially when these processes result in interpersonal self-fulfilling prophecies, and some of these have been discussed. Finally, there are some possible implications for the educational enterprise, and some of these will be suggested briefly.

Over time, our educational policy question has changed from "who ought to be educated" to "who is capable of being educated." The ethical question has been traded in for the scientific question. For those children whose educability is in doubt there is a label. They are the educationally, or culturally, or socioeconomically deprived children and, as things stand now, they appear not to be able to learn as do those who are more advantaged. The advantaged and the disadvantaged differ in parental income, in parental values, in scores on various tests of achievement and ability, and often in skin color and other phenotypic expressions of genetic heritage. Quite inseparable from these differences between the advantaged and the disadvantaged are the differences in their teachers' expectations for what they can achieve in school. There are no experiments to show that a change in pupils' skin color will lead to improved intellectual performance. There are, however, the experiments described in this paper to show that change in teacher expectation can lead to improved intellectual performance and related behaviors.

In none of the relevant experiments was anything done directly for the "disadvantaged" child. There were no crash programs to improve his school achievement, no trips to museums or art galleries. There was only the belief that the children bore watching, that they had intellectual competencies that would in due course be revealed. What was done in these programs of educational change was done directly for the teacher, only indirectly for her pupils. Perhaps, then, it is the teacher to whom we should direct more of our research attention. If we could learn how she is able to effect dramatic improvement in her pupils' competence without formal changes in her teaching methods, then we could teach other teachers to do the same. If further research shows that it is possible to select teachers whose untrained interactional style does for most of her pupils what teachers did for the allegedly special children described in this paper, it may be possible to combine sophisticated teacher selection and placement with teacher training to optimize the learning of all pupils.

As teacher training institutions begin to teach the possibility that teachers' expectations of their pupils' performance may serve as self-fulfilling prophecies, there may be a new expectancy created. The new expectancy may be that children can learn more than had been believed possible, an expectation held by many educational theorists, though for quite different reasons (e.g. Bruner, 1960; Skinner, 1968). The new expectancy, at the very least, will make it more difficult when they encounter the educationally disadvantaged, for teachers to shrug and say or think, "Well, after all, what can you expect?" As Lenore Jacobson has said: "The man on the street may be permitted his opinions and prophecies of the unkempt children loitering in a dreary schoolyard. The teacher in the schoolroom may need to learn that those same prophecies within her may be fulfilled; she is no casual passerby. Perhaps Pygmalion in the classroom is more her role."

## REFERENCES

ADAIR, J. G. and J. S. EPSTEIN, Verbal cues in the mediation of experimenter bias. *Psychological Reports*, 1968, 22, 1045–53.

ALLPORT, G. W., The role of expectancy. In H. Cantril (ed.), *Tensions that cause wars*. Urbana, Illinois: University of Illinois Press, 1950. Pp. 43–78.

ANDERSON, D. F., and R. ROSENTHAL, Some effects of interpersonal expectancy and social interaction on institutionalized retarded children. *Proceedings of the 76th Annual Convention of the American Psychological Association*, 1968, 479–80.

BEEZ, W. V., Influence of biased psychological reports on teacher behavior and pupil performance. *Proceedings of the 76th Annual Convention of the American Psychological Association*, 1968, 605–6.

BIEGEN, D. A., Unpublished data. University of Cincinnati, 1968.

BRUNER, J. S., *The process of education*. Cambridge, Mass.: Harvard University Press, 1960.

BURNHAM, J. R., Experimenter bias and lesion labeling. Unpublished manuscript, Purdue University, 1966.

———, Effects of experimenter's expectancies on children's ability to learn to swim. Unpublished master's thesis, Purdue University, 1968.

———, and D. M. HARTSOUGH, Effect of experimenter's expectancies ("the Rosenthal effect") on children's ability to learn to swim. Paper presented at the meeting of the Midwestern Psychological Association, Chicago, May, 1968.

CLAIBORN, W. L., An investigation of the relationship between teacher expectancy, teacher behavior and pupil performance. Unpublished doctoral dissertation, Syracuse University, 1968.

CLARK, K. B., Educational stimulation of racially disadvantaged children. In A. H. Passow (ed.), *Education in depressed areas*. New York: Bureau of Publications, Teachers College, Columbia University, 1963. pp. 142–62.

CONN, L. K., C. N. EDWARDS, R. ROSENTHAL, and D. CROWNE, Perception of emotion and response to teachers' expectancy by elementary school children. *Psychological Reports*, 1968, *22*, 27–34.

COOPER, J., L. EISENBERG, J. ROBERT, and B. S. DOHRENWEND, The effect of experimenter expectancy and preparatory effort on belief in the probable occurrence of future events. *Journal of Social Psychology*, 1967, *71*, 221–26.

FLANAGAN, J. C., *Test of general ability: technical report*. Chicago: Science Research Associates, 1960.

FLOWERS, C. E., Effects of an arbitrary accelerated group placement on the tested academic achievement of educationally disadvantaged students. Unpublished doctoral dissertation, Teachers College, Columbia University, 1966.

HEISERMAN, M. S., The relationship between teacher expectations and pupil occupational aspirations. Unpublished master's thesis, Iowa State University, Ames, 1967.

JOHNSON, R. W., Subject performance as affected by experimenter expectancy, sex of experimenter, and verbal reinforcement. Unpublished master's thesis, University of New Brunswick, 1967.

LARRABEE, L. L., and L. D. KLEINSASSER, The effect of experimenter bias on WISC performance. Unpublished manuscript, Psychological Associates, St. Louis, 1967.

MARWIT, S. J., An investigation of the communication of tester-bias means of modeling. Unpublished doctoral dissertation, State University of New York at Buffalo, 1968.

MEICHENBAUM, D. H., K. S. BOWERS, and R. R. ROSS, A behavioral analysis of teacher expectancy effect. Unpublished manuscript, University of Waterloo, 1968.

MERTON, R. K., The self-fulfilling prophecy. *Antioch Review*, 1948, *8*, 193–210.

PFUNGST, O., *Clever Hans (the horse of Mr. von Osten): a contribution to experimental, animal, and human psychology*. (Translated by C. L. Rahn) New York: Holt, 1911. Republished by Holt, Rinehart and Winston, 1965.

PITT, C. C. V., An experimental study of the effects of teachers' knowledge or incorrect knowledge of pupil IQ's on teachers' attitudes and practices and pupils' attitudes and achievement. Unpublished doctoral dissertation, Columbia University, 1956.

RAFFETTO, A. M., Experimenter effects on subjects' reported hallucinatory experiences under visual and auditory deprivation. Paper presented at the meeting of the Midwestern Psychological Association, Chicago, May, 1968.

ROSENTHAL, R., Clever Hans: a case study of scientific method. Introduction to Pfungst, O., *Clever Hans: (the horse of Mr. von Osten)*. New York: Holt, Rinehart, & Winston, 1965. Pp. ix-xlii.

————, The effect of the experimenter on the results of psychological research. In B. A. Maher (ed.), *Progress in experimental personality research*. Vol. 1. New York: Academic Press. 1964, Pp. 79–114. (a)

————, Experimenter outcome-orientation and the results of the psychological experiment. *Psychological Bulletin*, 1964, *61*, 405–12. (b)

————, *Experimenter effects in behavioral research.* New York: Appleton-Century-Crofts, 1966.

————, Interpersonal expectations: Effects of the experimenter's hypothesis. In R. Rosenthal and R. L. Rosnow (Eds.) *Artifact in behavioral research.* New York: Academic Press, 1969.

————, and D. F. ANDERSON, Teacher behavior and the mediation of teacher expectancy effects. Unpublished data, Harvard University, 1969.

————, and J. EVANS, Unpublished data, Harvard University, 1968.

————, and K. L. FODE, The effect of experimenter bias on the performance of the albino rat. *Behavioral Science,* 1963, *8,* 183–89. (a)

————, and ————, Three experiments in experimenter bias. *Psychological Reports,* 1963, *12,* 491–511. (b)

————, and L. JACOBSON, *Pygmalion in the classroom: Teacher expectation and pupils' intellectual development.* New York: Holt, Rinehart and Winston, 1968.

SKINNER, B. F., Teaching science in high school—What is wrong? *Science,* 1968, *159,* 704–10.

ZOBLE, E. J., Interaction of subject and experimenter expectancy effects is a tone length discrimination task. Unpublished AB thesis, Franklin and Marshall College, 1968.

## APPENDIX A   EXPERIMENTER EXPECTANCY EFFECTS OBTAINED IN 33 LABORATORIES

| *Investigator*[a] | *Location* | *Number of Studies* | *Overall z*[b] | *Percentage of Studies with $p < .10$ (One-tail)* |
|---|---|---|---|---|
| 1. Adair | Manitoba | 6 | +2.04[c] | 50% |
| 2. Adler | Wellesley | 3 | 0.00 | 33% |
| 3. Barber | Medfield[d] | 5 | 0.00[c] | 00% |
| 4. Becker | Saskatchewan | 3 | 0.00 | 00% |
| 5. Bootzin | Purdue | 3 | 0.00[c] | 67% |
| 6. Burnham | Earlham | 1 | +1.95 | 100% |
| 7. Carlson | Hamline | 2 | 0.00[c] | 00% |
| 8. Cooper | C C, CUNY | 1 | +3.37 | 100% |
| 9. Getter | Connecticut | 1 | 0.00 | 00% |
| 10. Harrington | Iowa State | 2 | +2.54 | 100% |
| 11. Hartry | Occidental | 2 | +6.15 | 100% |
| 12. Horn | George Washington | 1 | +2.01 | 100% |
| 13. Ison | Rochester | 2 | +5.11 | 100% |
| 14. Johnson | New Brunswick | 1 | +3.89[c] | 100% |
| 15. Kennedy | Tennessee | 2 | +1.61[c] | 50% |
| 16. Larrabee | South Dakota | 1 | +1.60 | 100% |
| 17. Marcia | SUNY, Buffalo | 2 | +3.58 | 100% |
| 18. Masling | SUNY, Buffalo | 2 | +1.45[c] | 50% |
| 19. McFall | Ohio State | 2 | 0.00[c] | 00% |
| 20. Minor | Chicago | 4 | 0.00[c] | 25% |
| 21. Moffat | British Columbia | 1 | 0.00 | 00% |
| 22. Peel | Memphis State | 1 | +3.58 | 100% |
| 23. Persinger | Fergus Falls[d] | 2 | +2.50[c] | 100% |

APPENDIX A (Cont'd)

| Investigator[a] | Location | Number of Studies | Overall $z$[b] | Percentage of Studies with $p < .10$ (One-tail) |
|---|---|---|---|---|
| 24. Raffetto | San Francisco State | 1 | +5.24[c] | 100% |
| 25. Rosenthal | Harvard | 35 | +4.83[c] | 49% |
| 26. Silverman | SUNY, Buffalo | 1 | +1.88[c] | 100% |
| 27. Timaeus | Cologne | 3 | 0.00[c] | 33% |
| 28. Uno | Keio (Tokyo) | 5 | −1.86[c] | 00% |
| 29. Wartenberg-Ekren | Marquette | 1 | 0.00 | 00% |
| 30. Weick | Purdue | 1 | +2.33 | 100% |
| 31. Wessler | St. Louis | 3 | 0.00[c] | 33% |
| 32. Zegers | Illinois | 1 | 0.00 | 00% |
| 33. Zoble | Franklin & Marshall | 2 | +4.06 | 100% |
| | Total | (103) | +57.86 | |
| | Combined $z$ | — | +10.08 | ($p$ infinitely small) |
| | Mean $p$ | | .040 | |
| | Median $p$ | | .054 | |

a For references to specific experiments see Rosenthal (1969).
b Standard normal deviate associated with overall $p$ per laboratory.
c Indicates that experimenter expectancy interacted with other variables at $z > /1.28/$.
d Indicates a state hospital. All other locations are colleges or universities.

FRED L. STRODTBECK

# 5. THE HIDDEN CURRICULUM IN THE MIDDLE-CLASS HOME

One alarming social problem in America today concerns those families who, despite our present efforts to help them, are still unable to rear their children in a way that will make them self-sufficient as adults. *Time* magazine expresses it this way:

> The tragedy of Harlem is that yet another generation of such men is being bred because they cannot break out of the vicious cycle of the ghetto: poor

Reprinted from *Urban Education and Cultural Deprivation*, C. D. Hunnicutt (ed.) (Syracuse, N.Y.: Syracuse University Division of Summer Sessions, 1964), by permission of the publisher.

schooling, leading to a low-paying job or no job at all, leading to housing in a rundown neighborhood, leading anew to poor schooling for the children (*Time,* July 31, 1964, p. 16).

A generation ago, the comparable popular explanation would have started the cycle with reference to poverty; today it is started with a reference to poor schooling. It is no longer believed that the central problem is poverty because, in its grosser economic aspects, poverty alone could be remedied. Morgan (1962) has pointed out that for about ten billion dollars a year the income of every family in the nation now below the subsistance level could be raised to it. Morgan views the problem of poverty as having become the dilemma of giving aid without creating continuing dependency upon governmental support.

At this moment, perhaps for the first time in the history of our nation, one can look objectively at the economic cost of maintaining the poor and know that we can afford this expenditure—if there is no long-range alternative. Most would be willing, however, to spend even more than that amount in efforts to discover an alternative which would reduce the magnitude of the long range problem. As the *Time* quotation indicates, in Harlem and elsewhere in the great cities, it is to education that America is turning for a solution.

In such matters, one must find for himself the balance of optimism or pessimism which is best matched to his own involvement, but judging from past efforts, the chances of failure are great. Our most recent well-intentioned and single-minded effort to solve such problems has involved housing. As a prelude to the discussion of education, let me comment upon a recent study of the effects of public housing. I draw upon a "before and after" study of a carefully chosen sample of 600 persons who were moved from crowded tenements to public housing. The investigators, Wilner and others, regretfully concluded in their 1962 report that:

> In general...it is not clear...that the change from bad to good housing has brought...distinguishable alteration in relations among persons within the family.

There was no greater freedom from illness, no difference in the rate of pregnancies, no improvement in the children's mean arithmetic and reading test scores. There was no change in concern for the larger community, no improvement in self-concept, and very little heightening of aspiration for the husband's job or the children's education. This study does report that the rehoused group liked the space they occupied better and their neighbors more—findings which, though positive, certainly fall below the community's expectations for what might be accomplished by improving housing at great public expense.

The mushrooming Aid to Dependent Children Program (hereafter called ADC) is assumed to function like improved housing—it is supposed to provide partial rehabilitation by meeting short-run needs so that the families involved can later assume responsibility for their own welfare. Burgess and Price (1963), in a study of a national sample of 5,398 ADC cases reach very pessimistic conclusions as to the effectiveness of the rehabilitation. At the time their cases were closed, 68 per cent of all families in the sample earned less than 60 dollars per month. Forty-seven per cent of ADC children were either educationally retarded or out of school between the ages of 14 and 17. By 18 years of age, only 25 per cent had completed high school. Long-term evidence for failure of rehabilitation was provided by the large number of cases in which relief was a family tradition. Forty per cent of the recipients had grown up in homes which had received public assistance. Here again, one can only conclude that the combined efforts of public relief and the schools fall below reasonable expectations.

It is my fear that despite the limited success of housing and public assistance programs, there is still a disposition to see the problems of the dependent poor as if they were self-evident. Given the multiple handicaps of being fatherless, poor, and Negro, it scarcely seems necessary to call in a social scientist to see precisely why dependency results. Yet direct attacks on housing and supplementation of low income have not improved the situation. The schools have admittedly done poorly with the population in question, so why is it believed that they will be able to launch a more fundamental attack upon their problem? The current answer is that the schools are expected to modify their traditional methods. But is it self-evident that we know what modifications to make?

If one reasons that the curriculum of the school supplements the curriculum of the home, then the compensatory preparation of students from culturally deprived families may require an analysis of what is learned in the middle-class home.

## THE ZACHARIAS REPORT

Despite the considerable sophistication of current approaches, the "hidden curriculum" I have in mind is often overlooked. To illustrate, I shall comment upon the recommendations for the education of the deprived and segregated made by the Panel on Educational Research and Development of the President's Science Advisory Committee (1964) often known as the Zacharias Committee. The population the Committee had in mind is the "difficult thirty per cent," a population larger than the children of the dependent poor, but inclusive of them. The suggestions of the Committee tended to be focused upon amelioration of the language deficit and included the following:

> 1. Special programs are needed for helping deprived children learn to read. One approach may be to concentrate first on spoken English, encouraging children to talk in school rather than constantly admonishing them to listen, and then encourage them in reading when they take it up.

One might guess that the Committee wishes to encourage spoken-aural techniques for transforming direct, perhaps nonsyntactic and dialectical speech into standard English before taking up the problems of a written language.

The Committee suggests that unreal situations be avoided, presumably in order to make the conditions of performance less discriminatory against lower-class children. This is elaborated as follows:

> 2. The culturally-deprived child may become frustrated when he reads about middle-class privileges (such as a boy having his own room in the house). The answer may be to let the child develop his own story materials, thus giving him the freedom to shape the manner of his learning.

In repeating these recommendations, I do not mean to infer that they are all especially good. Concerning this one, I must say that having been frustrated when I read the *Just So Stories* (for not only did I not own a mongoose, I had never seen one) I am ill prepared to think about life protected from the knowledge of such relative deprivations. Carried to an extreme, being restricted to current reality could in itself be very unreal.

> 3. The deprived child should be taught arithmetic and science in intuitive, nonbookish ways.

The Committee wishes science and arithmetic to be taught in ways that will increase readiness to read, rather than making these subjects dependent upon reading skill.

> 4. Curriculum units can be designed which are self-contained and self-demonstrative; that is, units should be structured in a way which enables deprived children to discover things for themselves.

This suggestion possibly grows out of the conviction that children, engaged in building the highest possible tower out of Plasticene, can see the results of their efforts immediately. The teacher can then present the theory of Calder's "stabiles" or some other exciting engineering perspectives. The Committee believes that such approaches will keep student interest high primarily because of the intrinsic stimulation of the materials and secondarily by avoidance of the ill effects of passive listening. Both curricular objectives may well increase the school adjustment of the deprived child without affecting his position relative to nondeprived children for, if these work as most reforms do, they will elicit even better response from the middle-class child.

> 5. The teacher should aim at developing "self-scrutiny, honesty, and careful observation" through social studies to the deprived. What the child needs is a growing knowledge of who he is and what kind of a world he is living in; much effort in this area is now destroyed by irrelevance, hypocrisy, and misplaced emphasis.

The Zacharias Committee apparently assumed that they would need to work largely with persons who were not professional educators in order to gain support for this simple, uncamouflaged indictment of the current social studies curriculum. The Committee may well have identified an area in which the schools have needlessly lagged behind what the community would accept. It cannot be denied that there are "hot" topics relating to stratification which all children could better understand. But without greater specification, their brief statement is not too helpful in anticipating what the effects might be on the culturally deprived.

> 6. Deprived children should be encouraged to develop entrepreneurial skills and industry, such as those related to commerce. It is not enough just to understand the world in which they live; they should also be taught the need for inventiveness in developing new enterprises.

This suggestion I view as a kind of Bank Street Ben Franklinism. The economic part of the message does not seem sensitive to the contribution which civil service or similar bureaucratic employment makes to Negro adjustment. Opportunities which provide an organizational structure and require little capital on the part of the new recruit are of increasing importance to our economy.

The Committee apparently believes that deprived children need more unconditional demonstrations of affection from the teacher, perhaps to compensate for a harsh home life. However, if the suggestion that the teacher relate to deprived children warmly is interpreted to encourage relating as a parental surrogate, this may be inappropriate preparation for later nonfamilial roles. More generally, throughout the Zacharias report, there is little emphasis upon personality theory, the facilitation of learning through identification, or the social psychology relevant to development.

The Committee, perhaps wisely, gives more emphasis to the feasibility of institutional innovations such as keeping the school open on what amounts to a settlement house schedule, schools—not custodial nurseries—for the three- to six-year-old children of the culturally deprived, expanding facilities into buildings not designed as schools, and zoning schools with sufficient flexibility so that changes in residence will not inevitably result in changes in enrollment. They further suggest using enthusiastic amateurs in voluntary programs, promotion according to need in a nongraded elementary system, and teaching in teams to increase specialization of teachers. The schools should have music and art centers, the teachers more resource and conference rooms, and the students a $10 yearly book allowance to be used for paperbacks in whatever subject the student may be engaged. The Committee suggests that preservice teacher training internships of six months could be alternated with six-month study periods which, on occasion, could be used for special preparation related to curricular innovations.

The Committee is convinced that a school system is the "natural unit" for reform. Hence subsystems comprising about 20,000 pupils and 30 principals would be the model size unit within a big city. The audacity of this suggestion, which might lead to a great university taking over such a segment, probably justifies the existence of the Committee. We will all be interested to see how well this one works out.

The Committee takes a somewhat radical but currently popular position on testing. The Committee is convinced that "whatever the shortcoming of tests as a means of grouping children in the more fortunate segments of the population, they are slight as compared with the tests for grouping the deprived and segregated." The Committee here alludes to their belief that abilities and achievement are more complex and subtle than any qualities the tests have been able to measure. There is very little research, they believe, on the nature of complex educational attainments, on acquisition of political ideals, style in writing, mechanical comprehension, etc. Given this state of affairs, the use of tests for guidance, college entrance, and job selection may unduly (perhaps "unfairly") fix the classification of a student. As a remedy, the Committee suggests that testing be made a matter of "local option," not an item to be required by the Superintendent. At the same time, they believe it would be good to devise tests which distinguish quickly between mental retardation and what for slum children can be regarded as pseudoretardation.

This treatment of testing is to my mind an intellectually inferior answer to the question, "Are Intelligence Tests Unfair to Culturally Deprived Children?" (Ausubel, 1963). Let us hope that America can be taught that tests measure achieved functional capacity. The earlier belief that they measure *innate* potentiality should be changed. The lower-class child's failure to develop test-taking skills, responsiveness to speed requirements, and familiarity with the specific vocabulary required should not be discounted as a matter of error in testing. These lacks are realities which affect the child's classroom performance, his future job performance, and his test score. The Committee, and all persons fundamentally concerned with the education of the culturally deprived, face a dilemma which grows from this reality. Should the school environment be engineered so as to filter away the importance of verbal intelligence, or should the school environment be modified so as to cultivate verbal intelligence more effectively?

In fairness to the Committee, they have probably reasoned that deprived persons can, with proper instruction, learn reading skills later and have concluded that it is a shame to impede the growth of mechanical and related competence by relying so heavily upon reading as a tool in the lower grades. Even so interpreted, it still seems to me that the Committee may inadvertently aggravate the problem it seeks to correct. They do not have any explicit premises about the different styles of language or the social organizational context which facilitates the development of particular verbal skills. In their emphasis upon the cognitive aspects of learning, they place little importance upon the role of verbal skills in maintaining interpersonal relations and motivation.

Not only are verbal skills of importance in the complex functioning of relatively established groups, they are also important in increasing one's vulnerability to involvement in group activities and, through this, to the shaping of motivation which group activity contributes. I believe that there are general linkages between organizational structures and verbal skill and that the understanding of such linkages, if they exist, is essential to the theory of compensatory education. More particularly, it is my guess that the conditions which facilitate the development of verbal ability in children relate much less to curricular stimulus material than to power differentials and organizational considerations.

## THE CONCEPT OF PUBLIC
## AND FORMAL LANGUAGE

I am most particularly indebted to Basil Bernstein who, in his analysis of the difference between working-class and middle-class speech in England, elaborated the difference between so-called public and formal language. In our country, the gradients of usage may not be so sharply defined. For this reason, Bernstein's formulation is to be viewed as no more than a provocative hypothesis for the lower classes as a whole, but is probably much more descriptive of the difference between the language of the dependent poor and the middle classes. Thus public language is characterized by short, grammatically simple sentences which have poor syntax and are often unfinished. There is a repetitive use of conjunctions ("then," "and," "because"), and the verb is in the active mood. There are many short commands and questions, a rigid and limited use of adjectives and adverbs, and an avoidance of impersonal pronouns (such as "one" and "it") as subjects of sentences (Bernstein, 1959).

In a public language, Bernstein suggests, idiomatic phrases operate on a low level of causal generality in which descriptive, visual, and tactile symbols are frequently employed more to carry emotive impact than to develop meaning logically. In contrast, a formal language has accurate grammatical order and syntax. Logical modifications and stress are mediated through a grammatically complex sentence structure, especially through use of a range of conjunctions and relative clauses. Impersonal pronouns are frequently used as subjects of sentences. Logical relationships and temporal and spatial contiguity are carefully indicated by the frequent use of the appropriate prepositions. A wide range of adjectives and adverbs is used, and sequences of sentences are organized so that there are qualifications *between* as well as *within* them.

The difference between saying "Shut up" to a child in contrast to "Johnny dear, mother would prefer that you not make that noise just now" is the essential element of the style difference under consideration. The second version makes it clear to the speaker of formal language that the mother regarded Johnny as a good person, that she wanted him to stop but recognized that he might not if making noise were really important to him, and that making loud noises might be allowable at some other time than the present. The admonition to "Shut up" might not necessarily lead the child to conclude that he wasn't loved. The child might reason that the mother was feeling bad. However, he could hardly conclude that there might be some situation in which he could legitimately make noise. He would more than likely conclude that there were some persons with whom he might get away with it. Thus, while one can't identify how many of the contingencies are left open for interpretation after the first message, there are probably fewer after the second. Imbedded in the broader information set of formal language are premises about interpersonal relations which are different from those included in the public language in that they motivate further verbal exploration.

Bernstein assumes that public language is more appropriate for some purposes—all formal language speakers use public language on occasions. But not all public language speakers master formal speech. Some people do not have the skill to categorize by multiple criteria and indicate subtle gradations of relationships. Without this ability, reliance on public speech is absolute. There seems to be a disposition for the speaker restricted to public language to interpret or "translate" formal language communication into less precise public terms. A public language speaker may respond to a formal clarification simply by stating, "That's what I said," being unwilling to admit the importance of an alternate phrasing, which, when translated in his mind, is in fact no more precise. It is also possible for many lower-class persons to read for pleasure without modifying their spoken vocabulary, in part because they do not catch the subtleties of what they read, in part because they have so few opportunities to play roles in which they can comfortably respond in formal language. Expressed in terms of life styles, lower classes ask their visitor to take off his jacket and speak public language, the middle classes put on formal language when jackets are required, and the elite classes tend to talk formally at play and at work—and frequently even when drunk.

If one asks whether it is true that lower-class persons are more frequently limited to public speech, the answer would again seem to be yes. It is the next question that contains the catch: Why is this distinction maintained? Is it enough to say that lower-class children speak public language because their parents do, or because they, and their parents, have less education? Both are true, but do we make an error in assuming that because higher education and formal speech capacity are so often associated, it is education, particularly the bookish kind, which creates it? If we take the middle-class mother's elaborated suggestion that her child be quiet as simply an instance in which she is socializing her child to participate in a polite middle-class interaction, we may be correct. But we need a more analytic explanation if we are to identify fully the conditions which promote maximum refinement of verbal skills.

## COMMUNICATION AND POWER RELATIONS

Consider for a moment two functions of the group, sociability and work. In sociability groups like cocktail parties, the importance of expressive gratification is high. The smaller the group, the greater the participation of each person; for this reason, people tend to break into groups of two or three. The conversation tends to be linked together only to the extent that it is necessary to build upon, or relate in a slight degree to, the remarks of the other. The conversation is thus continuously divergent (Riesman, Potter, and Watson, 1960). The topics frequently have the function of establishing the identity of the participant, or establishing the solidarity and value consensus of those present—frequently by judicious gossip about the behavior of persons who are mutually known. Such sociable interaction illustrates conditions under which participants are motivated to talk, and their remarks are under very mild review as to their relevance or accuracy.

Sociability groups may be compared with work groups in which problems of a routine nature are reiteratively present. When such problems are handled by something like a family unit, the respective duties soon fall into patterned allocation and the resources for conversation are produced by the unfolding events of daily life. In such groups, if there is a democratic atmosphere, a consensus will grow about agreed-upon premises or norms. These serve as a kind of shorthand reference to previous conversations and conserve the time of the participants as they face daily decisions. The patent familiarity of this process sometimes hides from recognition the very complicated social behavior which is involved.

For example, the presence of both a father and a mother who are relatively equal in power provides a child with a motivation to attend closely to the state of normative integration. If he knows that the value emphasis of one parent is slightly different from that of the other, he is provided an incentive to act so as to win advantages from this insight. The task is made more complicated and challenging when there are great warmth and consensus between the parents. A child not only has to make his move at the right time with a strong case, he must also be sure that the ensuing action does not exceed the threshold of protest of the other parent, who might then, through the parental solidarity relation, object as a point of privilege. The existence of two persons of power with small value differences, yet parallel commitment to a core of common values, creates a situation in which careful use of language and recognition of subtle difference are required to attain personal goals.

More generally, secure membership in a relatively stable group creates motivation to attain collective goals which require further communication. The middle-class family needs a car which is clean, appropriate, and not too expensive, and a home in a neighborhood with good schools and similar people. Yet the new home must not entail an imprudent sale of the old house or the disruption of the adolescent children's high-school associations. The children must have many dates but not become too intimate. Commitments to bowling as opposed to work on the church newsletter must be balanced. These and things like them all proceed under the discipline of two economic processes. First, there is the economic allocation of money, second, there is the economic allocation of time.

So long as coparticipants have slightly different utilities to be achieved from expenditures of resources, the requirements for carefully monitored discussion are present. A premium is set upon accuracy in the description of the external world, consistency in argument, and, most importantly, awareness of the degree to which a given action impinges upon others.

In this somewhat ideal-typic description of the middle-class home, we do not imply that because of the surface appearance of equalitarian functioning, one cannot recognize the greater essential power of the parents. Parental pressure exceeds the resistance most children can mobilize but, importantly, only in those rare circumstances which require full mobilization of power. Role induction in operating social systems can take place under conditions in which the full mobilization of power is only rarely required.

One important meaning of there being a correspondence between the norms of a family and the norms of the larger community relates to the absolute power of each member of the family. With the increase of integration into the larger community, there is an expansion of the gradations of inducement and resistance the participants can use as they argue the relevance of various norms for the action in question. The time required to review these considerations is democratizing because during the longer period required to reach a full showdown, extraneous events often produce some other challenge to the system of relationships. Such challenges may distract attention from the controversy by requiring a collective response which, if successful, adds to the solidarity of the system. A long-standing argument between a boy and his father over the boy's choice of a university may be more easily resolved after the two of them have worked together to paint the garage.

The importance of the duration of the period of assumed equality before a show of power may be illustrated by the example of a system in which the low-power person has little strength in the larger community and is convinced that his life opportunities depend upon his relationship with the stronger. When the tensions of the relation mount, the typical response of the low-power person is to escape by disengagement. To state the point in still another way, a low-power person will talk longest and most inventively in resistance to another's inducement when both are near middle rank in a system with normative consensus and when compliance with the other's inducement would reduce the actor's rank.

In family interaction studies (Strodtbeck, 1951; Strodtbeck, 1954) it is our observation that the ultimate disposition of the revealed difference is recognized by the three family members after about one-third of the conversation. The remaining two-thirds of the discussion is devoted to explaining how the original difference did not arise from a difference in values but rather from the different interpretations of the particular example. The family appears to act as if having the ultimate decision follow from previously agreed-upon norms produces a solution in which there is no loss of rank (in this instance the term "face" is also appropriate) as a result of the concession of one member to achieve consensus. The family's disposition to play and replay the game of verbal flourishes in the defense of rank is the source of the urge to talk well.

From this point of view one would avoid overestimating the importance of the sheer mass of printed and visual stimulus material which is found in a middle-class home. There are histories of isolated children having read themselves into a degree of specialization that formed the basis of their later career. This, obviously, could not have taken place if the materials were not present. But to a degree that few have recognized, good readership is motivated by the anticipation of the relevance that such information will have to later interaction. The problem encountered in the home and solved by reference to the encyclopedia both effects a change in information state which permits all participants to know what was decided and at the same time reassures the child that what he learns can be relevant to what he does. The relevance of an external and validated source of knowledge to the increase of an individual's absolute power is dependent upon the consensus in the group that validated knowledge can be the basis of action. This is particularly true for knowledge which has relevance for gratifications of the family at some time in the future. If a family's wherewithal to respond to expectations lags no more than might be made up by careful attention to detail, then it is possible to argue about and select the validated plans of actions which are believed to best meet family needs. Whenever it is clear that no matter how hard a family tries they cannot at the same time replace the car, have dental work done, rent extra space, etc., then an important tension goes out of the system. The motivation for verbal flourishes is lost. The delay to consider all factors is purposeless.

## THE SITUATION OF
## THE DEPENDENT POOR

The stable lower class, who still meet necessary demands of a somewhat more limited spectrum of institutional expectations, tend to do so at the cost of expending their reserve. Their security system then becomes a set of social relationships in which the common themes communicated by public language prevail. Muir and Weinstein (1962) describe the attempt of the lower-class person

> to evolve a way of life that will reduce his insecurity and enhance his power in ways that do not depend on achievement in the universalistic sector and on command of a rich and sophisticated variety of perspectives. He can do this by forging a network of relationships, with people similarly circumstanced, that is in some ways like a mutual insurance scheme. People linked by such a network provide one another with a sense of status and worth, and also with aid and support in time of need.... Such a network differs from a conventional insurance scheme in that the kinds of benefits to which one is entitled are not specified in advance...but consist broadly of "help in time of trouble"...and of "doing whatever he can" when another is in need.

> If one has a sufficiently extensive network of such obligations, and he has honored his obligations in the past, there is probably some one he can turn to if ever he should need help...until he is "back on his feet." Title to these benefits is not tied to incumbency of specific roles, approaches through prescribed channels, or conformity to legalistic requirements. On the contrary the relationships are valued precisely because they are not hedged about by such conditions...they are diffuse, reciprocal, durable and particularistic.

In contrast with lower-class persons, the dependent poor in the great cities suffer the even greater deprivation of being reduced to fearfulness of their neighbors. Let me illustrate this concretely with comments elicited from Negro mothers who are receiving Aid to Dependent Children. The comments were elicited by having the mothers listen to recordings of other Negro women's spontaneous comments upon what it means to be on ADC, how hard it is for a Negro man to get a job, why one doesn't want a man in the house if there are daughters, why it's foolish to think of marriage or divorce, etc. The mothers talked from five to seven minutes after each stimulus recording—their interviewer rarely spoke. She just nodded with interest as the remarks were recorded.

This is a free response of one mother talking about the threat of rape. The sentence structure has been slightly clarified and the dialect eliminated, but otherwise the respondent is quoted in the public language she used on the threat of rape as she experienced it:

> We had that two times since I've been in the building, but that's in the back apartment where you can see the husband, or whatever man is sleeping in, leave. The first time the man came on the first floor. He came through her kitchen window and he had a knife against her child and told her if she said anything he was going to kill her and so he tried to do it to the mama and she screamed and he went to get the child and that's when she got to the door. When she got to the door she left him in there with her child and that's the part I wouldn't have done. He'd just have had to kill me. She got the girl across the hall's husband to go down there and get that man out of her house. So when they got down there, he was gone.

The meaning of the triple locks Chicago Negroes place on their doors may be inferred from the following comments on transiency and fear of disasters.

As soon as someone moves out, someone else moves in. Before you can get acquainted with them, they're moved out. They don't be there long enough for you to know their names. But all the old tenants from when I moves in there are gone.

And another mother commented:

Because so much fires breaking out, I don't want to leave the children. It's hard to get somebody to keep them, it's dangerous to leave them by themselves. So that means I don't hardly get a chance to go nowhere. I'm scared to leave them at the house by themselves because so much fire breaking out. I just sit at the house all day long with the children. I just never go nowhere. I suspect that when I get around people I get nauseated, just nauseated. I just can't stand a crowd of people. I would like to go back to school, but my nerves are too bad. I don't think I could take it. If I was there, my mind would be right back at home with my girl, she's a young lady now, and I'd be afraid to leave her in the house by herself.

To support the thesis that the isolated Negro mother's socialization strategy is designed to cope with violence from hostile neighbors, consider this mother's comment upon her style of child-rearing.

When I go to the store I tell the children, don't open that door for Jesus. And they won't 'cause I know my worker came and he wouldn't let her in and she said but I'm Mrs. X and he said I'm sorry, but you can wait outside, and she'll be back and sure enough, I came in before she left the building and she said he wouldn't let her in and I said if he lets you in he might let someone else in. I told him don't open that door for Jesus. You know what that means. He's a spirit and that's the only thing that can go through. Anybody can say I'm the case worker.

The uneasy strategy that emerges is one of not getting too involved. One ADC mother stated it very reflectively: "I just visit a few people. If the group gets too big there's confusion. I have coffee every couple mornings with just two now. I used to be guilty of visiting around out of loneliness and lack of self-control. You need people around to do favors and fight loneliness." If you are too close to people, you can become overwhelmed by demands they might make in times of great need. A child can be taken care of while a friend comes in for a "nap," but more complicated actions relating to guard rails, letter boxes, or signal systems at the door, seem bafflingly difficult to arrange.

The way in which distrust of others prevents the growth of institutions which capitalize on cooperation was illustrated by the mothers' reactions to a hypothetical cooperative housing project. This project would have involved private apartments for the mothers and their small children, and dormitories for the older children. A common kitchen would have reduced the labor of food preparation. The negative reactions given revealed the mothers' lack of trust. They were concerned about the stealing of food and the possibility that some people would fail to carry their share of the responsibilities. Seven of the nine also rejected having their older children sleep away from them on the grounds that they would learn bad practices from others, it would lead to fights between the parents, and it would require excessive supervision. One mother felt that it might not be sanitary. Only one mother thought the children might not like it.

The rudimentary simplicity of the systems of relations of the ADC family starts of course with the absence of a continuously visible and effective father. Dealing with sexually differentiated adults who are in some degree in league with one another provides experience which helps one with a self-definition and also probably provides a sensible preparation for talking one's way through the complex bureaucracies of adult life. Just as the absence of membership in larger collectivities deprives the mother of external support, it also deprives a child of his family-based introduction to the complexity of role relations. Since mother's brothers are not important, the deprivation which attends the absence of a father is not compensated for. It is my guess that in the absence of such experiences with organizational complexity, an individual does not learn to see the actions of others as arising from organizational role expectations. Negro corner boys report no clear notion of who was boss on jobs from which they have withdrawn after having been placed by an employment counselor (Short & Strodtbeck, 1965). Persons who knock at a door are reacted to as if they loomed up out of a cloud; there is no premise about the organization which sponsored the visitors (Wilson, 1960). There is a disposition to assume that relations can continue so long as they are closely balanced as to the satisfactions provided. This implies that if either person chooses, the relation may be terminated and thereby cease to exist. There is no thought that a relationship bond will sustain an exchange which is seriously imbalanced over a protracted period. This is the crucial mechanism by which the reduction of absolute power undercuts the motivation for protracted verbal exploration of action possibilities.

One rarely goes into an ADC home without encountering another adult there. Yet in the interviews, many of the respondents insist that there is no one to whom they can turn if they are in trouble. There is widespread evidence of an uneasy tension between the need to affiliate and fear of involvement. There is a code of cooperation against the threat of collectors and investigative agents, but the rapid shift in residence erodes the sense of security. If you have made friends once, you don't want to try again, at least not every six months.

The most profound insight we have won into the recurrence of the syndrome of poverty and low-educability is through the linkage of Negro mothers' sense of threat and their actions to socialize their children. In some practices they appear to set up in their children certain expectations which are sharply frustrated. They wean children later, but more abruptly; they feed on demand and report few feeding problems; and they start bowel training later but take less time than the Sears, Maccoby, and Levin (1957) middle- and lower-class mothers. Their children are more frequently eneuretic and continue to be so at later ages. Negro ADC mothers are less responsive to crying and less punitive toward dependency. They exert strong pressure against masturbation and sex play and are strict in modesty training. They are not permissive of aggression toward parents and siblings, and they place more restrictions upon physical mobility. Although they expect less of the children in terms of performance of household tasks, they are more strict about obedience.

The ADC mothers' training techniques include more physical punishment and little use of praise, positive models, and reasoning. Isolation and withdrawal of privileges are rare. They reward and punish their children immediately and their children are rarely required to delay gratification. The failure to discipline in terms of language symbols as well as the related dependence upon physical means of punishment reduces the necessity for cognitive mediation in impulse control. The child gets much less assistance in discovering the relationship between his behavior and the responses it is likely to elicit.

A middle-class mother would be surprised by the amount of the Negro ADC mother's energies which go into admonishing the child to "be good" instead of rewarding and punishing for acts freely entered into. In the context of an overcrowded living space, "being good" means being physically inactive, verbally nonparticipative, and nonobservant. It is not that the achievements of the child are negatively viewed; rather, it is the "trouble" that achievement activity may lead to that is so consistently avoided. The mothers are extremely vulnerable to threat which is serious and unpredictable, and their children—above all else—are taught to be generally fearful rather than selectively cautious.

## IMPLICATIONS FOR INTERVENTION

The conclusion to be drawn from this analysis is that in the degree the Negro ADC mothers and Negro gang boys studied in Chicago are representative of culturally deprived persons, the educational intervention must reduce fear and motivate verbal participation by increasing the absolute power of the child in the school setting. Middle-class educational objectives cannot be seriously undertaken in the absence of some equivalent of stable lower-class security systems.

Beyond this, the children must be given the opportunity to make decisions and then be permitted to suffer the consequences of their decision. If they have book stamps which may be spent for classroom material, each student must have some say as to how his stamp is used. If every child chooses to buy the same book, the class must be given the opportunity to see how much better another class has done in obtaining a variety of books. If the class chooses to decorate their room in a garish way, they must live in it also. If factions grow concerning the allocation of resources, they should be encouraged to test alternatives which do not lead to the immediate amalgamation of the factions.

There should be student organizations broader than a given classroom. Through these organizations, the students must be given the opportunity to make suggestions for administrative consideration which are not cleared by their teachers. Each child should have a friendly contact with an adult in the school who is as powerful as the child's teacher, but who has no authority over the child. Older children should be given the motivation of reducing the length of their school day by getting their work done early. They should be permitted to organize so as to participate in the determination of what is a fair day's work.

These suggestions may never be tried, or, if they are tried, they may be defective in detail, but the underlying principle should be clear. The broader a range of problems an individual approaches as a member of a group, and the larger the number of working groups participated in, the greater his experience in explaining the external situation and in taking the role of the other in order to increase the relevance of his attempt to get the group to follow a given course of action. Though the implications of this process are profound, the preparation for it occurs almost unconsciously in primary groups whose members have different skills, work to do, and a concern about consensus, that is, in groups like the middle-class family. It is this hidden curriculum, which is absent from both the schools and the culturally deprived family, which must be added to accomplish the objectives of compensatory education.

## REFERENCES

Ausubel, D. P. The influence of experience on the development of intelligence. Paper read at a conference on Productive Thinking in Education, Washington, D.C., 1963.

Bernstein, B. A public language: Some sociological implications of a linguistic form. *Brit. J. Sociol.*, 1959, **10**, 311–26.

Burgess, M. Elaine, and D. O. Price. *An American dependency challenge.* Chicago: American Public Welfare Association, 1963.

Henry, J. Spontaneity, initiative, and creativity in suburban classrooms. In G. D. Spindler (Ed.), *Education and culture.* New York: Holt, Rinehart and Winston, 1963. Pp. 215–33.

Morgan, J. N., et al. *Income and welfare in the United States.* New York: McGraw-Hill, 1962.

MUIR, D. E., and E. A. WEINSTEIN. The social debt: An investigation of lower class and middle class norms of social obligation. *Amer. Sociol. Rev.,* 1962, **27,** 532–39.

Panel on Educational Research and Development of the President's Science Advisory Committee. *Innovation and experiment in education.* Washington, D.C.: U.S. Government Printing Office, 1964.

RIESMAN, D., R. J. POTTER, and JEANNE WATSON Sociability, permissiveness, and equality: A preliminary formulation. *Psychiatry,* 1960, **23,** 323–40.

SEARS, R., ELEANOR MACCOBY, and H. LEVIN. *Patterns of child rearing.* Glencoe, Ill.: Row, Peterson, 1957.

SHORT, J. F., and F. L. STRODTBECK. *Group process and gang delinquency.* Chicago: University of Chicago Press, 1965.

STRODTBECK, F. L. Husband-wife interaction over revealed differences. *Amer. Sociol. Rev.,* 1951, **16,** 468–474.

STRODTBECK, F. L. The family as a three-person group. *Amer. Sociol. Rev.,* 1954, **19,** 23–29.

WILNER, D. M. *The housing environment and family life.* Baltimore: Johns Hopkins Press, 1962.

WILSON, J. Q. *Negro politics: The search for leadership.* Glencoe, Ill.: The Free Press, 1960.

FRANCES L. ILG and
LOUISE BATES AMES

# 6. YOUR CHILD MAY BE IN THE WRONG GRADE AT SCHOOL

Here is a fact about our educational system that may shock you as much as it did us when we discovered it. If you have a child in school today, the chances are about 50-50 that he is at least a grade ahead of the one he should be in. More, the consequences of this misplacement may follow him through his entire school career, even in college.

The reason is simple. Almost all our schools use two largely inadequate measurements to determine whether children are ready for kindergarten or

Reprinted from the *Reader's Digest* (August 1966), by permission of the authors and the publisher. Copyright 1966 by The Reader's Digest Assn., Inc.

first grade: chronological age and I. Q. They ignore the most significant measure of all: the child's maturity, or behavior age. Yet this can be the crucial factor in determining whether a child will perform according to his ability. If it is disregarded, the child can suffer serious harm.

Our eyes were opened to this in the mid-1950's when we made the discovery that many of the "problem children" who came to our clinic in New Haven, Conn., had only one major problem: they were adjusting badly to school. And in almost every such case we found that the child had been started in school too soon.

We are able to make such a flat statement because we had given each child a test designed specifically to reveal his readiness for the work or grade he was in.

### BLOCK BANGERS

To understand how such tests work, review for a moment the basic discovery of the late Dr. Arnold Gesell at the Yale Clinic of Child Development.[1] Over a period of 40 years, Dr. Gesell and his staff minutely observed and recorded on film the behavior of hundreds of children as they grew from infancy to ten years of age. They documented the basic discovery that behavior develops in as patterned and predictable a way as does the physical organism itself.

For instance, just as the infant creeps before he walks, so he also pounds a block vertically on the table (at six months) before he can bang two blocks together horizontally (at nine months). Most four-year-old boys draw a circle from the bottom up, in a clockwise direction; but by five-and-a-half or six they draw it in the opposite direction—from the top, counterclockwise.

From such observations, Gesell devised a group of simple tests that can tell the skilled examiner just how far a child has come in his behavior. Gesell's infant and preschool tests have been translated into more than two dozen languages and are standard tools of psychologists and pediatricians throughout the world. The school-readiness tests, a direct outgrowth of Gesell's tests, extend the range into the school-age years of five to ten. Though more complex than the preschool tests, basically they are the same in concept and intent.

These readiness tests showed conclusively that the children in our clinic had been over-placed in school. However, we realized that the children brought to us were those already in trouble. What would tests show for a cross section of average children? To find out, we obtained a grant from the Ford Foundation's Fund for the Advancement of Education, and from

---

[1] For 20 years Drs. Ilg and Ames were associates of the late Dr. Arnold Gesell at his famed Yale Clinic of Child Development. In 1950, after his retirement, they founded the Gesell Institute of Child Development to continue his work. Of their many books, the most recent is *School Readiness* (Harper & Row, 1964).

1957 to 1962 made an intensive study of some 1000 kindergarten-through-second-grade children in three elementary schools near New Haven.

## "NOVEMBER BOY"

The results, we are convinced, reflect what is happening throughout the country. Only about a quarter of the children examined were definitely ready for the grades in which they had been placed. A quarter were definitely unready. The rest were at best questionable: they might or might not be able to make it.

If these figures are as hard for you to believe as they were for us, come inside the classroom and observe some of the children we saw. There was John, who as a "November boy" was a classic victim of the archaic chronological-age standard. In Weston, Conn., where John was in kindergarten, the legal readiness requirement is typical: a child is considered ready for kindergarten if his fifth birthday falls on or before December 31 of that school year. John's birthday fell in late November, so when he started he was only four years and ten months old. Poor John was unquestionably too young for school—and his behavior showed it. He spent much of the time in tears, did not enjoy group activities, and folded up from exhaustion long before the morning was over.

On our first visit to one classroom we sat in the back of the room and made a chart of the desks, marking with an X those children whose behavior was most obviously heading them for trouble. Checking later, we discovered that *every one* of our eight X marks was for a November or December child!

A New England primary-school principal told us: "I can almost predict which children will have to repeat, even before the teachers turn in their reports. They will be mostly boys, and will have an October, November or December birthday." Why mostly boys? Because boys this age are about six months behind girls in their development. Yet school-readiness requirements make no allowance at all for this known difference.

## SMART AS A WHIP

Margaret was a good solid seven years and six months when she entered second grade. She had an extremely high I. Q. and stood at the top of her class academically. But she was unhappy in school and had turned sour and disobedient at home. In her relations with other seven-year-olds she was a classic six-year-old: unpleasantly competitive about her marks and in her play, frequently bursting into displays of temper when she felt "her rights" were being violated. Her only friend in school was the teacher. Like John, she was over-placed, but for different reasons.

She was a type so common that we have coined a term to describe it: "superior-immature." You undoubtedly know children like this: smart as whips, with minds that sometimes seem to outrace your own—but with behavior that is babyish for their age.

Among the children we tested there were dozens of Johns and Margarets. In first grade, they were the fidgeters and gigglers and constant walkers to the pencil sharpener or the bathroom. In second grade, they were the daydreamers. By third grade, with the pattern of failure and unhappiness already beginning to harden, they had learned to hate school. One common symptom was that they had few school friends or none at all.

### NOTHING FAILS LIKE FAILURE

To prevent this continuing damage to so many children, we must dispel two common misconceptions. Myth No. 1 is that the symptoms of immaturity are so obvious that most children are eventually placed in the proper grade. Unfortunately, our experience is that this is rarely the case. Particularly with the "superior-immatures"—since their high I. Q.'s so delight both parents and teachers—the real problem is overlooked.

Even when immaturity is discovered, too often the child is *still* not held back. Various social and professional pressures work on parents and teachers alike to keep children "moving ahead and learning." The easier thing to do, and the tendency, is to keep a child going along in the wrong grade indefinitely, in the hope that "he'll catch up later on."

That is Myth No. 2. Most unready children do *not,* in our experience, catch up. To do so, they would at some point have to mature abnormally fast. Instead, what almost always happens is that, having started school a year too early, the child moves rung by rung up the grade ladder, always a year behind in maturity and behavior. Having learned early that school is an unhappy place, he becomes accustomed to failure.

And this pattern builds on itself year after year. In fact, we are convinced that early over-placement in school is one of the prime reasons for the "under-achievers" who crowd our classrooms today—the ones who fail to live up to their potential and, in too many cases, ultimately drop out.

Colleges increasingly are recognizing the need for more growing up by many students. Since the early 1950's, many colleges have been encouraging some freshmen to take a year or two off and then start again. A professor recently told us, "The best teaching years of my life were the ones just after World War II, when we started getting the G.I. Bill students whose education had been interrupted by the war. Those boys, as a group, were the first students I ever had who were mature enough."

### FROM TEARS TO CHEERS

How, then, can our schools properly match the child to the grade? Each child, before entering school, should be given an individual behavior test.

Since our original findings, we have trained some 200 teachers, school psychologists and guidance counselors to give school-readiness tests. And for the past year, with Ford Foundation support, we have been working intensively with three school systems, in California, Connecticut and Vermont, to help them grade their children on a developmental basis.

Earnest C. Imbach, school psychologist and guidance director of the Visalia, Calif., schools, reports: "Last year, when we gave developmental tests to the kindergarten-through-second-grade children in our Mountain View Elementary School, we found that *more than half* were being forced to work at a level for which they weren't ready. We've replaced most of them according to behavior age, and the results have been almost unbelievable. The kids are happier and much more involved in their work, and many are already showing a measurable increase in achievement. The teachers say they're now able to spend more time in creative teaching; the parents tell us the children are more enjoyable to live with. Now the parents and principals of other schools are asking us when they can start developmental placement."

## FIGHT FOR HIS RIGHTS

Your own school, like the vast majority, probably still uses the age-and-I.Q. standards. What, then, can you do to make sure your child is on the right rung of the educational ladder?

First, don't regard it as a stigma on your child if he is held back. The stigma, if any, belongs with the school or his parents for having put him in the wrong grade to begin with. And don't assume that replacing him will necessarily do emotional harm. It depends largely, we believe, on how the matter is explained to the child.

Second, keep in mind that it is *never* too late to put your child in the proper grade. Unfortunately, the older the child, the more bitterly he may protest being re-placed. But over-placing is too potentially damaging to ignore, and chances are—if there are no other complicating factors—that tears will be replaced by happiness as he begins to experience success and find friends in the new grade.

One frequently heard objection to behavioral placement is that a high-I.Q. child may suffer from academic boredom when put in a class with younger children. But in our experience this is far less of a problem than most people make it.

Third, if you are convinced your child is wrongly placed, and if the school resists making a change, *fight for his rights*. Putting yourself in your child's shoes may help.

"You would have to live through it to realize the tearing away of your confidence and the humiliation it brings," says a young woman recalling her own experience as an over-placed child. "My first two years in school

I cried each day. I couldn't eat. I sat with my head on my desk. I couldn't concentrate. The teacher screamed at me, and my mother blamed one teacher after another for my unhappiness. It was hell."

In every school there are children who are suffering this same agony. It is time we relieved them of the terrible, unnecessary pressure.

IRA J. GORDON

# 7.   ARE WE READY AS TEACHERS?

As a child growing up in New York City, like generations of children before me (and some since) I played "Hide and Seek." The one who was "It" counted to ten, then issued his challenge, "Ready or not, here I come!" Readiness to us (the hiders) meant a good hiding place. But even in the game world of childhood, one had eventually to come out of hiding and race to get home "free." In the grown-up world, it would still be nice if one could be ready for the challenge by hiding from it. However, here too real readiness means the ability to take the risk and race for the goal. Are we ready as teachers for changes which surround and come toward us, "ready or not"?

What does readiness mean for us as teachers?

These past 60 years have brought us from Kitty Hawk to Venus.
The future is not just a fresh page on the calendar, but a time when things are basically different and it is arriving at a voracious speed whether we like it or not, whether we are ready for it or not.
What will it be like? Take the wildest speculation you can imagine and then square it and then cube the result and the answer still won't be big enough to match the truth.[1]

If these changes are as profound as experts believe, are we ready for the changes in role that follow? Are we ready for children who will be different

Reprinted from *Childhood Education,* Vol. 43, No. 8 (April 1967), 444–47, by permission of Ira. J. Gordon and the Association for Childhood Education International, 3615 Wisconsin Avenue, N. W., Washington, D. C. Copyright © 1967 by the Association.

[1] Congressional Record, Senate Document 106, 89th Congress, August 30, 1966, pp. 20176-86, "Where the Votes Are."

from those we taught before? Will we be ready to interpret what we believe and know to the community at large and to the children's parents? Will we get home free?

## READY FOR THE CHILD

We in ACEI have long prided ourselves on being "child-centered," even in the face of new waves of educational thought and pressure. But is our image of the child accurate? Are our concepts of how to relate to him valid? Many of our ideas of childhood were shaped both by our own growth experiences and by the body of research literature mostly based on middle-class white children living in stable families during somewhat stable times. Our notions of intelligence, motivation and emotion, goal-orientation, parent-child relationships generally proved useful with these children. But we were, and are, ill-prepared for the slum child, the child from the broken home, the suburban TV-oriented child, the child from the highly mobile (both horizontal and vertical) home. We are ill-prepared for the child whose value system and cognitive style are alien to us.

Research literature now suggests that even the image that worked is no longer valid. Concepts of intelligence have been revolutionized in the last five years, concepts of motivation and emotion are going through a revolution at the present time, and the concept of cognitive style, the way an individual approaches his world, is just moving into focus. Even views concerning teacher and pupil self-concepts, especially as they relate to the disadvantaged child, require further thought. The teacher deemed effective by our current views of adequacy may not be effective with certain categories of children.

If Marshall McLuhan is right, in that children today are growing up in a nonlinear, instant total-message world whereas we grew up in a linear, printed-word sequential one, the gap between the generations may be wider than that which separated us from our parents. Some of the problems with teaching reading may be related to this difference in how one "gets the message" rather than in our classical explanations of reading difficulty.

If J. McV. Hunt is right, the problem of the match requires that we understand the cognitive and motivational system of the child, and that we bring our academic expectations into juxtaposition with this. If we are out of phase, if we expect too little or too much or present our expectations in ways which have little meaning, we shall have created the mismatch.

Being ready for the child, then, requires us to engage in *two* pursuits. We must:

- become more aware of new research literature, the new normative data on children
- look more closely at the children in school

- learn to assess them in keeping with the new concepts of their potentials, styles, views of self and world.

To treat the child as a known entity, to hold our view of him constant, to see him only as he was, is to continue to hide. Are we ready to come out and take this new look at the new child?

## READY FOR THE SCHOOL

In a recent Orwellian forecast, John Carroll wrote: "Somewhere a child is being born today who will have just passed his 18th birthday when, in the year 1984, he steps onto a moving walkway that will conduct him automatically to the LE (Learning Environment) booth in the LAG (Learning Activities Guider) Processing Building of Olympic State University, which has been pre-programed to give him the sequential combination of experiences and activities that will furnish the final modifications to his repertoire of knowledges, skills and attitudinal dispositions in such a way that he can become an I-LAG; i.e., Learning Activity Guider for the infants of the time."[2]

A LAG is Carroll's name for teacher. Are we disposed to be LAGs, or do we see a different future for ourselves? How shall we preserve the humanness in education?

Louis Bright, Associate U.S. Commissioner of Education, has indicated that computers for classroom use will be economically possible within a short span of years. The new educational technology is being produced at a rapid rate. What does this do to the teacher? Does the teacher become merely a skilled technician, plugging in the right units at the recommended time? Does the teacher become a unit in a man-machine system, in which the work of the teacher is as automatic and subject to programing as the work of the machine? The Charlie Chaplin film, "Modern Times," showed a worker on the assembly line; a revised version would show a worker watching a machine for lights to flash. A "Modern Times" classroom has been seen as an analogy to the factory of its day. Would a future classroom model show the teacher in a role analogous to the worker, waiting for the lights to flash?

## WHO MAKES DECISIONS?

Only as we take leadership in guiding change, as we learn to use the new aids (both personnel and hardware) as *aids* can we win the game. To be truly professional requires the rapid development of categories of subprofessionals and an understanding of the ways in which we can utilize tech-

---

2 John B. Carroll, "The Future of Educational Psychology," *Educational Psychologist*, Vol. 4, No. 1, November 1966, p. 1.

nology and technicians to accomplish our purposes. Just as the physician employs the X-ray machine and its operator and the computer and its programer to assist him in diagnosis and treatment, we need to use assistants —human and electronic—to aid in diagnosis and instruction. But the critical point is *who* makes the decision. Neither the X-ray technician nor the computer specialist decides for the physician; neither the teaching assistant nor the programer should decide for the teacher.

The technological revolution in the classroom requires a careful consideration of emerging roles for teachers. We have often talked of teachers as diagnosticians, guidance counselors, discussion leaders, group-process experts enabling students to explore the personal meanings of the information they are receiving from books, tapes, TV and other media. We have often deplored our ability to play these diverse roles because of the many other demands on our time. Now these other demands may be met through human and technological aids. Are we ready to play the roles we've said are ours to play?

Are we ready to play this new role of captain of an educational team? We are ill-prepared by education, experience and perhaps by personality organization to play such roles now. We have been taught to work with children; we often gain our professional satisfaction from close, personal relations with them. The picture of a young child holding a teacher's hand is likely to evoke a warm feeling in us. We have not seen our task as working with other adults except in committees or faculty meetings where we did not have to share the children with them. We react strongly to departmentalization in the intermediate grades not only because of our intellectual concepts of what children need but also because of our own personality needs for close ties with a group of children. We react to computer-assisted instruction not only because of theories of learning but also because we do not know how to cope with what it may require of us in new ways of relating to our task as teachers. We can neither be Luddites seeking to destroy technology, nor can we hide and believe it will go away. We cannot continue to talk about the diverse needs of children and their increased heterogeneity of background without modifying our notion of pupil-teacher ratios. We need to reduce such ratios by the increased use of subprofessionals, by a clarification of what can only be done by the professional, well-educated teacher and what can be delegated to the technician.

Readiness requires of us that we engage in study of our own classroom and school operations. We need to define those aspects of the instructional process which can perhaps be supported by the use of technology, those aspects of the classroom operation which are not instructional at all, those aspects which require a high level of on-the-spot professional judgment, those aspects which require careful and prolonged investigation outside the classroom before instruction begins, but which, because of this investigation, can then be accomplished in the room either by gadget or a subprofessional.

We need to modify our teacher education programs so that the new teacher is a professional in the fullest sense. He:

is able to make decisions about individual children from a considerable background of knowledge about children in general and much information about this child in particular

possesses a considerable knowledge about existing curricula and materials available for planning purposes, including skill in the analysis of material as to its goals, relevance, assumptions and specified content

has knowledge of ready access to information systems and instructional materials for individual children in his room.

This new teacher, to be ready for the new school, should have been educated in how to work effectively with peers in planning and evaluating the instructional program and how to supervise others in the execution of the program. This cannot be left to slapdash, haphazard inservice education.

Are we ready or not? I feel we are not ready either for the new child or the new school. But I believe we have taken or can easily take the first step toward readiness. We can stop hiding and begin running toward the base. Running is wearying, but it's better than being caught. We can begin by:

investigating the newer concepts of children and asking ourselves how to implement these concepts

finding out all we can, in responsible ways, about proposed technology and organizational systems for schools.

When we have begun this, we can make recommendations, suggest decisions and play active roles in shaping the new education and the new teacher education. Failure to do this means that we will be bypassed, left in hiding, and that the future will be left to those who may not really understand either children or the educative process.

CHAPTER 2

# DIMINISHING
# OBSTACLES
# TO ACHIEVEMENT

JACK R. FRYMIER

# 8. EDUCATIONAL PREMISES AND PRACTICES

In the middle 1950's, when *Harper's Magazine* columnist Bernard De Voto died, one of the *Harper's* editors pointed out that De Voto was an exceptionally perceptive observer of the social scene and a relentless critic of everything he saw. He criticized America, the editor maintained, because he loved it and because he believed in its ideals and in its total way. America was a vibrant, healthy, growing thing to Bernard De Voto. He wanted to make it stronger and better in every possible way. To accomplish this end, he used his pen to criticize the unjust and evil, the silly and pretentious.

These comments are made because some of my observations are also going to be critical. In the same manner that De Voto believed in America, I believe in education. I am committed to it.

I feel that it is our only hope for both preserving and improving the lot of all mankind. No other institution could even attempt, let alone hope to achieve, such a monumental undertaking. The future is truly in our hands. If we can rise to the occasion—and rise we must—then the "Great Society" might actually be realized. But not if we stay the same. So, I intend to criticize both what we do and what we are. As I raise the questions which follow, please bear in mind that my fundamental concerns revolve around a powerful belief in, and love for, the educational enterprise.

Let's look at some of the practices of city schools, big and small, and ask ourselves: What purposes do the practices serve? Are we actually accomplishing our objectives—or at least moving in that general direction? Are we doing things in education which are predicated upon fallacious logic, ancient data, or false analogies? Could we be doing things in our schools that are, in actuality, negating the very ends we seek because the premises are like a mountain of sand—immense, but extremely unstable? In the name of education, are we perverting educational goals to serve the institution's ends?

---

Reprinted from *Problems of School Men in Depressed Urban Centers,* Arliss Roaden (ed.) (Columbus, Ohio: The Ohio State University College of Education, 1969), pp. 11–23, by permission of the publisher.

These are serious questions, and the remainder of this paper will be devoted to a consideration of such questions, with a look at some of the common and not so common existing practices giving rise to my concerns. Let me try to outline several areas of educational practice and then attempt to push the premises upon which these rest as far as I can. In this process I will exercise the prerogative of extending an idea to its logical extreme to test its worth and to expose its scheme.

### PERSEVERATION AND CHANGE

Schools, school systems, and schoolmen exist to help children learn; however, organizations, like people, both *serve* and *have* particular needs. That is, although teachers work to help youngsters learn, teaching also helps the teacher. He makes a salary, buys the groceries, and pays the bills—not an unimportant set of needs. If it can be assumed that schools and schoolmen do, indeed, have particular needs of their own, then it becomes possible to ask: What kinds of needs are these?

This question can be approached in many ways, but I prefer the general concepts of Combs and Snygg,[1] who suggest that human needs might all be included in concepts of maintenance and enhancement of the phenomenal self. In other words, anything which people do is directed towards self-preservation and improvement. Though these needs are obviously different, they do have some similarities. Organismic needs can pertain to one or both of these basic human needs, for maintaining the organism involves existence and preservation kinds of activities. Enhancement, on the other hand, presupposes activity aimed at improvement and positive kinds of change for the person involved. To think of individual or organizational needs in such a framework suggests that whatever people or organizations do might be viewed in terms of either continuing, existence-type, or changing, improvement type activities.

Such conceptual categorization is arbitrary. These things cannot be separated except at any given point in space or time. But assuming that it is a useful model, the actions of schools and schoolmen may be viewed in these terms.

In first observing the educational enterprise, one is firmly convinced that just about everything is a preservation-type activity from the organization's point of view. From the learner's however, we can see another posture— most of the actions of school people and school systems are directed primarily toward "keeping the ship in operation."

There are classes to be taught and floors to be swept, teachers to be hired and reports to be filed, buildings to be built and payrolls to be met, curricu-

[1] Combs, Arthur W., and Snygg, Donald. *Individual behavior,* (Revised Edition). New York: Harper and Brothers, 1959.

lum materials to be prepared and parents to be placated, phone calls to be answered and a myriad of never-ending routine operations.

Just as the human organism continuously seeks water, food, and air from its environment to ensure its survival, so too does a school system have a never-ending list of activities which keep it functioning. They are maintenance, preservation, or existence-type activities. Enhancement, improvement, and change can occur only if existence is assured.

While many persons in the school system may actually want to make changes, work for improvements, and enhance the total operation in many ways, there are some who want things to stay the same. Indeed, many conflicts and power struggles revolve around basic issues related to maintenance, improvement, and change. Everybody cannot have his own way, and, thus, the struggle is born. Some are determined to preserve and perpetuate the present operation because it seems to work in meeting most of youth's learning needs. Others, however, feel the need to strike out in new directions, testing new truths in their search for "educational breakthroughs" to improve education. Some are caught squarely in between.

The picture, then, is one of three groups, all working hard in directions they believe most fruitful and true, but not always pulling together in a vital or coordinated way.

This picture, described so effectively by Prestheus[2] in his investigations of bureaucracies, can be important in thinking about education in big cities. Urban school systems are bureaucracies, and if basic patterns of behavior are discernible at the bureaucratic level, they need to be understood for what they indicate about the problems and possibilities in city schools. Prestheus maintains that bureaucratic operations are beset with conflicting interests and notes three types of visible functionaries.

First, are those whose allegiances lie within the organization itself. They seek to rise within the existing framework and policies. Sometimes, they work to modify things for a particular inclination, but they are generally of the administrative type—specialists in processing and facilitating actions falling within predetermined confines of administrator-set policies and lines. Their major concerns are financial status, prestige, and power; they seek to further themselves by adhering to the "organizational line."

Second, are those whose competencies and interests lie primarily within their own particular technical and knowledge areas. These are the scientists, scholars, and technicians committed to the truth, rather than to organization, per se. They seek their satisfactions from and render their loyalties to a particular discipline. As such, their views often conflict with those devoted to keeping the ship under way. These men often irritate their administrative superiors to whom they insist on relating as intellectual peers.

[2] Prestheus, Robert V. *The organizational society.* New York: Alfred A. Knopf, Inc., 1962.

Finally, there is the great body of workers who at one time started down one of the former two roads, but got sidetracked somewhere along the way. They are the tireless workers who do a steady job but seek their satisfactions outside of work. They simply do not care—let the administrators push for power and the scientists, scholars, and technicians press for change. Let the other two groups claw at each others' throats. The commitments of these workers lie beyond the bureaucratic ends; they do a day's work for a day's pay.

If these descriptions are accurate and, if those who work in large school systems fit the general pattern of participants in bureaucratic operations, it may be possible to look at education and identify who does what and why.

Any careful assessment of educational practice or of the kinds and results of educational experimentation over the years gives two general conclusions. First, those oriented toward maintenance or preservation-type activities have ruled the day. Second, experimentation and change which have taken place in the schools have consistently produced no significant change. These two factors are unquestionably related.

To listen to educational administrators express their concerns and suggestions for handling the complex problems of today's educational world gives one the definite feeling that what these men really want is more and more of what they already have—more buildings, teachers, books, supervisors, money, and time. In one sense, these concerns for "more and more of the same" strike one as curiously similar to an interesting psychological phenomenon, *perseveration*. When someone repeatedly works at doing the same wrong thing and is so tied to his convictions that he is unable to change, he is said to perseverate. He perseveres but in an uncreative and nonproductive way. He needs to step back, reexamine the whole problem, and develop a different approach to solve the problems with which he is faced.

To avoid perseverating, and, in order to enhance the general effort implicit in educating youth today, innovation and change have been initiated by those attempting to give perspective and leadership.

A study of the experimentation in big city schools is most discouraging. On the one hand, evidence indicates that "tinkering" is about all that has been encouraged or indeed allowed. One can "monkey" with the basic operation a little bit, but dares not go too far. Also, nearly all of the tested innovations involve what I would call "nonhuman" variables: class size, length of period, bases for grouping, instructional materials, textbooks, films, and personal factors which readily lend themselves to manipulation and change.

Almost all of the research with which I am familiar, however, suggests that "human" variables are far more important than "nonhuman" ones. Changing the length of a class period, textbook, or grouping procedures makes little if any difference in children's learning compared to the growth and development when the teacher is changed in some meaningful way. Teachers are the *key* ingredient and the most powerful variable in the educational process. For example, even though the PSSC physics program initiated in the late 1950's captured the imagination of the nation, the proportion of students enrolled in high school physics has consistently declined.[3] Furthermore, in spite of the tremendous national concern and support for engineering and scientific-type careers, the most able youth in America are steadily moving in nonengineering and nonscientific directions.[4]

These two ideas—perseveration in educational practice and changes in unimportant variables—raise a very fundamental question. What motivates teachers to change? If true that most school systems are primarily aimed at helping the professionals keep their heads above water, then change is needed now. Maneuverability is essential. Those working with public schools must uncover ways of working which will be more than professional preseveration. The problems facing educators today stem from many sources. They march in endless parade—more knowledge, more children, more social concern, and more pressure for equalization and fairness—all irrespective of the multiplicity of factors concerned.

The question is not *whether* the schools can meet the challenge, but *how*. How can we teach more children more things more effectively? How can we cope with the outside pressures and still be true to our own philosophy? Are there basic assumptions that have not been brought into the open or that we seek to avoid? I believe there are, and, in the remainder of this paper, I will explore some of these propositions as I believe they exist.

## SOME QUESTIONABLE PRACTICES

Some assumptions implicit in our operations are related to economic principles and practices. For example, the grading system seems predicated upon the idea that there must be some kind of distribution of grades—there are not enough "A's" and "B's" to go around. If a teacher were to give every student an "A," someone would raise his eyebrows and assert that this had to be changed. "I do not insist that my teachers grade on a curve," one principal told me, "but they must have some kind of reasonable distribution of grades."

If this idea is pressed further, most persons would agree, theoretically at least, that everyone ought to learn everything. In other words, the very thesis of education is founded upon the commitment of schools to help every youngster to learn as much as he possibly can. If successful, then,

---

3 Walsh, John. Curriculum reform, *Science,* May 8, 1964, *144,* 642–46.
4 Nichols, Robert C. Career decisions of very able students, *Science,* June 12, 1964, *144,* 1315–19.

every child should receive an "A." Therefore, assuming that there must be a distribution of grades is actually operating in accordance with the principle of scarcity in economics: there is not enough to go around.

Children do differ in learning rates and abilities, but devising a grading system that guarantees the failure of some makes no sense at all. Ideas are not property, the purpose of education is to maximize the sharing of information and experience. To accept the fact that youngsters differ in their accomplishments is one thing, but to construct an evaluation relegating a third or more to "poor" or "failure" labels is to confuse scarcity in economics disastrously with individual differences in growth and learning.

Another idea rooted in fact but greatly mistaken in practice is the grade level concept. Junior or senior high school teachers constantly repeat to visitors that "too many children here are too far below grade level for me to teach them much in this class." Teachers yearn to go to "better" schools and teach kids "who really want to learn." Some maintain that a child should not be allowed to progress until he is at, or beyond, grade level. In other words, grade level is being used as a philosophical "standard," an "ought to be achieved" level, assessed by standardized test scores, graded texts, and other devices.

Grade level, however, is a statistical, not a philosophical concept, as it is typically determined. It represents the midpoint at which some representative group achieves. In other words, it is the mean, median, or modal value for any particular standardizing sample, and, as such, represents that point which divides the sample approximately in half. Fifty percent of the norming group achieved at that point or above, and fifty percent achieved at that point or below. Grade level is, by definition, a midpoint, and any teacher or administrator expecting most or all of his students to be "up to grade level or beyond" may just as well expect everybody who gets married to be a woman. It cannot be. Although, to my knowledge, there are no studies on the matter, three-fourths or more of the teachers and administrators with whom I have had contact view grade level as achievement level to be expected of almost every child. Grade level is a statistical concept and to translate a statistical description of what is into a philosophical pronouncement of what ought to be is a mistake of the most serious order. The assumptions underlying this practice are flimsy beyond belief.

The notion of "seniority" as practiced in big city schools provides still another example. Teachers are hired by the central office staff and assigned to a school. If they want to move out of a slum area, say, to the plush suburb, length of service, rather than actual need of service, prevails. Central office hiring is an industrial technique, and seniority is a laboring man's way of solving his working problems. To assume that these make sense in an educational situation is to assume that education problems are similar to those of industry and the workingman.

One gets the feeling, especially in the larger cities, that seniority, efficiency, bargaining, and productivity—all economic concepts—constitute one major way of thinking about problems of education. Callahan's[5] study of the efficiency movement in America and its relationship to educational practice further proves this idea. Grading on the curve, paying teachers according to length of service, and using public relations to "sell education"—all are illustrations of the extent to which our culture's materialistic and economic aspects permeate educational practice.

Or, consider how school children are admonished to "work hard" and "compete." Conant[6] insists that youngsters should experience "hard homework." Critics of education blast the "easy courses" and maintain that schools must "toughen up" their courses and tighten their standards.

What do we see in the culture at large? Labor-saving devices are everywhere. Snap-open beer cans; tear-open cigar, cigarette, and gum packages; electric can openers; automatic gear shifts; power brakes; power seat adjustments; self-dimming lights; automatic clothes dryers; and premixed cakes are just a few examples. How can a culture, clearly committed to reducing both the kinds and degrees of work, expect its youth to be caught up in the spirit of hard work? Our society is dedicated to minimzing work and maximizing leisure and play. Such a complete reversal of roles between youth and adults is hardly possible in a very short time, if, indeed, desirable. Educators might well ask themselves how realistic is this insistence on hard work? Certainly, hard work for its own sake makes no sense at all. Since the work which children carry home from school is labeled "homework," perhaps, those household chores children do while they are in school might be "schoolwork."

These absurd illustrations have been used to raise a very crucial and encompassing question. School people themselves work hard. Overwhelmed with expanding enrollments, pressures, and noise, they perseverate, doing more and more of the same wrong things. Throughout these activities, one can repeatedly see economic concepts applied to essentially noneconomic entities.

We are committed to improvement, so we try to change, for change we must. We experiment with this technique or that procedure, or this innovation or that kind of reorganization—all upon a most questionable assumption. Every effort presupposes that teachers will accept and put to good use a particular change *if they get increased satisfaction from the change involved.* In an enterprise permeated with economic principles and affected by economic factors, it is interesting that we presuppose altruism as an adequate basis for improvement in educational practice today.

What happens if we try out some new scheme, procedure, or textbook?

5 Callahan, Raymond E. *Education and the cult of efficiency.* Chicago, Ill.: University of Chicago Press, 1962.

6 Conant, James B. *The American high school today.* New York: McGraw-Hill Book Co., Inc., 1959.

Suppose it does work better. So what? What does the teacher gain? Greater satisfaction, and that is all. No matter how effectively or ineffectively he serves, the teacher has nothing to look forward to or little to fear except greater or lesser satisfaction.

Teachers are altruistic. One city school system recently paid its teachers in scrip for twenty-six out of twenty-nine consecutive pay periods, and they still taught each day. This is altruism beyond compare. However, this is the big question which I want to pose directly: Is altruism and increased satifaction an adequate base for seeking improvements in schools today? I doubt it, very much.

Very few teachers stay in public school teaching because of the pay. Like it or not, our culture is built upon the idea that if a man does a more effective job, he can improve his lot. Nowhere is this thesis expressed in public school teaching. A man can try to do a better job, but to increase his pay, he has to leave public school teaching for administration or college work, or some other field. Looking at the proportion of older men in public school teaching clearly shows that building an educational effort with a base guaranteeing only increased satisfaction is grossly inadequate. I have had students in college classes who *never* had a male teacher in their twelve years of public school education. We all know what psychology and sociology say about the importance of male models in the lives of youth. School systems, especially in the cities, must find ways to reward teaching proficiency in more material ways.

This is the dilemma and because city educational groups are increasingly being affected by labor and other nonprofessional influences, the chance to modify the altruistic base steadily grows slimmer. Labor unions are not concerned with effectiveness of instruction; their primary concern is with leisure and pay. Unless improved teaching is rewarded in some way other than through general increases in personal satisfaction, no major gains will probably be made. Perhaps "holding our own" and "doing what we can" is in itself a noble goal. If there were no schools, things would be much different, but undoubtedly not better, than they are today. Doing "more of the same," somehow strikes me as the antithesis of education. Has education been institutionalized along the wrong dimensions? Are we espousing one doctrine while basing our practices upon another? Have we gone astray?

## QUESTIONS THAT NEED ANSWERING

Let me now raise a number of questions, which will probably sound rhetorical, but they reveal important problems. Since I am not certain which are actually more demanding, some may appear of little consequence, but I feel that each raises important considerations for educators concerned with depressed-area schools.

1. With children in the slums outnumbering those on the farms by more

than a million,[7] why is it that universities do not prepare teachers for depressed-area schools as they do those for vocational agriculture? Why are more student teachers not assigned to slum area schools?

2. Why is it that, in some areas where factory employment is down, but finance, real estate, insurance, and construction have more than doubled,[8] we do not devise programs preparing youth for work? Why are the vocational shops standing idle or partly used in our city schools? Why do we allow minimum state-supported programs to become ceilings instead of floors, as maintained by law?

3. If we know that basic patterns of academic achievement are fairly well fixed by grade three,[9] that academic motivations derive more from personality structure and value commitment learned at home rather than at school,[10, 11, 12] why attempt to motivate students with grades, honor rolls, or fear of punishment? Or, if failure is viewed as being good, why don't we fail everybody so that no one will be deprived of a good thing? With more than 700 cases of suicides among school age youth in America in 1963,[13] and with clear indications that some resulted directly from grading practices in schools, why is it that no one has studied the relationship of suicide to grades in school? Why do incomprehensible grading practices still exist? Why do public schools let college admissions officers set their basic evaluation policies by insisting on class rank? Why is it that we try to describe all that we know about the richness of human learning and growth with the barest element of the total language at our disposal—a single letter? Why do we assume that drastic changes in the grading system or revisions in notions of motivation are actually more difficult than getting a man to the moon?

4. With evidence clearly indicating fundamental differences between boys and girls in reading achievement, delinquency, stuttering, epilepsy, basal metabolic rate, mental retardation, grades received, motivation, and language development,[14] why do schools insist on the same kinds of educational experiences? Why is it assumed that all students should be treated exactly

7 Dodson, Dan W. Education and the powerless, paper prepared for Third Work Conference on Curriculum and Teaching, Columbia University, June 1964 (Mimeographed).

8 Papier, William. Manpower and employment trends in Ohio, Columbus, O.: Ohio Bureau of Unemployment Compensation, 1964 (Mimeographed).

9 Bloom, Benjamin, *Stability and change in human characteristics.* New York: John Wiley and Sons, Inc., 1964.

10 Arnold, Magda. *Story sequence analysis.* New York: Columbia University Press, 1962.

11 Lichter, Solomon O., *et al. The drop outs.* New York: The Free Press of Glencoe, 1962, Chapter V.

12 McClelland, David C. *et al. The achievement motive.* New York: Appleton-Century-Crofts, Inc., 1953.

13 *Vital Statistics of the United States, 1962.* Vol. II, Mortality, Part A.

14 Waetjen, Walter B., and Grambes, Jean D. Sex differences: case of educational evasion, *Teachers College Record,* December 1963, *65,* 261–71.

the same in order to be fair? Would we want our doctor to give us the same prescription he gave everyone else? Can we solve educational ills by treating everyone exactly alike?

5. If more than 64 per cent of high school seniors attended a college less than 100 miles from home,[15] why aren't educators working to expand the public junior college idea? In view of the percentage of students enrolled in Ohio colleges out of the total population (1.9 percent) as compared to California (3.4 percent),[16] why do educators accept cutbacks in allocations and curtailed expansion except when financed by federal funds?

6. Why do we confuse legal authority and professional competence on problems related to helping youngsters learn? Why are we unable to distinguish administrative prerogatives from teachers' areas of concern? Why is it that in a time of tremendous teacher shortage and with tenure assured, teachers fear taking a stand or asserting themselves on important professional problems that affect how students learn?

7. When we know that power politics, rather than reason and facts, alone, influence legislators and other political leaders,[17] why do schoolmen insist on the begging and "we'll take what you can spare" approach when requesting public funds? Why not work to get people emotional about the facts like all other effective groups competing for the public dollar? Why do we believe that petitions, position papers, or resolutions will make things better in any way?

8. Why don't we answer positively the question: Should we lead or follow? Are we willing to trust the important decisions to those inhabiting state legislatures without trying to become a major political force in our communities? It is professional, ethical, and true to the children we serve to allow pressure groups to dictate educational policies and practice?

9. Can ways be found to revise metropolitan area school districting to use all the cultural and economic resources in the city area effectively? Are we wasting time reorganizing the small rural districts, when the major inequities are actually between the many districts and schools in the metropolitan areas? Is it useful to allocate funds on present foundation formulae when the school systems needing the funds most have the greatest difficulty keeping a high ADA? Is the neighborhood school concept in any way viable?

10. Why are administrators so uncreative and restrictive in their views? Why are the defiant and "far out" so few? Why does every high school

[15] Flanagan, John C., *et al. Project talent: the American high school student* (U.S. Office of Education Cooperative Research Project 635). Pittsburgh: University of Pittsburgh, Project Talent, 1964, pp. 10–29.

[16] Computed on basis of number of students enrolled in all of the colleges in the state as described in *Education Directory, Part 3, Higher Education*, 1962, (Washington, D.C.: U.S. Department of Health, Education, and Welfare) and total population of the state as described in *Statistical Abstract of the United States*, 1962.

[17] Kimbrough, Ralph. *Political power and education decision-making.* New York: Rand McNally and Co., 1964.

schedule look the same, wherever you go? Why is the proportion of students in advanced algebra, French, or business courses about the same anywhere? Why is it that with 26,000 high schools and thousands of so-called local units having separate controlling boards, educational programs are almost the same everywhere?

11. What is the process of educational change? Who is holding change back? Is it teachers, administrators, school boards, legislatures, the general public? Is inbreeding in city school systems harmful? How necessary or damaging is it for one to "come up through the system?" What are the consequences of not regularly "going outside" for talent? Can we clarify our concepts of effectiveness and loyalty? What is disloyalty and unprofessional behavior?

12. Why do we assume that college and public school people can communicate on problems related to city schools? Do these two groups really have a broad enough body of understanding to hear what the other has to say? Can college people accept that more than 45 per cent of some students in certain city schools[18] achieve below the second percentile on national achievement norms? Do they have reasonable and practical suggestions for the administrators and teachers in these schools? Do they adequately prepare prospective teachers for such situations? Why do we keep trying to find logical answers to psychological and sociological problems?

13. Why must all research in education be original? Why do we not replicate studies again and again? Why don't school systems and universities unite to conduct major studies on such a massive scale that there can be no question about the meaning of the results? Why not use samples of 50,000 students, in twenty or more school systems, on simple but important problems, such as the relationship of reading achievement to class size in the early elementary grades? Are we more concerned with powerful statistics than rigorous and powerful design? Are we more obsessed with obtaining outside money for research than in trying to get the job done? Does it really take extra money or just a basic change of heart?

14. Why does teaching appear the same wherever we go, be it slum or plush school, fast group or slow? Why does the overriding concern seem to be memorization of more and more facts? Why do classroom examinations all look the same—straight recall and recognition for almost all subject areas? Will "discovery learning" and the "structure of the discipline" be useful for those in the lower half on any achievement or ability scale? Can we really accept the fact that over 90 million Americans have IQ's of 99 or below?

15. Have those of us in schools ever been out in the real world? Or, have we grown through school, gone to college, gone back and taught school,

---

[18] Illustration drawn from data in author's files which originally came from a system-wide testing program conducted in a school district of approximately 60,000 pupils.

and never left the confines of the school at all? Do we then assume that because we liked school all others do, too? Have we tried to use those methods and procedures which we enjoyed and from which we benefited? Are we actually projecting here in certain ways?

16. Why are we so reluctant to accept that education means purposeful change in behavior, and that this means control? Do we so fear control that we do not even try to measure accomplishments accurately? Do we have some hidden concern not allowed to come directly to grips with problems of educational objectives and purposes? Are we really rationalizing or just "begging off" when we say that "learning is so complex we cannot possibly be aware of and measure and control all the variables at any one time?"

> Our teachers were absolute tyrants. They had no sympathy with youth; their one object was to stuff our brains and turn us into erudite apes like themselves. If any pupil showed the slightest trace of originality, they persecuted him relentlessly.[19]

The person who said this was, to be sure, a dropout. But, this could have been said by any one of a million who have left school early. For example, in Ohio there are more than 825,000 with less than an eighth-grade education and under 45 years of age.[20] If just one of those dropouts moves in the same direction as the author of the statement above, then we are in for real problems—Hitler said it in 1942.

We are living in an era of revolutions. Sweeping changes in religion, transportation, communication, and social relations demand that we clarify our purposes and build our practice on a solid philosophical and empirical base. No one really believes in *regressive* education, even though *progressive* education is a bad word today.

Out of the existing ferment, if public school and university men can come together in new and more powerful working patterns and relationships, then, perhaps, we can conceptualize some bold new alternatives to the followership and emergency procedures so prevalent today. We need ideas more than money, and more brave men, rather than an isolated few. The overwhelming problems in urban school education are really opportunities in disguise, if we can learn to think that way.

---

[19] Shirer, William L. *The rise and fall of the Third Reich.* New York: Simon and Schuster, Inc., 1959, p. 12.

[20] Computed from data in *Educational attainment of unemployed beneficiaries in Ohio,* Columbus, Ohio: Bureau of Unemployment Compensation, 1964.

WILLIAM C. KVARACEUS

# 9. SOCIAL STRESSES AND STRAINS ON CHILDREN AND YOUTH: SOME IMPLICATIONS FOR SCHOOLS

The most dangerous occupation to be found in any community today is to be a teen-ager.

Adolescence is a time when youngsters make minor decisions that have major consequences. The wrong subject elected in the ninth grade can slide the youngster into a course of study which may restrict post-high school education or deny him entrée to a college of his choice. The decision to "go steady" may restrict the range of social participation and serve to limit the field of choice of a suitable mate. At the same time this is a period when popularity with one's pals is of paramount importance. Many maturing youngsters find it more comfortable to be wrong with their pals than right with the parents, teachers, or adult community. This is a period of worship of minor—if not false-gods. Dress, beauty, conformity and athletics dominate the everyday life of many teen-agers to the exclusion of more permanent and vital values. And last, this is a period when the youngsters can easily be caught up in the web of adult exploitation. After all, the young have served from time immemorial as the best institutional scapegoat on the market. If the Soviet system spurts ahead in the race to the moon, the adults can always blame the ninth grade pupils who have failed to elect mathematics or science for our lag. To be a youth is to live dangerously.

One of the important functions that all children and youth must assume in our social system is to be a learner or a student. This function will be more easily played out by middle-class youngsters and by upwardly mobile lower-class boys and girls. For the downwardly mobile middle-class pupil and the stable and staying lower class youngster the school can become a harsh and meaningless place of confinement envenomed by every subject in the curriculum. This educational pressure cooker can easily emit a school drop-

Reprinted from *The High School Journal*, Vol. 47, No. 4 (January 1964), 140–45 by permission of the publisher.

out or delinquent. But let us take a closer look at curriculum pressures as they relate to the class status of the learner.

For many lower-class and even some middle-class youngsters, most curriculum experiences appear irrelevant and pointless. There is very little apparent connection between what goes on in school and the present or future life of the learner. In addition to the traditional function of transmitting the culture, school activities must connect with the child's present and his future. To ensure relevancy, school goals must be specified in terms of expected changes or modifications in behavior or in terms of the acquisition of new and desirable modes of behavior. As the behavior of masses of children undergoes modification, it may thus be possible to change the way of life and to improve the less effective cultural practices of the disadvantaged. School attendance and involvement in learning activities should make a discernible difference. This difference, broadly speaking, should be observable in the acquisition of new behavior or the changes in behavior of the learner. Such changes might be seen in the pupil's leisure-time activities, in his job competencies, in the management of his day-to-day home economics activities, in his decision-making and problem-solving behavior, in his maintenance of health and physical well-being, in the reading he does for information or pleasure, and in his capacity for further learning. Unless the pupil's behavior has been modified and improved and unless new and desirable behavior has been established, learning cannot be said to have taken place.

To illustrate this principle, consider first the traditional learning experience in English literature in the high school. A youngster is required to read carefully (if not with pleasure) a number of books from the "recommended reading list." A detailed appraisal of his reading reveals his recall of plot, character, setting, and theme. Having answered all or a sufficient number of questions to the satisfaction of the teacher, the young learner seldom or never reads another book. Yet he may receive a "passing mark" in literature, although his nonreading behavior has not changed. Or consider the pupil in social studies who has learned to recite the Bill of Rights, chapter and verse, but whose behavior and conduct as a youth now or as an adult later reflect no understanding of the meaning or implications of these articles in his personal, political, social, or business life. The expected and desired change in behavior has not taken place. The youngster has not learned.

To reiterate, in planning a variegated curriculum to meet the different needs of all pupils, the course objectives in so far as possible should be stated as concrete and visible modes of new behavior or as improvements or changes in established and less effective ways of behaving. As this is done, curriculum planners will need to consider three related problems.

First, there is the current danger, already cited, of mass education that will lead to a standardization of the lower-class learner (Negro, Puerto

Rican, etc.) in the stereotype of the "middle-class citizen and parent" or into a regimented array of "correct" opinions, purchases, leisure-time pursuits, and occupations. Stated conversely, the maverick, the independent thinker or performer, or the divergent creator should be carefully sought out among children and youth who are born and who live within the estate of lower-classness. How to educate—literally, to lead out or draw out—the Negro child from his subculture into middle-class milieu if the school's objectives so demand and yet preserve and develop elements of individuality, divergency, and independence represents a major problem facing the curriculum planners. Unfortunately the curriculum planners seldom consult with youth—white or nonwhite—nor with their parents either in curriculum implementation.

On this point, Anna Freud has made an astute observation:

> Educators, that is to say those adults who form the environment of the child, always want to make him what suits them, which consequently differs according to the century, position, rank, class, etc. of the adults. But all these varying aims have one feature in common. The universal aim of education is always to make out of the child a grown-up person who shall not be very different from the grown-up world around him.[1]

What the dominant society demands for and of the Negro often makes little sense to him or to his parents. This is especially true of the nonmobile Negro who is stable and is staying in the subculture. Inarticulate and nonverbal as the youngster may appear (yet note the richness and creativity of his own hipster tongue), the dialogue concerning the aims and objectives of the school and the aims and objectives of the youngster and his family must be started even before he comes to school.

Anna Freud also indicated that an educator—unlike the childcaring mother——always wants something from the child. Many lower-class children perceive this, and they appear afraid, unwilling, or unable to give back to the demanding authority. We need to inquire in schools why this is so.

Second, there is the constant threat of confining the lower-class student and the potential or actual dropout to those educational experiences aimed exclusively in the direction of objectives that are immediate, extrinsic, utilitarian, and practical.[2] Preoccupation with these goals runs the risk of placing a low ceiling on courses offered or chosen. The danger to the upwardly mobile lower-class youth, whether on their way or in ferment, is great. This is not to overlook what Riessman[3] has on several occasions

[1] Anna Freud, *Psychoanalysis for Teachers and Parents*, (Barbara Low, translator) Boston, Massachusetts: Beacon Press, p. 45.

[2] See for example the very heavy work-study emphasis placed on programs for "alienated youth" by the Phi Delta Kappa Commission on the Role of the School in Prevention of Juvenile Delinquency.

[3] Frank Riessman, "Teaching the Culturally Deprived," *NEA Journal* (April, 1963), p. 22.

pointed out—the need for concreteness and "down-to-earth learning by doing," especially in the initial stages and with the culturally less mobile student. Although accent on self and creativity may be alien to the culture of many deprived children, ideational goals should be held aloft and clearly visible, especially for the upwardly mobile and ultimately, through progression, for the less mobile. To diminish in any way the ideational goals in the education of Negro youth, for example, is to derogate. The current emphasis on expansion of occupational training programs and on the development of marketable skills in many schools, as valuable as they may be, can in the long run further disadvantage the disadvantaged whose educational sights may be lowered or whose stay in school may be shortened through the pursuit of terminal courses. Equal emphasis must be given to the development of school programs that place the accent on cultural enrichment, general education, and instructional improvement. Implicit in the differential student-course matching is the need for pupil personnel services, including counseling, testing, and job placement.

Third, to ensure desirable modifications in behavior or the development of new and improved modes of behavior, the school must provide richer opportunities to *practice* these behaviors as a part of the learning experience and as an expression of the product of learning. This calls for the development of practice opportunities and laboratory experiences in school and community. Too much of school experience is theoretical, abstract, or, at best, vicarious. What is sorely needed in the curriculum of the secondary school is a graduated series of real-life experiences in problem solving and decision making, in participation within the social, political, and economic life of the in-school and out-of-school society. Most youth are cut out of the main stream of community activities. They have minimal function. The exile, the disenfranchisement, the rejection are most severe and complete with Negro youth. At least white youth have some cosmetic value in the dominant adult community. In contrast, few adults swell with pride at the sight of norm-conforming Negro youth. To be a nothing, to have no function, is hard for all youth; but it is doubly hard for Negro youth.

Courses of study in problems of democracy, for example, should be centered on the study, planning, and solution of local community problems. It is true that only youth can solve the youth problem. The energies of American youth, white and nonwhite, have seldom been tapped for social and civic benefit. That Negro youth have the initiative, the inspiration, and the commitment to high social purpose cannot be questioned as one views their strong role now in the steady drive to freedom and job opportunity. Energies expended in demonstrations, sit-ins, freedom marches can also be directed to goals of self-realization and social betterment. The question to be explored here is: "What kind of laboratory experiences and practices can the local schools establish as an integral part of the regular curriculum to lend reality, meaning, and significance to the focus of learning and to fix habits of behavior as explicated in the educational goals of the school?"

Now to point up our discussion of educational goals stated in terms of behavioral outcomes. The objectives of the school should be established and revised through continuous discussion with parents and with lower-class youth themselves. These dialogues between school and home must be carried on a bivariate screen. Figure 1 presents an opportunity to scale the objectives

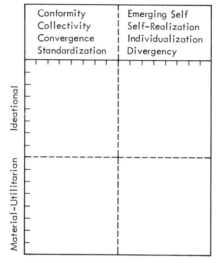

FIGURE 1. Goals of Education as Projections of Self-Image

of the school and of lower-class youth on two dimensions. The horizontal axis represents a bipolar dimension of objectives on a scale ranging from conformity to divergency; the vertical axis represents a scale ranging from material-utilitarian to ideational. The bivariate chart invites consideration of current emphasis in programs now being offered to culturally deprived youth; it also offers reflection for curriculum planners as well as for those who run the courses. It is suggested that the recorder plot the objectives of current school programs that have been implemented, using the suggested schemata or some adaptation of the two dimensions. The implications will soon become apparent.

But the goals of the school curricula are more than ordinary goals. They are projections of the future self-concept; they can promise a better future and a better self-concept; and they can beckon the learner to run the hard course of change.

PHILIP W. JACKSON

# 10.  ALIENATION IN THE CLASSROOM

Every child experiences the pain of failure and the joy of success long before he reaches school age, but his achievements, or lack of them, do not really become official until he enters the classroom. From then on, however, a public record of his progress gradually accumulates, and as a student he must learn to adapt to the continued and pervasive spirit of evaluation that will dominate his school years. For most, the adaptation is not too difficult. Ideally, they will experience far more success than failure, and will feel appropriately elated or depressed depending on the judgment their work receives. But, naturally, the ideal is not always realized. Many students do less well than they should and, more important, many—including some of the most able—do not seem to care, one way or the other, how they are doing. Although the two forms of difficulty—the academic and the motivational—are inter-related and both are serious, the apathetic student (irrespective of his achievement status) is a more disturbing example of classroom failure than is the youngster who is not doing well but who cares deeply about his lack of progress. The student who is willing but unable to do his work indicates, most frequently, the breakdown of a particular instructional sequence; but the student who no longer cares how well he does or who otherwise gives signs of being dissatisfied with school life, may signal the breakdown of social identification—a much more serious state of affairs. The remarks that follow focus chiefly on this second type of classroom failure: the student who cannot or will not respond appropriately to the values, the rewards, and the expectations, that combine to form the culture of the school.

Our understanding of social and psychological problems has been enhanced in recent years by the development of the concept of alienation. As the term was originally used by social theorists, such as Marx and Weber, alienation referred to the psychological discomfort suffered by the worker in an industrialized society. Cut off from both the means and the ends of production, the industrial worker lost the feeling of pride and commitment

Reprinted from *Psychology in the Schools*, Vol. 2, No. 4, (1965), 299–308, by permission of the publisher.

that had characterized the earlier craftsman. Labor, which was once a unified and intrinsically satisfying activity, had become fragmented and meaningless. The link between the product and the producer was broken, and with nothing to sell but himself, the worker began to feel curiously adrift in a world that seemed to be fashioned increasingly by and for the desires of others.

That which began as a theoretical description of the worker's plight has since been verified empirically, and as it is used today, the concept of alienation has been broadened to include not only the factory worker, but, to some extent, all who live in today's industrialized urban societies. The estrangement of modern man from himself and from others is viewed by many as the major psychological problem of our time. In the present paper ideas derived from empirical and theoretical studies of alienation will be applied to the examination of classroom problems.

## SIGNS OF ALIENATION IN THE SCHOOL

As a group, educators are highly achievement-oriented. And understandably so. Not only have their own academic careers been relatively successful—indicating that typically they have embraced the school's values from the beginning—but, in addition, their professional energies are focused almost exclusively on the promotion of achievement in others. It is hardly surprising, therefore, that many teachers view scholastic success as an all-encompassing good, and have a difficult time understanding people who do not share this basic value. Normally the teacher expects the student to be delighted by high grades and deflated by low ones (as he himself was when he was a student). Even when the rewards and punishments of grades are not operating, the student is thought to be gaining personal satisfaction from the growth of his own ability (as the teacher supposedly did), and, therefore, he is expected to undertake school tasks eagerly. When these expectations are not met, the teacher may become puzzled or annoyed by what he perceives as a complete disregard for an obvious virtue. Yet as the statistics on dropouts and delinquents, and the extensive literature devoted to the topic of classroom boredom indicate, there are many students who do not , share the teacher's enthusiasms.

One of the first and most important signs of disturbance in a social unit—and, hence, one of the most reliable indicators of alienation—appears when individuals or subgroups within the unit hold fundamentally different views of either the value of the rewards dispensed to group members or the conditions under which the rewards are distributed.

It is commonly recognized that there are two major reward systems operating in the classroom: the "intrinsic," which arises naturally from the growth of ability, and the "extrinsic," which comprises the evaluations given by teachers, fellow students, and outsiders. When either of these systems begins to misfire, the danger signals of more serious difficulties have been sounded. As has been suggested, the misfiring may occur in two ways: through the devaluation of the reward system or through its misapplication (either real or fancied).[1]

The student who gets no pleasure from his own progress has devaluated the *intrinsic* reward system. Similarly, the student who doesn't care what the teacher or others think has devaluated the *extrinsic* reward system. If the student is unable to see his own progress (or sees some when there is none) the *intrinsic* reward system is being misapplied. Similarly, if the student deserves praise or punishment from others (or thinks he does) and it is not given, the *extrinsic* reward system is being misapplied.

These two forms of malfunctioning—the devaluation and the misapplication of the school's rewards—are clearly interrlated. Indeed, in many instances there seems to be a causal relationship between the two. Devaluation (in the form of student indifference) is often a reaction to the suspicion of unfairness or illogic in the handling of rewards. The student who thinks he is being treated unfairly and who feels unable to do anything about it learns to remain detached and uninvolved. The possibility of there being this kind of causal link is important because it implies that beneath the student's bland indifference harsher feelings may lurk. These feelings may stem from a basic distrust of the classroom environment in general and of school authorities in particular.

A first step, then, in the diagnosis of alienation is to examine the degree of concordance between the objective and the subjective aspects of evaluation, between what society thinks of a person and what he thinks of himself. A lack of agreement in these matters would be interpreted as a serious danger signal. Even when there is a perfect agreement, however, and the reward system appears to be operating flawlessly, the search for symptoms of alienation cannot be abandoned. A second important diagnostic query focuses on the person's perception of the powers that give direction to his life. The important question here is how the individual believes his successes and failures come about. Who is responsible?

Basically, there are two sources of action—the self and the non-self—to which the burden of responsibility can be affixed. In extreme terms, we can believe either we are what we are because of our own actions or because of what others, or fate, or "Lady Luck," did to us. In the first instance, we feel in control of our life, as if we are masters of our destiny. In the second instance, helpless and victimized, as if our destiny is in the hands of forces over which we have little or no control. The beliefs of most people are

---

[1] Rewards may also be overvalued and, thus, sought more fervently than some people think they should be. The "money-hungry" adult and the "grade-hungry" student are two examples of such overstriving. These forms of pathological motivation will not be discussed in the present paper.

commonly somewhere between these two extremes, although one point of view may be more dominant than the other.

The student who does not accept personal responsibility for his achievement status is the educational equivalent of society's alienated man. Both his gains and his losses are a function of what others have done to him. Therefore, he cannot honestly feel pride in his achievements or shame for his failures.

Of the many manifestations of alienation, the one dealing with the assignment of responsibility has received the greatest amount of attention from researchers. An example of how this psychological condition is translated into empirical terms and used in studies of children is contained in an investigation by Crandall, Katkovsky, and Preston (1962). These researchers studied a group of forty primary grade children for whom they constructed a special test, called the Children's Intellectual Achievement Responsibility Questionnaire (abbreviated by the letters IAR). This questionnaire was designed to assess the degree to which the children believed their successes and failures to be the results of their own efforts or to be caused by what others did. The questionnaire contains descriptions of several common experiences of grade school children—some involving success and praise, others involving failure and criticism—and asks the child to tell whether these experiences, when they happen to him, are usually the result of what he does or of what others do. An example of a success item is: "Suppose you did better than usual in a subject at school. Would it probably happen (a) because you tried harder or (b) because someone helped you?" The following is a failure item: "When you make a mistake on a school assignment, is it usually (a) because the assignment the teacher gave was a particularly hard one or (b) because you were careless?" A high self-responsibility score is obtained by choosing the alternatives that imply the acceptance of personal blame or credit for failure or success.

Scores on the IAR were essentially unrelated to achievement behavior for girls, but not for boys. Indeed, the correlations between IAR scores and achievement were positive consistently for boys and were higher than similar statistics obtained with other predictor variables, including measures of need for achievement and general manifest anxiety.

An investigation of a similar phenomenon was conducted by Battle and Rotter (1963) who administered a newly designed projective test of internal-external control to a group of sixth and eighth grade students. The test consists of 29 cartoon items about which subjects are questioned concerning the assignment of responsibility for the conditions depicted (e.g., Why is she always hurting herself? Why is her mother always hollering at her?). The most important finding to come out of this study was that differences in attitudes toward internal and external control were related to social class and ethnic group. Lower-class Negroes were significantly more external than were middle-class Negroes or whites. Middle-class children, in general, were significantly more internal than were lower-class children.

A recent study by Bialer (1961) provides a third illustration of how the assignment of personal responsibility is used as a variable in research on children. Bialer developed a scale consisting of 23 questions of the following sort: "Do you really believe a kid can be whatever he wants to be?" "When nice things happen to you, is it only good luck?" "Do you often feel you get punished when you don't deserve it?" He administered this questionnaire, together with other tests, to a combined group of 89 mentally retarded and normal children selected from special classes and from regular elementary classrooms of a public school system. The tendency to perceive events as being under internal control (the opposite of being alienated) increased with age and was positively related, in particular, to the mental age of children. Bailer suggests that in the early stages of development there is no conception of the relationship between the outcome of events and one's own behavior. Consequently, he argues, young children, as a group, tend to view all of their experiences, as being controlled by the whims or fancies of fate, other people, and other external forces. Young children tend, then, to perceive events hedonistically, as merely pleasant or unpleasant, without considering whether or not their own actions might have contributed to the outcome.

The brief descriptions of these three studies give a general impression of how the concept of alienation is being used in studies of children. They also highlight the major findings with respect to assignment of personal responsibility. They indicate that the tendency to perceive success and failure as being bestowed by outside forces (a) is more characteristic of those who fail in school than of those who succeed; (b) is likely to occur more frequently among lower class than among middle class children; (c) is associated with other types of psychological disability, such as anxiety; and (d) is particularly evident in very young and mentally immature persons.

A logical reaction to a life over which one has little control would be to withdraw or to become resigned to the inevitable. It would seem, then, that an attitude of indifference might flow as naturally from the denial of personal responsibility as from the perception of injustice in the distribution of life's rewards. This indifference—which students sometimes describe as "playing it cool"—is the most important single indicator of alienation in the classroom. Underlying it are likely to be found feelings of being mistreated or manipulated by school officials.

## THE PERVASIVENESS OF ALIENATION

Only the surface manifestations of alienation have been treated thus far. To probe more deeply requires a consideration of how the syndrome of alienation may permeate many areas of behavior. Also, to this point, alienation has been described more as an individual psychological ailment, than as a shared mode of adaptation to some of the harsher features of social reality. In the comments that follow, the adaptive aspects of this behavioral strategy will be emphasized.

Social theory and research of the last few decades emphatically warns us not to assume that the alienated person is sick, and society well. Indeed, many social analysts believe that the opposite is true. This being so, when the sign of alienation appears in a student it is imperative to determine to what extent the symptoms arise from a unique personal history, and to what extent they stem from the reality of present school and home conditions. Sometimes, for example, the reward system of the school does operate illogically, and sometimes teachers do exert so much control that their students no longer have a feeling of personal power. When these conditions hold it is not surprising to find indifference or apathy in the classroom. Also, many children live in homes and neighborhoods in which there is little or no support for academic values. Small wonder that such students have difficulty working up more than lukewarm enthusiasm over the tasks and the rewards of school life. The badly functioning school and the unsupportive home environment are part of the everyday experience of many children. For these youngsters the syndrome of alienation is more understandable and the steps that might be taken to eliminate it are more obvious than is true for students who do not suffer from such immediate environmental disadvantages.

As he confronts an indifferent student, then, the teacher or counselor must ask whether the signs of motivational withdrawal are situationally confined or whether they pervasively color the student's view of the world. There is a difference between the student who is apathetic during his hours in the classroom, but engrossed in other contexts, and the one who is as indifferent to life outside the classroom as he is to life inside.

Two major difficulties, however, are connected with attempts to determine whether or not alienated behavior is situationally confined. The first arises from the fact that even when the behavior seems to occur only within clearly specified limits—such as a classroom—the question of how much the present situation contributes to the student's attitude is still to be answered. Although our typical reaction might be to place blame for the condition on the immediate setting, the student's present attitudes may be almost exclusively the result of his previous experience. Consider the high school student whose poor attention in mathematics classes stems from bad experiences with arithmetic instruction during his grade school years.

A second difficulty involved in fixing the limits of alienation derives from the fact that the disorder tends to spill over from one area of behavior to another. A major assumption underlying much of the theoretical writing is that when alienation arises in connection with the performance of a person's major social roles—such as worker, or mother, or soldier—it tends to spread to the performance of other roles as well. The alienation of the factory worker, arising out of conditions of the assembly line and mass production, shows up in his home life and his leisure hours as well as in his behavior on the job. In other words, alienation, even when situationally aroused, is not like a set of dirty coveralls that can be left behind when the whistle blows. Rather, it is an enduring perceptual set, which, if unchecked, may be expected to affect larger and larger portions of a person's life. Therefore, when students are identified whose total world view seems to be described appropriately as "alienated" it is unreasonable to assume that the source of this alienation is as diffuse as the symptom itself, although it might be quite difficult to identify the specific area of experience that served as the origin of the general ailment.

One way, then, of thinking about the degree or seriousness of a person's feeling of alienation is to consider the spread of the feeling in time and space; to ask, in effect, in how many different settings does he feel like this, or how many of his waking hours are tainted by these feelings? Another way is to consider the social or psychological depth, so to speak, at which the feeling seems to operate. In this regard, a helpful set of distinctions is suggested by Scott (1964), who argues that the condition of alienation may stem from four major "social sources." In order of increasing seriousness, these are: facilities, roles, norms, and values.

At the most rudimentary level, alienation consists of being unable to control facilities. Among the working class, with whom it was first identified, this feeling of powerlessness was created by the fact that the laborer no longer was able to control the speed of production (because of assembly line production) and was heightened as other major decisions concerning the means and ends of production were taken from him. At the second level, that of role, the alienated person no longer feels the need to adhere to the set of expectations society holds for him. Some of the many roles each person is expected to perform carry more status than others and, hence, are felt to be more important. The failure to accept responsibility for these "primary status-carrying roles" is naturally more serious psychologically and sociologically, than is a comparable failure with respect to more peripheral expectations.

Alienation from norms—Scott's third level—is reflected in the refusal to conform to the rules and regulations by which goals are obtained. The condition of being separated from the norms of society has received the label "anomie" from social theorists, notably Durkheim and Merton. The victim of this condition shares the values of most other men, but he cannot or will not use the normal channels for obtaining them. For such a person the usual relationship between means and ends has undergone a radical change. This change often brings with it a distrust of others, for when the means-ends relationship is altered a person can no longer believe that the motives of others are what they seem to be.

The fourth and most serious source of alienation occurs when the individual rejects, or simply fails to develop a commitment to one or more fundamental values of his society. The person who is alienated in this sense not only rejects the means of his fellows; he rejects the ends as well. In the most extreme case he does not transfer his allegiance to a set of substitute goals but, instead, turns away from all values. When this "devaluation of valuation" begins, the victim of alienation has entered upon the final separation that threatens to cut him off from all others, and, ultimately, from himself.

There are certain important and perhaps obvious resemblances between recurring forms of student behavior and the four types of alienation suggested by Scott. It is dangerous, however, to assume that these signs of difficulty have the same meaning when observed in students as when observed in adults. It may be, for example, that the separation between the world of children and the world of adults creates strains that produce, in turn, signs of a temporary alienation that will disappear by the time the child becomes an adult. It is equally possible, of course, that the greater social dependency of the child may make it more difficult for him than for the adult to turn away from the expectations and values of other people. Consequently, the behavioral indicators of alienation may signify a much more serious condition when observed in young people than when observed in adults. A variant of the latter argument is offered by Bettelheim (1961), who points out that "with the whole pressure of school, parents, educational system, and society at large favoring success in learning, it often takes a great deal more determination on the part of the non-learner to fail than for the good learner to do well in school." The comparison between adult and juvenile forms of alienation requires much more study than it has been given to date and must, therefore, be made with caution. Nonetheless, the resemblances are there and deserve comment.

The student who is separated from the facilities of scholarship (the first level of alienation in Scott's conceptual scheme) is the one who does not know how to handle the basic tools of learning. With respect to a particular subject (and possibly to all of his work) he may feel "lost" or "at sea." This student might also be overwhelmed by the amount of work he is expected to do and may despair of ever being able to catch up with his classmates.

The classroom equivalent of the adult's separation from role would be the young person's struggles with the responsibility of being a student. It is generally overlooked that the student role involves much more than the satisfactory performance of specific academic skills. A student is expected to maintain severe restrictions on his physical movement and his speech (even in the most "progressive" classroom!); he is expected to show the proper deference to the teacher and other authorities, while demonstrating, at the same time, his growth in autonomy and independence; he is expected to become intensely absorbed in the subject of the teaching session, but he is also expected to shift his interest and his focus of concern at the sound of a bell. He is expected to compete for the approval of the teacher and other educational rewards, but he is also admonished not to be a "show-off," for the reputation he earns in the classroom has to be lived with on the playground and in the dormitory. Given these varied and, at times, conflicting demands, it is hardly surprising that some people find the role of student difficult to perform.

The goals of the school, broadly considered, have to do with learning how to become a productive member of a particular segment of society. But the school is not alone in contributing to this end. Family, friends, and other formal agencies also play a part, and, depending on the particular group in which a person is seeking acceptance, the school's contribution may be great or small compared with that from other sources. It is possible, in other words, for a person to be highly achievement-oriented (in the general sense), to have an intense desire to learn certain things, and to care very much about his status in the eyes of others without at the same time viewing the school as instrumental in helping him to attain these goals. Such a person may be forced, of course, to be in school and while there his condition might best be described as alienation from a set of norms. For him the entire education institution, not just the role of student, is senseless. He may seek the same general goals as his classmates, but he does not perceive the classroom as a place where they may be obtained.

Separation from values, the most serious form of alienation in Scott's view, may show up in the classroom in two ways. First, some students may fail to shift from the value system of children—with its hedonistic orientation—to the value system of adults—with its emphasis on the virtues of responsibility, the control of impulse, and the like. Second, some students may fail to shift from the value system of their family and friends to the value system espoused by the school. The school, in other words, extols the virtues that characterize the mature middle-class adult (or are supposed to). Students who are uninterested or unable to become either mature or middle class might exhibit signs of this fourth form of alienation. Such students need not be openly defiant, although rebellion often springs from this condition; they may, instead, behave as if the "proper" values guided their action, but their lack of commitment rarely escapes the eye of the watchful teacher.

The four levels of alienation suggested by Scott—from facilities to values— do then, seem to be crudely identifiable within the classroom. Also, although much more needs to be known about the relationship between juvenile and adult froms of alienation, the increasing seriousness as the source of the separation moves from facilities to values seems to be as applicable to students as to adults. The task remaining is to consider, even though it can only be at the level of conjecture, some of the steps the school might take to check or reverse the progress of this disorder.

## THE TREATMENT OF ALIENATION

First, we must admit that no one really knows what to do about the alienated student. At best we can point to some of the common sources of classroom difficulty that seem to be related logically to the development of alienation and trust that improvement in these area will have beneficial results. Second, we must recognize that extreme forms of alienation may be too difficult for teachers to handle and may require outside help. The student who is extremely disgruntled with school life may also be disgruntled with life in general, and may need individual therapy if he is to begin to change his perceptions of himself and others.

One of the most badly needed changes in school practice is that of broadening our conventional definition of achievement. At present the assessment of achievement typically involves a normative judgment. That is, the student's work is compared with the achievement of his peers, locally and nationally, rather than with some absolute criterion or with his own previous level of performance. The normative approach is unavoidable in those school subjects where a precise statement of objectives is impossible—and there are many such subjects. But this type of evaluation often puts the student at the mercy of his classmates. If, on the one hand, he is "lucky" enough to have fellow students who do not want to work or who are not too bright, he can emerge successful from the experience. If, on the other hand, he happens to be among brilliant, hard-working students, he emerges looking a bit like a dolt. Either way, the student's evaluation is independent, to some extent, of his own efforts. Like the factory worker, he has little to do with setting the standards by which his work is judged.

If, however, some measure of growth were used or some absolute criteria set, the standards of achievement might not be as capricious as they now must seem to some students. The establishment of specific criteria of achievement is an extremely difficult job. Not enough is known about the structure of most school subjects to set anything but arbitrary standards. The use of gain scores as measures of achievement also presents problems. The interpretation of the size of gains, for instance, almost invariably reintroduces the concept of norm. Despite these difficulties, it is likely that any improvement in the variety and the logical compellingness of our achievement measures would help to reduce one of the common sources of discontent in the classroom.

Closely related to the goal of improving the assessment of achievement is the goal of clarifying academic expectations and the methods of attaining them. Students not only need to know far they have come; they also need to know where they are headed, and precisely how to get there. Yet scholastic goals and the best methods of reaching them are anything but clear in many classrooms. The clarification of ends and means does not require necessarily that students have a hand in setting their own goals, although it is probable that in some instances student planning would increase the appeal of educational objectives. In many instructional areas, however, it is doubtful that the students are capable of establishing their own goals or of determining how best to achieve them. Clear goals, regardless of how they are set, would help to reduce some of the uncertainty that likely contributes to the development of student indifference.

Academic standards are not the only expectations that operate in the classroom. In addition, there are the requirements that have to do with performing the role of student, and, as indicated earlier, these requirements are often ambiguous and conflicting. Most of the overt disturbances in the classroom appear to result from failure to meet student role expectations rather than from failure to meet academic standards. Therefore, efforts to clarify the student role or to decrease the internal conflict among the various role expectations would almost certainly make life in the classroom easier and more attractive.

Evidence in support of the benefits of greater clarity in the definition of the student role is presented by Kounin and Gump (1958) who conducted an observational study of kindergartens. They found that when teachers made their expectations clear, defined rules precisely, and suggested positive actions the misbehaving child might take, the incidence of unruly behavior diminished. Even when it occurred under these conditions, the misbehavior did not seem to have a negative effect on the rest of the children.

The student is not alone, of course, in his discomfort. The role of the teacher contains its own peculiar stresses, which serve indirectly as an additional source of classroom difficulty. Because teaching is a moral enterprise, the teacher often is encouraged to maintain a public image that is more virtuous, more omniscient, and more altruistic than is humanly possible. When students perceive the discrepancy between what the teacher professes to be and what he truly is, they are likely to charge the teacher with being "a phony." It is not difficult to understand why the student who perceives the teacher as being a bit of a fraud might feel disillusioned and might have some difficulty remaining involved in his role. In modern fiction many of the characters of J. D. Salinger—Holden Caulfield and Fanny Glass, in particular—reflect the disillusionment and disgust (harbingers of alienation) that accompany the perception of the "phony" teacher.

Contradictions between preaching and practicing are not new, and teachers are surely not the only offenders. Furthermore, in many instances the charge of phonyness is a bit too severe. As long as people strive to better themselves, a gap of some kind will exist between the real and the ideal. Failure to live constantly in accord with the ideal hardly provides grounds for applying the label "phony." Nonetheless, when students behave as if they believe such a label is appropriate, teachers must be alert enough to recognize this major sign of difficulty and to take steps to remedy it.

The classic educational solution for dealing with chronically failing students is to shower them with "success experiences." The engineering of success is certainly an important remedial strategy, but it is not the all-purpose palliative some educators believe it to be. First, if it is to be effective, the success must be in an area that is significant to the student. Success in building a doorstop or in winning a footrace is not very likely to ease the pain of failing to learn how to read, no matter how much we might believe in the benefits of compensation. The student cannot, in other words, make up for important failures by experiencing trivial successes. Second, success, if it is to have its expected therapeutic impact, must not only be perceived by the student as important, it must also be seen as resulting directly from something the student does. Success may be preplanned, but it must not be rigged. Educational handouts are of doubtful value to the alienated student.

In summary, the prevention and remediation of alienation involves first and foremost the clarification of the school environment. Students need to have a clearer picture of how they are doing, they need to understand the school's expectations and they need to be shown exactly how those expectations can be fulfilled. They need help in resolving the ambiguities of the student role and they need to be surrounded by teachers and administrators who are unequivocal in the perception of their own adult roles.

Finally, a repeated word of caution. Despite the similarities that have been discussed here, the alienated student and the alienated adult are really two distinct phenomena. It would be a mistake, therefore, to exaggerate the prognostic significance of signs of alienation in young people; to imagine, for example, that every indifferent student will become an indifferent adult. Fortunately, many of our least promising students turn out to be models of self-fulfillment when they mature. Not all, however, overcome the stresses of their student days, and others show no signs of difficulty until many years after they have left the classroom. Consequently, although we should not become prophets of despair each time we encounter a student who is less enthusiastic about schooling than we are, neither should we ignore early signs of danger that might erupt into a serious form of classroom failure.

## REFERENCES

BATTLE, ESTHER S., and J.B. ROTTER Children's feelings of personal control as related to social class and ethnic group. *Journal of Personality*, 1963, *31*, 482–90.

BETTELHEIM, B. The decision to fail. *School Review*, 1961, *69*, 377–412.

BIALER, I. Conceptualization of success and failure in mentally retarded and normal children. *Journal of Personality*, 1961, *29*, 303–20.

CRANDALL, V. J., W. KATKOVSKY, & ANNE PRESTON. Motivational and ability determinants of young children's intellectual achievement behaviors. *Child Development,* 1962, *33,* 643–61.

KOUNIN, J., and P. GUMP. The ripple effect in discipline. *Elementary School Jounal,* 1958, *59,* 158–62.

SCOTT, M. B. The social sources of alienation. In I. F. Horowitz (Ed.) *The new sociology: essays in honor of C. Wright Mills.* Oxford Univer. Press, 1964. Pp. 239–52.

RAPHAEL O. NYSTRAND

# 11. HIGH SCHOOL STUDENTS AS POLICY ADVOCATES

High school students are making unprecedented efforts to influence educational policy in American cities. Students across the country recently have used boycotts, demonstrations, and in some cases violence to protest local school conditions. Participants in these events often have been minority group students who charge that the school system has not treated them fairly. In some instances protests have erupted from student allegations that the curriculum is inadequate and/or that teachers or administrators are racially prejudiced. In other instances the precipitating incidents have been much more specific. For example, mass demonstrations have been provoked in some school districts by disagreements surrounding representation on the cheerleading squad, procedures for selecting a homecoming queen, or the suspension of a student for refusing to shave his mustache. A common theme in these events has been student advocacy of changes in school policies and procedures. In the disorders which sometimes have accompanied student protests, people have been injured, property has been destroyed, and schools have become staging centers for broader community conflict.

---

Reprinted from *Student Unrest in the Public Schools,* (Worthington, Ohio: Charles A. Jones Publishing Company, 1969), by permission of the publisher.

---

Editor Note: The inclusion of Nystrand's article is intended to reflect positively upon student activism as a strategy through which the conditions for achievement can be improved. Given this constructive prospect, it would seem unwise to always label dissent as an obstacle to achievement.

This emerging picture of American high school students as group activists, participating in collective protest and sometimes resorting to violence, contrasts markedly with the role usually ascribed to them. Student behavior in public schools has characteristically been that of obedient clients. According to the conventional view, students attend schools to receive educational benefits which are specified by parents, other citizens, and professionals. To be sure, these experiences frequently include student government and similar activities designed to sharpen student interactive and decision making skills. Testimony about the benefits of student government is ample and such activities have no doubt constituted a means for communicating the views of at least some students on some issues to school authorities. There are many indications, however, that student leaders frequently have been coopted by their faculty sponsors and that on matters which challenge traditional school procedures and/or are of educational significance, students usually have had little voice.

Student unrest in high schools is not in itself a new phenomenon. Any educator with responsibility for student discipline can cite numerous examples of students who show disrespect for authority. The vast majority of these examples, however, are of individual students who have created discipline problems, failed to do their homework, cut classes, or ultimately dropped out of school. Previous manifestations of group unrest have been limited almost exclusively to fights between rival student groups or destructive but essentially purposeless acts against school property by student gangs. Many of these rebellious acts have been products of student frustration and dissatisfaction with school authority systems but few have been a part of a conscious effort to change those systems.

There are indications that a new era in high school student-administration relations might be forthcoming. Students in many schools have recently attempted to bring about modifications in existing school policies by acting outside traditional school channels. The distinguishing feature of these incidents has been that students have organized themselves to aggregate their power in attempts to force changes by school authorities. The fact that these students have sought policy-oriented confrontations with school officials sets them apart from others in the past who have rebelled as individuals or who have worked through student government channels.

Participants in a recent seminar at Ohio State University prepared a series of case studies of incidents in which dissatisfied high school students advocated changes in school policies.[1] Incidents were selected in which students attempted to influence school policies by acting collectively outside

[1] These cases are presented and analyzed in Raphael O. Nystrand, editor, *Student Unrest in Public Schools* (Worthington, Ohio: Charles A. Jones Publishing Co., 1969). The names of all local people, places and organizations have been disguised in these cases and this paper. Any similarity of these names to actual people, places or organizations or to pseudonyms used in other case accounts is purely fortuitous.

traditional school authority structures. We identified and visited five cities across the nation in which such events had occurred. We will refer to them as Metropolis, Riverview, Central City, Elmwood and Big City. In each of these cities we sought to determine the reasons for student protests and demonstrations and the nature and consequences of these events. The remainder of this paper reports some findings from these case studies with regard to participants in student unrest, what students want, precipitating events and underlying causes, and the strategy of protest.

## PARTICIPANTS IN STUDENT UNREST

Participation in each of the five cases centered among minority group students. In no instance, however, did the situation appear to be one in which minority group (black or Mexican American) students were aligned against their white Anglo American counterparts. Indeed, white students actively supported the minority group cause in some instances.

We found little evidence that students who were leaders in the protests were recalcitrant trouble-makers of long standing. Indeed, the key figures in these incidents often were students who might just as well have been leaders in athletics, debate, student government or other traditional status activities in high schools. The original issue in Big City, for example, focused upon a star athlete. A principal in Metropolis emphasized that student leaders in his school were some of the smartest pupils. The Metropolis student activists disassociated themselves from other students who during a scheduled walkout broke school windows and destroyed other property. The way in which student activists coordinated their activities testified to the leadership skills which many possess. They generally defined and focused upon particular goals, spoke to school authorities with one voice, and planned their walkouts, meetings, and confrontations.

While participation was widespread in most instances, student support for the activists was by no means unanimous. Not all students joined the demonstrations and some of them expressed disdain for the demonstrators. For example, a student council member at the high school at which events centered in Central City criticized the activists for not working through established channels. Similarly, a student body president in Riverside presented a petition to the board of education in which more than two thousand students denounced the local student walkouts.

The evidence on this point is very sketchy but the cases suggest that student unrest may be more popular among underclassmen than it is with seniors and traditional student body leaders. Likewise, there is some evidence that students who oppose or are neutral toward the protestors initially can be won over by some small successes. For example, this apparently occurred in Elmwood when the response of school officials gave legitimacy to the protestors and subsequently enhanced the status of a group of sophomore negotiators with the student body.

WHAT STUDENTS WANT

Consideration of the demands enunciated by the students in the respective cities indicated similarity among them. For example, matters of dress and grooming were an issue in at least four of the cities, and students in all five called for more attention to minority culture on the part of school authorities. Useful distinctions can be made among three types of student demands which were encountered.

The first type includes matters which grow out of specific situations or a set of events, and for which students demand immediate and specific redress. School people sometimes regard such items as "things which bug kids now" and express the view that other concerns will supplant them soon. Examples of such items include demands to fire a particular teacher, retain a coach, reinstate certain students, change cafeteria menus and change the time of sock hops. Many principals undoubtedly recall numerous student petitions on such subjects which they merely set aside until student interest in them waned.

To dismiss all contemporary demands as being of this type grossly misinterprets and underestimates the importance of what students are saying. A second and more basic type of student demand is that which calls for recognition of student dignity and self worth. The central thrust of minority student demands is to achieve recognition and acceptance of the absolute equality of minority groups in American society. An essential theme in that context is that minority culture is the equal of white Anglo American culture. Therefore, the argument runs, schools should not force minority group students to forsake their own heritage for the standards of white, middle-class America. Calls for Afro or Mexican American history courses, the employment of minority group teachers and administrators, more student voice in school activities and greater sensitivity on the part of teachers and administrators exemplify this type of demand.

A third category of student demands includes those which call for improving educational programs as school people have traditionally defined them. In the instances which were studied, students called for smaller class sizes, more counselors, improved library facilities, bilingual instruction, remedial courses in some areas, and other types of curricular reform. These demands reflect consumer dissatisfaction in its most usual form. In effect, the students are saying that their schools are not doing what they are supposed to do as well as they should. An underlying theme in most protests seemed to be insistence that school personnel be more responsive to curriculum needs felt by students. In the cases which were studied support for students in these demands came not only from local citizens but in some instances from some administrators and teachers as well.

### PRECIPITATING EVENTS AND
### UNDERLYING CAUSES

The question of what actually sets off a student demonstration or a period of unrest is difficult to answer. In most of the cases, it is possible to point to a specific incident or series of incidents which preceded the statement of demands and student pursuit of them. In Riverview, for example, the cancellation of a school sponsored drama at the last minute prompted students to walk out in protest. An unproductive meeting between a local social worker and the school principal set things in motion at a high school in Central City. In Metropolis and Big City the suspension of students served as a rallying point for student unrest. It is more difficult to identify a single precipitating event at Woodruff High School in Elmwood where a series of events led some students to challenge the administration publicly.

It was clear in each of the cities, however, that the underlying causes of student actions were much more complicated than dissatisfaction over any single incident or set of events. These events seemed only to provide an exploitable opportunity for bringing basic dissatisfactions into the open.[2] Not only were there latent grievances apparent in all of the cities, students in at least four of them apparently spent some time planning their protest before it became public.

The search for underlying causes of student unrest must begin with the history of grievances that students believe they have endured previously without serious complaint. The cases indicated a few such conditions and there probably were others. But students like persons engaged in other pursuits always have been able to find fault with their institutions. Why do they act now and not before?

At least part of the answer relates to events in the larger society. Student leaders who were interviewed spoke forcefully about the importance of education in the modern world. As a statement by a student to the Central City board of education noted, they are interested in the best possible education. Second, the capability of schools to serve minority group students has been the subject of increasing criticism in recent years. This is true both for the nation and the specific cities which were visited. Students have noted this criticism particularly as it seems relevant to their own experience. Thus a climate has developed in which students appreciate the importance of education perhaps more than ever before, but simultaneously have become more sensitive to school weaknesses.

A third factor is that contemporary society has generated an action ethic.

[2] Similar tendencies have been noted in other settings. See, for example, James S. Coleman, *Community Conflict* (New York: The Free Press of Glencoe, 1957).

An important reaction to the growing industrialization and depersonalization of many societal processes has been emphasis upon organizing persons of like interests to control their own destiny.[3] Nowhere has the lesson of organize to make your interests known been taught more effectively in recent years than in matters related to schools and minority group affairs. In the former instance, teacher organizations have become a potent force in school policy making in many locales. In the latter case, new breed social workers, community organizers and other social actionists have helped ghetto residents organize everything from pleas for job training to rent strikes. Parents in some minority communities have learned that they, as well as teachers, can aggregate their power to have impact upon school policy making processes.[4] Students have observed these events and internalized the action ethic.

### THE STRATEGY OF PROTEST

The most important commonality among student strategies observed in the cases is that they were directed toward changing their respective educational systems. The students who developed them are activists not aliens. They differ from the dissatisfied students of previous generations who manifested their displeasure with the system by dropping out of it. They appear to differ also from some of the current breed of college students whose contempt for the system is so great that they urge its destruction.

Students in each of the cities emphasized the importance of unity and coordinating activities in support of their leaders. Actions which would reflect negatively upon the cause with which the students identified were often frowned upon and dissidents were sometimes disciplined. Thus, for example, East Riverview students postponed their walkout hoping to make it clear that the issues were more important than long hair and mini-skirts. Similarly the Metropolis student leaders disciplined a few students who destroyed local property while others carried out a planned march on the board of education. While many students in all of the cities did not associate themselves with the activists, those who did choose to challenge the system appeared to spend remarkably little energy arguing among themselves about goals and tactics. Indeed, the degree to which the respective student groups were able to mobilize and coordinate their resources contrasts sharply with the efforts of many adult groups involved in school affairs.

Students frequently sought assistance from outside their ranks. They often turned to adults for help in locating a place to meet, distributing informa-

[3] The literature on this point is extensive. A collection of relevant articles is Philip S. Olson, editor, *America as a Mass Society* (New York: The Free Press of Glencoe, 1963).

[4] The evidence of this lesson is seen most clearly in the emerging demands for community control. Probably the best-known examples are those associated with the I. S. 201 and Ocean Hill-Brownsville experimental districts in New York City.

tion, or refining goals and strategies. In more than one instance, they sought and received such assistance from teachers at their schools. Once they had formulated a set of grievances, the next step of the students usually was to attempt to talk with school officials about them. In most instances, these discussions began at the building level and moved progressively to the central administration and the board of education.[5]

It was not uncommon for the list of grievances or demands submitted by the students to grow in this process.[6] In Central City, for example, the issues expanded from one of grooming rules to the area of curriculum and student rights. In Elmwood a series of demands was presented in sequential fashion, and the ultimate issue turned upon the rights of students to plan two assemblies, a demand which came up very late in student-administrator discussions. Shifts which took place in student grievances tended to be from ones which were specific and based upon a particular incident (e.g., reinstatement of particular students) to those which were (1) harder to define but more basic to school activities (e.g., more sensitivity on the part of teachers) and, (2) of greater status value (e.g., freedom of dress or the right to plan an assembly).

Status demands appear to be of strategic importance to student efforts. In the first place, the achievement of status goals reinforces the feeling of self pride which is the central theme of contemporary thought within minority groups. Achievement of the right to display the symbols of a movement encourages more people to affect them. In the case of the student power movement, the display of such symbols also served to remind students of the success their leaders have enjoyed in negotiating with school officials. Equally important, the achievement of such visible goals indicates to school people and the general public alike that the distribution of power in school affairs has been altered. More than anything else student unrest reflects concerted efforts to loosen the controls which professional educators have maintained over students in virtually every important dimension of school life.

Student tactics in negotiating with school officials have included giving publicity to their grievances in the hope of enlarging their base of support, staging demonstrations, and boycotting classes. The latter two tactics are disruptive of the orderly processes typically associated with schooling, are given much publicity by the media, and almost always prompt a response from school officials. In the cases we observed it appeared that the primary purpose of such disruptive tactics was to force school officials to negotiate seriously with student leaders.

In conclusion, it should be noted that the students we have been talking

[5] The negotiation of school-community grievances presented by adults tends to follow a similar pattern. See Luvern L. Cunningham and Raphael O. Nystrand, *Citizen Participation in School Affairs* (Washington, D. C.: The Urban Coalition 1969).

[6] This is consistent with James S. Coleman's discussion of the dynamics of community conflict. James S. Coleman, *Community Conflict,* (New York: The Free Press of Glencoe, 1957) pp. 9–14.

about experienced varying degrees of success with respect to achieving policy changes. The incidents made the point that students can organize themselves to present demands to school officials and that at least some of the things which they call for can be negotiated successfully. These findings make it difficult to consider student unrest as merely a passing fad. The lesson is clear that students acting together can influence decisions about school programs and procedures. The question for the future is not whether student unrest will continue but what form it will take.

JOHN C. FLANAGAN

# 12.   IMPLEMENTING RECENT RESEARCH FINDINGS IN SECONDARY EDUCATION

Secondary education in the United States has not kept pace with its changing problem. The 1960 United States Census reports that the number of students enrolled in the four grades 9 through 12 was 87 percent of the total number of young people in the four age groups 14 through 17. In contrast, this ratio was 13 percent in 1900 and only 32 percent in 1920.

This has produced a situation in which the most noticeable single characteristic of today's school students is *individual differences.* The 1960 national survey known as Project TALENT found that 25 to 30 percent of the students in the 9th grade had already reached a higher level of ability and achievement in most of the common school subjects than had been attained by the average 12th grade student. Similarly it was found that the top 5 percent of the students in the 12th grade can learn the English equivalents of twice as many words in a foreign language in a given period of time as the average 12th grade student can. Students whose reading comprehension scores are in the top five percent of twelfth graders are able to answer correctly 8.5 of 10 five choice questions about the various ideas communicated by Jules Verne in typical paragraphs from his novels.

Reprinted from *The High School Journal,* (March 1965), pp. 377–82, by permission of the publisher.

Students with reading comprehension scores in the bottom five percent of twelfth graders answer less than 2 of 10 correctly. For typical paragraphs from children's adventure stories such as *Treasure Island* and *The Black Arrow* by Robert Louis Stevenson, those students with reading comprehension scores in the bottom five percent of twelfth graders answered only 2.7 of 10 questions correctly. The top five percent again answered 8.5 of 10 correctly. For typical paragraphs from the *Saturday Evening Post* the results were quite similar with the high group answering 8 to 10 questions correctly and the low group answering 2.7 of 10 correctly.

It is important to know just what types of material American twelfth graders can read with a satisfactory degree of understanding. If graduating high school seniors are designated as unsatisfactory readers who cannot answer correctly at least 5 of 10 items on paragraphs from Louisa May Alcott, 4 of 10 on paragraphs from Robert Louis Stevenson, 3 of 10 on paragraphs from Jules Verne, 6 of 10 from *Modern Screen,* 4 of 10 from the *Saturday Evening Post,* and 3 of 10 on paragraphs from the *Reader's Digest,* about 15 percent of twelfth grade students would be so designated.

Clearly all twelfth grade students should not be given the same textbooks and novels to read. Both teachers and administrators contribute to the conspicuous failure to suit instruction to the individual student. Many specific examples could be cited. To illustrate, consider the following:

1. A sophomore girl in a high school serving a professional clientele is not allowed to write a book review on the book she selected because it is on the junior reading list. Other sophomores who find the books on the sophomore list too difficult are not allowed to select easier ones.

2. As an example of the use of homogeneous grouping, it was found that none of the students assigned to the lowest of three sections of a ninth grade World History class could read and understand the text, but the teacher was required to use the same text as the other World History sections.

3. In a large city system a student who was erroneously assigned to study algebra and failed was required to repeat the course rather than substitute a more suitable general mathematics course. The administrative rule was that all failures must repeat the course until they pass or they were not allowed to graduate.

4. In the Project TALENT survey it was found that while two-thirds of the high schools in the large cities (250,000 or more), make some provision for bright students to complete their secondary schooling in less than four years, only a quarter of the other schools in the country permit any acceleration.

5. In the Project TALENT survey more than a third of the twelfth grade students said that about half the time or more often, "I read material over and over again without really understanding what I have read."

6. More than 53 percent of the twelfth grade boys and 37 percent of the twelfth grade girls said that about half the time or more often, "Lack of

interest in my school work makes it difficult for me to keep my attention on what I am doing."

To provide meaningful educational experiences for all of our school students, administrators and teachers must provide more flexible rules and more flexibility in course materials. They must once and for all discard the fiction that all entering ninth grade students are alike in knowledge and abilities and that all twelfth grade graduates must be expected to meet the same set of standards.

The high schools in the large cities and many other individual high schools throughout the country have set the pattern for caring for the academically bright. The formula varies from special schools such as the Bronx High School of Science, to special classes, to the procedures of individual teachers. As an example of the latter, in one high school in a college town, a mathematics teacher picked five students out of his class of 30 early in the eighth grade course. He gave them seats together in the back of the room and told them to pay attention to class discussions and his teaching only when it sounded interesting and to go on through the text book doing every other problem in the exercises. He suggested they check their answers with each other and when they finished the book he'd provide another. Although he offered to help if they had difficulties, he primarily agreed to set aside the strict rules and routines and let these students learn at their own rate. By the time they were juniors in high school they had completed college calculus and made outstanding scores on the advanced mathematics test of the College Entrance Examination Board.

It is clear that if the administrative and traditional obstacles are taken out of their way, the bright students can learn. In some fields such as English composition, supervision can be of more help than in others. However, teachers can be free to help students learn only if traditional procedures, requirements, and administrative "red tape" are removed. Unfortunately, improved opportunities for the education of the academically less apt are not so easily arranged. In many cases new types of instructional materials need to be developed for these students. Only by having many instructional resources immediately available can the teacher hope to cope with the great variety of educational needs presented by today's students. In the meantime, teachers and administrators must be resourceful in using and adapting the types of instructional materials now available to meet the needs of their students.

A second important characteristic of today's secondary school students is their *lack of positive motivation*. A large proportion of high school students have either no educational and occupational goals or inappropriate goals. For example, in the Project TALENT survey 53 percent of the 12th grade boys indicated they expected to graduate from a four year college. It is clear now that only a little more than half this number will obtain this amount of education.

The lack of realism with respect to the occupations 12th grade students expect to follow as a career is illustrated by the fact that 44 percent of the boys who expect to make a career in accounting are in the lower half in general academic aptitude. Similarly, 18 percent of all 12th grade boys plan engineering as their career. More than half of them fall below the 70th percentile in general academic aptitude which is likely to be the lower limit for successful completion of a college course in engineering. Of those planning a career in law, 30 percent are below the 20th percentile in general academic aptitude. It seems even more surprising to find that more than a third of the 12th grade boys who indicate they expect to make a career as a mathematician are below the average of all boys in this class in general academic aptitude. On the opposite side, 10 percent of the boys in this group who expect to make a career as an enlisted man in the armed forces and 10 percent of those who expect to make a career as a skilled worker are in the top 30 percent in general academic aptitude.

The career plans of many of the girls are similarly unrealistic. More than two-thirds of the 12th grade girls who expect to become accountants are in the lower half of the group in general academic aptitude. Half of these girls who plan careers as social workers are in the lower half of 12th grade girls in general academic aptitude. More than 20 percent of the girls who expect to become high school teachers are in the lower half of this group in general academic aptitude. On the reverse side, 20 percent of the 12th grade girls who are above the 70th percentile in general academic aptitudes expect to be secretaries, typists, and office clerks and an additional 12 percent of this high aptitude group are planning to be nurses.

Although the career plans of the students in the 12th grade are drastically changed from their plans in the 9th grade, well over half of those entering college will change their occupational plans during their college years. The plans of an even larger proportion of those not entering college change in the first years after completing high school.

The reasons for these changes have not been systematically analyzed yet. Certainly part of the reason is easily found. Students late in the 12th grade were asked how many times they had discussed colleges or college plans with their school counselor. More than 51 percent said either "none" or that they had "no school counselor." In reply to a similar question asking about their discussion of jobs or occupations, 62 percent reported either "no discussion" or "no school counselor available." Apparently teachers and principals were more available than counselors, since 63 percent of the 12th grade students reported at least one discussion regarding jobs and occupations with either a teacher or the principal.

It is clear that students are being given very inadequate assistance in making their educational and career plans. Their lack of realistic and definite direction is basic to the problems of dropouts, lack of interest in school work, and the floundering typical of many of today's young people.

The third characteristic of the present secondary school program is the inadequacy of procedures for *evaluating the effectiveness and quality of educational programs.* The first step in establishing evaluation procedures is to define and describe educational objectives in behavioral terms. Most statements of educational objectives are in broad general terms. To be useful for evaluation purposes the definition of educational objectives must be in terms of precise descriptions of observable changes to be produced in the behavior and performance of individual students. In accordance with the initial point regarding individual differences, it is completely unthinkable to develop a single set of educational objectives for secondary school students. There must be a separate and distinct set of educational objectives for each student.

To develop educational objectives appropriate to the needs of today's youth, it is essential to make a systematic study of these needs. The time when a few wise and experienced people can sit down and develop a set of educational objectives on the basis of their personal knowledge and observations is long past. No matter how wise and experienced the group is they must be provided systematic facts regarding the activities, obligations, and needs for effective participation in today's and, to the extent it can be foreseen, tomorrow's world. These needs are usually thought of in terms of two fundamental types. The first of these is the maximum realization of the individual's potential both in terms of vocational and avocational activities. The second relates to his effective participation in social groups of various types ranging from the family to international federations.

To collect these types of information as a basis for formulating detailed behavioral descriptions of effectiveness in these areas, empirical research to establish requirements must be carried out. Techniques such as task analysis and the collection of behavioral descriptions in the form of critical incidents are available for developing the systematic factual basis essential to preparing detailed statements of educational objectives.

In evaluation the definition of objectives is the first step. The second step is developing measurement and evaluation procedures. There are satisfactory procedures currently available for evaluating only a few types of educational objectives. Much developmental work remains to be done but this work is essential to evaluating the educational programs.

It is clear that there is a great deal of room for improvement in present educational programs. To distinguish mere change and innovation from genuine improvements, administrators and teachers must have clear statements of objectives and procedures for evaluating the progress of their students with respect to these objectives. Finally, the student, himself, must be made an important part of the process of establishing his personal objectives and evaluating his progress toward attaining them. Education in the secondary schools can become an effective aid to America's youth in their personal programs of self-development rather than retain its present image among many secondary school students as something to be endured.

PHILIP W. JACKSON

# 13.  THE STUDENT'S WORLD

When you were a child, how many times did you find yourself cornered by an adult, usually a strange aunt or uncle, who opened the conversation with that oldest of all gambits: "Well, how do you like school?" As an adult how often have you been left alone with someone else's child and, not knowing what else to say, found yourself falling back on some variant of the standard query: "How's school?" If you have not had both of these experiences, and each of them several times, you must be something of a recluse, for talk about school, when the dialogue is between an adult and a child, is almost as popular a social maneuver as talk about one's health or the weather.

Yet such talk, despite its popularity, rarely yields much information about what life in school is really like or how that life is experienced by the student to whom we are speaking. There seem to be two major reasons why this is so. First, in most instances neither the child nor the adult takes the query seriously. Both know that questions about school, like questions about personal health, are polite social gestures and usually are not intended to be answered fully or honestly. Thus, when asked about his classroom experiences, the fourth-grader who is having a miserable time with long division and who hates his teacher with a deep and abiding passion knows that he is expected to respond in much the same way as the victim of a migraine headache whose health is inquired into. Custom requires both sufferers to grin and say, "Fine, thank you."

A second limit to what we can learn about school life by talking to students arises from the fact that students may themselves not be acutely aware of what is happening to them in the classroom. Or, more precisely, they may never have tried to express the vague feelings and intuitive knowledge engendered by that experience. School life, like life in the military service, is not easy to describe to outsiders. You have to have been there.

But even being there is not enough, for when fellow students, or army veterans, discuss their common experience they often overlook or fail to

---

Reprinted from *The Elementary School Journal*, (April 1966), pp. 345–57, by permission of The University of Chicago Press and the author.

mention some of the obvious and pervasive aspects of that experience. And often it is these familiar and seemingly trivial features of life that are the most revealing when it comes to capturing the flavor or unique quality of membership in a social institution. Accordingly, the remainder of this essay will focus on some aspects of school life that students rarely talk about in the presence of adults or even, in all probability, in the presence of other students.

The subjects to be discussed are not dramatic, or even intrinsically interesting, though I shall do my best to keep them from becoming deathly dull. What is more important, they concern things we all know, even though we do not think about them too much. My only justification for asking you to attend to such mundane matters is my hope that a consideration of these trivial but neglected events will deepen our insight into the character of the student's world and, hence, might lead us to ask new questions about our responsibility for establishing and maintaining that world.

Two warnings are necessary. First, I do not bring words of uplift and inspiration. In fact, some of the things I am going to say about schools and schooling will not be pleasant. They may even sound harsh. But I am convinced that educators are ready for such talk, provided it stems from good intentions, and that they prefer frankness, even though it may hurt, to the sticky sentiment and clichés that have come to characterize educational discussions from college courses to inservice workshops. Second, I am not going to present a plan of action for your consideration. Indeed, I am going to raise many more questions than I shall answer. Here again, I believe that more and more teachers are becoming tired of hearing experts, whether from the university or the central office, hand out the latest panacea for eliminating our educational woes. For a change, therefore, I will ask you to do nothing but think. If there are practical implications that follow from what I have to say, it is up to you to find them.

## THE SOCIAL TRAFFIC OF
## THE CLASSROOM

Anyone who has ever taught knows that the classroom is a busy place, even though it may not always appear so to the casual visitor. Indeed, recent attempts to describe that busyness have yielded data that have proved surprising even to experienced teachers. For example, we have found in our studies of elementary-school classrooms that the teacher engages in as many as a thousand interpersonal interchanges each day. No comparable data are available for high-school teachers, but there is reason to believe that the interpersonal demands are equally severe at that level. A look at these and other demands is instructive as we try to understand what life in the classroom is really like.

First, consider the rapidity of the teacher's actions. What keeps her hopping from Jane to Billy to Sam, and back again, in the space of a few seconds? Clearly much of this activity is done in the interest of instruction. In most classrooms the teacher acts as a gatekeeper who manages the flow of interaction. When more than one person wishes to say something (a common condition in educational gatherings), it is the teacher who decides who will speak and when. Or we might turn our observation around and say that it is the teacher who determines who will not speak, for usually the number of students who want to say something exceeds the number who are granted the privilege.

### SUPPLY SERGEANT

Another time-consuming task for the teacher, at least in the elementary school, is that of serving as a supply sergeant. Classroom space and material resources are limited, and the teacher must allocate these resources judiciously. Not every student can use the big scissors at once; only one child at a time can look through the microscope or drink from the drinking fountain or use the pencil sharpener. Again, it is important to recognize that the number of students who want to use these resources at any given moment is often greater than the number that can use them.

Closely related to the job of doling out material resources is that of granting special privileges to deserving students. The teacher frequently must decide whether a student is to be allowed to hand in his homework paper late or make up a quiz that he missed or have an extra day to finish his laboratory assignment. In elementary-school classrooms it is usually the teacher who assigns coveted duties, such as serving on the safety patrol, running the movie projector, or clapping the erasers. Students soon learn that in school, as in life in general, many are called, but few are chosen.

### OFFICIAL TIMEKEEPER

A fourth responsibility of the teacher, and one that calls our attention to another important aspect of classroom life, is that of serving as an official timekeeper. The teacher sees to it that things begin and end on time, more or less. He determines the proper moment for switching from discussion to workbooks, or from spelling to arithmetic. He decides whether a student has spent too long in the washroom or whether those who take the bus may be dismissed. In many schools the teacher is assisted in this job by elaborate systems of bells and buzzers, but even when the school day is mechanically punctuated by clangs and hums, the teacher is not relieved of his responsibility for watching the clock. School is a place where things often take place not because people want them to, but because it is time for them to happen.

Our concern here is with the student and the quality of his life in the classroom. Therefore, the frenetic activity of the teacher, as she goes about calling on people, handing out supplies, granting privileges, and turning activities on and off, is of interest to us only insofar as the student experiences that behavior. We are interested, in other words, in what it is like to be on the receiving end of the teacher's action.

To begin, it is safe to say that for most students, some of the time, and for some students, most of the time, the classroom is a great place to be. When new insights are formed and mastery is achieved, when the teacher's queries can be answered with confidence, when privileges are granted and praise bestowed, when natural interests and desires coincide with institutional expectations—at such moments (and such moments do occur more or less regularly for many students) life at school must be extremely satisfying. A sufficient number of such experiences might well create the desire for further education and could set the stage for a lifetime of scholarship and academic pursuits.

But it is probably also true that for most students, some of the time, and for some students, most of the time, the classroom comes close to resembling a cage from which there is no escape. When activities are dull and repetitious, when the student is not called on even though he has signalled the desire to be heard, when privileges are not granted and blame, rather than praise, is bestowed, when natural interests and desires are antithetical to the demands of the institution—at such moments (and such moments probably occur more or less regularly for many students) life in school must be extremely irksome.

The important point is that these unpleasant aspects of school life are experienced not only by those who are failing in their schoolwork (although students with low achievement might receive more than their share of these discomforts). Nor are they simply a function of the cantankerousness or maladroitness of particular classroom teachers (although poor professional preparation and psychological disorders of teachers may well add to the student's burden). It would seem, in other words, that much of the pain of school life is a natural outgrowth of the problems of institutional living and the management of social traffic. Given the arrangement in which one person is chiefly responsible for serving the educational needs of thirty or thirty-five others and for articulating the demands of this group with those of several other groups in the same building, three of the most salient features of school life—delay, denial, and interruption—are almost inevitable.

### DELAY

Consider for a moment the frequency of delay. When we examine the details of classroom life carefully, it is surprising to see how much of the student's time is spent in waiting. In the elementary school, the students often line up for recess, for lunch, and for dismissal, and they frequently have to wait for the lines to be straight before they move. During individual seatwork they wait for the teacher to come around to their desk to inspect their work. When the whole class is working together, there is the waiting for the slower pupil to finish the work that the faster ones have completed. During discussion there is the waiting for fellow students to answer the teacher's query. When motion pictures or slides are shown, there is usually a delay as the room and the equipment are made ready. As time for the bell approaches, students are waiting for it to ring, even though they may still have their eyes on the teacher.

No one knows for sure how much of the student's time is spent in neutral, as it were, but it is certainly a memorable portion. How many of us who have lived thousands of days in schools can remember waiting anxiously for the minutes to tick away until the dismissal bell freed us? How many of us whose lungs are lined with chalk dust can recall the hours spent looking out the classroom window as we waited for the group in which we were imbedded to move sluggishly along? How many of us respond sympathetically to the following image of school life presented by George Santayana, as he describes his student days at Boston's Boys Latin School: "No blackboard was black; all were indelibly clouded with ingrained layers of old chalk; the more you rubbed it out, the more you rubbed it in. Every desk was stained with generations of inkspots cut deeply with initials and scratched drawings. What idle thoughts had been wandering for years through all those empty heads in all those tedious school hours! In the best schools almost all schooltime is wasted."[1]

Idleness, unfortunately, is only part of the picture, and perhaps not even the most important part. Waiting is not so bad and may even be beneficial when the things we are anticipating ultimately happen. Indeed, Longfellow was probably speaking with the voice of wisdom when, in his *Psalm of Life,* he advises us to "Learn to labour and to wait." But he was just a shade too optimistic when, in another poem (the title of which ironically is *The Student's Tale*), he promises his reader that "All things come round to him who will but wait." At least it is doubtful that Longfellow was referring to things that go on in classrooms, for there the waiting is sometimes in vain.

### DENIAL

The denial of desire is commonplace in school, and likely it has to be. Not everyone who wants to speak can be heard, not all the students' queries can be answered to their satisfaction, not all their requests can be granted. It is true that, considered individually, most of these denials are psychologically trivial; but considered cumulatively, their significance increases. Part of learning how to live in school involves learning how to give up desire as well as waiting for its fulfilment.

Typically, things happen on time in school, and, as a result, activities are often begun before interest is aroused and terminated before interest wanes. Once again, there is probably no alternative to this unnatural state of affairs.

---

[1] From George Santayana, "The Latin School" in *Unseen Harvests,* edited by Claude M. Fuess and Emory S. Basford. (New York: Macmillan, 1947), p. 487.

If we were to wait until students requested a history class on their own, as an instance, we would have a long wait. Similarly, if we allowed students to remain in their physical education classes until they grew tired of the game, there likely would not be time for other things. There seems to be no alternative, therefore, but to stop and start things on time, even though it means constantly interrupting the natural flow of interest and desire for at least some students.

### INTERRUPTIONS

But interruptions in the classroom are not confined to the beginning and ending of subject-matter periods. There are also more subtle ways in which activities are broken into. The irrelevant comment during class discussion, as an instance, often breaks the spell created by the relevant remarks that have preceeded it. When the teacher is working individually with a student while others are present—a common arrangement in elementary-school classrooms—petty interruptions, in the form of minor misbehavior or students coming to the teacher for advice, are the rule rather than the exception. In countless small ways the bubble of reality created during the teaching session is punctured, and much of the teacher's energy is spent in patching up the holes, just as much of the student's energy is spent in attempting to ignore them. Students are constantly "turning back" to their studies after their attention has been momentarily drawn elsewhere.

Here, then, are three of the unpublicized features of school life: delay, denial, and interruption. As educators what do we make of them? Or better, what should we make of them? Let's dispense with extreme reactions first.

On the one hand, there is the temptation to ignore these aspects of classroom experience. After all, delay, denial, and interruption are features of life in several other settings. Why pay particular attention to these petty annoyances when they occur in school? Students themselves do not seem to be too upset by these occurrences, the argument continues; therefore, it is probably safe to ignore them, with perhaps a passing cluck of disapproval, and move to more pressing educational problems.

On the other hand, there is the temptation to magnify these undesirable events until they become all that can be seen of school life. This alternative, which might be called the school-is-hell approach, seems to be dominant on many of our college campuses these days. It is the credo of the new undergraduate religion: anti-establishmentarianism.

The trouble with these extreme positions, as with most, is that they can be maintained only by choosing to ignore certain salient features of our educational scene. Defenders of the optimistic leave-well-enough-alone point of view preserve their calm by remaining blind to the fact of widespread discontent in our schools. Defenders of the school-is-hell point of view must keep the edge on their fury by failing to acknowledge that there is massive satisfaction as well as massive dissatisfaction in our classrooms.

A more dispassionate point of view, although one that is unlikely to capture newspaper headlines, might lead us to examine the strategies that students develop to adapt to these mundane features of school life. What must be done, in other words, if the student is to live a large portion of his life in an environment in which delay, denial, and interruption are inevitable? Further, how do the strategies for adapting to these demands combine with, complement, or contradict the strategies for acquiring knowledge and developing intellectual mastery?

## PATIENCE AND RESIGNATION

The quintessence of virture in an institutional setting is contained in the single word: *patience*. Without that quality life can be miserable for those who must spend time in our prisons, our hospitals, our corporation offices, and our schools. But virtue can become soured if tested too severely. And the conditions that lead to the development of patience can also, if carried too far, set the stage for the development of resignation—a much less virtuous condition. Indeed, the distinction between the patient person and the resigned person is not always easy to make on the basis of surface appearances, even though there is a world of difference in the psychological strength of the two.

While the patient person maintains a firm grasp on his own plans for the future and, hence, retains a sense of integrity, the resigned person does not. Resignation involves an act of psychological surrender in which one's own desires, plans, and interests are abandoned and action is taken on the basis of the desires, plans, and interests of others. The resigned person has not only given up hope, he has given up many other linkages between his motives and his actions. Resignation involves, in other words, a loss of feeling and a sense of no longer caring about what happens.

Returning to the situation in our schools, we can see that if students are to face the demands of classroom life with equanimity—rather than with disappointment, anger, and rebellion—they must learn to be patient. This means that they must be able to disengage, at least temporarily, their feelings from their actions. The hope is that the disengagement will not become permanent, that patience will not fade imperceptively into resignation. Yet in expressing this hope we acknowledge a real danger, for the one condition lies just beyond the other, along the same path. The problem for the teacher is to help students become uninvolved when conditions demand it, but not too uninvolved. We want students to be calm in the face of some of the frustrations caused by collective life in an institution, but we do not want them, in the jargon of adolescence, to "cool it."

## MASQUERADE

The second-grader who groans with disappointment when an enjoyable classroom activity is terminated, and the fourth-grader who zestfully waves his hand while his classmate is struggling to answer the teacher's question, both will likely be transformed by the time they reach high school or college into the jaded "professionals" of the classroom—those living inkblots whose enigmatic silence and languid slouch effectively mask both the presence and the absence of enthusiasm for educational affairs. Which ones are merely being patient, and which resigned? It is sometimes hard to tell.

Students also know that teachers like to see evidence of enthusiasm and involvement, and this knowledge causes alertness and other signs of interest to be worn as masks in much the same way as signs of indifference. Classroom courtesy demands that you keep your eye on the teachers and frown intensely at appropriate times even though your mind may be miles away. Again the teacher is faced with the problem of deciding which students are really with her as she goes about her work and which ones just appear to be with her.

The business of faking involvement and of masking withdrawal is not limited to the simple procedure of showing signs of attention when class is in session. These are not the only strategies by which students adapt to classroom demands. Nor are delay, denial, and interruption the only unpleasant aspects of school life with which the student must cope. The classroom, it must be remembered, is an evaluative setting in which the student must learn not just to comply with commands, but to comply in a way that yields a positive evaluation.

Thus arises the common practice of giving the teacher what she wants on written assignments and test questions, even though the assignments seem meaningless and the questions inane. Along with this practice goes the technique of disguising ignorance, of responding to the teacher's queries with sufficient ambiguity or with only thinly veiled flattery so that she will not discover and no longer care whether the student knows anything or not. (When I was a high-school student, this ploy was known as giving the teacher a "snow job." I do not know what name it goes under these days, but I am fairly confident that it is still being practiced.)

These forms of student behavior may be laughed off as harmless pranks, and sometimes they are nothing more than that. But all these acts of detachment and deception, each of which might be considered harmless, or even "cute," when used in moderation, grow out of attempts to deal with institutional constraints. When used excessively and in combination, they are the marks of the educational con-man, the student who has learned to size up teachers and give them what they want with all the shrewdness and feigned sincerity of a dishonest secondhand car dealer.

## THE TWO CURRICULUMS

Much that has been said up to this point can be summarized by suggesting that every school and every classroom really has two curriculums that the students are expected to master. The one that educators traditionally have

paid the most attention to might be called the official curriculum. Its core
is the three R's, and it contains all of the school subjects for which we
produce study guides and workbooks and teaching materials. It is the
curriculum that all the curriculum reform groups are shouting about
these days.

The other curriculum might be described as unofficial or perhaps even
hidden, because to date it has received scant attention from educators. This
hidden curriculum can also be represented by three R's, but not the familiar
one of reading, 'riting, and 'rithmetic. It is, instead, the curriculum of
rules, regulations, and routines, of things teachers and students must learn
if they are to make their way with minimum pain in the social institution
called *the school*.

## THE REWARD SYSTEM

Two or three important observations might be made about the relationship between these two curriculums. One is that the reward system of the
school is tied to both. Indeed, many of the rewards and punishments that
sound as if they are being dispensed on the basis of academic success and
failure are really more closely related to the mastery of the hidden curriculum. Consider, as an instance, the common teaching practice of giving a
student credit for trying. What do teachers mean when they say a student
tries to do his work? They mean, in essence, that he complies with the
procedural expectations of the institution. He does his homework (though
incorrectly), he raises his hand during class discussion (though he usually
comes up with the wrong answer), he keeps his nose in his book during free
study period (though he does not turn the page very often). He is, in other
words, a "model" student, though not necessarily a good one.

It is hard to imagine any of today's elementary-school teachers failing a
student who tries, even though his mastery of course content is slight.
And elementary-school teachers are not alone in this respect. At higher
levels of education as well rewards go to the solid citizen as well as to the
budding scholar. Surely many of our valedictorians and presidents of our
honor societies owe their success as much to institutional conformity as to
intellectual prowess. No doubt that bright-eyed little girl stands trembling before the principal on graduation day arrived there at least partly
because she typed her weekly themes neatly and handed her homework
in on time.

This manner of talking about educational affairs may sound cynical and
may be taken as a criticism of teachers or as an attempt to subvert the virtues
of neatness, punctuality, and courteous conduct in general. But nothing of
that kind is intended. The point is simply that in schools, as in prisons,
good behavior pays off.

Just as conformity to institutional expectations can lead to praise, so can the lack of it lead to trouble. As a matter of fact, the relationship of the hidden curriculum to student difficulties is even more striking than is its relationship to student success. Consider, as an instance, the conditions that lead to disciplinary action in the classroom. Why do teachers scold students? Because the student has given the wrong answer? Or because, try as he may, he fails to grasp the intricacies of long division? Not usually. A student is more likely to be scolded for coming into the room late or for making too much noise or for not listening to the teacher's directions or for pushing while in line. The teacher's wrath, in other words, is commonly triggered by violations of institutional regulations and routines rather than by the student's intellectual deficiencies.

Even with the more serious difficulties that clearly entail academic failure, the demands of the hidden curriculum lurk in the shadows. When Johnny's parents are summoned to school because their son is not doing too well in arithmetic, what explanation will be given for their son's poor performance? More than likely blame will be placed on motivational deficiencies in Johnny rather than on his intellectual shortcomings. The teacher may even go so far as to say that Johnny is *un*motivated during arithmetic period. But what does this mean? It means, in essence, that Johnny does not even try. And not trying, as we have seen, often boils down to a failure to comply with institutional expectations, a failure to master the hidden curriculum.

There is a further question that must be asked about the relationship between the official and the unofficial curriculums in our schools: To what extent does the mastery of one interfere with the mastery of the other? In other words, how do the demands of intellectual achievement relate to the demands of institutional conformity? Are they complementary or contradictory?

We have already seen that many features of classroom life call for patience, at best, and resignation, at worst. As the student learns to live in school, he learns to subjugate his own desires to the will of the teacher and to subdue his own actions in the interest of the common good. He learns to be passive and to acquiesce to the network of rules, regulations, and routines in which he is imbedded. He learns to tolerate petty frustrations and to accept the plans and the policies of higher authorities, even when their rationale is unexplained and their meaning unclear. Like the inhabitants of other institutional settings he learns that he must frequently shrug and say, "That's the way the ball bounces."

But the personal qualities that play a role in intellectual mastery are of a very different order from those that characterize the Company Man. Curiosity, as an instance, that most fundamental of all scholarly traits, calls forth the kind of probing, poking, and exploring that is almost antithetical to the attitude of passivity that has just been described. The productive scholar must develop the habit of challenging authority and of questioning the value of tradition. He must insist on explanations for things that are unclear. The scholar must certainly be a disciplined man, but his discipline is developed in the service of his scholarship, rather than in the service of other people's wishes and desires. In short, intellectual mastery calls for sublimated forms of aggression rather than submission to constraints.

## DOCILE SCHOLARS

These brief descriptions exaggerate the real differences between the demands of institutional conformity and the demands of scholarship, but they do serve to call our attention to points of possible conflict between the two sets of demands. Can both sets be mastered by the same person? Apparently so. Certainly not all our student council presidents and valedictorians are academic Uriah Heeps. Some have clearly managed to retain their intellectual aggressiveness while at the same time acquiescing to the laws that govern the social traffic of our schools. Apparently it is possible, under certain conditions at least, to breed docile scholars, even though the expression might appear at first glance to be a contradiction in terms. But how are these successes achieved? At what cost? And how many fail to achieve the synthesis of the so-called well-rounded student?

## A SOCIAL PRICE

The cost of scholastic success must be measured not only in terms of the intellectual energy expended or the non-academic gratifications denied. For many students there is also a social cost. The students who accede willingly and sincerely to both the intellectual and the institutional demands of the school run the risk of being perceived as defectors by their peers. At the lower levels of education these students are likely to be called *goody-goodies, tattletales,* and *teacher's pets;* at the upper levels they are called *greasy grinds, eager beavers,* and *squares.* In the eyes of many of their classmates the students who receive the highest praise from the authorities of the school are the ones who have sold out to the system. For many students this kind of name-calling, which is often correctly perceived as reflecting envy, is not difficult to endure and is a small price to pay for the admiration of adults whom they respect. For other students it is more important to appear to be a "regular guy." Many would rather be seen as a "buddy" than as a "brain."

The number of failures in our schools is much larger than the number of students who do not come up to snuff on our achievement tests or final exams. The failures include an untold number who seemingly succeed but who turn off their intellectual motors when the dismissal bell rings. These children have learned how to give the teacher what she wants all right, but in the process they have forgotten how to use their mental powers to give themselves what they want when the teacher is not around. This group includes the students who make the honor rolls and the dean's lists during the school year but who do not know what to do with themselves during the summer vacation. It includes the thousands who, after their formal schooling is finished and diploma hung on their wall, will never again be stirred by the quest for knowledge. It includes the millions for whom a childhood of teacher-watching is followed by an adulthood of television-viewing, with hardly a change of postures or facial expression to mark the transition. One almost expects them to raise their hands and ask Johnny Carson if they can go to the bathroom. Adequate as students? Yes. Adequate as adults? No.

### TWO WORLDS

And who is to blame for these failures? The schools? The society? The individual? All three share the responsibility, I suppose, but it is the school's role with which we are particularly concerned at present. The school, it would seem, asks the student for a commitment to two worlds—the world of the institution and the world of scholarship. Unfortunately, it often succeeds in obtaining only a feigned commitment to either one.

What about our own commitment to these two worlds? How have we partialled out our own loyalty? How much have we ourselves become Company Men, more interested in an up-to-date register than an up-to-date idea, more concerned with straight lines than with straight thinking? After all, we too, like our students, are rewarded for doing things neatly, and on time, with a minimum of fuss and bother. How often have we received compliments from our principals for the surface show of scholarship, for the attractiveness of our bulletin boards rather than for the vigor and imaginativeness of the ideas we present to our pupils? Nor are our administrators the villains of the piece, for they, in their turn, are caught in the same bind. The public wants its institutions to be run quietly, efficiently, and economically. The best-attended school-board meeting is almost always the one at which the budget is discussed. And who is this elusive public but the very people we educators had yesterday in our classrooms. So the circle is complete. No one is responsible, yet everyone is.

What, then, is life like in school? It would seem to be a life of contradictory demands and competing tendencies, a life in which discovery and disappointment go hand in hand, where the unpredictable and the routine are combined daily. These monotonous settings of desks and blackboards and books provide a stage for the cyclic enactment of a dull drama, a play that is at once boring and exciting. No wonder our young friend only says, "Fine!" when we ask him how things are going in the classroom. School is a puzzling place, and the puzzles are not all intellectual ones.

ROBERT BUSH

# 14. REDEFINING THE ROLE
# OF THE TEACHER

The necessity for a redefinition of the role of the teacher is upon us and may well shape the content and procedures of teacher education for decades to come. As big business and the Federal Government, with their formidable battery of modern technology crashes in upon our schools, classrooms, and teaching with rising crescendo, a permeating sense of disquietude stirs within us.

The public is uneasy, all the way from the parent and the citizen in the local community to the highest echelons of power in Washington. We in the profession are uneasy, too. New and higher than ever demands are being made upon the schools. At the same time, we are confronted with serious shortages of teachers and dollars. With the "knowledge explosion," curriculums are almost out of date before the ink on them is dry. Yet, we are expected to work miracles. These and other factors have conspired to produce a genuine educational crisis and, unless we have a vigorous and creative response to this crisis, the quality of our schools and, indeed, of our whole life will deteriorate.

The Federal Government has entered the arena because our leaders are convinced that the national welfare is at stake—education has moved from the sidelines to become a major productive force, an investment rather than a consumer item in the economy. One of the critical questions is: "Can the computer, automation, and modern technology help solve some of the critical problems in education?"

Big business, mass media, and the Federal Government are all converging to move into a sphere which, traditionally, has been one for local option and in which individual teachers have been relatively free to cope with their own problems. Nevertheless, in the face of teacher shortages and financial crises, school boards and taxpayers are intrigued with the economies that might be achieved if modern technology could be moved into the schools. Employers in all fields have always wanted to use machines when they could,

Reprinted from *Theory Into Practice,* (December 1967), pp. 246–51, by permission of the editor.

despite the fact that employees have always been suspicious of them and have even tried to destroy them. There is great beauty in the machine: the machine has no temper; it does what it is told with no argument; it has endless energy and never gets tired; it will endlessly repeat dull routine tasks without becoming bored and dissatisfied; it has no prejudice; it will treat equally the slum child in the central city and the affluent child. Most important, it can be junked, thrown away when it's worn out or when it becomes obsolete. These are an attractive set of propositions for the school administrator, the board of education, and the public.

Interesting experiments with the machines are being conducted here and abroad. For example, in American Samoa where education has been shamefully neglected for so long, we are testing whether or not a handful of excellent teachers can, through the use of television programs, radically improve the entire educational system. In Colombia, Alfonso Ocampo, the Rector of the University de Valle in Cali, recently pointed out:

> ...we are falling behind. With all of the additional monies that are being poured into this country, we are literally falling behind in education. Unless there is some radical application of technology to overcome the snail-like pace at which we are producing teachers and manning our schools, the result is going to be disastrous. If it's disastrous for us, it is going to be disastrous for you. [American educational system].[1]

We are further troubled because of radical changes taking place in our society in general. New and troublesome concepts are already beginning to affect the way in which we have organized our society. Margaret Mead points to the fact, not yet considered seriously, that we are no longer confronted mainly with a production problem, that distribution is more crucial today. The cost of preserving an affluent society is to get over the outworn idea of an industrializing society, i.e., that in order to share in society's wealth, one must do productive work. The idea that one must work in order to be able to live and to share in the wealth produced is an idea which Mead avers we must change if we are to preserve affluence. This means that a smaller and smaller percentage of highly skilled people will do more and more of the productive work of the world and that larger and larger numbers will stay in school longer, have a shorter work life, retire earlier, do less productive work, and still share fully in the fruits of society. These are bothersome concepts. We have been taught that you not only must but *should* work hard in order to share in the fruits of society. But, now, with automation lifting heavy production off our backs, we may at long last have enough people freed to care for other people—personal service for everyone. Automation can, however, be dehumanizing unless it is managed sensibly. The radical nature of technology is such that there will be fewer jobs and less work for human beings, not more as has been claimed. Further, adjust-

[1] From notes taken during a personal interview with Dr. Ocampo in Cali, Colombia, March 1967.

ment must also be made to the obsolete idea that once trained, we are trained for life. Many, perhaps most, occupations will require retraining two or three times. We shall have to rid ourselves of the idea that it is impossible to re-learn. This applies forcibly to what I wish to say about teachers: we need to establish the habit of going to school, of learning new roles and new ways of teaching things.

## THE ROLE OF THE TEACHER TODAY

To contrast the role of the teacher today with what I think it may become, I will draw on findings of some studies made over the last decade. Classrooms in public schools were studied with an interdisciplinary team to delineate the teacher's role as perceived by the teacher, by the administrator, and by selected persons in the community, and the role of the administrator was studied as perceived by the teacher, the administrator himself, and by selected laymen in the community.

According to the research, the teacher perceives his main role to be that of purveying knowledge to students, directing their learning—important work, which he felt was often disrupted by many irrelevant things imposed by administrators and laymen and parents. He also perceives that he should keep youngsters under direct control at all times—so does society, for we pass laws to ensure that no pupil shall be out from under the eye of a fully qualified teacher at any time during the day.

The teacher is taught to, and tends to believe, that he should do the whole job by himself, i.e., make the tests, grade the tests, return the results, interpret them, mark all the English themes, and teach all of the subjects. While he will accord others some say in the selection of what is to be taught, how it is to be taught is strictly his own affair, not subject to scrutiny by anyone else. The classroom is his castle. The administrator tends to accept most of this view held by the teacher, but he adds one important proviso: it is important for the teacher to teach youngsters, to teach them well, and to teach them something that is important, but, he should do it in such a way that *everybody is happy about it*. In this, he transfers his own role function as a harmonizer to that of the teacher. The administrator does not seem to care so much what the teacher teaches or how he teaches it as long as all teachers do it in approximately the same way. It is much easier to coordinate, another administrative function, if this is so.

The teacher also believes, and administrators and the community instruct him thus, that he should motivate and discipline the pupils. He should be a model of good behavior and conduct, thereby helping to shape the character and the moral structure of the individual pupil. It is furthermore conceived, particularly in the primary school, that the teacher will teach all the subjects for a whole year, with students moving the following year to another teacher who will teach all of the subjects. In the high school, the teacher is to teach one subject at a time, in a fairly standard period of fifty minutes, to be repeated five days a week for a semester or a year.

There is much wisdom bound up in all of this, and it should not be discarded lightly. But, I submit that it is conventional, and it is culture bound. For example, high schools abroad are not organized as American high schools, and, in elementary schools in some parts of the world, teachers stay with pupils for several years.

The established roles which I have delineated are now being challenged. A new order seems to be in the offing. We hear reports of teachers harmoniously dividing up the labor in wall-less carpeted rooms which are filled with accoustical perfume. What is going to happen? What should happen? What genuine possibilities exist in the new technologies and resources now available and appearing just over the horizon? What new attitudes should be adopted and what demands ought to be made on these developments?

The attitude we take toward the new technology may substantially affect what can be achieved. It is my conviction, not too strong as yet, that we may, at long last, be able to teach and to organize schools as we have really wanted and known how to for a long time. Consider for a moment the computers. At least three ways may be noted in which computers are beginning to be used:

*The Field of Data Processing.* Computers are being used to make report cards, registration, class lists, test scoring and reporting, processing of pupil personnel data, copying, record keeping, clerical work, attendance, etc. All of these matters have been a heavy burden, all must be well done, and all can be done much better by the computer and other data processing machines. We would be well rid of these tasks. These machines are still not being used widely, but they can and should be.

*Building the School Schedule.* Work on this problem has been under way for several years at Stanford. As we began study a half dozen years ago to see how well some of the new curriculums were being adopted, almost everywhere we encountered the reaction: "Yes, this is a great idea, but it can't be scheduled." We asked our industrial engineers, "Can the computer help us?" Now, five years and a half million dollars later, we can report that the problem has been licked in the sense that we can now get the schedule off the backs of the school personnel. In our first operational year, we demonstrated modular scheduling in four schools; this has steadily gone up each year. In 1967 we scheduled over one hundred schools. We could have five hundred, but we are still working on different kinds of problems. It is now possible to divide pupils into a variety of groups, have them meet for shorter or longer periods of time, in larger groups and smaller groups, once a week, or three times a day, in as many combinations as desired. It is now possible to unlock the school. But, the computer will not tell us a single thing about what to do with this unleashed potential. It has been interesting to note that in some schools where the computer schedule has been introduced, even though the computer schedule allows for more flexible scheduling, the schools are following precisely what they have for years. However, it is possible, with this potential, to realize Davies' idea of giving students responsibility for their own learning, putting them on their own for a substantial part of time so that they have time to read, write, think, and perform many other tasks without teacher supervision. At the same time we also provide relief for the unbearable load of the classroom teacher and give him some time to read, think, plan, and do many other things, handled more effectively when relieved of the task of supervising the pupil.

*Computer Assisted Instruction.* On the front page of its August 1966 issue, *Fortune* magazine carried a picture of the school of the future—a handsome young boy, a typewriter keyboard, a television monitor, but look as you will, no teacher. The Ravenswood Schools, in a suburb of Palo Alto, began teaching beginning arithmetic and beginning reading to first graders by computer and with no teacher present. Each pupil has an individual station. The lessons are individually paced and the pupils receive immediate feedback. Learning difficulties can be diagnosed, errors corrected, and extensive research on learning never before possible is taking place. At this time, the process is frightfully expensive and still frightfully frightening to many.

I have cited examples of things that are here now. With teachers freed from the bulk of the routine and with pupils spending substantial time each day on the machines, what will be left? What will teachers do? Much of what the teacher has formerly spent his time doing and what he has been expected to spend his time doing, namely the purveying of knowledge, may be better done with the new technology. The teacher's new and emerging role is going to lie elsewhere, mostly in the realm of interpersonal relationships.

## WHAT WILL TEACHERS DO?

If the teacher's role emerges as it should and can, the teacher will be able to view the process of education as a whole and to understand each individual child in his setting. The teacher will have an opportunity to confer and work with individual pupils and to confer and work closely with parents, something never really accomplished. Teachers have been a little more successful in working with parents in the elementary school than in the secondary school, but even in the elementary school the prevailing attitude is one of "toleration." Teachers will be free to work with pupils in small groups and to teach in small groups, e.g., in groups of five, eight, and ten, where I predict some of our most important redefinitions of the teacher's role may take place.

Another important change is that the teacher, instead of doing everything for everyone—feeling he must succeed with everyone and feeling guilty if he does not—is going to become the captain of a team rather than a lone operator and the sole arbiter and judge of everything that goes on. He will have machines, tools, materials, and other kinds of assistance available at his call and direction. He will be at the top of the educational pyramid rather than at its bottom, where he has remained for these many years. There will be greater specialization and use of assistance. With greater specialization at all levels, we shall need to guard against mechanization, to keep the process human and flexible. To self-guard against this, a central role of the teacher will be to work with youngsters in small groups.

Some troublesome questions arise concerning the ways in which teachers have been trained. My point of view is that much, if not most, of the current training of teachers is antithetical to effective teaching in small groups. Most of what trainees are taught to do, and most of what they are learning to do is exactly what they should not be doing if they are conducting small group teaching as it should be carried out. In the first place, we have assumed that teacher and student behavior is different from that which occurs in other contexts when the small group is genuinely operating for the correct purposes. Video tape recordings in classrooms where teachers now are teaching in small groups have been made. As anticipated, the teaching is almost identical with that which takes place in regular-sized groups and in large groups. The main role is as purveyor of knowledge, lecturer. It is mostly teacher talk. What is the appropriate purpose of teaching in small groups if the assumption that it is different from that which goes on in large groups is accepted? As a beginning, in our study of teaching in small groups at Stanford, we have identified two unique purposes: (1) to open up wide the channels of communication among the members of the group on an emotional and social as well as an intellectual level between pupil and pupil as well as between teacher and pupil; and (2) to provide an opportunity for individuals to apply knowledge and experience gained elsewhere to new situations, the old problem of transfer: to increase the ability to apply knowledge and experience to new problems.

With this as a beginning, we have been attempting to identify the kinds of pupil behavior which we want to foster in these small groups and that are uniquely appropriate for the small group. The next step is to identify the kind of teacher behavior which might reasonably be expected to produce the kind of pupil behavior desired and then to determine the kind of training programs which may be capable of producing teachers who can behave in the appropriate manner.

*Pupil Behaviors.* We want pupils to become genuinely involved in the activity. We want the individual pupil to be willing to put his ideas on the table, to be able to listen to what other pupils and teachers say about his contributions, both positively and negatively, and not react defensively when his ideas are criticized. It is important to be able and willing to put your ideas on the table and to listen to what others say and then to be able and willing to speak responsibly about another's ideas, to probe, approve, argue, and disagree.

We want to have the pupil behave not just for the teacher. According to almost all of the records we collected, this seems to be most of what goes on in school—we call it "playing school." The pupils are trying to find out what the teacher wants and generally to give it to him or in some cases to cause him difficulty in getting it. We have lucid examples. In one recording, we were trying to model the behavior of the teacher who was trying to get pupils genuinely involved and reacting because of the relevancy of the situation. The situation was defined as: "We are going to select what we want to study in social studies. And, after we have selected what we want to study, we'll then select one of the topics and go ahead and study it." The group leader stopped after this brief definition. It was quiet for fifteen or thirty seconds. The video tape records show the students beginning to squirm. The teacher sits quietly. After about forty-five seconds, one compulsive person who could no longer keep quiet says, "Well, uh, what about studying the origin of ancient civilizations?"

The teacher replies, "Well?"

Another fifteen or twenty second period of silence and another compulsive student responds, "Well, what about studying the origins of American civilization in Europe?"

Is more necessary? They tried repeatedly to find out what the teacher wanted. Only very skillful teacher behavior finally brought them to the point where they were discussing drugs, the war in Vietnam, and other matters that were uppermost in their minds.

The example illustrates that most of the behavior observed in small groups, and in all others, represents kids "playing school" rather than being genuinely involved, in listening thoughtfully to one another. They hide. They do not feel free to express their ideas. They want to dominate or be dominated. Thus, a further behavior we aim for is to help the pupil to perceive himself accurately—who he is. We aim to help him to learn to feel comfortable in the face of uncertainty, ambiguity, and change and, in the face of such circumstances, to act constructively.

If these are the kinds of pupil behavior desired, then what are the teacher behaviors that are most likely to produce the desired pupil behaviors?

*Teacher Behaviors.* For the pupil behaviors we have been discussing, the teacher behaviors needed appear to be almost exactly the opposite of most of what we are trying even with our experimental programs in teacher training at Stanford, where the aim in developing the technical skills of teaching is to teach teachers to reinforce specific kinds of student behavior in the Skinnerian model. Instead of giving positive reinforcement for every "proper" behavior, the teacher takes a nonevaluative stance toward pupils' comments. In other ways, he also tries to bring about an open environment for the group to operate in. In an appropriate small group setting, the teacher needs to react sensitively to the ideas, the feelings, and the actions of group members and to convey to each member of the group and to the group, itself, the worthwhileness of all contributions. It is also important in small group interaction for the teacher to alter his behavior appropriately for each phase in the development of the life history of the group. In the beginning, the teacher behaves in one way; as he reaches a certain point, he behaves in another fashion; and, as he comes to the end, he reacts in still another manner. This is not solely "group dynamics" or "sensitivity training," where a small group is thrown together to work out its problems. Here the emphasis is upon responsible professional teachers in small groups. The mode varies. It may at one point be necessary to get out of the way in order to get back in. Some teachers, for example, mistakenly aver that, if they talk too much they must move over to the side and let pupils take over. This is not the responsible role of which we speak. At this point, we are grasping for ways to train teachers to behave differently. We are groping in the dark in new territory, for the most part.

I have illustrated some of the directions we are now considering, but one troublesome problem is: Who sets the task in the small group? How do you modify it? Still another problem is: How do you evaluate work in the small group? The chief characteristic activity in a small group is discussion—not reading, not writing, not lecturing, not memorizing, not taking examinations.

There are certain things which should not be expected to appear in small groups, even though they often do: for example, we shouldn't assume that what has happened in a previous large group meeting will be immediately transferred into the small group. Another expectation is not to find discipline problems in small groups. When small groups are well run discipline problems simply do not appear. One of the most difficult lessons to learn is that everything that happens in a small group is revelant. If the topic gets off what you think is the main track, why did it get off? Who brings it back, why, and in what form? The *modus operandi* of teaching in small groups is more like that of modern jazz improvization than a Mozart concerto. Unfortunately, too many teachers try to conduct small groups in a style of a Mozart concerto. For large group instruction this is appropriate, but small group teaching properly proceeds from the nature of the group and the problems and the ideas that emerge from the group.

CONCLUSION

We could end this and the next decade with little or no change in the teacher's role. Those who believe this reflect the old proverb: this old anvil laughs at many broken hammers. I am inclined otherwise—if we are cooperative, helpful, and positive in our attitude and seize the opportunity, some exciting achievements are bound to occur. Recently, a national leader, speaking of the situation in the Far East, suggested that we must take a *positive* approach to our position on international affairs. He asserted, "You cannot bomb communism to death, you must feed it to death and clothe it to death and heal it to death. Where there is ignorance you must bring knowledge and where there is poverty you must bring relief. Most important, where there is oppression you must bring justice." Our attitude must be positive, for, if we continue to pursue our traditional pathways, we are like lemmings on our way to the sea.

CHAPTER 3

# RELATING
# AS A
# PROFESSIONAL

ARTHUR W. COMBS

# 15.  WHAT CAN MAN BECOME?

In his inaugural address President Kennedy said to us, "Ask not what your country can do for you. Ask, rather, what you can do for your country?"

This eloquent plea was immediately met with an answering cry from millions of Americans. "Tell us what we can do," we cried. We long for a goal to live for and die for. We long for goals that will define for us where we should stand, what we should work for, what we can commit our lives and fortunes to. These are not idle questions. They are deeply serious ones, for upon our answers to these questions will rest the outcome of the great ideological struggle in which we are now engaged. In such a struggle it is the beliefs, convictions, values we hold that will determine whether we win or lose. We simply cannot sit down at the same table to bargain with adversaries who have already decided before they begin, that they are willing to die for their beliefs unless we have an equally firm commitment. A man without conviction, engaged in discussion with one whose convictions are practically a religion, is a sitting duck to be changed. This is one of the things we learned from our research on the "brain-washed" soldiers who returned from Korea.

Well, what is our commitment? What do we stand for? Freedom, we have said, is our goal. For our forefathers this was easy to define. It was freedom from the tyranny of the British kings, freedom from religious persecution, freedom from want, freedom for the slaves. Even in our own times when we have been attacked we have risen magnificently to defend ourselves against outside aggressors. But what shall be our goals in times of peace and plenty or when outside forces do not press upon us? Goals for the have-nots are self-evident. Goals for those whose basic needs are satisfied are more difficult to define and less pressing to pursue.

Reprinted from the *California Journal for Instructional Improvement*, Vol. 4, (1961), pp. 15–23, a quarterly publication of the California Association for Supervision and Curriculum Development, by permission of the publishers.

REDEFINING FREEDOM IN
TERMS OF BECOMING

We all recognize that meaning and character come from striving. We are most alive when happily engaged in the pursuit of a goal. Freedom, we have said, is our goal—but freedom for what? What does freedom mean in a nation of incredible wealth? It is apparent we need a redefinition of freedom translatable into action, not in a time of crisis alone, but applicable as well in times of peace and security.

We have stated our fundamental belief in democracy in these terms: "When men are free, they can find their own best ways." But what is a free man? A man with a full belly? A man without problems? A man with no pressures? Free to do as he pleases? When such things are achieved, a man is still no more than a vegetable. It is not enough to be free to *be*. We need freedom to *become*.

But what can man become? What is the ultimate in human freedom? What does it mean for a man to achieve the fullest possible fulfillment of his potentialities? This is a question which a number of psychologists, sociologists, educators, and humanitarians have been asking for a generation. What does it mean to be a fully-functioning person, operating at the highest peak of his potentialities? What does it mean to be self-actualizing, self-realizing, a truly adequate person in the fullest possible sense of the word?

It would be hard to overestimate the importance of this search. For whatever we decide is a fully functioning, self-actualizing human being must, automatically, become the goal for all of us engaged in the helping relationships. These are the kinds of people we are trying to produce. It is to produce such people that our public schools exist, and the descriptions of these people provide us with the criteria in terms of which we can measure our success or failure.

As a result of the thinking and study of scholars and researchers, little by little, the picture begins to unfold. We begin to get some inkling of what the fully functioning person is like. This is no average man they are describing. Who, after all, wants to be average? This is a Free man with a capital F. This is a goal for us to shoot for, a picture of what can be and might be. Here is a concept of a free man that lifts our sights to what, perhaps, one day man may become.

What is more, a study of the characteristics emerging from the studies provides us with a blueprint for education practice. I believe the work of these people in defining the nature of self-actualization is certainly among the most exciting steps forward in our generation. For me, it has provided new meaning in life. It provides new goals and direction for me, not just in times of crisis, but in the quiet hours between, and in my professional work as well.

I cannot discuss all of the characteristics of these fully functioning, self-actualizing people which have now been described. Let me describe only two or three of these characteristics and go on to discuss what these characteristics seem to me to mean for education. Each of the characteristics of these people could be spelled out in many aspects of curriculum in terms of what we need to do to produce that kind of characteristic.

## SELF-ACTUALIZING PEOPLE SEE
## THEMSELVES IN POSITIVE WAYS

Highly free people, the studies seem to show, see themselves as liked, wanted, acceptable, able, dignified, and worthy. Feeling this way about themselves, moreover, they are likely to have a deep feeling of personal security which makes it much easier to confront the emergencies of life with far less fear and trembling than the rest of us. They feel about themselves that they are people of dignity and worth and they *behave* as though they were. Indeed, it is in this factor of how the individual sees himself that we are likely to find the most outstanding differences between well-adjusted and poorly adjusted people. It is not the people who feel about themselves that they are liked and wanted and acceptable and able and so on who fill our jails and mental hospitals. Rather, it is those who feel themselves deeply inadequate, unliked, unwanted, unacceptable, unable, and the like.

This characteristic of fully functioning personalities, it seems to me, has at least four distinctly important implications for us in education.

In the first place, it seems to me, it means *we must regard the individual's self as a recognized part of the curriculum.* People learn who they are and what they are from the ways in which they are treated by those who surround them in the process of their growing up. What we do in class, therefore, affects the individual's ways of seeing himself whether we are aware of our impact or not. We *teach* children who they are and what they are by the kinds of experiences we provide. Many school deficiencies we now know are the result of a child's *belief* that he cannot read, write, or do math. A child may be taught that he cannot read from the impatience and frustration among those who sought to teach him.

We cannot rule the self out of the classroom, even if we wanted to. A child does not park himself at the door. The self is the dearest thing he owns, and he cannot be induced to part with it for any reason. Even a poor, ragged, and unhappy self must be dragged along wherever he goes. It is, after all, the only one he owns. The self, we now know, determines even what we see and what we hear.

For some time now it has been a part of our education in philosophy that we need to be concerned about the learner as well as the subject. Consequently, we have emphasized the importance of the child in the process and have developed a so-called, child-centered school. Indeed, we have sometimes carried this so far that the general public has sometimes become concerned lest we get so involved in understanding the child that we forget to teach him something!

Sometimes this has been expressed in the question, "Are you educating for intellect or educating for adjustment?" Such a dichotomy is, of course, ridiculous. Surely, we are not seeking to produce either smart psychotics, on the one hand, nor well-adjusted dopes, on the other! The fact of the matter is, we simply cannot separate what an individual learns from the nature of the individual himself. Indeed, we do not have to. This is nicely demonstrated in a recent experiment by Staines in New Zealand.

As you know, at the end of the fourth year under the British system children take an examination which determines the direction of their educational program from that point on. Staines studied two groups of fourth-grade children preparing for these examinations. One group was taught by a teacher who paid no attention to the self-concepts of the children. The other class was taught by a teacher who was simply aware of and thinking about the self-concepts of the children, although he did nothing specifically planned to make changes in these matters. At the end of the year the two groups of children did about equally well on the academic aspects of the examination they took.

The adjustment level of the children in the two grades, however, was quite different. Adjustment levels in the classes taught by the teacher who was interested in the youngsters' self-concepts rose, while the adjustment level of the youngsters taught by the teacher who had ignored this factor actually decreased. Being concerned about the child's self-concept does not mean in any sense of the word that it is necessary for us to teach him any less.

Learning, itself, is a highly personal matter. Whether or not any given piece of information will be really learned by a youngster, we now know, is dependent upon whether or not he has discovered the personal meaning of that bit of information for him. It is the personal feeling I have about information, the personal commitment I have with respect to it that determines whether or not I behave differently as a result of having that information. Learning is not the cold, antiseptic examination of facts we once considered it. This is perhaps nowhere better illustrated than in the matter of dietetics. Dietitians have at their fingertips vast stores of information about what people *ought* to eat. Even you and I who are far less well informed know a good deal about what we ought to eat—but don't eat that! We go right on eating what we *want* to eat and *like* to eat, in spite of our information about the matter, until one day we cannot get into our favorite dress or a son says, "Gee, Mom, you're getting fat" or when, perhaps, like me, you visit your doctor for your annual checkup and, poking his finger in your stomach, he says, "Blubber! Sheer blubber!" Then, suddenly the information you have had all along takes on a new meaning and may even, just possibly, begin to affect your behavior.

Learning only happens to people. To ignore the presence of the person in the process simply runs the risk of failing to accomplish anything of very much importance. We cannot afford to ignore this important aspect of our problem. To do so runs the risk of making ourselves ineffective. The self is a part of the learning process and to ignore it is about as silly as saying, "I know my car needs a carburetor to run, but I think I'll run mine without one!"

Since the self is what matters to each of us, if we cast this out of school, we run the serious danger of teaching children that school is only about things that don't matter. If we are totally preoccupied with teaching subject matter, we may miss entirely the child to whom we are trying to teach it. We are all familiar with the examination time "boners." These represent the way the things we taught were seen by those whom we tried to teach.

Secondly, it seems to me, *the need for people who see themselves positively means that whatever diminishes the child's self has no place in education.* Humiliation, degradation, and failure are destructive to the self. It is commonly assumed in some places that shame and guilt are good for people, but this is rarely true, for the people who feel these things the most are the people who need them least.

Whatever makes the self smaller and meaner is not just bad for mental health. It undermines confidence and produces fear and withdrawal. It cuts down freedom of movement, the possibilities of intelligent behavior. What diminishes the self is stupefying and stultifying. Such people are a drag on the rest of us. Even worse are those who see themselves in negative terms as unliked, unwanted, unacceptable, unable, undignified, unworthy, and so on. These are the dangerous people of our society.

A positive self calls for success experience for everyone. People learn they *can* by succeeding, not by failing. There is a general feeling abroad in some places that failure is good for people, but nothing could be further from the truth. Self-actualizing people see themselves in positive ways, and you do not get this from having failures. If we teach a child he is a failure, we have no one to blame but ourselves if he comes to believe us and after that behaves so.

I do not believe it is an accident that for most children, after the third grade, there is very little variation in their grades for the rest of the time they are in school. It is as though, by the time a child reaches the third grade, he has discovered what his quota is, and after that he lives up to it. One learns he is *able* only from his successes. Even the "self-made man" who beats his chest and says, "What a fine fellow I am! I came up the hard way. Kids ought to have it hard," got this way precisely because he did *not* fail. He is a walking example of the man who did not fail.

But failure and success are feelings. They have to do with how the person to whom something happens sees the situation, not how it seems to those who look on from the outside. Success or failure does not happen unless the individual thinks it so. If a child believes he has failed, it doesn't make much difference whether other people think so or not. The important thing is what *he* believes, not what someone else does.

The provision of success for all students obviously calls for widespread curricula changes. Some sixty years ago we decided to educate everyone in this country, but we are still a long ways from discovering how to carry that out. We are still spending vast amounts of money, time, and energy trying to find ways to treat everyone alike. This, despite the fact that the most outstanding thing we know about human beings is that they are almost infinitely different. We are still providing many children with experiences of failure and self-reduction, not because we want to but because we seek to force them into a common mold which they do not fit.

*We must provide for individual differences.* We have talked now for a generation or more about individual differences, but we have made only a little progress in this direction. We see little in our elementary schools, practically none in our secondary schools, and in our colleges we are not even sure it is a good idea in the first place. Despite all our talk about individual differences we still continue to insist upon group goals and standards, to organize our schools around age groups with thirty students to a class. Many teachers are fearful and insecure when they leave the familiar territory of the textbook or traditional methods and the familiar lockstep of lecture, recitation, and grades. Even our beautiful new buildings are often no more than a dull series of similar boxes, light and airy and cheerful to be sure, but still designed for fixed-size groups.

What would it mean, I ask myself, if we were to organize in such a fashion as to *really* give each child an experience of success? We have talked about it, discussed it, even advocated it on occasion, but mostly we have been too timid and fearful to put it into effect.

The plain fact of the matter is we often impose failure on students by the kind of structure upon which we insist. Many a child in our large modern high school gets lost in the shuffle. What high school teacher can know all 300 students drifting through his class in the course of the day? Adolescence is lonely enough without further subjecting the child to this kind of experience.

We have decided that rich curricula require schools of large size. But people can and do get lost in large schools, and we run the risk of losing on the bananas what we made on the oranges. I recall the snow sculpture standing on the lawn of one of our dormitories at Syracuse University some years ago, a kind of cartoon in 3-D. It had a freshmen student jauntily walking into the University on one side and walking out the other side was, not a student, but an IBM card fully equipped with diploma and all his holes in the right places!

Surely it must be possible to organize our schools in such a way that somebody, somewhere in a junior or senior high school, is in contact with a child for a sufficiently long time to really get to know him. Guidance counselors who see him only an hour or two each semester are no solution. There is no substitute for the classroom teacher. The guidance function cannot be turned over to specialists. One good reason for this is the fact that adolescents simply do not take their problems to strangers. Adolescence is a deeply sensitive time of life, and the persons such children seek out for help are those with whom they have a continuing contact and that usually means a teacher, not a specialist. Some of the world's best guidance is done by coaches, advisers of the HiY, and even by the detention room keeper. The responsibility for knowing and understanding a child cannot be sloughed off. It remains the primary responsibility of the classroom teacher.

*We must apply our criteria for self-actualization to every educational experience.* Truly free, self-actualizing, fully-functioning people, we are told, are people who see themselves as liked, wanted, acceptable, able, dignified, worthy, and so on. Seeing oneself like this, however, is something one learns as a result of his experience during the years of his growing up. People *learn* that they are liked, wanted, acceptable, able from the things that happen to them and from the important people in their lives. In these statements we find the criteria for what we need to do in order to produce freer, more fully functioning people for our society. Let us apply these criteria to every aspect of educational experience. Let us ask about this school, this program, this policy, this method, this action, plan, or curriculum—does this help our students to feel more liked, wanted, acceptable, able, dignified, worthy, important, and so on? I have tried this with my own classes at the University with fascinating results. It has led me in some cases to reject time-honored methods and procedures. In others, it corroborated things I have known and believed for a long time. But perhaps best of all, it has led me in new directions, to new techniques, new principles. It has not always been easy, for sometimes I have had to give up cherished beliefs, to tread on unfamiliar paths with fear and trembling. Sometimes, even, I have gotten into trouble. I can only conclude, however, that despite the difficulties and tribulations the experimenting has been eminently worthwhile, and certainly never dull!

*It is necessary for us to learn how things seem to our pupils.* To produce the kinds of people the experts tell us we need and to do the kinds of things we have been talking about here require that we learn to understand how things look from the point of view of our students. Since students behave just as we do, according to how things seem to them, it follows that it is necessary for us to learn how things seem to our pupils. This, however, is not easy for two reasons: We have been taught for so long the importance of being objective, "of getting the facts," that for many of us it is a difficult thing to give up this scientific way of looking. On the other hand, how things seem to each of us seems so right and so *so* that it is a very difficult thing to understand that it may not be. Indeed the way things seem to us seems so certain that when other people do not see them the way we do we jump to either one of two conclusions: Either they must be very stupid or they are being perverse. Phyllis McGinley once expressed it very nicely when she said,

> I think we must give up the fiction
> That we can argue any view
> For what in me is pure conviction
> Is simply prejudice in you!

We need to develop a sensitivity to how things seem to the people with whom we are working. For a long time we have advocated in teacher-training institutions the idea that teachers need to understand the child. What has often happened, however, is that we have confused understanding *about* a child with understanding the child *himself*. Even when I know a great deal about human growth and development I may fail to understand a given child. When I have made a careful study of him, when I have interviewed his parents, searched his school records, looked over his health and physical records, tested and examined him fore and aft, I still may not understand him. I do not really understand him until I have learned to see how he sees himself and how he sees the world in which he lives. All this information about him will be of limited value until I have come to understand the way he sees things in his private world of meaning and feeling. There is a world of difference between understanding a *person* and understanding *about* him.

The kind of understanding we are talking about here is not a *knowledge about,* but a *sensitivity* to people. It is a kind of empathy, the ability to put oneself in another's shoes, to feel and see as he does. All of us have this ability to some extent, but good teachers have a lot of it.

In some research we have been carrying on at the University of Florida we find that we cannot tell the difference between good teachers and poor teachers on the basis of the methods they use. One of the differences that does seem to exist, however, between good and poor ones has to do with this question of sensitivity. Good teachers seem to be much more sensitive to how things seem to the people with whom they are working. In fact, this sensitivity seems so important that apparently intelligent people who have it can do pretty well at teaching without any instruction in methods whatever. With such sensitivity they find their own methods. On the other hand, equally intelligent people with much instruction in methods may do very badly because they are unable to assess the effect of their methods upon the people they are trying to teach.

### SELF-ACTUALIZING PEOPLE ARE
### OPEN TO THEIR EXPERIENCE

Let us turn now to a second characteristic of these highly self-actualizing, fully functioning personalities. All such people seem to be characterized by a high degree of openness to their experience. That is to say, they are people who are able to look at themselves and the world about them openly and without fear. They are able to see themselves accurately and realistically. Psychologists have sometimes called this the capacity for "acceptance" by which they seem to mean the ability to confront evidence.

Highly self-actualizing people seem to have such a degree of trust in themselves that they are able to look at any and all data without the necessity for defending themselves or distorting events in ways they would like them to be. They are able to accept the facts about the world and about themselves, and because they are able to do this, they are people with a high degree of autonomy. They are free wheelers able to move off in new directions, and this of course is what is meant by creativity. Believing and trusting in themselves, they are able to move out in new directions. What is more, because they are more open to data they are much more likely to have right answers than other people and consequently are much more likely to behave intelligently and efficiently than are the rest of us.

Self-actualizers enjoy exploring; they enjoy discovering. They are not thrown by their experience or defensive against it. They are able to accept what is and to deal with it effectively. Please note that acceptance in the sense we are using it here means the willingness to confront data. It does not mean that acceptance and resignation are synonymous. Because an individual is willing to say, "Yes, it is true I am a stinker," does not mean that he is necessarily resigned to that fact!

This capacity for acceptance, trust in oneself, and openness to experience points to at least three important principles for us in educational practice.

*The kind of openness to experience we have been talking about calls for rich opportunities for individuals to explore and test themselves.* Such openness comes from opportunities to permit oneself 'to get involved in events. Like learning to swim, one needs sufficient help to be sure that he does not drown. On the other hand, one can *never* learn to swim if he never goes near the water. Such openness to experience comes about as a consequence of being sufficiently secure where one is that he is able to branch out into new events with courage and determination. This is the road to creativity, so needed in this generation.

One cannot be creative, however, without opportunities to get into difficulties. Indeed, it has been said that the characteristic of genius is the enjoyment of getting into difficulties for the sheer pleasure of getting out of them. Creativity calls for breaking with tradition, going out in the blue, trying one's wings, breaking out of the established ruts. Creativity is bound to be accompanied with a high amount of disorder. A creative class will not be a quiet one, and a rigidly ordered class will not be a creative one. An overemphasis upon order, procedure, custom, tradition, the "right" may actually destroy the kind of openness we are talking about.

This is a strange profession we are in. It is a profession built upon right answers. We pay off on right answers and discourage wrong ones at every level of the teaching profession. Now it is certainly a good thing to be right, but if we are so preoccupied with "being right" that we have no room for people to make mistakes, we may rob them of their most important learning experience. People learn from their mistakes. Some of the most important learnings that most of us have ever had probably came about as a consequence of our mistakes, much more than those instances where we were right.

The fear of making mistakes is almost a disease of our profession. However, an overemphasis on the importance of being right and insistence upon perfection may boomerang to discourage people from trying at all. We need a great deal more freedom to look, to try, to experiment, to explore, to talk about, to discuss. We need to open up our curricula to things we do not grade for. This was beautifully stated by a little boy in the fifth grade who wrote to his teacher after they had had a discussion about love in his classroom: "I was very surprised when we talked in our class about love yesterday. I learned a lot of things and I found out about how lots of others feel. But I was surely surprised because I never knew you could talk about things in school that you didn't get grades for."

*The kind of openness called for by the experts requires of us that we help young people to cut loose from dependency far earlier than they do.* One of the criticisms we hear most often these days about our public schools is that we are producing a generation of irresponsibles. Like many of the criticisms leveled against us, I do not believe it is by any means as serious as that. I do believe, however, there is a germ of truth to be given some real consideration. The continued extension of childhood, characteristic of every phase of our modern life, tends to keep young people dependent far longer than they need be. Most of this dependency comes about as a consequence of our fear that young people may make mistakes if we set them free. The kind of openness characteristic of self-actualization, however, does not come about as a consequence of increased dependency. Quite the contrary, it comes about as a consequence of responsibility.

There are some who feel the setting up of a separate society by our adolescents is a consequence of this fear. The word "teenager" is practically a cuss word in our society. We simply do not like teenagers. They are permitted no real worthwhile place. We have built a world where there is little or no opportunity for them to have any feeling that they belong or are part of the larger society in which they live. They have little or no voice in what happens to them. They long for a feeling of importance and meaning, something to commit themselves to.

But the usual adult approach to these young people is to build them a new playground or Teen-Town where they are told to "go and play" some more. The plain fact of the matter is they are often an embarrassment to us. Consequently, we treat them as outsiders. It should not surprise us then if they build their own society. Look around you, and you will see that that is precisely what they have done—with their own language, their own customs, traditions, codes of values, even their own music, ways of dress, and symbols of status and prestige. They have done this because we have made no real place for them in our society.

This kind of separation of young people from their culture has the potentiality for great danger. They are people who do not feel they belong, do not feel under any necessity to pay their dues or look out for the members. Membership in a society is not felt by those who are cast out from it. Feelings of belonging and responsibility come about only as a consequence of feeling a part of and being given responsibility for other people.

Responsibility and independence, we need to remind ourselves, are not learned from having these things withheld. Take the case of the teacher who believes her class, for example. The teacher leaves her class telling the group, "I am going down to the office for a few minutes. I want you to be good kids until I get back." She goes to the office and returns to find the room in bedlam. Seeing this, she enters the room and says to her youngsters, "I will never leave you alone again!" If she means this, she has thereby robbed these youngsters of their only opportunity to learn how to behave when the teacher is not there. You cannot learn how to behave when the teacher is not there if the teacher never leaves you!

We do the same thing in the high school with student government. We are so afraid the youngsters might make a wrong decision that we do not let them make any. Whenever they make a decision, we veto that, and it doesn't take long before they get the idea that student government is only a game. Having come to this conclusion, they then tend to treat it like a game, and this infuriates us. We then cry out in despair, "See there, they do not even treat their government as anything but a game!" Perhaps, if they treat it like a game, we have no one to blame but ourselves for teaching them that that is what it is. In order to try one's wings there must be freedom of movement and opportunity to look and explore. If the fears of adults prevent this exploration, we have no one but ourselves to blame.

Let us not be misled by the cries of the young people themselves in this connection. I have often had teachers say to me, "But I want to give them responsibility and they don't want to take it!" This, of course, is often true, but should not discourage us from giving youngsters responsibility. It is only another indication that they are fearful of it because they had so little successful experience with it. The youngster who has not had much responsibility is quite likely to be frightened by having a large dose given to him before he is ready to assimilate it.

The rules of readiness that apply to everything else we know in education apply to learning about responsibility as well. Opportunities have to be paced to capacities. Readiness and capacity, however, are achieved from experience. You cannot expect a child to read if you never let him try, and you cannot expect him to be responsible without some successful experience with it. This is beautifully illustrated in the two old sayings: "If you want something done, get a busy man to do it" and "The rich get richer and the poor get poorer."

## WHEN MEN ARE FREE,
## THEY FIND THEIR OWN WAYS

It is a basic principle of democracy that "when men are free, they can find their own best ways." Modern psychology tells us that in each of us there is a deep and never-ending drive to become the very most we can. Despite the assurances of the psychologists about man's basic nature and the beliefs we ourselves so glibly state about the nature of democracy, nevertheless, most of us still approach children with serious doubts and misgivings. We don't *really* believe they can find their own best ways if we provide the proper conditions.

Recently I have been reading A. S. Neill's fascinating book, *Summerhill*. This is a description of a school in England run by a headmaster who believes in giving children freedom, even to the extent of deciding for themselves whether they will go to class at all. (They do!) The lengths he has gone to in giving personal responsibility are fascinating, even shocking, to many people. Certainly he goes far beyond what I have been willing to do in my teaching. The fascinating thing is this: He has been doing this for forty years *and it works!* Here is a living demonstration that individual freedom can work, that we do not need to be afraid as we have been, that maybe, if we can really have the courage to try, it will work out all right.

In recent years I have been trying to place more responsibility and trust in my students. One thing I have done is to use a method of grading that places most of the responsibility for planning, study, and evaluation on the student. This has been much criticized by my colleagues, but the results it gets in more and better work, in individual commitment, in increased freedom for the student, in more reading and thought and effort are well worth the price. Besides, as one of my students expressed it, "Well, Dr. Combs, sure, some students take advantage of your method of grading, but then the old method took advantage of the student!"

The production of openness and responsibility in students requires courage and trust on the part of teachers. If we ourselves are afraid to try and let others try, if we are so fearful they may make mistakes, we may rob them of their most priceless opportunities to learn and will defeat ourselves as well. We need to remind ourselves of Roosevelt's "The only thing we have to fear is fear itself."

## WHEN AN INDIVIDUAL FINDS INNER SECURITY, HE CAN BECOME OPEN TO HIS EXPERIENCE

The kind of openness characteristic of the truly adequate, full functioning personality the experts are describing for us comes about as a consequence of the individual's own feeling of security in himself. It is a product of his feeling that he is important, that he counts, that he is a part of the situation and the world in which he is moving. This feeling is created by the kind of atmosphere in which he lives and works. It is encouraged by atmospheres we are able to create in the classroom and the halls and laboratories that help young people to develop a feeling of trust in themselves.

What causes a person to feel outside undermines and destroys his feelings of trust. Differences must be respected and encouraged, not merely tolerated. As Earl Kelley has told us, the goal of education must be the increasing uniqueness of people, not increasing likeness. It is the flowering of individuality we seek, not the production of automatons. This means differences of all kinds must be encouraged, appreciated, valued. Segregation is not only socially undesirable; it is demoralizing and diminishing as well. We need to remind ourselves there is segregation on a thousand other bases than segregation of white and Negro that can equally as well get in our way. There is segregation, too, on the basis of age, social status, athletic prowess, dress, language, and religion, to name but a few.

The kind of openess we seek in the free personality requires a trust in self, and this means, to me, we need to change the situations we sometimes find in our teaching where the impression is given the student that all the answers worth having lie "out there." I believe it is necessary for us to recognize that the only important answers are those which the individual has within himself, for these are the only ones that will ever show up in his behavior. Consequently, the classroom must be a place where children explore "what I believe, what I think, what seems to me to be so" as well as what other people think and believe and hold to be true.

Since most human behavior is the product of beliefs, values, and convictions, it is these values that must make up a larger and larger part of our educational experience. We have been in the grip of a concept of teaching that worships objectivity for a long time now. Objectivity is of value to be sure, but objectivity requires looking at events with cold and dispassionate regard. People simply do not behave objectively. They behave in terms of their feelings, attitudes, and convictions even about the most scientific matters. I can be objective about your child; I cannot be objective about my own! The things that affect my behavior most importantly and most closely are those things in the realm of values and beliefs. An education system which does not permit me to explore these or which regards these vital aspects of life as unimportant or inadmissible to the classroom runs the risk of making itself an esthetic exercise valuable to only a few, having little to do with life, and making little impact upon the generations it hopes to affect.

DON HAMACHEK

# 16. CHARACTERISTICS OF GOOD TEACHERS AND IMPLICATIONS FOR TEACHER EDUCATION

It is, I think, a sad commentary about our educational system that it keeps announcing both publicly and privately that "good" and "poor" teachers cannot be distinguished one from the other. Probably no issue in education has been so voluminously researched as has teacher effectiveness and considerations which enhance or restrict this effectiveness. Nonetheless, we still read that we cannot tell the good guys from the bad guys. For example, Biddle and Ellena[2] in their book, *Contemporary Research on Teacher Effectiveness,* begin by stating that "the problem of teacher effectiveness is so complex that no one today knows what *The Competent Teacher* is." I think we *do* know what the competent—or effective, or good, or whatever you care to call him—teacher is, and in the remainder of this paper I will be as specific as possible in citing *why* I think we know along with implications for our teacher-education programs.

## WHAT THE RESEARCH SAYS

By and large, most research efforts aimed at investigating teacher effectiveness have attempted to probe one or more of the following dimensions of

Reprinted from *Phi Delta Kappan,* (February 1969), pp. 341–45, by permission of the author and publisher.

teacher personality and behavior: 1) personal characteristics, 2) instructional procedures and interaction styles, 3) perceptions of self, 4) perceptions of others. Because of space limits this is by no means an exhaustive review of the research related to the problem, but it is, I think, representative of the kind and variety of research findings linked to questions of teacher effectiveness.

*Personal Characteristics of Good Versus Poor Teachers.* We would probably agree that it is quite possible to have two teachers of equal intelligence, training, and grasp of subject matter who nevertheless differ considerably in the results they achieve with students. Part of the difference can be accounted for by the effect of a teacher's personality on the learners. What kinds of personality do students respond to?

Hart[7] conducted a study based upon the opinions of 3,725 high school seniors concerning best-liked and least-liked teachers and found a total of 43 different reasons for "liking Teacher A best" and 30 different reasons for "liking Teacher Z least." Not surprisingly, over 51 percent of the students said that they liked best those teachers who were "helpful in school work, who explained lessons and assignments clearly, and who used examples in teaching." Also, better than 40 percent responded favorably to teachers with a "sense of humor." Those teachers assessed most negatively were "unable to explain clearly, were partial to brighter students, and had superior, aloof, overbearing attitudes." In addition, over 50 percent of the respondents mentioned behaviors such as "too cross, crabby, grouchy, and sarcastic" as reasons for disliking many teachers. Interestingly enough, mastery of subject matter, which is vital but badly overemphasized by specialists, ranked sixteenth on both lists. Somehow students seem willing to take more or less for granted that a teacher "knows" his material. What seems to make a difference is the teacher's personal style in *communicating* what he knows. Studies by Witty[14] and Bousfield[3] tend to support these conclusions at both the high school *and* college level.

Having desirable personal qualities is one thing, but what are the results of rigorous tests of whether the teacher's having them makes any difference in the performance of students?

Cogan[4] found that warm, considerate teachers got an unusual amount of original poetry and art from their high school students. Reed[10] found that teachers higher in a capacity for warmth favorably affected their pupils' interests in science. Using scores from achievement tests as their criterion measure, Heil, Powell, and Fiefer[8] compared various teacher-pupil personality combinations and found that the well-integrated (healthy, well-rounded, flexible) teachers were most effective with *all* types of students. Spaulding[12] found that the self-concepts of elementary school children were apt to be higher and more positive in classrooms in which the teacher was "socially integrative" and "learner supportive."

In essence, I think the evidence is quite clear when it comes to sorting out good or effective from bad or ineffective teachers on the basis of personal characteristics. Effective teachers appear to be those who are, shall we say, "human" in the fullest sense of the word. They have a sense of humor, are fair, empathetic, more democratic than autocratic, and apparently are more able to relate easily and naturally to students on either a one-to-one or group basis. Their classrooms seem to reflect miniature enterprise operations in the sense that they are more open, spontaneous, and adaptable to change. Ineffective teachers apparently lack a sense of humor, grow impatient easily, use cutting, ego-reducing comments in class, are less well-integrated, are inclined to be somewhat authoritarian, and are generally less sensitive to the needs of their students. Indeed, research related to authoritarianism suggests that the bureaucratic conduct and rigid overtones of the ineffective teacher's classroom are desperate measures to support the weak pillars of his own personality structure.

*Instructional Procedures and Interaction Styles of Good Versus Poor Teachers.* If there really are polar extremes such as "good" or "poor" teachers, then we can reasonably assume that these teachers differ not only in personal characteristics but in the way they conduct themselves in the classroom.

Flanders[6] found that classrooms in which achievement and attitudes were superior were likely to be conducted by teachers who did not blindly pursue a single behavioral-instructional path to the exclusion of other possibilities. In other words, the more successful teachers were better able to range along a continuum of interaction styles which varied from fairly active, dominative support on the one hand to a more reflective, discriminating support on the other. Interestingly, those teachers who were *not* successful were the very ones who were inclined to use the same interaction styles in a more or less rigid fashion.

Barr[1] discovered that not only did poor teachers make more assignments than good teachers but, almost without exception, they made some sort of textbook assignment as part of their unyielding daily procedure. The majority of good teachers used more outside books and problem-project assignments. When the text was assigned they were more likely to supplement it with topics, questions, or other references.

Research findings related to interaction styles variously called "learner-centered" or "teacher-centered" point to similar conclusions. In general, it appears that the amount of cognitive gain is largely unaffected by the autocratic or democratic tendencies of the instructor. However, when affective gains are considered, the results are somewhat different. For example, Stern[13] reviewed 34 studies comparing nondirective with directive instruction and concluded:

> Regardless of whether the investigator was concerned with attitudes toward the cultural out group, toward other participants in the class, or toward the

self, results generally have indicated that nondirective instruction facilitates a shift in a more favorable, acceptant direction.

When it comes to classroom behavior, interaction patterns, and teaching styles, good or effective teachers seem to reflect more of the following behaviors:

1. Willingness to be flexible, to be direct or indirect as the situation demands
2. Ability to perceive the world from the student's point of view
3. Ability to "personalize" their teaching
4. Willingness to experiment, to try out new things
5. Skill in asking questions (as opposed to seeing self as a kind of answering service
6. Knowledge of subject matter and related areas
7. Provision of well-established examination procedures
8. Provision of definite study helps
9. Reflection of an appreciative attitude (evidenced by nods, comments, smiles, etc.)
10. Use of conversational manner in teaching—informal, easy style

*Self-Perceptions of Good Versus Poor Teachers.* We probably do not have to go any further than our own personal life experiences to know that the way we see, regard, and feel about ourselves has an enormous impact on both our private and public lives. How about good and poor teachers? How do they see themselves?

Ryans[11] found that there are, indeed, differences between the self-related reports of teachers with high emotional stability and those with low emotional stability. For example, the more emotionally stable teachers 1) more frequently named self-confidence and cheerfulness as dominant traits in themselves, 2) said they liked active contact with other people, 3) expressed interests in hobbies and handicrafts, 4) reported their childhoods to be happy experiences.

On the other hand, teachers with lower emotional maturity scores 1) had unhappy memories of childhood, 2) seemed *not* to prefer contact with others, 3) were more directive and authoritarian, 4) expressed less self-confidence.

We can be even more specific. Combs,[5] in his book *The Professional Education of Teachers,* cites several studies which reached similar conclusions about the way good teachers typically see themselves, as follows:

1. Good teachers see themselves as identified with people rather than withdrawn, removed, apart from, or alienated from others.
2. Good teachers feel basically adequate rather than inadequate. They do not see themselves as generally unable to cope with problems.
3. Good teachers feel trustworthy rather than untrustworthy. They see themselves as reliable, dependable individuals with the potential for coping with events as they happen
4. Good teachers see themselves as wanted rather than unwanted. They see

themselves as likable and attractive (in a personal, not a physical sense) as opposed to feeling ignored and rejected.

5. Good teachers see themselves as worthy rather than unworthy. They see themselves as people of consequence, dignity, and integrity as opposed to feeling they matter little, can be overlooked and discounted.

In the broadest sense of the word, good teachers are more likely to see themselves as good people. Their self-perceptions are, for the most part, positive, tinged with an air of optimism and colored with tones of healthy self-acceptance. I dare say that self-perceptions of good teachers are not unlike the self-perceptions of any basically healthy person, whether he be a good bricklayer, a good manager, a good doctor, a good lawyer, a good experimental psychologist, or you name it. Clinical evidence has told us time and again that *any* person is more apt to be happier, more productive, and more effective when he is able to see himself as fundamentally and basically "enough."

*Perceptions of Others by Good Versus Poor Teachers.* Research is showing us that not only do good and poor teachers view themselves differently, there are also some characteristic differences in the way they perceive others. For example, Ryans[11] reported several studies which have produced findings that are in agreement when it comes to sorting out the differences between how good and poor teachers view others. He found, among other things, that outstandingly "good" teachers rated significantly higher than notably "poor" teachers in at least five different ways with respect to how they viewed others. The good teachers had 1) more favorable opinions of students, 2) more favorable opinions of democratic classroom behavior, 3) more favorable opinions of administrators and colleagues, 4) a greater expressed liking for personal contacts with other people, 5) more favorable estimates of other people generally. That is, they expressed belief that very few students are difficult behavior problems, that very few people are influenced in their opinions and attitudes toward others by feelings of jealousy, and that most teachers are willing to assume their full share of extra duties outside of school.

Interestingly, the characteristics that distinguished the "lowly assessed" teacher group suggested that the relatively "ineffective" teacher is self-centered, anxious, and restricted. One is left with the distinct impression that poor or ineffective teachers have more than the usual number of paranoid defenses.

It comes as no surprise that how we perceive others is highly dependent on how we perceive ourselves. If a potential teacher (or anyone else for that matter) likes himself, trusts himself, and has confidence in himself, he is likely to see others in somewhat this same light. Research is beginning to tell us what common sense has always told us; namely, people grow, flourish, and develop much more easily when in relationship with someone who projects an inherent trust and belief in their capacity to become what they have the potential to become.

It seems to me that we can sketch at least five interrelated generalizations from what research is telling us about how good teachers differ from poor teachers when it comes to how they perceive others.

1. They seem to have generally more positive views of others—students, colleagues, and administrators.
2. They do not seem to be as prone to view others as critical, attacking people with ulterior motives; rather they are seen as potentially friendly and worthy in their own right.
3. They have a more favorable view of democratic classroom procedures.
4. They seem to have the ability and capacity to see things as they seem to others—i.e., the ability to see things from the other person's point of view.
5. They do not seem to see students as persons "you do things to" but rather as individuals capable of doing for themselves once they feel trusted, respected, and valued.

### WHO, THEN, IS A GOOD TEACHER?

1. A good teacher is a good person. Simple and true. A good teacher rather likes life, is reasonably at peace with himself, has a sense of humor, and enjoys other people. If I interpret the research correctly, what it says is that there is no one best better-than-all-others type of teacher. Nonetheless there are clearly distinguishable "good" and "poor" teachers. Among other things, a good teacher is good because he does not seem to be dominated by a narcissistic self which demands a spotlight, or a neurotic need for power and authority, or a host of anxieties and tremblings which reduce him from the master of his class to its mechanic.

2. The good teacher is flexible. By far the single most repeated adjective used to describe good teachers is "flexibility." Either implicitly or explicitly (most often the latter), this characteristic emerges time and again over all others when good teaching is discussed in the research. In other words, the good teacher does not seem to be overwhelmed by a single point of view or approach to the point of intellectual myopia. A good teacher knows that he cannot be just one sort of person and use just one kind of approach if he intends to meet the multiple needs of his students. Good teachers are, in a sense, "total" teachers. That is, they seem able to be what they have to be to meet the demands of the moment. They seem able to move with the shifting tides of their own needs, the student's, and do what has to be done to handle the situation. A total teacher can be firm when necessary (say "no" and mean it) or permissive (say "why not try it your way?" and mean that, too) when appropriate. It depends on many things, and good teachers seem to know the difference.

### THE NEED FOR 'TOTAL' TEACHERS

There probably is not an educational psychology course taught which does not, in some way, deal with the highly complex area of individual differences. Even the most unsophisticated undergraduate is aware that people differ in readiness and capacity to handle academic learning. For the most part, our educational technology (audiovisual aids, programmed texts, teaching machines, etc.) is making significant advances designed to assist teachers in coping with intellectual differences among students. We have been making strides in the direction of offering flexible programs and curricula, but we are somewhat remiss when it comes to preparing flexible, "total" teachers. Just as there are intellectual differences among students, there are also personality and self-concept differences which can have just as much impact on achievement. If this is true, then perhaps we need to do more about preparing teachers who are sensitive to the nature of these differences and who are able to take them into account as they plan for their classes.

The point here is that what is important for one student is not important to another. This is one reason why cookbook formulas for good teachers are of so little value and why teaching is inevitably something of an art. The choice of instructional methods makes a big difference for certain kinds of pupils, and a search for the "best" way to teach can succeed only when learners' intellectual *and* personality differences are taken into account. Available evidence does not support the belief that successful teaching is possible only through the use of some specific methodology. A reasonable inference from existing data is that methods which provide for adaptation to individual differences, encourage student initiative, and stimulate individual and group participation are superior to methods which do not. In order for things of this sort to happen, perhaps what we need first of all are flexible, "total" teachers who are capable of planning around people as they are around ideas.

## IMPLICATIONS FOR TEACHER EDUCATION

Research is teaching us many things about the differences between good and poor teachers, and I see at least four related implications for teacher education programs.

1. If it is true that good teachers are good because they view teaching as primarily a human process involving human relationships and human meanings, then this may imply that we should spend at least as much time exposing and sensitizing teacher candidates to the subtle complexities of personality structure as we do to introducing them to the structure of knowledge itself. Does this mean personality development, group dynamics, basic counseling processes, sensitivity training, and techniques such as life-space interviewing and encounter grouping?

2. If it is true that good teachers have a positive view of themselves and others, then this may suggest that we provide more opportunities for teacher candidates to acquire more positive self-other perceptions. Self-concept research tells us that how one feels about himself is learned. If it is learned,

it is teachable. Too often, those of us in teacher education are dominated by a concern for long-term goals, while the student is fundamentally motivated by short-term goals. Forecasting what a student will need to know six months or two years from now, we operate on the assumption that he, too, perceives such goals as meaningful. It seems logical enough, but unfortunately it doesn't work out too well in practice. Hence much of what we may do with our teacher candidates is non-self-related—that is, to the student it doesn't seem connected with his own life, time, and needs. Rather than talk about group processes in the abstract, why can't we first assist students to a deeper understanding of their own roles in groups in which they already participate? Rather than simply theorize and cite research evidence related to individual differences, why not also encourage students to analyze the individual differences which exist in *this* class at *this* time and then allow them to express and discuss what these differences mean at a more personal level? If one values the self-concept idea at all, then there are literally endless ways to encourage more positive self-other perceptions through teaching strategies aimed at personalizing what goes on in a classroom. Indeed, Jersild[9] has demonstrated that when "teachers face themselves," they feel more adequate as individuals and function more effectively as teachers.

3. If it is true that good teachers are well-informed, then it is clear that we must neither negate nor relax our efforts to provide them with as rich an intellectual background as is possible. Teachers are usually knowledgeable people, and knowledge inculcation is the aspect of preparation with which teacher education has traditionally been most successful. Nonetheless, teachers rarely fail because of lack of knowledge. They fail more often because they are unable to communicate what they know so that it makes a difference to their students. Which brings us to our final implication for teacher-education programs.

4. If it is true that good teachers are able to communicate what they know in a manner that makes sense to their students, then we must assist our teacher candidates both through example and appropriate experiences to the most effective ways of doing this. Communication is not just a process of presenting information. It is also a function of discovery and the development of personal meanings. I wonder what would happen to our expectations of the teacher's role if we viewed him less as dispenser, answerer, coercer, and provoker and more as stimulator, questioner, challenger, and puzzler. With the former, the emphasis is on "giving to," while with the latter the focus is on "guiding to." In developing ability to hold and keep attention, not to mention techniques of encouraging people to adopt the reflective, thoughtful mood, I wonder what the departments of speech, theater, and drama on our college and university campuses could teach us? We expose our students to theories of learning and personality; perhaps what we need to do now is develop some "theories of presentation" with the help of those who know this field best.

This paper has attempted to point out that even though there is no single best or worst kind of teacher, there are clearly distinguishable characteristics associated with "good" and "bad" teachers. There is no one *best* kind of teaching because there is no *one kind* of student. Nonetheless, there seems to be enough evidence to suggest that whether the criteria for good teaching is on the basis of student and/or peer evaluations or in terms of student achievement gains, there are characteristics between both which consistently overlap. That is, the good teacher is able to influence both student feeling and achievement in positive ways.

Research is teaching us many things about the differences between good and bad teachers and there are many ways we can put these research findings into our teacher-education programs.

Good teachers do exist and can be identified. Perhaps the next most fruitful vineyard for research is in the classrooms of good teachers so we can determine, by whatever tools we have, just what makes them good in the first place.

## REFERENCES

1. A. S. BARR, *Characteristic differences in the teaching performance of good and poor teachers of the social studies.* Bloomington, Ill.: The Public School Publishing Co., 1929.
2. B. J. BIDDLE and W. J. ELLENA, *Contemporary research on teacher effectiveness.* New York: Holt, Rinehart, and Winston, 1964, p. 2.
3. W. A. BOUSFIELD, Student's rating on qualities considered desirable in college professors. *School and Society,* February 24, 1940, pp. 253–56.
4. M. L. COGAN, The behavior of teachers and the productive behavior of their pupils, *Journal of Experimental Education,* December, 1958, pp. 89–124.
5. A. W. COMBS, *The professional education of teachers.* Boston: Allyn and Bacon, 1965, pp. 70–71.
6. N. A. FLANDERS, *Teacher influence, pupil attitudes and achievement: studies in interaction analysis.* University of Minnesota, U. S. Office of Education Cooperative Research Project No. 397, 1960.
7. W. F. HART, *Teachers and teaching.* New York: Macmillan, 1934, pp. 131–32.
8. L. M. HEIL, M. Powell, and I. Feifer, *Characteristics of teacher behavior related to the achievement of children in several elementary grades.* Washington D.C.: Office of Education, Cooperative Research Branch, 1960.
9. A. T. JERSILD, *When teachers face themselves.* New York: Bureau of Publications, Teachers College, Columbia University, 1955.
10. H. B. REED, Implications for science education of a teacher competence research, *Science Education,* December, 1962, pp. 473–86.
11. D. G. RYANS, Prediction of teacher effectiveness, *Encyclopedia of Educational Research,* 3rd Edition. New York: Macmillan, 1960, pp. 1,486–90.
12. R. SPAULDING, Achievement, creativity, and self-concept correlates of teacher-pupil transactions in elementary schools. University of Illinois, U. S. Office of Education Cooperative Research Project No. 1352, 1963.
13. G. C. STERN, Measuring non-cognitive variables in research on teaching, in

*Handbook of Research on Teaching,* N. L. Gage (ed.). Chicago: Rand McNally, 1963, p. 427.

14. P. WITTY, An analysis of the personality traits of the effective teacher, *Journal of Educational Research,* May, 1947, pp. 662–71.

NED A. FLANDERS

# 17. INTENT, ACTION AND FEEDBACK: A PREPARATION FOR TEACHING

## THE PROBLEM

The point is that much of what is learned in education courses is neither conceptualized, quantified, nor taught in a fashion that builds a bridge between theory and practice. Education students are only occasionally part of an exciting, systematic, exploration of the teaching process, most infrequently by the instructor's example. How can we create, in education courses, an active, problem-solving process, a true sense of inquiry, and a systematic search for principles through experimentation? At least one factor favors change and that is the lack of solid evidence that anything we are now teaching is clearly associated with any index of effective teaching, with the possible exception of practice teaching.

A great many factors resist curriculum change in teacher education. Perhaps the most important is that genuine curriculum innovation, to be distinguished from tinkering with content and sequence, would require that existing faculty members, old and new alike, think differently about their subject matter, act differently while teaching, and relate differently to their students. For some this is probably impossible, for all it would be difficult. Yet changes do occur when enough energy is mobilized and convictions are strongly held.

It is a serious indictment of the profession, however, to hear so many education instructors say that their students will appreciate what they are learning *after* they have had some practical teaching experience. What hurts

Reprinted from the *Journal of Teacher Education.* Vol. 14 (1963), pp. 251–60, by permission of the publishers.

is the obvious hypocrisy of making this statement and then giving a lecture on the importance of presenting material in such a way that the immediate needs and interests of the pupils are taken into consideration. Such instances reveal a misunderstanding of theory and practice. To be understood, concepts in education must be verified by personal field experiences; in turn, field experiences must be efficiently conceptualized to gain insight. With most present practices, the gorge between theory and practice grows deeper and wider, excavated by the very individuals who are pledged to fill it.

One stumbling block is our inability to describe teaching as a series of acts through time and to establish models of behavior which are appropriate to different kinds of teaching situations. This problem has several dimensions. First, in terms of semantics, we must learn how to define our concepts as part of a theory. We also need to organize these concepts into the fewest number of variables necessary to establish principles and make predictions. Too often we try to teach the largest number of variables; in fact, as many as we can think of for which there is some research evidence. Second, in terms of technology, we must develop procedures for quantifying the qualitative aspects of teaching acts so that our students will have tools for collecting empirical evidence. Third, in terms of philosophy, we must decide whether our education students are going to be told about teaching in lectures and read about it in books or if they are going to discover these things for themselves. This paper will be devoted to these three issues, in reverse order.

## A PHILOSOPHY OF INQUIRY

When Nathaniel Cantor (5) published his nine assumptions of orthodox teaching, there was little evidence to support his criticisms. Must pupils be coerced into working on tasks? In what way is the teacher responsible for pupils acquiring knowledge? Is education a preparation for later life rather than a present, living experience? Is subject matter the same to the learner as it is to the teacher? The last decade has provided more evidence in support of Cantor's criticism than it has in defense of existing practice.

H. H. Anderson and his colleagues (1, 2, 3, 4) first demonstrated that dominative teacher contacts create more compliance and resistance to compliance, that dominative teacher contacts with pupils spread to the pupil-to-pupil contacts even in the absence of the teacher, and that this pattern of teaching creates situations in which pupils are more easily distracted and more dependent on teacher initiative.

Flanders and Havumaki (8) demonstrated that dominative teacher influence was more persuasive in changing pupil opinions but that such shifts of opinion were not stable since inner resistance was so high.

A research team in Provo, Utah (9) believes that patterns of spontaneous teacher action can be identified and that more effective patterns can be distinguished from less effective patterns. The difference is that more dominative patterns are less effective.

Our own eight-year research program which involved the development of interaction analysis as a tool for quantifying patterns of teacher influence lends further support to Cantor. The generalizations to follow are based on all teachers observed in our different research projects. This total is only 147 teachers, representing all grade levels, six different school districts in two countries; but these teachers came from the extremes of a distribution involving several thousand teachers. The total bits of information collected by interaction analysis are well in excess of 1,250,000.

The present, average domination of teachers is best expressed as the rule of two-thirds. About two-thirds of the time spent in a classroom, someone is talking. The chances are two out of three that this person is the teacher. When the teacher talks, two-thirds of the time is spent by many expressions of opinion and fact, giving some direction and occasionally criticizing the pupils. The fact that teachers are taking too active a part for effective learning is shown by comparing superior with less effective classrooms. A superior classroom scores above average on constructive attitudes toward the teacher and the classwork. It also scores higher on achievement tests of the content to be learned, adjusted for initial ability. In studies (7) of seventh grade social studies and eighth grade mathematics, it was found that the teachers in superior classrooms spoke only slightly less, say 50 to 60 percent of the time, but the more directive aspects of their verbal influence went down to 40 to 50 percent. These teachers were much more flexible in the quality of their influence, sometimes very direct, but on more occasions very indirect.

To describe the classrooms which were below average in constructive pupil attitudes and in content achievement (they are positively correlated), just change the rule of two-thirds to the rule of three-fourths plus.

The foregoing evidence shows that no matter what a prospective teacher hears in an education course, he has, on the average, been exposed to living models of what teaching is and can be that are basically quite directive. After fourteen or so years he is likely to be quite dependent, expecting the instructor to tell him what to do, how to do it, when he is finished, and then tell him how well he did it. Now it is in this general context that we turn to the question of how we can develop a spirit of inquiry with regard to teaching.

Thelen (10) has described a model of personal inquiry, as well as other models, and the question is whether teacher education can or should move toward this model. He describes this model as follows (*ibid.*, p. 89):

> ...(personal inquiry) is a process of interaction between the student and his natural and societal environment. In this situation the student will be aware of the process of which he is a part; during this process he will be aware of many choices among ways he might behave; he will make decisions among

these ways; he will then act and see what happens; he will review the process and study it with the help of books and other people; he will speculate about it, and draw tentative conclusions from it.

Returning to the education course, the student will be aware of the learning process of *that* classroom, he will confront choices, he will make decisions among the choices, he will act and then evaluate his actions, and then he will try to make some sense out of it with the help of books, the instructor, and his peers. This is a tall order, but who knows, it may be the only route to discovery and independence for the prospective teacher.

Occasionally we hear of exciting learning experiences in which education students attain a sort of intellectual spirit of inquiry. A unit on motivation can begin with an assessment of the motivation patterns of the education students. The same assessment procedures can then be used at other grade levels, permitting comparisons and generalizations. Principles of child growth and development can be discovered by observation and learned more thoroughly, perhaps, than is possible with only lecture and reading. But this is not what is meant by inquiry.

Inquiry in teacher education means translating understanding into action as part of the teaching process. It means experimenting with one's own behavior, obtaining objective information about one's own behavior, evaluating this information in terms of the teacher's role; in short, attaining self-insight while acting like a teacher.

Procedures for obtaining self-insight have been remarkably improved during the last decade in the field of human relations training. Two characteristics of these training methods seem relevant to this discussion. First, information and insights about behavior must become available in a way that can be accepted and in a form that is understood. Second, opportunities to utilize or act out these insights must be provided. Our ability to accept information about ourselves is a complex problem, but it helps if we believe the information is objective, valid, and given in an effort to help rather than hurt. Our understanding of this information will depend a great deal on our ability to organize the information conceptually. Freedom to act at least requires freedom from threat or embarrassment.

From all of these things, a spirit of inquiry develops.

## THE TECHNIQUE OF INTERACTION ANALYSIS

Interaction analysis is nothing more and nothing less than an observation technique which can be used to obtain a fairly reliable record of spontaneous verbal statements. Most teacher influence is exerted by verbal statements, and to determine their quality is to approximate total teacher influence. This technique was first developed as a research tool, but every observer we ever hired testified that the process of learning the system and using it in classrooms was more valuable than anything else he learned in his education courses. Since interaction analysis is only a technique, it probably could be applied to teacher education in a fashion that is consistent or even totally inconsistent with a philosophy of personal inquiry. How it is used in teacher preparation is obviously as important as understanding the procedure itself.

The writing of this manuscript followed the completion of a terminal contract report of a U.S. Office of Education-sponsored, inservice training program based on interaction analysis as a tool for gathering information. How we used interaction analysis is illustrated by the conditions we tried to create for the fifty-five participating teachers, most of whom represented about one-half of the faculties of two junior high schools:[1]

1) Teachers developed new (to them) concepts as tools for thinking about their behavior and the consequences of their behavior. These concepts were used to discover principles of teacher influence. Both types of concepts were necessary: those for describing actions and those for describing consequences.

2) Procedures for assessing both types of concepts in practical classroom situations were tried out. These procedures were used to test principles, to modify them, and to determine when they might be appropriately applied.

3) The training activities involved in becoming proficient in the assessment of spontaneous behavior, in and of themselves, increased the sensitivity of teachers to their own behavior and the behavior of others. Most important, teachers could compare their intentions with their actions.

4) By avoiding a discussion of right and wrong ways of teaching and emphasizing the discovery of principles of teacher influence, teachers gradually became more independent and self-directing. Our most successful participants investigated problems of their own choosing, designed their own plans, and arranged collaboration with others when this seemed advantageous.

Five filmstrips and one teacher's manual have been produced and written. These materials would have to be modified before they could be used with undergraduate students. Before asking how interaction analysis might be used in teacher preparation, we turn next to a description of the procedures.

## THE PROCEDURE OF OBSERVATION

The observer sits in a classroom in the best position to hear and see the participants. At the end of each three-second period, he decides which category best represents the communication events just completed. He writes

---

[1] Interaction analysis as a research tool has been used ever since R. F. Bales first developed a set of categories for studying groups. Most of our research results can be found in the references at the end of this paper. Its use as a training device is more recent. Projects have taken place in New Jersey, Philadelphia, Chicago, and Minneapolis. Systematic evaluation is available in only the Minneapolis project.

this category number down while simultaneously assessing communication in the next period and continues at a rate of 20 to 25 observations per minute, keeping his tempo as steady as possible. His notes are merely a series of numbers written in a column, top to bottom, so that the original sequence of events is preserved. Occasionally marginal notes are used to explain the class formation or any unusual circumstances. When there is a major change in class formation, the communication pattern, or the subject under discussion, a double line is drawn and the time indicated. As soon as the total observation is completed, the observer retires to a nearby room and completes a general description of each separate activity period separated by the double lines, including the nature of the activities, the class formation, and the position of the teacher. The observer also notes any additional facts that seem pertinent to an adequate interpretation and recall of the total visit.

The ten categories that we used for interaction analysis are shown in Table 1.

The numbers that an observer writes down are tabulated in a $10 \times 10$ matrix as sequence pairs, that is, a separate tabulation is made for each overlapping pair of numbers. An illustration will serve to explain this procedure.

> *Teacher:* "Class! The bell has rung. May I have your attention please!" [6]
> During the next three seconds talking and noise diminish. [10]
> *Teacher:* "Jimmy, we are all waiting for you." [7] Pause.
> *Teacher:* "Now today we are going to have a very pleasant surprise, [5] and I think you will find it very exciting and interesting. [1] Have any of you heard anything about what we are going to do?" [4]
> *Pupil:* "I think we are going on a trip in the bus that's out in front." [8]
> *Teacher:* "Oh! You've found out! How did you learn about our trip?" [4]

By now the observer has written down 6, 10, 7, 5, 1, 4, 8, and 4. As the interaction proceeds, the observer will continue to write down numbers. To tabulate these observations in a $10 \times 10$ matrix, the first step is to make sure that the entire series begins and ends with the same number. The convention we use is to add a 10 to the beginning and end of the series unless the 10 is already present. Our series now becomes 10, 6, 10, 7, 5, 1, 4, 8, 4, and 10.

These numbers are tabulated in a matrix, one pair at a time. The column is indicated by the second number, the row is indicated by the first number. The first pair is 10-6; the tally is placed in row ten, column six cell. The second pair is 6-10; tally this in the row six, column ten cell. The third pair is 10-7, the fourth pair is 7-5, and so on. Each pair overlaps with the next, and the total number of observations, "N," always will be tabulated by N-1 tallies in the matrix. In this case we started a series of ten numbers, and the series produced nine tallies in the matrix.

Table 2 shows our completed matrix. Notice that in a correctly tabulated matrix the sums of the corresponding rows and columns are equal.

Table 1   CATEGORIES FOR INTERACTION ANALYSIS

| | | |
|---|---|---|
| Teacher Talk | Indirect Influence | 1.* Accepts Feeling: accepts and clarifies the feeling tone of the students in a nonthreatening manner. Feelings may be positive or negative. Predicting or recalling feelings are included.<br>2.* Praises or Encourages: praises or encourages student action or behavior. Jokes that release tension, not at the expense of another individual, nodding head or saying, "um hm?" or "go on" are included.<br>3.* Accepts or Uses Ideas of Student: clarifying, building or developing ideas suggested by a student. As teacher brings more of his own ideas into play, shift to category five.<br>4.* Asks Questions: asking a question about content or procedure with the intent that a student answer. |
| | Direct Influence | 5.* Lecturing: giving facts or opinions about content or procedures; expressing his own ideas, asking rhetorical questions.<br>6.* Giving Directions: directions, commands, or orders with which a student is expected to comply.<br>7.* Criticizing or Justifying Authority: statements intended to change student behavior from nonacceptable to acceptable pattern; bawling someone out; stating why the teacher is doing what he is doing; extreme self-reference. |
| Student Talk | | 8.* Student Talk—Response: talk by students in response to teacher. Teacher initiates the contact or solicits student statement.<br>9.* Student Talk—Initiation: talk by students which they initiate. If "calling on" student is only to indicate who may talk next, observer must decide whether student wanted to talk. If he did, use this category. |
| | | 10.* Silence or Confusion: pauses, short periods of silence and periods of confusion in which communication cannot be understood by the observer. |

*\* There is no scale implied by these numbers. Each number is classificatory; it designates a particular kind of communication event. To write these numbers down during observation is to enumerate, not to judge a position on a scale.*

Table 2

| Category | 1 | 2 | 3 | 4 | 5 | 6 | 7 | 8 | 9 | 10 | Total |
|---|---|---|---|---|---|---|---|---|---|---|---|
| 1 | | | | 1 | | | | | | | 1 |
| 2 | | | | | | | | | | | 0 |
| 3 | | | | | | | | | | | 0 |
| 4 | | | | | | | | 1 | | 1 | 2 |
| 5 | 1 | | | | | | | | | | 1 |
| 6 | | | | | | | | | | 1 | 1 |
| 7 | | | | 1 | | | | | | | 1 |
| 8 | | | 1 | | | | | | | | 1 |
| 9 | | | | | | | | | | | 0 |
| 10 | | | | | | 1 | 1 | | | | 2 |
| Total | 1 | 0 | 0 | 2 | 1 | 1 | 1 | 1 | 0 | 2 | 9 |

The problem of reliability is extremely complex, and a more complete discussion can be found in two terminal contract reports (6, 7) one of which was published as a research monograph in the 1963 series of the Cooperative Research Program. Education students can learn how to make quick field checks of their reliability and work toward higher reliability under the direction of an instructor.

## THE INTERPRETATION OF MATRICES

A matrix should have at least 400 tallies, covering about twenty minutes or more of a homogeneous activity period, before attempting to make an interpretation.

Certain areas within the matrix are particularly useful for describing teacher influence. Some of these areas will now be discussed by making reference to Table 3.

The column totals of a matrix are indicated as Areas "A," "B," "C," and "D." The figures in these areas provide a general picture by answering the following questions: What proportion of the time was someone talking compared with the portion in which confusion or no talking existed? When someone was talking, what proportion of the time was used by the students? By the teacher? Of the time that the teacher talked, what proportion of his talk involved indirect influence? Direct influence?

The answers to these questions form a necessary backdrop to the interpretation of the other parts of the matrix. If student participation is about 30 or 40 percent, we would expect to find out why it was so high by studying the matrix. If the teacher is particularly direct or indirect, we would expect certain relationships to exist with student talk and silence.

The next two areas to consider are areas "E" and "F." Evidence that categories 1, 2, and 3 were used for periods longer than three seconds can be found in the diagonal cells, 1-1, 2-2, and 3-3. The other six cells of Area E indicate various types of transitions between these three categories. Sustained praise or clarification of student ideas is especially significant because such elaboration often involves criteria for praise or reasons for accepting ideas and feelings. The elaboration of praise or student ideas must be present if the student's ideas are to be integrated with the content being discussed by the class.

Area F is a four-cell combination of giving directions (category 6) and giving criticisms or self-justification (category 7). The transition cells 6-7 and 7-6 are particularly sensitive to difficulties that the teacher may have with classroom discipline or resistance on the part of students. When criticism follows directions or direction follows criticism, this means that the students are not complying satisfactorily. Often there is a high loading on the 6-9 cell under these circumstances. Excessively high frequencies in the 6–6 cell *and* 7–7 cells indicate teacher domination and supervision of the stu-

Table 3  MATRIX ANALYSIS

| Category | Classification | | Category | 1 | 2 | 3 | 4 | 5 | 6 | 7 | 8 | 9 | 10 | Total |
|---|---|---|---|---|---|---|---|---|---|---|---|---|---|---|
| Accepts Feelings | Teacher Talk | Indirect Influence | 1 | | | | | | | | | | | |
| Praise | | | 2 | | Area E | | | | | | | | | |
| Student Idea | | | 3 | | | | | | | | | | | |
| Asks Questions | | | 4 | | | | | | | | | Area I | | |
| Lectures | | Direct Influence | 5 | | | | "Content Cross" | | | | | | | |
| Gives Directions | | | 6 | | | | | | Area F | | | | | |
| Criticism | | | 7 | | | | | | | | | | | |
| Student Response | Student Talk | | 8 | | Area G | | | | Area H | | Area J | | | |
| Student Initiation | | | 9 | | | | | | | | | | | |
| Silence | | | 10 | | | | | | | | | | | |
| Total | | | Total | | Area A | | | Area B | | | Area C | | Area D | |
| | | | | | Indirect Teacher Talk | | | Direct Teacher Talk | | | Student Talk | | | |

183

dent's activities. A high loading of tallies in the 6-6 cell alone often indicates that the teacher is merely giving lengthy directions to the class.

The next two areas to be considered are Areas G and H. Tallies in these two areas occur at the instant the student stops talking and the teacher starts. Area G indicates those instances in which the teacher responds to the termination of student talk with indirect influence. Area H indicates those instances in which the teacher responds to the termination of student talk with direct influence. An interesting comparison can be made by contrasting the proportion G to H versus the proportion A to B. If these two proportions are quite different, it indicates that the teacher tends to act differently at the instant a student stops talking compared with his overall average. Often this is a mark of flexible teacher influence.

There are interesting relationships between Area E and Area G and between Area F and Area H. For example, Area G may indicate that a teacher responds indirectly to students at the instant they terminate their talk, but an observer may wish to inspect Area E to see if this indirect response is sustained in any way. The same question with regard to direct influence can be asked of Areas F and H. Areas G and H together usually fascinate teachers. They are often interested in knowing more about their immediate response to student participation.

Area I indicates an answer to the question, What types of teacher statements trigger student participation? Usually there is a high tally loading in cells 4-8 and 4-9. This is expected because students often answer questions posed by the teacher. A high loading on 4-8 and 8-4 cells alone usually indicates classroom drill directed by the teacher. The contrast of tallies in columns 8 and 9 in this area gives a rough indication of the frequency with which students initiate their own ideas versus respond to those of the teacher.

Area I is often considered in combination with Area J. Area J indicates either lengthy student statements or sustained student-to-student communication. An above-average frequency in Area C, but not in Area J, indicates that short answers, usually in response to teacher stimulation, have occurred. One would normally expect to find frequencies in Area E positively correlated with frequencies in Area J.

We turn next to concepts and principles of teacher influence before speculating about how this technique can be applied to teacher education.

## CONCEPTS AND PRINCIPLES
## OF TEACHER INFLUENCE

It may be too early to determine what are the *fewest* number of concepts which, if organized into logically related principles, can be used by a teacher to plan how he will use his authority. Surely he will need concepts that refer to his authority and its use. He will need concepts to describe learning goals and pupil tasks. He will need concepts to classify the responses of

students. He may also need concepts to characterize class formations and patterns of classroom communication. These concepts are at least the minimum.

## CONCEPTS THAT REFER
## TO TEACHER BEHAVIOR

*Indirect Influence.* Indirect influence is defined as actions taken by the teacher which encourage and support student participation. Accepting, clarifying, praising, and developing the ideas and feelings expressed by the pupils will support student participation. We can define indirect behavior operationally by noting the the percent of teacher statements falling into categories 1, 2, 3, and 4.

*Direct Influence.* This concept refers to actions taken by the teacher which restrict student participation. Expressing one's own views through lecture, giving directions, and criticizing with the expectation of compliance tend to restrict pupil participation. We can define direct behavior operationally by noting the percent of teacher statements falling into categories 5, 6, and 7.

Other concepts which we do not have the space to discuss include: flexibility of teacher influence, dominance or sustained direct influence, and intervention.

## CONCEPTS THAT REFER TO
## LEARNING GOALS

*Clear Goals.* Goal perceptions are defined from the point of view of the pupil, not the teacher. "Clear goals" is a state of affairs in which the pupil knows what he is doing, the purpose, and can guess at the first few steps to be taken. It can be measured by paper-and-pencil tests, often administered at different points in a problem-solving sequence.

*Ambiguous Goals.* "Ambiguous goals" describes a state of affairs in which a pupil is not sure of what he is expected to do, is not sure of the first few steps, or is unable to proceed for one reason or another. It can be measured as above.

Other concepts in this area include: attractive and unattractive clear goals, pupil tasks, task requirements, and similar concepts.

## CONCEPTS THAT REFER
## TO PUPIL RESPONSES

*Dependent Acts.* Acts of dependence occur when a pupil not only complies with teacher influence but solicits such direction. A pupil who asks a teacher to approve of his work in order to make sure that it is satisfactory, before going on to the next logical step, is acting dependently. This type of response

can be measured by observation techniques and by paper-and-pencil tests on which he indicates what kind of help he would like from the teacher.

*Independent Acts.* Acts of independence occur when the pupils react primarily to task requirements and are less directly concerned with teacher approval. The measurement of this concept is the same as for dependent acts.

Other concepts include: dependence proneness—a trait, compliance, conformity, counter-dependence, and similar concepts.

### SOME PRINCIPLES THAT CAN
### BE DISCOVERED

We discovered in our research (7) that, during the first few days of a two-week unit of study in seventh grade social studies and when introducing new material in eighth grade mathematics, superior teachers (as previously defined, page 177) are initially more indirect, becoming more direct as goals and associated tasks become clarified. We also suspect that these same teachers are more indirect when helping pupils diagnose difficulties, when trying to motivate pupils by arousing their interest, and in other situations in which the expression of pupil perceptions is helpful. On the other hand, the average or below average teacher did exactly the opposite.

Now the problem in teacher education is not only to create a situation in which education students could verify these relationships but could practice controlling their own behavior so as to become indirect or more direct at will. One place to begin is to have two, six-man groups work on a task under the direction of a leader. One task is something like an assembly line; it has a clear end product and sharp role differentiation. The other task is much more difficult to describe and does not have clear role differentiation. Now let the class superimpose different patterns of leader influence. Let them interview the role players, collect interaction analysis data by some simplified system of categories, and discuss the results. When undergraduate students first try to classify verbal statements, it sometimes helps to use only two or three categories. In one instance, the issue was the effect of using broad questions versus narrow questions. A broad question was one to which it was hard to predict the type of answer. A narrow question was one to which it was easy to guess at the type of answer. Which type of question was more likely to increase pupil participation? The students role-played this and kept a record of broad questions, narrow questions, and the length of the response. The fact that they verified their prediction correctly for this rather superficial problem was much less important compared with the experience that they gained. They learned how to verify a prediction with empirical evidence, and some had a chance to practice control of their own behavior for professional purposes.

There is no space here to list a complete set of principles that can be investigated by systematic or intuitive data-collecting procedures. The following questions might stimulate useful learning activities. Does dependence

always decrease as goals become clear? Is the final level of dependence determined by the pattern of teacher influence when goals are first formulated? Are measures of content achievement related to the pupils' attitudes toward the teacher and the schoolwork? What effects can you expect from excessive and pedantic clarification of pupil ideas and feelings? And many others.

## APPLICATIONS OF INTERACTION ANALYSIS TO TEACHER EDUCATION

Suppose that before education students were given their practice teaching assignment, they had been exposed to a variety of data-collecting techniques for assessing pupil perceptions, measuring achievement, and quantifying spontaneous teacher influence. Suppose, further, that these skills had been taught in a context of personal inquiry as described earlier. What effect would this have on their approach to practice teaching?

One of their suggestions might be that two students should be assigned as a team to the first assignment. While one took over the class the other could be collecting information; the next day or so, the roles could be reversed. Together they would work out a lesson plan, agree on the data to be collected, go over the results with the help of the supervising teacher who might also have the same data-collecting skills. This situation could approach the inquiry model described earlier. The practice teacher might discover that his failure to clarify the pupils' ideas restricted the development of curiosity or that his directions were too short when he was asked for further help; both of these inferences can be made from an interaction matrix with reasonable reliability and objectivity.

Later on a student may wish to take a practice teaching assignment by himself and turn to the supervising teacher for aid in feedback. In either case, the requirement is that the learner be able to compare his intentions with feedback information about his actions and analyze this information by using concepts which he found useful in his earlier courses in education.

There are some precautions that can already be stated with regard to the use of interaction analysis in such a situation.

First, no interaction analysis data should be collected unless the person observed is familiar with the entire process and knows its limitations.

Second, the questions to be answered by inspecting the matrix should be developed before the observation takes place.

Third, value judgments about good and bad teaching behavior are to be avoided. Emphasis is given to the problem being investigated so that cause-and-effect relationships can be discovered.

Fourth, a certain amount of defensive behavior is likely to be present at the initial consultation; it is something like listening to a tape recording for the first time.

Fifth, a consultation based on two observations or at least two matrices

helps to eliminate value judgments or at least control them. Comparisons between the matrices are more likely to lead to principles.

Just how experiences of the type we have been discussing will fit into the present curricula is difficult to know. If activities of the sort described in this paper are valuable, are they to be superimposed on the present list of courses or is more radical surgery necessary?

Perhaps this is the point to risk a prediction, which is that teacher education will become increasingly concerned with the process of teaching itself during the next few decades. Instead of emphasizing knowledge which *we think* teachers will need in order to teach effectively, as we have in the past, we will turn more and more to an analysis of teaching acts as they occur in spontaneous classroom interaction. We are now at the point in our technology of data collecting at which procedures for analyzing and conceptualizing teaching behavior can be developed. Systems for doing this will become available regardless of whether they are similar or dissimilar to the procedures described in this paper. When this fine day arrives, the role of the education instructor will change, and the dichotomy between field and theory will disappear. The instructor's role will shift from talking about effective teaching to the rigorous challenge of demonstrating effective teaching. The process of inquiry will create problem-solving activities that will produce more independent, self-directing teachers whose first day on the job will be their worst, not their best.

These changes will be successful to the extent that the graduates of teacher education can learn to control their own behavior for the professional purpose of managing effective classroom learning. It will be the responsibility of the education instructor to help prospective teachers discover what their teaching intentions should be and then create training situations in which behavior gradually matches intentions with practice. Teaching will remain an art, but it will be studied scientifically.

## REFERENCES

1. Anderson, Harold H. The measurement of domination and of socially integrative behavior in teachers' contacts with children. *Child Development* 10: 73–89; June 1939.
2. ———, and Helen M. Brewer. *Studies of teachers' classroom personalities, I: dominative and socially integrative behavior of kindergarten teachers.* Applied Psychology Monographs of the American Psychological Association. No. 6. Stanford, California: Stanford University Press, July 1945.
3. ———, and Joseph E. Brewer. *Studies of teachers' classroom personalities, II: effects of teachers' dominative and integrative contacts on children's classroom behavior.* Applied Psychology Monographs of the American Psychological Association. No. 8. Stanford, California: Stanford University Press, June 1946.
4. ———, J. E. Brewer, and M. F. Reed. *Studies of teachers' classroom personalities, III: follow-up studies of the effects of dominative and integrative*

*contacts on children's behavior.* Applied Psychology Monographs of the American Psychological Association. No. 11. Stanford, California: Stanford University Press, December 1946.

5. CANTOR, NATHANIEL. *The teaching-learning process.* New York: Dryden Press, 1953. Pp. 59–72.

6. FLANDERS, N. A. A terminal contract report on using interaction analysis for the inservice training of teachers. To be submitted to the U.S. Office of Education, N.D.E.A., Title VII. Available from the author, University of Michigan.

7. ———. *Teacher influence, pupil attitudes, and achievement.* Dittoed manuscript, published in 1963 as a Research Monograph. Cooperative Research Program, U.S. Office of Education. Available from author, University of Michigan, 176 pp.

8. ———, and S. HAVUMAKI. Group compliance to dominative teacher influence. *Human Relations* 13:67–82.

9. ROMNEY, G. P., M. M. HUGHES, and others. *Progress report of the merit study of the Provo City Schools.* Provo, Utah, August 1958. XIX + 226 pp. See also *Patterns of effective teaching: second progress report of the merit study of the Provo City Schools.* Provo, Utah, June 1961. XII + 93 pp.

10. THELEN, H. A. *Education and the human quest.* New York: Harper Brothers, 1960. Pp. 74–112.

CHARLES GALLOWAY

# 18. NONVERBAL COMMUNICATION

When second-grade teacher Ruth Harris was getting dressed for school one dull Monday, she hesitated between a black suit and a bright print dress. Choosing the print, she thought, "It will brighten the day for me and the children." Things did seem to go well all day. . . .

As Paul Trask entered the school building, he saw the principal at the end of the hall. Expecting a smile and a wave, he was surprised to get a curt nod and the sight of a disappearing back. Paul wondered what could be wrong. . . .

Annette Webster looked at her fourth-year arithmetic group as they bent over the problem she had presented to them. She noticed Chris scowling at his paper and biting his lip and moved to help him. . . .

Reprinted from *The Instructor,* (April 1968), pp. 37–42, by permission of the publishers.

What happened with these teachers? Each one either sent or received a message without saying or hearing a word. What happened was nonverbal communication.

Nonverbal communication is behavior that conveys meaning without words. It can be symbolic or nonsymbolic, spontaneous or managed. It can be expressive, transmitting emotion; or it can be informative, transmitting facts. It can be as specific as a gesture or as general as the atmosphere of a room. It can be either dynamic or static.

Nonverbal communication takes a certain amount of time and occurs at a certain tempo. It can be quick or slow. It can be negative or positive— something that doesn't happen as well as something that does. Or it can be a combination of any of these—and there's even a nonverbal component in verbalisms.

All human beings are compelled to send and receive messages. They try constantly to discover information which lessens confusion or increases understanding. When messages are carried by words, the participators are consciously aware of hearing or seeing the words. But nonverbal communication is given much less conscious thought. The operations of giving information through nonverbal action and reading the meaning of another person's nonverbal behavior usually occur without deliberate reflection.

The clothing you wear, your posture, or how you walk transmits a message to others. You may be saying, "I am a teacher; I am meeting your expectations (and mine) of how a teacher should look." Depending on your emotional needs, you may also be trying to say, "I am an alert, modern teacher," or even, "I may be a teacher, but at heart I'm a swinger!"

So we can say that nonverbal clues are evident in any situation where people are with other people. In fact, the most subtle and covert kinds of information can be discovered in this way. Here are three examples:

*Nonverbal phenomena establish the status of interaction.* At a party you are talking to someone, but his eyes are following someone else around the room. His posture and manner indicate his desire to be off. What conclusion do you come to?

*Nonverbal behavior indicates what the other person thinks of us.* You are discussing a controversial topic with a small group. Everyone is reacting politely, but you are aware of those who approve of your ideas and those who disagree. How do you know?

*Nonverbal clues are used to check the reliability of what is said.* You had mailed a coupon indicating interest in an expensive set of books. The man who shows up at your door is poorly groomed and shifty-eyed. Although his credentials seem in order, you hesitate even to let him in.

The significance of nonverbal behavior in the classroom is an idea about teaching that is growing in importance. Until now, it has seldom been recognized or understood, at least in a formal, specific way. Now, persons interested in improving the teaching act are studying the implications of

nonverbal communication—implications that are important for you to understand.

1. Think of at least one classroom situation in which of each the three conditions described above occurred.

2. Review the last two days of school. Can you recall an incident in which a child's behavior belied his remarks?

3. When a nonverbal cue disagrees with or contradicts a verbal remark, we tend to accept the nonverbal message as representative of the real meaning. Discuss why this occurs.

NONVERBAL PHENOMENA

Nonverbal behavior consists of such events as facial expression, posture, gestures, movement, even the arrangement of space or objects around the behaver. It involves use of the body, use of space, and even the use of time.

Although we are often unaware of the process, we are very conscious of the eloquence of nonverbal cues. We all agree that "actions speak louder than words," and realize that *how* we say something can be as important as *what* we say. We also know the feeling of being "in tune" with someone— immediately understanding him and having him understand us.

Most of us believe that the most personal and valid kinds of information are discovered by what we call intuition. What really happens is that we subconsciously respond to nonverbal clues transmitted by other persons.

During the school day, many graphic portrayals of nonverbal phenomena occur. Here are some common ones, and as you read them, think about your class. Undoubtedly you will recall many examples like them, and will be able to add others.

*Substitute Expression.* A child shrugs his shoulder in an "I don't know" manner after being accosted in the hallway for running. Probably this means he feels guilty at being caught, yet he hesitates to engage the teacher in a verbal debate. This is especially true if his verbal defense is likely to be employed against him later in the conversation. One of the places events like this occur repeatedly is in inner-city schools, where children are already conditioned to express their frustrations and defiance in a non-verbal way.

*Qualifying Expression.* Ann says, "I don't sing well," but what does she mean? Stated one way, it suggests that she *does* sing well; or it may mean that she *would like* to sing well; or, that she truly *does not* sing well. The intent of verbal remarks is usually qualified through intonation and inflection. Facial expressions and gestures also qualify verbal language.

*Nonverbal Symbolic.* John observed the teacher watching him. Now he is

painting with large dramatic strokes, one eye on the teacher, hoping she will look his way again. When we know we are being observed, our behavior is designed to have intent or purpose for the observer. It symbolizes our thoughts or intentions. Eyes alone may beckon or reject. Many gestures and facial expressions symbolize our deepest feelings.

*Nonverbal Nonsymbolic.* You are watching a child who is observing another child, totally unaware that you are watching him. His behavior is considered nonsymbolic since it is free of overt intent. When you observe the unobserved observer, it is a profound process—for his reactions are genuinely his own with no desire to create an impression. Observing a person who is unaware of our presence is both informative and fun.

*Attentive or Inattentive.* Your students are pretending to listen while their minds wander in fields of fantasy, and when they respond it is in a bored fashion. Nonverbally they are being inattentive. As an experienced teacher, you are able to detect such reactions and use them to change the pace and direction of what is being taught. Observing when students are involved and interested and when they are not is a skill that teachers learn. But teachers vary widely in their ability or willingness to use these pupil reactions as directions for their own behavior.

There are other nonverbal occurrences, but these are good ones to start with. Undoubtedly you can add other specific types from your own experiences.

### ASSIGNMENTS

1. Identify children in your class who typically react nonverbally to either reprimand or approval. Do you know what they are really trying to communicate?

2. Experiment with positive body and facial qualifying expressions, especially when you feel a need to support a request or judgment you are making.

3. Think of a nonsymbolic situation in which your observation was later confirmed; another one which later proved wrong.

### CLASSROOM CUES

Nonverbal behavior is not limited to personal practices. Many classroom phenomena serve as nonverbal communicators. Their impact on the course and direction of an activity can strongly affect the contextual meaning that is derived from it.

Methods of distributing materials can affect the activity that follows; the way a group is formed influences its practices; even the degree of neatness required suggests behavior to the pupil.

Nonverbal cues either reinforce or minimize verbal messages. They become the focus of attention and *carry conviction that lingers long after the verbal*

*event has passed.* Why this is so is difficult to answer, but the strong influence of nonverbal cues is unmistakable.

Classroom phenomena often play a more significant role in students' learning than the formal teaching which takes place. In any classroom, the extent and duration of teacher-pupil contacts are great. It is vital to have mutual understanding in the exchange of the messages that are nonverbal in character and import.

Consider phenomena that are typical of any classroom:

*Use of Space.* Classrooms are divided into territories. Both teacher and students occupy space. Some arrangements of territorial rights are traditional, with the teacher's desk at the front of the room and students seated in rows. Other arrangements are more imaginative. Some uses of space are fluid, others are static.

Space arrangement shows the teacher's priorities—what she thinks important; what she thinks about her children; how she envisions her own position. A change in a spatial arrangement influences the potential meaning of a learning context.

*Teacher Travel.* Where and when a teacher chooses to travel in a classroom is significant. In the past, teachers usually moved around their own desks as if they were isles of security. They rarely ventured into territories of student residence, unless they wished to check up on or monitor seatwork. Today that picture has changed. Some teachers have done away with desks; others have put them in less focal places.

To move toward or away from students signifies relationships. Teachers may avoid some students or frequent the work areas of others. All of those movements have meaning that students recognize.

*Use of Time.* How teachers use their time indicates the value and importance they place on types of work, on subject areas, and on acceptable activities. Spending little or no time on a topic indicates a lack of interest in or knowledge about it so that even little children are aware of teachers' preferences.

Teachers often fail to recognize the implications of their use of time. One teacher spends two hours marking papers. A teacher in the next room spends the same amount of time in helping children mark their own papers. Certainly these teachers have different concepts of evaluation, and it is revealed by their uses of time.

*Control Maneuvers.* Teachers engage in various nonverbal tactics to control the behavior of students. These silent expressions serve as events reminding students of teacher expectations. Some typical examples of nonverbal maneuvers: the teacher indicates inability to hear due to classroom noise; places finger to lips; stands with hands on hips and stares in silence; scans room to see who is not working; records in grade book while student is making a report. Negative maneuvers tend to "put children in their place." Similarly, positive maneuvers can give encouragement, help a child overcome fear, put a nervous child at ease, or resolve a tense situation.

As the teacher works to establish better classroom phenomena, he must be careful to avoid *incongruity*. This is an event where there is a contradiction between what is said and what is done, and it may occur many times in a day. The thing to remember about an incongruity is that it is nonverbal behavior that makes the impression that is most lasting and most difficult to overcome.

Incongruous behaviors occur frequently during times of praise or encouragement. Teachers use words such as "good" or "nice job" but the praise can appear false or unbelievable. When we are not honest with children, it is the nonverbal clues that trip us up.

Nonverbal phenomena should not be thought of primarily in negative terms. Many classrooms are well arranged. The teacher's approach to an activity provides excellent motivation. Or, through meeting a child's eyes or with a small gesture, a teacher builds confidence. Such nonverbal events can be highly conducive to good classroom climate.

Nonverbal qualities that contribute to effective classroom interaction are suggested:

*Attention.* The event of listening to pupils when they talk. This is essential. When a teacher fails to listen, a pupil is likely to believe that what he says is unimportant.

*Reception.* Behavioral evidence that a teacher is listening, by maintaining eye contact while a pupil is talking. The event of attending to pupils when they talk assures pupils and encourages them to believe that their verbal communication is valued by the teacher.

*Reinforcement.* A look or gesture to reinforce approval of an act by a student. Not only the timid but also the seemingly forward child may need reinforcement if he is to go ahead on his own.

*Facilitation.* A movement toward a student for the purpose of helping or assisting. Teachers quite often detect needs or unexpressed feelings by students, and initiate a move toward the student to alleviate his concern. Teachers engage in such events because, either consciously or subconsciously, they have become sensitive to the nonverbal cues given by their students.

We all recognize that expressive cues are fleeting and transitory. Nonetheless, they transmit emotion and feeling, and are detected as indications of meaning far more quickly than speech. *It is the appearance of such cues that especially suggests to others the attitudes we hold at a given time.* Therefore, they are particularly important in establishing the classroom environment and in working out good rapport with each child.

### ASSIGNMENTS

1. Draw some alternate layouts for your classroom. List changes in nonverbal phenomena that each layout would imply.

2. Make a two-day study of how often you contact each child in any of many ways. Keep a list of children's names and devise a simple code to

indicate times of approving or disapproving, individual or group sharing, listening, or other interaction.

### FEEDBACK

Improving classroom nonverbal behavior is not easy, especially in discovering incongruity. Yet we probably all agree that such improvement should be a conscious goal for any teacher.

One enlightening and sometimes disconcerting way to check your present behavior is by watching yourself on film or video-tape. Another way is to listen to the comments and suggestions of an observer whose judgment you trust. *A teacher's major source of feedback, however, is the responses of students.*

To become more knowledgeable about the nonverbal reactions of your youngsters to your behavior is a difficult quest. Even when you begin to recognize the reactions, it is naïve to believe that change is imminently possible. Most of us have been observing and behaving in patterned ways for a long time. Ridding oneself of past habits and attitudes is a difficult undertaking and must be a continuing process.

The best way to start is to develop an attitude of *openness.* Openness to one's experience and the realization that a rich and available source of data exists in the classroom is crucial. Openness is necessary if an improvement of perceptual skills and style of behaving is to be effected.

Assuming that a teacher has an open attitude toward self and others, the steps for becoming better informed involve *awareness, understanding,* and *acceptance.* To be aware is to observe more fully and to be open to the nonverbal reactions of others and oneself. To understand implies the need to analyze the meaning of your observations and to suspend judgment until you are reasonably certain of their real meaning. To accept is to acknowledge that your behavior means what it does to students, even though the meaning is not what you intended to imply.

This last step is especially difficult because most of us do not like to admit even to ourselves that others perceive us differently. But once you can accept what your behavior represents to others, the door is open to behaving differently. (Does it seem odd to be talking about the *behavior* of teachers? That is a word usually reserved for children, yet the teacher's conduct in the classroom is of vital importance to every child.)

In being open to nonverbal cues, it is useful to recognize behavior as a cultural, social, and psychological phenomenon. The behavior of a teacher or of students arises from experiences that have been learned over a period of time. Here are some points to consider as you view students' reactions:

*Similar Experiences Can Mean Different Things.* A pat on the back to one child may imply friendliness and support, whereas to another exactly the same behavior may be interpreted as an aggressive and threatening gesture. Similarly, an aggressive act by a child may be in defiance of controls, or in response to something in your classroom climate that has encouraged him to go ahead on his own.

*Reaction to Physical Contact Varies.* To some children who are accustomed to adults maintaining a physical distance from them, too close a proximity by the teacher might well stifle and embarrass. Conversely, other children prefer the close contact and warmth of teacher-pupil contacts. One broad cultural understanding among us that you may not have realized is that we do not stand too close to one another while talking in public. When the appropriate distance is broken, talking ceases.

*Nonverbal Expressions Among Racial, Ethnic, and Social Classes Can Differ Markedly.* Similarly, the behaviors of suburban, rural, and inner-city children vary. The teacher must be sensitive to behavior differences and seek to learn what they imply rather than coming to premature conclusions.

*Meeting Expectations Appears to be a Development Ability.* If meeting expectations is a learned process, it explains why the behavior of young children appears so unaffected and natural. Much of their behavior is spontaneous and unrehearsed. With older children, activities of pretending to listen in class, appearing busy during seatwork assignments, and putting on a front of seeming to be interested, may all be games that they have learned to play.

There are perhaps many such games that children learn to play in school, and the longer they go to school the better their skills develop. This is a necessary step in preparing for adult roles; but on the other hand, children who do need help may be able to conceal their need.

*Responsiveness May Be Misleading.* Parents who want their children to succeed often stress the importance of "pleasing the teacher." In actuality, the student less overt in his responsiveness may be more receptive to what is going on. Nonverbal clues are the best way to judge responsiveness.

*Deprived Children May Be Incapable of Meeting the Behavioral Expectations of the Teacher.* They may neither understand the rules of the school game nor be able to control their behavior satisfactorily. Indeed, many teachers do not facilitate their fumbling efforts, but, rather, try to catch them in the act. Such students need practice in what it means to be a student.

Awareness of the behavior of yourself and your students and what it means does not come all at once. Interpretations change as realization increases. But the processes of awareness and realization are concomitant. You perceive to greater depths, you are more attuned to those around you, and you begin to employ nonverbal clues for positive purposes. Having opened the door, you realize you have the ability to change and improve.

### ASSIGNMENTS

1. A company selling video-tape recorders may be willing to give a demonstration of its product in your school. Volunteer to be photographed. It may

take courage! Or make a class movie, letting children take footage with a movie camera. (Don't try to be in the film. Chances are you will be automatically included.) Study it to see how your nonverbal behavior could improve.

2. Make a study of the feedback at times when you are an observer—for example, of children's reactions to the librarian, music teacher, or other classroom visitors.

3. Discuss feedback in a teachers' meeting. Let teachers anonymously mark profile sheets showing impressions they have of other teachers, including yourself. (The results may amaze you.)

### EXPERIMENTING

Since nonverbal communication is so basic and certainly old as mankind, why the recent interest in its role in education? Are teachers now expected to search for hidden meanings behind everything that happens in their classrooms? Must they become overly sensitive to ordinary behavior? Not at all.

Teachers need not set out to discover meanings that lurk in the subterranean caverns of the mind. Indeed, they shouldn't. Instead, the purpose is to become more aware of nonverbal cues because they operate as a silent language to influence teacher-student understandings and interactions. And it is through these understandings and interactions in the classroom that the business of teaching and learning goes forward.

Your final assignment in your nonverbal course is an invitation to experiment in every phase of classroom nonverbal communication. The possibilities are limitless:

1. If you customarily work with small groups of children, experiment with the spread of the chairs. When the chairs are touching each other, do children react differently from when they are a foot apart? What about two feet? Does it make a difference whether you sit on a higher chair or one the same height?

2. Nonverbal acts are often preferable to words, and many studies show that the teacher's voice is heard far too often. Without telling the children of your intentions, experiment with giving nonverbal instead of verbal directions. Use devices such as a tap of a bell to tell children you want their attention, or the flick of lights to show that a period is about to end.

3. Make a definite attempt to react more effectively to signals. A kindergarten teacher found that she could avoid calamity by observing more closely a boy with bathroom problems. The child chewing his pencil may be hoping you will come to his desk. Or, the one wanting to sharpen his pencil may be lacking an idea to write about.

4. Try to match your degree of nonverbal behavior to the child's and examine the results. For instance, sometimes teachers tend to be over-

articulate with a nonarticulate child, subconsciously compensating for his lack. In contrast, a child who sits quietly beside the teacher may be getting warmth and comfort from the teacher's sitting quietly beside him. Matching the nonverbal behavior of a child is a kind of approval.

5. Experiment with light and heat—both important factors in classroom climate. Some teachers flick the switch as soon as they open the door, yet in most classrooms, any artificial light is not necessary on a normal day. Light affects mood, and so does heat. Deliberate changes in temperature can also be an effective device for changing classroom atmosphere.

6. Use nonverbal displays. The old adage that a picture is worth a thousand words applies in establishing classroom climate, especially if you employ humor and relaxation. One teacher experimented with two signs. The first said, "Pick up paper and put it in the wastebasket." The second was a silhouette of a child neatly dropping paper in the wastebasket. The second proved to be by far the better reminder.

7. Provide opportunities for children to express emotions by nonverbal means. Pantomimes are not only highly expressive for the actors but also give teachers insight into their feelings and emotions. Various forms of rhythm and creative dance are good nonverbal expressions, and so of course are all types of art work.

8. Talk about nonverbal patterns with your children, but do it astutely. Give them the opportunity to express themselves about nonverbal behavior on the part of adults that gives them pleasure or causes them frustrations.

9. Increase your practice of looking students in the eye. Experiment with glance exchanges for individual-to-individual contact.

10. Increase the frequency of your relevant gestures. They are an excellent way of underlining points you are trying to make.

11. Check your relevancy by checking your degree of effectiveness in transmitting ideas. This is not easy to do but it is especially important. Do you often feel misunderstood? Does a particular point you tried to make fail to get across? Your nonverbal behavior may have an incongruity that cancels out the effectiveness of your words.

12. Experiment with new movement patterns. Things you have been doing, do differently for a while. You may be making yourself too available or not available enough. Be sure, however, that your accessibility is not just a sneaky way to maintain close supervision.

13. Let children experiment with furniture arrangement that involves group interaction. One teacher tried putting desks in groups of four with the children facing each other. Two days later the desks were reversed so that this time the children faced away from each other.

14. Individualize your attention. You can't listen to all of the children all of the time, so experiment with listening very intently to a child for a brief period. As long as he is talking, look directly at him.

These suggested experiments aren't new. You've known about them all before. What's new is the emphasis on their nonverbal aspects. Considering them from this new point of view can help you understand their impact. Your goal is to use nonverbal communication more effectively in your quest for better ways of teaching.

DONALD R. CRUICKSHANK

# 19. TEACHER v. TEACHER: A PROPOSAL FOR IMPROVING RELATIONSHIPS

Now all the evidence of psychiatry...shows that membership in a group sustains a man, enables him to maintain his equilibrium under the ordinary shocks of life.... If his group is shattered around him, if he leaves a group... and finds no new group to which he can relate himself, he will, under stress, develop disorders of thought, feeling, and behavior.

George C. Homans
Harvard University

## THE PROBLEMS

Each year, approximately 150,000 teachers enter classrooms for the first time. At the same time, countless experienced teachers are moving from one teaching position to another. Both groups share the problem of adjusting to environments which are strange and, at times, even hostile. In each case, new and satisfying relationships must be formed if the individual teacher is to function as a mature human being and an effective teacher. Unfortunately, little time or conscious effort is given to helping teachers, both newcomers and old-timers, to know, understand and work with each other.

As the recent arrival strives to meet his new needs, he sometimes unintentionally manifests behavior which has unanticipated consequences. For example, because a new teacher seeks the acceptance of his students, he may indulge them in ways which disturb old-timers. Again seeking professional recognition, he may appear too eager in his relationship with superiors. In both cases, personal needs and lack of understanding of the norms of

---

Reprinted from *The Clearing House,* Vol. 41 (January 1967), 304–7, by permission from the publisher.

"acceptable teacher behavior" in the new setting place the newcomer in jeopardy. In short, his behavior is incompatible with that which would be accepted by his peers.

### SELF-EVALUATION

Some of the more common "mistakes" made which disturb relationships with other teachers are cited in a study by Allen.[1] Teachers were asked to report behavior they found unacceptable in their colleagues. The kinds of behavior mentioned most frequently as being undesirable in a classroom teacher are arranged below in checklist form. Each item requires a yes or no response.

(1)  Do I criticize or report fellow teachers to the principal?
(2)  Am I inconsiderate of pupils?
(3)  Am I inconsiderate of my colleagues?
(4)  Do I gossip about other teachers?
(5)  Do I interfere in another teacher's work?
(6)  Do I complain constantly about students?
(7)  Do I complain constantly about school conditions?
(8)  Do I complain constantly about school duties?
(9)  Do I engage in petty arguments?
(10) Am I intolerant of others?
(11) Do I criticize the former teacher's achievement with children?
(12) Am I unsympathetic with other teacher's problems?
(13) Am I jealous of other teacher's success?
(14) Do I expect special privileges?
(15) Am I *constantly* talking shop?
(16) Do I take out personal feelings on children?
(17) Do I criticize or gossip about children in front of others?
(18) Do I belittle my co-workers?
(19) Do I belittle my supervisors?
(20) Am I sarcastic with my pupils?
(21) Do I fail to settle complaints in a professional manner?
(22) Am I "cliquish" with other teachers in the building?
(23) Do I go to the principal with petty problems?
(24) Do I spread rumors?
(25) Do I borrow materials and not return them?
(26) Do I borrow without asking?
(27) Am I unable to take criticism or suggestions?
(28) Do I discipline other teacher's pupils without informing him?
(29) Do I snoop?
(30) Do I dwell on personal troubles?

Obviously the affirmative responses are seen as least desirable by fellow teachers.

A self rating might tell us, to some extent, how our colleagues look upon our behavior which affects our acceptance and effectiveness in the faculty group.

[1] Ruth A. Allen, "And How About You," *National Elementary Principal* (February 1959), pp. 37–40.

Another way we might look at "acceptable v. unacceptable teacher behavior" is by noting *how* teachers react when they are in conflict situations with fellow staff members. Spector[2] has provided us with a continuum of courses of action a teacher may take in a conflict situation. They are arranged from the immature physical exchange of blows to the objective attempt to determine the cause of the irritation as follows:

(1) a. Exchange blows
    b. Threaten with fists
    c. Curse vocally
(2) a. Talk back
    b. Bluster
    c. Threaten or curse under the breath
(3) a. Laugh it off
    b. Placate by smiling
    c. Be coldly polite
(4) a. Remain calm and silent
    b. Ignore
    c. Walk away
(5) a. Feel annoyed
    b. Feel resentful
    c. Feel hurt
(6) a. Discuss calmly
    b. Stick to the facts of the situation
    c. Try to determine the cause of irritation

The subjects in Spector's study were asked to react to school conflict situations by selecting a course of action from the possibilities above. One conflict situation to which an action was requested was, "You have been accused of spreading gossip about another teacher. You are entirely innocent. The teacher confronts you and berates you. What would you do?"

## SOME CAUSES OF FRICTION

It has been noted that, among other things, our degree of acceptance by other teachers is affected by our behavior in relatively unstructured situations and by our reactions in the face of conflict. Since behavior is symptomatic, it is incumbent upon us to understand better the causes of any behavior. Since behavior is dynamic, it is possible that this increased understanding of the causes of behavior may lead to increased personal effectiveness and provide better understanding of others.

Initially, it was noted that the growth of the teaching force and its increasing mobility cause a teaching faculty to be composed of newcomers and old-timers. Empirically it could be argued that age differences among staff members might affect teacher relationships. Some support for this

2 Samuel I. Spector, "Teacher Reactions to Conflict Situations," *Journal of Educational Psychology* (November 1955), pp. 437–45.

supposition is found in the work of Havighurst.[3] According to his classification, members of each age group have different needs. For example, the new teacher—as a young adult—generally is occupied with selecting a mate, learning to live with a marriage partner, starting a family, rearing children, managing a home, getting started in an occupation, taking on civic responsibility, and finding a congenial social group.

In contrast the old-timer, having accomplished these tasks to some extent, is confronted with a different array of needs such as achieving adult civic and social responsibility, establishing and maintaining an economic standard of living, assisting teen-age children to become responsible and happy adults, developing adult leisure time activities, relating one's self to one's spouse as a person, accepting and adjusting to the psychological changes of middle age, and adjusting to aging parents.

Lack of understanding of the needs and behavior of those of a different age group well may contribute to discord among faculty. At the same time the very nature of the differences sometimes are difficult to accept. For example, while the newcomer is at her aesthetic best, the old-timer may increasingly be aware of and concerned with her vanishing youth.

Beside the differences in needs which may contribute to poor teacher-to-teacher relationships, at least one other cause may be speculated here. Perception of the role of the teacher varies widely, as shown in studies of teacher effectiveness. We all are convinced we can tell a good teacher when we see one. Thus, we judge our colleagues on the basis of *our* perception of what *they should* do as professionals. When they behave as we would wish, they are "good teachers." Good teaching, then, is value loaded. Our failure to recognize this leads us all to set up personal models to which we expect others to conform. Seeking a common denominator for the teaching behavior of our colleagues is a mistake we cannot afford.

### POSSIBLE SOLUTIONS

After noting the problems and discussing some possible causative factors, our attention must focus on alternative solutions.

It has been illustrated that knowledge of the causes of ineffective teacher-to-teacher relationships is imperative. Such diagnosis makes progress possible, for the causes and not the symptoms must be treated. It is only a first step albeit an important one, to recognize that one "gossips about other teachers" or "is cliquish." The fundamental question is *why* one behaves so. This question is indicative of a desire to understand the forces that shape our behavior. Unfortunately, few of us are willing to commit our personal behavior to discussion or inspection by others. Opportunities to discuss the problems collected by Allen as problems of a "third person" might prove fruitful. Case studies have an advantage for this purpose.

[3] R. J. Havighurst, *Developmental Tasks and Education* (New York: Longmans, Green), 1952.

Awareness of our reactions to conflict situations is commendable, but achieving better self control or more objective behavior is a more difficult task.

Possibly the most fruitful avenue for increasing positive teacher-to-teacher relationships is suggested by Homans,[4] who hypothesizes that the oftener people do things together the more they will tend to like each other; the more they like each other, the oftener they will tend to do things together. If this is true, it is incumbent upon the school leader to provide satisfying opportunities for staff members to relate to one another. Efforts might be worthwhile which would enable teacher isolates and stars, newcomers and old-timers, to work together.

Interclass visitations are one way in which teachers can better get to know and understand each other. Several studies report this as a successful technique for improving teacher interrelationships.

In the final analysis, however, our ability to relate successfully within our professional peer group seems to be in direct proportion to our ability to accept ourselves and others. The ability to do this may come only late in life, if at all, for some. However, we must be diligent in our efforts for our happiness and effectiveness depend a great deal upon whether we can say, "I like myself, I like others, and others like me."

DORWIN CARTWRIGHT

# 20. ACHIEVING CHANGE IN PEOPLE: SOME APPLICATIONS OF GROUP DYNAMICS THEORY

We hear all around us today the assertion that the problems of the twentieth century are problems of human relations. The survival of civilization, it is said, will depend upon man's ability to create social inventions capable of harnessing, for society's constructive use, the vast physical energies now at

From *Human Relations,* 4:1951, pp. 381–92. Reprinted by permission of the Plenum Publishing Corporation and the author.

[4] George C. Homans, *The Human Group* (New York: Harcourt, Brace and World, Inc.), 1950.

man's disposal. Or, to put the matter more simply, we must learn how to change the way in which people behave toward one another. In broad outline, the specifications for a good society are clear, but a serious technical problem remains: How can we change people so that they neither restrict the freedom nor limit the potentialities for growth of others; so that they accept and respect people of different religion, nationality, color, or political opinion; so that nations can exist in a world without war, and so that the fruits of our technological advances can bring economic well-being and freedom from disease to all the people of the world? Although few people would disagree with these objectives when stated abstractly, when we become more specific, differences of opinion quickly arise. How is change to be produced? Who is to do it? Who is to be changed? These questions permit no ready answers.

Before we consider in detail these questions of social technology, let us clear away some semantic obstacles. The word "change" produces emotional reactions. It is not a neutral word. To many people it is threatening. It conjures up visions of a revolutionary, a dissatisfied idealist, a trouble-maker, a malcontent. Nicer words referring to the process of changing people are education, training, orientation, guidance, indoctrination, therapy. We are more ready to have others "educate" us than to have them "change" us. We, ourselves, feel less guilty in "training" others than in "changing" them. Why this emotional response? What makes the two kinds of words have such different meanings? I believe that a large part of the difference lies in the fact that the safer words (like education or therapy) carry the implicit assurance that the only changes produced will be good ones, acceptable within a currently held value system. The cold, unmodified word "change," on the contrary, promises no respect for values; it might even tamper with values themselves. Perhaps for this very reason it will foster straight thinking if we use the word "change" and thus force ourselves to struggle directly and self-consciously with the problems of value that are involved. Words like education, training, or therapy, by the very fact that they are not so disturbing, may close our eyes to the fact that they too inevitably involve values.

Another advantage of using the word "change" rather than other related words is that it does not restrict our thinking to a limited set of aspects of people that are legitimate targets of change. Anyone familiar with the history of education knows that there has been endless controversy over what it is about people that "education" properly attempts to modify. Some educators have viewed education simply as imparting knowledge, others mainly as providing skills for doing things, still others as producing healthy "attitudes," and some have aspired to instil a way of life. Or if we choose to use a word like "therapy," we can hardly claim that we refer to a more clearly defined realm of change. Furthermore, one can become inextricably entangled in distinctions and vested interests by attempting to distinguish sharply between, let us say, the domain of education and that of therapy. If we are to try to take a broader view and to develop some basic principles that promise to apply to all types of modifications in people, we had better use a word like "change" to keep our thinking general enough.

The proposal that social technology may be employed to solve the problems of society suggests that social science may be applied in ways not different from those used in the physical sciences. Does social science, in fact, have any practically useful knowledge which may be brought to bear significantly on society's most urgent problems? What scientifically based principles are there for guiding programs of social change? In this paper we shall restrict our considerations to certain parts of a relatively new branch of social science known as "group dynamics." We shall examine some of the implications for social action which stem from research in this field of scientific investigation.

What is "group dynamics"? Perhaps it will be most useful to start by looking at the derivation of the word "dynamics." It comes from a Greek word meaning force. In careful usage of the phrase, "group dynamics" refers to the force operating in groups. The investigation of group dynamics, then, consists of a study of these forces: what gives rise to them, what conditions modify them, what consequences they have, etc. The practical application of group dynamics (or the technology of group dynamics) consists of the utilization of knowledge about these forces for the achievement of some purpose. In keeping with this definition, then, it is clear that group dynamics, as a realm of investigation, is not particularly novel, nor is it the exclusive property of any person or institution. It goes back at least to the outstanding work of men like Simmel, Freud, and Cooley.

Although interest in groups has a long and respectable history, the past fifteen years have witnessed a new flowering of activity in this field. Today, research centers in several countries are carrying out substantial programs of research designed to reveal the nature of groups and of their functioning. The phrase "group dynamics" has come into common usage during this time and intense efforts have been devoted to the development of the field, both as a branch of social science and as a form of social technology.

In this development the name of Kurt Lewin has been outstanding. As a consequence of his work in the field of individual psychology and from his analysis of the nature of the pressing problems of the contemporary world, Lewin became convinced of society's urgent need for a *scientific approach* to the understanding of the dynamics of groups. In 1945 he established the Research Center for Group Dynamics to meet this need. Since that date the Center has been devoting its efforts to improving our scientific understanding of groups through laboratory experimentation, field studies, and the use of techniques of action research. It has also attempted in various ways to help get the findings of social science more widely used by social management (2).

For various reasons we have found that much of our work has been devoted to an attempt to gain a better understanding of the ways in which people change their behavior or resist efforts by others to have them do so. Whether we set for ourselves the practical goal of improving behavior or whether we take on the intellectual task of understanding why people do what they do, we have to investigate processes of communication, influence, social pressure—in short, problems of change.

In this work we have encountered great frustration. The problems have been most difficult to solve. Looking back over our experience, I have become convinced that no small part of the trouble has resulted from an irresistible tendency to conceive of our problems in terms of the individual. We live in an individualistic culture. We value the individual highly, and rightly so. But I am inclined to believe that our political and social concern for the individual has narrowed our thinking as social scientists so much that we have not been able to state our research problems properly. Perhaps we have taken the individual as the unit of observation and study when some larger unit would have been more appropriate. Let us look at a few examples.

Consider first some matters having to do with the mental health of an individual. We can all agree, I believe, that an important mark of a healthy personality is that the individual's self-esteem has not been undermined. But on what does self-esteem depend? From research on this problem we have discovered that, among other things, repeated experiences of failure or traumatic failures on matters of central importance serve to undermine one's self-esteem. We also know that whether a person experiences success or failure as a result of some undertaking depends upon the level of aspiration which he has set for himself. Now, if we try to discover how the level of aspiration gets set, we are immediately involved in the person's relationships to groups. The groups to which he belongs set standards for his behavior which he must accept if he is to remain in the group. If his capacities do not allow him to reach these standards, he experiences failure, he withdraws or is rejected by the group and his self-esteem suffers a shock.

Suppose, then, that we accept a task of therapy, of rebuilding his self-esteem. It would appear plausible from our analysis of the problem that we should attempt to work with variables of the same sort that produced the difficulty, that is to work with him either in the groups to which he now belongs or to introduce him into new groups which are selected for the purpose and to work upon his relationships to groups as such. From the point of view of preventive mental health, we might even attempt to train the groups in our communities—classes in schools, work groups in business, families, unions, religious and cultural groups—to make use of practices better designed to protect the self-esteem of their members.

Consider a second example. A teacher finds that in her class she has a number of trouble-makers, full of aggression. She wants to know why these children are so aggressive and what can be done about it. A foreman in a factory has the same kind of problem with some of his workers. He wants the same kind of help. The solution most tempting to both the teacher and the foreman often is to transfer the worst trouble-makers to someone else, or if facilities are available, to refer them for counselling. But is the problem really of such a nature that it can be solved by removing the trouble-maker from the situation or by working on his individual motivations and emotional life? What leads does research give us? The evidence indicates, of course, that there are many causes of aggressiveness in people, but one aspect of the problem has become increasingly clear in recent years. If we observe carefully the amount of aggressive behavior and the number of trouble-makers to be found in a large collection of groups, we find that these characteristics can vary tremendously from group to group even when the different groups are composed essentially of the same kinds of people. In the now classic experiments of Lewin, Lippitt, and White (7) on the effects of different styles of leadership, it was found that the same group of children displayed markedly different levels of aggressive behavior when under different styles of leadership. Moreover, when individual children were transferred from one group to another, their levels of aggressiveness shifted to conform to the atmosphere of the new group. Efforts, to account for one child's aggressiveness under one style of leadership merely in terms of his personality traits could hardly succeed under these conditions. This is not to say that a person's behavior is entirely to be accounted for by the atmosphere and structure of the immediate group, but it is remarkable to what an extent a strong, cohesive group can control aspects of a member's behavior traditionally thought to be expressive of enduring personality traits. Recognition of this fact rephrases the problem of how to change such behavior. It directs us to a study of the sources of the influence of the group on its members.

Let us take an example from a different field. What can we learn from efforts to change people by mass media and mass persuasion? In those rare instances when educators, propagandists, advertisers, and others who want to influence large numbers of people, have bothered to make an objective evaluation of the enduring changes produced by their efforts, they have been able to demonstrate only the most negligible effects (1). The inefficiency of attempts to influence the public by mass media would be scandalous if there were agreement that it was important or even desirable to have such influences strongly exerted. In fact, it is no exaggeration to say that all of the research and experience of generations has not improved the efficiency of lectures or other means of mass influence to any noticeable degree. Something must be wrong with our theories of learning, motivation, and social psychology.

Within very recent years some research data have been accumulating which may give us a clue to the solution of our problem. In one series of experiments directed by Lewin, it was found that a method of group decision, in which the group as a whole made a decision to have its members change their behavior, was from two to ten times as effective in producing actual change as was a lecture presenting exhortation to change (6). We have yet to learn precisely what produces these differences of effectiveness, but it is clear that by introducing group forces into the situation a whole new level of influence has been achieved.

The experience has been essentially the same when people have attempted to increase the productivity of individuals in work settings. Traditional conceptions of how to increase the output of workers have stressed the individual: select the right man for the job; simplify the job for him; train him in the skills required; motivate him by economic incentives; make it clear to whom he reports; keep the lines of authority and responsibility simple and straight. But even when all these conditions are fully met we are finding that productivity is far below full potential. There is even good reason to conclude that this individualistic conception of the determinants of productivity actually fosters negative consequences. The individual, now isolated and subjected to the demands of the organization through the commands of his boss, finds that he must create with his fellow employees informal groups, not shown on any table of organization, in order to protect himself from arbitrary control of his life, from the boredom produced by the endless repetition of mechanically sanitary and routine operations, and from the impoverishment of his emotional and social life brought about by the frustration of his basic needs for social interaction, participation, and acceptance in a stable group. Recent experiments have demonstrated clearly that the productivity of work groups can be greatly increased by methods of work organization and supervision which give more responsibility to work groups, which allow for fuller participation in important decisions, and which make stable groups the firm basis for support of the individual's social needs (3). I am convinced that future research will also demonstrate that people working under such conditions become more mature and creative individuals in their homes, in community life, and as citizens.

As a final example, let us examine the experience of efforts to train people in workshops, institutes, and special training courses. Such efforts are common in various areas of social welfare, intergroup relations, political affairs, industry, and adult education generally. It is an unfortunate fact that objective evaluation of the effects of such training efforts has only rarely been undertaken, but there is evidence for those who will look that the actual change in behavior produced is most disappointing. A workshop most generally develops keen interest among the participants, high morale and enthusiasm, and a firm resolve on the part of many to apply all the wonderful insights back home. But what happens back home? The trainee discovers that his colleagues don't share his enthusiasm. He learns that the task of changing others' expectations and ways of doing things is discouragingly difficult. He senses, perhaps not very clearly, that it would make all the difference in the world if only there were a few other people sharing his enthusiasm and insights with whom he could plan activities, evaluate consequences of efforts, and from whom he could gain emotional and motivational support. The approach to training which conceives of its task as being merely that of changing the individual probably produces frustration, demoralization, and disillusionment in as large a measure as it accomplishes more positive results.

A few years ago the Research Center for Group Dynamics undertook to shed light on this problem by investigating the operation of a workshop for training leaders in intercultural relations (8). In a project, directed by Lippitt, we set out to compare systematically the different effects of the workshop upon trainees who came as isolated individuals in contrast to those who came as teams. Since one of the problems in the field of intercultural relations is that of getting people of good will to be more active in community efforts to improve intergroup relations, one goal of the training workshop was to increase the activity of the trainees in such community affairs. We found that before the workshop there was no difference in the activity level of the people who were to be trained as isolates and of those who were to be trained as teams. Six months after the workshop, however, those who had been trained as isolates were only slightly more active than before the workshop whereas those who had been members of strong training teams were now much more active. We do not have clear evidence on the point, but we would be quite certain that the maintenance of heightened activity over a long period of time would also be much better for members of teams. For the isolates the effect of the workshop had the characteristic of a "shot in the arm" while for the team member it produced a more enduring change because the team provided continuous support and reinforcement for its members.

What conclusions may we draw from these examples? What principles of achieving change in people can we see emerging? To begin with the most general proposition, we may state that the behavior, attitudes, beliefs and values of the individual are all firmly grounded in the groups to which he belongs. How aggressive or cooperative a person is, how much self-respect and self-confidence he has, how energetic and productive his work is, what he aspires to, what he believes to be true and good, whom he loves or hates, and what beliefs and prejudices he holds—all these characteristics are highly determined by the individual's group memberships. In a real sense, they are properties of groups and of the relationships between people. Whether they change or resist change will, therefore, be greatly influenced by the nature of these groups. Attempts to change them must be concerned with the dynamics of groups.

In examining more specifically how groups enter into the process of change, we find it useful to view groups in at least three different ways. In the first view, the group is seen as a source of influence over its members. Efforts to change behavior can be supported or blocked by pressures on members stemming from the group. To make constructive use of these pressures the group must be used *as a medium of change*. In the second view, the group itself becomes the *target of change*. To change the behavior of individuals, it may be necessary to change the standards of the group, its style of leadership, its emotional atmosphere, or its stratification into cliques and hierarchies. Even though the goal may be to change the behavior of *individuals,* the target of change becomes the group. In the third view, it is recognized that many changes of behavior can be brought about only by the organized efforts of groups *as agents of change*. A committee to combat intolerance, a labor union, an employers' association, a citizens' group to increase the pay of teachers—any action group will be more or less effective depending upon the way it is organized, the satisfactions it provides to its members, the degree to which its goals are clear, and a host of other properties of the group.

An adequate social technology of change, then, requires at the very least a scientific understanding of groups viewed in each of these ways. We shall consider here only the first two aspects of the problem: the group as a medium of change and as a target of change.

## THE GROUP AS A MEDIUM OF CHANGE

*Principle No. 1.* If the group is to be used effectively as a medium of change, those people who are to be changed and those who are to exert influence for change must have a strong sense of belonging to the same group.

Kurt Lewin described this principle well: "The normal gap between teacher and student, doctor and patient, social worker and public, can... be a real obstacle to acceptance of the advocated conduct." In other words, in spite of whatever status differences there might be between them, the teacher and the student have to feel as members of one group in matters involving their sense of values. The chances for re-education seem to be increased whenever a strong we-feeling is created (5). Recent experiments by Preston and Heintz have demonstrated greater changes of opinions among members of discussion groups operating with participatory leadership than among those with supervisory leadership (12). The implications of this principle for classroom teaching are far-reaching. The same may be said of supervision in the factory, army, or hospital.

*Principle No. 2.* The more attractive the group is to its members the greater is the influence that the group can exert on its members.

This principle has been extensively documented by Festinger and his co-workers (4). They have been able to show in a variety of settings that in more cohesive groups there is a greater readiness of members to attempt to influence others, a greater readiness to be influenced by others, and stronger pressures toward conformity when conformity is a relevant matter for the group. Important for the practitioner wanting to make use of this principle is, of course, the question of how to increase the attractiveness of groups. This is a question with many answers. Suffice it to say that a group is more attractive the more it satisfies the needs of its members. We have been able to demonstrate experimentally an increase in group cohesiveness by increasing the liking of members for each other as persons, by increasing the perceived importance of the group goal, and by increasing the prestige of the group among other groups. Experienced group workers could add many other ways to this list.

*Principle No. 3.* In attempts to change attitudes, values, or behavior, the more relevant they are to the basis of attraction to the group, the greater will be the influence that the group can exert upon them.

I believe this principle gives a clue to some otherwise puzzling phenomena. How does it happen that a group, like a labor union, seems to be able to exert such strong discipline over its members in some matters (let us say in dealings with management), while it seems unable to exert nearly the same influence in other matters (let us say in political action)? If we examine why it is that members are attracted to the group, I believe we will find that a particular reason for belonging seems more related to some of the group's activities than to others. If a man joins a union mainly to keep his job and to improve his working conditions, he may be largely uninfluenced by the union's attempt to modify his attitudes toward national and international affairs. Groups differ tremendously in the range of matters that are relevant to them and hence over which they have influence. Much of the inefficiency of adult education could be reduced if more attention were paid to the need that influence attempts be appropriate to the groups in which they are made.

*Principle No. 4.* The greater the prestige of a group member in the eyes of the other members, the greater the influence he can exert.

Polansky, Lippitt, and Redl (11) have demonstrated this principle with great care and methodological ingenuity in a series of studies in children's summer camps. From a practical point of view it must be emphasized that the things giving prestige to a member may not be those characteristics most prized by the official management of the group. The most prestige-carrying member of a Sunday School class may not possess the characteristics most similar to the minister of the church. The teacher's pet may be a poor source of influence within a class. This principle is the basis for the common observation that the official leader and the actual leader of a group are often not the same individual.

*Principle No. 5.* Efforts to change individuals or subparts of a group which, if successful, would have the result of making them deviate from the norms of the group will encounter strong resistance.

During the past few years a great deal of evidence has been accumulated showing the tremendous pressures which groups can exert upon members to conform to the group's norms. The price of deviation in most groups is rejection or even expulsion. If the member really wants to belong and be accepted, he cannot withstand this type of pressure. It is for this reason that efforts to change people by taking them from the group and giving them special training so often have disappointing results. This principle also accounts for the finding that people thus trained sometimes display increased tension, aggressiveness toward the group, or a tendency to form cults or cliques with others who have shared their training.

These five principles concerning the group as a medium of change would appear to have readiest application to groups created for the purpose of producing changes in people. They provide certain specifications for building effective training or therapy groups. They also point, however, to a difficulty in producing change in people in that they show how resistant an individual is to changing in any way contrary to group pressures and expectations. In order to achieve many kinds of changes in people, therefore, it is necessary to deal with the group as a target of change.

### THE GROUP AS A TARGET OF CHANGE

*Principle No. 6.* Strong pressure for changes in the group can be established by creating a shared perception by members of the need for change, thus making the source of pressure for change lie within the group.

Marrow and French (9) report a dramatic case-study which illustrates this principle quite well. A manufacturing concern had a policy against hiring women over thirty because it was believed that they were slower, more difficult to train, and more likely to be absent. The staff psychologist was able to present to management evidence that this belief was clearly unwarranted at least within their own company. The psychologist's facts, however, were rejected and ignored as a basis for action because they violated accepted beliefs. It was claimed that they went against the direct experience of the foremen. Then the psychologist hit upon a plan for achieving change which differed drastically from the usual one of argument, persuasion, and pressure. He proposed that management conduct its own analysis of the situation. With his help management collected all the facts which they believed were relevant to the problem. When the results were in they were now their own facts rather than those of some "outside" expert. Policy was immediately changed without further resistance. The important point here is that facts are not enough. The facts must be the accepted property of the group if they are to become an effective basis for change. There seems to be all the difference in the world in changes actually carried out between those cases in which a consulting firm is hired to do a study and present a report and those in which technical experts are asked to collaborate with the group in doing its own study.

*Principle No. 7.* Information relating to the need for change, plans for change, and consequences of change must be shared by all relevant people in the group.

Another way of stating this principle is to say that change of a group ordinarily requires the opening of communication channels. Newcomb (10) has shown how one of the first consequences of mistrust and hostility is the avoidance of communicating openly and freely about the things producing the tension. If you look closely at a pathological group (that is, one that has trouble making decisions or effecting coordinated efforts of its members), you will certainly find strong restraints in that group against communicating vital information among its members. Until these restraints are removed there can be little hope for any real and lasting changes in the group's functioning. In passing it should be pointed out that the removal of barriers to communication will ordinarily be accompanied by a sudden increase in the communication of hostility. The group may appear to be falling apart, and it will certainly be a painful experience to many of the members. This pain and the fear that things are getting out of hand often stop the process of change once begun.

*Principle No. 8.* Changes in one part of a group produce strain in other related parts which can be reduced only by eliminating the change or by bringing about readjustments in the related parts.

It is a common practice to undertake improvements in group functioning by providing training programs for certain classes of people in the organization. A training program for foremen, for nurses, for teachers, or for group workers is established. If the content of the training is relevant for organizational change, it must of necessity deal with the relationships these people have with other subgroups. If nurses in a hospital change their behavior significantly, it will affect their relations both with the patients and with the doctors. It is unrealistic to assume that both these groups will remain indifferent to any significant changes in this respect. In hierarchical structures this process is most clear. Lippitt has proposed on the basis of research and experience that in such organizations attempts at change should always involve three levels, one being the major target of change and the other two being the one above and the one below.

These eight principles represent a few of the basic propositions emerging from research in group dynamics. Since research is constantly going on and since it is the very nature of research to revise and reformulate our conceptions, we may be sure that these principles will have to be modified and improved as time goes by. In the meantime they may serve as guides in our endeavors to develop a scientifically based technology of social management.

In social technology, just as in physical technology, invention plays a crucial role. In both fields progress consists of the creation of new mechanisms for the accomplishment of certain goals. In both fields inventions arise in response to practical needs and are to be evaluated by how effectively they satisfy these needs. The relation of invention to scientific development is indirect but important. Inventions cannot proceed too far ahead of basic scientific development, nor should they be allowed to fall too far behind. They will be more effective the more they make good use of known principles of science, and they often make new developments in science possible. On the other hand, they are in no sense logical derivations from scientific principles.

I have taken this brief excursion into the theory of invention in order to make a final point. To many people "group dynamics" is known only for the social inventions which have developed in recent years in work with groups. Group dynamics is often thought of as certain techniques to be used with groups. Role playing, buzz groups, process observers, post-meeting reaction sheets, and feedback of group observations are devices popularly associated with the phrase "group dynamics." I trust that I have been able to show that group dynamics is more than a collection of gadgets. It certainly aspires to be a science as well as a technology.

This is not to underplay the importance of these inventions nor of the function of inventing. As inventions they are all mechanisms designed to help accomplish important goals. How effective they are will depend upon how skillfully they are used and how appropriate they are to the purposes to which they are put. Careful evaluative research must be the ultimate judge of their usefulness in comparison with alternative inventions. I believe that the principles enumerated in this paper indicate some of the specifications that social inventions in this field must meet.

## REFERENCES

1. Cartwright, D. Some principles of mass persuasion: selected findings of research on the sale of United States War Bonds. *Human Relations,* 1949, 2, No. 3, 253–67.
2. ———. *The research center for group dynamics: a report of five years' activities and a view of future needs.* Ann Arbor: Institute for Social Research, 1950.
3. Coch, L., and J. R. P. French, Jr. Overcoming resistance to change. *Human Relations,* 1948, 1, No. 4, 512–32.
4. Festinger, L., *et al. Theory and experiment in social communication: collected papers.* Ann Arbor: Institute for Social Research, 1950.
5. Lewin, K. *Resolving social conflicts.* New York: Harper and Brothers, 1948, 67.
6. ———. *Field theory in social science.* New York: Harper and Brothers, 1951, 229–36.
7. ———, R. Lippitt, and R. K. White. Patterns of aggressive behavior in experimentally created 'Social climates'. *Journal of Social Psychology,* 1939, 10, 271–99.
8. Lippitt, R. *Training in community relations.* New York: Harper and Brothers, 1949.
9. Marrow, A. J., and J. R. P. French, Jr. Changing a stereotype in industry. *Journal of Social Issues,* 1945, 1, 3, 33–37.

10. NEWCOMB, T. M. Autistic hostility and social reality. *Human Relations,* 1947, 1, No. 1, 69–86.

11. POLANSKY, N., R. LIPPITT, and F. REDL. An investigation of behavioral contagion in groups. *Human Relations,* 1950, 3, No. 4, 319–48.

12. PRESTON, M. G., and R. K. HEINTZ. Effects of participatory vs. supervisory leadership on group judgment. *Journal of Abnormal and Social Psychology,* 1949, 44, 345–55.

# 21. THE CODE OF ETHICS OF THE EDUCATION PROFESSION

### PREAMBLE

The educator believes in the worth and dignity of man. He recognizes the supreme importance of the pursuit of truth, devotion to excellence, and the nurture of democratic citizenship. He regards as essential to these goals the protection of freedom to learn and to teach and the guarantee of equal educational opportunity for all. The educator accepts his responsibility to practice his profession according to the highest ethical standards.

The educator recognizes the magnitude of the responsibility he has accepted in choosing a career in education, and engages himself, individually and collectively with other educators, to judge his colleagues, and to be judged by them, in accordance with the provisions of this code.

### PRINCIPLE I
### COMMITMENT TO THE STUDENT

The educator measures his success by the progress of each student toward realization of his potential as a worthy and effective citizen. The educator therefore works to stimulate the spirit of inquiry, the acquisition of knowledge and understanding, and the thoughtful formulation of worthy goals.

In fulfilling his obligation to the student, the educator—

1. Shall not without just cause restrain the student from independent action in his pursuit of learning, and shall not without just cause deny the student access to varying points of view.

---

Adopted by the Representative Assembly of the National Education Association, July 5, 1968. Reprinted by permission.

2. Shall not deliberately suppress or distort subject matter for which he bears responsibility.
3. Shall make reasonable effort to protect the student from conditions harmful to learning or to health and safety.
4. Shall conduct professional business in such a way that he does not expose the student to unnecessary embarrassment or disparagement.
5. Shall not on the ground of race, color, creed, or national origin exclude any student from participation in or deny him benefits under any program, nor grant any discriminatory consideration or advantage.
6. Shall not use professional relationships with students for private advantage.
7. Shall keep in confidence information that has been obtained in the course of professional service, unless disclosure serves professional purposes or is required by law.
8. Shall not tutor for remuneration students assigned to his classes, unless no other qualified teacher is reasonably available.

## PRINCIPLE II
## COMMITMENT TO THE PUBLIC

The educator believes that patriotism in its highest form requires dedication to the principles of our democratic heritage. He shares with all other citizens the responsibility for the development of sound public policy and assumes full political and citizenship responsibilities. The educator bears particular responsibility for the development of policy relating to the extension of educational opportunities for all and for interpreting educational programs and policies to the public.

In fulfilling his obligation to the public, the educator—

1. Shall not misrepresent an institution or organization with which he is affiliated, and shall take adequate precautions to distinguish between his personal and institutional or organizational views.
2. Shall not knowingly distort or misrepresent the facts concerning educational matters in direct and indirect public expressions.
3. Shall not interfere with a colleague's exercise of political and citizenship rights and responsibilities.
4. Shall not use institutional privileges for private gain or to promote political candidates or partisan political activities.
5. Shall accept no gratuities, gifts or favors that might impair or appear to impair professional judgment, nor offer any favor, service or thing of value to obtain special advantage.

## PRINCIPLE III
## COMMITMENT TO THE PROFESSION

The educator believes that the quality of the services of the education profession directly influences the nation and its citizens. He therefore exerts every effort to raise professional standards, to improve his service, to promote a climate in which the exercise of professional judgment is encouraged, and to achieve conditions which attract persons worthy of the trust to careers in education. Aware of the value of united effort, he contributes actively to the support, planning, and programs of professional organizations.

In fulfilling his obligation to the profession, the educator—

1. Shall not discriminate on grounds of race, color, creed, or national origin for membership in professional organizations, nor interfere with the free participation of colleagues in the affairs of their association.
2. Shall accord just and equitable treatment to all members of the profession in the exercise of their professional rights and responsibilities.
3. Shall not use coercive means or promise special treatment in order to influence professional decisions of colleagues.
4. Shall withhold and safeguard information acquired about colleagues in the course of employment, unless disclosure serves professional purposes.
5. Shall not refuse to participate in a professional inquiry when requested by an appropriate professional association.
6. Shall provide upon the request of the aggrieved party a written statement of specific reason for recommendations that lead to the denial of increments, significant changes in employment, or termination of employment.
7. Shall not misrepresent his professional qualifications.
8. Shall not knowingly distort evaluations of colleagues.

PRINCIPLE IV
COMMITMENT TO PROFESSIONAL
EMPLOYMENT PRACTICES

The educator regards the employment agreement as a pledge to be executed both in spirit and in fact in a manner consistent with the highest ideals of professional service. He believes that sound professional personnel relationships with governing boards are built upon personal integrity, dignity, and mutual respect. The educator discourages the practice of his profession by unqualified persons.

In fulfilling his obligation to professional employment practices, the educator—

1. Shall apply for, accept, offer, or assign a position or responsibility on the basis of professional preparation and legal qualifications.
2. Shall apply for a specific position only when it is known to be vacant, and shall refrain from underbidding or commenting adversely about other candidates.
3. Shall not knowingly withhold information regarding a position from an applicant, or misrepresent an assignment or conditions of employment.
4. Shall give prompt notice to the employing agency of any change in availability of service, and the employing agent shall give prompt notice of change in availability or nature of a position.
5. Shall not accept a position when so requested by the appropriate professional organization.
6. Shall adhere to the terms of a contract or appointment, unless these terms

have been legally terminated, falsely represented, or substantially altered by unilateral action of the employing agency.

7. Shall conduct professional business through channels, when available, that have been jointly approved by the professional organization and the employing agency.

8. Shall not delegate assigned tasks to unqualified personnel.

9. Shall permit no commercial exploitation of his professional position.

10. Shall use time granted for the purpose for which it is intended.

# CHAPTER 4

# LEARNING
# THEORY,
# A RESOURCE FOR
# METHOD

ERNEST R. HILGARD

# 22. A PERSPECTIVE ON THE RELATIONSHIP BETWEEN LEARNING THEORY AND EDUCATIONAL PRACTICES

The relationship between learning theory and educational practices is that between any pure science and its technological applications. In the process of application something more than the theory is always involved. Thus, one does not move directly from astronomy to navigation without concern for tides, prevailing winds, and the location of lighthouses; investigations of heredity in fruitflies do not lead immediately to applications in animal husbandry without concern for the resistance of cattle to disease, the desirable characteristics determined by the market, and many other considerations; advances in the chemistry of fuels do not automatically determine whether a manufacturer will favor compact cars or full-sized ones, with engines in the front or in the rear. It is no different with educational practices, for these practices are determined by educational objectives, by the demands of mass education, by community resources, as well as by the teachings of psychology. In this article, I propose to examine some aspects of the contribution of learning theory and of experimentation on learning to the technology of education.

## SOME FAULTY CONJECTURES

First, I should like to dispose of some assertions which, if not often made, are sometimes implied.

*1. "We cannot expect to have instruction scientifically based as long as learning theorists are not in agreement."* If one were unable to proceed without a learning theory upon which all agreed, the situation would indeed

Reprinted from *Theories of Learning and Instruction*, 63rd Yearbook of the National Society for the Study of Education, Part I, Ernest R. Hilgard (ed.), (Chicago: The Society, 1964), pp. 402–15, by permission of the author and publisher.

be frightening. At least two things need be said. For one thing, the disagreement among theorists may be in respect to the interpretation of a set of facts upon which, as facts, all agree; in this case, the issue often is not one to trouble the practical person at all. Thus rewards may control learning in a given situation and be interpreted in contiguity terms, in reinforcement terms, or in information terms. While eventually the correct interpretation might make some difference, it often makes little difference at the present stage of technology. Thus Lumsdaine points out that *fading* in programing can be supported by Guthrie's contiguity theory, although it is advocated by Skinner as in accord with his theory of *shaping* through reinforcement. Second, the technology of instruction rests on much more than learning theory.

2. *"Once learning theory is in order, the principles of instruction will flow from it."* Technology must respect theory, in that it cannot violate fundamentally established principles, but theory never dictates technology directly. Learning theory will not dictate instructional practices any more than the principles of thermodynamics dictate whether airplanes shall be driven by propellers or jets.

It is only at the most advanced stages of theory construction, and usually after considerable interplay with technology, that greater reliance comes to be placed upon theory. Thus, computations of the orbits of space vehicles make use of advanced theory; at the same time the materials used, the fuels employed, and the like, have in them a large measure of empiricism.

3. *"The learning theorists are quarrelsome, but psychological experimentation is sound. If we know the experimental literature, then we can base our instruction upon it."* This is a tricky matter, for several reasons. For one thing, experiments are often guided by (and limited by) theory. That is, a test of a given theory is usually conducted with the constraints appropriate to that theory, and may not be fair to other theories that would favor different constraints. Hence, the facts do not "speak for themselves." For another, experimentation goes on at various levels and at various degrees of relevance to educational practices. Even those experiments which appear to be most closely related to instruction may not be generalizable to other instructional situations. Ignorance of the literature is not, therefore, the trouble in trying to apply learning theory to education.

4. *"Because we can't wait for the learning theorist to finish his job, and because learning theory will not in any case tell us what to do, we might as well ignore the learning theorist."* Things are not as white or black as this; learning theory is quite likely to be useful even if it is not directly determinative of practice. One can think of other parallels. Historians, for example, despair of finding general lessons of history, yet they argue fervently that a political leader is better off if he is informed about history, for he can, in fact, learn something from it. Learning theory is likely to produce some

economy in educational experimentation by suggesting directions in which answers can be sought, thus saving a wasteful empirical search. In the end, a practice must work, but if we guide our search for workable practices by theoretical considerations, we may save a great deal of time and effort along the way.

5. *"Psychologists know plenty about learning; educators know the problems of the schools. If only we could get them together, to talk to each other, most of our problems would be solved."* How many half-truths there are! Collaboration is needed, but its terms have to be specified. A few week-end conferences between psychologists and educators are not going to do the trick. The collaboration must be on long-range investigations, in which the search is conducted together. We do not know the best specifications for team research, but a variety of skills and experiences have to be brought together among people who understand each other as they face a common task. They have to learn from each other, so that part of the synthesis goes on in individual minds.

6. *"Teaching is an art, and we can learn more from good teachers than from any experiments we are likely to design, or from what any psychologist says about teaching."* Of course we can learn from skilled teachers, and it is true that some good instructional practices are invented rather than discovered in a laboratory. As Woodring points out, many reform movements in education are essentially inventions, without much benefit of psychological theory. But to throw away all the possibility of improving instruction through carefully designed studies would be like returning medical practice to the prescientific physician because we still value the bedside manner.

These assertions are highlighted to show that a problem exists and that we should try to think as clearly as we can about it in our attempt to establish a sounder relationship between theory and research in psychology and educational practices.

STEPS ON THE ROAD
FROM PURE-SCIENCE RESEARCH
TO ESTABLISHED EDUCATIONAL PRACTICES

In order to avoid the sharp distinction between pure and applied research, I find it convenient to break up the stages from the "purest" of research on learning to the most "applied" research (that concerned with the adoption of an approved practice) into six steps according to their relevance to the educational enterprise. Three of these are placed within the "pure science" end of the continuum, three of them in the "educational technology" end, as shown in Figure 1. The steps are abstracted from what is, in fact, a continuum; any one investigator may work at once upon several of the steps, or in the areas in which the steps shade into each other. The roles become increasingly diverse as the steps become farther apart. While the diagram is self-explanatory, its two halves call for some added comments.

## PURE-SCIENCE RESEARCH ON LEARNING

By pure-science research is meant that which is guided by the problems which the investigator sets himself, without regard for the immediate applicability of the results to practical situations. This does not mean that the investigator has no practical interests, or that he does not want his results used; it is only that he is patient and uses the methods and procedures appropriate to the topic on which he works. Within learning research we may divide the stages of relevance to learning into the following three, expanding somewhat the left three boxes of Figure 1.

Step 1. Research on learning with no regard for its educational relevance, e.g., animal studies, physiological, biochemical investigations. Learning in the flatworm and learning in the rat with transected spinal cord classify here.

Step 2. Research on learning which is not concerned with educational practices but which is more relevant than that of Step 1 because it deals with human subjects and with content that is nearer to that taught in school, e.g., nonsense syllable memorization and retention. The principles being tested are likely to be theoretical ones, such as the relative importance of proactive and retroactive inhibition.

Step 3. Research on learning that is relevant because the subjects are school-age children and the material learned is school subject matter or skill, though no attention is paid to the problem of adapting the learning to school practices, e.g., foreign language vocabulary learned by paired-associate method with various lengths of list and with various spacing of trials.

These three steps of relevance all classify as pure-science research because the problems are set by the investigators in relation to some theoretical issues and do not arise out of the practical needs of instruction. Of course there may be bridges from any pure-science project to a practical one: perhaps drugs discovered in brain studies of rats may aid remedial reading, studies of interference may suggest intervals between classes or what should be studied concomitantly, and language-vocabulary results in a pure context may guide language acquisition in schools. The main point is that the scientist has not committed himself to relevance. He may even disavow it, in line with a cult of pure science that seems to have been developing. According to this view, something is valuable precisely because it is remote from application; so long as it is precise, it does not matter how trivial it is. This is a faulty conception of pure science, and for the investigator to escape responsibility for the relevance of his work by falling back upon this "pure science" is as likely to be a sign of weakness as of strength. . . .

A further word on Step 3 is in order. The best work will be done at this

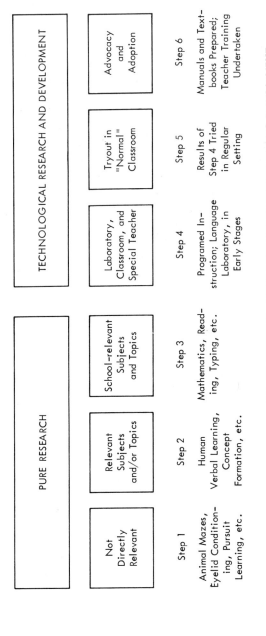

FIGURE I. STEPS IN RESEARCH ON LEARNING—PURE RESEARCH TO TECHNOLOGICAL DEVELOPMENT

stage by combining the skills of the subject-matter specialist with those of the experimenter upon learning. I have in mind combining the work of linguist and psychologist, as in the use of Hockett's linguistic analysis by Gibson, Gibson, Danielson, and Osser,[1] and in the combination of experts in mathematical learning theory and linguists in the work of Suppes, Crothers, Weir, and Trager.[2]

A brief characterization of the report by Suppes and others will be useful in showing some of the characteristics of Step 3 investigations. The authors consist of a logician sophisticated with respect to mathematical models, a psychologist whose work lies particularly in the field of mathematical learning, and two linguists. The studies, which concern the teaching of the Russian language, used actual language students, working in the familiar setting of the language laboratory in one of the local junior high schools. The material to be studied was prepared with the aid of a linguist familiar with the structure of the Russian language, so that certain conjectures about linguistics could be studied at the same time that learning theory was being investigated. The discriminations called for were real ones—Russian words being spoken into the tape by someone fluent in Russian. Contrast this with the usual preparation of a list to be memorized in the laboratory! Without going into detail, let me indicate the kinds of things that come from such a study:

1. Linguists have offered some conjectures about which combinations of phonemes can be most easily identified and how easily allophones can be recognized. (An allophone is a phoneme that is acoustically a variant: the phoneme that is represented by the letter *p* in English is not equally explosive in *speech*, *peach*, and to*p*most. Hence these three *p's* are allophones.) The investigation gave evidence that most of the conjectures of the linguist were indeed correct. A native speaker has no trouble in hearing two allophones as the "same" phoneme, but the student hearing a foreign language has a great deal of trouble, and in constructing a good program these details are important.
2. The effort to work up by small steps from the easier combinations to the more difficult ones, which seemed plausible enough from the theory of programing, turned out not to be advantageous. The students who received random presentations from the start did somewhat better than those who had the orderly progression from easy to difficult.
3. The mathematical model that proved to fit these data best was a two-stage model, as though learning took place in two jumps from no learning through an intermediate stage to mastery. What this means in terms of the underlying processes is not yet clear; it may mean that first comes a stage of discriminating the stimuli and responses, and then a stage of connecting them.

[1] Eleanor J. Gibson, J. J. Gibson, A. Danielson, and H. Osser, "A Developmental Study of the Discrimination of Letter-like Forms," *Journal of Comparative and Physiological Psychology*, LV (December, 1962), 897–906.

[2] Patrick Suppes, E. Crothers, Ruth Weir, and Edith Trager, *Some Quantitative Studies of Russian Consonant Phoneme Discrimination*. Stanford, California: Stanford University, Institute for Mathematical Studies in the Social Sciences, Technical Report No. 49, September 14, 1962.

My reason for placing this investigation at Stage 3 is that it is essentially a pure-science project, concerned with phoneme-allophone discrimination, on the one hand, and mathematical models of learning, on the other. Its relevance to classroom learning comes about because of its choice of subjects, laboratory conditions, and subject matter. It is close to the technology of instruction but is not yet designed to indicate just how Russian should be taught. The order of presentation (increasing difficulty *vs.* random difficulty) is the most technologically relevant of the suggestions coming from the study, but this has to do with only a small aspect of learning Russian and requires more substantiation before it can be generalized. At the same time, it is fairly obvious that experimentation closely related to the instructional task is likely to bear educational fruit more quickly than experiments classifiable within Steps 1 and 2.

### APPLIED OR TECHNOLOGICAL
### RESEARCH AND DEVELOPMENT

We are ready to consider what happens on the right-hand side of Figure 1, in the steps having to do with applied rather than pure-science research. The steps may be described as follows:

Step 4. Research conducted in special laboratory classrooms, with selected teachers, e.g., bringing a few students into a room to see whether or not instruction in set theory or symbolic logic is feasible, granted a highly skilled teacher.

Step 5. A tryout of the results of prior research in a "normal" classroom with a typical teacher. Whatever is found feasible in Step 4 has to be tried out in the more typical classroom, which has limited time for the new method, and may lack the special motivation on the part of either teacher or pupil.

Step 6. Developmental steps related to advocacy and adoption. Anything found to work in Steps 4 and 5 has to be "packaged" for wider use, and then go through the processes by which new methods or procedures are adopted by those not party to the experimentation.

It is evident that the mood has changed in the transition from pure-science research to technological research, although the distinction between Steps 3 and 4 may be slight under some circumstances, as indeed in the experiment by Suppes and others used in illustration of Step 3.

If one were to review the relationship between experimentation on learning by psychologists in its relation to education over the past several decades, it would be fair to say that too much of the research has rested at Steps 1 and 2 to be educationally relevant; educational psychologists, too, have tended to work at this end of the spectrum and then to jump, by inference, to Step 6, without being sufficiently patient about Steps 4 and 5. In this respect the introduction of programed learning has been helpful, because of the serious concern both with the structure of subject matter and with the individual learner for whom the program is designed.

It is fruitful to compare educational measurement with the psychology of learning according to the steps of Figure 1. Educational measurements have been improved through the "pure-science" researches in statistics, theory of scaling, factor analysis, and so on; at the same time, the arranging of materials and the development of norms have been very careful, so that the better intelligence and achievement tests are well prepared and well accepted. Until the advent of the teaching machine there was little such processing of teaching materials, except for some rather spurious use of word counts in editing spellers and readers. A psychological speculation was for many years permitted to guide practice in the production of teaching materials, without the serious tryouts that would have been given to educational measurement materials. One consequence is that the prestige of educators who worked in the area of measurements was of high order among their psychological colleagues, while this has not been as true of those working in the field of learning. There are signs that this is now changing; what the steps of Figure 1 say, among other things, is that there are important tasks to be done all along the way. Many indicators point to a much healthier situation today than a few years ago in that the attention of scholars is being attracted to all steps along the way from pure science to technological application.

## A SET OF STRATEGIES FOR INTEGRATING THE PSYCHOLOGY OF LEARNING WITH THE TECHNOLOGY OF INSTRUCTION

Dividing the spectrum of pure and applied research into the six steps, three "pure" and three "technological," is descriptive of a problem, but it does not prescribe a program, except to invite good work all along the line. I wish to consider the same set of problems from a slightly different vantage point: the strategies that are involved with the aim of emerging with a scientifically based technology of instruction.

### STRATEGY OF DISCOVERY AND INVENTION

Discovery is the task of pure science, and the scientist in his laboratory must be free to perform this task in his own way. From the point of view of education, we need to make the approach in the spirit of pure science but need to direct it to relevant contents. There is no reason why we should not seek to have more experimentation on school children in the learning of subject matters or necessary skills or the kinds of problem-solving that are likely to go on in school.

While assigning *discovery* to the pure-science end of our continuum of relevance, we must not overlook *invention*, which is by no means limited to scientists. Some promising advances in education have come about as the inventions of skilled teachers, and a technology of instruction needs to examine and conserve the values of these inventions. I think, for example, of the augmented Roman alphabet being tried out in England in order to gain the advantages of a purely phonetic reading and writing in English. This seems to be meeting with great success; I should call it an invention rather than a discovery. One might say the same of O. K. Moore's use of an electric typewriter with beginners in reading and writing. Pure scientists are inventive in the realm of ideas but not always in the realm of technologies. As one of my colleagues is fond of pointing out, an Einstein does not take out patents; an Edison does. We need both kinds, and this is an added reason why the psychologist whose work is to be relevant to education needs to be close to educators and teachers.

### STRATEGY OF DEVELOPMENT OF METHODS, MATERIALS, AND PROCEDURES

At another level of science, this time applied science, we need those who will be concerned with the utilization of the discoveries and tested inventions from the investigations that have been described. This is not a matter of taking some principle and applying it in cookbook fashion to the subject matter of schools. We have had too much of this in the past. For example, when Thorndike emphasized the significance of word counts as giving order to what is taught in reading, the very plausible notion that the more frequent words should be taught first became a fetish in the construction of some elementary-school readers. This was a scientific aid to textbook construction, to be sure, but the further steps in development were not taken. Whenever they *were* taken it was found that, in context, pupils could learn words that were considered too difficult on the basis of the frequencies from word counts. Now there is a kind of revolt against the artificiality that has crept into the substance of much of our reading material, and an effort is being made to revitalize it.

As soon as the more practical step is taken seriously, it becomes obvious that the psychologist cannot work alone. There is a structure to knowledge, so that later steps depend in part upon earlier ones. There are discriminations to be made. Theories gain their support from selected facts of a particular kind, so that what kinds of facts are taught may establish the readiness for theoretical interpretations. Much of this lies outside the psychology of learning and in the realm of the subject-matter expert—the mathematician, the physicist, the biologist, and sociologist, the historian, the artist, the musician, the linguist. The serious interest being taken in the schools today by the scholars within the various disciplines is encouraging, but they can no more go it alone than the psychologists can go it alone. The emphasis upon the intellectual in education is fine, but it can easily produce, in new form, the old misunderstandings that gave rise to exaggerated theories of formal discipline. The subject-matter specialist is likely to think that his material is fundamentally so interesting that as long as it is arranged logically, and is comprehensible, the psychological problems will take care of themselves. This is no more true today than it ever was. This subject-matter expert has an essential role, but his collaboration with the learning expert is equally essential.

As long as the experimenter upon learning used artificial tasks, such as mirror-drawing, finger-mazes, pursuit rotors, and lists on memory drums, he could suit his own convenience; once he decides to program symbolic logic or the Russian language or the appreciation of poetry, he has additional constraints upon him. He finds it necessary to collaborate not only with subject-matter experts but to make use of the experience of skilled teachers. One of the first lessons of program development is this: A good program is not developed out of the mechanics of program construction or out of familiarity with the psychology of learning; it is not developed out of subject-matter expertness, nor through the sheer artistry of an able teacher; it requires the collaborative effort contributed by the various expertnesses. Once a reasonably promising program is developed, it has to be tried out in a classroom, perhaps a laboratory-type classroom, but with real school children taught by a real teacher. Then, before the development is completed, it has to be tried out in a regular classroom, where other obligations also exist. A teacher has many responsibilities, and children have diverse interests; whatever is new has to be fitted in somehow within an existing set of classroom procedures. These steps are all rather foreign to the typical experimental student of learning, but they are essential if the educational program is to be sound. I would argue for a division of labor and prestige, so that those who take on the developmental task are recognized and honored for the ingenuity they display, which must be at least equal to that of the pure scientist.

## STRATEGY OF INNOVATION

In something as complex as a school system, we need another level of research strategy, which I shall call *the strategy of innovation*. The best of equipment may lie idle, the best of resources remain unused, the best of techniques sabotaged, if there is not care in introducing the new methods or new materials to all concerned. Once the pure-science principles have been established and the applications validated in practice schoolrooms, the more widespread adoption is by no means guaranteed or, if the adoption is forced there is no assurance that the desired results will be forthcoming. Abstractly, the steps of innovation are clear enough: Provide (*a*) a sound research-based program, validated in tryout, (*b*) the program packaged in such a way as to be available, as in good textbooks, supplementary readings in the form of pamphlets, films, programs for teaching machines, and guides for the teacher, (c) testing materials by which it can be ascertained if the objectives of the program have indeed been realized, with appropriate normative data on these evaluative instruments, (d) in-service training of the teacher to overcome the teacher's resistance to something new and to gain his enthusiastic acceptance of the program as something valuable as well as to train him in its use, and (e) support for the program from the community, school boards, parents, and others concerned with the schools.

It is my feeling that we have not done very well in appraising carefully our strategies of innovation. We have sometimes gone overboard for the novel and untried, just to keep up with the Joneses ("we have teaching machines, too"); at other times we have been very resistant. Commercialism and vested interests enter in unpleasant ways, sometimes supported, unfortunately, by factions of the educational profession itself. Here, then, is a task calling for wisdom and sensitivity. The psychological contributions may come more from social psychology than from the psychology of learning, because the processes are those of social control and attitude change; but unless there is serious concern about the appropriate ways in which to bring innovation about, schools are likely to be the victims of whims, rather than the heirs of the best tradition we can establish through co-operative effort.

There are some specific suggestions that might be given consideration. It would be desirable, for example, for every school system, of whatever size, to have somewhere within it a school building, or at least a set of school-rooms, devoted to in-service training of teachers and to innovation; these are on-going matters important at the community level and cannot be left to teacher-training colleges or universities. Both children and teachers could be rotated through these rooms in order to try out innovations before there is firm commitment to them. Thus, a few teaching machines or closed-circuit television projectors could be tried out without investing in them for a whole school system; teachers could have a voice in saying whether or not they wanted the new devices, or in selecting among various possibilities. Usually no harm would be done in waiting for a while if teachers were not ready, for methods imposed on teachers are unlikely to prove successful. Some of the innovations to be tried out might be those of successful local teachers themselves, here given the opportunity to show their colleagues how they do it in their own classrooms. Members of the school board and representatives of the parents could be brought in also to see things being tried out. The principles of tryout before acceptance, of choice by those who are to use the method, seem to me sound ones. If the new methods are indeed good, they will find acceptance.

The remarks that I have made reduce to this: In order to build a sound bridge from the experimental studies of learning to the classroom, we need a series of steps, for applied science consists of more than applying principles to practice. The main points are that in the research and development phases a collaboration is called for between psychologist, subject-matter specialist, and teacher; beyond this, careful consideration has to be given to techniques of innovation. If we achieve success in integrating these phases, we will move toward that improvement of education which will be satisfying to us all.

B. F. SKINNER

# 23. WHY WE NEED TEACHING MACHINES

Current suggestions for improving education are familiar to everyone. We need more and better schools and colleges. We must pay salaries which will attract and hold good teachers. We should group students according to ability. We must bring textbooks and other materials up to date, particularly in science and mathematics. And so on. It is significant that all this can be done without knowing much about teaching or learning. Those who are most actively concerned with improving education seldom discuss what is happening when a student reads a book, writes a paper, listens to a lecture, or solves a problem, and their proposals are only indirectly designed to make these activities more productive. In short, there is a general neglect of education method. (Television is no exception, for it is only a way of amplifying and extending *old* methods, together with their shortcomings.)

It is true that the psychology of learning has so far not been very helpful in education. Its learning curves and its theories of learning have not yielded greatly improved classroom practices. But it is too early to conclude that nothing useful is to be learned about the behavior of teacher and student. No enterprise can improve itself very effectively without examining its basic processes. Fortunately, recent advances in the experimental analysis of behavior suggest that a true technology of education is feasible. Improved techniques are available to carry out the two basic assignments of education: constructing extensive repertoires of verbal and nonverbal behavior and generating that high probability of action which is said to show interest, enthusiasm, or a strong "desire to learn."

From *Harvard Educational Review* (Fall 1961), pp. 377–98. Copyright (c) 1961 by the President and Fellows of Harvard College. Reprinted by permission of the author and publisher.

The processes clarified by an experimental analysis of behavior have, of course, always played a part in education, but they have been used with little understanding of their effects, wanted or unwanted. Whether by intention or necessity, teachers have been less given to teaching than to holding students responsible for learning. Methods are still basically aversive. The student looks, listens, and answers questions (and, incidentally, sometimes learns) as a gesture of avoidance or escape. A good teacher can cite exceptions, but it is a mistake to call them typical. The birch rod and cane are gone, but their place has been taken by equally effective punishments (criticism, possibly ridicule, failure) used in the same way: the student must learn, or else!

By-products of aversive control in education range from truancy, early dropouts, and school-vandalism to inattention, "mental fatigue," forgetting, and apathy. It does not take a scientific analysis to trace these to their sources in educational practice. But more acceptable techniques have been hard to find. Erasmus tells of an English gentleman who tried to teach his son Greek and Latin without punishment. He taught the boy to use a bow and arrow and set up targets in the shape of Greek and Latin letters, rewarding each hit with a cherry. He also fed the boy letters cut from delicious biscuits. As a result, we may assume that the boy salivated slightly upon seeing a Greek or Latin text and that he was probably a better archer; but any effect on his knowledge of Greek and Latin is doubtful.

Current efforts to use rewards in education show the same indirection. Texts garnished with pictures in four colors, exciting episodes in a scientific film, interesting classroom activities—these will make a school interesting and even attractive (just as the boy probably liked his study of Greek and Latin), but to generate specific forms of behavior these things must be related to the student's behavior in special ways. Only then will they be truly rewarding or, technically speaking, "reinforcing."

We make a reinforcing event contingent on behavior when, for example, we design a piece of equipment in which a hungry rat or monkey or chimpanzee may press a lever and immediately obtain a bit of food. Such a piece of equipment gives us a powerful control over behavior. By scheduling reinforcements, we may maintain the behavior of pressing the lever in any given strength for long periods of time. By reinforcing special kinds of responses to the lever—for example, very light or very heavy presses or those made with one hand or the other—we "shape" different forms or topographies of behavior. By reinforcing only when particular stimuli or classes of stimuli are present, we bring the behavior under the control of the environment. All these processes have been thoroughly investigated, and they have already yielded standard laboratory practices in manipulating complex forms of behavior for experimental purposes. They are obviously appropriate to educational design.

In approaching the problem of the educator we may begin by surveying available reinforcers. What positive reasons can we give the student for studying? We can point to the ultimate advantages of an education—to the ways of life which are open only to educated men—and the student himself may cite these to explain why he wants an education, but ultimate advantages are not contingent on behavior in ways which generate action. Many a student can testify to the result. No matter how much he may *want* to become a doctor or an engineer, say, he cannot force himself to read and remember the page of text in front of him at the moment. All notions of ultimate utility (as, for example, in economics) suffer from the same shortcoming: they do not specify effective contingencies of reinforcement.

The gap between behavior and a distant consequence is sometimes bridged by a series of "conditioned reinforcers." In the laboratory experiment just described a delay of even a fraction of a second between the response to the lever and the appearance of food may reduce the effectiveness of the food by a measurable amount. It is standard practice to let the movement of a lever produce some visual stimulus, such as a change in the illumination in the apparatus, which is then followed by food. In this way the change in illumination becomes a conditioned reinforcer which can be made immediately contingent on the response. The marks, grades, and diplomas of education are conditioned reinforcers designed to bring ultimate consequences closer to the behavior reinforced. Like prizes and medals, they represent the approval of teachers, parents, and others, and they show competitive superiority, but they are mainly effective because they signalize progress through the system—toward some ultimate advantage of, or at least freedom from, education. To this extent they bridge the gap between behavior and its remote consequences; but they are still not contingent on behavior in a very effective way.

Progressive education tried to replace the birch rod, and at the same time avoid the artificiality of grades and prizes, by bringing the reinforcers of everyday life into the schools. Such natural contingencies have a kind of guaranteed effectiveness. But a school is only a small part of the student's world, and no matter how real it may seem, it cannot provide natural reinforcing consequences for all the kinds of behavior which education is to set up. The goals of progressive education were shifted to conform to this limitation, and many worthwhile assignments were simply abandoned.

Fortunately, we can solve the problem of education without discovering or inventing additional reinforcers. We merely need to make better use of those we have. Human behavior is distinguished by the fact that it is affected by small consequences. Describing something with the right word is often reinforcing. So is the clarification of a temporary puzzlement, or the solution of a complex problem, or simply the opportunity to move forward after completing one stage of an activity. We need not stop to explain *why* these things are reinforcing. It is enough that, when properly contingent upon behavior, they provide the control we need for successful educational design.

Proper contingencies of reinforcement, however, are not always easily arranged. A modern laboratory for the study of behavior contains elaborate equipment designed to control the environment of individual organisms during many hours or days of continuous study. The required conditions and changes in conditions cannot be arranged by hand, not only because the experimenter does not have the time and energy, but because many contingencies are too subtle and precise to be arranged without instrumental help. The same problem arises in education.

Consider, for example, the temporal patterning of behavior called "rhythm." Behavior is often effective only if properly timed. Individual differences in timing, ranging from the most awkward to the most skillful performances, affect choice of career and of artistic interests and participation in sports and crafts. Presumably a "sense of rhythm" is worth teaching, yet practically nothing is now done to arrange the necessary contingencies of reinforcement. The skilled typist, tennis player, lathe operator, or musician is, of course, under the influence of reinforcing mechanisms which generate subtle timing, but many people never reach the point at which these natural contingencies can take over.

A relatively simple device supplies the necessary contingencies. The student taps a rhythmic pattern in unison with the device. "Unison" is specified very loosely at first (the student can be a little early or late at each tap) but the specifications are slowly sharpened. The process is repeated for various speeds and patterns. In another arrangement, the student echoes rhythmic patterns sounded by the machine, though not in unison, and again the specifications for an accurate reproduction are progressively sharpened. Rhythmic patterns can also be brought under the control of a printed score.

Another kind of teaching machine generates sensitivity to properties of the environment. We call an effective person "discriminating." He can tell the difference between the colors, shapes, and sizes of objects, he can identify three-dimensional forms seen from different aspects, he can find patterns concealed in other patterns, he can identify pitches, intervals, and musical themes and distinguish between different tempos and rhythms—and all of this in an almost infinite variety. Subtle discriminations of this sort are as important in science and industry and in everyday life as in identifying the school of a painter or the period of a composer.

The ability to make a given kind of discrimination can be taught. A pigeon, for example, can be *made* sensitive to the color, shape, and size of objects, to pitches, and rhythms, and so on—simply by reinforcing it when it responds in some arbitrary way to one set of stimuli and extinguishing responses to all others. The same kinds of contingencies of reinforcement are responsible for human discriminative behavior. *The remarkable fact is that they are quite rare in the environment of the average child.* True, children are encouraged to play with objects of different sizes, shapes, and colors, and are given a passing acquaintance with musical patterns; but they are seldom exposed to the precise contingencies needed to build subtle discriminations. It is not surprising that most of them move into adulthood with largely undeveloped "abilities."

The number of reinforcements required to build discriminative behavior in the population as a whole is far beyond the capacity of teachers. Too many teachers would be needed, and many contingencies are too subtle to be mediated by even the most skillful. *Yet relatively simple machines will suffice.* [One such apparatus] is adapted from research on lower organisms. It teaches an organism to discriminate selected properties of stimuli while "matching to sample." Pictures or words are projected on translucent windows which respond to a touch by closing circuits. A child can be made to "look at the sample" by reinforcing him for pressing the top window. An adequate reinforcement for this response is simply the appearance of material in the lower windows, from which a choice is to be made.

The child identifies the material which corresponds to the sample in some prescribed way by pressing one of the lower windows, and he is then reinforced again—possibly simply because a new set of materials now appears on the windows. If he presses the wrong window, all three choices disappear until the top window has been pressed again—which means until he has again looked at the sample. Many other arrangements of responses and reinforcements are, of course, possible. In an auditory version, the child listens to a sample pattern of tones and then explores other samples to find a match.

If devices similar to these were generally available in our nursery schools and kindergartens, our children would be far more skillful in dealing with their environments. They would be more productive in their work, more sensitive to art and music, better at sports, and so on. They would lead more effective lives. We cannot assert all this with complete confidence on the present evidence, but there is no doubt whatsoever *that the conditions needed to produce such a state of affairs are now lacking.* In the light of what we know about differential contingencies of reinforcement, the world of the young child is shamefully impoverished. And only machines will remedy this, for the required frequency and subtlety of reinforcement cannot otherwise be arranged.

The teacher is, of course, at a disadvantage in teaching skilled and discriminative behavior because such instruction is largely nonverbal. It may be that the methods of the classroom, in which the teacher is said to "communicate" with the student, to "impart information," and to build "verbal abilities," are better adapted to standard subject matters, the learning of which is usually regarded as more than the acquisition of forms of behavior or of environmental control. Yet a second look may be worthwhile. Traditional characterizations of verbal behavior raise almost insuperable problems for the teacher, and a more rigorous analysis suggests another possibility. We can define terms like "information," "knowledge," and "verbal ability" by reference to the behavior from which we infer their presence. *We may then teach the behavior directly.* Instead of "transmitting information to the student" we may simply set up the behavior which is taken as a sign that he possesses information. Instead of teaching a "knowledge of French" we may teach the behavior from which we infer such knowledge. Instead of teaching "an ability to read" we may set up the behavioral repertoire which distinguishes the child who knows how to read from one who does not.

To take the last example, a child reads or "shows that he knows how to read" by exhibiting a behavioral repertoire of great complexity. He finds a letter or word in a list on demand; he reads aloud; he finds or identifies objects described in a text; he rephrases sentences; he obeys written instructions; he behaves appropriately to described situations; he reacts emotionally to described events; and so on, in a long list. He does none of this before learning to read and all of it afterwards. To bring about such a change is an extensive assignment, and it is tempting to try to circumvent it by teaching something called "an ability to read" from which all these specific behaviors will flow. But this has never actually been done. "Teaching reading" is always directed toward setting up specific items in such a repertoire.

It is true that parts of the repertoire are not independent. A student may acquire some kinds of responses more readily for having acquired others, and he may for a time use some in place of others (for example, he may follow written directions not by responding directly to a text but by following his own spoken instructions as he reads the text aloud). In the long run all parts of the repertoire tend to be filled in, not because the student is rounding out an ability to read, but simply because all parts are in their several ways useful. They all continue to be reinforced by the world at large after the explicit teaching of reading has ceased.

Viewed in this way, reading can also be most effectively taught with instrumental help. A pupil can learn to distinguish among letters and groups of letters in an alphabet simply as visual patterns in using the device and procedures just described. He can be taught to identify arbitrary correspondences (for example, between capitals and lower-case letters, or between handwritten and printed letters) in a more complex type of stimulus control which is within reach of the same device. With a phonographic attachment, correspondences between printed letters and sounds, between sounds and letters, between words and sounds, between sounds and printed words, and so on, can be set up. (The student could be taught all of this without pronouncing a word, and it is possible that he would learn good pronunciation more quickly if he had first done so.)

The same device can teach correspondences between words and the properties of objects. The pupil selects a printed or spoken word which corresponds in the language to, say, a pictured object or another printed or spoken word. These semantic correspondences differ in important respects from formal matches, but the same processes of programming and reinforcement can—indeed, must—be used. Traditional ways of teaching reading establish all these repertoires, but they do so indirectly and, alas, inefficiently. In "building a child's need to read," in motivating "his mental readiness," in "sharing information," and so on, the teacher arranges, sometimes almost surreptitiously, many of the contingencies just listed, and these are responsible for whatever is learned. An explicit treatment clarifies the program, suggests effective procedures, and guarantees a coverage which is often lacking with traditional methods. Much of what is called reading has not been covered, of course, but it may not need to be taught, for once these basic repertoires have been established, the child begins to receive automatic reinforcement in responding to textual material.

The same need for a behavioral definition arises in teaching other verbal skills (for example, a second language) as well as the traditional subjects of education. In advancing to that level, however, we must transcend a limitation of the device [described]. The student can *select* a response without being able to speak or write, but we want him to learn to *emit* the response, since this is the kind of behavior which he will later find most useful. The emission of verbal behavior is taught by another kind of machine. A frame of textual material appearing in the square opening is incomplete: in place of certain letters or figures there are holes. Letters or figures can be made to appear in these holes by moving sliders (a keyboard would be an obvious improvement). When the material has been completed, the student checks his response by turning a crank. The machine senses the settings of the sliders and, if they are correct, moves a new frame of material into place, the sliders returning to their home position. If the response is wrong, the sliders return home, and a second setting must be made.

The machine can tell the student he is wrong without telling him what is right. This is an advantage, but it is relatively costly. Moreover, correct behavior is rather rigidly specified. Such a machine is probably suitable only for the lower grades. A simpler and cheaper procedure, with greater flexibility, is to allow the student to compare his written response with a revealed text. [A device using this principle exists.] It is suitable for verbal instruction beyond the lower primary grades—that is, through junior high school, high school, and college, and in industrial and professional education. Programmed material is stored on fan-folded paper tapes. One frame of material, the size of which may be varied with the nature of the material, is exposed at a time. The student writes on a separate paper strip. He cannot look at unauthorized parts of the material without recording the fact that he has done so, because when the machine has been loaded and closed, it can be opened only by punching the strip of paper.

The student sees printed material in the large window at the left. This may be a sentence to be completed, a question to be answered, or a problem to be solved. He writes his response in an uncovered portion of a paper strip at the right. He then moves a slider which covers the response he has written with a transparent mask and uncovers additional material in the larger opening. This may tell him that his response is wrong without telling him what is right. For example, it may list a few of the commonest errors. If the response he wrote is among them, he can try again on a newly uncovered portion of the paper strip. A further operation of the machine covers his second attempt and uncovers the correct response. The student records a wrong response by punching a hole alongside it, leaving a record for the instructor who may wish to review a student's performance, and operating a counter which becomes visible at the end of the set. Then the student records the number of mistakes he has made and may compare it with a par score for the set.

Exploratory research in schools and colleges indicates that what is now taught by teacher, textbook, lecture, or film can be taught in half the time with half the effort by a machine of this general type.[1] One has only to see students at work to understand why this is a conservative estimate. The student remains active. If he stops, the program stops (in marked contrast with classroom practice and educational television); but there is no compulsion for he is not inclined to stop. Immediate and frequent reinforcement sustains a lively interest. (The interest, incidentally, outlasts any effect of novelty. Novelty may be relevant to interest, but the material in the machine is always novel.) Where current instructional procedures are highly efficient, the gain may not be so great. In one experiment[2] involving industrial education there was approximately a 25% saving in the time required for instruction, something of the order of a 10% increase in retention, and about 90% of the students preferred to study by machine. In general, the student generally likes what he is doing; he makes no effort to escape—for example, by letting his attention wander. He need not force himself to work and is usually free of the feeling of effort generated by aversive control. He has no reason to be anxious about impending examinations, for none are required. Both he and his instructor know where he stands at all times.

No less important in explaining the success of teaching machines is the fact that each student is free to proceed at his own rate. Holding students together for instructional purposes in a class is probably the greatest source of inefficiency in education. Some efforts to mechanize instruction have missed this point. A language laboratory controlled from a central console presupposes a group of students advancing at about the same rate, even

---

[1] Under the direction of Allen Calvin of Hollands College, an 8th grade class in the Roanoke School System completed all the work of a 9th grade class in algebra in one term. Test scores were comparable with a normal 9th grade performance, and a test nine months later showed a retention of at least 90% of the material learned.

[2] More recent results with the same material improved in the light of the earlier experiment were reported by J. L. Hughes and W. J. McNamara at the Annual Meeting of the American Psychological Association in New York, September, 1961. Their work concerned the use of programmed texts in industrial education.

though some choice of material is permitted. Television in education has made the same mistake on a colossal scale. A class of twenty or thirty students moving at the same pace is inefficient enough, but what must we say of all the students in half a dozen states marching in a similar lock step?

In trying to teach more than one student at once we harm both fast and slow learners. The plight of the good student has been recognized, but the slow learner suffers more disastrous consequences. The effect of pressure to move beyond one's natural speed is cumulative. The student who has not fully mastered a first lesson is less able to master a second. His ultimate failure may greatly exaggerate his shortcoming; a small difference in speed has grown to an immense difference in comprehension. Some of those most active in improving education have been tempted to dismiss slow students impatiently as a waste of time, but it is quite possible that many of them are capable of substantial, even extraordinary, achievements if permitted to move at their own pace. Many distinguished scientists, for example, have appeared to think slowly.

One advantage of individual instruction is that the student is able to follow a program without breaks or omissions. A member of a class moving at approximately the same rate cannot always make up for absences, and limitations of contact time between student and teacher make it necessary to abbreviate material to the point at which substantial gaps are inevitable. Working on a machine, the student can always take up where he left off or, if he wishes, review earlier work after a longer absence. The coherence of the program helps to maximize the student's success, for by thoroughly mastering one step he is optimally prepared for the next. Many years ago, in their *Elementary Principles of Education,*[3] Thorndike and Gates considered the possibility of a book "so arranged that only to him who had done what was directed on page one would page two become visible, and so on." With such a book, they felt, "much that now requires personal instruction could be managed by print." The teaching machine is, of course, such a book.

In summary, then, machine teaching is unusually efficient because (1) the student is frequently and immediately reinforced, (2) he is free to move at his natural rate, and (3) he follows a coherent sequence. These are the more obvious advantages, and they may well explain current successes. But there are more promising possibilities: the conditions arranged by a good teaching machine make it possible to apply to education what we have learned from laboratory research and to extend our knowledge through rigorous experiments in schools and colleges.

The conceptions of the learning process which underlie classroom practices have long been out of date. For example, teachers and textbooks are said to "impart information." They expose the student to verbal and nonverbal material and call attention to particular features of it, and in so doing they

---

3 Thorndike, Edward, and Arthur Gates. *Elementary Principles of Education.* (New York: B. Macmillan Co., 1929).

are said to "tell the student something." In spite of discouraging evidence to the contrary, it is still supposed that if you tell a student something, he then knows it. In this scheme, teaching is the transmission of information, a notion which, through a false analogy, has acquired undue prestige from communication engineering. Something is undoubtedly transmitted by teacher to student, for if communication is interrupted, instruction ceases; but the teacher is not merely a source from which knowledge flows into the student. We cannot necessarily improve instruction by altering the conditions of transmission—as, for example, by changing to a different sensory modality. This is a mistake made by some so-called teaching machines which, accepting our failure to teach reading, have tried to restore communication by using recorded speech. The student no longer pores over a book, as in the traditional portrait; he stares into space with earphones on his head. For the same reasons improvements in the coding of information may not be immediately relevant.

The student is more than a receiver of information. He must take some kind of action. The traditional view is that he must "associate." The stream of information flowing from teacher to student contains pairs of items which, being close together or otherwise related, become connected in the student's mind. This is the old doctrine of the association of ideas, now strengthened by a scientific, if uncritical, appeal to conditioned reflexes; two things occurring together in experience somehow become connected so that one of them later reminds the student of the other. The teacher has little control over the process except to make sure that things occur together often and that the student pays attention to them—for example, by making the experiences vivid or, as we say, memorable. Some devices called teaching machines are simply ways of presenting things together in ways which attract attention. The student listens to recorded speech, for example, while looking at pictures. The theory is that he will associate these auditory and visual presentations.

But the action demanded of the student is not some sort of mental association of contiguous experiences. It is more objective and, fortunately, more controllable than that. To acquire behavior, *the student must engage in behavior.* This has long been known. The principle is implied in any philosophy of "learning by doing." But it is not enough to acknowledge its validity. Teaching machines provide the conditions needed to apply the principle effectively.

Only in the early stages of education are we mainly interested in establishing *forms* of behavior. In the verbal field, for example, we teach a child to speak, eventually with acceptable accent and pronunciation, and later to write and spell. After that, topography of behavior is assumed; the student can speak and write and must now learn to do so appropriately—that is, he must speak or write in given ways under given circumstances. How he comes to do so is widely misunderstood. Education usually begins by establishing so-called formal repertoires. The young child is taught to "echo" verbal behavior in the sense of repeating verbal stimuli with reasonable accuracy. A little later he is taught to read—to emit verbal behavior under the control of textual stimuli. These and other formal repertoires are used in later stages of instruction to evoke new responses without "shaping" them.

In an important case of what we call instruction, control is simply transferred from so-called formal to thematic stimuli. When a student learns to memorize a poem, for example, it is clearly inadequate to say that by reading the poem he presents to himself its various parts contiguously and then associates them. He does not simply read the poem again and again until he knows it. (It is possible that he could never learn the poem in that way.) Something else must be done, as anyone knows who has memorized a poem from the text. The student must make tentative responses while looking away from the text. He must glance at the text from time to time to provide fragmentary help in emitting a partially learned response. If a recalled passage makes sense, it may provide its own automatic confirmation, but if the passage is fragmentary or obscure, the student must confirm the correctness of an emitted response by referring to the text after he has emitted it.

A teaching machine facilitates this process. It presents the poem line by line and asks the student to read it. The text is then "vanished"—that is, it becomes less and less clear or less and less complete in subsequent presentations. Other stimuli (arising from the student's own behavior in this case) take over. In one procedure a few unimportant letters are omitted in the first presentation. The student reads the line without their help and indicates his success by writing down the omitted letters, which are confirmed by the machine. More of the line is missing when it again appears, but because he has recently responded to a fuller text, the student can nevertheless read it correctly. Eventually, no textual stimulus remains, and he can "recite" the poem.

(If the reader wishes to try this method on a friend or member of his family without a machine, he may do so by writing the poem on a chalk board in a clear hand, omitting a few unimportant letters. He should ask his subject to read the poem aloud but to make no effort to memorize it. He should then erase another selection of letters. He will have to guess at how far he can go without interfering with his subject's success on the next reading, but under controlled conditions this could be determined for the average student quite accurately. Again the subject reads the poem aloud, making no effort to memorize, though he may have to make some effort to recall. Other letters are then erased and the process repeated. For a dozen lines of average material, four or five readings should suffice to eliminate the text altogether. The poem can still be "read.")

Memorized verbal behavior is a valuable form of knowledge which has played an important role in classical education. There are other, and generally more useful, forms in which the same processes are involved. Consider, for example, a labeled picture. To say that such an instructional device "tells the student the name of the pictured object" is highly elliptical—and dangerous if we are trying to understand the processes involved. Simply showing a student a labeled picture is no more effective than letting him read a poem. He must take some sort of action. As a formal stimulus, the label evokes a verbal response, not in this case in the presence of other verbal behavior on the part of the student, but in the presence of the picture. The control of the response is to pass from the label to the picture; the student is to give the name of the pictured object without reading it.

The steps taken in teaching with labeled pictures can also be arranged particularly well with a machine. Suppose we are teaching medical-school anatomy at the textbook level. Certain labeled charts represent what is to be learned in the sense that the student will eventually (1) give the names of indicated parts and describe relations among them and (2) be able to point to, draw, or construct models of parts, or relations among them, given their names. To teach the first of these, we induce the student to describe relations among the parts shown on a fully labeled chart. One effect of this is that he executes the verbal behavior at issue—he writes the names of the parts. More important, he does this while, or just after, looking at corresponding pictured details. He will be able to write the names again while looking at a chart which shows only incomplete names, possibly only initial letters. Finally, he will be able to supply the complete names of parts identified only by number on still another chart. His verbal responses have passed from the control of textual stimuli to that of pictured anatomical details. Eventually, as he studies a cadaver, the control will pass to the actual anatomy of the human body. In this sense he then "knows the names of the parts of the body and can describe relations among them."

([A device may be] designed to skip one or two steps in "vanishing" textual stimuli. A fully labeled chart may be followed by a merely numbered one. The student writes the name corresponding to a number in the first space. If he cannot do this, he operates the machine to uncover, not merely some indication that he is right or wrong, but additional help—say, a few letters of the correct response.)

Learning a poem or the names of pictured objects is a relatively straight-forward task. More complex forms of knowledge require other procedures. At an early point, the main problem becomes that of analyzing knowledge. Traditionally, for example, something called "a knowledge of French" is said to permit the student who possesses it to do many things. One who possesses it can (1) repeat a French phrase with a good accent, (2) read a French text in all the senses of reading listed above, (3) take dictation in French, (4) find a word spoken in French on a printed list, (5) obey instructions spoken in French, (6) comment in French upon objects or events, (7) give orders in French, and so on. If he also "knows English," he can give the English equivalents of French words or phrases or the French equivalents of English words or phrases.

The concept of "a knowledge of French" offers very little help to the would-be teacher. As in the case of reading, we must turn to the behavioral repertoires themselves, for these are all that have ever been taught when education has been effective. The definition of a subject matter in such terms may be extraordinarily difficult. Students who are "competent in first-year college physics," for example, obviously differ from those who are not—but in what way? Even a tentative answer to that question should clarify the problem of teaching physics. It may well do more. In the not-too-distant future much more general issues in epistemology may be approached from the same direction. It is possible that we shall fully understand the nature of knowledge only after having solved the practical problems of imparting it.

Until we can define subject matters more accurately and until we have improved our techniques of building verbal repertoires, writing programs for teaching machines will remain something of an art. This is not wholly satisfactory, but there is some consolation in the fact that an impeccable authority on the excellence of a program is available. The student himself can tell the programmer where he has failed. By analyzing the errors made by even a small number of students in a pilot study, it is usually possible to work a great improvement in an early version of a program. ([A machine may be] designed to supply the necessary feedback to the programmer in a convenient form. When a student punches an error, he marks the back of the printed material, which eventually carries an item-by-item record of the success or failure of the programmer. This is obviously valuable during the experimental stages of programming, but it will also be desirable when machines are widely used in schools and colleges, since publishers can then periodically call in programs to be studied and improved by their authors. The information supplied might be compared to a record showing the percentage of students who have misunderstood each sentence in a text.)

The teaching machine [described above] falls far short of the "electronic classrooms" often visualized for the schools and colleges of the future. Many of these, often incorporating small computers, are based on misunderstandings of the learning process. They are designed to duplicate current classroom conditions. When instruction is badly programmed, a student often goes astray, and a teacher must come to his rescue. His mistakes must be analyzed and corrected. This may give the impression that instruction is largely a matter of correcting errors. If this were the case, an effective machine would, indeed, have to follow the student into many unprofitable paths and take remedial action. But under proper programming nothing of this sort is required. It is true that a relatively important function of the teacher will be to follow the progress of each student and to suggest collateral material which may be of interest, as well as to outline further studies, to recommend changes to programs of different levels of difficulty, and so on, and to this extent a student's course of study will show "branching." But changes in level of difficulty or in the character of the subject need not be frequent and can be made as the student moves from one set of material to another.

Teaching machines based on the principle of "multiple choice" also often show a misunderstanding of the learning process. When multiple-choice apparatuses were first used, the organism was left to proceed by "trial and error." The term does not refer to a behavioral process but simply to the fact that contingencies of reinforcement were left to chance: some responses happened to be successful and others not. Learning was not facilitated or accelerated by procedures which increased the probability of successful responses. The results, like those of much classroom instruction, suggested that errors were essential to the learning process. But when material is carefully programmed, both subhuman and human subjects can learn while making few errors or even none at all. Recent research by Herbert S. Terrace,[4] for example, has shown that a pigeon can learn to discriminate colors practically without making mistakes. The control exerted by color may be passed, *via* a vanishing technique, to more difficult properties of stimuli —again without error. Of course we learn something from our mistakes—for one thing, we learn not to make them again—but we *acquire* behavior in other ways.

The teaching machines of S. L. Pressey,[5] the first psychologist to see the "coming industrial revolution in education," were mechanical versions of self-scoring test forms, which Pressey and his students also pioneered. They were not designed for programmed instruction in the present sense. The student was presumed to have studied a subject before coming to the machine. By testing himself, he consolidated what he had already partially learned. For this purpose a device which evaluated the student's selection from an array of multiple-choice items was appropriate. For the same purpose multiple-choice material can, of course, be used in all the machines described above. But several advantages of programmed instruction are lost when such material is used in straightforward instruction.

In the first place, the student should *construct* rather than *select* a response, since this is the behavior he will later find useful. Secondly, he should advance to the level of being able to emit a response rather than merely recognize a given response as correct. This represents a much more considerable achievement, as the difference between the sizes of reading and writing vocabularies in a foreign language demonstrates. Thirdly, and more important, multiple-choice material violates a basic principle of good pro-

---

[4] Terrace, Herbert S. Discrimination Learning With and Without Errors (unpublished Ph.D. Dissertation, Department of Psychology, Harvard University, 1961).

[5] Pressey, S. L. A simple apparatus which gives tests and scores—and teaches. *School and Society*, 1926, *23*, 373–76. This article and other articles concerning teaching machines by S. L. Pressey are included in Lumsdaine, A. A., and Glaser, Robert (eds.), *Teaching Machines and Programmed Learning: A Source Book* (Washington, D.C.: National Education Association, 1960).

gramming by inducing the student to engage in erroneous behavior. Those who have written multiple-choice tests know how much time, energy, and ingenuity are needed to construct plausible wrong answers. (They must be plausible or the test will be of little value.) In a multiple-choice *test,* they may do no harm, since a student who has already learned the right answer may reject wrong answers with ease and possibly with no undesirable side-effects. The student who is *learning,* however, can scarcely avoid trouble. Traces of erroneous responses survive in spite of the correction of errors or the confirmation of a right answer. In multiple-choice material designed to teach "literary appreciation," for example, the student is asked to consider three or four plausible paraphrases of a passage in a poem and to identify the most acceptable. But as the student reads and considers unacceptable paraphrases, the very processes which the poet himself used in making his poem effective are at work to destroy it. Neither the vigorous correction of wrong choices nor the confirmation of a right choice will free the student of the verbal and nonverbal associations thus generated.

Scientific subjects offer more specific examples. Consider an item such as the following, which might be part of a course in high school physics:

As the pressure of a gas increases, volume decreases. This is because:
(a) the space between the molecules grows smaller
(b) the molecules are flattened
(c) etc. . . .

Unless the student is as industrious and as ingenious as the multiple-choice programmer, it will probably not have occurred to him that molecules may be flattened as a gas is compressed (within the limits under consideration). If he chooses item (b) and is corrected by the machine, we may say that he "has learned that it is wrong," but this does not mean that the sentence will never occur to him again. And if he is unlucky enough to select the right answer first, his reading of the plausible but erroneous answer will be corrected only "by implication"—an equally vague and presumably less effective process. In either case, he may later find himself recalling that "somewhere he has read that molecules are flattened when a gas is compressed." And, of course, somewhere he has.

Multiple-choice techniques are appropriate when the student is to learn to compare and choose. In forming a discrimination . . . an organism must be exposed to at least two stimuli, one of which may be said to be wrong. Similarly, in learning to "troubleshoot" equipment there may be several almost equally plausible ways of correcting a malfunction. Games offer other examples. A given hand at bridge may justify several bids or plays, no one of which is wholly right and all the others wrong. In such cases, the student is to learn the most expedient course to be taken among a natural array of possibilities. This is not true in the simple acquisition of knowledge —particularly verbal knowledge—where the task is only rarely to discriminate among responses in an array. In solving an equation, reporting a fact of history, restating the meaning of a sentence, or engaging in almost any of the other behavior which is the main concern of education, the student is to *generate* responses. He may generate and reject, but only rarely will he generate a set of responses from which he must then make a choice.

It may be argued that machines which provide for branching and decision making are designed to teach more than verbal repertoires—in particular, that they will teach thinking. There are strategies in choosing from an array, for example, which require kinds of behavior beyond the mere emission of correct responses. We may agree to this without questioning the value of knowledge in the sense of a verbal repertoire. (The distinction is not between rote and insightful learning, for programmed instruction is especially free of rote memorizing in the etymological sense of wearing down a path through repetition.) If an "idea" or "proposition" is defined as something which can be expressed in many ways, then it may be taught by teaching many of these "ways." What is learned is more likely to generalize to comparable situations than a single syntactical form, and generalization is what distinguishes so-called deeper understanding.

But not all thinking is verbal. There are, first of all, alternative, parallel nonverbal repertoires. The mathematician begins with a verbal problem and ends with a verbal solution, but much of his intervening behavior may be of a different nature. The student who learns to follow or construct a proof entirely by manipulating symbols may not engage in this kind of thinking. Similarly, a merely verbal knowledge of physics, as often seen in the student who has "memorized the text," is of little interest to the serious educator. Laboratories and demonstrations sometimes supply contingencies which build some nonverbal knowledge of physics. Special kinds of teaching machines could help, for machines are not only not confined to verbal instruction, they may well make it possible to reduce the emphasis on verbal communication between teacher and student.

A more clear-cut example of the distinction between verbal and nonverbal thinking is musical composition. The composer who "thinks musically" does more than perform on an instrument or enjoy music. He also does more than use musical notation. In some sense he "thinks" pitches, intervals, melodies, harmonic progressions, and so on. It should not surprise us that individuals differ greatly in their "abilities" to do this, since the necessary contingencies are in very short supply. One might attack the problem by setting up an explicit kinesthetic repertoire in which "thinking a pitch" takes the form of identifying a position on a keyboard. A device which arranges the necessary contingencies is under development. With its help we may discover the extent to which students can in general learn (and at what ages they can learn most effectively) to strike a key which produces a tone which has just been heard. Similar devices might generate important forms of nonverbal mathematical behavior or the behavior exhibited, say, by an inventor conceiving of a device in three dimensions, as well as creative repertoires in other forms of art. Here is an extraordinary challenge to the technology of instrumentation.

There is another sense in which the student must learn to think. Verbal and nonverbal repertoires may prepare him to behave in effective ways, but he will inevitably face novel situations in which he cannot at first respond appropriately. He may solve such problems, not by exercising some mental ability, but by altering either the external situation or the relative probabilities of parts of his own repertoire. In this way he may increase the probability of an adequate response.

In this sense, thinking consists of a special repertoire which we may call self-management. For example, the student may alter the extent to which the environment affects him by "attending" to it in different ways. As one step in teaching thinking we must teach effective attending. The phrase "Pay attention!" is as common on the lips of teachers as "Open, please" on those of dentists—and for much the same reason: both phrases set up working conditions. The student may pay attention to avoid punishment and in doing so may learn to pay attention, but where aversive sanctions have been given up, teachers have resorted to attracting and holding attention. The techniques of the publication and entertainment industries are extensively invoked. Primers are usually decorated with colored pictures, and high school textbooks are sometimes designed to resemble picture magazines. Films dramatize subject matters in competition with noneducational films and television.

Attention which is captured by attractive stimuli must be distinguished from attention which is "paid." Only the latter must be learned. Looking and listening are forms of behavior, and they are strengthened by reinforcement. A pigeon can learn to match colors, for example, only if it "pays attention to them." The experimenter makes sure that it does so, not by attracting its attention, but by reinforcing it for looking. Similarly, a well-taught student pays attention to sentences, diagrams, samples of recorded speech and music, and so on, not because they are attractive but because something interesting occasionally happens *after* he has paid attention.

Most audio-visual devices fail to teach attention because they stimulate the student *before* he looks or listens closely. No matter how well a four-colored text or a dramatically filmed experiment in physics attracts attention, it prepares the student only for comics, advertising, picture magazines, television programs, and other material which is *interesting on its face*. What is wanted is an adult who, upon seeing a page of black-and-white text, will read it because it may *prove* interesting. Unfortunately, the techniques associated with captured and paid attention are incompatible. Whenever a teacher attracts the attention of a student, he deprives him of an opportunity to learn to pay attention. Teaching machines, with their control over the consequences of action, can make sure that paying attention will be effectively reinforced.

Another activity associated with thinking is studying—not merely looking at a text and reading it but looking and reading *for the sake of future action.* Suppose we show a child a picture and later, in the absence of the picture, reinforce him generously for correct answers to questions about it. If he has done nothing like this before, he will probably not be very successful. If we then show him another picture, he may begin to behave in a different way: he may engage in behavior which will increase the probability that he will later answer questions correctly. It will be to his advantage (and to ours as educators) if this kind of behavior is taught rather than left to chance. We teach a student "how to study" when we teach him to take notes, to rehearse his own behavior, to test himself, to organize, outline, and analyze, to look for or construct mnemonic patterns, and so on. Some of these behaviors are obvious, but others are of more subtle dimensions and admittedly hard to teach. Machines have an advantage in maintaining the contingencies required for indirect or mediated reinforcement.

Other aspects of thinking, including the solution of personal problems, can also be analyzed and directly programmed. This is not current practice, however. Students are most often "taught to think" simply by thrusting them into situations in which already established repertoires are inadequate. Some of them modify their behavior or the situation effectively and come up with solutions. They may have learned, but they have not necessarily been taught, how to think.

Logicians, mathematicians, and scientists have often tried to record and understand their own thinking processes, but we are still far from a satisfactory formulation of all relevant behaviors. Much remains to be learned about how a skillful thinker examines a situation, alters it, samples his own responses with respect to it, carries out specific verbal manipulations appropriate to it, and so on. It is quite possible that we cannot teach thinking adequately until all this has been analyzed. Once we have specified the behavior, however, we have no reason to suppose that it will then be any less adaptable to programmed instruction than simple verbal repertoires.

Teaching machines and the associated practices of programmed instruction will have proved too successful if their practical consequences are allowed to overshadow their promise for the future. We need teaching machines to help solve a very pressing problem, but we also need them to utilize our basic knowledge of human behavior in the design of entirely new educational practices.

Teaching machines are an example of the technological application of basic science. It is true that current machines might have been designed in the light of classroom experience and common sense, and that explanations of why they are effective can be paraphrased in traditional terms. The fact remains that more than half a century of the self-conscious examination of instructional processes had worked only moderate changes in educational practices. The laboratory study of learning provided the confidence, if not all the knowledge, needed for a successful instrumental attack of the *status quo.*

Traditional views may not have been actually wrong, but they were vague and were not entertained with sufficient commitment to work substantial technological changes.

As a technology, however, education is still immature as we may see from the fact that it defines its goals in terms of traditional achievements. Teachers are usually concerned with reproducing the characteristics and achievements of already educated men. When the nature of the human organism is better understood, we may begin to consider not only what man has already shown himself to be, but what he may become under carefully designed conditions. The goal of education should be nothing short of the fullest possible development of the human organism. An experimental analysis of behavior, carried out under the advantageous conditions of the laboratory, will contribute to progress toward the goal. So will practical experiments conducted in schools and colleges with the help of adequate instrumentation.

SIDNEY L. PRESSEY

# 24.   TEACHING MACHINE
# (AND LEARNING THEORY) CRISIS

For several years now, all over the country, learning theorists have been programing books and other matter into numerous little "frames" each consisting of a very easy question or statement with space for writing a one or two word "constructed" response, to be verified by turning a page or turning up a "teaching machine" roll. One learned by responding (the theory was) and the more responding the more adequate the learning. In preparing each question the effort was not so much to contribute to a larger meaning as to assure that the student "emitted" the desired response, on the ground that he learned by making correct responses and an error would tend to recur. Multiple-choice questions are not used, because they involve the presentation of wrong alternatives, and also call merely for discrimination. All this has seemed plausible theoretically, and hopes have been high for extraordinary educational advances.

Reprinted from *Journal of Applied Psychology*, (February, 1963), pp. 1–6, by permission of the author and the publisher.

## NOT GAIN BUT CONFUSION

Instead, evidence has been accumulating that the above hypotheses on which the programing was being based were, *for human learning of meaningful matter,* not so!˙ Such learners dealing with such materials may profit by seeing not only what a thing is but what it is not, may profit by mistakes, may learn to recall from learning to discriminate. Further, some half-dozen investigators have reported that as much may be learned in a given time simply by reading, as by reading *and* responding (Pressey, 1962; Silberman, 1962). In short, these theorists have independently discovered what educators have known about and been investigating for over 40 years—silent reading! Further, as programed matter has been used over a period of time, it has been realized that for skimming for main ideas, for review—for any use except that initial go-through—the programed book is almost impossible and the teaching-machine roll entirely so. Mostly, even for the first go-through, they are unsatisfactory, because most important matter to be learned has structure, which the programing destroys except the serial order, and most important learning is integrative and judgmental, so requires a looking about in what is being studied; for all such purposes a teaching machine seems about as hampering as a scanning device which requires that one look at a picture only 1 square inch at a time, in a set order. Much seems very wrong about current attempts at autoinstruction.

A possible basic factor is suggested by Hilgard (1956) when he questions

the generalization from comparative studies that there are no differences, except quantitative ones, between the learning of lower mammals and man. . . . It is strange that the opposite point of view is not more often made explicit—that at the human level there have emerged capacities not approached by the lower animals, including other primates. . . . Language in man is perhaps the clearest of the emergents which carries with it a forward surge in what may be learned. . . . There are probably a number of different kinds of learning, following different laws. [Further, in man] the ceiling of ability itself may be modified by training. [Thus after acquiring] appropriate linguistic or mathematical tools [he can solve problems previously impossible] (pp. (460–461).

Surely that now taken-for-granted but really marvelous skill, silent assimilative reading, is such a tool. Also more important than often recognized are a variety of skills and strategies in learning usually grouped together as methods of study.

With Hilgard's position the writer would agree. He would say that the learning theorists have with notable vigor and consistency applied "generalizations from comparative studies" to problems of learning in school, and that the results have shown, more adequately than ever before, the unsatisfactoriness of those generalizations for that purpose. For a learner with reading-study skills, conventional textual matter orders and structures its contents in paragraphs and sections and chapters, exhibits that structure in headings and table of contents, makes all readily available in index with page headings and numbers. The learner thus has multiple aids to the development and structuring of his understanding. If need be he can, with a flick of the finger, move about in the material; he can skip the already known, turn back as a result of a later felt need, review selectively. As a way to present matter to be learned, the average textbook may not be best. But thousands of frames on a teaching-machine roll or strung through a programed book would seem close to the worst. To make a very bad pun, the programers have "framed" the textbook. Instead of trying to improve their programs, they might better consider very broadly how best to present matter for learning. The opinion is ventured that the best will be found closer to texts than to their programs.

But did not Socrates so teach the slave boy? The boy could not read. What about the often-cited skillful tutor? He assumed that the student had done some reading. However, both Socrates and the tutor did further learning by asking questions. The writer would contend that neither simply presented an idea and then reinforced it. Brownell's (1928) early research regarding primary school children's learning of arithmetic here seems relevant. Simply telling them that $2 \times 3 = 6$ did *not* bring about real learning of that number combination. These sturdy little empiricists had not merely to be *told*; they had to be shown, as by putting out two sets each of three pennies and demonstrating that they did indeed count to six. They had similarly to verify, and to differentiate, that $2 + 3$ was 5 and $3 - 2$ was only 1. As Piaget (1954) and others have described, children gradually develop a number system, also cognitive schema as of space, causality; and they do this not by so crude a rote process as the accretion of bit learnings stuck on by reinforcements, but by progressive processes of cognitive integration and clarification.

Moreover, such clarification is commonly by differentiation, and multiple-choice items involve just such processes. The three-choice question $2 \times 3 = 1$, 5, or 6 differentiates the correct answer from answers got by wrongly subtracting or adding. In this one concise little item are thus packed three arithmetic processes and three number combinations, and study of the item might well involve all six issues, with autoinstructional dealing with the item clarifying of all. The point will be returned to.

But first a brief summary of the position so far. The past decade has seen an extraordinary "boom" in autoinstruction; most of this work has been dominated by concepts of operant conditioning deriving directly from animal experimentation and has become stylized in terms of initial presentation of tasks in numerous frames with immediate constructed response. Because thus so special in origin and nature, as well as yielding often question-raising results, a basic critical review of current autoinstructional concepts seemed called for. Doubts have been raised as to whether human learning of meaningful material can be adequately accounted for by animal based theory, programed matter is satisfactory for such learning, and reinforcement adequately accounts for the process (Gagné, 1962).

## BUT WHERE FROM HERE?

When in doubt about such a theory-dominated situation, it is sometimes well to pull back and see whether a very practical analysis may helpfully reconstrue issues. If this be done, an obvious early question is this: what is the best way *initially* to present matter to be learned? The programers have been cutting it into little pieces each responded to, but now recognize that one may learn from reading without responding. Then how big may the piece be? The writer has stressed that the bigger piece may have structure which should be made evident, and that first consideration as well as review or selective use may make it desirable that the learner can move about freely in the material. Perhaps it would be granted that a questioner who interrupted the reading of this paper should be asked to wait until it was all before him—that it would be then that the discussion could be most profitable. Surely it will be granted that the paper can best be understood if seen in print so that one can glance about and see headings; rather than if heard, when one cannot thus study—as one cannot study a teaching-machine roll. So the suggestion is: that the initial presentation might most often best be a very well organized and well written substantial statement much like a chapter in a good textbook! And the autoinstruction should follow and should be like a series of questions in a very good discussion of such a chapter.

Some "autopresentation" might be helpful: a teaching-machine roll might picture two groups each of three pennies and then six and so make clear to the child mind that $2 \times 3$ does make six. *After* his number system has been somewhat established, there may be automatized drill. The printed word "house" may be thus associated with a picture of one. Sundry sorts of detail-learning and of drill may be dealt with piecemeal. But mostly (the writer believes) initial presentation of what is to be learned will be in field trip, demonstration or experiment, or most commonly a substantial unit like an incisive textbook chapter, *not* all mixed up with autoinstruction. The "autodiscussion" would follow, and its function would be (to paraphrase a statement in Ausubel's 1961 review) to enhance the clarity and stability of cognitive structure by correcting misconceptions, and deferring the instruction of new matter until there had been such clarification and elucidation.

In difficult matter such as a science text or industrial or military training manual, bits of autoinstruction may be needed more frequently; each step in the solution of a difficult problem may need such autoelucidation. But the manual or text need not be fragmented into thousands of frames. Problems may be explicated in autoinstructional matter supplementary to the text; and there, or perhaps every 3 or 4 pages in the book, clusters of autoexplicating queries may keep check on understanding. But a book's structured coherence and orderliness of presentation, and its convenience for overview, review, and reference, can be kept.

If the autoinstruction is thus to *follow* presentation of what is to be learned, then (like a good tutor or teacher) it will deal only with issues which need further clarification or emphasis. Such adjunct autoelucidation will *not* cover everything, may jump from one point to another or even back and forth. It will be very much shorter than present "programs," which attempt both to present matter to be learned and autoinstruct about it in the same aggregate. Being so different, such supplemental autoinstruction might well be given a different name, as autoelucidation or explication.

But how would matter for adjunct autoinstruction or explication be selected? Experienced teachers would have many suggestions as to points needing special elucidation. They would be indicated in published research regarding pupils' learning of and difficulties in spelling, arithmetic, algebra, composition, science, and history. Additional research, for development and trial of such elucidative material, would suggest more items and better ways of presenting them. Some could be cleared up by making the initial presentation more lucid. But some students would still have difficulty with some items; perhaps those troubling 10% of the pupils or more would be dealt with in the adjunct autoinstruction.

The items should usually there appear (the writer is convinced) as multiple-choice questions with only such wrong alternatives as express common misunderstandings and a right answer notably clear. There is evidence that, contrary to theoretical inference, students do, after auto-instruction with such items, *less* often make the so-labeled mistakes, more often get things right, and transfer or generalize so that the gains appear on recall and yet other types of end tests (see for instance Jones, 1954; Lumsdaine & Glaser, 1960, pp. 52–93). Only half the students in a class may get such an item right on a pretest, but almost all of them do so on an end test a month later. In striking contrast, the perverse requirements of the orthodox programer make any such effectiveness impossible: the item is initially supposed to be so easy that at least 95% pass it, errors cannot be identified as such because they must not be shown, and right statements are limited to such as the student can be maneuvered into hastily formulating himself. And orthodox improvement consists of making the items yet easier! In contrast, improvement of such an item as here urged would involve making wrong alternates clearer expressions of common misconceptions and the right more clearly right so that gains would be yet greater. In addition, the ease of checking objective items, with immediate indication of correctness (as by instant change of color of the check mark on a "chemo-card" or turn to next question on a key machine) makes possible going through many more items in a given time—so presumably more learning.

### RANGE OF EVALUATIONS

But what of the argument that orthodox programs have been found greatly to save time, so that for instance a college course was finished in the first 2 months of a semester, or an industrial training course similarly shortened? Independent study plans have made possible marked reduction of time in class without any such programs (Baskin, 1960). The average class and the average business training session may be very time wasting and otherwise inefficient, and a number of alternatives may be shown to be better. In a college or secondary school course with several sections, it should be feasible to have one or more taught in conventional fashion, one or more use an orthodox program, a similar number try what the writer has called adjunct autoinstruction, another venture a planned independent study procedure, and outcomes on a carefully made final examination compared. If so made, such examinations can yield some analysis of outcomes; does one method or another bring more recall, transfer, application? Experiments of this type under the writer's direction have shown adjunct autoinstruction superior to conventional classes in all these respects.

These experiments also showed the adjunct materials very useful in planned independent study: in a room set aside for such use and having all the readings, laboratory material, and adjunct autoinstructional sheets available but looked after by an assistant, the students came in and worked when they wished, in small groups or individually, consulting the assistant when they so desired. All finished the 11-week course within 6 weeks. All did well on midterm and final examinations. But informal reports and interviews indicated yet other values, as gains in ability to work independently—though the students became better acquainted than in formal classes! The opportunity to save time was motivating. Several of these students took another course by independent study during the second half of the quarter.

More broadly, appraising experiments involving considerable numbers of students with different instructors over considerable periods of time—preferably a whole school or business training course—have yet other values. Methods have to be tolerable in long continued and routine, not simply brief and special, use. In the work just described, the best all-purpose "teaching machine" was judged to be a 3 x 5 chemo-card having 30 lines each of four squares: on this answer card the student checked his choice of answer to each of 30 four-choice questions on a teach-test sheet, using a special red ink which instantly turned black when he marked in the right answer-box (because of an invisible chemical printed there). The student kept trying on each question until this color-change feedback told him he had the correct answer. For remedial review he had only to note where his red marks were, the sum of them was his error-score; the instructor had only to note where he saw most red on the cards for a given day to see where some corrective discussion might be desirable, and for both him and the students the cards were a compact easily-filed record.[1] In the writer's adjunct autoinstructional procedure, everything except the cards could be used over and over again, easily returned to again as for review. For long-continuing flexible use and re-use, it seemed apparent that a text or business manual plus perhaps 50 adjunct autoinstructional sheets (and some chemo-cards) was far more practicable than that manual or text cut up into 3,000 frames on a teaching-machine roll (with the machines) or strung through a programed book.

## RESUME AND RECOMMENDATIONS

Teaching machines and programed materials are now being used all over the country in schools and colleges and in industrial and military training. Manufacture and sale of such products are a major enterprise of many publishers and equipment makers. Ambitious young people are embarking on careers in such work. The whole subject has become an accepted topic of everyday talk. However, there is disturbing evidence that current autoinstruction is *not* up to the claims made for it, that the current "boom" might be followed by a "bust" unfortunate for those involved—and for psychology. This paper is first of all a plea that to guard against such a danger the whole situation be soon given close critical inspection, and not merely to assure (as is now being attempted) that programs are good; but critically to consider whether the whole current concept of programing may be at fault, and an almost totally different approach than now orthodox to all ideas about autoinstruction be called for.

The archvillain, leading so many people astray, is declared to be learning theory! No less a charge is made than that the whole trend of American research and theory as regards learning has been based on a false premise— that the important features of human learning are to be found in animals. Instead, the all-important fact is that human has transcended animal learning.[2] Language, number, such skills as silent reading, make possible facilitations of learning, and kinds of learning, impossible even for the apes. Autoinstruction should enhance such potentials. Instead, current animal derived procedures in autoinstruction destroy meaningful structure to present

---

[1] Yet more convenient autoinstructional cards are possible. Instead of a pen with special ink, only a pencil may be needed; a mark with it, or a stroke of its eraser, breaks through an overprint to reveal a "c" underneath when the right answer is found. For 30-item 3-choice teach tests, a device little larger than a stopwatch, and less complicated, may both teach and keep score. An apparatus little larger than an electric desk clock may both teach and provide selective review.

[2] For this conclusion there is no less evidence than the whole history of civilization! Basically more significant than Skinner's brilliant research regarding animal learning may well be the almost forgotten finding of Kellogg and of Cathy Hayes that even if an ape be raised in a home like a child, it can never learn to talk. Far more remarkable than Skinner's pigeons playing ping pong is the average human scanning a news-

fragments serially in programs, and replace processes of cognitive clarification with largely rote reinforcings of bit learnings.

An "adjunct autoinstruction" is urged which keeps, makes use of, and enhances meaningful structure, the autoinstruction serving to clarify and extend meaningfulness. Texts, manuals, laboratory exercises, instructional moving pictures and television would be kept (though often improved), and the autoinstruction would aid in their use and increase their value. The materials would be perhaps only a tenth as bulky as present programs; and being objective, their use could be greatly facilitated by automating devices.

Evaluations should not merely (as is now projected) compare the merits of various "orthodox" programs. Those should be compared with such adjunct autoinstructional materials as here advocated. Adaptability should be compared for use with other media as books and movies and other methods as guided independent study. Convenience and cost for continuing general use should be hard-headedly appraised. The prediction is ventured that in all respects adjunct autoinstruction will be found far superior: time and work saving will be great yet more will be accomplished—courses often completed in half the usual time, years saved but nevertheless more accomplished in school and college, industrial and military training tasks reduced perhaps a third in length and all with great time and trouble saved instructional staffs. Then at long last the "industrial revolution" in education may come about which the writer predicted (Pressey, 1932) just 30 years ago. Further, somewhat as the practical testing movement from the First World War on greatly stimulated and aided research and theorizing regarding abilities, so autoinstruction may get research on learning out from under its long dominance by comparative psychology and confinement in the laboratory and evolve vigorous new theory.

---

paper—glancing about to find matter of interest to him, judging, generalizing, reconstruing, all in silent reading without overt respondings or reinforcings. Most remarkable of all is it to see learning theorists, hypnotized by the plausibilities of a neat theory, trying to teach that human as if he were a pigeon—confining his glance to the rigid slow serial peep show viewing of innumerable "frames" each demanding that he respond and be reinforced.

N. L. GAGE

# 25.  THEORIES OF TEACHING

The thesis of this article is that theories of learning will have greater usefulness to education when they are transformed into theories of teaching.[1]
This thesis rests upon an assumption as to the present usefulness of learning
theory in education and upon a distinction between theories of learning
and theories of teaching. Let us examine each of these ideas.

First, the limited usefulness of learning theory in education has long been
acknowledged. Estes, writing on "Learning" in the *Encyclopedia of Educational Research,* judged that "no convergence is imminent between the
educator's and the laboratory scientist's approaches to learning," and he
was able to report little progress "toward bridging the gap between laboratory psychology and the study of school learning."[2] Near the close of his
*Theories of Learning,* Hilgard stated, "...It is not surprising, therefore,
that the person seeking advice from the learning theorist often comes away
disappointed."[3] Educational psychology textbooks usually include treatments
of learning that draw in general terms upon learning theories. But these
treatments bear only slight resemblance to the elaborations of the theories
as portrayed in Hilgard's book.

Second, our thesis embodies a basic distinction between theories of learning and theories of teaching. While theories of learning deal with the ways
in which an organism learns, theories of teaching deal with the ways in
which a person influences an organism to learn.

To rephrase the thesis: Although theories of learning are necessary to
the understanding, prediction, and control of the learning process, they

---

Reprinted from *Theories of Learning and Instruction,* 63rd Yearbook of the
National Society for the Study of Education, Part I, Ernest R. Hilgard (ed.),
(Chicago: The Society, 1964), pp. 268–85, by permission of the author and
publisher.

1 The author is very grateful to Philip W. Jackson and Romayne Ponleithner for
valuable editorial suggestions.
2 William K. Estes, "Learning," in *Encyclopedia of Educational Research,* p. 767.
Edited by Chester W. Harris. New York: Macmillan Co., 1960 (third edition).
3 Ernest R. Hilgard, *Theories of Learning,* p. 485. New York: Appleton-Century-
Crofts, 1956 (second edition).

cannot suffice in education. The goal of education—to engender learning in the most desirable and efficient ways possible—would seem to require an additional science and technology of teaching. To satisfy the practical demands of education, theories of learning must be "stood on their head" so as to yield theories of teaching.

In this chapter, we shall attempt to support this thesis by considering (*a*) the need for theories of teaching, (*b*) the need for analysis and specification of teaching in developing such theories, (*c*) some illustrative analyses and specifications of teaching, and (*d*) the kinds of research that might yield improved empirical bases for theories of teaching.

## THE NEED FOR THEORIES OF TEACHING

That theories of teaching are needed in addition to theories of learning may seem in the main to require no argument. Yet, the development of theories of teaching has been neglected. In comparison with learning, teaching goes almost unmentioned in the theoretical writings of psychologists. Many signs of this disregard can be observed. For example, *Psychological Abstracts* contains large sections on laboratory learning and school learning but only a small section on teaching, and that within the section on "Educational Personnel." The *Annual Review of Psychology* usually includes a chapter on learning but seldom more than a few paragraphs on teaching. Volumes have been devoted to theories of learning, but not a single book deals exclusively with theories of teaching. Textbooks of educational psychology give much more space to discussions of learning and the learner than to methods of teaching and the teacher. *A Comprehensive Dictionary of Psychological and Psychoanalytical Terms* has three pages, containing 50 entries, concerned with learning but devotes only five lines to "Teaching" as follows: "The art of assisting another to learn. It includes the providing of information [instruction] and of appropriate situations, conditions, or activities designed to facilitate learning."[4]

### REASONS FOR THE NEGLECT

The reasons for the neglect of theories of teaching are in themselves of interest. Examining these reasons may help determine whether such theories are possible of formulation and are desirable.

*Art vs. Science.* Sometimes the attempt to develop theories of teaching is seen as implying the development of a science of teaching. Yet, some writers reject the notion of a science of teaching. Highet entitled his book *The Art of Teaching,*

---

[4] Horace B. English and Ava C. English, *A Comprehensive Dictionary of Psychological and Psychoanalytical Terms.* New York: Longmans, Green & Co., 1958.

...because I believe that teaching is an art, not a science. It seems to me very dangerous to apply the aims and methods of science to human beings as individuals, although a statistical principle can often be used to explain their behavior in large groups and a scientific diagnosis of their physical structure is always valuable. . . . Of course it is necessary for any teacher to be orderly in planning his work and precise in his dealing with facts. But that does not make his teaching "scientific." Teaching involves emotions, which cannot be systematically appraised and employed, and human values, which are quite outside the grasp of science. "Scientific" teaching, even of scientific subjects, will be inadequate as long as both teachers and pupils are human beings. Teaching is not like inducing a chemical reaction: It is much more like painting a picture or making a piece of music, or on a lower level like planting a garden or writing a friendly letter.[5]

Highet's argument would, of course, also militate against the development of a science of learning. His argument against a science of teaching need not be considered to apply to a theory of teaching. We should not equate the attempt to develop a theory about an activity with the attempt to eliminate its phenomenal, idiosyncratic, and artistic aspects. Painting and composing, and even friendly letter-writing and casual conversation, have inherent order and lawfulness that can be subjected to theoretical analysis. The painter, despite the artistry immanent in his work, often can be shown by students of his art to be behaving according to a theory—of color, perspective, balance, or abstraction. The artist whose lawfulnesses are revealed does not become an automaton; ample scope remains for his subtlety and individuality. His processes and products need not remain immune to attempts at rational understanding on the part of critics and scholars.

So it is with teaching. Although teaching requires artistry, it can be subjected to scientific scrutiny. The power to explain, predict, and control that may result from such scrutiny will not dehumanize teaching. Just as engineers can still exercise ingenuity within the theory of thermodynamics, teachers will have room for artistic variation on the theory that scientific study of teaching may establish. And for the work of those who train, hire, and supervise teachers, theory and empirical knowledge of teaching will provide scientific grounding.

Even if it had no practical value, a scientific understanding of teaching should still be sought. Like interstellar space and evolution, learning has been studied for its own sake. So teaching can be studied as a phenomenon of interest in its own right. Theories of teaching are desirable because of their practical value if it is forthcoming, but desirable in any case.

*Presumed Adequacy of Learning Theory.* The need for theories of teaching stems also from the insufficiency *in principle* of theories of learning. Theories of learning deal with what the learner does. But changes in education must

5 Gilbert Highet, *The Art of Teaching,* pp. vii–viii. New York: Vintage Books, 1955.

depend in large part upon what the teacher does. That is, changes in how learners go about their business of learning occur in response to the behavior of their teachers or others in the educational establishment. Much of our knowledge about learning can be put into practice only by teachers. And the ways in which these teachers would put this knowledge into effect constitute part of the subject of theories of teaching. Our position is that practical applications have not been gleaned from theories of learning largely because theories of teaching have not been developed. The implications of learning theory need to be translated into implications for the behavior of teachers. Teachers will then act on these implications in such ways as to improve learning. Theories of teaching and the empirical study of teaching may enable us to make better use of our knowledge about learning.

Is there any room for theory of teaching? Or, on the other hand, is theory of learning and behavior so all-encompassing as to preclude any valid concern with theory of teaching? Hilgard pointed out that Hull "scarcely distinguishes between a theory of learning and a theory of behavior, so important is learning in his conception of behavior. . . . Hence the systematic aspects of learning theory have come to be important to all psychologists interested in more general theories."[6] Because teaching is a form of behavior, adequate theories of learning, or general theories of behavior, would, in this view, encompass teaching as well. But this view applies only to teaching considered as the "dependent variable," the thing to be explained. In this sense, the behavior of teachers will indeed be understood by the same theories that apply to the behavior and learning of pupils. The kind of theory of teaching with which we are concerned places the behavior of teachers in the position of "independent variables" as a function of which the learning of pupils is to be explained. That is, theories of teaching should be concerned with explaining, predicting, and controlling the ways in which teacher behavior affects the learning of pupils. In this perspective there is ample room for theories of teaching. Such theories would deal with a whole realm of phenomena neglected by theories of learning.

It might be objected that, with learning as the dependent variable, theories of teaching become only a subclass of theories of learning: a subclass in which the independent variables consist of the behavior and characteristics of teachers. Such a conception of theories of teaching seems altogether admissible within the thesis of this chapter; it would not change the major argument. Theories of teaching would still need to be developed as a substantial discipline, even if not co-ordinate with theories of learning.

The two kinds of theory must ultimately, of course, be strongly connected; theories of learning will have many implications for theories of teaching. But that is another matter. These implications will become clear as the study of teaching develops. As will be illustrated, the psychology of learning

6 Hilgard, *op. cit.*, p. 2.

has much to offer the person who attempts to formulate the ways in which teaching proceeds.

## THE DEMANDS OF TEACHER EDUCATION

Explicit concern with the theory of teaching should benefit teacher education. In training teachers, we often seem to rely on mere inference from theory of learning to the practice of teaching. Yet, what we know about learning is inadequate to tell us what we should do about teaching. This inadequacy is clearly evident in our educational psychology courses and textbooks. The irrepressible question of students in educational psychology courses is, "How should I teach?" While they may infer a partial answer from a consideration of how pupils learn, they cannot get all of it in this way. Much of what teachers must know about teaching does not directly follow from a knowledge of the learning process. Their knowledge must be acquired explicitly rather than by inference. Farmers need to know more than how plants grow. Mechanics need to know more than how a machine works. Physicians need to know more than how the body functions. Teachers need to know more than how a pupil learns.

Teachers must know how to manipulate the independent variables, especially their own behaviors, that determine learning. Such knowledge cannot be derived automatically from knowledge about the learning process. To explain and control the teaching act requires a science and technology of teaching in its own right. The student of educational psychology who complains that he has learned much about learning and learners, but not about teaching, is asking for the fruits of scientific inquiry, including theories of teaching.

## THE NEED FOR ANALYSIS
## AND SPECIFICATION

How should work toward such theory proceed? In this section, we advocate the analysis and specification of teaching. Then we consider some sketches of what such analysis and specification might lead to.

## THE MISLEADINGLY GENERIC
## TERM, "TEACHING"

As a concept, teaching sorely needs analysis. Such analysis should clarify the concerns of theories of teaching. For "teaching" is a misleadingly generic term; it covers too much. It falsely suggests a single, unitary phenomenon that may fruitfully be made the subject of theory development.

It may fairly be argued that learning theory has long been hung up on a similar fallacy. Because the term "learning" has been applied to an enormous range of phenomena, psychologists have been misled into believing that a single theory can be developed to explain all these phenomena. Animal learning in puzzle boxes and Skinner boxes, human learning of nonsense syllables and eyelid responses in the laboratory, and the learning of school subjects in classrooms have all been termed "learning." And, because all these activities have been given the same name, psychologists have attempted to account for all of them by a single, unified, general theory.

Yet, as is well known, after more than a half-century of effort, no such unification of learning theory has materialized. Research and theorizing on learning have had three main foci—animal learning, human learning in the laboratory, and human learning in the classroom. (In recent years, a fourth focus has developed: programed learning. In time this new development may strengthen the connection between the laboratory and the school.) The various kinds of learning have not been embraced successfully by any single learning theory. And this failure may well stem from the false belief that a single term, "learning," guarantees that a single, universally applicable theory of learning can be found.

Some analogies to other processes may clarify this point. Medicine does not search for a single theory of illness or healing. Physicians long ago discovered that people can get sick in several basically different ways, such as being infected with germs or viruses, having organic malfunctions, suffering traumatic impacts of energy, or experiencing environmental deprivations. And, rather than a general theory of healing, physicians use several different approaches, such as giving medicines, using surgery, improving environments, or changing diets.

Another example is "getting rich," which is, like learning, concerned with the acquisition of something. Getting rich also takes place in many different ways—inheriting, gambling, stealing, making profits, or earning wages—and no one has tried to develop a general, unified theory of how to get rich. The concept of "getting rich" simply has no scientific value; it covers too many different processes. Perhaps we should consider the possibility that, as a unitary concept, school learning has no scientific value either, because it covers too many distinct phenomena and processes.

The same then might be said of teaching. The term "teaching" should not be taken to imply that teaching is a basic process to which a general theory may apply. For "teaching" embraces far too many kinds of process, of behavior, of activity, to be the proper subject of a single theory. We must not be misled by the one word, "teaching," into searching for one theory to explain it.

## WAYS OF ANALYZING
## THE CONCEPT OF TEACHING

If this argument is valid, the concept of teaching must be analyzed to reveal processes or elements that might constitute the proper subject of theories. What kinds of analysis can be made? Several can be suggested.

First, teaching can be analyzed according to types of teacher *activities*.

Teachers engage in explaining activities, mental hygiene activities, demonstrating activities, guidance activities, order-maintaining activities, housekeeping activities, record-keeping activities, assignment-making activities, curriculum-planning activities, testing and evaluation activities, and many other kinds of activities. If everything a teacher does *qua* teacher is teaching, then teaching consists of many kinds of activity. It is unreasonable to expect a single theory to encompass all of these.

Second, teaching can be analyzed according to the types of *educational objectives* at which it is aimed; examples of major types are affective, psychomotor, and cognitive objectives. Thus, teaching processes can be classified according to the domain of objectives to which they seem primarily relevant. When the teacher uses words to define, describe, or explain a concept, such as "extrapolation," his behavior may be primarily relevant to cognitive objectives. When he offers warmth and encouragement, we may consider him to be acting in ways primarily relevant to the affective domain. When he demonstrates the correct way to write a capital *F*, his behavior may be primarily relevant to psychomotor objectives. At any given moment, more than one of these domains of objectives may be affected. It may sometimes be difficult to distinguish the teacher's influence on cognitive change from his influence on affective change in pupils. So, when the teacher fails to explain something clearly, the pupil may become not only confused (cognitively) but discouraged (affectively) as well. Nonetheless, analyses of this kind may have strategic value. At any rate, we should not assume that a single theory of teaching will apply to all kinds of objectives.

A third way to analyze teaching stems from the notion that teaching can be viewed as the obverse, or "mirror image," of learning and therefore has *components corresponding to those of learning*. If the learning process can be analyzed into basic elements or components—let us use Neal Miller's "drive," "cue," "response," and "reward" as examples—then teaching can be analyzed similarly. Corresponding components of teaching might be "motivation-producing," "perception-directing," "response-eliciting," and "reinforcement-providing." For some elements of Miller's analysis of learning, there are well-established separate domains of theory, such as theories of motivation and theories of perception. Similarly, theories of motivating, perception-directing, response-eliciting, and rewarding, corresponding to such elements of the teaching process, may develop. In any event, it is questionable whether a single theory of teaching should be sought to encompass all these components of the teaching process.

A fourth way to analyze teaching, not entirely distinct from those already mentioned, derives from *families of learning theory*. These families may be illustrated by "conditioning theory," "identification theory," and "cognitive theory." Some theorists (e.g., Mowrer[7]) conceive learning, in all its forms,

---

[7] O. Hobart Mowrer, *Learning Theory and Behavior*, p. 213. New York: John Wiley & Sons, 1960.

to be a matter of conditioning with punishment or rewards consisting of primary or secondary reinforcements associated with independent or response-dependent stimulation. Such a conditioning theory of learning may imply a corresponding kind of theory of teaching. Other theorists (e.g., Bandura[8]) emphasize that learning consists, at least in major part, of the learner's identification with a model, whom the learner imitates. In this case, a second kind of theory of teaching is implied. A third kind of theorist (e.g., Luchins[9]) holds that learning consists of the cognitive restructuring of problematical situations. Here, a third kind of theory of teaching is suggested.

It is conceivable that all three of these major families of learning theory are valid, for different kinds of persons learning different things in different situations. Any reductionism, or attempt to derive the other two from any one of these, may yield only a spurious parsimony. The three kinds of theory seem at present to be compatible, in the sense that they at least do not lead to different predictions about the same data. Rather, they seem to have been developed to account for different data—for the learning of different kinds of things in different situations. If so, all three approaches to the development of theory of teaching should be of some value.

### ILLUSTRATIVE SPECIFICATIONS

We have suggested the bases for four different analyses of teaching: (*a*) types of teacher activities, (*b*) types of educational objectives, (*c*) components of the learning process, and (*d*) families of learning theory. We have also suggested that no single theory of teaching should be offered that would attempt to account for all activities of teachers, would be aimed at all objectives of education, and would involve all components of the learning process, in a way that would satisfy all theories of learning. To comply with our call for specification, we should now at least sketch what a theory of teaching might be concerned with, if it is to become specific. To do so, we shall make various selections from among the products of our analyses.

*Selection One.* From the teacher's activities, let us select the one called explaining, leaving aside for the moment the mental hygiene, demonstrating, and other activities. Of the types of objectives, let us choose to focus on the cognitive domain, and, even more specifically, on the student's ability to extrapolate trends beyond the given data. Of the components of the learning process, let us choose the perceptual, or the teacher's corresponding function of directing the student's perceptions to the salient part of his environment, which, in the present instance, consists of the kinds of trends in data that we want him to learn to extrapolate. And finally, of the families

---

8 Albert Bandura, "Social Learning through Imitation," in *Nebraska Symposium on Motivation.* Edited by M. R. Jones. Lincoln: University of Nebraska Press, 1962.

9 Abraham S. Luchins, "Implications of Gestalt Psychology for AV Learning," *AV Communications Review,* IX, No. 5 (1961), 7–31.

of learning theory in accordance with which we wish to derive a theory of teaching, let us choose the cognitive restructuring approach.

At this point, having made these choices, we should be in a better position to develop a theory of teaching. Having eliminated many realms of phenomena from our concern, we have cut the problem down to size. We may still be a long way from our goal, but not so far as before.

Of the several choices we have made, the most arguable one is that of the congnitive restructuring as against the conditioning or the identification paradigms of learning and, hence, of teaching. The cognitive restructuring paradigm of learning holds that the learner arrives at knowledge and understanding by perceiving the situation (the problem) before him and then rearranging it, through central cognitive processes, in ways that yield meaning of a rational, logically consistent kind. The teacher can engender this restructuring by pointing to, either physically or verbally, and by manipulating the parts of the cognitive configuration so as to make the structure he wants learned stand out as a kind of figure against the ground of irrelevancies and distractions. The teacher manipulates the cognitive field in accordance with laws of cognition—analogous to the laws of perception governing the constancies, groupings, and whole-qualities in visual and auditory stimuli. Then the pupil apprehends the cognitive structure to be learned. He can no more avoid learning in this instance than he can avoid seeing the phi-phenomenon (the appearance of motion when two lights are flashed in brief succession) under proper conditions.

This conception of teaching follows the metaphor of the manipulator of stimuli who *compels* perceivers to see the stimuli in certain ways. Following certain principles of, say, similarity and proximity, we can compel a person to see a configuration of dots as falling into rows rather than columns. Similarly, following certain principles of cognitive structure, the teacher can "compel" his students to understand the principles of extrapolation.

Can we justify the rejection of the conditioning and identification paradigms for this kind of teaching? The conditioning paradigm seems to fall short simply because such teaching does not proceed by successive approximation of responses to the objective, as is implied by the term "shaping behavior." The teacher does not get the pupil to move gradually toward correct extrapolating behavior by feeding him stimuli that gradually take on the form of the problem to be understood, eliciting responses that gradually approximate what is correct, and providing reinforcement appropriately along the way. Rather, the teacher can often produce the desired behavior all at once by judiciously restructuring the student's cognitive field.

As for the identification paradigm in this instance, it would hold that the teacher gets his results by being prestigious or positively cathected. Why do we reject this approach to understanding the teaching of a logically consistent set of ideas? The identification approach implies that prestigious models can succeed in teaching even logically inconsistent or invalid ideas. But it is unlikely that the model can get a learner to imitate behavior that the learner can plainly perceive to be logically or cognitively inconsistent. (Asch's conformity-producing group-pressure situations seem to produce mere compliance rather than learning, since much of the yielding disappears in private retests.[10]) Much of what we teach has an iron logic of its own; mathematics is a prime example. *To the degree that the content is logically structured,* the learner will be influenced by the structure rather than by his human model.

*Selection Two.* Let us now try another fairly likely combination of the components resulting from our analyses. From the teacher's activities, let us select his mental-hygiene function. From the types of educational objectives, let us select one from the affective domain, such as the pupil's emotional security in the classroom situation. Of the components of the learning process, let us choose the motivational one, or the teacher's corresponding function of arousing in the pupil a desire to learn what the teacher wants him to learn. And finally, of the families of learning theory, let us choose conditioning.

For this particular selection of specifications, we should pay particular attention to the teacher's acts of rewarding the pupil's provisional tries. Dispensing praise and warmth, almost without regard to what the pupil does so long as it remains within classroom requirements, the teacher positively reinforces the pupil's efforts to comply with the teacher's demands for effort and activity. Basking in a shower of laudatory remarks and approving glances, the pupil gradually comes out of his shell. He shows evidence of improved security.

Why do we select the conditioning approach here and reject cognitive restructuring or identification? In this instance, what has to be learned has no particular cognitive structure. No set of logically organized ideas has to be grasped by the pupil. The goal of getting the pupil to feel secure enough to respond in the classroom cannot readily be achieved, as we all know, through any process of rational explanation or intellectual argument.

We reject the identification approach because the goal in this instance is not to get the pupil to behave the way the teacher does. The kinds of emotional security and activity that the pupil should exhibit in the classroom cannot be achieved through a process of imitating the teacher's security and activity. Indeed, the teacher's confidence and high activity may be precisely what overwhelms the pupil and causes him to withdraw into nonparticipation. For this particular combination of (*a*) mental-hygiene activity, (*b*) affective objective, and (*c*) motivational component of the learning process, it is not the pupil's identification with the teacher that will bring about the

---

10 David Krech, Richard S. Crutchfield, and Egerton L. Ballachey, *Individual in Society*, pp. 504–29. New York: McGraw-Hill Book Co., 1962.

security we want. It is rather the teacher's consistent reinforcement, by the conditioning paradigm of the teaching process, that will gradually "shape" the pupil's behavior into a form bespeaking emotional security.

*Selection Three.* A third selection from the components of our analyses of teaching will illustrate a still different version of a theory of teaching. Suppose we select the teacher's demonstrating activities, aimed at psychomotor objectives, with special concern for the response component of the learning process. For example, let us consider the teacher's activity in demonstrating the proper way to write the capital letter *F* in attempting to teach handwriting. Here it seems appropriate to emphasize the identification-imitation paradigm of the teaching process. The teacher goes to the blackboard and writes the letter *F* with the motions that he wants his pupils to adopt as their own. The teacher's prestige makes his way of performing this task unquestionably correct in the eyes of his pupils. His pupils watch him do it and then do it themselves. Depending on the maturity of their psychomotor skills, their success may be complete or partial. But given sufficient maturity, the pupils will write the letter *F* with the motions that the teacher wants them to use. The pupils make responses matching those of the teacher. Their imitation involves combining responses into relatively complex new patterns solely by observing the performance of another person.

In this instance, let us again assume that what is to be learned has no necessary logic. Many different ways of writing the letter *F* could be defended on rational grounds. Thus, the teacher does not carry out his task by explaining the reasons for a particular solution of the problem of how to write the letter. He does not derive his solution by building on earlier conclusions or premises. He has no ideational structure for his pupils to incorporate into their own thinking. Hence, the notion of teaching by cognitive restructuring does not seem to apply to this particular form of teaching.

We reject the conditioning approach here because it would entail a highly inefficient kind of gradual approximation to the desired behavior. To proceed through a painstaking process of response differentiation and extinction, gradually reinforcing desired bits of writing behavior and extinguishing the undesired ones, would be a wearisome and ineffective undertaking. It seems better to characterize the teaching process in this instance as a matter of inducing imitation of what is demonstrated by a prestigious model with whom the pupil identifies.

The foregoing may not represent the most fruitful ways of analyzing the concept of teaching. Other analyses, yielding different components, are clearly possible. Other combinations of resulting components may be more interesting to other persons seeking to develop theories of teaching. The point is that some such analyses and choices must be made before the properly specified concern of a theory can be isolated. Otherwise, attempts to develop theories of teaching will founder on excessive generality. To avoid such analyses and choices is to assume that the single word *teaching* denotes a single process amenable to a single, general theory. That kind of assumption has led to the present chasm between the purportedly general theories of learning developed in psychological laboratories and the kind of learning that goes on in schools. Although learning the Morse code, learning political attitudes, and learning mathematics are all called "learning," they do not necessarily involve the same kind of process. And, because the teaching of all these things is called by the one name of teaching, it does not follow that a single theory of teaching will account for how the teacher does his work.

## CONNECTIONS BETWEEN THEORY
## AND RESEARCH ON TEACHING

Theories not only reflect past experience but also shape future research. Often the main value of a theory lies in the new kinds of research it generates. Throughout the history of psychology, new empirical work, revealing new phenomena and processes, has followed upon new theories. Theories of motivation, perception, and learning have had this effect, and, similarly, the development of theories of teaching may stimulate new kinds of research with variables that have been neglected previously.

This kind of development can be seen in current research on programed learning. Many new variables have been given experimental attention in studies of programed learning as a result of the development of reinforcement theory. Prompting, construction versus selection of responses, overtness of response, and a variety of reinforcement techniques are now being studied. Some of these variables had been identified previously, but they now take new forms, more relevant to meaningful learning in classrooms.

What impact will the development of theories of teaching have on research? Only research effort will tell. But some conjectures may be warranted. Such conjectures are intended to stimulate explicit concern with theories of teaching of the kind urged in this chapter. Some of the new research movements briefly described below are already under way and serve as illustrations of promising developments.

*Teaching as Cognitive Restructuring.* Theories of teaching as cognitive restructuring focus on the teacher's behavior as a manipulator of ideas. Such theories concentrate research attention on the intellectual structures that characterize what is to be taught. This emphasis was occasionally evident in the research on teaching done in the 1930's and '40's. Studies of cognitive development and learning, such as those by Piaget, have long been available. But manifestations of a growing concern with the teacher's role in fostering such learning have only recently begun to appear. As Ausubel and Fitzgerald put it, "The importance of cognitive structure variables has been generally underestimated in the past because preoccupation with noncognitive, rote, and motor types of learning has tended to focus attention on such current situational and intrapersonal factors as task, practice, drive, incentive, and reinforcement variables."[11]

Some recent research on teaching conceived as cognitive restructuring may be mentioned to illustrate the kinds of variables brought to the fore by such an orientation. Smith has directed a study[12] of the logical operations of secondary-school teachers and students; he and his co-workers have described and analyzed such logical operations as defining, designating, classifying, explaining, and evaluating.

Another kind of research concerned with cognitive variables in teaching is illustrated by the work of Runkel,[13] who was concerned with a relationship, termed "collinearity," between the teacher's dimensions of thought and those of his students. Collinearity differs from similarity in that it indicates whether the dimensions or factors used in evaluating a set of objects might be the same even though the rank order of the objects in the evaluations given by two persons might be quite different. For example, two persons might evaluate a number of suits of clothing on the same bases (color, cut, and price) as underlying dimensions, even though they assign quite different rank orders to the suits. Runkel found evidence that, the greater the collinearity of students and teachers, the higher the achievement of the students as judged by the teachers. The finding was attributed to better communication between teachers and students when their cognitive structures were collinear.

A third style of research on cognitive variables in teaching is exemplified in studies by Suchman, who has been developing methods of training children in scientific inquiry,[14] that is, methods of increasing the number of valid questions children ask in seeking explanations of elementary scientific phenomena demonstrated in a film.

A final example is provided by the work of Ausubel,[15] who used organizers (i.e., "advanced introductory material at a high level of abstraction, generality, and inclusiveness") to influence various attributes of cognitive structure and then ascertained the influence of this manipulation on learning, retention, and problem-solving.

11 David P. Ausubel and Donald Fitzgerald, "Meaningful Learning and Retention: Interpersonal Cognitive Variables," *Review of Educational Research*, XXXI (December, 1961), 500–510.

12 B. Othanel Smith and Milton O. Meux, with the collaboration of Jerrold Coombs, Daniel Eierdam, and Ronald Szoke, *A Study of the Logic of Teaching.* Urbana: Bureau of Educational Research, University of Illinois, 1962 (mimeographed).

13 Philip J. Runkel, "Cognitive Similarity in Facilitating Communication," *Sociometry*, XIX (1956), 178–91.

14 J. Richard Suchman, "Inquiry Training in the Elementary School," *Science Teacher*, XXVII (November, 1960), 42–47.

15 Ausubel and Fitzgerald, *op. cit.*, p. 505.

*Teaching as Model-Providing.* As for research illustrating the identification approach to teaching, Bandura's recent work[16] seems noteworthy. He has conducted experiments dealing with (*a*) the effects on imitation of pairing a model with generalized reinforcers, (*b*) delayed imitation in the absence of the model, (*c*) the influence of the behavior of models in shaping frustration-reactions, and (*d*) the influence of social reinforcement and the behavior of models in shaping children's moral judgments. Bandura offers cogent arguments for greater concern with what we would characterize as teaching by model-providing than with teaching by conditioning.

*Teaching as Conditioning.* The conditioning approach to teaching has been studied extensively in recent years—primarily through research on teaching machines and programed learning. Krumboltz's review[17] organized recent findings under four headings: (*a*) evoking the desired response, (*b*) reinforcing the desired response, (*c*) maintaining and improving the desired response, and (*d*) eliminating the undesired response. To the degree that such research can be translated into implications or teacher behavior rather than merely the design and administration of programed learning materials, it will bear upon theories of teaching conceived according to the conditioning approach.

## SUMMARY

This article has developed the thesis that theories of learning will become more useful in education when they are transformed into theories of teaching. In support of this thesis, we examined the need for theories of teaching and sought to counter the arguments that teaching is an art and that learning theories make theories of teaching unnecessary. The demands of teacher education make theories of teaching especially important. In developing theories of teaching, a major step is analysis and specification. We offered analyses on the basis of (*a*) types of teacher activity, (*b*) types of educational objective, (*c*) components of the learning process, and (*d*) families of learning theory. Then we examined several selections of components from these analyses to illustrate how theories of teaching might be formulated when they were aimed at different combinations of *a, b, c,* and *d,* above. The sketches of these selections indicate that no single, unified, general theory of teaching should be sought to account for the various processes by which teachers engender learning. Rather, a number of theories of teaching, corresponding to major families of learning theory, will be necessary. Finally, the various approaches to the development of theories of teaching will

16 Bandura, *op. cit.,* pp. 256–64.
17 John D. Krumboltz, "Meaningful Learning and Retention: Practice and Reinforcement Variables," *Review of Educational Research,* XXXI (December, 1961), 535–46.

influence research on teaching. Such influence has already appeared in a number of research movements that can be classified according to the three families of theory of teaching employed in the earlier discussion: cognitive structure theories, identification theories, and conditioning theories.

NED A. FLANDERS

# 26. TEACHER INFLUENCE
# IN THE CLASSROOM

Most of the research reviewed in this article makes use of observational techniques to assess the spontaneous behavior of the teacher. The analysis of spontaneous teacher behavior involves the development and standardization of a system of categories that an observer can use to note the frequency of qualitatively different acts. Systematic observation produces a frequency distribution within discrete categories that can be drawn as a histogram profile covering short or long periods of observation. Profiles from long periods of observation ignore variability of teacher influence that is easily seen if profiles of the same teacher over short time periods are compared.

The ultimate goal of the study of teacher influence in the classroom is to achieve understanding of teacher-pupil interaction, and, in particular, to specify conditions in which learning is maximized. The research on classroom climate that is reviewed here contributes to a general understanding of teacher influence over long time periods, but it ignores short-term influence patterns of the teacher and changes in classroom conditions that occur as a result of learning.

## RESEARCH ON CLASSROOM CLIMATE

The words *classroom climate* refer to generalized attitudes toward the teacher and the class that the pupils share in common in spite of individual differences. The development of these attitudes is an outgrowth of classroom social interaction. As a result of participating in classroom activities, pupils

Reprinted from *Theory and Research in Teaching*, Arno A. Bellack (ed.), (New York: Teachers College, Columbia University, Bureau of Publications, 1963), pp. 37–52, by permission of the author and the publisher.

soon develop shared expectations about how the teacher will act, what kind of a person he is, and how they like their class. These expectations color all aspects of classroom behavior, creating a social atmosphere or climate that appears to be fairly stable, once established. Thus the word *climate*[1] is merely a shorthand reference to those qualities that consistently predominate in most teacher-pupil contacts and contacts between pupils in the presence or absence of the teacher.

The earliest systematic studies of spontaneous pupil and teacher behavior that relate directly to classroom climate are those of H. H. Anderson and his colleagues Helen and Joseph Brewer, and Mary Frances Reed (1939, 1945, 1946), and are based on the observation of "dominative" and "integrative" contacts. It is essential to understand the qualitative differences between an integrative and a dominative social contact because most of the research on classroom climate makes similar behavioral distinctions.

> A preliminary study showed that it was possible to devise reliable measures of the behavior of young children. Behavior was recorded as "contacts" and divided into two groups of categories. If a child snatched a toy, struck a playmate, or commanded him, or if he attempted to force him in some way, such contacts were included under the term "domination." By such behavior he ignored the rights of the companion; he tended to reduce the free interplay of differences and to lead toward resistance or conformity in responding or adapting to another.
> Other contacts were recorded which tended to increase the interplay of differences. Offering a companion a choice or soliciting an expression of his desires were gestures of flexibility and adaptation. These tended in the direction of discovering common purposes among differences. Such contacts were grouped under the term "socially integrative behavior" (Anderson *et al.*, 1946, p. 12).

The findings of Anderson *et al.* are based on the study of preschool, primary, and elementary school classrooms involving several different teachers and extending over several years. Taken altogether, their imaginative research has produced a series of internally consistent and significant findings. First, the dominative and integrative contacts of the teacher set a pattern of behavior that spreads throughout the classroom; the behavior of the teacher, more than that of any other individual, sets the climate of the class. The rule is that when either type of contact predominates, domination incites further domination, and integration stimulates further integration. It is the teacher's tendency that spreads among pupils even when the teacher is no

---

[1] Climate is assessed either by analysis of teacher-pupil interaction and inference of underlying attitudes, or by the use of a pupil attitude inventory and prediction of the quality of classroom interaction. Its precise meaning, when commonly used, is seldom clear, just as its synonyms "morale," "rapport," and "emotional tone" are also ambiguous. To have any meaning at all, the word must always be qualified by an adjective, and it is in the choice of adjectives that researchers reduce their scientific integrity by losing their objectivity; e.g., Lippitt and White's choice of "authoritarian" and "democratic" to describe climate.

longer in the room. Furthermore, the pattern a teacher develops in one year is likely to persist in his classroom the following year with completely different pupils. Second, when a teacher's integrative contacts increase, pupils show an increase in spontaneity and initiative, voluntary social contributions, and acts of problem-solving. Third, when a teacher's dominative contacts increase, the pupils are more easily distracted from schoolwork, and show greater compliance to, as well as rejection of, teacher domination.

A year or so after Anderson started his work, Lippitt and White (1943), working with Kurt Lewin, carried out laboratory experiments to analyze the effects of adult leaders' influence on boys' groups. The laboratory approach used had certain advantages (or disadvantages, depending on your point of view) in studying the effects of the adult leader's behavior. First, the contrasting patterns of leader behavior were purified and made more consistent as a result of training and role playing. Second, differences in the underlying personalities and appearances of the adult leaders were minimized through role rotation. Third, since there were only five boys to a group, the effect of the pattern of leader behavior was greater than it would have been in a classroom. Roughly speaking, the pattern Lippitt and White named "authoritarian leadership" consisted of dominative contacts, "democratic leadership" consisted of integrative contacts, and "laissez-faire leadership" consisted of irregular and infrequent integrative contacts with an element of indifference to the total group that is seldom found in a classroom and was not present in the studies of Anderson et al.

Most of the conclusions of the study by Lippitt and White confirm or extend the general conclusions of Anderson et al. with some semantic modification but very little change, if any, in behavioral meaning. From the point of view of classroom teaching, one interesting extension was the conceptualization of "dependence on the leader" by Lippitt and White. This is a state of affairs in which group members are unable to proceed without directions from the leader. Anderson et al. used the category "conforming to teacher domination," and thus noted its occurrence, but in the more concentrated social climates of the laboratory experiments it was clearly seen that extensive compliance occurs when there is a generalized condition of dependence.

As a result of these two basic and independent studies that produced mutually supportive results, the notion of social climate was established. Additional research revealed minor variations of the central theme already established. Withall (1949) showed that a simple classification of the teacher's verbal statements into seven categories produced an index of teacher behavior almost identical to the integrative-dominative (I-D) ratio of Anderson et al. Flanders (1951) created laboratory situations in which contrasting patterns of teacher behavior were exposed to one pupil at a time. A sustained dominative pattern was consistently disliked by pupils, reduced their ability to recall later on the material studied, and produced disruptive anxiety as indicated by galvanic skin response and changes in the heartbeat rates. Pupil reactions to integrative contacts showed these trends reversed. Perkins (1951), using Withall's technique, studied groups of teachers organized to study the topic of child growth and development. He found that greater learning about child growth and development occurred when group discussion was free to focus on that topic; groups with an integrative type of leader were able to do this more frequently than were groups led by a dominative type of leader. In a large cross-sectional study that did not use observation of spontaneous teacher behavior, Cogan (1956) administered a single paper-and-pencil instrument containing three scales to 987 eighth-grade students in 33 classrooms. On one scale, student perceptions of the teacher were assessed; on another scale, students reported how often they did required schoolwork; on the last scale, students reported how often they did extra, nonrequired schoolwork. Cogan's first scale assessed traits one would associate with the behavior patterns observed in the research already cited, although it was developed in terms of Murray's list of major personality needs (1938). The items of one pattern were grouped as "dominative," "aggressive," and "rejectant"; these correspond to Anderson's dominative and integrative patterns. Cogan found that students reported doing more assigned and extra schoolwork when they perceived the teacher's behavior as falling into the integrative pattern rather than the dominative pattern.

Altogether, these research projects support the statements about classroom climate that appear in the first paragraph of this section. The two teacher behavior patterns that create the contrasting classroom climates have been well established.

| *The integrative pattern*[2] | *The dominative pattern*[2] |
|---|---|
| a) Accepts, clarifies, and supports the ideas and feelings of pupils. | a) Expresses or lectures about own ideas or knowledge. |
| b) Praises and encourages. | b) Gives directions or orders. |
| c) Asks questions to stimulate pupil participation in decision making. | c) Criticizes or deprecates pupil behavior with intent to change it. |
| d) Asks questions to orient pupils to schoolwork. | d) Justifies his own position or authority. |

| *Associated attitudes of teacher (suggested by Cogan)* | | *Associated attitudes of teacher (suggested by Cogan)* | |
|---|---|---|---|
| Outgoing | Patient | Antisocial | Impatient |
| Good-natured | Self-effacing | Surly | Self-assertive |
| Friendly | Self-submissive | Spiteful | Self-centered |
| Cheerful | Responsive | Dour | Aloof |
| Trustful | | Hostile | |

2 Most of the researchers cited have their own favorite words to describe essentially the same behavior patterns. Anderson *et al.:* "dominative vs. integrative"; Lippitt and White: "authoritarian vs. democratic vs. laissez-faire"; Withall, Flanders, Perkins: "teacher-centered vs. student-centered"; and Cogan: "preclusive vs. inclusive." For the sake of simplicity, Anderson's terms have been used in the first section of this paper; the concepts of "direct influence" and "indirect influence" will be introduced later.

These research results should be interpreted with caution. They do not suggest that there is a single pattern of teacher behavior that should be continually maintained in the classroom. Anyone with teaching experience recognizes that there are situations in which an integrative teacher behavior pattern is less appropriate than a dominative pattern; furthermore, it is possible that identical acts by the teacher may in one situation be perceived by pupils as dominative and in another situation as integrative. These research results do show that, over a period of time, more integrative than dominative teacher-pupil contacts will establish desirable pupil attitudes and superior patterns of work. The work of Anderson *et al.* and Cogan presents evidence that a desirable climate results in more learning, although additional evidence is needed to confirm the conclusion.

### THE IMPLICATION OF RESEARCH ON
### CLASSROOM CLIMATE FOR
### A THEORY OF INSTRUCTION

Research on classroom climate is incomplete because it does not contribute to the question, "Why and when should a teacher react in either a dominative or integrative manner?" An adequate theory of instruction should specify the effects of integrative or dominative contacts for different types of situations that occur frequently in the classroom. In other words, there is a need for a dynamic explanation of how short-term patterns of teacher influence affect momentary situations so that the flexibility of the teacher's behavior is taken into account.

One clue that supports the notion that teachers probably are flexible in exerting dominative and integrative influences over short periods of time appears in the work of Mitzel and Rabinowitz (1953), who used Withall's technique to assess the classroom climate of four teachers. Their observation data were organized to permit an analysis of variance between teachers, visits, and observers. Since the median length of an observer's visit was about 20 minutes, the finding of statistically significant, wide variability among visits to the same teacher suggests that teachers adapt their influence to the immediate situation. There may be several reasons for the flexibility of teacher influence.

Teachers may adapt their influence to fit different phases of problem-solving that probably occur in the classroom. Bales and Strodtbeck (1951) have found that, in group problem-solving discussion, the quality of verbal interaction changes as the discussion progresses through phases of orientation, evaluation, and control.

Teachers may also adapt their influence to fit the needs of the individual pupil in contacts with single pupils. In two different studies involving college-age students, Wispe (1951) and Smith (1955) have shown that psychologically different types of students, identified by personality tests, have different reactions to the same teacher-behavior patterns. This was equally true of the two contrasting patterns used in each study, and, while the patterns were by no means identical to Anderson's dominative-integrative contrast, they were in many ways similar. Gage *et al.* (1956), in a study of elementary school children, found that pupils' perceptions of the same teacher were different according to whether the pupil could be classified as tending to seek "affective" or "cognitive" responses from a teacher.

Even though research on climate tends to ignore flexibility of teacher influence and is restricted to generalized, broad patterns of teacher behavior, it does make a fundamental contribution to a theory of instruction. This contribution consists of identifying general patterns of the teacher's influence that produce predictable pupil responses. Thus it establishes cause-and-effect principles that are true in the long run. However, the task of investigating flexibility of influence remains uninvestigated.

## TENTATIVE HYPOTHESES OF TEACHER INFLUENCE

The purpose of this section is to develop hypotheses of teacher influence that are consistent with generalizations about classroom climate but which account for flexibility of teacher influence. Most of the hypotheses are not yet supported by research evidence. If future experimentation provides evidence in support of the hypotheses, they may contribute to a theory of instruction.[3]

In the classroom, teacher-pupil relationships are essentially superior-subordinate in quality. The responsibility for classroom activities is the teacher's, and both the teacher and the pupils expect the teacher to take charge, to initiate, and to control the learning activities. The freedom to direct or not to direct the activities of others is initially given only to the teacher; whatever freedom pupils have in this respect results from the actions of the teacher. No pupil can consistently ignore the authority of the teacher, and it is most difficult and sometimes impossible for a pupil to escape from the teacher's control. In the discussion that follows, the word *dependence* refers to these essential qualities of a superior-subordinate relationship. The presence of dependence has already been noted in the work of Anderson and of Lippitt and White.

The opposite of dependence is *independence,* and since various degrees of dependence or independnce exist, they must be distinguished in the discussion that follows. *High dependence* refers to a condition in which pupils voluntarily seek additional ways of complying with the authority of the teacher. This condition has aptly been described by Lewin (1935, p. 132) as, "at every point within his (the pupil's) sphere of action he is internally controlled by the wishes of the adult (teacher)." He adds, later, that a pupil might even anticipate these wishes. *Medium dependence* refers to the

---

[3] For an initial consideration of a "theory of instruction" the author is indebted to Professor Herbert A. Thelen, University of Chicago. See "Toward a Theory of Instruction" (entire issue), *J. Educ. Res.,* Oct., 1951.

average classroom condition in which teacher direction is essential to initiate and guide activities but the pupils do not voluntarily solicit it. When it occurs they comply. *Low dependence* refers to a condition in which pupils react to teacher directions if they occur, but their present activities, usually teacher initiated, can be carried on without continued teacher direction. In the face of difficulties pupils prefer the teacher's help. *Independence* refers to a condition in which the pupils perceive their activities to be "self-directed" (even though the teacher may have helped create the perception) and they do not expect directions from the teacher. In the face of difficulties pupils prefer to at least try their own solutions before seeking the teacher's help. If teacher direction is given, pupils feel free to evaluate it in terms of the requirements of the learning activities.

Underlying the entire discussion that follows is the basic assumption that the learning potential of pupils is inversely related to their level of dependence within reasonable and practical limits of classroom organization. In a condition of high dependence a pupil is too concerned with his relationship to the teacher to be completely objective about the learning task. "Objectivity cannot arise in a constraint situation; it arises only in a situation of freedom." (Lewin, 1935, p. 178) No doubt there are philosophical values at issue here, but it is psychologically sound and logically self-evident to point out that the learning experience is distorted to the extent that the dependence present in the learning situation is not present in the situation in which the learning is applied. No pupil is ever completely independent of the teacher's authority, nor is anyone completely independent in society, but there are certain types of desirable educational objectives that can be achieved only in a situation involving the degrees of independence defined in the preceding paragraph. It is equally true that there are some limited objectives that can best be achieved in a condition of medium dependence, also defined above.

Conditions of dependence or independence are created by the teacher's choice of influence. One can conceive of *direct influence* and *indirect influence* which, under appropriate circumstances, determine the degree of dependence. These two kinds of influence can be defined, in terms of verbal behavior, as follows:

*Direct influence* consists of stating the teacher's own opinion or ideas, directing the pupil's action, criticizing his behavior, or justifying the teacher's authority or use of that authority.

*Indirect influence* consists of soliciting the opinions or ideas of the pupils, applying or enlarging on those opinions or ideas, praising or encouraging the participation of pupils, or clarifying and accepting their feelings.

It has been shown that the teacher's direct and indirect influence can be reliably assessed by observation in spontaneous classroom situations and that the dependence of pupils can also be assessed by observation or paper-and-pencil techniques.

If the flexibility of teacher influence is to be understood, a theory of teacher influence should explain why direct influence may increase or maintain dependence in one situation, and increase or maintain independence in another. The cues used consciously or unconsciously by a teacher to guide his choice of influence may arise from a *Gestalt* so complex as to defy conceptualization. In order to be parsimonious, the theory about to be conceptualized will employ the fewest number of variables that seem necessary to predict and understand the teacher's choice of influence.

One aspect of the classroom situation that should make a difference in the pupil's reaction to teacher influence is his perception of the learning goal and the methods of reaching that goal. One can conceive of a situation in which the goal and the methods of reaching the goal are clear to the pupil and another situation in which these are unclear. Certainly, when a student knows what he is doing, his reactions to teacher influence will not be the same as when he isn't sure of what he is doing. In order to distinguish between these two situations in the discussion that follows, references will be made to *clear goals* and *unclear goals*.

Another aspect of the goal in a learning situation is whether or not the goal is perceived by the student as desirable or undesirable. The attraction of a goal determines motivation[4] and this attribute of a goal has been designated by Lewin (1935, p. 77) as *positive valence* or *negative valence*. In the discussion that follows, a positive valence is assigned to goals that satisfy the interests of pupils *and* require goal activities that match their abilities. A negative valence is assigned to goals that fail to satisfy the interests of pupils and/or require activities that do not match their abilities.

By logical convention, an unclear goal has an unknown or neutral valence.

It should now be clear that the theory about to be developed will suggest that direct and indirect influence will have a different but predictable effect in situations in which (a) the goal is unclear, (b) the goal is clear with a positive valence, and (c) the goal is clear with a negative valence. The operational differences between these three situations, necessary for experimentation, are that (a) the pupils do not know what goal will develop, (b) the pupils know what the goal is, know what steps they will take to reach the goal, see necessary actions as matching their ability, and are very interested and satisfied to be working toward that goal, and (c) the pupils know what the goal is, what steps are necessary to reach the goal, may or may not see necessary actions as matching their ability, and are very uninterested and dissatisfied to be working toward that goal.

### SITUATIONS IN WHICH GOALS ARE UNCLEAR

Suppose one makes the following assumptions:

> *Assumption A:* There exists a drive in both the teacher and the pupils to establish a learning goal in the classroom and work toward that goal.

---

[4] Whether one refers to motivation as a "drive toward" or an "attraction to" a goal is irrelevant to the present discussion.

*Assumption B:* When the goal is unclear, the behavior of pupils participating in identifying and clarifying a goal is determined by the real or imagined restraints of the teacher's control.

This is to say that most pupils expect to work on "schoolwork" in the classroom; that in order to get started, they expect the teacher to initiate activities that will clarify a learning goal and spell out the steps required to reach the goal. In short, in a classroom with unclear goals, there exists a state of medium dependency.

*H 1.00* Indirect influence increases independence, when goals are unclear, by reducing the real or imagined restraints[5] of the teacher's control. ("H" will refer to "hypothesis"; "SH" to "sub-hypothesis.")

*SH 1.10* When restraints are at the barest minimum needed to coordinate class activity, pupils will have the maximum opportunity to express their interests in the goals suggested and to compare their abilities with the activities required.

*SH 1.20* Pupils who tend to be uncomfortable with minimum teacher restraints will need considerable support and encouragement, as part of the teacher's indirect influence, in order to continue to express their interests and to compare their abilities.

These hypotheses suggest that, when goals are unclear, the effect of indirect influence is to stimulate the expression of the pupils' interest, curiosity, and appreciation of several possible learning goals, and to evaluate these goals in terms of the methods required to reach them. To be realistic, the goals requirements should be within range of the abilities of the pupils. During this activity the teacher takes an active part by asking questions, praising and encouraging pupil participation, and expressing his own opinions primarily in terms of pupil ideas. In practice, the more mature judgment of the teacher is expressed by what he chooses to praise and the particular ideas he chooses to question or develop.

*H 2.00* Direct influence increases dependence, when goals are unclear, by maintaining or increasing the restraints of the teacher's control.

*SH 2.10* With high dependence or increasing medium dependence, direct influence results in overt compliance.

*SH 2.11* If the goals subsequently prove interesting and match the pupils' ability, the overt compliance will occur with inner acceptance.

---

5 "Restraints" is a word originally used by Lewin to refer to barriers. Here it refers to barriers the teacher sets to pupil behavior or that pupils imagine that the teacher sets. Included would be prohibitions, admonitions and imposed directions. The author recognizes that every teacher must set "minimum restraints," but he believes that if they are set reasonably, pupils will perceive a degree of freedom that permits disciplined self-direction. Technically, restraints refer to forces which exist in the pupil's social environment (life space).

*SH 2.12* If goals subsequently prove uninteresting or do not match the pupils' ability, the overt compliance will occur with inner resistance.

*SH 2.13* Either type of compliance maintains the restraints of the teacher's control and pupils will be more dependent throughout the entire process of reaching the goal, compared to goals identified with direct influence.

*SH 2.20* Pupils who are more comfortable in a dependent teacher relationship will actively solicit the teacher's direct influence when goals are unclear.

These hypotheses suggest that the effect of direct influence, when goals are unclear, is to increase, or at least maintain, the existing dependence of pupils on the teacher's control. Under these circumstances, direct influence restricts the alternative reactions of pupils to overt compliance. Festinger (Sherif and Wilson, 1953, pp. 232–256) has suggested that public compliance to group pressures can occur with private acceptance or without private acceptance; with a slight change in words, his analysis is adapted here as a reasonable outcome of direct influence. The notion that either type of compliance maintains a dependent relationship is, perhaps, most questionable in the case of overt compliance with inner acceptance. However, it can be argued that compliance is not so much a matter of working on an interesting or uninteresting goal as it is perception of the pupil that he must work on that goal only if he is to receive the approval of the teacher, who holds ultimate authority. The consequences of this perception will be discussed later.

Both SH 1.20 and SH 2.20 are tentative extensions of the work of Wispe, Smith, and Gage, whose studies of individual pupil reactions to various types of teacher influence have already been mentioned.

The hypotheses stated are presumed to hold whenever goals are unclear either for individual pupils or for the class as a whole, whether this occurs at the beginning, at the middle, or near the end of a particular learning cycle. Goals are most likely to be unclear for the total class during the initial phases of a learning cycle. However, it is a common experience to be working toward what appears to be a clear goal only to find, after some progress, that the original picture of the goal has become unrealistic. Barriers to progress lower goal clarity by changing the steps required to reach the goal. The incidence of unclear goal perceptions among pupils may be far more frequent at the beginning of a school year when pupils, teacher, subject, and methods are less understood. In general, unclear goals become clear with the passage of time, either suddenly or gradually, so long as efforts to reach the goal are maintained. Since perceptions of the goal are subject to individual differences, and some goals are more difficult to understand than others, a teacher must assume that there is a range of goal perceptions in a class at any given moment.

The development of positive or negative valence occurs simultaneously with the clarification of goals and methods of reaching goals. As soon as a pupil imagines a relationship between his interests and abilities and the nature of a goal, positive or negative valence is anticipated. Many pupils bring into the classroom a generalized anticipation of goal valence based on past experience, the previous class, or their attitudes toward the teacher. Indirect influence is particularly useful for clarifying such feelings and relating them to the present goal activities.

In the next two sections consideration is given to situations in which the goal and the goal activities are sufficiently clear for pupils to have definite positive or negative reactions toward the goal. But before these situations are discussed, it is necessary to examine more closely the meaning of dependence and independence when goals are clear.

As a goal becomes clear with a positive valence, a force toward the goal develops, action becomes rewarding, and the resultant pupil behavior is usually classified as "self-motivated." As a goal becomes clear with a negative valence, a force away from the goal develops, action becomes unrewarding, and if the resultant pupil behavior is oriented toward the goal, it is usually the result of a force created by the teacher through the use of reward or punishment. In this latter situation, medium or high dependence exists and pupils comply with forces that stem from teacher's authority. In the case of a clear, positive goal, dependence exists to the extent that the pupil reacts, either consciously or unconsciously, to forces that stem from the teacher's authority. This latter case is most clearly illustrated by the pupil who senses that his present enjoyment in working on a rewarding task is a "gift," or is permitted by the teacher. He expresses his dependence by appreciating the teacher as well as the nature of the task. In a practical problem-solving sense, his objectivity is distorted, since his decisions include judgments of what the teacher will approve or disapprove, as well as the more objective requirements of the problem. His behavior is the resultant of both the restraining forces set by the teacher and the force that results from the positive goal valence.

## SITUATIONS IN WHICH THE GOAL
## IS CLEAR WITH A POSITIVE VALENCE

With a clear, positive goal there is a strong force toward the goal which will be stable as long as the action satisfies the pupil's interests and his ability permits him to proceed. If the restraining forces set by the teacher are small compared with the valence force, the pupil's behavior will be relatively independent. If the restraining forces approach significance compared with the valence force, the dependence of the pupil will increase. The proportional balance of these two sets of forces depends on the use of direct or indirect influence when the goals are initially clarified and upon subsequent influence that the teacher provides.

*H 3.00* When the initial positive valence of a goal is clarified with indirect influence, the effect of subsequent direct or indirect influence on the existing independence is insignificant.

*SH 3.10* The tendency of subsequent direct influence to increase dependence, and indirect influence to decrease it, is greater when the influence is initiated by the teacher, compared with being solicited by pupils.

*SH 3.20* Independent progress toward a clear, positive goal reenforces the valence and provides pupils with objective criteria with which to evaluate teacher influence.

These hypotheses emphasize the primary goal orientation of an independent pupil moving successfully toward a clear, positive goal. Teacher influence solicited by pupils is likely to have a goal orientation and, as such, will not affect independence. Influence initiated by the teacher is unlikely to affect independence unless the pupil fails to see a relationship between such influence and the goal; e.g., when the teacher attempts to change to a completely different goal. Under these conditions, which include a maximum of independent goal orientation and a minimum of teacher restraints, barriers to progress are more likely to appear as an intellectual challenge. With proper teacher stimulation and direct challenge there will be an opportunity to enrich the problem-solving experience by stretching the goal requirements to the limit of pupil ability without loss of positive valence.

In the case of a clear goal with a positive valence that was developed with direct influence, the restraining forces set by the teacher would be of sufficient magnitude to affect the pupil's behavior. However, successful progress toward a positive goal may modify the original dependence. This modification is probably due to the development of the valence force, and not to a decrease in the restraining forces; on this point, however, different interpretations are certainly possible. Lewin (1935, p. 169) would suggest that the decrease in restraining forces would be more likely to occur with younger children, provided that the goal activities are truly rewarding. With older children, the realization that the original direct influence was, in a sense, unjustified would increase the pupil's awareness of the restraining forces. Although the dynamics of this situation are not yet clear, the author is disposed to suggest the following hypotheses, primarily because dependence is easier to create during initial stages than it is to diminish in later stages.

*H 4.00* When the initial positive valence of a goal is clarified with direct influence, subsequent direct influence maintains or increases existing dependence, and subsequent indirect influence decreases existing dependence only slightly, if at all.

*SH 4.10* If a goal that is initiated with direct influence develops a positive valence, the existing dependence of the pupils is reenforced by the rewarding experience.

*SH 4.20* Direct influence during initial clarification of positive goals, followed by indirect influence, maintains existing dependence if pupils become aware of the inconsistency in the teacher's influence.

These hypotheses suggest, in effect, that once dependence is established, under conditions of H 2.00, it is not likely to decrease even if the learning goal develops a positive valence.

## SITUATIONS IN WHICH THE GOAL
## IS CLEAR WITH A NEGATIVE VALENCE

In this situation the actions of both the teacher and pupils are limited. The teacher usually attempts to maintain the restricted learning possibilities by exerting direct influence through either reward or punishment. The only other alternative is to attempt to change the valence of the goal. This second alternative will be considered first.

Dislike of a goal or the activities required to reach a goal depends on the total perceptual field of the pupil. He may think the task too difficult, too tedious, of no future value, or he may simply dislike the teacher. The reorganization of the pupil's perceptual field is best facilitated by indirect influence that clarifies and supports the pupil's diagnosis of his own difficulties. Successfully carried out, the process is very similar to initiating a new goal. A resourceful teacher recognizes that it is the pupil's perception that must be changed, that only he can change it, and that the change can often occur with only minor alterations in the nature of the goal or goal activities. In fact, the same task, imbedded in a different perceptual organization, may take on a completely different valence. (Lewin, 1935, p. 168)

*H 5.00* A shift from negative to positive goal valence is most likely to occur in response to indirect influence by the teacher.

The analysis of situations involving reward and punishment has already been carried out by Lewin (1935, pp. 114–170) and an analysis of compliant behavior has been published by Festinger (Sherif and Wilson, 1953, pp. 232–256). In both references there are many principles which apply directly to the classroom and are related to direct influence, compliance, and dependence. In nearly every classroom, reward or punishment is never used alone; instead, the two are used in combination. The essence of direct influence with the threat of punishment or possibility of reward is the creation of a conflict situation which restricts the pupil's freedom and narrows the alternative actions of the pupil to one or two that the teacher desires. The maintenance of these restrictions requires alert and active surveillance of pupil behavior by the teacher because there are usually a few pupils who are willing and able to test the limits of their freedom in imaginative and unusual ways. With negative goal valence, if the threat of punishment is relaxed or if rewards are unfulfilled, action toward the goal decreases or stops. Thus, high dependence is maintained at all times.

## SUMMARY AND CONCLUSIONS

The major purpose in reviewing research on classroom climate and in developing hypotheses about the effects on direct and indirect teacher influence is to explain variability of teacher influence. In considering, first, situations in which goals are unclear, and, second, situations in which goals are clear, different effects of the same teacher behavior were hypothesized.

A general assumption underlying the discussion is that in the control of classroom learning, there are times when direct influence is most appropriate and other times when indirect influence is most appropriate. At first glance, this assumption may appear to conflict with the findings of research on classroom climate. However, a careful study of the data collected indicates that in all types of classroom situations, both direct and indirect influence occurred. A widespread misinterpretation of research on classroom climate has been that direct influence should be avoided in the classroom. H 3.00 suggests that there will be no change in dependence when direct influence is exerted during periods when goals are clear. In fact, direct influence related to a clear goal may provide opportunities to challenge the ideas and conclusions of the pupil and to enrich the learning process.

The contrast between the predictions of H 1.00 and H 2.00 and those of H 3.00, provides a tentative explanation of why direct or indirect influence may have different outcomes in different situations.

Many factors have been ignored in this initial statement of teacher influence. Some data have already been collected suggesting that younger pupils, ages five through seven, do not react to direct influence in the same way as older pupils. If this trend is supported, some modification of H 1.00 and H 2.00 will be required that takes into account the age of the pupils. Data from the classrooms of older pupils also suggest that certain kinds of learning activities can be introduced into classrooms with what appears to be almost instantaneous goal clarity. If this is true, such activities may be unrelated to H 1.00 and H 2.00. Data from high school classes suggest that certain topics such as mathematics and science are normally associated with a higher proportion of direct influence, although, at the moment, this should be considered as no more than a commentary on current school practice.

No effort has been made in the present article to indicate how patterns of direct influence can be modified by using group activities in the classroom. It may be that the teacher who uses group methods can control dependence by making appropriate shifts in the classroom group organization. Finally, there are certain obvious relationships between the hypotheses of teacher influence, principles of counseling, and the trainer's role in group therapy that have not been developed.

## REFERENCES

ANDERSON, H. H., et al., 'Studies of teachers' classroom personalities,' III. (Follow-up of the effects of dominative and integrative contacts on children's behavior.) Stanford: Stanford University Press, 1946.

BALES, R. F., and F. L. STRODTBECK, Phases in group problem solving, *Journal of Abnormal and Social Psychology*, 1951:46, 458–96.

COGAN, M. L., Theory and design of a study of teacher-pupil interaction, *Harvard Educational Review*, 1956:26, 315–42.

Flanders, N. A., Personal-social anxiety as a factor in experimental learning situations, *Journal of Educational Research,* 1951:45, 100–10.

Gage, N. L., et al., Teachers' understanding of their pupils and pupils' ratings of their teachers, *Psychological Monograph: General and Applied,* 1956: 406–21.

Lewin, K., *Dynamic Theory of Personality.* New York: McGraw-Hill, 1935.

Lippitt, R., and R. K. White, The 'social climate' of children's groups, in *Child Behavior and Development,* R. G. Barker, J. S. Kounin and H. F. Wright (eds.). New York: McGraw-Hill, 1943.

Mitzel, H. E., and W. Rabinowitz, Assessing social-emotional climate in the classroom by Withall's Technique, *Psychological Monographs,* 1953:67, No. 18.

Murray, H. A., *Explorations in Personality.* New York: Oxford University Press, 1938.

Perkins, H. V., Climate influences group learning, *Journal of Educational Research,* 1951:45, 115–19.

Sherif, M., and M. P. Wilson (eds.), *Group Relations at the Crossroad.* New York: Harper, 1953.

Smith, D. E. P., Fit teaching methods to personality structure, *High School Journal,* 1955:39, 167–71.

Wispe, L. G., Evaluating section teaching methods in the introductory courses, *Journal of Educational Research,* 1951:45, 161–86.

Withall, J., The development of a technique for the measurement of social-emotional climate in classrooms, *Journal of Experimental Education,* 1949:17, 347–61.

R. D. KITCHEN

# 27.   JEAN PIAGET AND THE TEACHER

## INTRODUCTION

For the past forty years Jean Piaget, a Swiss psychologist, has carried out numerous experimental studies into the processes of children's intellectual development. His published works range over the language and thought of children,[1] their ability to reason and form judgments about their physical

Reprinted from *The Forum of Education,* Vol. XXVIII, No. 1 (March 1969), by permission of the author and publisher.

[1] Piaget, J.: *The Language and Thought of the Child.* London: Routledge and Kegan Paul, 1926.

world,[2] their conception of number[3] and reality,[4] and other mental operations. All these studies provide mutually supporting evidence for his belief that intellectual growth[5, 6] stems from an individual's active interaction with his environment. Unlike many of his contemporaries, who have seen intelligence as a fairly fixed and rather undefinable quantity, Piaget elaborates upon a number of major stages in intellectual growth; the sensori-motor period, preoperational and intuitive thought, and concrete and formal operations in thinking.

His original and stimulating work and the supporting results of further studies are having a considerable effect on curricula content and teaching methods, particularly in mathematics. It is being increasingly recognized that children, especially at the primary stage, need a variety of experiences with tangible and visible objects to help them build up the essential basic concepts for an understanding of their environment. This kind of practical and active experience appears necessary as a basis for the development of more difficult and abstract modes of thinking at the adolescent and adult stages.[7]

## INTELLECTUAL GROWTH

According to Piaget, the starting point of a child's intellectual development is not sensory perception or anything pressed upon him from outside, but is an internal and continuous growth, stemming from his own actions. In the most literal and physical sense of the term, these actions govern his life from the very beginning. It is through his own activities that he gains new and ever widening experiences of his surroundings. Each child takes a controlling hand in procuring and organizing his contact with the outside world. A baby in a cot, for example, turns his head, moves his eyes and explores with them. He grips with his hands, lets go, pushes and gains knowledge of the objects around him. Through constant repetition of these same actions, he builds up internally mental structures of his environment. In fact, it is his actions which fashion and shape his viewpoint, support it, and provide him with the essential key to his understanding.

As the baby grows, he becomes involved in more and more complex procedures, partly to fit himself into this world, and partly to fit it to himself. It is an adaptive process whereby he "assimilates," or takes in mentally his

2 Piaget, J.: *Judgment and Reasoning in the Child.* London: Routledge and Kegan Paul, 1928.

3 Piaget, J.: *The Child's Conception of Number.* London: Routledge and Kegan Paul, 1952.

4 Piaget, J.: *The Construction of Reality in the Child.* London: Routledge and Kegan Paul, 1954.

5 Piaget, J.: *The Psychology of Intelligence.* London: Routledge and Kegan Paul, 1950.

6 Piaget, J.: *The Origins of Intelligence in Children.* London: Routledge and Kegan Paul, 1952.

7 Piaget, J.: *Les Mécanismes Perceptifs.* Paris: Universitaires de Paris, 1961.

surroundings, like an organism assimilating food. He also fits himself to his environment. That is, he "accommodates" himself to the objects and people outside himself. He has to learn, for example, that some things are hard, others soft; some small, others big; and each needs to be handled in a particular way. These distinguishing features he accepts and acknowledges as he adapts himself to the nature of his surroundings.

These patterns and processes of assimilation and accommodation are, for Piaget, chief factors in intellectual growth, and both functions are present in every intellectual act. They both lead towards a "state of equilibrium" in the human being. That is, in simplest terms, each individual strives to arrive at a meaningful and realistic understanding of his environment. This is attained when a balance, or state of equilibrium, prevails between assimilation and accommodation.

Experiments with young babies led Piaget to state that, in the earliest months, they have no awareness of the world outside themselves. A young baby has sensations and is capable of making movements, but has no knowledge of the objects or things that surround him. He has no awareness of their existence as something permanent outside himself. In the earliest months, a baby reacts to objects presented to him as a rattle, doll, or feeding bottle, but if these same objects are placed out of sight, he gives no indication of being aware of their existence and makes no attempts to search for them.

At this time, however, the constant appearance of the same object gives a baby opportunity and experience in acquiring movements of touch, feeling and seeing. These repeated actions with the same objects allow him to build up an awareness of them. The process has to continue for many months, for it is not until about the age of two years that a child appears capable of accepting the existence of an object and looks for it if out of sight. Piaget maintains that children build up an internal structure of objects in gradual sequential stages over these first two years. Perhaps the playful child who throws an object from his pram for others to pick up, and return to him, is confirming his recent achievement. He has come to realize that objects have a permanence, identity and existence of their own.

Following upon the sensori-motor stage of the first two years, a young child gradually becomes able to identify different objects and separates them to some extent from each other. He begins to place objects into groups, as apple, pear, and orange under "fruit", but he has not yet the means of grouping objects into sub-groups. Each of his judgments at this stage, the preoperational, is isolated and self-sufficient. For example, if some wooden beads which may be brown in colour with a few white beads added are given to a child, he may judge that there are more brown beads than wooden beads. He finds it impossible at this period to reason about the whole (in this instance, wooden beads) and its parts (the two colours) at the same time.

With increasing age and experience; through looking, handling, manipulating; through striving to walk, talk and through the mastery of every kind of new activity, a child enlarges and organizes internally his view of the world. His actions become progressively internalized through learning of language and his expanding experience in play till they culminate in a more organized scheme of mental operations. A child builds up within him a kind of working model of his surroundings to which he refers in his thinking. This structure remains basically the same, but he enriches it and enlarges upon it. He draws upon it in his thinking and behaviour, and relies upon it when he has to think out a course of action. It is his internal model of the real world.

### PRIMARY SCHOOL AGE

A young child of about school age continues incessantly expanding, enriching, organizing and re-organizing this inward model of his surroundings. He develops konwledge by experimenting, through combining questions with listening and talking. He extends his world by being able to walk further, manipulate paper, cloth and other materials. He is beginning to extend his activities through more contact with children of his own age; with them he explores. He is constantly repeating actions and gaining greater confidence in his physical and mental abilities. Yet, most of his thoughts and ideas tend to be vague and unstable. His thinking depends upon present activities, upon the "here and now" situation, and he is lost if he moves away from the visible and tangible objects before him. According to Piaget, a child's mind at this period of growth is in a stage of flux; nothing is clear or stays put. The judgments of most five year old children are uncertain, fragmentary and lack clear settled notions. Their thoughts are "intuitive". If, for example, a child at this stage is presented with two balls of plasticine made up of equal amounts he will admit they are equal. But if one of them is drawn out to sausage shape, he will probably say that the sausage shape has more plasticine because it is longer or thinner.

It is a period of half-truths, for he is able to count and give an impression of being number-wise, but he most likely cannot match two groups of objects, arrange members of a class in order of size, judge two amounts of beads in a jar as equal, even after counting them one by one into the jar. In other words, a child of around five years old, may have learnt to count correctly ten bricks or other objects when placed before him. But, if these same objects are piled up together, or re-arranged in a more complex pattern of say four together, another four, then two, he will not always give the correct total answer of ten objects. Piaget[3] has shown repeatedly that "there is no connection between the acquired ability to count and the actual operations of which the child is capable." That a child can count is no sure sign that he understands the principles of number essential to a fundamental knowledge of mathematics.

To count intelligently, a child must first understand the one-to-one correspondence between one object and another object; to understand the oneness of one, and its relationship to another object. It is obvious that until children do fully understand the relationship of objects to each other, calculations on a blackboard or on paper with the symbols "4" plus "4" plus "2," or any other combination have only very limited meaning. An understanding of the underlying principles in mathematics cannot be implanted by rote-learning into a individual child, like an imprint upon a plastic record. Children need time and opportunity to compare and contrast objects of different size and shape. They have to learn by their own actions, through manipulations and seeing for themselves, the meaning of "much," "less," "less than," "more than," "equal to," and other basic mathematical notions.

It is during the primary stage that a child's actions on the environment becomes more and more internalized, resulting in an ability to classify objects into size, shape, and work with numbers. His mental system of operations (internalized actions) begins to take on a simple logical basis that gives order to his world. He attains "reversibility" of thought, that is, when he is faced with such problems as the "sausage" problem mentioned earlier, he is no longer led astray by perceptual features. Mental operations can revert back, stabilizing his judgments. He can now "conserve" the quantity and know that whatever the shape of a ball of plasticine may be pulled into, it remains the same in quantity. A child's intellectual structure at this period is defined as a "concrete" operation, that is a reversible internalized action.

These new achievements appear to be the direct result of playing and working with real objects, particularly in school. Beard,[8] testing children's conceptions of conservation in primary schools, concluded that experience and opportunity to play with water, see-saw balances and other play objects are an important part of helping a child to obtain an understanding of conservation. On the other hand, a recent attempt[9] in Canada to develop formal "training techniques" in school to encourage the development of conservation and reversibility were not successful.

Not all children attain conservation and reversibility at the same age. Lovell,[10] reporting research in an English junior school, examined 322 children individually to study the growth of the concept of conservation of substance. He noted that at an age of seven years plus, only 36 percent of the total number of children tested had attained the concept of conservation, and that even at the age of 10 years plus, 14 percent had no understanding that quantity remained the same, whatever the change in shape. His results

[8] Beard, R. M.: The order of concept development in two fields. Section I, *Educational Review*, 15.2, Section II, *Educational Review*, 15.3., 1963.

[9] Mermelstein, E. and others: The training techniques for the concept of conservation. Edmonton: *Alberta Jour. Educ. Research*, XIII. 3., 185–200, September, 1967.

[10] Lovell, K.: *The Growth of Mathematical and Scientific Concepts in Children*. London: University of London, 1961.

would seem to suggest that there lies a wide difference in individual attainment in the understanding of the concept of conservation.

It is highly probable that slower learning children fail to achieve real understanding of their school work, and merely follow the rote-learning processes of habit and repetition. Academic instruction can go beyond a child's actual intellectual growth, so that he counts and writes without fully grasping the essential basis of his work. He performs a school task like a "good boy"—or like a good parrot! The mind of a child can only deal effectively with a quantity of material, a glass of water, or a number of objects, if they are understood to remain permanent in amount and independent of any re-arrangement of their individual parts.

Peel[11] quotes an experimental study on Piagetian lines to test children's logical judgments. A number of questions, based on simple historical passages, were graded to different levels of mental growth. From the children's answers, it was evident that a young child is unable to reason about or explain set passages, except within the contents of the passages themselves, and is not able to see causal relationships. Peel argues that the results obtained imply, "...more active questioning, answering and discussion in relation to reading in History and English would do much more than passive reading in providing concrete experience (parallel to that of handling models and materials in arithmetic, geography and simple science) necessary for a child to progress to the stage of being able to reason more formally."

If we agree with Piaget's insistence that intellectual growth depends upon an individual's active interaction with his environment, then children must be given more opportunity in our primary schools to learn for themselves the basic principles, the master ideas, that underlie the world in which they live and play. Teachers need greater freedom to provide for the right kind of learning-teaching situations within the classroom and school. Piaget's work emphasizes again and again, how necessary it is to understand the laws of a child's internal growth, and by cooperating with these laws, draw upon them to lead him on, and guide him through his active interest. By so doing, teachers can then give opportunity for real understanding to take place.

Churchill,[12] summing up the results of a teachers' conference, wrote, "It was generally agreed that one of the problems even today, is still that too many teachers see their role as one of imparting information and that it would be very useful if more headteachers could be persuaded to release teachers from a syllabus to be covered and a standard to be reached. What

11 Peel, E. A.: Experimental examination of some of Piaget's schemata concerning children's perception and thinking, and a discussion of their educational significance. *Brit. J. Educ. Psychol.* XXIX. 89–103, 1959.

12 Churchill, E. M.: *Piaget's Findings and the Teacher*. London: National Froebel Foundation, 1961, pp. 12–13.

matters is that children are active, inquiring and experimenting and that where this is happening teachers learn as well as the children and come in time to provide increasingly challenging and satisfying experience for them."

The new approach to science in the primary school is essentially an active way of finding out about the immediate environment, and often forms the basis of what goes on at other times in reading, writing, talking, art and other subjects. According to one science teacher's experience[13] in an English junior school, this approach allows children to learn more effectively, because they become involved in practical problems which arise from their own questions and enquiries. He tells us that he "...does not decide in advance what will be studied and then proceeds to direct the children along preconceived paths." Rather he encourages discussion and offers suggestions towards further discovery on active lines. Some of his children, for example, finding that the cog in the centre of a bicycle wheel would turn only in one direction, got together as a group to investigate gears, ball bearings and other related items. There followed a lively amount of mathematics. This kind of activity supports one of Piaget's major tenets, stressed from his earliest writings, that group activities liberate the child from his egocentricism. Social cooperation is one of the principal formative factors in intellectual growth.

During most of the primary stage, a child's thinking is limited by being tied to tangible and visible objects, for he can only deal satisfactorily with a "real" world. He is unable to consider possible explanations and form hypotheses. In addition, his thought processes do not form as yet an integral comprehensive mental system of operations for general application. It is not until he attains the next stage in thinking, the "formal" stage, that he begins to work out problems on lines similar to that of the adult.

### SECONDARY SCHOOL AGE

Towards the beginning of the secondary school stage pupils start to carry out logical operations on symbolic and abstract material. They can refer to objects that are not visible to them and classify them into sub-groups. For example, they can understand "fruit" as a collective term, and relate it to apple, orange, pear; sweet, sour; cooking; eating; large, small and other distinguishing features. They can make decisions as a result of their mental abstract operations. The arithmetical calculations at the earlier stage which were carried out best on actual quantities of material and objects, can be coped with at this later period in arithmetical symbols of quantities. The underlying process is the capacity to operate internally with abstract entities.

Piaget and a colleague Inhelder[14] have demonstrated that young adoles-

---

13 Rose, A. J.: The science scene. *New Education*, 2.4., 10–13, April, 1966.
14 Inhelder, B. and Piaget, J.: *The Growth of Logical Thinking*. London: Routledge and Kegan Paul, 1958, p. 72.

cents begin to be concerned with possibilities and probable explanations. They start to free their thinking from slavish concern about "real" things, and become involved in trying to envisage relationships which might or might not be true to data. They begin to grope with possible answers, and from manipulations of their mental operations, deduce certain conclusions. They calculate with more variables, and know that if they fill, for example, a kettle with water, place it on a stove, and according to the heat applied and quantity of water, it will boil in so many minutes.

An essential element of this hypothesis formulation is an ability to create in the mind relationships between symbolic representations. Young children at the primary stage would have no difficulty in saying who was the fastest runner in a race, but not until the "formal" stage of thinking is reached, would they be able to reason out in a formal way, the following problem. "John runs faster than Bill. Tom runs slower than Bill. Who runs the fastest?"

Formal operations are ways of transforming propositions about reality so that the relevant variable can be isolated and relations between them deduced. They enable a student to combine propositions internally, and to isolate in an abstract way those which confirm his hypothesis. For instance, a young adolescent can find out a certain number of facts about rods of metal and formulate them as propositions from which to hypothesise about the determinants of flexibility. He maybe says to himself; "This rod is made of steel. It is long. This rod is steel, but shorter" and then on to, "This rod is made of brass" and so on. From experiments with such rods, a student can discover that long steel rods bend, but a short brass rod does not. According to Piaget, it is an adolescent's combinatorial system of mental structures which enable him to manipulate a combination of facts.

To gain further information about adolescents' capacity to reason and note differences from young children, Piaget and Inhelder carried out many experiments. One of the better known is the "Oscillation of a Pendulum." The problem utilizes a simple apparatus consisting of string which can be shortened or lengthened and a set of varying weights. The other variables that might be considered relevant by the student are the height of the release point and the force of the push given to the weight to make is swing. The subject is asked to explain the varying frequency of oscillation. That is, what makes the pendulum go fast or slow—the weight, the push, the height, or the length of string?

The solution to the problem lies in isolating the length of string from the other variables, and thereby gaining an understanding of the principle involved. When, however, this experiment is given to a child at the "intuitive" stage of thinking the subject's physical action dominates his mental operations, and nearly all his explanations imply the real cause of the variations in frequency of the oscillations is due to his pushes. The child at this stage is unable to give an objective account of the experiment or give consistent explanations.

At the "concrete" stage, subjects can vary the length of string serially, and judge differences in oscillations. That is, they generally achieve correspondence, but are unable to separate the variables and draw conclusions. Inhelder and Piaget[14] state that at this stage "...it is evident that the subjects still lack some logical instrument for interpreting the experimental data and that their failure to separate out the factors is not simply the result of mental laziness." The thinking of adolescents differs fundamentally from that of the child.

The formulation of hypotheses and the testing of them against actual data appears to form an essential part of adolescent thinking. Adolescents seek explanations, reasons and answers to the many problems that daily confront them, and school subjects appropriately taught can form a strong link with the environment in which they live.

Progress in school depends much upon pupils' capacity to think, and as teachers we ought to promote intellectual growth at all levels of school work. We need to give ample opportunity for effective mental operations. Piaget's studies emphasize the psychological gulf that lies between "true learning" that is "growth", and the so-called learning that comes from mere verbal training, habit formation, and the mechanical mastery of skills. True learning develops through "doing" and genuine understanding.

Possibly the new science projects at secondary level[15] are beginning to give a lead for "discovery through doing" is their keystone. Many science teachers are guided by the belief that "...the best way to awaken original thinking in children studying science is to engage them in experiments and practical enquiry." Traditional science tends to confirm foregone conclusions which, according to one writer[16] is "damaging to lively minds."

## CONCLUSIONS

Jean Piaget, possibly more than any other writer, has shown how children build up a structural model of the world in their minds as they interact with their environment. He has demonstrated that children are not born with this knowledge, nor is it an automatic growth, but has to be constructed internally piece by piece from birth on a very active basis. Thought processes evolve in accord with an identifiable developmental direction which he prescribes into major stages.

During the first two years, a child learns to coordinate sense and movement, and give direction to his movements. Through active manipulation of objects and substances, there comes knowledge of some of the fundamental concepts in his environment. These processes form the basis for the growth of

[15] Nuffield Foundation, *Science Teaching Report*. Longmans-Penguin Books, October, 1964, p. 15.
[16] Schools Council, *Science for the Young School Leaver*. Working Paper No. 1. London: H.M.S.O., 1966.

abstract and propositional thinking with symbolic material at the formal stage in adolescence.

The educational implications of Piaget's studies are many. For teachers concerned with curricula planning and methodology, his work provides a detailed normative frame of reference about cognitive structures. If a teacher has an idea of what and how children are likely to think at a given stage, some idea of children's possibilities and limitations, whether they are likely to understand their school work, then much greater harmony and achievement between child and teacher must ensue.

One of the most important aspects of Piaget's teaching is that a child must experience and manipulate material objects and substances to develop his intellectual powers. Stable and enduring learning about the world in which he lives comes about only through a very active intercourse with the world on the part of the learner. The teacher's task is to give pupils at all stages of learning opportunity for them to learn from their own experiences. What matters most is not verbal learning of rules and facts but growth of complex functional structures or internal organizations that permit children to understand their environment in a meaningful way.

JEROME S. BRUNER

# 28.  LEARNING AND THINKING

I

I have been engaged, these last few years, in research on what makes it possible for organisms—human and subhuman alike—to take advantage of past learning in attempting to deal with and master new problems before them now. It is a problem with a deceptively simple ring to it. In pursuit of it, my colleagues and I have found ourselves observing children in schoolrooms, watching them learning. It has been a revealing experience.

We have come to recognize in this work that one of the principal objectives of learning is to save us from subsequent learning. This seems a

Reprinted from *Harvard Educational Review,* Vol. 29, No. 3 (Summer 1959), 184–92, by permission of the author and publisher. Copyright © 1959 by the President and Fellows of Harvard College.

paradox, but it is not. Another way of putting the matter is to say that when we learn something, the objective is to learn it in such a way that we get a maximum of travel out of what we have learned. A homely example is provided by the relationship in arithmetic between addition and multiplication. If the principle of addition has been grasped in its deeper sense, in its generic sense, then it is unnecessary to learn multiplication. For, in principle, multiplication is only repeated addition. It is not, as we would say in our curricula, another "unit."

Learning something in a generic way is like leaping over a barrier. On the other side of the barrier is thinking. When the generic has been grasped, it is then that we are able to recognize the new problems we encounter as exemplars of old principles we have mastered. Once over the barrier, we are able to benefit from what William James long ago called "the electric sense of analogy."

There are two interesting features in generic learning—in the kind of learning that permit us to cross the barrier into thinking. One of them is *organization;* the other is *manipulation.* If we are to use our past learning, we must organize it in such a way that it is no longer bound to the specific situation in which the learning occurred. Let me give an example from the history of science. It would have been possible for Galileo to have published a handbook of the distances traversed per unit time by falling bodies. School boys for centuries thereafter could easily have been tortured by the task of having to remember the Galilean tables. Such tables, cumbersome though they might have been, would have contained all the necessary information for dealing with free-falling bodies. Instead, Galileo had the inspiration to reorganize this welter of information into a highly simplified form. You recall the compact expression $S = \frac{1}{2}gt^2$: it not only summarizes all possible handbooks but organizes their knowledge in a way that makes manipulation possible. Not only do we know the distances fallen, but we can use the knowledge for bodies that fall anywhere, in any gravitational field—not just our own.

One of the most notable things about the human mind is its limited capacity for dealing at any one moment with diverse arrays of information. It has been known for a long time that we can deal only with about seven independent items of information at once; beyond that point we exceed our "channel capacity," to use our current jargon. We simply cannot manipulate large masses of information. Because of these limits, we must condense and recode. The seven things we deal with must be worth their weight. A simple formula that can regenerate the distance fallen by any free body, past or future, is under these conditions highly nutritious for its weight. Good organization achieves the kind of economical representation of facts that makes it possible to use the facts in the future. Sheer brute learning, noble though it may be, is not enough. Facts simply learned without a generic organization are the naked and useless untruth. The proper reward of learning is not that it pleases the teacher or the parents, nor is it that we become "quiz kids." The proper reward is that we can now use what we have learned, can cross the barrier from learning into thinking. Are we mindful of these matters in our conduct of teaching?

What has been said thus far must seem singularly lacking in relevance to magic, to art, and to poetry. It appears to relate principally to the learning of mathematics, science, and the social studies. But there is an analogous point to be made about the learning of the arts and literature. If one has read literature and beheld works of art in such a way as to be able to think with their aid, then one has also grasped a deeper, simplifying principle. The underlying principle that gives one the power to use literature and the arts in one's thinking is not of the order of a generic condensation of knowledge. Rather it is metaphoric in nature, and perhaps the best way of describing this class of principles is to call them guiding myths.

Let me take an example from mythology. Recall when you read for the first time the story of Perseus slaying the hateful Medusa. You recall that to look directly upon the Medusa was to be turned to stone. The secret of Perseus was to direct the killing thrust of his sword by the reflection of Medusa on his polished shield. It is an exciting story, full of the ingenuity that Hercules had taught us to expect. Beneath the story, beneath all great stories, there is a deeper metaphoric meaning. I did not understand this meaning for many years, indeed, not until my son asked me what the myth of Perseus "meant." It occurred to me that the polished shield might symbolize all of the devices by which we are able to take action against evil without becoming contaminated by it. The law suggested itself as one such device, enabling us to act against those who trespassed against morality without ourselves having to trespass in our action. I do not wish to hold a brief for my interpretation of the Perseus myth. But I would like to make one point about it.

Man must cope with a relatively limited number of plights—birth, growth, loneliness, the passions, death, and not very many more. They are plights that are neither solved nor by-passed by being "adjusted." An adjusted man must face his passions just as surely as he faces death. I would urge that a grasp of the basic plights through the basic myths of art and literature provides the organizing principle by which knowledge of the human condition is rendered into a form that makes thinking possible, by which we go beyond learning to the use of knowledge. I am not suggesting that the Greek myths are better than other forms of literature. I urge simply that there be exposure to, and interpretation of, literature that deals deeply with the human condition. I have learned as much from Charley Brown of *Peanuts* as I have learned from Perseus. The pablum school readers, stripped of rich imagery in the interest of "readability," stripped of passion in the erroneous belief that the deeper human condition will not interest the child—these are no more the vehicles for getting over the barrier to thinking than are the methods of teaching mathematics by a rote parroting at the blackboard.

II

I should like to consider now some conditions in our schools today that promote and inhibit progress across the barrier from learning to thinking. I should point out in advance that I am not very cheerful on this subject.

### THE PASSIVITY OF KNOWLEDGE-GETTING

I have been struck during the past year or so, sitting in classrooms as an observer, by the passivity of the process we call education. The emphasis is upon gaining and storing information, gaining it and storing it in the form in which it is presented. We carry the remainder in long division so, peaches are grown in Georgia, transportation is vital to cities, New York is our largest port, and so on. Can the facts or the methods presented be mimicked? If so, the unit is at an end. There is little effort indeed which goes into the process of putting the information together, finding out what is generic about it. Long division is a skill, like threading a needle. The excitement of it as a method of partitioning things that relates it to such matters as subtraction is rarely stressed. One of the great inventions of man—elementary number theory—is presented as a cookbook. I have yet to see a teacher present one way of doing division and then put it squarely to the class to suggest six other ways of doing it—for there are at least six other ways of doing it than any one that might be taught in a school. So too with algebra. Algebra is not a set of rules for manipulating numbers and letters except in a trivial sense. It is a way of thinking, a way of coping with the drama of the unkonwn. Lincoln Steffens, in his *Autobiography,* complains upon his graduation from the University of California that his teachers had taught him only of the known, how to commit it to mind, and had done little to instruct him in the art of approaching the unknown, the art of posing questions. How does one ask questions about the unknown? Well, algebra is one technique, the technique for arranging the known in such a way that one is enabled to discern the value of an unknown quantity. It is an enriching strategy, algebra, but only if it is grasped as an extended instance of common sense.

Once I did see a teacher specifically encourage a class to organize and use minimal information to draw a maximum number of inferences. The teacher modeled his technique, I suppose, on the tried method of the storyteller. He presented the beginnings of the Whiskey Rebellion and said to his pupils, much in the manner of Ellery Queen speaking to his readers, "You now have enough to reconstruct the rest of the story. Let's see if we can do it." He was urging them to cross the barrier from learning into thinking. It is unhappily true that this is a rare exception in our schools.

So knowledge-getting becomes passive. Thinking is the reward for learning, and we may be systematically depriving our students of this reward as far as school learning is concerned.

One experiment which I can report provides encouragement. It was devised and carried out by the research group with which I am associated at Harvard in collaboration with teachers in the fifth grade of a good public school. It is on the unpromising topic of the geography of the North Central States and is currently in progress so that I cannot give all of the results. We hit upon the happy idea of presenting this chunk of geography not as a set of knowns, but as a set of unknowns. One class was presented blank maps, containing only tracings of the rivers and lakes of the area as well as the natural resources. They were asked as a first exercise to indicate where the principal cities would be located, where the railroads, and where the main highways. Books and maps were not permitted and "looking up the facts" was cast in a sinful light. Upon completing this exercise, a class discussion was begun in which the children attempted to justify why the major city would be here, a large city there, a railroad on this line, etc.

The discussion was a hot one. After an hour, and much pleading, permission was given to consult the rolled up wall map. I will never forget one young student, as he pointed his finger at the foot of Lake Michigan, shouting, "Yipee, *Chicago* is at the end of the pointing-down lake." And another replying, "Well, OK: but Chicago's no good for the rivers and it should be here where there is a big city (St. Louis)." These children were thinking, and learning was an instrument for checking and improving the process. To at least a half dozen children in the class it is not a matter of indifference that no big city is to be found at the junction of Lake Huron, Lake Michigan, and Lake Ontario. They were slightly shaken up transportation theorists when the facts were in.

The children in another class taught conventionally, got their facts all right, sitting down, benchbound. And that was that. We will see in six months which group remembers more. But whichever does, one thing I will predict. One group learned geography as a set of rational acts of induction— that cities spring up where there is water, where there are natural resources, where there are things to be processed and shipped. The other group learned passively that there were arbitrary cities at arbitrary places by arbitrary bodies of water and arbitrary sources of supply. One learned geography as a form of activity. The other stored some names and positions as a passive form of registration.

## THE EPISODIC CURRICULUM

In a social studies class of an elementary school in a well-to-do suburb of one of our great eastern cities, I saw groups of twelve-year-old children doing a "project" on the southeastern states. Each team was gathering facts that might eventually end up on a map or a chart or some other graphic device. The fact-gathering was atomized and episodic. Here were the industrial products of North Carolina. There was the list of the five principal cities of Georgia. I asked the children of one team what life would be like and what people would worry about in a place where the principal products were peanuts, cotton, and peaches. The question was greeted as "unfair." They were gathering facts.

It is not just the schools. The informational environment of America seems increasingly to be going through such an atomization. Entertainment is in fifteen minute episodes on TV, to be taken while sitting down. The school curriculum is built of episodic units, each a task to itself: "We have now finished addition. Let us now move to multiplication." Even in our humor the "gag" threatens to replace the shrewd observer of the human comedy. I have seen an elementary school play fashioned entirely on a parody of radio commercials. It was a brave effort to tie the 10-second atoms together.

I do not wish to make it seem as if our present state of education is a decline from some previous Golden Age. For I do not think there has ever been a Golden Age in American public education. The difference now is that we can afford dross less well than ever before. The volume of positive knowledge increases at a rapid rate. Atomizing it into facts-to-field is not likely to produce the kind of broad grasp that will be needed in the world of the next quarter century. And it is certainly no training for the higher education that more and more of our children will be getting.

I have not meant the above as a plea for the "central subject" or the "project" method of teaching. It is, rather, a plea for the recognition of the continuity of knowledge. One hears professional educators speak of "coverage," that certain topics must be covered. There are indeed many things that must be covered, but they are not unconnected things. The object of learning is to gain facts in a context of connectivity that permits the facts to be used generatively. The larger the number of isolated facts, the more staggering the number of connections between them—unless one can reduce them to some deeper order. Not all of them can be. Yet it is an ideal worth striving for, be it in the fifth grade or in graduate school. As Robert Oppenheimer put it in a recent address before the American Academy, "Everything cannot be connected with everything in the world we live in. Everything can be connected with anything."

## THE EMBARRASSMENT OF PASSION

I should like to consider now the guiding myth. Let me begin with a summary of the young Christopher Columbus as he is presented in a popular social studies textbook. Young Chris is walking along the water front in his home town and gets to wondering where all those ships go. Eventually he comes back to his brother's cobbler shop and exclaims, "Gee, Bart, I wonder where all those ships go, whether maybe if they just kept going they wouldn't come back because the world is round." Bart replies with pleasant brotherly encouragement. Chris is a well-adjusted kid. Bart is a nice big brother. And where is the passion that drove this obsessed man across uncharted oceans? What impelled this Columbus with such force that he finally enlisted the aid of Ferdinand and Isabella over the protest of their advisors? Everything is there in the story except the essential truth—the fanatical urge to explore in an age of exploration, the sense of an expanding world. Columbus did not have a schoolboy's whim, nor was he the well-adjusted grownup of this account. He was a man driven to explore, to control. The justification for the pablum that makes up such textbooks is that such accounts as these touch more directly on the life of the child.

What is this "life of the child" as seen by text writers and publishers? It is an image created out of an ideal of adjustment. The ideal of adjustment has little place for the driven man, the mythic hero, the idiosyncratic style. Its ideal is mediocentrism, reasonableness above all, being nice. Such an ideal does not touch closely the deeper life of the child. It does not appeal to the dark but energizing forces that lie close beneath the surface. The Old Testament, the Greek Myths, the Norse legends—these are the embarrassing chronicles of men of passion. They were devised to catch and preserve the power and tragedy of the human condition—and its ambiguity, too. In their place, we have substituted the noncontroversial and the banal.

Here a special word is needed about the concept of "expressing yourself," which is our conception of how one may engage the deeper impulses of the child. I have seen a book review class in a public school in which the children had the choice of reporting on any book they wished to choose, in or out of the school library, and where the discussion by the other children had to do entirely with the manner in which the reciting child presented his material. Nothing was said about the book in the discussion. The emphasis was on nice presentation, and whether the book sounded interesting. I have no quarrel with rewarding self-expression. I wonder simply whether it is not perhaps desirable, too, to make known the canons of excellence. The children in this class were learning to be seductive in their recounting; they were not concerned with an honest accounting of the human condition. The books they had read were cute, there was no excitement in them, none to be extracted. Increasingly the children in American elementary schools grow out of touch with the guiding myths. Self-expression is not a substitute. Adjustment is a worthy ideal, if not an ennobling one. But when we strive to attain it by shutting our eyes to the turmoils of human life, we will not get adjustment, but a niggling fear of the unusual and the excellent.

### THE QUALITY OF TEACHERS

I do not wish to mince words. The educational and cultural level of the majority of American teachers is not impressive. On the whole they do not have a good grasp of the subject matter that they are teaching; courses on method will not replace the absent subject matter. In time and with teaching experience this deficiency is often remedied. But in so many cases there is no time: the turnover in the teaching profession as we all know is enormous; the median number of years of teaching before departure for marriage or motherhood is around three.

This leaves us with a small core of experienced teachers. Do we use them to teach the new teachers on the job? No. The organization of the school with respect to utilization of talent is something short of imaginative. It consists of a principal on top and a group of discrete teachers beneath her, and that is all. In large metropolitan high schools this is sometimes supplemented by having departments at the head of which is an experienced teacher. The communication that goes on between teachers is usually at a highly informal level and can scarcely be called comprehensive. It is usually about problem-children, not about social studies or mathematics or how to bring literature alive.

I would urge, and I believe that educators have taken steps in this direction, that we use our more experienced teachers for on-the-job training of less experienced, new teachers. I would also urge that there be established some means whereby the substantive topics taught in our elementary and high schools be included in some kind of special extension program provided by our eighteen hundred colleges and universities in the United States for the benefit of teachers. I am not speaking only of teachers colleges, but rather of all institutions of higher learning. Institutions of higher learning have a responsibility to the lower schools, and it can be exercised by arranging for continuous contact between those, for example, who teach history at the college level and those who are teaching history or social studies at the lower levels. And so, too, with literature or mathematics, or languages. To assume that somehow a teacher can be "prepared" simply by going through teacher training and then by taking courses on methods in summer school is, I think, fallacious. Often it is the case that the teacher, like students, has not learned the material well enough to cross the barrier from learning to thinking.

### III

It is quite plain, I think, that the task of improving the American Schools is not simply one of technique——however comforting it would be to some professional educators to think so. What is at issue, rather, is a deeper problem, one that is more philosophical than psychological or technological in scope. Let me put it in all innocence. What do we conceive to be the end product of our educational effort? I cannot help but feel that this rather overly simplified question has become obscured in cant. There is such an official din in support of the view that we are "training well-rounded human beings to be responsible citizens" that one hesitates to raise the question whether such an objective is a meaningful guide to what one does in classroom teaching. Surely the objective is worthy, and it has influenced the techniques of education in America, not always happily. For much of what we have called the embarrassment of passion can, I think, be traced to this objective, and so too the blandness of the social studies curriculum. The ideal, sadly, has also led to the standardization of mediocrity by a failure of the schools to challenge the full capacity of the talented student.

Since the war, there has been a perceptible shift in the problems being faced by schools and parents alike. It is the New Competition. Will Johnny and Sally be able to get into the college of their first choice or, indeed, into any college at all? The origins of the concern are obvious enough—the "baby bulge" has made itself felt. The results are not all bad, I would urge, or need not be. There are, to be sure, severe problems of overcrowding that exacerbate the difficulties already inherent in public education. And it is true that parental pressures for grades and production are increasing the proportion of children with "learning blocks" being referred to child guidance clinics.

But the pressures and the competition are also rekindling our awareness of excellence and how it may be nurtured. The shake-up of our smugness by the evident technical thrust of the Soviet Union has added to this awareness. Let me urge that it is new awareness that requires shaping of expression in the form of a new set of ideals. Grades, admission to college, followed by admission to graduate school—these are surely not the ideals but, rather, the external signs.

Perhaps the fitting ideal is precisely as we have described it earlier in these pages, the active pragmatic ideal of leaping the barrier from learning into thinking. It matters not *what* we have learned. What we can *do* with what we have learned: this is the issue. The pragmatic argument has long been elaborated on extrinsic grounds, that the higher one has gone in the educational system the greater the economic gain. Indeed, at least one eminent economist has proposed that parents finance college education for their children by long-term loans to be repaid by the children on the almost certain knowledge that higher earning results from such education. All of this is the case, and it is indeed admirable that educational progress and economic success are so intimately linked in our society. I would only suggest that the pragmatic ideal be applied also to the intrinsic aspects of education. Let us not judge our students simply on *what* they know. That is the philosophy of the quiz program. Rather, let them be judged on what they can generate from what they know—how well they can leap the barrier from learning to thinking.

CHAPTER 5

# EDUCATING
# FOR
# CREATIVE
# BEHAVIOR

J. P. GUILFORD

# 29. CREATIVITY: YESTERDAY, TODAY, AND TOMORROW

The launching of a new journal devoted to the subject of creativity is an appropriate occasion for considering how the study of creativity has evolved, how matters in that subject stand, and what its future may be. The trail of the past is largely on the record, and also some aspects of the present status. The promise for the future can only be inferred from present trends found outside the field of creativity as well as within its borders. Interpretations and predictions are demanding mental exercises, and must inevitably reflect subjective impressions and judgments. And no one who undertakes these exercises is omniscient.

### FROM GALTON TO 1950

Although geniuses in various fields of human affairs have always been recognized and usually highly valued, it was not until Galton's studies of men of genius (1869) that the eyes of natural science were turned upon them. Galton did not seriously attempt to understand the mental operations by which distinguished leaders produce their novel ideas, but rather he tried to understand the hereditary determination of creative performances. His study became a classic, but he failed to reach uncontestable conclusions.

Reaching an understanding of exceptionally creative people and of the mental operations by which creative productions are achieved should have been the responsibility of psychologists. But early scientific psychologists were having such difficulty with more simple mental events such as sensation, perception, and memory that they had neither time nor the courage to tackle problems of creativity. If anything at all related to the subject was mentioned in the textbooks, it was under the mysterious label of "imagination" or "creative imagination". Usually only passing mention was made of the concept. Then behaviorism swept the field of psychology—in the USA at least—and such mentalistic concepts were commonly forced off the pages

Reprinted from *Journal of Creative Behavior*, Vol. 1, No. 1 (Winter 1967), 3–14, by permission of the author and the publisher.

of psychological writing. Only two writers (Schoen, 1930; Guilford, 1939, 1952), each devoting a chapter to the subject, have had much to say about creativity to the beginning student of psychology.

## PSYCHOMETRIC INTERESTS IN CREATIVITY

One kind of psychologist could not avoid the problem of creativity completely, for he dealt with the many characteristics in which one person differs from another. Among these characteristics are those that prepare some individuals for higher levels of performance including invention and innovation. The first successful tests of intelligence, from Binet to Terman and others, were aimed at prediction of academic achievement at the elementary level, where almost no attention was given to self-initiated ideas when it came time to evaluate achievement. The selection of abilities to be measured in the first Stanford revision of the Binet scale omitted those especially relevant to the assessment of creative potential, due to an incidental result in a faulty experiment. Terman (1906) had administered to two extreme groups (of seven each, out of 500 subjects who had been ranked for brightness *versus* dullness by their teachers) a set of experimental tests, one of which he recognized as a test of ingenuity. The ingenuity test failed to discriminate the extreme groups, but all the other tests were successful in doing so. Thus, over the years, tests of creative qualities have been almost nonexistent in intelligence scales.

The lack of correlation between tests recognized as belonging in the creative category and tests common to intelligence scales has been noted in isolated studies over the years. Even before Terman's experience with an ingenuity test, Dearborn (1898) had found this relative independence to be true for his tests involving "productive imagination". Over the years, replications of such findings have been reported by Chassell (1916), Andrews (1930), and Welch (1946). Terman could have used Dearborn's finding as evidence supporting his own conclusion that inventive qualities were outside the realm of intelligence, where the latter pertains only to basic academic potential. Or he could have reached the more recently demonstrated conclusion that intelligence, broadly conceived, embraces several components, some of which, at least, do not correlate very much with others. But the prevailing notion was that intelligence was a monolithic ability, all-relevant and unanalyzable.

## ANECDOTAL STUDIES OF CREATIVE PERFORMANCE

While psychologists were doing very little to attempt to understand creative people and creative production, others, not willing to wait for enlightenment from that source, proceeded to do something about the matter. They recorded instances of discoveries in science, literary productions, and other examples of output from recognized creative geniuses. Samples of this kind of investigation may be seen in the books by Wallas (1926, 1945), Hadamard (1945), and Ghiselin (1952). Rossman (1931) made a more systematic study of inventors, utilizing a questionnaire approach.

The weaknesses of anecdotal methods for the purposes of extracting generalizations are well known. Still, such information can be fruitful by suggesting hypotheses that can be explored further by means of more rigorous scientific procedures. The most fruitful outcome of the study of creative episodes was a list of the stages of thinking that a creator typically exhibits in the total process, beginning with the realized need for creative effort to the "wrapping up" of the final product. Both Wallas and Rossman proposed steps that take place in the course of the total creative event—Rossman for inventors, specifically, and Wallas for creative production in general.

### EXPERIMENTAL STUDIES
### OF CREATION

A few, but very few, investigators took seriously the creative steps proposed by Wallas—preparation, incubation, illumination, and elaboration. One of them was the psychologist Patrick (1935, 1937, 1938, 1941), who attempted to determine by experiments, mostly within the psychological laboratory, whether the Wallas processes could be identified, whether they run their courses in the given order, and what roles each of them play in a complete creative event. She found the process concepts relevant, but that the steps show many departures from the 1-2-3-4 order given by Wallas. The latter conclusion has been supported by similar findings of Eindhoven and Vinacke (1952).

### CREATIVE PRODUCTION
### IN RELATION TO AGE

A more lively and more extensive area of investigation regarding creativity was that pertaining to the ages of life at which the highest quality of creative performances is most likely to occur, and to quantity of creative production as related to age. Studies by Lehman culminated in a book (Lehman, 1953). This kind of study has also been conducted by Dennis (1956).

This thumbnail sketch of the fate of the subject of creativity to mid-century has emphasized only a few points. The subject was almost entirely ignored by psychologists. Psychometric psychologists ruled creative potential out of intelligence, and behaviorism adopted a general viewpoint from which creativity could not be seen. Non-psychologists made a few attempts to fill the gap, utilizing an anecdotal approach. One beneficial consequence was the suggestion of stages in creative production, which implied hypotheses that could and were investigated experimentally in a preliminary way.

Genetic studies, utilizing biographical information gave attention to the ages at which different degrees of quality and quantity of creative production occur. Almost nothing was learned about the nature of creative thinking itself, except that studies on such rare topics as insight have been shown to be relevant (Guilford, 1967).

## CREATIVITY SINCE 1950

Although the year 1950 is generally regarded as the turning point with respect to interest in creativity, and sometimes the writer's APA address (Guilford, 1950) is cited as a stimulus, there were indications of other trends in our *Zeitgeist* that converged upon the same effects. The number of publications on the subject had shown some positive acceleration in the 30's and 40's, consistent with the explosive rate of activity of this sort since 1950.

A number of forces were undoubtedly at work. The second World War had called forth great efforts toward innovation in research and development, culminating in the atomic bomb. The coming of peace that was no peace left us in the cold war, which called for ever-accelerating efforts in a contest of intellects. Inventive brains were at a premium, and there were never enough. We were on the eve of the space age, and rockets were already taking trial flights, stirring our imaginations of things to come. The stage was well set, then, ready for the psychologist to play his proper role in trying to fathom the creative person and his creative processes.

As more tangible evidence of the stirrings of interest in creativity, Alex F. Osborn had written his book on *Applied Imagination* which was ready for publication in 1953. The book was immediately popular, and has gone through numerous printings. The fact that it has been translated into a number of languages indicates that the new attention to the subject has become world wide. Osborn also founded the *Creative Education Foundation* and the annual *Institute for Creative Problem Solving,* which has been held for twelve years at what is now the State University of New York at Buffalo. The Creative Education Foundation has initiated and is sponsoring this journal.

## *NEW INVESTIGATIONS*
## *OF CREATIVITY*

The lively research activity since 1950 has been variously motivated and has used several different approaches. There has been much theoretical interest, which leads to asking the questions of what, how, and why. There have been efforts to solve certain practical problems, some of them utilizing information derived from basic studies and some not.

*Basic Information on the Nature of Creativity.* New research in an area where there has been little precedent is likely to be exploratory, involving little or no hypothesis testing. Such is the case with a number of investigations of the characteristics of people of recognized creative performance, as the study of outstanding scientists by Ann Roe (1952) and the studies of recognized creative writers, architects, and mathematicians, by MacKinnon and Barron, and their associates in the Institute for Personality Assessment and Research at The University of California in Berkeley (MacKinnon, 1960). With a psychoanalytic theoretical bias, these studies emphasized motivational and temperamental characteristics. Some of the salient findings were that highly creative persons, at least in the groups examined, are inclined to be strongly interested in esthetic and theoretical matters and that they tend to be highly intuitive and introverted. As to intellectual status, most of the individuals were in the upper ranges of IQs, and within this range there was practically no correlation between IQ and level of creative performance.

Another major approach, which has emphasized the intellectual qualities that might contribute to creative thinking and creative performance, has been made through application of multivariate methods of factor analysis. The locale of this research has been the Aptitude Research Project at the University of Southern California, under the writer's direction. Rejecting the prevailing doctrine that intelligence is a single, monolithic ability, and also the view that creative talents are something outside the realm of intelligence, the studies began with the assumption that there are several, perhaps many, distinguishable abilities involved. It was also assumed that creative talents are not confined to a favored few individuals, but are probably widely distributed to different degrees throughout the population. Creative talents could therefore be investigated without being restricted to observation of the gifted few.

The initial factor analysis started with a prior hypothesis as to what distinctions were to be expected among abilities that should be relevant to creative performance. Most of the hypothesized abilities were demonstrated by a factor analysis (Wilson, *et al.,* 1954).

Within a setting of exploration of other hypothesized intellectual abilities, a general theory of intelligence and its components known as the "structure of intellect" was developed. This theory forecast many distinguishable abilities yet to be demonstrated many of which could be especially relevant for creative performance. Subsequent factor analyses have supported all the hypothesized abilities that have been investigated. The outcomes of all these studies are summarized, and their implications treated in the writer's volume on *The Nature of Human Intelligence* (Guilford, 1967).

Briefly, the abilities believed to be most relevant for creative thinking are in two categories. One category is "divergent-production" (DP) abilities. DP abilities pertain to generation of ideas, as in solving a problem, where variety is important. Some DP abilities have been characterized as kinds of fluency, some as kinds of flexibility, and others as elaboration abilities. The varieties of abilities within the DP category depend upon the kind of information with which the person is dealing. This circumstance strongly suggests that creative talents depend upon the media in which the person is working —for example, whether he deals with lines and colors, sounds, or words, as in the various arts.

The other potential source of creative talents is in the category of "transformation" abilities, which pertain to revising what one experiences or knows, thereby producing new forms and patterns. Readiness to be flexible is a general characteristic of this group of talents, where flexibility leads to reinterpretations and reorganizations. Again, the variety of transformation abilities depends upon the kind of information or media with which creators deal.

An important advantage of analyzing creative disposition in terms of abilities is that kinds of abilities also imply kinds of mental functions. Having taken this logical step, we are ready to talk about the processes of creative thinking, as such. Discovery of the intellectual factors or abilities answers the question what; applying these answers to operations that the individual performs answers questions of how. Thus, the study of how a creative thinker operates is opened to us, for we have the concepts that we need—the handles that we can grasp in further research efforts.

*Some Conditions of Creative Performance.* Other traditional research approaches have been used for the problems of creative development and its promotion. Using tests of the kind developed through factor analysis, Torrance (1962) has examined the question of how creative potential changes as a function of age in children and adolescents. He has found that development does not occur at a uniform rate; the most significant departure is the "fourth-grade slump" at about the age of nine. Although the same tests show a leveling-off of averages in the late teens, other tests have shown further development even to the age of 30 (Trembly, 1964). The latter result supports the findings of Lehman, that quality of production commonly reaches its maximum in the early thirties. It is likely, however, that growth curves will be found to differ, depending upon which of the factorial abilities is being measured.

In line with the general optimism about improving abilities through favorable environmental conditions, some studies have been designed to assess improvement in creative activity as a result of various kinds of practice. From the factorial-theory viewpoint, we may regard the relevant abilities as being intellectual skills with some degree of generality. This means that exercises of appropriate kinds should yield improved performance in the abilities concerned. Most of the studies have shown that changes in performance can be assessed and that improvements with some degree of durability do occur. Many of these studies have been conducted by Sidney Parnes and his associates at SUNY Buffalo, and by Irving Maltzman and his associates at UC Los Angeles.

Other experiments have concerned the nature of creative thinking and problem solving, which extensively overlap, to say the least, and with the conditions affecting those phenomena. For example, Torrance and his associates have examined the effects of criticism and other conditions of motivation upon creative performances of school children (Torrance, 1965). Other experimental studies have examined conditions affecting insight or intuition.

As stated earlier, the relation of creative potential and creative production to the traditional IQ has been found close to zero where groups of superior IQ are concerned. This finding has been verified by a number of investigations (e.g., Getzels and Jackson, 1961). But in the lower ranges of IQ there is a substantial correlation. When the whole range of IQ is included, say from 62 to 150, there is a characteristic scatter plot. This plot shows that when the IQ is low, scores on tests of creative potential can only be low. When the IQ is high, there can be a wide range in performance on creative tasks.

Assuming that IQ tests are very much confined to cognitive abilities (and this means essentially to amount of basic information possessed), IQ appears to set an upper limit on creative potential. The relationship described suggests that we have numerous creative underachievers but very few over-achievers. A question of utmost educational import is whether ways can be found to bring creative underachievers up to cognitive potential, and whether the latter can also be raised by educational procedures. This is the great educational challenge of the immediate future.

## SOME TECHNOLOGICAL PROBLEMS

The pressing needs for more creative personnel, especially in the research and development arena, naturally directed considerable effort to finding more creative scientists and engineers, and to conditions in their working milieu that affect performance. The most outstanding example of this kind of effort has been the series of conferences on "The Identification of Creative Scientific Talent," sponsored by the University of Utah, under the leadership of Calvin W. Taylor. Six of these conferences have been held, culminating thus far in the publication of three books of proceedings (Taylor and Barron, 1963; Taylor, 1964; Taylor, 1966). The conferences included reports of basic research as well as technological matters. In pursuit of the main goal of these conferences, Taylor and his associates have tried to develop criteria for evaluating creative-research performance and to design a biographical-data scale for predicting research performance. McPherson and others have given much attention to the circumstances under which research scientists do their work, including problems of supervision.

Torrance and others have studied problems of creative teaching and procedures for developing creative behavior in the classroom. Getzels and

Jackson (1961) and others have looked into the relation between scores on creative-thinking tests and measures of achievement in education. The problems of creativity in the educational setting are endless, and the scope of research in this area is rapidly spreading. It is quite appropriate that this new journal should have a strong interest in problems of creative education and education for creativity.

## CREATIVITY'S FUTURE

There seems little doubt that considerable momentum has been generated in investigations of creativity and consequent implementations in education and elsewhere. So many new avenues of theory and of ways of investigation have been opened that there should be little loss of momentum; there should, instead, be some continuation of the acceleration that has already been evident. Let us consider next some of the remaining problems, especially in the basic-research setting.

### NEEDS FOR MORE
### BASIC RESEARCH

Basic future investigations will probably take two major directions: toward a more detailed and complete understanding of the processes of creative thinking, and toward a survey of the conditions that influence creative thinking, positively or negatively.

*The Nature of Creative Thinking.* It is desirable to conceptualize the roles of fluency, flexibility, and elaboration in the operations of creative production and problem solving in general, in ways that suggest investigative operations. Fluency, for example, is largely a matter of retrieval of information from one's memory store, and comes under the historical concept of recall of learned information. Psychologists have studied the storing of information intensively; they have given relatively little attention to the *uses* of stored information. What little effort has been evident treats only what this writer (Guilford, 1967) has called "replicative recall." Not much has been done with the much more important "transfer recall." How does one get at one's stored information and use it in new connections and in novel ways?

As a deduction from structure-of-intellect theory regarding mental functions, one kind of flexibility is a matter of transformations of information. How are transformations brought about? How is information reinterpreted or redefined so as to adapt it resourcefully to new uses? Another type of flexibility concerns reclassifications. No doubt the classification of items of learned information has much to do with their efficient retrieval. Class ideas determine the areas of search. Each item of information has its "address" or "addresses," to use computer terminology, which help to locate it. Failure to recall may be due to persistence in the use of wrong addresses, a persistence within wrong or too limited classes.

What are the processes of elaboration, and how may they be facilitated? Structure-of-intellect theory conceives of elaboration as a matter of producing implications. What are the various kinds of connections by which one item of information comes to imply another, and produces chain-like thinking, each link bringing into view the next? This is really the old problem of association in new dress, envisaged in a way that should be more fruitful in accounting for thinking.

Transformations offer an important key to the understanding of insights or intuitions. The latter are often recognized as sudden changes, and changes are transformations. What are the principles or laws of transformation?

And what of the phenomenon of incubation, on which only one intentional study can be cited? Note that it is classed as a phenomenon rather than a process. It involves a period of relaxation of effort in the total event of solving a problem or producing a creative product. There is no doubt that the phenomenon exists and that some creators use it effectively. Why do some individuals keep a problem open, and keep coming back to it, when others regard early attempts as closed events? What kinds of mental processes occur during incubation? To say that unconscious thinking is going on tells us practically nothing. We have to infer what thinking events took place from the observed behavior of the individual before, during, and after the period of incubation.

*Conditions Affecting Creative Thinking.* Some of the questions just raised imply that there are determining conditions that affect creative-thinking processes, by way of facilitation or inhibition. Effects of evaluation, critical or otherwise, were touched upon earlier. Absence of self-evaluation while generating ideas has been known as "suspended judgment." There is still much to be learned about when and where evaluation should be applied, for evaluation of some kind there must be, if the end product is to be satisfying in certain respects.

A general source of determination of creative events lies in the area of motivation. In general, what motivates individuals to creative production? To make the question somewhat more specific which needs, interests, and attitudes help the individual to be productive creatively and which put blocks in his way? How do certain attitudes and emotions affect various steps in the entire creative event? What are their influences upon recall, insight, and elaboration? The answers to all such questions provide bases for increased control over creative events.

## SOCIAL CONSEQUENCES

The consequences on the future of mankind of present and future efforts to gain understanding and control of creative performance are incalculable. It is apparent that the solutions to numerous human problems are dependent upon education of the world's population, both extensively and intensively. An informed people, with skills in using its information, is a creative, problem-solving people. In a real sense, mankind is involved in a race between expanding education on the one hand, and threatened disaster, perhaps oblivion, on the other.

To live is to have problems, and to solve problems is to grow intellectually. It is probably safe to say that at no time has a large number of informed and otherwise intellectually able individuals lived on this planet, yet the problems to be solved seem almost overwhelming—how to keep the peace, how to feed and clothe an expanding population, how to keep the population from expanding too rapidly, and how to educate it. Education in the more enlightened countries has been rather successful in transmitting to younger generations the accomplishments of older generations. But as Torrance (1962) has pointed out, teaching has been much too authoritative. It has not given the younger generation instruction in how to use information in creative ways, or even the opportunity to do so in many cases. Creative education, on the other hand, aims at a self-starting, resourceful, and confident person, ready to face personal, interpersonal and other kinds of problems. Because he is confident, he is also tolerant where there should be tolerance. A world of tolerant people would be peaceful and cooperative people. Thus creativity is the key to education in its fullest sense and to the solution of mankind's most serious problems.

## REFERENCES

Andrews, E. G. The development of imagination in the perschool child. *Univ. Iowa Stud. Character*, 1930, *3* (4).

Chassell, L. M. Tests originality. *J. Educ. Psychol.*, 1916, 7, 317–29.

Dennis, W. Age and productivity among scientists. *Science*, 1956, *123*, 724–25.

Eindhoven, J. E. and W. E. Vinacke.Creative process in painting. *J. Gen. Psychol.*, 1952, *47*, 139–64.

Galton, F. *Hereditary genius: An inquiry into its laws and consequences.* New York: Appleton, 1869.

Getzels, J. W. and P. W. Jackson.*Creativity and intelligence.* New York: Wiley, 1961.

Ghiselin, B. *The creative process.* Berkeley: Univ. of California Press, 1952; New York: Mentor, 1955.

Guilford, J. P. Creativity. *Amer. Psychol.*, 1950, *5*, 444–54.

Guilford, J. P. *General psychology.* Princeton, N.J.: D. Van Nostrand, 1939, 1952.

Guilford, J. P. *The nature of human intelligence.* New York: McGraw-Hill, 1967.

Hadamard, J. S. *An essay on the psychology of invention in the mathematical field.* Princeton, N.J.: Princeton Univ. Press, 1945.

Lehman, H. C. *Age and achievement.* Princeton, N.J.: Princeton Univ. Press, 1953.

MacKinnon, D. W. The highly effective individual. *Teachers Coll. Rec.*, 1960, *61*, 367–78.

McPherson, J. H. Environment and training for creativity in C. W. Taylor (Ed.). *Creativity: Progress and potential.* New York: McGraw-Hill, 1964, 130–53.

Osborn, A. F. *Applied imagination.* Rev. ed. New York: Scribners, 1963.

Patrick, C. Creative thought in poets. *Archives Psychol.,* N.Y., 1935, *26,* 1–74.

Patrick, C. Creative thought in artists. *J. of Psychol.,* 1937, *4,* 35–73.

Patrick, C. Scientific thought. *J. of Psychol.,* 1938, *5,* 55–83.

Patrick, C. Whole and part relationship in creative thought, *Amer. J. Psychol.,* 1941, *54,* 128–31.

Roe, Anne. *The making of a scientist.* New York: Dodd, Mead, 1952.

Rossman, J. *The psychology of the inventor.* Washington, D.C.: Inventors Publishing Co., 1931.

Schoen, M. *Human nature. A first book in psychology.* New York: Harper, 1930.

Taylor, C. W. (ed.). *Instructional media and creativity.* New York: Wiley, 1966.

Taylor, C. W. *Widening horizons in creativity.* New York: Wiley, 1964.

Taylor, C. W., and F. Barron. *Scientific creativity: Its recognition and development.* New York: Wiley, 1963.

Terman, L. M. Genius and stupidity: A study of some of the intellectual processes of seven "bright" and seven "stupid" boys. *Ped. Sem.,* 1906, *13,* 307–73.

Torrance, E. P. *Guiding creative talent.* Englewood Cliffs, N.J.: Prentice-Hall, 1962.

Torrance, E. P. *Rewarding creative behavior.* Englewood Cliffs, N.J.: Prentice-Hall, 1965.

Trembly, D. Age and sex differences in creative thinking potential. *Amer. Psychol.* 1964, *19,* 516. (Abstract)

Wallas, G. *The art of thought.* London: C. A. Watts, 1945.

Welch, L. Recombination of ideas in creative thinking. *J. Appl. Psychol.,* 1946, *30,* 638–43.

Wilson, R. C., J. P. Guilford, P. R. Christensen, and D. J. Lewis. A factor-analytic study of creative-thinking abilities. *Psychometrika,* 1954, *19,* 297–311.

JOHN KORD LAGEMANN

# 30. HOW WE DISCOURAGE CREATIVE CHILDREN

If your child gets a high score on one of the IQ tests that are usually given between kindergarden and third grade, he will have a considerable advantage in preparing for college and a career. Teachers and school administrators will rightly put him in the "gifted" category and make a special effort to help him develop his abilities.

Reprinted from *Redbook Magazine,* (March 1963), pp. 44, 123–25, by permission of the author and the publisher. Copyright © 1963 by McCall Corporation.

But suppose your child gets only an average or a slightly above average IQ score? Does this mean that he isn't gifted? That's the general assumption, not only among teachers but among parents as well. According to Dr. E. Paul Torrance, one of the nation's foremost authorities on creativity and intelligence, no fallacy has done more harm to children or robbed society of more creative talent.

"Children are apt to be far more gifted than their parents or teachers realize—and in different ways," Dr. Torrance told me when I visited him recently. "IQ tests do not measure creative talent. By depending on them we miss seventy percent of our most gifted youngsters."

During the past six years, Dr. Torrance and his associates at the Bureau of Educational Research have studied over 15,000 boys and girls from nursery school to the sixth grade. Their findings show that most children start life with valuable creative potential and that most of them have it knocked out of them by the time they reach the fourth grade. It is not that parents and teachers deliberately squelch creativity; it is rather that they fail to recognize it. Often they mistake it for unruliness, eccentricity and even stupidity.

There is no question that "creativity involves getting away from the obvious, safe and expected and producing something which—to the child, at least—is new," says Dr. Torrance. This makes extra trouble for teachers and parents. The child's constant questioning, experimenting and exploring can make him trying to other people.

In most elementary classrooms the good pupil is the one who repeats what he is told and makes pictures like the ones in the book. The creative youngster, on the other hand, wants to make up his own stories. He draws what he actually sees the way *he* sees it and not necessarily the way he is supposed to see it. The child in the fairy story who blurted out, "But the emperor has no clothes!" was undoubtedly the creative type and undoubtedly he was royally squelched.

The creative child is constantly asking questions because he wants to make sense out of what he sees and hears.

"Which is more," asks four-year-old Danny, "twelve miles or twelve hours?" His mother says, "Don't be silly." Actually Danny's question is highly intelligent. So far in his young life the number 12 has always been connected with something—miles, hours, marbles or eggs. Now it is beginning to dawn on Danny that 12 is a number with an identity of its own. With this discovery he takes his first step into mathematics.

A father tells of reading *Mother Goose* to his highly inquisitive four-year-old. "You try something simple and straightforward like 'Tom, Tom, the Piper's Son.' Right away he starts interrupting: 'Was Tom about my age? What is a piper? Was Tom's father poor? Is that why Tom stole the pig? If Tom was my age, how did he carry a pig? If the pig was so small, how did it kill the goose? What's a calaboose? You mean they put little boys in jail?'"

Another father tells of answering as best he could his seven-year-old son's questions about "what things are made of." The next day he got a call from the second-grade teacher, complaining of Tommy's disruptive behavior. "I'm afraid he's being overstimulated at home," she said. "When he came into class today he said, 'You're nothing but a bunch of molecules.' "

What is creativity? How does it differ from the kind of mental ability that is measured by IQ?

"Suppose the problem was to improve oil lamps," Dr. Torrance explains. "The IQ mentality would apply all the known facts about oil lamps to build a better model. The creative mentality would invent the electric light."

When your child takes an IQ test he is called on to solve a variety of problems like these:

How many weeks in a year? How many hours in a day? Where is Peru? If you start with ten newspapers and sell four, how many are left? What is a shovel? A bowl? A lake?

How are an apple and a plum alike? Why do we have congressmen? What should you do if you step on a nail? Why is it better to make buildings of brick than of wood?

Some of the questions have a single predetermined "right" answer. Others have a single "best" answer, with half credit for a limited range of "acceptable" answers. The child who makes an ingenious, imaginative or unusual reply that is not in the manual is penalized in the scoring of the test. Thus the expected answer to why it is better to use brick than wood as a building material is that brick is stronger, longer-lasting, safer and provides better insulation. A child who mentioned at least two of these factors would get full credit; the child who could muster only one of these reasons would get half credit. But the child who answered that it was better to use brick "to save our national forests" or "so we can use the wood for newspapers" would get no credit. Neither would the child who argued that brick *wasn't* the better material "because brick is cold and ugly and wood is warm and beautiful."

Creative thinking, like the thinking required in the IQ tests, is a problem-solving process. But it is one that calls on the individual to use his own knowledge and experience to work out an answer that satisfies a deeply felt need for self-expression. The problems that call for creative thinking are the kind that have more than one right answer—and this category includes practically all the basic problems we face in growing up, marrying, rearing a family, earning a living and finding order and beauty and meaning in life through science, art and religion.

The problems in the creativity tests devised by Dr. Torrance and his associates have no predetermined right answers. They are as much fun as parlor games, which they resemble. In a "Product Improvement" test the youngster is handed a toy—say a stuffed, plastic dog—and asked to think of as many ways as possible for changing it to make it "more fun to play with."

A conventional-minded child made three suggestions: shorten the nose, lengthen the tail and change the color. A highly creative child made over a dozen suggestions, including: "a spring so he can do back flips...sew fleas on his back...flashlight bulbs for eyes...give him claws so he can dig a real hole...a balloon inside so he can bark and drink out of a bowl... a magnet in his nose he can chase a rabbit with a magnet in its tail...."

Another test directs the child to "list all the uses you can think of for empty tin cans." For the conventional thinkers the cans retain their character as containers—as flowerpots, drinking cups or receptacles for odds and ends. The creative child breaks free of the container idea with suggestions for using old cans as cookie cutters, toy telephones, xylophones, metal roof shingles, stilts to walk on, rockets to explode into the air and "something on which you could paint a picture that would go all the way around."

One of the test materials is a piece of paper filled with 26 circles. The child is asked to see how many things he can make out of the circles with a pencil or crayon, using the circle itself as the main part of his drawing. The time limit is ten minutes.

"You have only ten seconds left," Dr. Torrance once told a class of second graders. One little girl, still with two rows of circles to go, immediately drew a girl blowing bubbles and made the unused circles serve as the bubbles. This kind of last-minute improvisation is characteristic of creative children.

Unlike IQ, creative potential can't be measured by totaling the number of right answers a child gets on a standardized test and comparing this with the number of right answers obtained by a majority of children his age. "There will never be a CQ, or 'creativity quotient,'" Dr. Torrance told me. "Sizing up a child's creative gifts will always be a matter of individual judgment." But simply by observing the child at work and at play you may detect creativity easily enough if you know what to look for. Here are the key signs that Dr. Torrance and his coworkers have found most reliable:

1. Curiosity. The child's questioning is persistent and purposeful. He is not content with glib explanations but digs under the surface. Curiosity isn't always oral. A baby handles things, shakes, twists and turns them upside down. A youngster takes things apart, not destructively but to see "how it works" or what is inside. The creative boy or girl experiments with words and objects and ideas, always trying to wring new meaning out of them.
2. Flexibility. If one approach doesn't work, he quickly thinks of another. To some older boys trying in vain to throw a rope over a high tree branch to make a swing, eight-year-old Jackie suggested, "Why not fly a kite over it and then pull up the rope with the string?"
3. Sensitivity to problems. He is quick to see gaps in information, exceptions to the rules, and contradictions in what he hears or reads.
4. Redefinition. He can see hidden meanings in statements that others take at face value, find new uses for familiar objects and see connections between things that seem unrelated to others. It was a creative child who said, "Eternity is a clock without hands."
5. Self-feeling. He has a feeling of being somebody in particular. He is self-

winding, self-directed and can work alone for long periods—provided it's on his own project. Merely following directions bores him.

6. Originality. He has surprising, uncommon, interesting ideas. His drawings and stories have a style that mark them as his own. Even the most creative child, of course, is unlikely to make any really new discoveries—it is the spontaneous rediscoveries that count. Have you ever watched a three-year-old mix blue and yellow and discover that they make green?

7. Insight. He has easy access to realms of the mind which noncreative people visit only in their dreams. He toys with ideas that just come to him. As one five-year-old girl told Dr. Torrance at a birthday party where she reached into a grab bag for favors, "That's how I get ideas—just reach in and scrunch around in my mind till I feel like pulling something out."

Qualities like these count very little on IQ tests, which measure memory, vocabulary, number ability and general reasoning. These IQ abilities are valuable, and the creative child usually has them too. Outstanding creativity is very seldom found among children of below-average IQ. But Dr. Torrance's research shows that above 115 or 120, IQ scores have no bearing on creativity. This means that if a child is normally intelligent, his potential for achievement in school and in life is not limited by his IQ score.

The numerical scoring of tests has left the impression that giftedness is distributed according to an ascending IQ scale, with imbeciles at the bottom and geniuses at the top. The truth is, however, that creative giftedness may be found anywhere along the scale except, possibly, at the bottom. The child with a so-called genius IQ of 180 is in reality no more likely to be a genius than the child with a slightly above average IQ of around 120. In fact, there is evidence that some very high IQ children may develop memory and logical reasoning powers at the expense of insight, imagination and adventurousness—qualities that are essential to genius.

In one of the great studies of intelligence, the Stanford University psychologist Dr. Lewis Terman followed a group of 1,500 exceptionally high IQ boys and girls from childhood well into adulthood. While a high proportion grew up to be intellectually competent and valuable citizens, none made outstanding, original contributions to the arts, literature, science, business or statesmanship.

More recently Dr. Catherine M. Cox, of Stanford, studied the lives of 300 acknowledged geniuses and estimated their probable IQ on the basis of early mental traits. The estimates covered a wide range, from average to Olympian. Molière, Heine, Balzac and Sir Isaac Newton got estimated IQs of roughly 120 to 130—ratings that are surpassed by a large proportion of freshmen in a number of our colleges and universities. If a very high IQ equaled creative talent or contributed to it in a particularly significant way, we would graduate thousands of Sir Isaac Newtons every year.

"Creativity is pretty nearly universal," says Dr. Torrance. "All of us share to some extent in the creative ability we admire in Shakespeare, Da Vinci and Einstein. The difference is that these men had a great deal more of it."

The qualities that make us creative are the same no matter where you find them—in children or adults, in art, science, politics or industry.

"Because children's creativeness so often comes out in painting or sculpturing doesn't mean that they are going to grow up to be painters or writers, or even that they have exceptional artistic talent. It simply means that they are expressing with paint and clay the qualities of mind that may someday make them creative as doctors, scientists, businessmen—and as husbands and wives, parents and friends."

Everyone acknowledges, in principle, that we need creative intelligence as we never needed it before to cope with change, explore the mysteries of space and find new meaning and value in life on this planet. But in actual practice, Dr. Torrance has found, "society is down-right savage in its treatment of creative people, particularly when they are young."

In a number of first-, second- and third-grade classrooms, the Minnesota researchers asked teachers and pupils to nominate those children who talked most, those who had the most good ideas, those with the most ideas for being naughty and those with the silliest ideas. Teachers and pupils voted pretty much alike. They credited the "best ideas" to youngsters who tested low on creativity and near the top in IQ. The boy who was cited for having the "silliest" ideas and the most ideas for being naughty proved in subsequent testing to be the most creative member of the class.

In another experiment first-, second- and third-grade children were organized into teams of five with just one highly creative boy or girl in each. Teams were given a time limit to examine and manipulate science toys to try to find out what could be done with them and what scientific principles they illustrated. There were prizes and the competition was intense. In every group, although the one highly creative member usually produced the best ideas, he seldom got credit. After ridiculing his ideas, teammates often adopted them. When the creative member was a girl, she was likely to pass her ideas along to some boy, who then got credit.

In school after school, Dr. Torrance and his associates found that teachers almost invariably favor the high-IQ child over the highly creative one—despite the fact that the highly creative child actually learned as much as the high-IQ child when measured on such standard achievement tests as the Iowa Basic Skills battery and the Gates Reading Test.

Why this prejudice against the highly creative child? Why this favoritism shown the high-IQ child? In large part it's a matter of personality. The abilities that make a child creative also make him "different."

Dr. Torrance, reviewing scores of personality studies, listed the characterizations that have been found to describe creative children: "accepts disorder...attracted to the mysterious...playful...likes to toy with ideas... offbeat ideas...emotionally sensitive...a fault finder...spirited in disagreement...courageous...takes risks...energy to burn...."

To find out the qualities teachers prefer—and reward—Dr. Torrance asked several hundred to rate a list of character traits in order of preference. Toward the top of the list teachers placed such traits as "promptness, courtesy, popularity, receptivity to ideas of others, ability to take criticism and good memory." Toward the bottom of the list, in the category of least desirable, they put "adventurous, always asking questions, courageous, unwilling to accept say-so, willing to take risks, and visionary."

At the heart of the creative child's problem in finding acceptance is the fact that he is never content to learn only by authority but persists in finding out for himself through constant questioning, probing and experimenting. To a large extent he is the victim of his virtues. His independence may make him appear rebellious. His capacity for complete absorption in his work may give the impression that he is antisocial. His humor and playfulness combined with his cleareyed view of the world may strike grownups as mocking or disrespectful. His off-the-beaten-track ideas give him the reputation among his own contemporaries as a "screwball." No wonder his teachers and parents sometimes groan, "Why can't he be like other kids?"

Dr. Torrance and his associates at the University of Minnesota found that even parents who insisted they wanted their children to learn and think creatively were actually disturbed, irritated and embarrassed by the differences they observed in children who did so.

In reality, Dr. Torrance says, it is not the differences but the conformity of the creative child that should concern parents. "The exuberance and flexibility of the creative child are the surest sign of a healthy, fully functioning personality. It is not creativity but its suppression that parents need to worry about."

Under parental pressure, children themselves often feel guilty about their gifts. Instead of accepting themselves, they try to remake themselves into more conventional types and hide or destroy the talents that make them different. This guilt was frequently revealed in stories Dr. Torrance's young subjects were asked to make up about a monkey who could fly. One third-grade youngster wrote:

"Once there was a little monkey who was always doing what his mother told him not to. One day he told his sister, 'I can do something that you will never be able to do. I can fly.' His sister said he couldn't, so he climbed a tree, gave a leap and began to fly. His sister ran as fast as she could to the mother monkey. The mother was surprised and angry. She told the little monkey to go back to the house but he refused. So that night when father monkey came home she told him all about it. And he went and got the little monkey and said for him not to fly any more or the other animals would think he was crazy and out of his head."

Six years of testing by the Minnesota group has revealed ups and downs in creativity which can be charted chronologically. Three to five is a highly creative period. A sudden drop occurs when the child enters kindergarten or first grade. There is a period of creative thinking during the second and third grades. Then near the end of the third grade and the beginning of the fourth comes a sudden, drastic decline that Dr. Torrance has labeled the "Fourth-Grade Slump." Only a small minority of children resist pressure at this stage and go on to develop their own creative thinking powers.

Are these fluctuations an intrinsic part of growing up?

"Not at all," says Dr. Torrance. "We find whole groups of children who go through nursery school, kindergarten and the primary grades without a break in their creative development. When children give up their creative spark it is because of outside pressures."

What are these pressures? How can you as a parent eliminate them or mitigate their effects on your child? Here are Dr. Torrance's suggestions:

Don't discourage fantasy. One of the qualities of the creative person, young or old, is his ability to move freely back and forth between the world of facts and reason and the vast realms of the mind that lie just below the surface of consciousness. The creative person's greater flexibility, depth of feeling and keenness of insight come from being open to vague feelings and hunches that others dismiss as silly.

Don't hold him back. On the theory that nothing succeeds like success, American parents are so intent on sparing their children the hurt of failure that they deny them a chance to learn from their mistakes. American children are so conditioned to the idea of preventing emergencies that they are failing to learn how to cope with them. To learn creatively, children have to bite off more than they can chew, overestimate their capacities and take risks. "It's never too early for self-initiated learning," says Dr. Torrance. Educators have found that children can start learning long before they reach the supposed "readiness period." The trick is not to teach them creative thinking but to stop interfering with it.

Make creativity rewarding. Children, like adults, achieve most along whatever lines bring the most satisfaction. Dr. Torrance found that when eighth-grade children are rewarded for originality they produce about twice as many original ideas as when they are rewarded for sheer number of ideas regardless of quality. Sixth graders who are rewarded for originality and interest produce much better stories than children who are rewarded for correctness, but they also make many more mistakes in spelling and grammar.

Avoid sexual stereotypes. Don't let your boy feel that it is "sissy" to be open to feelings and interested in color, form, movement and ideas. Don't make your daughter feel that it is wrong for her to be intellectually curious, interested in exploration and experimentation—and competitive. Sexual stereotypes are destructive of creativity. In the Product Improvement test, elementary-school children were asked to think of ideas for improving, among other toys, a fire truck and a nurse's kit. Most of the boys Dr. Torrance tested refused even to touch the nurse's kit, protesting, "I'm a boy. I can't play with things like that." A few of the more creative males changed it into a doctor's kit before offering suggestions. The girls refused to interest themselves in the fire truck. That was officially a boy's toy.

Don't judge him by his reading and writing. Creative children often lag behind the group in verbal abilities. It is sometimes difficult for them to put their ideas down on paper. One nine-year-old boy, at the bottom of his class because of reading and writing problems, turned out to be near the top on creativity tests. The researcher who examined him wrote: "This boy impresses me as the kind of individual who will be able to dictate to five secretaries at the same time without becoming confused." Most children love to dictate stories to their parents, and this is an excellent way to keep their ideas flowing.

Allow freedom to experiment. To think creatively, a child needs to toy with the subject, play around with ideas, try out wild and farfetched guesses. Instead of laughing at him, encourage him to test his statements, imagine what the world would be like if they were true. Don't pin him down to "right" or "wrong." Parents and teachers both have a tendency to confuse getting right answers with being morally right. "In most schools," says Dr. Torrance, "the child takes a calculated risk every time he asks an unusual question or advances a new idea, for fear of ridicule by his classmates and sometimes his teacher." He has found that creative thinking in the lower grades takes a tremendous surge when children are told that what they are doing is just for fun, without any grades or criticism.

Help him use his creativity in social relations. One of his biggest problems in life will be getting along with others without sacrificing the qualities that make him creative and "different." Help him use his sensitivity to be kind, his insight to be understanding and tolerant of those who don't see things his way. Show him he can assert himself without being domineering, work alone without being withdrawn, be honest with others without being over-critical. Prepare him to accept the fact that anyone who has original ideas must be prepared to be a minority of one, at least for a time.

"I don't want my child to be a genius," many parents say. "I just want him to be a normal, happy, well-adjusted kid." But, as Dr. Torrance points out, happiness, normality and adjustment consist primarily of using one's capacity to the fullest. "Creative people," says Dr. Torrance, "are, in the final analysis, happy people—provided they are free to create."

ELLIOT W. EISNER

# 31. CREATIVITY AND PSYCHOLOGICAL HEALTH DURING ADOLESCENCE

The relationship between psychological health and human creativity is difficult to determine. Neither creativity nor psychological health are easily defined, measured, or related. Yet certain observations have been made about the relationship, some emanating from ordinary experience, others derived from empirical research.

Many of the men considered to be among the most highly creative the world has ever known—painters such as Vincent Van Gogh, Edvard Munch, and Amedeo Modigliani, writers such as Ernest Hemingway, Fyodor Dostoevsky, and Edgar Allan Poe, scientists such as Leonardo da Vinci, Sigmund Freud, and Isaac Newton—have been men who were not exactly paradigms of psychological health. If historians have been accurate in describing their behavior, these men seemed to display characteristics frequently associated with psychopathology. Observations such as these have led some people to believe that creativity and psychopathology are related; others seem to believe that one is a precondition for the other.

Some empirical studies as well as some theoretical positions have pointed to opposite conclusions, although these studies and positions are far from definitive. Terman,[1] for example, in describing the characteristics of the gifted students in his study, points out that they were healthier both mentally and physically than their "average" peers. Kubie, in an intriguing little book, *Neurotic Distortion of the Creative Process*,[2] argues that psychopathology does not facilitate, but rather hampers creative behavior. In Kubie's words,

---

Reprinted from *The High School Journal*, (May 1965), pp. 465–73, by permission of the publisher.

---

[1] Lewis M. Terman. *Genetic Studies of Genius.* Vol. 1. (Stanford: Stanford University Press, 1925).

[2] Lawrence Kubie. *Neurotic Distortion of the Creative Process.* (Lawrence: University of Kansas Press, 1958), 20–21.

The measure of health is flexibility, the freedom to learn through experience, the freedom to change with changing internal and external circumstances, to be influenced by reasonable argument, admonitions, exhortation, and the appeal to emotions; the freedom to respond appropriately to the stimulus of reward and punishment, and especially the freedom to cease when sated. The essence of normality is flexibility in all of these vital ways. The essence of illness is the freezing of behavior into unalterable and insatiable patterns. It is this which characterizes every manifestation of psychopathology, whether in impulse, purpose, act, thought, or feeling.

Arguments can be and have been drawn on each side of this issue, and as yet the question as to the relationship between creativity and psychological health is far from clear. What is clear is that psychopathology has been a characteristic of a great many creative people, but whether the former condition created the latter or whether the latter functioned in spite of the former remains to be determined.

The field of education has long been concerned with the psychological health of the student. Both Plato and Aristotle spoke of the relationship of the body to the mind and of the mind to learning. And the Progressives, during their heyday in the twenties and thirties, spoke of wholeness of the child and urged that teachers concern themselves with the mental and social well-being of the student as well as with traditional educational goals.

Surely one of the problems that faces anyone concerned with developing *both* the student's mental health and his creativity is one of identifying on the one hand the characteristics of psychological health and on the other, the behaviors that define creativity.

It is easy, I think, to mistakenly assume that social adjustment, if we take that to mean the congruence of individual behavior to the expectations of a criterion group, is synonymous with psychological health. And in the classroom it is easy to mistakenly assume that the obsequious student, the student who causes no difficulties, who hands in assignments on time, whose outward manner is always pleasant, is a person who is psychologically healthy. For while it may be true that psychologically healthy individuals tend to be socially adjusted, social adjustment does not insure psychological health. If we distinguish between psychological integration and social adjustment we might find that the student who is psychologically well-integrated is socially maladjusted, while the quiet, soft-spoken, obsequious student who is socially adjusted may, at the same time, be poorly integrated. Such a student may have a great many internal psychological difficulties but may lack the ego strength to be able to display them externally. The point is that overt behavior, whether acceptable or unacceptable to teachers is not, by itself an adequate index of psychopathology. And I would argue that if the school has a responsibility to contribute to the psychological well-being of the student it is his psychological health and not his social adjustment per se that the school should attend to.

I have mentioned these distinctions between psychological integration and social adjustment because they have special relevance for the highly creative adolescent.

The adolescent has special concerns with respect to group maintenance and social conformity that others do not have in as great a degree. The marginal character of the adolescent period—not a child and yet not an adult—creates in the adolescent a strong need for identification. The opportunities that were available in the past when America was primarily rural and when child labor laws were not in force, made it possible for the adolescent to emulate and identify with the role of the working father or mother. A young man of fourteen or fifteen could earn a day's wages by engaging in real work, he could develop a self concept by real production. Contemporary society has changed all of that. We now require that he stay in school and by law prohibit his working full time. The model of the working father is often far removed from his experience, and the world of work far removed from the sophomore year in high school.

To compensate for the functions these opportunities of the past performed, an adolescent society has been created here in America and in almost every other highly industrialized nation. Teenagers have their own economy—they spend millions of dollars annually in the United States—they have their own form of dress, and their own vocabulary and language systems. To secure a sense of identity and to provide cohesiveness for the groups that form within this society, values, behavior patterns, and role expectations are developed. Behaviors are sanctioned when congruent with the expectations of the group or punished when they threaten the activities or status of the groups within that society.

Any society or group that establishes fixed and rigid codes of behavior presents difficulties to individuals who engage in activities that threaten members of the group holding such codes. One characteristic of some types of creative behavior is that it deviates from the standards, values, or beliefs of the status quo. Societies or groups that encourage and provide for the ready assimilation of such new developments are more likely to develop as a society, to progress through the contributions of its highly creative members. Societies which punish such activity impede the highly creative individual, they make him an outcast or, as in the past, burn him at the stake for questioning dogma. One has only to recall the travails of Galileo, Copernicus, the Fauves, Freud, Socrates and Pasteur to recognize the difficulties that novel modes of creative productivity have heaped upon their creators.[3]

The highly creative adolescent who engages in novel modes of creative behavior or productivity may produce behaviors or products that are not acceptable to the standards of the group to which he belongs. If he belongs

---

3 For a fascinating discussion of creative productivity in the history of science, see Arthur Koestler, *The Sleepwalkers* (New York: The Macmillan Company, 1959).

to a group, for example, that values athletic achievement and if his talents lie in scientific or artistic activities such activities may become exceedingly difficult for him to engage in without feeling outside of the group and of risking its acceptance of him.[4] If a student sees alternatives to solutions arrived at in classroom discussion, say, in the social studies, if he feels the urge to state a rather new approach for dealing with social conflict, the United Nations, racial integration, or space exploration, he may be unable to express them because he may feel that his peers will frown upon an "argumentative attitude" or the display of a "queer set of ideas." Such a situation may create an extremely discomforting state of affairs for the adolescent. In such a situation the highly creative adolescent is faced with the problem of *somehow* resolving his inward need to express his new insight and the outward pressure that he believes he will face from his peers if he in fact does express it. If he has a strong ego and sense of who he is, he may be willing to face the expected criticism of his peers and present his novel point of view or if he feels he cannot risk loss of status or acceptance, he may repress thoughts and behaviors that he has constructed. By forgetting his novel idea he diminishes both his own development as an individual and that of the group in which he participates.

One might hope that such students would find support from the teacher but alas, this does not seem to be the case. Teachers do not seem to prefer the highly creative adolescent in their classrooms.[5] The teacher, too, has a set of values and role expectations for the student, and the student who challenges these values or upsets these role expectations too often, presents teaching difficulties for the teacher. And even if such support by the teacher were given, the adolescent secondary school student does not live alone; it is with his peers and not with his teachers that he must make his social life. Thus, the highly creative student who gives in to the expectations and pressures of his peer group may seem well adjusted by his conformity, but he may be undergoing a deep sense of frustration inside. While the student who is able to withstand such pressure may be considered maladjusted, perhaps even rejected, he might be personally well integrated as his ability to withstand such pressures may indicate. One important problem for the secondary school is to provide the type of educational milieu that facilitates the development of both creative behavior and psychological health. What is it that the secondary school can do to encourage and reward the highly creative student without jeopardizing the very real needs that are met by a cohesive adolescent society within the school?

Before identifying the practices secondary schools might employ to provide

4 Paul Torrance, in his study of creativity, reports that he frequently observes pressures placed upon highly creative children by their peers. See, for example, his book, *Guiding Creative Talent* (Englewood Cliffs, New Jersey: Prentice Hall, Inc., 1962).

5 Jacob Getzels and Philip Jackson. *Creativity and Intelligence: Explorations with Gifted Students.* (New York: John Wiley, 1962).

for the creative development of the adolescent while, at the same time, providing for his needs for identification and belonging, it might be well to describe some of the behaviors that characterize highly creative individuals.

It is possible to identify four types of creative behavior that individuals may display.[6] I have called these types boundary pushing, inventing, boundary breaking and aesthetic organizing. The first three types are characterized by the presence of novelty; in the fourth type no novelty is displayed. The boundary pusher is an individual who redefines or extends the uses to which ordinary objects or ideas may be put. Individuals who are not functionally fixed, who are able to employ objects in ways for which they were not originally intended, display this mode of creativity.

The inventor, however, is an individual who so combines objects that a new object is created. The inventor does not merely extend or redefine the use of the ordinary, he creates essentially new ideas or objects by using objects or ideas already available. In common discourse we consider individuals such as Edison, Gutenberg, and Whitney to be inventors, while the person who first thought of using rubber for the blades of electric fans, the individual who first thought of installing electric shaver outlets in automobiles, and the person who first used plastic for roller skates may be considered boundary pushers.

The boundary breaker is an individual who questions or rejects the very premises upon which major contemporary assumptions are made and in so doing reshapes our view of reality. Such people are very rare but highly provocative and have been the ones who have suffered the most because of their ideas. By asking "Where does blood go?" Harvey developed a conception of blood circulation; by asking "Do people really forget?" Freud developed a conception of the unconscious and of repression; by questioning a belief in a geocentric universe, Copernicus reshaped our view of the heavens and our place in it. Boundary breakers seem to threaten us the most because they question our most cherished beliefs. By doing this, they force us to reconstruct our view of reality or to chastise them for deviant behavior. Because each of these three types of creative behavior can threaten the group in which it may occur, each may provide special difficulties for the individual creating these behaviors.

Aesthetic organizing, the fourth type of creativity, is a mode of creative behavior in which novelty is *not* created. The aesthetic organizer is an individual who puts things together in a satisfying, harmonious and functional way. In the arts, for example, students may be highly creative in the way in which they organize qualities into aesthetic relationships but yet fail to produce aesthetic objects having novel characteristics. In the area of social organization it is not uncommon to find individuals who are creative in their

6 These types of creativity have been described in my series on creativity in *The Instructor,* Vol. 72 and empirical data can be found in my article, "A Typology of Creativity in the Visual Arts," *Studies in Art Education,* Vol. 4 (Fall 1962), 11–22.

ability to organize and to enable a group to function well. Such people are not likely to threaten a group but rather to win approval from the group since the ideas or qualities they work with are not redefined but organized in common yet satisfying ways. It is when new qualities are created—cacophony, dissonance, action painting—that the individual creator is likely to meet with resistance.

Given the distinction between psychological integration and social adjustment and between the types of creativity individuals may display and given the premise that schools should provide for the development of both creativity and psychological health, it seems appropriate to identify some of the conditions that might contribute to realization of such ends.

First, it seems that rather than to rely upon examinations which deal only with assessing the student's ability to provide answers, it might be well for teachers to construct examinations which tap the student's ability to raise significant questions. Answer-oriented tests too often encourage and reward premature closure. They tend to lay great premium on half-understood answers. Yet the conditions that seem to characterize creative behavior are those of openness to ideas and of playfulness with ideas and with alternative solutions to problems. What would happen to student behavior if instead of rewarding students for correct answers to questions, teachers constructed tests which rewarded students for imaginative questions? If it is true that behavior that is rewarded tends to persist, by rewarding the types of behaviors in the area of creativity that educators claim they value, such behaviors might be more likely to develop.

Second, because the adolescent seems to need approval and acceptance from his peers and because the school can influence his status with his peers (note the position of status secondary schools provide for outstanding athletes) the school might find ways to provide recognition for students who engage in activities of a highly creative variety. This means, for example, that students who function creatively in the arts as well as those who are highly creative in the sciences would be given their educational due by the school. It means further that the secondary school places value on creative thinking in curriculum areas that are now serving as last resorts for future dropouts.

Third, the conception of the balanced curriculum might need to undergo surgery. Perhaps what we need for students is an *un*balanced rather than a balanced curriculum. Perhaps it is not foolish to allow students with special interests or aptitudes to develop these at the risk of leaving others undeveloped. Why do all students need to spend almost the same amount of time studying the same subject matters? If we are serious about providing for the individual differences that we know we have, might we not allow students to develop educational programs that are uniquely suited to their talents? This will not be easy. On the one hand, we are guided by an image of education which considers "basic" education necessary for all youth—yet what is basic for who? On the other hand, secondary school programs are being increasingly restricted by the admission procedures established by the colleges. Thus, curricula differentiation and experimentation can occur only in schools where the students are so bright that they will be admitted to college no matter what is *not* done, or where the students are so culturally disadvantaged that they will not go to college no matter what *is* done.

Fourth, in addition to differentiating the curriculum in order to make the most of the unique talents of the student, the opportunity to work in depth on a project or in a domain should be encouraged. Working creatively in any area requires that an individual have control over the materials and ideas with which he is working. If a student is shuttled through a series of exercises quickly and then given another series having little relationship to the first, the likelihood that he will have an opportunity to develop the type of controls he needs for creative action will be diminished. If, for example, a writer needs to figure out how to spell each word he wants to use, it is unlikely that he will have enough energy left to use the words creatively. If a painter has to stop and think of the color he will get by mixing, say, yellow and blue or green and red, his concerns will be focused away from the expressive and upon the technical. In short, the opportunity to work in depth on a project or in a domain of inquiry is more likely to develop the type of controls needed for creative action than brief contact with a large area.[7]

Fifth, along with providing opportunities for students to raise and be rewarded for insightful questions, the threat of failure in classrooms and in school need to be reduced. Failure is essentially an educational concept. It is a concept which is based upon an assumption that the student should achieve a particular set of objectives within a specified period of time—either by the time of testing or by the end of the semester. If the student does not learn at the expected rate and to the expected degree, he fails. Yet, in our common assessment of learning we do not say that if a child does not learn to ride a bike as fast as his peers he fails. We merely recognize that it takes him longer. By utilizing the threat of failure as a social control the school also uses it as an intellectual control. Fear of failure breeds anxiety and with high levels of anxiety, especially on complex tasks, effectiveness in performance is diminished.[8] Developing a playful, exploratory attitude toward ideas is hardly possible if students are in dread of committing an error or risking a speculation.

The needs of students during adolescence are particular and acute. They need an opportunity to develop a sense of identity and to maintain the

---

7 Some empirical evidence for this was obtained in a study by Kenneth Beittel and Edward Mattil, "The Effect of a 'Depth' vs. a 'Breadth' Method of Art Instruction at the Ninth Grade Level," *Studies in Art Education*, Vol. 3 (Fall 1961), 75–87.

8 Britton E. Ruebush. "Anxiety," in *Child Psychology* (62nd Yearbook of the National Society for the Study of Education), Nelson B. Henry and Herman G. Richey, editors. (Chicago: University of Chicago Press, 1963).

sense of security that emanates from group acceptance. They also need to develop the type of cognitive functioning which seems to emerge for the first time during this period of human development. By providing for the development of intellectual and qualitative competence, in depth, in an area of interest and aptitude, the school may at the same time be contributing to the development of the dual educational goals of psychological health and creativity.

JEROME L. SINGER

# 32. EXPLORING MAN'S IMAGINATIVE WORLD

One of the apparently unique characteristics of man as a biological species is his capacity to provide himself with an extensive source of stimulation by means of images, fantasies, dreams, and related phenomena. This ability to project events, conversations, or abstract formulae onto a mental screen by means of an as yet unimagined neurophysiological process frees man to a remarkable degree from dependence on his external environment. By comparison, all other living species seem to manifest an almost complete dependence on concrete external stimuli or relatively fixed combinations of environmental patterns and fairly specific physiological mechanisms as guides to their movements and behavior patterns. The stimulus bondage of the animal world ranges from tropistic behavior to the releaser mechanisms that govern patterned instinctual performances in more complex species. While some animals seem capable of brief delayed reactions (largely through orienting responses) and some monkeys even show indications of rudimentary abstractions ability (after much training), man seems relatively alone in his capacity to generate within his "mind's eye" a sequence of stimuli to which he may then respond with as much complexity, affect, or directedness as he does to an objective stimulus in his environment.

Consider the situation of a man driving his car home from work. If traffic conditions are not hazardous, the driver is likely to be able to execute a series of fairly complex motor responses such as shifting, depressing clutch, chang-

Reprinted from *Teachers College Record*, Vol. 66, No. 2, (November 1964) 165–79, by permission of the author and publisher.

ing pressure on gas, steering, and watching the road relatively automatically with little if any need for concentration of attention on his motor movements. At the same time he may be listening to the radio, perhaps even humming along with the music, and, in addition, he may drift into a fairly complex daydream about the possible outcome of the project he is working on at his office. If the light turns red ahead and he is not too far lost in thought, he may react appropriately to this external signal by stopping the car with only a brief interruption of his reverie. As his train of images about his project continues, however, he suddenly envisions his desk, and an idea strikes him about a portion of the project which calls for his immediate attention. As soon as the light changes he whips the car around and heads in a different direction. An entire new sequence of behavior has thus been initiated by stimuli which are not observable to anyone else and which are completely independent of the external environmental cues or even of the physiological drive state of hunger which may be fairly high in him at this time of day.

### BLOOM AND HAMLET

This somewhat commonplace example serves to emphasize the general and widespread phenomenon involved in fantasy or imaginative behavior. The extensive literary concern with the "stream of consciousness" or the *monologue intérieur,* as well as the psychoanalytic use of free association, have led to an excessive glamorizing of what are actually quite general human phenomena. Indeed, one of the great masterpieces of "inner world" literature, Joyce's *Ulysses,* is designed to demonstrate the extremely complex and convoluted inner experience of an average man, Leopold Bloom, on his day's rounds in Dublin. The interior monologue of the contrasted character of Stephen Daedelus, the artist, are more literary and poetic, perhaps, but no more extensive or complex than Bloom's.

Concern with man's mental life formed an important part of early psychology. William James' great *Principles of Psychology* had chapters on the "stream of thought" and imagination, and it dealt at length with many issues of self-awareness and inner experience, albeit without much of the dynamic character which has been added by psychoanalysis. The powerful shift of emphasis towards objective behaviorism which characterized American psychology after 1910 led to a sharp diminution in interest in man's imagery, free-flowing thought, and daydreaming because they were not susceptible to measurement by the methods then being developed.

In a sense, the shift toward scientific objectivity in America was not the only factor in the lessened interest in imaginative processes. A more general sociological pattern was involved. America was interested in action and in "getting things done." Bertrand Russell made his brilliant comment that rats in American research laboratories learned by rushing about and active trial and error, whereas animals in German laboratories sat quietly, thought out the problem, then went directly to the goal. This action-oriented emphasis was evident in both theoretical developments, including the ideas of Watson, Thorndike, Hull, and Guthrie, and in the educational trends which represented Dewey's influence. Dewey himself had placed great emphasis on the formal cultivation of thought and had endorsed F. M. Alexander's training methods for "internal awareness" (1) as a basic element of all education. Nevertheless, the general atmosphere in the US stressed action to the neglect of introspection. The mental tests and questionnaires developed to detect the emotionally unstable all included items such as "I daydream frequently," and introversion and neuroticism were assumed to be highly correlated. In education the quiet, inactive child was often viewed critically as a "daydreamer." One of literature's great introverts, Hamlet, speaks disparagingly of himself as "John-a-dreams" and refers to the "native cast of resolution sicklied o'er with the pale cast of thought." Reading much of the American psychological literature of the '20s and '30s certainly confirmed this negative view of man's inner processes.

## NEW FOCUS ON DREAMS

Within psychoanalysis, which has, of course, relied heavily on dreams and fantasies, the emphasis has largely been upon the content of such material and their pathological implications. Freud (11) speculated that thought represented a form of experimental action accompanied by some discharge of energy that permitted the child to delay his attempts at need gratification. The daydream was viewed as continued manifestation of infantile hallucination when primitive impulses sought discharge. Eidelberg (7), recognizing the apparent contradiction between the emphasis on censorship and disguise in dream interpretation and the frequently naked wish fulfillment of daydreams, resolved the issue by suggesting that the actual content of a wishful daydream represents a disguised and more acceptable compromise solution for a still unconscious wish. Daydreaming was viewed by Anna Freud (10) chiefly in its defensive or compensatory role, and it has only been more recently in the new development of ego psychology that Hartmann (18) has considered the possibility of a more general function of daydreaming and fantasy processes.

Psychologists have now begun to reexamine the whole area of man's internal cognitive experience. Spurred in part by methodological developments in the field but also by increasingly important theoretical questions, investigators have begun a more systematic examination of the range, frequency, and function of daydreaming and reverie phenomena. Some of the kinds of questions that arise are basic ones: How does the brain represent images of things past, or how can assorted stored memories be combined into new daydream images or planful thought sequences? No theory of neurophysiology or brain function can be satisfactory until it can explain man's capacity to shift his attention away from ever-present external stimuli to an image only in the mind's eye. At a more obviously practical level are other questions: What degrees or patterns of daydreaming are pathological or maladaptive, or what is the significance for education of the differential development in children of an extensive inner life? Indeed, as one considers the subject in the light of a really surprising paucity of systematic evidence, a host of more specific questions floods to consciousness. To what extent do adults and children differ in the frequency of daydreaming or response to internally produced cognitive stimuli? Are these differences associated with any important definable personality characteristics? Do the reported differences in frequency of resort to inner experience reflect *actual* differences in the frequency of such activity, or do they represent, rather, differences between people in self-sensitivity or willingness to communicate private processes to others? To what extent does the occurrence of a fantasy serve to allay or increase anxiety, reduce drive (as Freud suggested), or arouse the organism to new activity? What factors in the developmental experience of a child lead to differences in the resort to or awareness of inner processes? Do particular patterns of the family constellation or sociocultural background influence the growth of inner life?

## AVENUES OF INQUIRY

Approaches to answering some of these questions have been made along four fronts. One calls for the acquisition of fairly basic knowledge concerning the nature of human differences in frequency and content of daydreaming and related processes. Questionnaire and interview methods have been employed with large samples of normal persons in order to provide some notion of the background factors which influence resort to inner processes. Factor analytic studies have been carried out to ascertain the dimensions of inner experience and also some of the relationships between other personality characteristics and fantasy behavior. A second approach calls for studies of the relationship between electrophysiological processes, attention, and alertness and daydreaming. Recent theory in the field of brain function has brought to the fore the issue of whether certain continuous stimulus activities are necessary to maintain a waking state or a sense of alertness. For example, under extended conditions of sensory deprivation, normal adults show great discomfort and an almost desperate need for some type of feed-in or stimulation. It seems possible that a continuous source of inner stimulation in the form of imagery and other thought processes may be an important aspect of alertness in situations where environmental stimuli are monotonous or greatly reduced. Experiments calling for normals to engage in varied or monotonous mental activity while attending to a flickering light in a darkened room or engaging in various types of mental activity while hooked up to electrophysiological measuring instruments are under way.

A third avenue for studying inner processes calls for studies of normal individuals under conditions of need deprivation, anxiety, anger, and other drive-related conditions. Thus, there is now some support for the notion that an opportunity to express anger through fantasy may reduce the strength of an aggressive drive induced through such means as insult or frustration (*8, 9*). At the same time, clinical experience and some evidence suggest that certain fantasies increase drive or emotional reactions (*34*). Certainly, inner experiences seem more complex than is suggested by the drive-reduction hypothesis. Studies of the relationship, for example, between time experience and fantasy are carried out to evaluate the possibility that persons who can enjoy fantasy or related inner-produced stimuli can tolerate delay or monotony better because they make the time pass more pleasurably and apparently faster. In an unpublished study by Moore, for example, adults, who had not eaten in ten hours felt that an interval of waiting just before receiving food was shorter when they engaged in a fantasy activity than did another group who were prevented from such fantasy.

### STYLES OF PLAY

Still another approach to the area of fantasy calls for the study of its development in children. If we observe a group of young children playing on the street, the style of play falls frequently into several types. Several children may be wholly involved in games that call for great physical activity, agility, or control, *e.g.*, bicycle riding, whereas others may introduce more imaginative elements into their play. The latter group may play "Pirates" or "Cops and Robbers"; they may introduce invisible figures into the game or change the scene to far-off places. Of course, most children play both types of games, but it does seem clear that some prefer fantasy games or develop them extensively in their play repertory without necessarily excluding such physical activities as baseball. Studies are now under way to clarify the process by which a child comes to focus more on fantasy play and how this becomes eventually internalized into daydreaming or inner cognitive experience. In one study, for example, children who were told that they were being considered as astronauts of the future were required to sit quietly for long periods of time in a simulated space-ship. It was found that children who reported more extensive fantasy play activities and greater parental contact through reading and story-telling were able to sit quietly for longer time periods (*30*).

These example represent only brief glimpses of the types of studies now being attempted. The technical difficulties of carrying out experiments in this area are great, particularly because mental activity is constant and fleeting. Rather than stress the methodological issues, however, it may be best to attempt a more general formulation of some of the findings as well as of some of the general impressions gained through an extensive exploration of the whole domain of imagination and daydreaming behavior. The summary offered here represents an extremely tentative statement, some of it supported by experimental findings, much of it reflecting more recent hunches and hypotheses suggested by a fresh look as this difficult research frontier.

## ORIGINS OF IMAGINATION

A major theoretical issue in any attempt at conceptualizing the role of imaginative processes in personality organization concerns the degree to which fantasy is to be viewed as a derived process, growing out of conflict or the frustration of a drive. More recently, there has been considerable criticism of theories that reduce most complex human behavior to the form of defenses or sublimations of certain appetitive or aggressive drives (36). Much more attention is now being paid to early patterns of curiosity and the apparent satisfaction and information an organism obtains from sheer intercourse with a variety of environmental stimuli. The important striving for self-development within particular organ-systems and the significance of developing and discriminating capacities, and of new skills related to them, are being increasingly recognized (18, 26, 36).

Wthin this conceptual framework it may be most useful to look on imaginative behavior in the same fashion as Bartlett (4) has regarded all thinking—as a skill. Fantasy, daydreaming, inner experience, and introspective capacity may all represent aspects of a dimension of internally produced cognitive processes whose growth and patterning, while probably limited by constitutional factors, may be greatly influenced by opportunities for learning and practice. If the ultimate origin of imagery as a brain process remains obscure, we may still entertain some fruitful notions as to the concatenation of conditions which foster its development differentially in man.

It seems likely that some basic symbolic or imagery capacity is an important component of all thought and certainly fantasy. There have been, of course, extensive studies of imagery types (12, 22), but these researches have emphasized the revival of recently perceived stimuli and have been less concerned with the day-to-day flow and pattern of inner experience. A recent study (31) has suggested that even reported daydreaming reflects a great deal of variation in the degree and type of imagery involved although visual and verbal imagery predominate. It certainly seems reasonable to expect that some basic capacity for symbolic capacity is involved in imagination. An intriguing experimental question in this connection is whether symbolic or imaginative thought can be learned through formal training procedures. The educational and philosophical implications of such a process, were it demonstrable, are manifold.

Allowing for initial differences in constitution, what factors in the early experience of a child may also account for the development of fantasy capacities? Present evidence points to the importance for the child of a close attachment or identification with at least one parent (*15, 29, 30*). In orthodox psychoanalytic theory itself, much emphasis is placed on the fact that a moderately successful handling of the Oedipal conflict in a child involves his inhibition of erotic and aggressive drives and, through identification with parental figures, incorporation of a set of values and internal controls on impulses. Indeed Arlow (*3*), in describing the theoretically presumed behavior of a child who has never had an Oedipal complex, presents a picture that corresponds to the impulsive, unimaginative, stimulus-bound behavior reported by Goldfarb (*15*) in his studies of children reared from early years in such impersonal institutional settings as orphanages.

### CONTROLS FROM LOVE

One need not accept the conception of a universal Oedipus complex, however, to recognize how the early experience of closeness to a parent may foster the development of inner controls and also internal cognitive processes. The child who has considerable contact with a parent is likely, on the one hand, to be required to control various childish impulses and motor behavior, whereas at the same time, he is provided with verbal content, with story-telling material, and with play-acting games by the adult and with encouragement to be like the adult. To a child, the attempt to simulate the adult's behavior or world and even to perceive it accurately requires a repetitious reconstruction of the stimulus in order to grasp its details. Schachtel (*26*) has made this point in explaining children's delight in rereading simple stories. A benign and interested parent establishes an atmosphere in which the child is likely to attempt, even in the parents' temporary absence, to reconstruct some of the pleasurable features of the contact. Thus, a reasonably positive and fairly intensive contact with at least one parent may be an important feature of the atmosphere conducive to fantasy development in the child. Mowrer (*23*) has pointed to the importance of such an affective tie even in the basic learning of language as well as in animal training. There are by now some indications that both normal and emotionally disturbed adults and children (*28, 29, 30*) who show more positive feelings about at least one parent also reveal more imaginative tendencies.

Which of the parents is more significant in this respect? The mother naturally comes to mind. Indeed Nunberg (*24*) quotes Goethe:

> From Father I have looks and build
> And the serious conduct of living.
> My mother gave me gaiety
> And zest for spinning stories.

Certainly, within many cultures, the mother's role in singing lullabies and telling bed-time stories or in presenting religious precepts may serve to foster imaginative thought either as a substitute or supplement to the child's physically active exploration of the environment. Most of the evidence available on this point tends to support this notion. Sharaf *(28)*, for example, found that a close attachment and even confiding relationship with the mother was associated with the development of what he called introceptive attitudes in a group of young men. Data from several questionnaire studies of reported daydream frequency in adult men and women indicate that those persons who tend to see themselves as rather more identified in interests with their mothers than their fathers report greater fantasy tendencies than more paternally oriented subjects *(32, 33)*. A more recent finding with a group of middle class seven-year-olds, however, raises a question about whether in the greater "togetherness" and father-child relatedness fostered by some suburban patterns, the situation may be changing *(30)*.

## PRACTICING FANTASY

Given the closeness to at least one adult who encourages verbal interchange or fantasy play, a child still requires some opportunity to practice such activities. Present indications are that extensive contact with other children is likely to provide less opportuinty for such fantasy play unless, of course, the other children are considerably older and play a quasi-parental role, e.g., a much older sister plays "house" or "school" with a younger sibling. By and large, the extensive and kaleidoscopic ebb and flow of motion and affective stimulation provided by a group of children is most likely to involve a child in the external situation and will minimize tendencies toward fantasy play. In one study *(30)*, children who reported more extensive fantasy play, for instance, also proved to have significantly fewer older siblings (*i.e.,* tended to be first-born or only children). It is of interest to note that studies of precocious children or of the childhood of geniuses have suggested in many instances only a minimal contact with other children and occasionally actually discouragement of such contacts by parents seeking to develop greatness in their children *(21)*. Bertrand Russell *(6)*, in an autobiographical note, provides a touching example of how loneliness, obvious intellectual giftedness, and curiosity combined in the development of his extensive inner capacities.

The instance of Russell points up, however, an issue as yet little touched by research. The inner world of man appears not to be a unitary phenomenon; daydreams and reveries vary greatly in content and general structure. It seems likely *(31)* that certain young people have in general more extensive inner activity of all types than do their more extroverted or externally responsive peers. At the same time, consistent differences in degree of interpersonal, abstract, or highly objective content occur. It seems reasonable to suppose that while men such as Russell, Tennessee Williams, or Beethoven may have had lonely childhoods and subsequently developed complex imaginations, they also developed rather strikingly different predominant patterns of content. Why a child should choose one of several options in his pattern of inner experience remains a fascinating question. A small clue is suggested by a finding by Roe (25) that biological scientists more frequently experienced an early loss of a parent than did psychologists.

Naturally, family interest patterns and the cultural atmosphere or early exposure to certain areas of success or to significant teachers may influence the direction of content of fantasy. Active curiosity, combining with the occurrence of some puzzling or unexplained family situation, has been offered as explaining particular developments of fantasy lives or scientific interests (20, 24). Early detection of such patterns of fantasy may be one avenue open to educators striving to improve capacities and motivation for qualitative excellence in particular subject areas.

### COGNITION AND INDEPENDENCE

It should be stressed at this point that the closeness with at least one parent mentioned above does not necessarily mean overdependence. If anything, because fantasy seems to require practice, the "smothering" mother, by providing constant help or gratification, may effectively limit opportunities for imaginative development or may enhance the development of a sexualized involvement with herself that leads to a narrowed and distressing fantasy life in the child. A popular joke tells of the aged mother who boasts of her closeness to her son, now a 40-year-old bachelor, by saying, "He still lives at home, sends me flowers, loves my cooking, and—you know what—he goes to this fancy psychoanalysis doctor about a nervous condition, and all he talks about to him every day is me!"

If anything, the development of an inner life of some complexity may increase the relative independence of a young person. The degree to which such a child or adolescent can find increased satisfaction in reading or in some symbolic or artistic experience greatly enhances both the fullness of his mental content and his behavioral repertoire. Such persons are likely to be less closely bound to the opinions of the mediocre norm of playmates or teachers. Their independence may present some difficulties for them socially or even educationally, as the recent work of Getzels and Jackson (13) has suggested. It should be noted, however, that development of an extensive inner life by no means excludes the possibility of enjoyment and skill in social experiences, group games, or sports. The recognition and acceptance of one's inner life merely gives one an additional medium for play and satisfaction.

In this connection a word may be said about the influence of television on the development of inner experience. Although there has yet been little systematic study here, one may surmise that by providing a varied and extensive content (humorous characters, far-off countries, adventurous incidents), TV may greatly increase the imaginative scope of a child. Certainly, the vocabularies and scientific knowledge of millions of children have been influenced by the vivid attraction provided by this visual and auditory medium. Its great hold via our most responsive sense, the visual, may be ultimately destructive of imaginative skill, however. As already stressed, development of the fantasy dimension requires active practice, and TV viewing, if permitted unchecked, becomes a substitute for such internal development. Even radio listening provided a somewhat better medium because the auditory medium alone was involved, and fantasy imagery was required by a child to follow the broadcast story. Extensive TV viewing may, therefore, prevent the full development of imaginative skills. The possible harmful influence of unchecked television-viewing on the development of thinking ability, however compelling a notion, nevertheless remains a hypothesis until some really extensive experimental studies are forthcoming. Observation suggests that children who show some early imaginative capacities are likely, even when viewing TV, to become involved in a game of their own which elaborates on the ongoing presentation or ultimately demands almost the full attention of the child.

## CULTURAL IMPACT

The influence of the immediate family constellation or the early childhood experiences do not appear to be completely sufficient bases for the development of an extensive inner dimension. Certain cultural or sociological factors also seem to play a role. Particular value systems within subcultural groups in the United States are transmitted through family and peer groups or early school experiences. There are, for example, some suggestions in the research that adults who have been reared in urban or rural settings report more daydreaming than persons reared in suburbs (32). In a sense, one can be more alone in a big city or a rural area than in the suburbs, where organizational activities, Cub Scouts, and planned "groupiness" have long flourished. Sociological factors like upward social mobility seem also related to reported daydreaming frequency (33); adults from Negro, Jewish, and Italian backgrounds revealed more frequent daydreaming than did persons whose subcultural backgrounds were Irish, German, and Anglo-Saxon. The daydreaming frequency was closely related to social status, immigration patterns, and general economic mobility. Undoubtedly, too, the more general American pattern, largely puritan and Anglo-Saxon with its emphasis on action and practical effectiveness, may play a role in the acceptability to a given person of an inner life.

For the adolescent, clinical indications suggest that much depends on the degree to which the teenager can find at least some social value or group support for his imaginative experience. A great many college freshmen, interviewed about their daydreaming patterns, reported a sharp drop in this activity after they entered college (*31*). Even so the evidence indicates that the college period is a peak for reported daydream frequency with a decline through the mid-fifties (*32*). Although no data on older age groups are available, one suspects that as the pressure of daily chores is lessened, the older person may begin to drift more and more into reminiscent daydreaming. If the adolescent finds a group of friends or teachers who value inner experience, or if he finds some sense of identification through a personal expression of this experience in scientific or aesthetic media, he is more likely to tolerate imaginative dimension. It is likely that at this period fantasy may begin to be crystallized more and more within particular subcategories such as the objective-rational or the interpersonal-fanciful.

### FANTASY IN ADAPTATION

What is the adaptive significance of a well developed fantasy life or an inner dimension of cognitive experience? Some obvious advantages need not be discussed here simply because no one will question that thinking represents a great evolutionary advance in living species. Man's capacity for long-range planning, the development of tools, and control of the physical environment chiefly results from his great superiority in the conception and communication of abstract symbols. Let us consider some other manifestations of imagination, however. The person who through reading and imaginative play has developed a considerable ability to picture events or scenes concerning people in his mind's eye has available a valuable tool for greatly increasing his own response repertory. The capacity to imagine a variety of social responses or to run through a sequence of alternative reactions to a stress situation may greatly enhance the ability of a person to deal with novel or difficult social demands. Actual practice in real situations is necessary too, but it is possible that such learning will come more quickly to a person who has engaged in prior fantasy.

An example may be cited in connection with a problem of increasing significance—relationships with persons from very different cultures. The person lacking much interest or fantasy play in envisioning himself in distant lands, among people with strange customs, may often, when actually confronted with such a foreigner, react with anxiety or aggression when an unanticipated response is made. The more imaginative individual whose combination of reading and reverie has prepared him for greater diversity of response, may not immediately know what is expected of him by the foreigner, but he may be less anxious and hence more willing to explore until a suitable communication is possible. Hall (*17*) has documented many instances in which an imaginative preparation for cultural diversity might have greatly eased communication between Americans and persons from different cultures.

The urban industrial civilization in which we live, with its institutionalized fantasy in the media of TV, movies, and advertising (27), actually demands greater capacity for flexible fantasy-like thinking in many of its work situations. The person who can enjoy the kaleidoscopic play of images and symbols that often characterize the stream of thought may find himself at an advantage in dealing with many work situations that call for a flexible use of symbolism or verbal fluency.

The role of imagination and daydreaming as a defense mechanism is stressed in most of the clinical literature and need not be dealt with at length here. The individual who can deal with anxieties and aggressive affect by means of the imaginative representation of situations which evoke them may often be better off than the person who lacks such capacity or who fears conscious symbolic representation of his distress. Playing some of one's anger or need out in fantasy may, indeed, as Freud suggested, reduce some of the drive; over and above this, however, it may, by its very flexibility, prevent an overt and irrevocable act and may also suggest new alternative routes for satisfying the arousal need. The fact that fantasy takes its origin in play brings it close to humor and wit and makes it possible for the person who employs fantasy when anxious or in conflict to see a humorous aspect to his dilemma or to play out the stress through a comical fantasy. Often enough, a husband who has been enraged by his wife's action and finds himself, in fantasy, playing out a symbolic and elaborate "perfect crime," may find a way to communicate his concerns with humor rather than rancor. Many of James Thurber's domestic vignettes have much of the quality of the exaggerated play of fantasy as a means of dealing with a frustrating situation.

## DREAMS, CREATIVITY, PATHOLOGY

At a somewhat more neurophysiological level, there is now sound preliminary evidence that the capacity for imaginal representations may be important for generally maintaining the alertness or homeostatic balance of the human being. Dement's work (5) on dream deprivation has suggested that awakening sleepers as soon as electrophysiological measures imply that a dream has begun leads to gross disturbances, irritability, and a desperate need to catch up on such imaginal activities. Similarly, studies of persons under sensory deprivation (14) or in situations calling for perceptual vigilance under prolonged monotonous conditions (2) strongly suggest that imaginative capacity is related to arousal processes in the brain. The person who can enjoy fantasy may be able to provide himself with a pleasurable and varied stimulus medium when external sensory experiences are greatly reduced; hence, he may be able to stay awake or alert where others drop off to sleep. Research in this area is only beginning, however.

The relation of imaginative capacity to creative activity has, of course, been widely discussed. Studies of creative persons in both the scientific and aesthetic fields suggest that a playful attitude, an acceptance of diverse or previously unconnected associations, is often one of their characteristics. Whether for artistic or scientific purposes or for creative living in interpersonal situations apart from vocation, the ability to employ imaginative means and the willingness to resort to that realm prior to an immersion in direct perceptual reaction or overt behavior seems necessary if not sufficient. Huxley (*19*) has presented many important examples of the value of such a development of man's inner dimension.

If it is clear that many aspects of daydreaming and fantasy can be viewed as adaptive, preparatory for effective functioning, and representative in some situations of man's highest capacities, there remain some pathological and maladaptive developments of fantasy. To the extent that daydreaming provides a functional stimulus world for the observer, it competes to some degree with the external stimulus field. To the extent that a person takes great pleasure in responding to internally produced cognitive stimuli, he is liable to overlook important signals from the outside world that demand immediate reactions. The absent-minded professor presents the most benign form of this maladaptive pattern. Lost in an inner contemplation of a mathematical derivation or the relative merits of two new translations of a Chinese classic, he enters his home, removes his coat, and having begun an unconscious habitual sequence, continues to undress as if for bed. Such excessive resort to an inner world is far more serious under circumstances where rapid response and perceptual discrimination are urgent. Our homebound motorist referred to earlier may become so involved in envisioning his work assignment that he misses a change in traffic lights—with potentially disastrous results. Similarly, the person who perhaps has developed an extreme reliance on fantasy as a defense mechanism may lose himself in artistic reverie during conversations and fail to respond appropriately to his companions or fail completely to observe the needs or desires of the other persons. Excessive reliance on fantasy may thus result in withdrawal from effective perception or social communication and may severely interfere with one's capacity for interpersonal intimacy.

## WITHDRAWAL AS DEFENSE

For the developing child, excessive resort to fantasy may become an almost complete substitute for social contact. The result may be failure to develop important social skills and sensitivity to the nuances of interpersonal communication. Much of our relating to other persons involves a good deal of nonverbal communication and the perceptive timing of affective reactions or direct communications. The child withdrawn completely into fantasy play may learn too late that he is lacking in such skills. He may be overly formal with peers or perhaps too literary in his conversation. The resulting embarrassment may force him more into his inner world, and as time passes, social intercourse may appear more and more like an alien activity fraught with danger. In some instances, this pattern may lead to a schizophrenic reaction. The loneliness and desire for contact with others is coupled with anxiety. Fantasies about the possible outcomes of interaction with others are carried out on an increasingly ethereal plane. The potentiality for social communication and abstract symbolism cannot be actualized by test in social situations, and an increasingly bizarre quality appears in the overt expressions of the adolescent—with consequent destructive feedback. A withdrawal into a total fantasy world may result.

Despite our popular conceptions, however, it is rare to find chronic schizophrenics with extensive daydream lives. The withdrawal of longstanding schizophrenic patients does not appear to be actually a removal to an extensive imaginative world. It is very likely that the fantasy defense still requires some external reinforcement or social approval to exist; and in the case of psychotic patients, it seems likely that the pleasure in daydreaming has long faded and that the fantasy response has been extinguished in favor of an almost contentless, unfocused perceptual blurring (much as occurs normally under great fatigue), or an obsessive perceptual concentration on minute internal bodily reactions or on external trivia like the slow burning of the ash on one's cigarette.

Somewhat less extreme, perhaps, is the development of a tendency toward obsessive rumination in persons who show many reasonably adaptive characteristics. These persons reflect more the characteristics attacked in himself by Hamlet—the hesitation about action because of preoccupation with manifold alternatives, the excessive preoccupation with clarifying one's own image while important matters wait, the failure to observe carefully what the external situation demands because of the predominance of an elaborate prior fantasy. Much attention has been given in psychoanalysis to the role of fantasy as part of the complex that characterizes certain masochistic sexual tendencies as well as certain more general self-harming social patterns.

Somewhat less dramatic but upsetting in its consequences is the pattern often observed when a person develops an elaborate fantasy prior to a much awaited event. A wife awaits her husband's return from work and constructs a pleasant fantasy of his romantic entrance and his passionate embrace and words of devotion and reassurance. The husband, on the other hand, having spent his day in numerous verbal exchanges, frenzied or anguished, may construct a fantasy of the relaxed quiet and good dinner that await him on his return. Both fantasies may be overly elaborate. When the husband enters, kicks off his shoes, and slumps wearily into a chair, the disappointed wife may launch into an angry recital of the day's appliance breakdowns and children's misfortunes which smashes the man's fantasy, and a bitter quarrel ensues. An important feature of psychotherapy is the clarification to a patient, through careful elucidation of the details of such a quarrel, of the manner in which his anger and destructive behavior may reflect distress over the failure of such a fantasy to materialize into reality. Very often, this close connection between frustrated fantasy and a subsequent outburst of anger is not perceived. One consequence of an effective psychoanalysis is a heightened awareness of the relationships among one's inner fantasies, affective reactions, and overt behavior.

## EDUCATIONAL IMPLICATIONS

It must be stressed that while the general advantages of assisting persons to increase their awareness of or capacity for internal experiences may be apparent, we still know little in a sufficiently precise fashion to set up rules of thumb in this domain. Huxley (*19*) has argued cogently that modern education neglects to our detriment our capacity for "elementary awareness." He believes both that sensitivity to external events can be greatly increased, and that we need training in the "wise passiveness" which, "followed in due course by wise hard work, is the condition of creativity" (*19*, p. 288). If children are properly trained he says, they can profitably use imaginative games as symbolic outlets for anger and frustration.

Granted the value of such an effort, the question of suitable techniques remains an open one and begs for systematic exploration. Pending such research, the type of radical revision of our curriculum that Huxley calls for seems far away. A first step, however, calls for the recognition of the adaptive and maladaptive facets of daydreaming or imaginative play. The alert teacher must be careful not to label the "daydreamer" as a problem child without more careful examination of what really underlies his apparent immersion in fantasy. Indeed, some children who are termed "daydreamers" because they are inattentive may actually suffer from a lack of capacity for such imaginative activity. Lacking an ability for sustained attention, they are a constant prey to changing environmental stimuli. Eventually, they may have to be helped to develop some inner dimension as a control mechanism to balance their external responsiveness.

The fantasy play patterns of children may also serve as an important guide to their interests. The child who shows a great deal of play involving historical figures may be become involved more readily in reading materials or related activities if they are associated with his fantasies. Our increasing knowledge also suggests some caution in the interpretation of the content of fantasy. The occurrence of much violence in the fantasy play of a child does not necessarily imply a danger of overt destructive behavior. Neither does aggressive fantasy preclude such overt violence. More important than content seems to be structure—the degree to which the child clearly sees it as play or fantasy, the degree to which a shift back to social responsiveness is possible, the degree of creative elaboration of the story-line as against crude expression of the content coupled with much overt physical action. All these are important clues as to the likelihood of overt antisocial reactions. Unusually idiosyncratic content of a bizarre nature or obviously related to disturbing family patterns may provide clues as to specific problems distressing a child; but generally speaking, the relationship of fantasy to emotional disturbance is more complex, and such interpretations can be misleading.

### FAMILY AND FANTASY

The extent to which children's fantasy or imaginative scope can be broadened remains an unanswered question. Certainly one may take a hint from the indications concerning the origins of fantasy in the family constellation. The teacher who establishes a strong positive bond with a child becomes a role-model. If the teacher herself has a capacity for a certain type of imaginative thought or play, children will seek to emulate it and incorporate it into their own role-repertory. A sense of humor about certain problems can be transmitted in this fashion. One teacher, much beloved for her warmth by her students, often used the phrase, "So I ask myself, sez I, 'Should I do it this way or the other?'" In this fashion, she seemed able to encourage a pattern of self-examination about alternatives.

Fantasy outlets, actual dramatic productions, and story-telling for cathartic purposes have been found to be clinically useful in dealing with children who bring insufficient inner controls to the classroom situation. One wonders to what extent a fairly active play-acting program, with educational materials deliberately and relevantly woven into the dramatic structure, might prove useful with certain acting-out children. The combination of some structural form and the content of the dramatic part might assist such children in the development of controls and of some broader role conceptions while also serving as an outlet for certain aggressive drives. The socialization of such drives through athletic activities has long been accepted and has provided our society with its major sport figures; a concomitant program for developing more imaginative capacity by fantasy play or dramatic activities has not been tried to the same degree.

It should be clear from this presentation that we stand only at the threshold of systematic knowledge concerning the nature and educational implications of man's inner dimension of experience. Much basic research along the lines suggested needs to be done, but it does not seem premature to begin applied studies of new techniques for heightening imaginative capacity in young people. Methods such as the fantasy games or the "synectics" techniques of Gordon (*16*) might be employed in formal controlled studies with children chosen as extremes along relevant dimensions, *e.g.,* inadequate inner controls or easy distractibility. Many possibilities beckon once one regards fantasy or daydreaming as a neutral dimension of experience and frees it from the opprobrium implied in "retreat from reality" or "defense mechanisms." Viewing our human capacity to daydream as a skill to be developed encourages an approach to both research and education that may prove richly rewarding.

## REFERENCES

1. ALEXANDER, F. M. *The use of the self.* New York: Dutton, 1932.
2. ANTROBUS, J. S., and J. L. SINGER Visual signal detection as a function of rate of stimulus presentation and sequential variability of simultaneous speech. *J. Exp. Psychol.*, 1964.
3. ARLOW, J. Psychoanalysis as scientific method. S. Hook (Ed.) *Psychoanalysis, scientific method, and philosophy.* New York: Grove Press, 1959. Pp. 201–211.
4. BARTLETT, F. M. *Thinking.* New York: Basic Books, 1958.
5. DEMENT, W. The effect of dream deprivation. *Sci.*, 1960, *131*, 1705–1707.
6. EGNER, R. E., and L. E. DENNON *The basic writings of Bertrand Russell.* New York: Simon & Schuster, 1962.
7. EIDELBERG, L. Contributions to the study of masturbation fantasy. *Int. J. Psychoanal.*, 1945, *26*, 127–137.
8. FESHBACH, S. The drive-reducing function of fantasy behavior. *J. Abnorm. Soc. Psychol.*, 1955, *50*, 3–11.
9. FESHBACH, S. The stimulating versus cathartic effects of a vicarious agressive activity. *J. Abnorm. Soc. Psychol.*, 1961, *55*, 381–385.
10. FREUD, ANNA. *The ego and the mechanisms of defense.* New York: International Univers. Press, 1946.
11. FREUD, S. Formulations regarding the two principles in mental functioning. *Collected Papers*, Vol. IV. London: Hogarth, 1925. Pp. 13–21.
12. GALTON, F. *Inquiries into the human faculty.* London: Macmillan, 1883.
13. GETZELS, J., & Jackson, P. W. *Creativity and intelligence.* New York: Wiley, 1962.
14. GOLDBERGER, L., and R. R. HOLT A comparison of isolation effects and their personality correlates in two divergent samples. *Progress report., Biomed. Lab.*, US Air Force, Wright-Patterson AFB, Ohio, 1961.
15. GOLDFARB, W. Effects of psychological deprivation in infancy and subsequent stimulation. *Amer. J. Psychiat.*, 1945, *102*, 18–33.
16. GORDON, W. *Synectics.* New York: Harper, 1961.
17. HALL, E. *The silent language.* New York: Doubleday, 1959.
18. HARTMANN, H. *Ego psychology and the problem of adaption.* New York: International Univers. Press, 1958.
19. HUXLEY, A. Education on the nonverbal level. *Daedalus*, 1962, *91*, 279–293.
20. JONES, E. *The life and work of Sigmund Freud.* New York: Basic Books, 1955.
21. McCURDY, H. G. The childhood pattern of genius. *Horizon,* 1960, *2*, 32–38.
22. McKELLAR, P. *Imagination and thinking.* New York: Basic Books, 1957.
23. MOWRER, O. H. *Learning theory and behavior.* New York: Wiley, 1960.
24. NUNBERG, H. *Curiosity.* New York: International Univers. Press, 1961.
25. ROE, ANNE. Analysis of group Rorschachs of psychologists and anthropologists. *J. Proj. Tech.*, 1952, *16*, 212–224.
26. SCHACHTEL, E. *Metamorphosis.* New York: Basic Books, 1959.
27. SCHRAMM, W., J. LYLE,and E. B. PARKER *Television in the lives of our children.* Stanford, California: Stanford Univers. Press, 1961.

28. SHARAF, M. R. An approach to the theory and measurement of introception. Unpublished doctoral dissertation, Harvard Univer., 1959.
29. SINGER, J. L. Delayed gratification and ego-development: implications for clinical and experimental research. *J. Consult. Psychol.,* 1955. *19,* 259–266.
30. SINGER, J. L. Imagination and waiting ability in young children. *J. Pers.,* 1961, *29,* 396–413.
31. SINGER, J. L., and J. S. ANTROBUS A factor analytic study of daydreaming and conceptually-related cognitive and personality variables. *Percept. Mot. Skills. Monogr. Suppl.,* 3v17, 1963, *17,* 187–209.
32. SINGER, J. L., and VIVIAN MCGRAVEN Some characteristics of adult daydreaming. *J. Psychol.,* 1961, *51,* 151–164.
33. SINGER, J. L., and VIVIAN MCGRAVEN. Patterns of daydreaming in American subcultural groups. *Inter. J. Soc. Psychiat.,* 1962, *8,* 272–282.
34. SINGER, J. L., and R. ROWE. An experimental study of some relationship between daydreaming and anxiety. *J. Consult. Psychol.,* 1962.
35. SINGER, J. L., and ROSALEA SCHONBAR. Correlates of daydreaming: a dimension of self-awareness. *J. Consult. Psychol.,* 1961, *25,* 1–6.
36. WHITE, R. W. Motivation reconsidered: the concept of competence. *Psychol. Rev.,* 1959, 66, 297–333.

MICHAEL A. WALLACH and
NATHAN KOGAN

# 33.   CREATIVITY AND INTELLIGENCE IN CHILDREN'S THINKING

While there has been a great deal of discussion in recent years concerning the importance of fostering "creativity" in our children, there is little solid evidence to support the claim that creativity can be distinguished from the more familiar concept of intelligence. To be sure, the word "creativity" has caught the fancy of the culture—frequent reference is made to creativity in contexts as diverse as education, industry, and advertising. Time and time again, however, the "proof" offered to support the existence of a type of cognitive excellence different from general intelligence has proven to be a will-o-the-wisp.

Reprinted from *Trans-action Magazine,* Vol 4, (1967), pp. 38–43, by permission of the authors and publisher. Copyright © 1967 by *Trans-action Magazine,* Rutgers University, New Brunswick, N. J.

The logical requirements for such a proof can be put as follows. The psychological concept of *intelligence* defines a network of strongly related abilities concerning the retention, transformation, and utilization of verbal and numerical symbols: at issue are a person's memory storage capacities, his skill in solving problems, his dexterity in manipulating and dealing with concepts. The person high in one of these skills will tend to be high in all; the individual who is low in one will tend to be low in all. But what of the psychological concept of *creativity?* If the behavior judged to be indicative of creativity turns up in the same persons who behave in the ways we call "intelligent," then there is no justification for claiming the existence of any kind of cognitive capacity apart from general intelligence. We would have to assert that the notion of greater or lesser degrees of *creativity* in people simply boils down, upon empirical inspection, to the notion of greater or lesser degrees of general *intelligence.* On the other hand, in order to demonstrate that there are grounds for considering creativity to be a kind of cognitive talent that exists in its own right, another kind of proof would be required. It would be necessary to demonstrate that whatever methods of evaluation are utilized to define variations in creativity from person to person result in classifications that are different from those obtained when the same individuals are categorized as to intelligence.

When we reviewed the quantitative research on creativity, we were forced to conclude that these logical requirements were not met. Despite frequent use of the term "creativity" to define a form of talent that was independent of intelligence, examination of the evidence indicated that the purported measures of creativity tended to have little more in common with each other than they had in common with measures of general intelligence. If one could do about the same thing with an IQ measure as one could with the creativity measures, (regarding who should be considered more creative and who should be considered less creative) it was difficult to defend the practice of invoking a new and glamorous term such as "creativity" for describing the kind of talent under study.

While varying conceptions of the meaning of creativity had been embodied in the measures used, they all shared one thing in common: they had been administered to the persons under study as *tests.* From the viewpoint of the person undergoing assessment, the creativity procedures, no less than an intelligence test, carried the aura of school examinations. They were carried out with explicit or implicit time limits in classroom settings where many students underwent the assessment procedures at the same time. Indeed, we even found that the creativity procedures had been described to the students as "tests" by the psychologists who gave them.

We were suspicious that such a test-like context was inimical to the wholehearted display of cognitive characteristics which could be correctly referred to as being involved in creativity. Hence we believed that creativity had not yet been given a fair chance to reveal itself as a different form of excellence than intelligence. These suspicions were reinforced when we considered what creative artists and scientists have said concerning creative moments in their own work.

## THEIR CREATIVE ELDERS

In their introspections one finds an emphasis upon the production of a free flow of ideas—the bubbling forth of varieties of associations concerning the matter at hand. Einstein, for example, refers to the need for "combinatory play" and "associative play" in putting ideas together. Dryden describes the process of writing as involving "a confus'd mass of thoughts, tumbling over one another in the dark." Poincaré talks about ideas as having "rose in crowds" immediately prior to his obtaining a significant mathematical insight. These associations, moreover, range with high frequency into the consideration of unique, unusual possibilities, but ones which are nevertheless relevant to the issue rather than just bizarre. When we look in to the conditions under which an abundant flow of unique ideational possibilities has been available, the artists and scientists indicate that the most conducive attitude is one of playful contemplation—if you will, of permissiveness. Creative awareness tends to occur when the individual—in a playful manner—entertains a range of possibilities without worry concerning his own personal success or failure and how his self-image will fare in the eyes of others.

With this in mind we formulated a research program that involved the extensive study of 151 fifth-grade children. They were of middle-class socio-economic status, and boys and girls were about equally represented in our sample. The work, which was supported in part by the Cooperative Research Program of the United States Office of Education, has been described in detail in our book, *Modes of Thinking in Young Children: A Study of the Creativity-Intelligence Distinction* (Holt, Rinehart and Winston, 1965).

From the introspections of scientists and artists arose some ground rules concerning what creativity might rightfully signify if in fact it constitutes a type of excellence different from intelligence. These ground rules might be put in terms of the following two injunctions:

First, study the flow of ideas—consider how unique and how abundant are the kinds of ideas that a child can provide when contemplating various sorts of tasks. One is talking here, of course, about relevant ideas, not about ideas that might earn the status of being unique only because they are so bizarre as to have no relevance at all to the task.

Second, provide an atmosphere that convinces the child that he is not under test—that the situation is one of play rather than one where his intellectual worthiness is under evaluation by others. This second injunction may be a particularly difficult one to fulfill on the American educational scene, where testing and the feeling of undergoing personal evaluation are ubiquitous. Yet if our considerations were correct, it obviously was essential to fulfill it if creativity was to receive a fighting chance to display itself.

Accordingly, we mustered every device possible to place the assessment procedures in a context of play rather than in the typical context of testing with which the children were all too familiar. There were no time limits on the procedures. They were administered to one child at a time rather than to groups of children seated at their classroom desks. The adults who worked with the children, moreover, had already established relationships in the context of play activities. We even took pains to avoid the customary vocabulary of tests and testing in connection with the research enterprise as a whole—in our talk with the children we described the work as oriented to the study of children's games for purposes of developing new games children would like.

CHILDREN'S RESPONSES TO ABSTRACT DRAWINGS

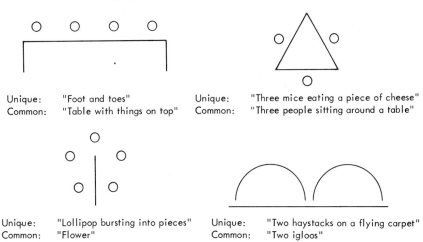

Unique:    "Foot and toes"
Common:   "Table with things on top"

Unique:    "Three mice eating a piece of cheese"
Common:   "Three people sitting around a table"

Unique:    "Lollipop bursting into pieces"
Common:   "Flower"

Unique:    "Two haystacks on a flying carpet"
Common:   "Two igloos"

Reprinted from *Modes of Thinking* by Michael A. Wallach and Nathan Kogan, (New York: © Holt, Rinehart and Winston, Inc., 1965) by permission of Holt, Rinehart and Winston, Inc.

The procedures involved such matters as requesting the child to suggest possible uses for each of several objects, or to describe possible ways in which each of several pairs of objects are similar to each other. For example, in one procedure the child was to suggest all the different ways in which we could use such objects as a newspaper, a cork, a shoe, a chair. "Rip it up if angry" was a unique response for "newspaper," while "make paper hats" was not unique. In another, he was to indicate similarities between, for example, a potato and a carrot, a cat and a mouse, milk and meat. "They are government-inspected" was a unique response for "milk and meat," while "they come from animals" was not unique. In yet another, he was to indicate all the things that each of a number of abstract drawings might be—such as the drawings shown in the illustrations. For the triangle with three circles around it, "three mice eating a piece of cheese" was a unique response, while "three people sitting around a table" was not unique. For the two half-circles over the line, "two haystacks on a flying carpet" was a unique response, while "two igloos" was not unique.

Our interests were in the *number* of ideas that a child would suggest, and the *uniqueness* of the suggested ideas—the extent to which a given idea in response to a given task belonged to one child alone rather than being an idea that was suggested by other children as well. In addition, we used a variety of traditional techniques for assessing general intelligence with the same children.

When the results of the creativity assessment procedures were compared with the results of the intelligence measures, a definite divergence was obtained—the kind that had not been found in earlier studies. They had already shown, and so did our study, that a child who scores at the high intelligence end of one intelligence test will tend to score that way in other intelligence tests as well. In addition, however, our research revealed two further facts which tended to be different from earlier studies:

The various measures of creativity that we utilized had a great deal in common with one another: a child who scored at the high creativity end of one of our creativity measures tended to score at the high creativity end of all the rest of these measures.

Of particular importance, the indices of creativity and the indices of intelligence tended to be independent of each other. That is to say, a child who was creative by our measures would just as likely be of low intelligence as of high intelligence. Likewise, a child who was relatively low in creativity by our measures would as likely be of high intelligence as of low intelligence.

In short, the obtained facts *did* support the view that in school children creativity is a different type of cognitive excellence than general intelligence. Such an outcome was especially striking in light of the fact that our procedures for assessing creativity of necessity called upon the child's verbal ability in some degree—and verbal ability is known to contribute substantially to performance on IQ tests. Despite this possible source of commonality, the chances that a child of high intelligence would also display high creativity by our measures were no more than about 50–50.

What are some of the characteristics, then, of children in our four categories: intelligent and creative; neither intelligent nor creative; intelligent but low in creativity; and creative but low in regard to intelligence? The composite pictures that emerged from the experiments and observations that we carried out are composites in the sense that some portions of the evidence upon which they are based were more clear for the boys, while other parts of the evidence were more clear for the girls. However, the general pictures that emerged for the two sexes tended to suggest the same underlying characteristics.

## HIGH CREATIVITY—HIGH INTELLIGENCE

In many respects these children earn the most superlatives of any of the four groups. For example, when they are observed in the classroom they tend to be particularly high in degree of attention span and concentration upon academic work. At the same time, their academic bent does not put them at a social disadvantage. Quite to the contrary, they are observed to be the most socially "healthy" of the four groups: they have the strongest inclination to be friends with others, and others also have the strongest inclination to be friends with them. (These observations were made during play periods as well as during class sessions.)

These children, in addition, are the least likely of all four groups to behave in ways that suggest disapproval or doubt concerning oneself, one's actions, and one's work. However, this isn't merely a question of behaving in a manner most in harmony with the society's expectations, for these children also demonstrate a strong inclination to engage in various sorts of disruptive activities in the classroom. It's as if they are bursting through the typical behavioral molds that the society has constructed.

What are some of the underpinnings of the general behaviors just described for this group? For one thing, they are likely to see possible connections between events that do not have too much in common. The members of this group, in other words, are more willing to posit relationships between events that are in many respects dissimilar. For another thing, these children are particularly good at reading the subtle affective or expressive connotations that can be carried by what goes on in the environment. These two matters are not entirely separate—a sensitive, aesthetic "tuning" to the possible expressive meanings conveyed by human gesture or by abstract design forms involves seeing possible linkages between quite different kinds of objects and events. The children high in both creativity and intelligence seemed to be most capable of all the groups regarding this kind of aesthetic sensitivity.

To illustrate how we studied the child's ability to read subtle expressive connotations, consider the following example. We confronted the child with a picture of a straight line and asked him to imagine that he was looking down from above at a path that someone had made. The child was to tell us what sort of person made this trail. Our interest was in determining whether the child's response conveyed information about the kinds of emotional experience that might characterize the person in question, or on the other hand conveyed information only about the superficial character of what the person did. An example of a response showing sensitivity to possible expressive meanings was: "Someone very tense; because if he were relaxed he might wander all over; somebody mad." On the other hand, here is an example of a response that did not show expressive sensitivity: "Man was traveling on a highway; he met people in a huge car; it had a lot of people and it was crowded; they traveled together and got food in restaurants; when they got where they were going, they had a nice vacation."

Turning finally to the way these children describe their own feeling states, we find a tendency for them to admit to experiencing some anxiety, some disturbance—neither a great deal nor very little. It may be that experiencing some anxiety serves an energizing function for them: it is not so much anxiety as to cripple them, and not so little anxiety as to leave them dormant. Also, their total mode of adaptation does not minimize the experience of anxiety for them.

## LOW CREATIVITY—HIGH INTELLIGENCE

In what respects are the children who are high with regard to general intelligence but low in creativity different from those who are high in both? Let us return first to behavior observed in classroom and play settings. While the high intelligence-low creativity children resembled the high creativity-high intelligence children in possessing strong capacities for concentration on academic work and a long attention span, in other respects they were quite different. Those of high intelligence but low creativity were least likely of all four groups to engage in disruptive activities in the classroom and tended to hesitate about expressing opinions. In short, these children seemed rather unwilling to take chances.

Parallel behavior was observed in their social relations with other children; while others had a strong inclination to be friends with them, they in turn tended to hold themselves aloof from interaction with other children. The high intelligence-low creativity children, therefore, seemed to be characterized by a coolness or reserve in relations with their peers. Others would seek out the high intelligence-low creativity children for companionship, possibly because of this group's high academic standing. The children in question, however, tended not to seek out others in return. Perhaps this group felt themselves to be on top of the social mountain, as it were—in a position where they could receive homage from others without any need for requital.

The observations regarding a tendency toward caution and reserve on the part of the high intelligence-low creativity children receive further corroboration in other areas of their functioning. For example, when asked to make arrangements and groupings of pictures of everyday objects in whatever ways they considered most suitable, they preferred to make groupings that were more conventional in nature. They tended to avoid making free-wheeling, unconventional arrangements in which there would be greater free play for evolving unique combinations of objects. For instance, a more conventional grouping would be assembling pictures of a lamppost, a door, and a hammer, and calling them "hard objects." A more unconventional grouping, on the other hand, would be putting together pictures of a comb, a lipstick, a watch, a pocketbook, and a door, and describing them as items that concern "getting ready to go out." It is as if a greater fear of error characterizes these children, so that when left to their own devices, they tend to gravitate toward ways of construing the world that are less open to criticism by others.

We also found out that if you *request* these children to try to behave in a manner that involves establishing more free-wheeling linkages among objects, they are capable of doing so. It is not that they lack the ability to look at the world in this manner, but the inclination. When an adult in their environment comes along and makes it clear that they are expected to consider unusual and possibly bizarre ways in which objects can be linked, they are able to conform to this task demand with skill. But most of the time, their environment tells them that the more unconventional ways of proceeding are more likely to lead them into error and be criticized as wrong. Since the possibility of error seems particularly painful to these children, their typical behavior is to proceed in a manner that is less likely, on the average, to bring them criticism.

Another example of the same sort of process is provided when we consider how the high intelligence-low creativity group reads the possible affective meanings that can be possessed by the behavior of others. As in the case of arranging objects into groups, one can contrast more conventional, expected ways and more unconventional, unusual ways of construing what the behavior of others may signify. For example, an angry figure can be described as "angry" with little risk of error. It requires acceptance of unconventional possibilities, on the other hand, for the child to admit the idea that this figure might be "peaceful" or might be "searching." It turns out that the group in question is least likely to entertain the possibility of the more unconventional, unusual kinds of meanings. They seem locked, therefore, in more conventional ways of interpreting their social world as well as their physical world. Again, fear of possible error seems to be at work.

Since the high intelligence-low creativity children seem to behave in a manner that should maximize correctness and minimize error, we can expect them to be in particularly good standing in their classroom environment. Given their apparent tendency to conform to expectations, their mode of functioning should be maximally rewarding and minimally punishing for them. In short, there should be a high degree of fit between customary environmental expectations and their way of conducting themselves. We find, in fact, that this group admits to little anxiety or disturbance when asked to describe their own feeling states. Their self-descriptions indicate the lowest levels of anxiety reported by any of the four creativity-intelligence groups. Since this group behaves in a manner that should minimize worry or concern for them, their minimal level of reported anxiety probably represents an accurate description of how they feel. But at a cost, as we have noted, of functioning in a constricted manner.

## HIGH CREATIVITY—LOW INTELLIGENCE

Turning to the group characterized by high creativity but relatively low intelligence, we find, first of all, that they tend to exhibit disruptive behavior in the classroom. This is about the only respect, however, in which their observable conduct in the usual school and play settings resembles that of the group high in both creativity and intelligence. Of all four groups, the high creativity-low intelligence children are the least able to concentrate and maintain attention in class, the lowest in self-confidence, and the most likely to express the conviction that they are no good. It is as if they are convinced that their case is a hopeless one. Furthermore, they are relatively isolated socially; not only do they avoid contact with other children, but in addition their peers shun them more than any other group. Perhaps, in their social withdrawal, these children are indulging fantasy activities. At any rate, they are relatively alone in the school setting, and in many respects can be characterized as worse off than the group low in both creativity and intelligence.

It should be borne in mind that the high creativity-low intelligence children nevertheless give evidence of the same kind of creative thinking capacities as are found in the high creativity-high intelligence group. Again, for example, we find a greater likelihood of seeing possible connections between events that do not share much in common. The high creativity children, whether high or low regarding intelligence, are more willing to postulate relationships between somewhat dissimilar events.

Apparently, the kinds of evaluational pressures present in the case of intelligence and achievement testing as well as in the typical classroom environment serve to disrupt cognitive powers which can come to the fore when pressure is reduced. An interesting complementarity seems to exist with regard to the psychological situations found for the high creativity-low intelligence group and the low creativity-high intelligence group: while members of the former seem to perform more effectively when evaluational pressures are absent, members of the latter seem to work more adequately when evaluational pressures are present. It is as if the former children tend to go to pieces if questions of personal competence and achievement enter the picture, while the latter children have difficulty if they are denied a frame-work of standards within which they can evaluate what is required of them if they are to seem competent in the eyes of adults.

## LOW CREATIVITY—LOW INTELLIGENCE

While the children in this group show the greatest cognitive deprivation of the four groups under study, they seem to make up for it at least to some degree in the social sphere. From observations of their behavior in school and at play they are found to be more extroverted socially, less hesitant, and more self-confident and self-assured than the children of low intelligence but high creativity. The members of the low-low group are particularly poor regarding the kinds of aesthetic sensitivity that were mentioned earlier —for example, they show the weakest tendencies to respond to the possible expressive meanings that abstract line forms may convey. Despite such deficiencies, however, this group does not seem to be the maximally disadvantaged group in the classroom. Rather, the low-low children seem to have worked out a *modus vivendi* that puts them at greater social ease in the school situation than is the case for their high creativity-low intelligence peers.

### THE MOTIVATIONAL HURDLE

Now that we have characterized the four groups of children, let us finally consider the implications of the relative roles played by ability and by motivational factors in a child's thinking. The only group that looks like it is in difficulty with regard to ability—and even in their case we cannot be sure—is the group low in both intelligence and creativity. In the cases of the two groups that are low regarding one cognitive skill and high regarding the other—the low intelligence-high creativity group and the high intelligence-low creativity group—our evidence suggests that, rather than an ability deficiency, the children in question are handicapped by particular motivational dispositions receiving strong environmental support. For the low intelligence-high creativity children, the difficulty seems to concern excessive fear of being evaluated; hence they perform poorly when evaluational standards are a prominent part of the setting. For the high intelligence-low creativity children, on the other hand, the difficulty seems to concern a fear of not knowing whether one is thought well of by significant others. The possibility of making mistakes, therefore, is particularly avoided. Further, if evaluational standards are not a clear part of the setting, so that the child does not know a right way of behaving in order to fulfill the expectations of others, performance will deteriorate because the problem of avoiding error becomes of prime importance.

In theory, at least, these kinds of motivational hindrances could be rectified by appropriate training procedures. If one could induce the low intelligence-high creativity children to be less concerned when evaluational standards are present, and the high intelligence-low creativity children to be less concerned when evaluational standards are absent, their thinking behavior might come to display high levels of both intelligence and creativity.

JOAN E. SIEBER

# 34. LESSONS IN UNCERTAINTY

One ability needed to solve problems creatively has received little consideration in modern educational practice. It is the ability to generate and handle
uncertainty (1).

Uncertainty, as the word is used here, means an awareness of two or
more possible courses of action, each of which is considered likely but not
certain to lead to a suitable solution. The more choices one considers, the
more uncertain one tends to feel.

It is important to recognize that someone who is uncertain about a
decision he faces is not necessarily indecisive. Decisions must often be made
without full information. Under these conditions, one is likely to be uncertain
about the outcome of a course of action.

It is also important to recognize that someone who is uncertain about a
decision is not necessarily lacking in self-confidence. One may be uncertain
that a chosen course of action will lead to a desired outcome and still feel
confident that the decision is the best possible, given the information
available.

Suppose that a teacher wants to improve the reading skill of an un-
motivated child. The teacher realizes that to promote the child to the top
reading group might challenge him—or might intimidate him. If careful
consideration of all evidence suggests that promotion is likely to have a
salutary effect on the pupil, the teacher would be warranted in feeling
confident that the best possible decision would be to promote the boy.
But the teacher would be unwarranted and naïve in feeling certain that the
promotion would improve the pupil's ability to read.

Uncertainty, or awareness of alternative courses of thought or action, is
useful both before and after a decision is made. The individual who is
trying to discover the correct thing to do may improve his chances of being
correct if he allows himself to become very uncertain—if he gives himself
a chance to discover and evaluate many possibilities. This course usually
improves the chances of being correct, because usually there are courses

Reprinted from *The Elementary School Journal,* (March 1969), pp. 304–12,
by permission of the University of Chicago Press and the author.

of action that can be taken that are not obvious. Sometimes the best courses are the least obvious.

Even though one may discover and evaluate many alternatives, one rarely has total information about a situation that requires a decision. Having made a decision despite incomplete information, one may find it useful to remain aware that the outcome of the decision is uncertain. By remaining uncertain, one remains receptive to information that does not support the decision and one is likely to learn from mistakes or to reverse poor decisions before too much damage has been done.

In most of our decisions, certainty is not warranted. For instance, to get along with others, we must make judgments about their personalities, but since we never have complete information about the habits and motives of others, there is no warrant for certainty. We may trust someone enough to lend him a book, believing on various grounds that the book will probably be returned. Yet we may be aware of a number of reasons why the book may never be returned.

Many of us are not always aware of when we should be uncertain. We generate only one hypothesis as to possible outcomes of a situation and feel (erroneously) certain of the correctness of our single hypothesis; we do not know that we do not know the correct answer (2, 3, 4). Ignorance is the state of not knowing; here I use the expression "secondary ignorance" to denote the state of not knowing that one does not know.

Some individuals consistently exhibit secondary ignorance: they rarely give any indication that they do not know. They score high on tests of dogmatism. They tend to make decisions quickly and tend not to expose themselves to new information or to be curious (4: 139–47). To illustrate, let us consider three familiar types of school children who often show secondary ignorance.

One type is the "genius," usually a socially inept child whose only distinction among his peers is that he seems to know almost everything. To support his reputation, he is usually the first to blurt out answers, though he may be at a loss to give reasons for his responses. The endless flow of facts that he hostilely barks out includes a strange mixture of misunderstood information and incorrect information. He may make extravagant assertions: "I understand relativity: $E = mc^2$."

Then there is the "true believer" who usually comes from a family of "true believers." His views—be they social, political, or religious—are emotion-laden and narrow. He tends automatically to reject information that does not support his views. He may declare: "I know that evolution doesn't happen, because my father said God made all people."

Finally, there are most of the other pupils in the class. They accept unquestioningly all they read and hear, and do not search for alternative interpretations, exceptions to rules, or new solutions to old problems. They make unquestioning statements such as: "I know it's going to rain because the weatherman said so." "All white people in the North fought in the Civil War to free all the black people from slavery."

It may seem reasonable to assume that individuals who can generate many possible solutions to problems are likely to be better problem-solvers than individuals who can generate few possible solutions. However, it is not necessary to rely on assumptions. Studies have been made, and findings are available.

Experiments have demonstrated that individuals who are able to generate many possible solutions and who tend to be willing to admit to being uncertain also tend to seek more information for evaluating alternatives and to spend more time considering their decisions. They are more likely to be correct in their final decisions than individuals who do not generate alternative solutions and who do not admit being uncertain (2, 5). Moreover, the ability to generate many alternative responses is known to be characteristic of creative persons (6).

In summary, in problematic situations effective problem-solvers tend to entertain much uncertainty. Individuals who are disposed toward "secondary ignorance" are apparently too sure they are right to discover otherwise.

## A STUDY OF CHILDREN'S UNCERTAINTY

In a classroom study, it was found that elementary-school children in a working-class neighborhood arrived at solutions to difficult problems quickly. The solutions were usually incorrect, though the children usually felt certain that they were correct.

One classroom each of first-, second-, fourth-, fifth-, and sixth-graders participated in this study. The problems were presented orally. The children were instructed to state what they believed to be the answer and to indicate on a five-point scale how certain they were that their answer was correct. Each child was given a five-point certainty scale similar to that shown in Figure 1 and instructed in its use. Here are three of the problems presented:

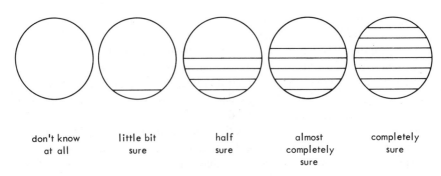

| don't know at all | little bit sure | half sure | almost completely sure | completely sure |

FIGURE I. UNCERTAINTY RATING SCALE

1. "Turn around and look at the back bulletin board. Now face the front of the room." After the children faced front, the title at the top of the bulletin board (*"Spring"*) was covered and the children were asked to recall a characteristic of the script used in the title. For example: "In the word *Spring* at the top of the bulletin board, is the g written like this: *q* or like this: *g?* How sure are you of your guess?"

2. "Suppose someone left the class and when he returned told you that the sidewalk outside was wet. Guess why it was wet, and tell how sure you are of your guess."

3. "Look at the coats hanging at the back of the room. Now look to the front of the room. What color is the coat on the end by the door? How sure are you of your guess?"

The results are simple to report. Every child who answered said that he was completely certain that he was correct. Children were eager to volunteer answers; many children answered every question. The answers varied widely, but no child admitted to uncertainty.

### TEACHING CHILDREN TO BE UNCERTAIN

The tendency to be certain may or may not be characteristic of children of elementary-school age. This tendency may or may not be a result of teachers' proneness to reward quick and confident answers. It is not important here for us to know precisely why children manifest secondary ignorance. It is important to know that this behavior can be changed. Ways of teaching children how to be uncertain can be described concretely and in detail and precise criteria can be stated for determining whether the desired learning has occurred.

It is possible to have clear-cut criteria for learning when to be uncertain. This fact is noteworthy, for it seems to be generally assumed that higher-order intellectual processes such as open-mindedness can be learned only through many complex interactions of an undescribable nature, between a pupil and an intellectually stimulating teacher. Throughout the controversy among educators about the merits of specifying educational objectives in behavioral terms, the opponents (7, 8) have pointed out that it is easy to be precise in specifying, producing, and measuring trivial behavior, but that it is difficult to be precise about higher-order intellectual processes in meaningful situations. The advocates of stating educational objectives in behavioral terms have not answered this objection. They have made only the counter-accusation that unspecified objectives are usually inadequately thought out and sometimes also trivial (9).

We shall examine three ways in which children can be taught to recognize situations in which it is appropriate to be uncertain. In the first approach, pupils are taught to estimate the likelihood that their answers are correct. In the second approach, pupils are taught to generate hypotheses concerning solutions. In the third approach, pupils are taught to discover available information and decide how it bears on their hypotheses.

### ESTIMATING UNCERTAINTY

A procedure for teaching pupils to estimate the likelihood that their answers are correct has been successfully used with elementary-school children. The first step in the procedure is to devise situations that, like the three problem situations described earlier, provide no basis for certainty. Next, problems of this type are interspersed with problems that have solutions that may be stated with relative certainty on the basis of the information available. The purpose of mixing the two types of problems is to help pupils learn to discriminate between them.

Then, as in the study described earlier, children are asked to suggest plausible answers to each problem and to state how certain they are of these answers. Each child is requested to write down his guess and to indicate his level of uncertainty. Children may rate their certainty on a five-point scale such as the one shown in Figure 1. Children in elementary school quickly learn how to use a scale of this kind and to apply it to a variety of tasks.

After the children have indicated their guesses and their uncertainty ratings, each problem is discussed in detail. The teacher asks various pupils to give their suggested answers and to describe the supporting evidence. During the discussion, the teacher tells the children that every hypothesis which is in any way warranted by evidence is worthwhile. She points out to the class that difficult problems are often best explored and solved by producing and evaluating many hypotheses about solutions. The teacher also tells the children that it is desirable to generate many hypotheses, and she warns them that it is foolish to be certain that a hypothesis is correct when there is evidence that partly supports other hypotheses as well, but does not completely support any one hypothesis. Finally, she encourages pupils to contribute information that bears on this idea.

After the children have generated various hypotheses and weighed their hypotheses against the available evidence, they should decide which hypotheses are the most reasonable and what degree of confidence is appropriate for each. It should be clear to the children that the object of the task is not to give the "correct answer." The object is to estimate uncertainty with all possible accuracy.

For evaluation purposes, teachers may want to measure how accurately pupils can estimate warranted uncertainty.

One measure of the accuracy with which a pupil can estimate warranted uncertainty is his "average deviation score." This is the average number of scale points by which his estimates of uncertainty deviate from the average level of uncertainty agreed on by a group of reasonable persons who have access to the same information as the learner. This "reasonable group" might consist of the entire class and the teacher. The group's level of uncertainty would be the level they agree on after considering all the hypotheses they can generate in the light of the relevant evidence they can discover.

The child's growth in the ability to estimate warranted uncertainty can be assessed by comparing the average deviation score obtained during his first lesson in estimating uncertainty with his average deviation score during subsequent lessons.

## GENERATING HYPOTHESES

A second means of teaching pupils when it is appropriate to be uncertain involves teaching them to increase the number of solution hypotheses they can generate for any given problem. Problems chosen for these lessons should be problems for which most children lack the knowledge to arrive at a correct answer. It should be clearly explained to the children that the task is to give all the possible solutions they can for each problem, and to give reasons for their hypotheses, if they can.

Unusual hypotheses should be encouraged. But what about bizarre hypotheses? And what about hypotheses for which children are unable to give a rationale? These are acceptable. It should be pointed out that a new idea which turns out to be useful is sometimes first arrived at intuitively—without a clear understanding of the reasons why it is a good idea. Intuitive ideas deserve tentative acceptance, though eventually a clear explanation of how an idea applies to a problem and why it provides a good solution must be found before it can be considered seriously.

After a number of hypotheses have been generated, pupils might follow the procedure for discussing evidence and assigning degrees of confidence described in the previous method.

After the teacher has taught pupils to generate hypotheses in a variety of simple classroom situations, the class may be required to apply its new skill. In a class that has been studying meteorology, the children may be given the following problem: "Suppose that when you went outside this morning you noticed that the sidewalk was wet. Why might it have been wet?" Each child should be encouraged to guess why the sidewalk might have been wet. The class should be encouraged to think of unusual, but plausible explanations. At first, the children will find it difficult to think of explanations, but if the teacher encourages and rewards originality the pupils' ability to produce good and unusual hypotheses will grow.

Finally, each hypothesis should be evaluated in terms of all the information that has been found. Often the information available does not provide conclusive evidence in support of any hypothesis. Pupils should learn to recognize when evidence is inconclusive and try to determine what kind of evidence would be convincing, even if such evidence cannot easily be obtained.

In this way, children can be led to understand three important things about problem-solving and decision-making. First, they can see that it is foolish to be certain of one's hypothesis when other reasonable hypotheses can be offered and supported by evidence. Second, they can see that it is often impossible or impractical to obtain evidence that will indicate, for certain, which of several hypotheses is correct. In such cases, the children learn that they must make whatever decision seems most likely to be right, realizing that there is no conclusive evidence to support any decision. Individuals who remain openminded are most likely to recognize evidence for other solutions when they see it.

Third, the integration of lessons on generating hypotheses with the study of science, social studies, and other subjects may lead pupils to understand that plausible explanations can be found for any given phenomenon.

Man has typically been intolerant of uncertainty. He has been very certain of many things—phlogiston, devils and gods, the flatness of the earth, the indivisibility of atoms, racial superiority, causes of illness, predictors of weather, causes of war and peace.

The desire for certainty has often been very costly. It has kept man in ignorance. It has prevented him from examining evidence supporting alternative views. It has caused the persecution or death of some who have questioned popular beliefs. Why are men afraid of uncertainty when it is certainty that can be so dangerous?

The study of history—social and scientific—offers countless opportunities to explore this question. History bears witness to the importance of being free to express uncertainty, to examine new hypotheses, and to encourage others to do so.

## DISCOVERING AVAILABLE INFORMATION

After pupils have begun to understand that many solutions may be generated for problematic tasks, and that certainty about any one solution is unwarranted if available evidence does not indisputably indicate that that solution is correct, a third means of teaching for uncertainty may be introduced: teaching pupils to discern all available evidence. It is desirable that children learn to make use of all available information when attempting to solve problems. Details that would normally go unnoticed are often helpful in generating and evaluating useful and creative hypotheses on solutions and in determining what level of uncertainty to attach to each hypothesis.

To teach children to use available information, they should first be required to describe everything they know about a problem. With practice children can become more attentive to subtle details. The ability to notice many details of the information presented may be measured by requiring pupils to list everything they have noticed about a problem.

Besides stating what information has been discerned about a problem, pupils may be required to tell how each bit of information bears on each hypothesis that has been generated. They may also be required to be alert to new hypotheses that the information suggests.

To return to the earlier example, pupils might inspect a wet sidewalk and the surrounding area for evidence to help determine why the sidewalk is wet. Is the explanation rain, dew, spilt water, a broken water main, runoff from a nearby bog? Or is there some other cause? The task is to describe a situation with the greatest detail and accuracy possible, rather than to give a solution.

Pupils may be evaluated objectively on the basis of the number of details they notice, the number of cues they use to evaluate hypotheses, and the number of hypotheses they think of on the basis of the details they have noticed. At first, the teacher may give hints, but hints will become unnecessary as pupils gain fluency in noticing and using details.

Children should be shown that as new information becomes available they may become either more certain or less certain about the correctness of a hypothesis. To demonstrate that new information can increase or decrease warranted certainty, pupils should be required to reassess their level of uncertainty after they have generated as many solutions and discerned as much relevant information as possible. It is important for pupils to realize that additional information may suggest more possibilities and thus increase uncertainty, but that this result is not undesirable. On the contrary, it may lead to a deeper understanding of a problem, and ultimately to a better chance of reaching a correct solution.

## CONTINUING LESSONS

It is unreasonable to expect that children will automatically apply these skills to other problems. While each of these skills can be taught to elementary-school children in a half hour or less, frequent practice is required if children are to learn, as a habitual intellectual process, to reasonably estimate when and to what degree they should be uncertain about their ideas.

Several steps are involved in creating situations conducive to increasing uncertainty or reducing secondary ignorance. First, in any lesson—be it arithmetic, meteorology, biology, social studies, or whatever—the teacher needs to identify problematic issues. The issues may be major ones built into the curriculum, such as identification of the causes of the Civil War. Or the issues may be problems devised by the teacher for classroom discussion, like the problem of identifying the source of the liquid on the sidewalk. Second, before the lesson the teacher should understand the basis for several hypotheses. He might use these hypotheses as examples to help pupils understand why any rational person should be uncertain about an answer given in such a situation. Third, problems should be presented and pupils should be asked to generate hypotheses and state how uncertain they are and their grounds for feeling that uncertain. Fourth, pupils should be helped in their hypothesizing and rewarded for their search for hypotheses and for discovery of confirming and disconfirming evidence. The teacher should acknowledge that reasonable hypotheses may be difficult to generate, since they are often not obvious. Certainly he should not assure the class that all reasonable hypotheses have been examined merely because he himself cannot think of any more. He should be genuine and sincere in his acceptance of pupils' hypotheses. Finally, he should help pupils decide which hypothesis seems most likely to be correct on the basis of the information they have amassed and the level of uncertainty that seems warranted for each hypothesis.

Are we trying to teach children to feel uncertain and to search for information whenever alternative solutions could possibly exist? No. Such an approach to life would be inefficient and neurotic. We are trying to teach children to consider reasonable alternative views even when such views conflict with firmly held beliefs. We are also trying to provide them with a set of intellectual skills and attitudes that they may use when they want to explore and solve problems creatively.

## USEFUL SIDE-EFFECTS

Some educators reject the practice of advance specification of educational objectives in behavioral terms. They offer two major objections to this practice. They argue, first, that it prevents teachers from taking advantage of instructional opportunities that occur unexpectedly in the classroom and, second, that the practice encourages only trivial behavior. I have argued that neither objection applies to lessons in warranted uncertainty.

Teachers can increase the likelihood that they will identify unexpected instances of dogmatism and produce habits of open-mindedness by taking the following four steps in designing and carrying out lessons: First, create or identify simple situations in which it can be demonstrated that the correct answer is not known for certain but that educated guesses can be made and that it is appropriate to be unsure about the correctness of such guesses. Second, require pupils to state their hypotheses as to the correct answer to such problems and to state how sure they are of their hypotheses. Third, reward the generation of various possible responses to given problem situations. Fourth, reward attention to a wide variety of information related to problems, especially information that leads to conflicting solutions.

The procedures described here can be made an integral part of specific areas of the curriculum and of teachers' classroom behavior. The procedures can be used on a planned basis as well as on a spontaneous basis. A not unlikely side-effect of such teaching is that the teacher himself may learn a bit more about when to be uncertain.

## REFERENCES

1. This is a slightly expanded version of a symposium paper presented at the Nineteenth Annual State Conference on Educational Research, California Teachers Association, San Diego, November, 1967.
2. J. M. DRISCOLL and J. T. LANZETTA. Effects of two sources of uncertainty in decision-making, *Psychological Reports, 17* (October, 1965), 635–48.
3. J. E. SIEBER and J. T. LANZETTA. Conflict and conceptual structure as determinants of decision-making behavior, *Journal of Personality, 32* (December, 1964), 622–41.
4. R. C. ZILLER and B. H. LONG. Some correlates of the don't know response in opinion questionnaires, *Journal of Social Psychology, 67* (October, 1965), 139–47.
5. J. E. SIEBER and J. T. LANZETTA. Some determinants in individual differences in pre-decision information processing behavior, *Journal of Personality and Social Psychology, 4* (November, 1966), 561–71.
6. S. A. MEDNICK. The associative basis of the creative process, *Psychological Review, 69* (August, 1962), 220–32.
7. E. W. EISNER. Educational objectives: help or hindrance? *School Review, 75* (Fall, 1967), 250–60.
8. P. W. JACKSON and ELIZABETH BELFORD. Educational objectives and the joys of teaching, *School Review, 73* (Autumn, 1965), 267–91.
9. W. JAMES POPHAM. Threat-potential of precision. Paper read at Nineteenth Annual State Conference on Educational Research, California Teachers Association, San Diego, November, 1967.

E. PAUL TORRANCE

# 35. EPILOGUE: CREATIVITY IN AMERICAN EDUCATION, 1865-1965

In a sense, "creativity" has always been an issue in education. Certainly it has been an issue in American education throughout the century from 1865–1965. Interest in creativity in American education however, has waxed and waned during this period and has been discussed under a variety of names. At different periods educators have used different ways of describing the status and role of creativity in education. See if you can guess the period in which the following description was published:

"A boy of good ability has just completed his high school course. In a conversation with a friend the question is raised about going to college. 'A man is a fool to go to college after he has had a good high school education. Haven't we learned everything there is any use of knowing? We have had astronomy and geology, chemistry and physics, botany and zoology, physiology, psychology and political economy, and a great many more, and I don't see as there is anything more to learn. And if we forget something, why, there are our books: we can learn it over again!'

"But suppose a youth in this condition be advised or constrained to go to a university and continue, if we may so designate the process, studies. . . . His instructor asks him for an account of the work he has done along the line he proposes to follow. Our student names over a number of books and courses he has taken. Very well. The professor next asks him whether he is especially interested in any particular problem that he wishes to solve. He evidently does not understand the question, and the professor puts it more plainly. Is there not some particular point in this whole field which you are conscious that you do not know and have not been able to find in books, and that you think may be worth your time and labor to investigate? No, he does not think of any such point. He has never been taught to look at the subject with a view of doing anything about it himself. . . .

"Finally the instructor shoulders the man bodily, gives him a problem that he is anxious to have worked out, gets all the material and apparatus ready

Reprinted from *Creativity: Its Educational Implications*, John C. Gowan, George D. Demos, E. Paul Torrance (eds.), (New York: John Wiley & Sons, 1967), by permission of the publisher.

to his hand and tells him to go to work. Next day he calls at the man's laboratory and finds him reading a book. Asks him what he has done? What observations he has made? What experiments he has tried? And finds that he has made no observations, done nothing, but has found a 'very interesting book.' "

Actually, this is a quotation from an article by C. F. Hodge and published in a 1900 issue of *Pedagogical Seminary*. In what ways are college students today different from the one described by Hodge? If I can judge by the college students that I know, the ones that my colleagues describe, and the ones described in the educational literature of 1965, they have much in common. Today's high school student would not say that "A man is a fool to go to college after he has had a good high school education." He realizes that he must go to college in order to get along in life and succeed in a vocation. He may believe that he has already learned everything there is any use of knowing, because apparently most high school students are still being taught as though knowledge is complete. The textbooks they have studied present knowledge in this way, as though all truths in the field are known. We do have new curricular materials that treat fields like physics, chemistry, biology, mathematics, and even social studies as incomplete and as ways of thinking. In Minnesota, for example, only 12 percent of the high schools use the newer curricular materials in physics and less than 15 percent use any of the newer curricular materials in chemistry (Kleeman, 1965). These newer curricular materials have now been available for several years.

Our entering college student would *not* be expected to answer the questions that Hodge in 1900 expected him to answer about choosing a problem for investigation. We college professors have long ago given up such expectations. We have even given up such expectations of graduate students until they pass their preliminary doctoral examinations. It is then that we start asking students the questions that Hodge's professor asked his entering freshman. It is then that we usually receive the same answers that Hodge's professor received.

It is not that high school graduates are incapable of meeting this expectation. They are. This has been abundantly demonstrated by the work of such men as Jablonski (1964) at the University of Pittsburgh. Jablonski first discovered the potential of high-school students participating in National Science Foundation Summer Science Programs. He encouraged his summer protégés to continue their research work the year round and solicited the help of personnel in Pittsburgh schools. Some of their experiments have been published in regular professional journals against the competition of mature and experienced scientists. Jablonski estimates that 25 percent of his high-school researchers are producing publishable material.

Jablonski wanted next to begin working with younger students. His colleagues told him that this was really getting ridiculous, but nevertheless he went ahead with projects with fourth-, fifth-, and sixth-grade students.

Jablonski admits that he had grossly underestimated the readiness of these children to do research. Groups of them have joined him in cancer research. They asked the meaning of words and soon mastered the technical language just as if they were learning English. As a result, these youngsters produced useful research ideas and discoveries.


## EDUCATIONAL EXPERIMENTATION

It is interesting to examine the ups and down of educational research and the experimental testing of creative ideas in education. Let us examine the following quotation from *Education,* a journal that has been published continuously from 1880 to the present time:

> "Our incessant experiments in educational reform serve only to interrupt the traditions, and therefore to lessen the prestige of our culture; they perplex teachers, scholars, and parents alike; they lead to doubt and hesitancy, and must all end in a simple return to the old system" (Marble, 1880, p. 176).

Although these words were written by A. P. Marble in 1880, they are words that have been shouted during every period in American education since 1865. In fact, they have been shouted so loudly and so effectively that one might wonder if Marble's prediction is not accurate—that is, that we continually return to the old system. Certainly, this is a loud and powerful voice in America today.

It has not mattered that the experimental methods, materials, or procedures frequently have been able to demonstrate their superiority to the "old system." For example, let us examine what happened to the curriculum that Francis Parker, one of the Progressive Educators, established at Quincy, Massachusetts, between 1875 and 1880. As the fame of Parker's methods spread, the attackers arose. They so disturbed the patrons of the Quincy schools that they demanded an evaluation. The children were then tested by the old tests, not by tests that would have assessed the objectives of the new curriculum. Nevertheless, the pupils in Parker's school came out ahead of pupils taught by the old methods, even on the old tests (Atkinson and Maleski, 1962).

These same loud cries are heard today. One reads that we do not know enough about creativity to increase the chances that creative behavior will occur, that anything learned in a creative way is superficial and of no value, that children who learn in creative ways will neglect the three R's, that the best way to produce creative individuals is to be rough with them and make school as unpleasant for them as possible. When we conduct controlled experiments to see what would happen, if we were to teach various kinds of subject matter creatively, these claims simply do not hold up. In one carefully-controlled and thrice replicated study, for example, Sommers

(1961) in a technical course found that students who learned in creative ways not only showed more signs of creative growth but also did better on the old tests than did their controls who learned under the old methods.

Have we achieved a more creative kind of education from 1865 to 1965? Let us examine in broad perspective the pulsations, the educational reforms, the innovations and experiments of the past 100 years and see what progress we have made and perhaps out of this reevaluation we may be able to avoid some of the mistakes of the future and not have to "return to the old system."

## STAGES OF AMERICAN EDUCATIONAL THOUGHT

Frederick Mayer (1964) maintains that American educational thought has passed through four identifiable periods. The first was dominated by Puritan ideas, authoritarianism, stress on the limitations of man, and the view of man as a sinner filled with evil. It made of the teacher a punitive disciplinarian. All dissenters were persecuted.

During the second period, we find a spirit of enlightenment and freedom. This is the period that gave us the Constitution and the Bill of Rights. Thinkers such as Franklin and Jefferson stressed creativity and the possibilities and freedom of man. Franklin said, "When a man ceases to be creative, he ceases to really live."

The year 1865 finds American educational thought moving into a third period. It was the time of Emerson, a thorough-going individualist, who believed in intellectual independence, the inadequacy of the scientific method, and the importance of intuition. He believed that though books can both stimulate and hinder man in the search for truth that there was too much conformity and too much respect in the United States for the printed word. He believed that one must be creative even to read well. He believed that the learner should be free and brave. Emerson's ideas, however, were ridiculed and ignored. They had little impact on the educators of his day.

Here and there, however, we find records that a few courageous and imaginative educators were trying to translate Emerson's ideas into educational methods and materials. For example, in 1865, Professor S. S. Greene at a meeting of the National Teachers Association reported on an innovation called "Object-Teaching." He is quoted as follows:

"Object-teaching is that which takes into account the whole realm of nature and art, so far as the child has examined it, and assumes as known only what the child knows, and works from the well known to the obscurely known, and onward and upward till the learner can enter the fields of science, or of abstract thought.... It is that which makes the school a place where the child comes in contact wih realities, just such as appeal to his common-sense when he roams at pleasure in the fields. It is that which relieves the child's school task by making it intelligent and possible. It bids him examine for himself, discriminate for himself, and express for himself, while the teacher stands to give hints and suggestions, not to relieve the labor" (Calkins, 1880, p. 170).

He describes something that comes quite close to what I have called the "responsive" or "creative" environment, a kind of teaching that stresses self-initiated learning and discovery but which combines with it the most sensitive and alert kind of guidance and direction—a kind of teaching that involved an absorbed kind of listening, fighting off criticism and disparagement, and making all sincere efforts to learn rewarding enough to keep up the zest and excitement of learning. Teachers often ask what they can do to stimulate creativity in the classroom and it is quite natural that teachers imbued with a stimulus-response psychology would count upon a stimulating environment to bring about creative growth. As a matter of fact, probably nothing could do more to discourage creative behavior than to stimulate original ideas, searching questions, invention, and the like and then not be respectful of these ideas, questions, and inventions.

The fourth period, known as the era of pragmatism, was represented by such eloquent spokesmen as William James, John Dewey, William Heard Kilpatrick, Francis Parker, Boyd Bode, George Counts, and others. This was the era of Progressive Education which centered on the interests of the child, emphasized democratic ways of behaving, made group standards important, and used problem-centered inquiry. Educational psychologists such as G. Stanley Hall and William James may be said to have supplied the educators of this period with many of their ideas, which were disbelieved then and are still disbelieved rather widely but many of which are being tested today and found to be accurate. For example, G. Stanley Hall (Mayer, 1964, p. 287) who stressed creativity placed emotions above intellect and intuition above reason. He believed, however, that too much analysis into the creative processes would destroy spontaneity and creativity and that we should not ask too many impertinent "how's" and "why's." Hall (1905) believed in the potentiality of man and that too much time is wasted in school training for orderliness in going, standing, and sitting and that teachers erred by helping children over difficulties instead of spurring them on to self-activity.

William James (1900), too, believed in potentiality. He recognized and respected individual differences, although he did not have a very clear idea about mental abilities and how different kinds of mental abilities are called into play by different ways of learning and by different kinds of tests. In his *Talks to Teachers* in 1900, he cautioned:

> "Be patient, then, and sympathetic with the type of mind that cuts a poor figure in examinations. It may, in the long examination which life sets us, come out in the end in better shape than the glib and ready reproducer, its passions being deeper, its purposes more worthy, its combining power less commonplace, and its total mental output consequently more important."

In general, however, history indicates that teachers have not been patient with this creative type of mind. In a study of over 400 eminent men and women, Goertzel and Goertzel (1962) estimated that at least 60 percent of them had serious difficulties in schools. Many of them did not make good grades on the examinations and many of them dropped out of school, at least for a time.

Francis Parker (1905) reacted against the Puritan tradition in education. He believed in man's goodness and potentiality. To the Puritan, education must be authoritarian; to Parker education has to be democratic. In Puritan education, the supernatural was all important; in Parker's curriculum, nature was the guide. To the Puritan, truth is absolute; to Parker, truth is discovered in the relativity of experience. He assigned roles of importance to curiosity, fantasy and imagination, intellectual courage, and observation. He believed in planning learning activities, methods, and materials in the light of information about developmental stages. He maintained, however, that there is no perfect method.

William Heard Kilpatrick (Van Till, 1963), is generally recognized as the leader of that wing of the Progressive Education movement that sought answers in the potential of the individual learner. He emphasized purposeful activity, intrinsic motivation, planning, open-mindedness, rigor, honesty, group action, and child-centeredness.

John Dewey, however, was one of the most prolific writers and thinkers associated with the Progressive Education movement. He was a spokesman of the rebellion against authority and showed how the scientific method can be applied to all realms of inquiry. He believed that the knowledge of the future must be functional, experimental, and subjected to the rigorous tests of laboratory methods. In *My Pedagogic Creed* in 1900, he stressed the importance of developmental processes, interests, and learning as an active rather than as a passive process.

According to Cremin (1961) and others, Progressive Education died in 1957 when the *Journal of Progressive Education* ceased publication two years after the Progressive Education Association had passed out of existence. Many say that it was dead long before this. Others point out that the issues raised by the leaders of progressive education have not died and that many of the ideas developed by them will never die. Progressive Education aroused so much controversy and still engenders such strong negative reactions that the label of Progressive Education is still used to damn educational innovations. Many of those who attack ideas directed to a more creative kind of education are trying to attach to them the label of "Progressive Education" as a way of damning them.

## LOOKING TO THE FUTURE

Let us examine the major precepts of Progressive Education and see if what we have learned during the ten years since the dissolution of the

Progressive Education Association in 1955 places us any nearer the achievement of the creative kind of education that will help us realize the American dream of a kind of education that will give every child a chance to grow and to achieve his potentialities. It is perhaps an oversimplification but it may be said that Progressive Education rested its case on the following six chief precepts:

1. Individual differences among children must be recognized.
2. We learn best by doing and by having a vital interest in what we are doing.
3. Education is a continuous reconstruction of living experience that goes beyond the four walls of the classroom.
4. The classroom should be a laboratory for democracy.
5. Social goals, as well as intellectual goals, are important.
6. A child must be taught to think critically rather than to accept blindly (Atkinson and Maleska, 1962, p. 78).

On the basis of what we have learned during the past ten years about the human mind and its functioning, mental abilities and their development, and the interaction of mental abilities and ways of learning and teaching, it would appear that all of these precepts are good as far as they go but that they do not go far enough. For example, examine the precept that "individual differences among children must be recognized." This precept cannot help us a great deal unless we know what individual differences are important in individualizing instruction and what individual differences in mental functioning, motivation, and personality are brought into play in various ways of learning. What we have learned during the past ten years has enabled us to remove much of the puzzlement experienced by educational researchers of the 1920's and 1930's.

We need no longer be puzzled by McConnell's finding in 1934 that mental age as measured by an intelligence test is more highly related to achievement in second grade arithmetic when taught by authoritative identification than when taught by the methods of discovery advocated by many of the Progressive Educators. Hutchinson in 1963 in a study involving learning in junior high school social studies also found that under traditional, authoritarian teaching, there is a statistically significant correlation between mental age and achievement but not between measures of creative thinking and achievement. In the experimental conditions where there was considerable opportunity for learning in creative ways the reverse was true. In another 1963 study involving fifth grade children using programmed instruction in language arts, Gotkin and Massa found significant negative relationships between measures of creative thinking and achievement. A year earlier, Stolurow (1962) had found higher correlations between measures of originality and achievement than between mental age and achievement with programmed materials in mathematics and statistics. The difference was that Gotkin and Massa used programmed materials that permitted only tiny mental leaps and gave no opportunity for making, identifying, and correcting errors, while Stolurow's programmed materials emphasize a trouble-shooting or hypothesis-making-and-testing approach that builds specific but multiple associations to a stimulus. MacDonald and Raths (1964) found that highly creative children are more productive on frustrating tasks than are less creative children. Furthermore, they enjoy such tasks more than do their less creative peers. The least creative children are less productive in open tasks and the most creative ones react less favorably to closed tasks. Thus, pupils of varying levels of creative thinking ability react differently to different kinds of curriculum tasks and are possibly best taught by varying procedures.

Perhaps the most exciting insight that has come from our research (Torrance, 1962, 1963, 1965) is that different kinds of children learn best when given opportunities to learn in ways best suited to their motivations and abilities. Whenever teachers change their ways of teaching in significant ways, a different group of learners become the stars or high achievers. This has far-reaching implications for educating a larger number of people to a higher level and for achieving a higher level of dignity and mental health in our society.

Regarding the second precept that "we learn best by doing and by having a vital interest in what we are doing," we recognize now that people do not learn automatically by doing. This type of learning requires the most sensitive and alert type of guidance and direction. Children must be taught the skills of inquiry and research—the spirit and skills of historiography, the concepts and skills of descriptive and experimental research. Curiosity and creative needs are strong enough and universal enough to make creative ways of learning useful for all individuals. Creative ways of learning should not be regarded as an exclusive way of learning for all children nor for any single child, even though he may prefer learning in creative ways and learn little when we insist that he learn exclusively by authority.

I see no real quarrel with the third precept that "education is a continuous reconstruction of living experience that goes beyond the four walls of the classroom." From an understanding of the creative process, we recognize that one thing must be permitted to lead to another. To accept such a precept requires a great deal of courage on the part of the teacher. Both teachers and pupils have to learn to think in terms of possible consequences. Too frequently, the educational system is unwilling to accept the consequences of this "continuous reconstruction of living experiences beyond the four walls of the classroom." To illustrate what I mean I would like to cite a couple of examples, since they also identify the potency of the threats that arise when schools accept the fourth and fifth precepts that the classroom should be a laboratory for democracy and that social goals, as well as intellectual goals, are important.

The first illustration (Courtis, 1964) involves a beginning fourth grade teacher who had received a directive to put aside the regular work of the day and devote time with the children to plan what they might do to make their city more beautiful. After some hesitation, one pupil reported that his alley was full of ashes and wondered if cleaning out the ashes in the alley would do. This struck a responsive chord and soon the children were inspecting the condition regarding ashes in 35 blocks around the school. Every child found that not only the alleys were full of ashes but that yards were overflowing with metal baskets, barrels, and ashes. From what their parents had said the children knew that the city should have collected the ashes. They asked why the ashes had not been collected and decided that it was probably because the city did not have enough money. One girl said that her father worked in city hall and thought she could find out. Her father found that the city had appropriated $30,000 for the purpose. Now, the children were really excited and made their reports to their parents. A day or two later, the principal of the school received a telephone call from the head of the Department of Public Works. He asked, "What are you doing up there? Your business is to teach reading, writing, and arithmetic. Lay off meddling in city affairs." Thus, the city beautiful project came to a sudden halt.

The second illustration (Courtis, 1964) was in the classroom of an able and experienced teacher. One of her brightest pupils reported from a local newspaper clipping that half of the people in their city live in substandard houses. They wanted to know what is a standard house and if they lived in one. No one knew what a standard house was and the teacher confessed that she did not know either. The quotation was from the State Commissioner of Housing so they wrote letters to him, using models found in their textbooks. The next day letters were passed from one to another and judged until the best one was selected. The Commissioner replied promptly. The material that he sent was studied avidly without any assignment from the teacher. Applying the criteria of a standard house to their own homes, the entire class reported that they all lived in standard houses. The teacher explained that they were fortunate people, but they insisted that they wanted to see some substandard houses. Together they planned, with some suggestions from the teacher, an extensive survey. They discovered a long strip of the city where the houses were mere shacks, with only one source of water, a small pipe coming out of the ground, outdoor privies, and a wide ditch that was an open sewer. They were indignant.

The father of one of the boys was so affected by his son's excitement that he went to the city hall to verify his son's statement. The city engineer showed him a map with well laid out streets and sewers, and laughed at the statement. The man was embarrassed and took his son to task for telling him such a story. The boy stood his ground and demanded that his father come with him and see for himself. After his visit he was more incensed than his son. The next day he gathered together a group of important citizens and took them along the entire length of the open sewer. The indignation of these men led to investigations that revealed much graft and dishonesty that had escaped public notice. Eventually, new elections were held and the grafters removed from office and the slum district uncovered by the class was greatly improved. Almost daily the class read the newspapers and covered the classroom board with clippings, feeling that they had had a part in the reforms. They read avidly in school and library books about civics, city management, etc. The teacher had never had a class so active in planning their own learning activities and asking for help when they ran into new problems.

From these illustrations, it seems clear that when these precepts are accepted, learning becomes alive, plenty of creative behavior occurs, there is cooperation with parents and action by them. It is also clear that the acceptance of these precepts can be very threatening to the security of the teacher and call not only for courage but for skills in group dynamics, creative problem-solving, and strategies for coping .with change and stress. We have now accumulated enough knowledge about group dynamics, creative problem-solving, and strategies for coping with change in stress to make these precepts meaningful. Even now, however, it is still a struggle to get such information into the textbooks and curricula of teacher education. Knowledge in these areas, however, has the potentialities of permitting us to stand on the shoulders of the Deweys and Kilpatricks and see further than they were able to see.

We are also beginning to understand the inadequacies of the sixth precept that "a child must be taught to think critically rather than to accept blindly." We know now through creativity research that it is not enough to be able to criticize the ideas of others. It is necessary that students be able to produce ideas of their own, to be critical of their own ideas, and to use tests that keep them from deceiving themselves. Furthermore, we have learned that in the production of ideas it may be necessary to suspend judgment temporarily to avoid unduly putting the brakes on our thinking (Osborn, 1963). After ideas have been accumulated, it is then necessary to formulate criteria for use in judging these ideas and making decisions. If knowledge is to be used constructively in solving problems creatively, the learner must have a constructive, though not uncritical, attitude towards information. He must be willing to entertain and test the possibility that the information may be true and useful. In two different experiments, I (1965) found that students who assumed a constructive rather than a critical attitude toward available information were able to produce a larger number of creative solutions and more original ones. One of these experiments involved the reading of research articles and a second, textbook material. In both, one group was asked to read material with a critical attitude, identifying defects; and the other was asked to read material with a creative or constructive attitude, thinking of other possibilities, applications and the like.

In a presentation of this type, it is possible to review only a very small percentage of the ideas and research information that has the potentiality of moving us ahead and of adding to the precepts of Progressive Education many of the missing elements required in the education demanded by our day. I would not venture to say whether or not education today is more creative than it was in 1865. I do believe that we have made enough advances in educational thinking to make possible a more creative kind of education. The big questions are: "Will we choose to use these advances in knowledge and thinking and will we choose in time?"

It seems to me that we have reached a stage in history when we *must* make such a choice. In the past, we have been able to survive with static goals and concepts. Things are changing so rapidly that we can no longer survive, if we insist on thinking and living in static terms. It seems to me that we cannot afford to return to the old ways. We must accept the creative challenge.

## REFERENCES

Atkinson, Carroll and E. T. Maleska. *The story of education.* Philadelphia: Chilton Books, 1962.

Calkins, N. A. Object teaching: its purpose and province. *Education,* 1880, *1,* 165–172.

Courtis, S. A. How to shift from teaching to serving. *Forward Look in Education,* 1964, Vol. 1, No. 5.

Cremin, L. A. *The transformation of the school: progressivism in American education.* New York: Alfred A. Knopf, 1961.

Dewey, J. *The child and the curriculum.* Chicago: University of Chicago Press, 1902.

Goertzel, V. and Mildred G. Goertzel. *Cradles of eminence.* Boston: Little, Brown, 1962.

Gotkin, L. G. and N. Massa. *Programmed instruction and the academically gifted: the effects of creativity and teacher behavior on programmed instruction with young learners.* New York: Center for Programmed Instruction, Inc., 1963.

Hall, G. S. *Aspects of child life and education.* Boston: Ginn and Co., 1907.

Hall, G. S. A German criticism of American schools. *Pedagogical Seminary,* 1905, *12,* 508–512.

Hodge, C. F. Foundations of nature study. *Pedagogical Seminary,* 1900, *7,* 95–110.

Hutchinson, W. L. Creative and productive thinking in the classroom. Doctoral dissertation, University of Utah, Salt Lake City, 1963.

Jablonski, J. R. Developing creative research performance in public school children. In C. W. Taylor (ed.), *Widening horizons in creativity.* New York: John Wiley & Sons, Inc., 1964. Pp. 203–219.

James, W. *Talks to teachers on psychology.* New York: Holt, Rinehart and Winston, 1900.

Kilpatrick, W. H. *Education for a changing civilization.* New York: Macmillan Co., 1926.

Kleeman, R. P. Survey finds most schools don't teach modern science. *Minneapolis Tribune,* February 2, 1965, p. 15.

McCONNELL, T. R. Discovery vs. authoritative identification in the learning of children. *University of Iowa Studies in Education*, 1934, *9(5)*, 13–62.

MacDONALD, J. B. and J. D. RATHS. Should we group by creative abilities? *Elementary School Journal*, 1964, *65*, 137–142.

McNEMAR, Q. Lost: our intelligence? why? *American Psychologist*, 1964, 19, 871–882.

MARBLE, A. P. Learning or training: which? *Education*, 1880, *1*, 173–176.

MAYER, F. *American ideas and education.* Columbus, Ohio: Charles E. Merrill Books, 1964.

PARKER, F. W. *How to study geography.* New York: Appleton-Century, 1905. (Copyright 1899)

OSBORN, A. F. *Creative imagination.* (Third Revised Edition) New York: Charles Scribner's Sons, 1963.

SOMMERS, W. S. The influence of selected teaching methods on the development of creative thinking. Doctoral dissertation, University of Minnesota, Minneapolis, 1961.

STOLUROW, L. M. Social impact of programmed instruction: aptitudes and abilities revisited. Paper presented at the American Psychological Association Annual Convention, St. Louis, Mo., September 2, 1962.

THAYER, V. T. *The role of the school in American society.* New York: Dodd, Mead and Co., 1960.

TORRANCE, E. P. *Guiding creative talent.* Englewood Cliffs, N. J.: Prentice-Hall, Inc., 1962.

TORRANCE, E. P. *Education and the creative potential.* Minneapolis: University of Minnesota Press, 1953.

TORRANCE, E. P. *Rewarding creative behavior: experiments in classroom creativity.* Englewood Cliffs, N. J.: Prentice-Hall, Inc., 1965.

VAN TILL, W. Is progressive education obsolete? In P. Woodring and J. Scanlon (eds.), *American education today.* New York: McGraw-Hill Book Co., 1963.

# CHAPTER 6

# EVALUATION
# IN THE
# CLASSROOM

ORVILLE G. BRIM, JR.

# 36. AMERICAN ATTITUDES
# TOWARD INTELLIGENCE TESTS

"Given tests as they are now, do you think it is fair (that is, just) to use intelligence tests to help make the following decisions?"

To decide who can go to certain colleges
To put children into special classes in school
To decide who should be hired for a job
To decide who should be promoted

If one asks a representative group of Americans over 18 these questions, he finds that many of them are against the use of intelligence tests. Forty-one percent are opposed to using tests to help decide on admission of students to colleges; 37% are against using tests in job selection, and 50% against their use to help decide on job promotions; about one-fourth are opposed to using intelligence tests to help establish special classes in school.

One might expect that a younger group of respondents, having had more experiences with tests, would be more favorable in their attitudes. This is not true. High school students in the United States are even more strongly opposed to the use of intelligence tests. Fifty-three percent are against using tests in job hiring; 62% against their use in deciding on promotion; and 54% think it unfair to use tests to help select students for colleges. Almost half are even opposed to using intelligence tests to help in establishing special classes in schools.

How are we to account for this opposition to the use of standardized ability tests by such a substantial number of Americans? Psychologists have the primary responsibility in this country for the development and use of tests in the national interest. Only by facing the existence of a strong antitesting sentiment in the population, by making a professional appraisal

Reprinted from *American Psychologist*, (February 1965), pp. 125–30, by permission of the author and publisher. This article is part of a research report: Brim, Orville G., Jr., (with David C. Glass, John Neulinger, and Ira J. Firestone), *American Beliefs and Attitudes About Intelligence,* (New York: Russell Sage Foundation), 1969.

of its causes, and by taking effective action will their responsibility be discharged.

Two years ago Russell Sage Foundation began a program of research on the social consequences of standardized ability tests. The data just reported come from two opinion surveys which are part of the program. In the first study a national sample of 1,500 adults was interviewed. In the second study a questionnaire was administered to 10,000 students in a national sample of 60 secondary schools; these included 40 public, 10 private, and 10 parochial schools. The data reported here are from the 40 public high schools, with over 5,000 respondents.

Results of the two surveys are only partially analyzed at this point, but they do provide some insights and hypotheses about antitesting sentiment. This report is divided into two parts. The first deals with five criticisms of tests. The second goes on to examine the basic sources of these criticisms as they arise from human nature and society.

## CRITICISMS OF TESTS

When we examine antitesting sentiment as expressed by both lay and professional groups today we find one or more of the following issues to be involved:

Inaccessibility of test data
Invasion of privacy
Rigidity in use of test scores
Types of talent selected by tests
Fairness of tests to minority groups

Consider the first, the inaccessibility of records. It is natural for a person to have an interest in any facts about himself. If someone else knows something about him that he, himself, does not know, then, of course, he will try to find it out, especially if it is something of such importance as his intelligence test score.

Most secondary school students believe that they should be told the actual scores they get on ability tests; but they are not getting this information now. Although almost all of them wish they had received specific, precise information about their test performance, 38% got no feedback at all, and another 24% got only a general idea. Adults, of course, are interested in their children's intelligence, yet 34% of those in our national sample reporting that their children took at least one test never got any information about their children's test performances.

I know the reasons we do not, routinely, give information to people about their test scores. One is that those who do poorly may find the information disturbing. Another is the possible misinterpretation of test scores, and their too rigid use by the inexperienced (a child may be labeled both in his own mind and his parents' as a result of his early test performance).

Even so, it seems to me to be callous on our part to go on ignoring the natural interest of the respondent in his performance, and denying him reasonable information. The American Psychological Association's Committee on Psychological Assessment has recommended that research be undertaken on the effects of communicating psychological information, including experimentation with different methods of feedback. But we cannot wait for research to be completed to start work on a coherent and sensible policy: Steps must be taken to establish a collaborative relationship between tester and respondent in which both gain information of value to them.

A second major criticism of testing is that it constitutes an invasion of privacy. This is a growing concern to many persons because test data are a key part of the new concept of the career record or dossier, which will accompany a person throughout his life. But, who is to keep the record and who is to have access to it? This criticism, to be sure, is directed more to tests of motives, beliefs, and attitudes than to tests of intelligence; but it is pertinent to our general theme, because if legislation is ever passed eliminating personality tests, intelligence tests could well be destroyed along with them.

Psychologists have defended the use of personality inventories by claiming that the data would be confidential, its access limited to competent research persons. The fact is that confidentiality cannot be protected. Psychologists are misinformed in thinking that test responses have the character of a privileged communication. Test results are subject to subpoena by any group with proper legal authority and easily can become a matter of public record.

Therefore, many are concerned about the legal rights of the individual to refuse to give out information about himself. The concern is legitimate and we must listen. The issue is: Under what conditions can the state invade an individual's right to privacy? Where national security is at stake, the state can invade; for instance, conscription, and the psychological testing associated with it, is legitimate. Also justified is the use of intelligence and achievement tests in the nation's public education system, for it is a valuable diagnostic device helping the school system do a better job of educating the students.

But, even though testing by psychologists often is justified on the ground that it benefits the respondents, there are many occasions when the use of tests by psychologists invades privacy without justification. Indeed, one could question the legitimacy of asking the questions reported on subsequently in this paper—questions which were asked of a "captive audience" of public high school students. Perhaps one justifies it because of its eventual contribution to knowledge, on the assumption that the growth of social science knowledge is a public good. But is this really sufficient? A serious matter is involved here, and psychologists must work through their moral philosophy on this point and chart a new section in our code of ethics.

A third objection to tests is their use early in the life of an individual to determine his life chances. Rigid use of tests makes no allowance for possible changes in either the person or his future environments. This is all the more a point for criticism because the public believes that intelligence increases throughout life, viewing it more as knowledge and wisdom than as a quality with a large genetic component.

The public attitude toward intelligence is shown by our survey data in a number of ways. Half of our high school respondents say intelligence tests measure mostly (or only) learned knowledge, while only 13% view tests as measuring mostly inborn talent. The high school students (three quarters of them) say that intelligence increases throughout life, that their older siblings are more intelligent than they, and that while they are not as smart as their fathers right now, they will be considerably smarter than their fathers 10 years from now.

No wonder, then, that with this concept of intelligence there is antagonism to the use of intelligence tests. Two actions are indicated: The public is not, of course, wholly right in its confusion of wisdom with intelligence; some education about the nature of intelligence tests and their value would be in order. But, on the other hand, there can be no doubt that actual use of test results in many schools (and other settings) is much too rigid, being at variance not only with these public views but with what we ourselves know about test reliability and predictive validity. What we need is provision for continuous appraisal of an individual's performance after he has been allocated to one or another environment: a special class in school, a certain college, a particular job. Psychometric theory permits one to appraise the probabilities of subsequent success, but we must not fail to safeguard ourselves from treating the probabilities as certainties. There are some test users—in schools, the Civil Service, the military establishment— who must be converted from their belief that once they have assigned an individual to a given path in life their work has ended. They must realize instead that they have a continuing responsibility to find out if their decisions prove to be right.

A fourth source of antagonism toward intelligence tests is that they deny opportunity to persons with different and possibly highly valuable talents. Since the opportunity structure in American education, and to some extent in occupations, is organized around intelligence tests, there will be resentment from those who do not think intelligence is very important.

Those who hold such a view maintain that intelligence tests are restricted in the talent they measure, and that the valued qualities of man are diverse and multiple in nature—creativity, ambition, honesty, concern for the general welfare of man. More studies on the independence of intelligence from commonly valued characteristics such as creativity, or altruism, or achievement would be of help in defining the degree to which the issue is a real one.

The fifth criticism of tests of ability is that they screen out from opportunities for advancement those individuals from a background of cultural deprivation, who because of the deprivation give an inferior performance on the tests. Fortunately Joshua Fishman and his colleagues (Deutsch, Fishman, Kogan, North, & Whiteman, 1964) have completed their analysis of this problem. Their action recommendations command the attention of all psychologists.

I would like just to add this observation. Those of culturally deprived backgrounds are frequently members of minority groups against which society discriminates. Minority groups, as such, should be favorably inclined to the use of ability tests, since tests constitute a universal standard of competence and potential. When tests are substituted for discriminatory methods of educational placement and discriminatory methods of job selection and promotion, they increase the opportunities of minority group members because they measure ability rather than social status. Tests therefore should be viewed with favor by this segment of the culturally deprived.

Our data seem to show this. A comparison of Negro and white adult respondents, controlled for social class, shows that at the lower social class levels Negroes have the more favorable attitude toward the use of tests in job selection and promotion (although no differences exist for higher social class levels).

Now, to conclude this part: Some criticisms can be met, I believe, by giving heed to familiar recommendations to psychologists. The criticisms involving too rigid usage and inappropriate interpretation of test results of deprived children can be dealt with directly by increased education, training, and supervision of those responsible for the use of tests. Since individuals themselves sometimes misinterpret the meaning of their test scores, an accompanying public education program would be desirable.

Other criticisms cannot be met this easily. I refer to the questions regarding the invasion of privacy, the inaccessibility of records, and the kinds of talent that psychologists want to nurture. These are not matters of educating others, or of technical improvements in tests, but of a carefully reasoned legal, moral, and scientific position which the American psychologist chooses to take.

If these five criticisms can be met by effective action then many critics will be quieted. There are many men of good will toward tests who favor their use, subject to improvements along the lines indicated.

## BASIC SOURCES OF CRITICISMS

I now want to go on to consider a sharply different group of issues: not the criticisms raised about tests, but the personal and social characteristics of some of the critics themselves. For a significant number of these critics, the familiar objections that I have just reviewed are often merely superficial expressions of their more fundamental opposition. The attempt to classify these deeper sources of antitest sentiment leads to noting at least four types of opposition.

First, there is opposition arising from one's general personality characteristics. Second, there is opposition arising from one's general system of values. Third, opposition develops as a consequence of the individual's experience with intelligence tests; antagonism is bred in the loss of self-esteem a person may have suffered as a result of poor performance. Last, opposition arises from the restrictions on one's life opportunities, which also result from poor performance on tests.

Although we do not as yet have data on all four of these I want to touch on each to give a full picture.

Those who object to psychological testing may do so by virtue of their personality characteristics. It is likely, for example, that strong opposition exists among those people who are distinctly hostile to any self-examination, introspection, or self-understanding. These are the people who are also authoritarian in interpersonal relations, intolerant of diversity in ideology or beliefs, and strongly opposed to most forms of social change. The association of this personality type with extremist groups in our country, especially the extreme rightwing political groups, is commonly recognized, and it is understandable that such groups are pushing for legislation banning the use of tests.

The personality syndrome of these persons might well be examined more carefully in our own studies. Although I have no data to report at this time, we did include several scales measuring defensiveness and anti-introspection in our study of the high school students. We are presently analyzing the relationship of these scales to attitudes toward psychological tests. It should be understood, moreover, that little is known about how "authoritarian" personality characteristics relate to the type of objection directed against psychological tests. Will the authoritarian person emphasize invasion of privacy or some other objection? The determining factors undoubtedly involve situational influences as well as personality characteristics. The important point to recognize, however, is that given the personality structure, one or more of the five objections mentioned above is sure to be raised.

The second source of opposition to ability tests is one's general belief about how a society should be organized. One's attitudes, favorable or unfavorable, are rooted in the basic and conflicting themes of American democracy—whether men really are equal, and if they are, what one is to do about the obvious differences between them. In his book entitled *Excellence,* John Gardner (1961) distinguishes between three ways in which societies can be organized: according to an equalitarian philosophy, or with an inherited aristocracy, or as a result of open competition. Which type of organization a person believes is best should strongly influence his attitudes toward the use of ability tests in his society.

From the equalitarian viewpoint men are equal, and differences in ability should be equalized by differential treatment. Ability tests are incompatible with this view because the rationale of ability tests is that there are individual differences of an important kind, and that tests are able to detect such differences.

In an aristocratic society one is given money, power, and prestige according to his parents' social position, and the aristocracy is maintained through ingroup marriage. The doctrine of opening avenues of achievement in a society according to biological inheritance, rather than to social inheritance, is a direct challenge to the established aristocratic social order, and the use of ability tests would not be condoned.

In contrast with these two value systems is the belief that open competition between different types and levels of ability is a social good. In each generation a talented elite should rise to the top, to be replaced next generation by others bearing no necessary blood relationship to them. Each individual has the right to contribute to society as much as he is able, according to his talents. Since tests identify the talented and make it possible to provide them with opportunities for full development of their capacities, a favorable view of intelligence tests should follow.

According to our two surveys, how do Americans feel about these questions? The data show that US students have a less aristocratic outlook than adults. The high school group more often says that parents should not be allowed to pass on their wealth and prestige and that people of wealth and position should not marry their own kind. For the high school students it is the equalitarian position, rather than the belief in open competition, which they take as their own. More high school students than adults say that everyone should go to college; more believe there is no difference in intelligence between social groups; and to back up this belief, more of them disagree with the view that the more intelligent should get better schooling and have the most opportunities. It should follow that the high school students are more opposed to the use of ability tests than are the adults; you will recall that this is the case.

There is other evidence of the linkage of these beliefs to test attitudes: Within the adult population our intragroup analyses show those adults who hold equalitarian views to be the ones who say most frequently that intelligence tests are unfair. (We have not yet completed our within-group analysis for the high school students, but I am certain that this result will hold up.)

If the difference in social philosophy between the generations reflects a historical change, then antitest sentiment is growing. If it is an age difference only, then expect to find most of the antitest sentiment in the younger population. In either event we see that there is a link between opposition to tests and one's general scheme of values.

A third important source of opposition to ability tests is the wounded self-esteem of those who may have done poorly on such tests. We are not ready with any full analysis, but have some suggestive data from the high school group. We note that there are several necessary conditions for test scores to have an impact on self-esteem.

First, one must believe intelligence itself is important. Among a long list of desirable characteristics, intelligence is rated as extremely important by the largest number of respondents with the exception of good health. Also, in another question, more than a third viewed intelligence as more important than any other thing for success in life.

Second, if test scores are to have an impact, one must view them as accurate. Again, the high school respondents included two-thirds who said tests are accurate, even highly accurate, with 18% holding the view that they are inaccurate.

Third, the respondents must have received information about their intelligence as a result of taking standardized ability tests. About 40% said they had received no such information from ability tests; the other three-fifths did.

Fourth, the test information received must present a picture of the respondent less desirable than the one he holds. In the normal course of things half the population would get test scores below normal. However, the self-descriptions of our high school respondents find 43% saying they are above average, another 33% saying they are average, and only 8% rating themselves below average at all. Thus, many of these must have been disappointed in the test information they received. We see, then, that all four conditions are met.

Now comes a curious fact. What is actually reported about the effects of receiving information is that 24% raised their intelligence estimate as a result of the test, 16% made no change, and 7% lowered it. Another one-third said it had no effect or could not remember. How is one to account for this preponderance of raised estimates? This suggests first that the test scores are misinterpreted. We know that the students report receiving only vague and general scores, subject to loose interpretation. Or, it may be a simple misunderstanding such as that a score of 90 is viewed as a high score when one starts with a base of 0, as they are used to in a school grading system.

But other data show that increasing self-estimates of intelligence are a general phenomenon not linked solely to receiving test data. Whatever the source of influence on intelligence, the influence is upward. When one asks whether the school marks they have received caused them to change their mind about how intelligent they are, the same thing occurs, 28% changing upward, and 10% changing downward. Moreover, changes resulting from any experience other than test scores or marks show 70% raising their estimate, 28% lowering it. This suggests a selective use of information designed to protect one's self-esteem, in which those who receive data which upgrades their ability estimates remember it and use it, and those who receive the contrary data forget it or explain it away. The disagreeable experience in the receipt of an unexpectedly low test score may be defended against by forgetting, but the residue of displeasure may well remain and be directed in general ways into resentment against tests. This would be particularly the case in the high school group because of their more frequent and near universal test experience.

The fourth major source of resentment against tests is any punishing effects they may have had on the individual's life chances. We asked both groups of respondents for their perceptions of the influence of tests on such things as educational, occupational, military, and other kinds of opportunities. Very few effects were reported by either group, and those that were mentioned were almost wholly positive. It may simply be that for the adults there has been little impact of tests, while the high school students have not yet entered into military or career choices; indeed, the tenth graders have not yet faced college entrance. Our high school group 10 years from now might report more negative experiences, but for now it appears that it is the impact of test scores on personal feelings rather than life opportunities which is a main matter of concern.

Our review of these four fundamental sources of opposition to tests leads to the conclusion that psychologists must be concerned about the society in which tests are used. Testing does not occur in isolation; there is always a social context. Test scores have a social meaning. They have impact on man's self-esteem; they influence his life chances; they engage his deepest political and social attitudes. These forces must be understood as part of the social setting in which intelligence testing is carried on.

### REFERENCES

DEUTSCH, M., J. A. FISHMAN, L. KOGAN, R. NORTH, and M. WHITMAN. Guidelines for testing minority group children. *Journal of Social Issues,* 1964, 22 (2, Suppl.), 127–45.

GARDNER, J. W. *Excellence.* New York: Harper, 1961.

GOSLIN, D. A. *The search for ability: Standardized testing in social perspective.* New York: Russell Sage Foundation, 1963.

ROBERT L. EBEL

# 37. SHOULD SCHOOL MARKS BE ABOLISHED?

School marks of some kind are a significant element in almost all formal programs of education. Yet there are few educational practices that have been attacked more persistently, or for which a wider variety of remedies have been proposed. Clearly, the problem of marking is one that merits careful consideration, not only by school administrators but also by teachers, students, and all others concerned with the processes of education.

## WHAT IS A SCHOOL MARK?

For the purposes of this discussion it may be helpful to define the term "school mark" rather specifically. *A school mark is a number or a letter that is used to express the level of a student's achievement in some subject of study.* At the beginning of this century numerical marks were prevalent. Usually the numbers purported to express the percent a student had learned of what he was expected to learn. Often a mark somewhere in the vicinity of 70 was regarded as the minimum passing mark.

Somewhat later, letter marks began to replace numerical marks in many schools and colleges. The system that became most popular made use of five letters, defined approximately in these terms:

A—excellent
B—good
C—average
D—poor
F—failing

This system, or some variant of it, is prevalent today.

## THE NEED FOR PERIODIC REPORTS

The case for school marks, as here defined, rests primarily on the validity of two propositions. Here is the first.

---

Reprinted from *Michigan Journal of Secondary Education,* (Fall 1964), pp. 12–30, by permission of the publisher.

*It is educationally useful to determine, and to report periodically, the level of a student's achievement in each of the major subjects he is studying.*

This proposition simply asserts that some kind of a determination of educational achievement should be made from time to time, and reported in some fashion to those who need to know it. It implies that if superior educational achievements are desired they must be defined, identified, and rewarded. The proposition suggests that those concerned with the processes of education ought to pay attention, systematically, to the results they are getting.

This seems to be a reasonable suggestion. Formal education is a purposeful activity. It is directed toward the attainment of certain goals. It requires the skillful management of complex processes. Things can go wrong, so that students sometimes fall far short of the desired levels of achievement. If these deficiencies are to be corrected, the first requirement is that they be clearly recognized. Periodic reports of levels of student achievement permit this recognition.

Formal education is an important activity. Communities go to a great deal of trouble to establish and maintain schools. Laws are passed, taxes are assessed, buildings are built, teachers are employed, courses are planned and taught, all for the purpose of promoting student learning. Is it reasonable to provide excellent facilities for learning without making some effort to assess what is being learned? Reports of student achievement provide one basis for this assessment.

Formal education is a cooperative activity. It requires the coordinated efforts, not only of students and teachers but also of school administrators and parents. All of them have a legitimate interest in the outcome of their efforts. They have a real need to know to what extent educational goals are being achieved, for if those goals are being attained badly they may need to change the nature and magnitude of their efforts. Reports on levels of student achievement can help to provide them with this knowledge.

## SOME APPARENT EXCEPTIONS

Can education occur in the absence of periodic evaluations? Indeed it can. A great deal of a person's education is gained informally or incidentally, not as a result of purposefully planned and carefully organized educational programs. While the extent and quality of a person's informal education will affect his success in formal schooling, it is not feasible or necessary to assess informal educational attainments separately and directly. The situations in which periodic determinations and reports of levels of achievement are most useful are those in which the educational experiences are planned and organized most purposefully to help students attain definite goals.

There are a few notable examples of educational programs, such as Sunday School programs, and certain educational-recreational programs for adults, in which formal efforts to evaluate student achievement are rare or absent altogether. In some of these no very definite goals for attainment are set. Continued attendance and participation is valued more highly than the achievement of any particular kinds or levels of competence. Learning unquestionably goes on, and in some instances it may go on very well. In other instances it appears to go very badly. Specific data on average levels of achievement are necessarily lacking. If no attempt is made to assess levels of achievement precisely and formally, no very specific or dependable data are likely to exist to show how good or poor the average level of achievement may be.

## SOME LOGICAL DILEMMAS

Those who claim that learning proceeds better in the absence than in the presence of systematic determinations of achievement encounter an interesting logical problem. They cannot provide evidence to support the claim without doing what they say ought not to be done. They must measure achievement to prove that learning is facilitated by not measuring achievement. It is impossible in principle to show that more will be learned when no attempt is made to determine how much has been learned. And there is something patently absurd in the assertion that the best progress will be made when no attention is paid to progress. It is like suggesting that a business will prosper best if it keeps no financial accounts, or that a driver will reach his destination most certainly if he drives with his eyes closed.

Somewhat the same logic applies to the suggestion that informal procedures for assessing and reporting student achievement provide better information than formal procedures. The only difference between the two is that the formal procedures are planned more carefully and purposefully, and executed more systematically. Surely careless, incidental, unsystematic determinations and reports cannot in the long run provide more useful information than can be obtained from purposeful, painstaking procedures. In almost all human activities, painstaking effort is a better recipe for success than casual indifference.

## SCHOOL MARKS AND PUPIL ADJUSTMENT

Thus far in this discussion our attention has been directed toward educational achievement, toward cultivation of the student's knowledge and development of his abilities. But what of his feelings? What of his adjustment? Is there no danger that our periodic reports of levels of achievement may have the effect of destroying self-confidence and discouraging educational efforts?

There is indeed, and recognition of this danger has been largely responsible for suggestions that precise, systematic reports on achievement ought to be abolished, or at least de-emphasized. But the suggestions are unsound. If adopted they tend to impair achievement without contributing much to improved adjustment. Let us explain.

A rational person living in a real world is bound to experience failure as well as success. What he regards as success, and what as failure depends largely on his own self concept, and his own level of aspiration. If that level is much too high, he may experience failure rather consistently. But if he has come to terms with himself, and with the demands of the world, most of his days will seem to be reasonably satisfactory. The occasional stunning defeats will be balanced by about an equal number of glorious successes.

Anyone who expects his own performances to be consistently above average *for him* is expecting the impossible. Anyone who expects to excel others in all lines of endeavor is expecting the improbable. Most of us manage to find a few things we can do a little better than most other people, and we concentrate on doing those things. We settle for near average performance in most other activities.

These considerations are relevant to educational programs too. A school that strives to avoid experiences of failure is not helping students to come to terms with themselves or with life. A school that tries to shield a student from knowledge that he does some things better than others, and that some others can do many things better than be can, is not contributing much to his adjustment either. On the other hand, a school whose programs offer nothing but a high probability of failure to some of its students in anything they attempt to learn can hardly qualify as a good school. But in such cases it is the school's program, not the reports of achievement that should be blamed and corrected. The reports did not create failure, and the failures would still be there, whether reported or not. In fact, systematic reports of student achievement can contribute to the solution of problems like this, by calling attention to their existence.

Thus even when the primary goal is adjustment rather than achievement, a good case can be made for periodic reports of student levels of achievement. To ignore differences in attainments, or to withhold information about them from those most concerned, the students and their parents, really solves no problems and helps no one in the long run. Ignorance is a poor ally to education, and the encouragement of ignorance has no place in the process of education. We need to know, and periodic determination and reporting of achievements help us to know how well our efforts are succeeding and in what ways they need to be redirected.

## THE CASE FOR SYMBOLIC MARKS

The second major proposition supporting the case for school marks is this. *A standard set of symbols, such as conventional letter or numerical marks, can provide a satisfactory means for reporting levels of student achievement.*

Symbols such as these have the useful virtues of simplicity, conciseness, and convenience. If properly used they can have the essential virtue of unequivocal meaningfulness. Of course they cannot communicate all that might be useful about a student's strong and weak points, or the reasons for his successes or deficiencies. They provide only a single over-all index of the general level of achievement. But this is by all odds the most important thing to communicate in the first instance. It provides an excellent starting point and stimulus for more detailed investigations of attainments, deficiencies, and possible corrective actions.

The two chief rivals of symbolic marks are individually written descriptive reports and oral interviews. Both of these are much more time consuming than symbolic marks to prepare or conduct. While they permit communication of many more different items of information, each of these items tends to be less specifically stated, and to be less well supported by specific evidence. In these reports and interviews teachers try to say mainly pleasing, general things, in the interests of good interpersonal relations. Many of the same things can be said, without serious falsification, of almost all their students. Hence it is not surprising that teachers sometimes report difficulty in finding different ways to express the same impressions they have about many of their pupils.

The time required to write reports and conduct interviews raises other serious questions. It may impose an extra burden on the teachers. In some schools classes are dismissed for half a day over a two week period to allow the teacher time to interview the parents of each child separately. Whether a child's educational development is promoted enough, as a result of one half-hour interview, to make up for the loss of ten half-days of school work may be open to question.

## THE MEANINGFULNESS OF MARKS

But, actually, how much meaning does a symbolic mark have? What does an A in first year French, or a D in beginning algebra, really signify?

To begin with, such marks have very little to say directly about how much French or how little chemistry the student knows. What they can say is that the student who got the A in French showed outstanding achievement, in comparison with his peers, all of whom were presumably seeking to attain the same goals. The D in chemistry reflects below average achievement. On the assumption that a reasonably good course was fairly well taught to moderately capable students, a well informed educator can make some pretty good guesses as to how much French or chemistry has been mastered in each case. But the meaning of the mark is essentially relative meaning, expressing the achievement of one student in relation to that of his classmates.

This is clearly limited meaning, but it is far from meaninglessness. It is about all the meaning one can reasonably ask of a standard set of symbols applied to all kinds of course content. Somewhat surprisingly, it may signify more with respect to actual content mastery than can be gleaned from the typical written report or oral interview.

To make a quantitative measure of achievement (i.e., a mark) *completely* meaningful with respect to content mastered, one would need a *complete* inventory of that content and all of its possible applications. This is a task so great as to be practically impossible of completion. The best one can hope for ordinarily is to approximate such an inventory with a sample of the items of knowledge and ability it ought to include. A good objective achievement test may provide such a sample. If one has a copy of the test before him, and knows what score a particular student made on it, he can form a reasonably accurate impression of what the student can or cannot do in that area of achievement.

The achievements of a group can often he reported meaningfully by indicating what proportion of its members can successfully complete each of a small number of representative tasks. During World War II, Admiral Nimitz used this technique effectively to report on the mathematical competence (or lack of it) of naval recruits. He presented a list of sixteen problems requiring fundamental arithmetical operations with whole numbers, common fractions and decimals, and reported that the average recruit could solve less than half of those problems correctly.

## LIMITATIONS OF MARKS

The second proposition said that symbolic marks *can* be satisfactory. Often, it must be admitted, they are not. In some cases the school faculty has not taken the trouble to define the marks clearly, and to supervise the use of the marking system so as to maintain the defined meanings. In other cases, and for various reasons, teachers do not secure enough reliable data on levels of student achievement to make the marks they issue reasonably accurate. But the logical remedy for these deficiencies is to correct them, not to abolish marks.

School marks have a limited but an important function. They sometimes need to be supplemented by written reports and oral interviews. On the grounds of convenience and meaningfulness, however, they have definite advantages over other forms of periodic reports. They merit the widespread use that is currently made of them in an overwhelming majority of schools and colleges.

A. HARRY PASSOW

# 38.  DIMINISHING TEACHER PREJUDICE

"By all known criteria, the majority of urban and rural slum schools are failures." This judgment by the President's Panel on Educational Research and Development (1964, p. 30) grew out of five indictments of current school practices: the severe scholastic retardation which progressively worsens as children grow older, a dropout rate which exceeds 50 per cent, fewer than five per cent of this group enrolling for some form of higher education, deteriorating IQ scores, and a distressing picture of adolescents leaving schools "ill-prepared to lead a satisfying, useful life or to participate successfully in the community."

The plight of the inner-city school (described in considerable, if depressing, detail elsewhere in this volume) is a pulsing tangle of academic retardation, pupil and staff transiency, racial imbalance, alienation, personnel and staff shortages, and general inadequacy of resources. What still is at issue, however, is the *why* of the inner-city school. The tough question, raised by social psychologists such as Goodwin Watson, is, "To what extent has the school itself cultivated the apathy, lack of self-confidence, absence of persistent effort, the evasions, the suspicions, defensiveness and hostility of slow learners?" (Watson, 1964.) Are the attitudes and biases of professional educators—conscious or not—responsible for the inferior attainments and expression of problems in inner-city schools, or are teachers being made scapegoats for the ills of school and society?

## ASSESSING CAUSE

The "educational deprivation vs. social deprivation" controversy continues. The former blames the massive academic retardation in depressed areas on the attitudes and behavior of the teachers and administrators; the latter attributes the large-scale underachievement to experiential deficits in early childhood, which fail to equip children to fit into and adapt well to school environments. Difficulties in adjusting to school tasks are predictable but

Reprinted from *The Inner-city Classroom: Teacher Behaviors*, Robert D. Strom, (ed.), (Columbus, Ohio: Charles E. Merrill Books, Inc., 1966), pp. 93–109, by permission of the publisher.

not yet explainable. Both rationales can be supported, and neither alone accounts for the academic malfunctioning in the inner-city school.

Kenneth B. Clark documents the inferior educational attainment of Negro pupils in Harlem's ghetto, but he rejects all explanations under the general heading of "cultural deprivation." Pointing to interview data from HARYOU, he underscores the significance of teacher attitudes in the success or failure of students. Crucial are the problems of white, middle-class teachers in identifying with, accepting, and achieving empathy with children deemed "unappealing or alien." The ghetto school, says Clark, is a scene of educational atrophy and class struggle. Most reprehensible is the practice of placing youngsters in tracks on the basis of invalid judgments of their ability to learn: the consequence is the self-fulfillment of prophecies of uneducability. "They induce and perpetuate the very pathology which they claim to remedy" (Clark, 1965, p. 128).

Even more pointed is Clark's description of the school system wherein power is vested in the hands of white, middle-class professionals:

> The clash of cultures in the classroom is essentially a class war, a socioeconomic and racial warfare being waged on the battleground of our schools, with middle-class and middle-class aspiring teachers provided with a powerful arsenal of half-truths, prejudices, and rationalizations, arrayed against hopelessly outclassed working-class youngsters. This is an uneven balance, particularly since, like most battles, it comes under the guise of righteousness (Clark, 1965, p. 129).

Martin Deutsch sees minority group and class status as hurting the lower-class child since he "enters the school situation so poorly prepared to produce what the school demands that initial failures are almost inevitable, and the school experience becomes negatively rather than positively reinforced." Deutsch sees experiential differentials as crucial and teachers poorly trained to understand and cope with cultural variations.

> School is an experience which for children in the experimental group (primarily Negro, lower-class children) is discontiguous with the values, preparation, and experience they receive from their homes and particular community; it represents society's demand that they bridge social-class orientations for a few hours a day, five days a week. No catalyst is provided for this transition, and few plans have been made to facilitate the child's daily journey across the chasm (Deutsch, 1960, p. 3).

These formulations by Clark and Deutsch are essentially critical of the predominantly white, middle-class oriented teacher and administrator—of what they do or do not do, of their attitudes and prejudices.

### RACIAL BIAS

Philip Freedman asserts that three assumptions can be made about educators, supported by empirical observation, anecdotal data, and common sense—the last two following logically from the first:

...The Caucasian population of the United States harbors a substantial amount of racial prejudice directed against Negroes.... The teaching staffs of our urban areas, drawn chiefly from the Caucasian, middle-class reservoir, share, in some measure, the negative racial attitudes of the communities from which they spring.... These negative attitudes impede the participation of the middle-class Caucasian teachers in programs for the deprived child, who is usually either Negro or Puerto Rican.

Freedman maintains that these unhealthy racial attitudes act as a barrier to both the recruitment of teachers for inner-city schools and the effectiveness of teachers assigned to classes consisting of minority group children.

David Gottlieb asserts that, despite considerable attention being given to the problems of racial integration, relatively little data have been gathered about the values, attitudes, and expectations of both Negro students and teachers: "We know even less about the differences and similarities between Negro and white students who find themselves in schools where there are variations in the racial composition of students and teachers" (1963, pp. 2–3).

However, considerable data clarify the consequences of discrimination and segregation on the ego development, motivation, and personality traits of minority group children. David Ausubel, writing particularly about the largest segment of the disadvantaged, the Negro, contends that certain distinctive properties undoubtedly result in significant differences:

> Negro children live in a predominantly lower-class subculture that is further characterized by a unique type of family structure, by specially circumscribed opportunities for acquiring status, by varying degrees of segregation from the dominant white majority, and, above all, by a fixed and apparently immutable denigration of their social value, standing, and dignity as human beings because of their skin color (Ausubel, 1963, p. 109).

Increasingly, educators are beginning to understand the meaning of this background which the Negro child (and his counterpart in every other minority group, with minor or major variations) brings into the classroom from the time he enters. The young Negro is fully aware of racial differences long before he enters school, and much of what goes on in the classroom extends and reinforces his feelings of inferiority. This is so, even when the teacher is basically sympathetic to the problems stemming from discrimination. However, too often teachers and administrators are consciously or unconsciously racially biased, lack understanding and insight into the bases for the child's reactions and behavior, are hostile and frustrated, and think and act in terms of stereotyped images.

On the other hand, Joseph Lohman maintains that most Negroes, as well as whites, think in terms of stereotypes. The Negro child and his parents view the teacher "not as an individual but as a representative of the group which has treated them as inferior and has discriminated against them."

While the teacher may in fact be unprejudiced, unless he can accept the pupil's right to these feelings of suspicion and hostility as valid and respond without becoming defensive, he will not be able to serve effectively.

## MIDDLE-CLASS ORIENTATION

Since the studies of the 1930's, the charge has been made that the school is a middle-class institution (Davis, 1948; Hollingshead, 1949; Stendler, 1949; Warner, *et al.,* 1944). From teachers and administrators whose value orientation is middle-class, through a curriculum and teaching materials which reflect the middle-class culture, to modes of discipline and control which are middle-class, the school presents a general climate which rewards and reinforces the behavioral patterns of the middle-class homes. As William Burton (1953) puts it, "The school has generally been geared to the aims, ambitions, moral or ethical standards of the white, prosperous, middle-class, Protestant, Anglo-Saxon population." Further, Burton observes, "Many lower-class children simply do not value the objectives and the processes of the school, hence do not try. The school immediately dubs these children 'unintelligent,' 'uncooperative,' or 'stubborn.' "

Deutsch's study indicated that as much as 80 per cent of the school day in the experimental classes went to disciplining and organizational details (i.e., collecting milk money, cookie funds, reports). In contrast, this figure never exceeded 50 per cent in the control classes. Deutsch suggests that these data imply that the lower-class Negro child is getting one-half to one-third the exposure to learning that children from more favored environments receive and, in all probability, does not get the same help or support at home that is common in the middle-class family. If these findings are consistent, Deutsch speculates, the teacher's role and self-concept are probably transformed from that of an instructor to that of a monitor who is likely to ask for transfer out of the lower-class school as soon as possible (1960, p. 23).

That the social origin of the classroom teacher influences his attitudes toward his pupils, their parents, his colleagues, and the administrators is backed up by several studies. Howard Becker's analysis of social-class variations in teacher-pupil relationships reveals that, by reacting to cultural differences, teachers "perpetuate the discrimination of our educational system against the lower-class child." Becker found that the amount of work and effort the teacher requires varies inversely with the pupil's social class. This aggravates the problem and widens the gap between what the child should know and what he does know in each grade. Children from lower-class families are considered more difficult to control, "being given to unrestrained behavior and physical violence." However, it is in the area that Becker calls "moral acceptability" that the slum child's actions and appearance are most distressing, managing "to give teachers the feelings that they are immoral and not respectable. In terms of physical appearance and condition they disgust and depress the middle-class teacher" (1952a).

Ulibarri's study of teacher awareness of sociocultural differences in New Mexico schools indicates that middle-class oriented teachers:

> Have little awareness of the "life space" of the minority group children in their classrooms. Though these teachers perceived their students' lack of motivation, difficulties with assigned texts, and language deficiencies, they did not perceive these problems to be related to differences in cultural backgrounds (Smiley, 1964, pp. 53, 54).

Examining children's perceptions of their teachers' feelings toward them and their self-concepts, scholastic achievement, and behavior, Helen Davidson and Gerhard Lang found a direct relationship between children's social class and teachers' ratings. Also, they found that children clearly sensed their teachers' attitudes toward them; those who felt their teachers ranked them low seemed to have lower self perceptions, achieved less well, and behaved less well in the classroom than did more favored classmates.

By Allison Davis' reckonings, ninety-five of every one hundred teachers are from middle-class origins, a way of life that differs sharply from that of the majority of their pupils. They often undergo an emotional trauma when beginning teaching in situations with lower-class pupils:

> Many new (and old) teachers find it impossible to understand the attitudes and values of these pupils; they are puzzled by the students' reactions to the material and to the instructor, and by their often sullen, resentful behavior... The result in many cases is bewilderment, followed by disillusionment and apathy (Davis, 1964, p. 15).

David Gottlieb reports on the differences and similarities between 36 Negro and 53 white teachers in outlook towards their work and their students (approximately 85 per cent Negro, from low-income families) in six inner-city elementary schools. More than 80 per cent of both groups were female, with the Negro teachers tending to be somewhat younger, more likely to be married, with fewer divorcees or widows. The Negro sample tended to come from larger communities and were twice as likely to have attended public colleges in urban centers. While the white teachers were generally raised in middle-class families, the Negro teachers came from lower-class families, primarily manual occupations. To Gottlieb, the fact that the Negro teachers, more often than the white, came from lower socioeconomic strata, from families headed by a woman, possibly explains the differences in the attitudes and perceptions of the two groups. Gottlieb concluded that white teachers are less well prepared than their Negro counterparts to work in the inner-city school. With respect to job satisfaction, the Negro teachers seemed less likely to voice their gripes. They tended to mention factors associated with the system (i.e., related to the physical or organizational structure), while the white teachers were more often critical of either students or their parents.

When selecting from a list of thirty-three adjectives those which most accurately described their pupils in the inner-city schools, Negro and white teachers differed in their choices. In order of importance, white teachers most frequently selected talkative, lazy, funloving, high strung, and rebellious. Negro teachers selected funloving, happy, cooperative, energetic, and ambitious. The white teachers tended to omit adjectives which are universal attributes of children and related to successful learning. Thus, the Negro teacher is less likely to list shortcomings which might be attributed to Negroes generally and point to deficiencies in the system to explain his dissatisfactions. Gottlieb observes:

> The individual whose own educational experience included being part of a middle-class culture where children were "well behaved," fairly sophisticated in the handling of materials and educational tasks, and socialized by parents who not only played an active role in the school through PTA activities and school-community programs, but saw to it that their children did do their schoolwork, would no doubt experience the greater feeling of "culture shock" when placed in the setting of the inner-city school (1963, p. 9).

## DISSONANT STANDARDS AND EXPECTATIONS

The effects of social stratification and segregation on the academic attainments of elementary school children have been studied by Alan Wilson, who analyzed achievement records of elementary school pupils in a district characterized by socioeconomic residential segregation. Expecting different achievements among children from varying ethnic and socioeconomic strata, Wilson found also that "the normalization of diverging standards by teachers" crystallized different levels of scholastic attainment. Teachers apparently adapt their norms of success and their concepts of excellence to the composition of their student bodies. They accept much less from the low-income children. The normalization of lower standards of performance in the less-favored socioeconomic group provides the same kind of circular reinforcement for the group that normalization of past performance does for the individual student.

Students who are considered outstanding in less-favored schools do not achieve as high as the average student in the more-favored schools, yet receive higher marks. However, as the students progress into secondary schools and junior colleges, uniform achievement criteria are applied to all, and those who have been overevaluated in the past fall behind and often drop out. Wilson observed that students from the "Hills" (more-favored) schools tend to be assigned to the academic streams while those from the "Flats" (least-favored) schools are assigned almost automatically to the general or vocational programs. He also found that although many of the working-class, and especially Negro, students entered the so-called open-door junior colleges, even at this late point they are "counseled or 'cooled out' into terminal vocational training."

Thus, by accepting and expecting lowered standards, teachers must bear some responsibility for the sharp differences between the disadvantaged youth's aspirations and achievements. Wilson comments that whatever educational adaptations need to be made for education of the underprivileged, "misguidance and obscurantism are surely not among them" (1963, p. 234). Arguing that these low expectations and standards on the part of teachers and administrators account for inferior achievement, Kenneth Clark asserts:

> A normal child who is expected to learn, who is taught, and who is required to learn will learn. . . . A single standard of academic expectations, a demanding syllabus, and skillful and understanding teaching are essential to the raising of the self-esteem of disadvantaged children, increasing their motivation for academic achievement and providing our society with the benefits of their intellectual potential (1963, p. 157).

But this matter has a second sharp edge. It is easy to see vindictiveness in high standards, as Eleanor and Leo Wolfe caution:

> The dilemma is reflected in the plaint frequently heard from teachers who work in schools in changing neighborhoods. They often report that if they adhere to the same grading standards they used with previous (more privileged) populations they may be accused of prejudice, or at least of harshness, as demonstrated by a larger number of failures and poor grades. But if they alter their grading system, they may be accused of relaxing standards to the detriment of their new pupils (1962).

## PERCEIVING THE JOB

The unwillingness of new teachers to accept appointments to inner-city schools and the tendency of experienced teachers to seek transfers or to leave teaching have been characterized by Harry Rivlin as a subtle, nation-wide teachers' strike which cannot be stopped by a court injunction. The major reason for this condition, Rivlin maintains, is fear:

> They [young teachers] are afraid they will be trapped in a blackboard jungle; they are afraid of possible physical attack; they are afraid that they cannot deal with the situations they will meet in the schools; and they are afraid that they will have to spend their days being policemen rather than teachers (1962).

At Hunter College, Harry Miller found that many education students had a crusading zeal for helping the disadvantaged child, and only a few were hostile. Most were unenthusiastic about the probability that they would be assigned to a difficult school, but accepted it as a fact of life. Whether the student was eager, accepting, or hostile, Miller found that the prospective teacher was unsure and fearful about the forthcoming first assignment: "Newspaper reports, student gossip, their parents' fears, the reports of friends who are already teaching, all have contributed to a body of beliefs about the schools in lower-class areas which build up their general apprehension" (1963, pp. 1, 2).

The high rate of rejection of appointments to depressed area schools by beginning teachers is due, Vernon Haubrich suggests, to the "inability to comprehend, understand, and cope with the multiple problems of language development, varying social norms, habits not accepted by the teacher, behavior which is often not success-oriented, lack of student cooperation, and achievement levels well below expectancies of teachers" (1963, p. 246).

At Queens College, the BRIDGE Project staff found that no matter how much the beginning teacher has read or heard about the low scholastic performance of children in the inner-city school, he apparently has no idea of what this actually means and how it will affect his teaching until he is on the job. The consequence often is a loss of self-confidence on the part of the teacher:

> They are bewildered and desperate, they feel they cannot reach these children, they clutch at the teaching choices mentioned (which their own experience and education contradict), they bitterly submit to a "trainer's" role or misguidedly try a clinician's role, and they no longer have faith that they can be teachers anymore—in these classrooms (Kornberg, 1963, p. 265).

Becker (1952b) found that the typical Chicago teacher's career consisted of shifting from one school to another, seeking a position where basic work problems—stemming from relationships with children, parents, principals and other teachers—were least aggravated and most susceptible of solution. Teachers felt that the nature and intensity of problems vary with the social-class background of the pupils. What comes out by implication is that teachers praise discipline and pliability above their pupils' other traits. The lowest group (slum children) is perceived as "difficult to teach, uncontrollable and violent in the sphere of discipline, and morally unacceptable on all scores, from physical cleanliness to the spheres of sex and 'ambition to get ahead'." Children from the better neighborhoods, on the other hand, are viewed as quick learners, easily taught, but spoiled and lacking such traits as politeness and respect for elders. The middle group (lower-middle and upper-lower class) is perceived as hardworking but slow learning, easy to control, and most acceptable to the teachers on the moral level.

The new teacher in the Chicago system, Becker found, typically begins her career in the least desirable kind of school and then follows one of two paths: she applies for a transfer to a better neighborhood school as soon as possible or she adjusts resignedly over a period of years to the unsatisfactory conditions and work problems of the lower-class school. Adjustment in the second pattern erases the teacher's restlessness and efforts at transfer. A change in the ethnic or racial composition of the neighborhood or in the administrative structure (e.g., arrival of a new principal) may result in the position's becoming unsatisfactory and the teacher's seeking a transfer to a nicer school.

Teaching in the inner-city school is perceived as an undesirable assignment, even as a "type of punishment or an initiation ritual that must be survived if one is to succeed in the city school system." Yet, some teachers do stay and some spend their entire careers there. To find out why, William Wayson studied a sample of forty-two teachers (twenty-seven white and fifteen Negro) who had remained in slum schools and twenty teachers (sixteen white and four Negro) who had transferred from these schools. The most apparent difference between white stayers and leavers was that a greater proportion of the former tended to be inert, rooted in the situation and unwilling to change jobs and face an unknown situation. The second greatest difference was in the liking for the autonomy enjoyed in the slum school— freedom from pressures or interference from outside the classroom, either from parents or administrators. Eighty-nine per cent of the stayers also expressed altruism and loyalty to an accommodating principal who catered to the needs and desires of the staff, while only 19 per cent of the leavers gave responses in one or more of these categories. All Negroes felt constrained by organizational rules and other external pressures, and their responses tended to agree with those of the white stayers more than with the white leavers. Wayson also observed:

> Stayers seemingly had internalized the role of teacher (which they defined broadly) to a greater degree than leavers (who defined teaching in terms of academic achievement). Stayers were more personally involved in the role and their satisfactions were more ego centered.
>
> Slightly more of the leavers had experienced shock when they first entered the slum school. The greatest shock was caused by the child's violation of middle-class standards. The second greatest source of shock was the child's inability to perform at the prescribed level of achievement.

Simply staying in a slum school cannot be construed as success, Wayson points out, for other criteria are needed to judge this. Unfortunately, some of the sources of satisfaction for the teacher in the slum school and some of the reasons for staying seem negative and unhealthy.

## A BETTER FOCUS

The foregoing survey of literature gives a bleak montage of teachers and administrators who are blinded by their middle-class orientation; prejudiced toward all pupils from lower-class, racial, and ethnic minority groups; culturally shocked and either immobilized or punitive in the classroom; and groping constantly for safer berths where success, in terms of academic achievement, is more likely. Some, not all, teachers are hostile, vindictive, inept, or even neurotic, but many more are compassionate and skillful. (Nor are the undesirable teachers found only in inner-city schools.) Even the HARYOU report (1964, p. 204), which lacerates the schools and their staffs, observes that "there are brilliant, dedicated, responsible teachers who are giving children the kind of academic guidelines and exposures which have made possible a degree of success, in spite of the present structure." Many disadvantaged children *do* achieve; many *do* have healthy self-images, high aspirations, and positive motivations; for many, the classroom is the most supportive element in their lives.

The picture of the biased teacher in a school system heavily stacked against the lower-class, minority-group child is both distorted and incomplete. It implies courses of action for the teacher which may be, to some extent, contradictory: to make the classroom a haven from the problems of depressed area living while giving full play to elements of the lower-class culture, to provide many essential social-wefare benefits while still increasing the time devoted to academic instruction. The picture ignores or dismisses as irrelevant the growing body of research which details the impact of poverty and unemployment, of segregation and discrimination, of all other aspects of the inner-city ghetto living on the mental, emotional, and physical development of the disadvantaged child. Having little or nothing to do with policy decisions regarding racial balance and desegregation, for instance, the teacher is called on to implement these policies and to effect ᴵᵗ· ration within the classroom. It is obvious that schools alone cannot deal satisfactorily with all the forces and factors which affect inner-city life—but it is equally clear that the schools (meaning really teachers, administrators, and other personnel) have a central role and a catalytic function to perform.

The classroom teacher creates the curriculum and the climate for learning. The two are, of course, tightly intermeshed. The teacher's attitudes toward and understandings of the inner-city child—a generic term for millions of different personalities—powerfully influence what is learned and the conditions under which it is learned. Concern with educational problems of the disadvantaged has promoted study and modifications of instructional content, teaching methods, resources, school organization, and special services. The elements of *compensatory* and *remedial* programs are being spelled out, although only a beginning has been made. Emerging techniques for diagnosing cognitive and language disabilities of disadvantaged children should help pinpoint curricular adaptations. New publications teach basic skills but they also aim specifically to raise self-confidence among minority groups, enhancing the self-concepts of students and extending understanding and appreciation among diverse cultural groups (Goldberg, 1964a; Passow, 1964). At both the preservice and in-service levels, teachers need the kinds of experiences which will acquaint them with the potential and applicability of new content, materials, and procedures. But techniques and materials need be accompanied by attitudes composed of such qualities as compassion, respect, reserved judgment, and patience. Writing about the successful teacher of disadvantaged pupils, Miriam Goldberg points out that this teacher:

> does respect his pupils—and not because he sees them through the rose-colored lenses of the romantic—finding "beauty" and "strength" where others see poverty and cultural emptiness. On the contrary, he sees them quite realistically as different from his children and his neighbors' children; yet like all children, coping in their own way with the trials and frustrations of growing up (1964b).

It does little good to belabor the middle-class teacher for having middle-class values; instead, the emphasis must be on knowing about and understanding the lower-class culture, especially when it collides with the culture that permeates our schools. Many of the differences involve relationships with peers, with adults, with authority figures, with culturally different individuals. The poignancy of Bel Kaufman's heroine in *Up The Down Staircase* (1964) reflects inner conflicts caused by her emotional involvement with her students. Miss Barrett is a teacher who cares deeply about her students, feels and expresses her real warmth toward them, and who is hurt by her inability to reach and be liked by each of her students.

These relationships, involving apathy and withdrawal, aggression and hostility, test the teacher constantly. Joseph Lohman suggests that the teacher must expect and be able to take either rejection or hostility without returning it.

> She is the adult and can expect a little more of herself than of a still maturing student. She must learn to live with frustration and not let it keep her from continued effort. She cannot expect results too soon, either in her own increased awareness of our culturally divergent children or in their reaction to her. She can demand certain standards of behavior; she cannot demand that children trust her or believe in her when they have had too much experience to the contrary (p. 25).

Patricia Sexton argues that middle-class culture, whatever its faults and virtues, differs substantially from lower-class culture. Since the lower-class child has difficulty adjusting to these differences, "we must learn new ways of reaching these groups, and we must provide rules to which they can adjust and rewards which will stimulate their interest in school" (1961, p. 79).

Social and behavioral scientists, together with insightful teachers, have provided analyses of the problems of the inner-city child. But, they have also identified variations from middle-class patterns which can be assets rather than liabilities. Leon Eisenberg advises that "the key issue in looking at the strengths of the inner-city child is the importance of not confusing difference with defect" (1964). Teacher education programs must provide experiences to enable personnel realistically to understand and accept various subcultures, recognizing strengths and positive aspects on which to build. Lohman stresses the need for the teachers to understand the cultures from which students come, without viewing the varying cultures as right or wrong, superior or inferior, but simply as different. To the extent that a teacher can really come to understand (not necessarily accept or approve of) the student's subculture, he can come to respect the person from that culture, without necessarily approving of his behavior (pp. 83–84).

## THE PREPARATION OF TEACHERS

Clearly, teacher education at both the pre-service and in-service levels needs modification if we are to recruit, train, and keep dedicated teachers who have the know how, insight, and commitment to extend educational opportunities to disadvantaged children. Changes are already being initiated in many teacher preparation programs. One of the more promising is that of Hunter College, whose project prepares teachers in the very school where they will eventually teach. The specific notions being tested by the Hunter program are:

> Student teaching can be both challenging and rewarding in a personal and professional sense; the apprehensions of prospective teachers are best alleviated and their perceptions modified by direct, wide contact with education and community workers and leaders; a team of professionals from the depressed-area school itself—such as subject matter specialists, curriculum experts, and social psychologists—is required for introducing the student teacher to the particular demands of these schools and for helping orient him to working with children in this special context; participation in a program for teaching in a depressed-area school should be voluntary on the student's part and must begin early in his college career (Passow, 1963, p. 238).

Any teacher program modifications being proposed at this time for inner-city school staffs are concerned with both curriculum and climate—with insights into teaching strategies and content adaptations as well as with understandings of cultural differences. Involvement of subprofessionals, teacher aides, and indigenous persons from the inner city in projects designed to help disadvantaged children has opened up new training programs, some of which have been as helpful for the trainers as for the trainees in altering attitudes toward the culturally different. With support of federal and foundation funds, numerous institutes and workshops have focused on helping staffs plan for integrated education, for preschool programs and for remedial projects of various kinds.

No radical innovations in teacher preparation programs have yet emerged, although some patterns seem to be forming. These include:

> (a) Early and continuous contact with children and adults in disadvantaged areas in a variety of school and non-school related activities. These range from one-to-one tutoring of pupils to supervising after-school activities to classroom observations and intensive classroom teaching. These experiences are carefully supervised and often analyzed in seminar or small group sessions afterwards.
> (b) Intensive involvement of behavioral and social scientists who apply research and theory from their disciplines to the specific needs and problems

of the disadvantaged area. These include cultural anthropologists, social psychologists, architects, city planners, historians and political scientists—many of whom are actively involved in field experiences with students.

(c) Intensive involvement of successful school practitioners—classroom teachers, principals, counselors and others—in working with the teacher education staff in planning, supervising, and evaluating experiences. The two-way flow of college and school staffs has been of considerable benefit to both. Rivlin has urged the use of affiliated schools as laboratories for urban teacher education—drawing the analogy to the teaching hospital attached to the medical school.

(d) Opportunities for pre-service teachers to work with non-school agencies, government and agency-sponsored, and to become actively involved in ongoing projects for overcoming poverty, extending civil rights, and generally "reversing the spiral toward futility." Aside from the insights acquired into the life styles of the inner-city families, such experiences are apparently instrumental in more positive attitude formation to the problems faced in such areas.

(e) Modification of college courses to develop those techniques and skills essential to teaching in depressed areas. These include help with diagnostic and remedial procedures, with methods and materials for individualization of instruction, with strategies for classroom control, and with personnel and material resources.

(f) Opportunity to examine, discuss, and plan local program adaptations to known situations, current research, and experimentation being reported by other education centers.

(g) Establishment of internships and other means for continuing relationships between the college and the teacher in-service so that the teacher has continuing supervisory aid as well as support.

Leon Eisenberg maintains that the effective teacher of inner-city children is one whose concern for their welfare goes far beyond the four walls of the classroom: "to citizen participation in efforts to upgrade the neighborhood, to abolish discriminatory practices, to provide more recreational facilities, to support social action for human betterment" (1964). Education in the inner-city school has dimensions which are less crucial in more-favored schools with more advantaged children. Teacher education must offer experiences which will help the teacher, both in preparation and in-service, to modify his behavior and attitudes for the sake of his pupils' healthy and successful learning. In doing so, the teacher will truly teach. Beyond that, as he devotes himself to the many children who are convinced that they have no share in the American Dream, he can help transform the idea of equality of opportunity into reality.

## REFERENCES

AUSUBEL, D. P., and P. AUSUBEL, Ego development among segregated Negro children, in *Education in Depressed Areas,* A. Harry Passow (ed.). New York: Teachers College, Columbia University, 1963, p. 109.

BECKER, H. S., Social-class variations in teacher-pupil relationships, *Journal of Educational Sociology,* April 1952a, 25, 452, 462.

————, The career of the Chicago public schoolteacher, *American Journal of Sociology,* March 1952b, Vol. 57, No. 5, 470–77.

BURTON, W. H., Education and social class in the United States, *Harvard Educational Review,* Fall 1953, Vol. 23, No. 4, 243–56.

CLARK, KENNETH B., *Dark Ghetto: Dilemmas of Social Power.* New York: Harper and Row Publishers, 1965, pp. 128–9.

DAVIS, ALLISON, *Social Class Influences Upon Learning.* Cambridge, Mass.: Harvard University Press, 1948.

DEUTSCH, MARTIN, *Minority Group and Class Status as Related to Social and Personality Factors in Scholastic Achievement.* Ithaca, N.Y.: Society for Applied Anthropology, Monograph No. 2., 1960, pp. 3, 23.

EISENBERG, LEON, Strengths of the inner-city child, *Baltimore Bulletin of Education,* Vol. 41, No. 2 (1963–1964), 10, 16.

FREEDMAN, P. I., Racial attitudes as a factor in teacher education for the deprived child. Unpublished paper, Hunter College, n.d.

GOLDBERG, MIRIAM L., Adapting teacher style to pupil differences: teachers for disadvantaged children, *Merrill-Palmer Quarterly,* Vol. 10, No. 2, 1964a, pp. 167–68.

————, Methods and materials for educationally disadvantaged youth. Paper prepared for the Post-Doctoral Seminar of the College of Education, The Ohio State University, Columbus, October 1964b.

GOTTLIEB, DAVID, Teaching and students: the views of Negro and white teachers. Unpublished paper, Michigan State University, August 1963, pp. 2–3, 9.

HARLEM YOUTH OPPORTUNITIES UNLIMITED, INC., *Youth in the Ghetto: A Study of the Consequences of Powerlessness.* New York: HARYOU, 1964, p. 204.

HAUBRICH, V. F., Teachers for big-city schools in *Education in Depressed Areas,* A. Harry Passow (ed.). New York: Teachers College, Columbia University, 1963, p. 246.

HOLLINGSHEAD, AUGUST B., *Elmtown's Youth.* New York: John Wiley & Sons, Inc., 1949.

KAUFMAN, BEL, *Up the Down Staircase.* Englewood Cliffs, N.J.: Prentice-Hall, Inc., 1964.

KORNBERG, LEONARD, Meaningful teachers for alienated children, in *Education in Depressed Areas,* A. Harry Passow (ed.). New York: Teachers College, Columbia University, 1963, pp. 265, 274.

LOHMAN, JOSEPH D., *Cultural Patterns of Differentiated Youth: A Manual for Teachers in Marginal Schools.* Berkeley, Calif.: University of California, n.d., pp. 24, 83–84.

MILLER, HARRY L., The effect of information on student beliefs about the slum school. New York: Hunter College Project TRUE, 1963, pp. 1–2.

PASSOW, A. HARRY, Instructional content for depressed urban centers: problems and approaches. A paper presented for the Post-Doctoral Seminar of the College of Education, The Ohio State University, October 1964.

————, Teachers for depressed areas, in *Education in Depressed Areas,* A. Harry Passow (ed.). New York: Teachers College, Columbia University, 1963, p. 238.

PRESIDENT'S PANEL ON EDUCATIONAL RESEARCH AND DEVELOPMENT OF THE SCIENCE ADVISORY COMMITTEE, *Innovation and Experiment in Education.* Washington, D.C.: U.S. Government Printing Office, 1964, p. 30.

RIVLIN, HARRY N., Teachers for the schools in our big cities. A paper prepared for the University of Pennsylvania Schoolmen's Week Program, October 12, 1962, p. 7.

Sexton, Patricia C., *Education and Income*. New York: The Viking Press, 1961, p. 79.

Smiley, Marjorie, Research and its implications, in *Improving English Skills of Culturally Different Youth in Large Cities,* Arno Jewett, Joseph Mersand, and Doris V. Gunderson (eds.). Washington, D.C.: U.S. Government Printing Office, 1964, pp. 53–54.

Stedler, Celia B., *Children of Brasstown*. Urbana, Ill.: University of Illinois Press, 1949.

Warner, W. Lloyd, Robert J. Havighurst, and Martin B. Loeb. *Who Shall Be Educated?* New York: Harper & Row, Publishers, 1944.

Watson, Goodwin B., (ed.) No Room at the Bottom. Washington, D.C.: National Education Association, 1964.

Wilson, Alan B., Social stratification and academic achievement, in Education in Depressed Areas, A. Harry Passow (ed.). New York: Teachers College, Columbia University, 1963, p. 234.

Wolf, Eleanor P., and Leo Wolf., Sociological perspective on education of culturally deprived children, *School Review,* Vol. 70, No. 4, Winter 1962, pp. 381–82.

ROBERT L. THORNDIKE

# 39. EDUCATIONAL DECISIONS AND HUMAN ASSESSMENT

When we speak of "measurement" in education, we can elect to use the term narrowly and rigorously in the way that the physical scientist and philosopher of science do when they speak of "fundamental measurement." We then must restrict ourselves to those attributes where we can establish both a zero point, meaning "exactly none of," and the equality of units, so that we can show in some meaningful way how X units of intelligence could be added to Y units of intelligence to yield Z units of intelligence. But a really rigorous definition of this sort would exclude all of the procedures and devices that we have developed in psychology and education. We have no way of identifying exactly zero intelligence, and we can't add one moron IQ of 70 to another moron IQ of 70 and get a genius IQ of 140. Our zero points and our units in educational and psychological measurement are at best arbitrary and somewhat elastic. So both by necessity and by choice,

Reprinted from *Teachers College Record,* Vol. 66, No. 2 (November 1964), by permission of the author and publisher.

we shall accept a much looser and more inclusive definition of measurement.

Going to the other extreme, we can mean by measurement any procedure that permits us to group specimens into distinct categories or arrange them in an ordered series with respect to some attribute, a procedure which permits us to say "Peter and Paul are alike, but Mary is different," or "Peter has the most; Mary is next, and Paul has the least." Of course, we would certainly welcome refinements that permitted us to assign numerical values to Peter, Paul, and Mary in a somewhat more discriminating way, but we recognize the usefulness of even rough classifications. The point is that this broader definition does not restrict us to formal tests, formally constructed and formally administered, but permits us to accept, with whatever weight and confidence it may deserve, any procedure by which we can make meaningful and consistent distinctions between persons. Teacher judgments, anecdotal observations, peer nominations, and evaluations of individual pupil products are all measurements in this sense, differing from formally planned, standardized, and distributed measurement devices only in degree of refinement and precision. For much of our thinking about educational measurement and evaluation, this is the most serviceable and appropriate definition. It is serviceable just because it emphasizes that the formal structure of educational and psychological testing differs from the broader foundation of pupil evaluation only in degree of refinement and not basically in kind.

## DECISION FROM PREDICTION

Decisions imply predictions. The decision to admit Jack Smith to Patchoula College is based upon the prediction that he is likely to be successful there. Depending upon our value system, success may mean that he will get all A's or that he will be all-Conference high scorer on the basketball team; but in either event, a prediction is involved. In the final analysis, a decision results from a complex and not always rational calculus, involving the interaction of predictions about facts and an existing framework of values. The values are numerous, though not always clear and explicit. Should Johnny take algebra in the ninth grade, or should he take general mathematics? A fact, which we would like to predict as accurately as we can, is how successful he will be in algebra. But the decision depends equally heavily upon the value that we place on algebra—as preparation for later mathematics courses, as a requirement for college admission, as a tool in various professions, as a component of our intellectual heritage. These values will enter into the picture with different weights depending upon all that we know about Johnny—his family setting, his educational goals, and his vocational aspirations.

Should Henry apply for admission to Wigwam University? One basic fact is his likelihood of being admitted, and a second is his probability of maintaining the required academic average once he is there. But a complex of values is also involved. Henry's rich Uncle Henry, for whom he was named, is an alumnus of Wigwam. Wigwam has a good program in forestry, in which Henry has expressed interest. Wigwam is over a thousand miles from Henry's home. Henry prefers a small college to a big university. The list of considerations which lend valence, positive or negative, to college in general and Wigwam in particular as Henry views them could be extended without limit. Whether Henry should apply is a resultant on the one hand of these values, and on the other hand, a best prediction of the facts concerning his acceptance and success.

Where measurement has a role is in making the predictions of fact more accurate. If measures are worth their salt, it is because they enable us to predict within a smaller margin of error that Jack Smith will achieve a C average, or that Mary Jones will improve in reading if put in a remedial section, or that the students in Indianapolis will learn more algebra if they work through a specific sequence of programed instruction, each at his own rate, or that Henry Schute will be happier as an electrician than as a bank clerk.

Let us see what some of the facts of life are about making predictions, and try to draw from a contemplation of these facts some principles to guide us on how best to use measurement in the decision-making process.


## OF PROBABILITY AND TIME

The first, the most fundamental and the most disheartening fact is that *all* predictions are fallible. All have a component of error. Even if the prediction is only from how well Johnny reads today to how well he will read tomorrow, there is still an element of indeterminacy. Changes in vocabulary and structure from one passage to another, changes in Johnny, and an element of sheer chance combine to produce unpredictable shifts from day to day, from one measurement to another. So all predictions must have an element of tentativeness about them, be couched in terms of probabilities rather than in absolutes! "If we were to give him the Gateford Reading Test, there are 2 chances in 3 that Johnny would fall between the 65th and 85th percentile."

Unfortunately, it is the nature of decisions that they *cannot* always or even usually be tentative. There comes a time when we must act. But many decisions *do* have an element of tentativeness. They are decisions to explore, decisions to try. They are revocable. The inescapable fact of the standard error of estimate in any prediction points out to us that we should cherish this tentativeness, where it is admissible, and view as many as possible of our decisions as hypotheses to be pursued and tested further, but to be abandoned if further evidence points to abandonment as desirable.

A second general point is that our predictions will typically become less accurate the greater the time span over which we attempt to extend them. The effect of increasing the time interval is marked when the time interval includes a large part, or the crucial part, of the growth span. Thus, if made at the pre-school level, even two-or three-year predictions of intellectual level are quite fallible, whereas in adult life, predictions of intellectual level can be made over 20 to 30 years with a fairly high degree of accuracy.

The decreasing accuracy of predictions with increasing time span has implications both for decision-making and information-seeking. On the one hand, especially at the earlier school ages, we should try to schedule our measuring so that the evidence will be as current as possible at those points at which crucial decisions are likely to be made. From another point of view, we should give relatively less weight to old than to recent information in the decision process. And thirdly, we should be more tentative about those decisions that have implications for the more remote future than about those whose reference is immediate. Thus, we might be quite ready to assign a pupil to the accelerated ninth-grade algebra section on the basis of an eighth-grade mathematics achievement test, but be quite unwilling to decide on that basis that this pupil should continue math through the twelfth grade.

## DETERMINERS OF THE PREDICTED

Principle number three states that predictions will, in general, be less accurate the more difference there is between the predictor and what is being predicted. In the 10-year-old, the best predictor of 12-year-old reading ability will be present reading ability. Prediction from a measure of verbal intelligence will be somewhat less good; prediction from a measure of nonverbal intelligence will be still less good, and prediction from the size of the pupil's head will be no good at all.

There are times when this principle does not hold. Thus, at the first-grade level, a good individual intelligence test will give a better long-range forecast of reading ability than will a beginning reading test. At this point, there has been so little development of reading, and the patterns are so unstable and rapidly changing, that they do not provide a solid basis on which to make extended forecasts. Other instances come easily to mind in which a particular ability has not yet been developed or is in so formative a stage that a direct measure of it provides little basis for extended predictions. But it is still a good working strategy to base educational predictions, and consequently decisions, on performances as much like the one in which we are ultimately interested as possible. Thus, achievement in arithmetic on the one hand and a miniature algebra-learning test on the other provide good bases for predicting achievement in algebra. High school rank in class remains the best single forecaster of college freshman grade-point average. A biographical inventory covering past mechanical or selling activities provides as good a basis as an ability test for judging future choice of a mechanical or sales occupation. It will, then, usually pay us, as educational decision makers to analyze presently available information with an eye to how closely it resembles that which we wish to forecast, and to start, at least, by "doing what comes naturally"—by using that present information which has the most evident relationship to the relevant outcomes.

A fourth principle asserts that all behavior is multiply determined. The progress that a six-year-old will make in learning to read depends not only upon his mental age, but also upon his specific stock of language experiences, the level and type of his home support, the security of his relationships with parent and teacher, the manner in which reading is taught, the skill with which his initial difficulties are identified and corrected, and a host of other components of him and his environment. The grade-point average that is made by a college freshman reflects his verbal and quantitative abilities as they have developed up to the time of college entrance, his background of educational skills and knowledge, his techniques of study and preparation, his level of interest and effort, his freedom from emotional stresses and strains that prevent him from mobilizing his resources for academic work, the courses he takes, and the instructors who teach them— to mention only a few of the components in an involved complex. The more of these determinants we can include in our prediction, the more accurate, in theory at least, our prediction can be and, consequently, the more informed our decision. Thus, as a general strategy of decision-making, we should recommend the measurement of a multitude of the factors that contribute to our prediction and are therefore relevant to our decision.

The simplest application of this principle would say, "The more we know about the individual, the better; and if we know enough, our predictions will approach perfection." This is the faith underlying the detailed, intensive case history as well as the multi-test aptitude battery. To what extent is it sound? What are its shortcomings? What factors limit the accuracy of our prediction even as we accumulate vast amounts of information about the individual? Let us examine four such factors.

## LIMITS ON FAITH

The first limiting factor is overlapping or redundancy in the various items of information. Take the prediction of freshman grade-point average as an example. Suppose we start with high school grades, which have generally appeared to be our most valid single predictor. Then we decide to add on a scholastic aptitude test because we have evidence that such tests correlate with grades in college. But only a part of the information that the scholastic aptitude test adds is really new information because scholastic aptitude also correlates with and is strongly represented in high school grades. So we try out a self-report inventory of study skills and attitudes. But the same thing is true here, for good or poor study skills and habits helped the pupil to get those good or poor marks in high school. All right then, let's have a go at measuring motivation to achieve, as best we can, by inventory or by projective device; and we find that such motivational measures *do* give some modest prediction of freshman GPA, but, alas, we also find that they too add little if anything new to the prediction from high school grades because grades are themselves indicators of level of academic motivation.

The situation is not *quite* as gloomy as I have pictured it, but it is certainly true that increments in predictive accuracy from the addition of predictors come only slowly and grudgingly because of the overlapping in the information that different predictors provide. Two or three predictor measures, chosen because they are each good predictors when taken singly and because they are as independent of one another as possible, each yielding new and different information, will usually do about as much for us as the most elaborate and extensive battery.

Increments in accuracy of prediction are held down, in the second place, because each additional fact that we consider about an individual introduces irrelevant information into the picture along with any new and relevant information. Thus, the aptitude test may place a premium on a type of facileness and a range of superficial acquaintance that is different from and does not contribute to ability to master college work. The report of study techniques may indicate what the individual thinks he *ought* to do, rather than what he does do. The motivational measure may be distorted by anxiety about being away from home or by last night's fight with the girl friend. The determinants of *test behavior* are also multiple, and only a fraction of these determiners are relevant to the life behavior that we are trying to predict. This is another way of saying that *all* tests fall short of perfection so far as validity and reliability are concerned, and that our tests and other indicators for some of the factors that we would like to measure are woefully imperfect.

The increment in accuracy of prediction from a complex of information may be held down, thirdly, by inappropriate weighting of the different component facts. In trying to understand Johnny's poor reading and thereby to predict what remedial steps are likely to be effective, we may be overly influenced by his rivalry with his little sister and give inadequate attention to a shift in schools and a change in the philosophy of instruction that took place at the second grade. We may be over-influenced by a low group-test IQ and insufficiently impressed by specific incapacities shown by a test of word-analysis skills. If a complex array of facts is to enable us to make the best possible prediction, each of the facts must enter into our awareness with the proper emphasis and weight. How is this to be achieved?

## ACTUARY VS. CLINICIAN

Basically, there are two ways in which a number of facts about an individual can be combined to yield a prediction relating to him. They may be combined actuarially, or they may be combined clinically. When we combine data actuarially, we combine them in accordance with a formula or table based upon extensive previous experience. Thus, experience accumulated over previous years may have indicated that in order to predict achievement in ninth-grade algebra, we should give a weight of three to achievement in eighth-grade arithmetic, a weight of two to the Orleans Algebra Prognosis Test, and a weight of one to the Numerical Ability test of the Differential Aptitude Tests. Proceeding actuarially, we would apply this formula to past records and prepare an expectancy table, showing what the probabilities are of different levels of success in algebra for any given composite score on the weighted team of predictors. To make our prediction concerning Johnny, we would apply the 3–2–1 formula to his grades and test scores, find the composite score, and look up the probabilities in our expectancy table. Our prediction for Johnny would be taken directly from this actuarial table of past experience.

Proceeding by the clinical approach, we would get the same three facts about Johnny—eighth-grade arithmetic grades, prognostic test score, and numerical ability test score—but we might also give some consideration, intentionally or inadvertently, to a variety of other facts about Johnny. We might know that his father is an engineer, that Johnny is tall for his age, that Johnny is an Eagle Scout, that Johnny is the oldest of four children, that Johnny won second prize in physical science in the school Science Fair, that Johnny is an engaging redhead. Programming this complex of data through that original electronic computer, the human brain, we would come out with a judgment as to how good a bet Johnny is for the algebra class.

Note that the "clinician," if we can apply this designation to any person who is called upon to digest a set of facts about a person and arrive at a decision about him, typically has a much larger number and wider range of data available than could be incorporated into an actuarial prediction equation. At the same time, the only weighting system that the clinician has is that somewhat unstable and untested one represented by his own fluctuating judgment. Theoretically, in view of the relative wealth of information available to him, it should be possible for the clinician to make much more accurate and discriminating predictions than can result from the mechanical combining of two or three measures into an actuarial prediction, but this potentiality can only be realized if he picks out the *right* components from the mass of available information and gives them the *right* weight. Those comparative studies that we have of clinical and actuarial prediction tend, by and large, to find more accurate results for actuarial than for clinical predictions. I hasten, however, to add that the conditions in these studies have generally been somewhat artificial, not giving full scope to the talents of the skilled clinician. The studies nevertheless point out that there is no guarantee that human judgment will use data optimally, and that even though it is possible to feed both more data and a wider variety of data into a human judge than into a prediction equation, the judge may process his information inappropriately or inefficiently and come out with generally inaccurate predictions.

### RECURRENCE AND UNIQUENESS

Of course, we can only use an actuarial approach to prediction and decision-making successfully if we have systematically accumulated the type of actuarial data that will permit us to select the most efficient team of predictors and determine the optimum weights to assign to each. This is possible only where the event to be predicted is a frequently occurring one—success in college, success in a particular course or program, or some such tangible and recurring item. The roles and settings under which this can occur are unfortunately limited. If we are in charge of admissions for a college, freshman grade-point averages at our institution can be accumulated in quantity, and expectancy tables for prediction can be developed if we wish. In the same way, a school or school system can develop expectancy tables for success in any of its own courses or programs. There are also possibilities for making such material more broadly available. Thus, in the state of Georgia, expectancy tables are published and made available to high school counselors, showing the probability of a grade-point average of C, of B, and of A at each of the colleges within the state for individuals with any given combination of high school grades and College Board Scholastic Aptitude Test scores. Again, hidden in the College Board's *Manual of Freshman Class Profiles,* there is material that would permit development of at least crude expectancy tables showing chance of admission to some hundreds of different colleges in relation to SAT scores and high school grades, and these tables should be quite useful to high school counselors.

But many events are relatively unique in the experience of the decision maker. As a high school counselor, you have never before had a student who wanted to go to Williwaw Tech, and you must synthesize as best you can any available information about the college and the student in order to arrive at an estimate of his prospects of success. No remedial reading teacher works with enough pupils, or with pupils enough alike in age, reading level, and type of difficulty, to have the possibility of assembling formal expectancy tables that could be applied in making a forecast about a new case. The range and individuality of the problems encountered by a school psychologist in working with the problems of individual pupils defy any accumulation of evidence of a formal actuarial nature. Research studies may have pointed out the factors that are relevant and the strength of general relationships that exist, but these general findings must be interpreted and applied in new combinations with the individual case.

For the vast numbers of situations in which we must make predictions concerning events that are of infrequent occurrence or that represent a new and somewhat different combination of familiar components, we necessarily rely upon the informal prediction equations that have accumulated in the neurones of the school psychologist, the remedial reading teacher, the guidance counselor, or the principal, based upon their knowledge of previous research and their background of experience. And then prediction is inaccurate to the extent that these prediction equations are inappropriate or unstable or both.

To recapitulate, (a) all events are multiply determined, so (b) our predictions can be improved by taking account of a number of determiners, but (c) the gain from adding on additional predictors is held down by the fact that our different predictors are redundant or overlapping and (d) by the difficulty of giving optimum weight to each component, especially (e) when the weighting is done intuitively on the basis of the fluctuating judgment of an individual "clinician." Thus, the accuracy of our predictions is limited in part by the information available to us and in part by our techniques for processing that information.


## PREDICTING CHANGE

A fifth fact of life, or principle underlying educational decision-making, is that change is much more difficult to predict than status. As I suggested earlier, we can make a very good forecast of where pupils will be in reading a year from now just by knowing where they are at the present time. Present educational status is the best single predictor of future educational status. But just in proportion as this is true, predicting who will gain most from initial test and who will gain least becomes impossible. To the extent that today's performance forecasts next year's performance, we are saying that gains will be uniform or differ only by chance and in unpredictable ways from one pupil to the next, and that individual differences in gain are essentially unpredictable. It is my impression that this is not far from the fact of the matter, at least in those educational achievements that have a continuous history of development through the school years.

I'm not certain how often educational decisions are based on the type of prediction that states that Mary can be expected to make rapid progress in reading this next year, but Helen can be expected to show less than average progress. I hope not too often, because I am sure that the batting average on such predictions is really low. But I suspect that we often have a feeling that we are predicting differential growth when we are really just predicting differences in future status from differences in present status.

A sixth principle, related to the one that I have just presented, but of more fundamental importance, is that differential prediction is more difficult and less accurate than absolute prediction. An example of absolute prediction is the assertion that Joe's freshman grade-point average will be C or lower. One type of differential prediction, on the other hand, asserts that Joe will do better in freshman math than in freshman English. Another type of differential prediction states that Joe will learn more English if he is put in a remedial section than if put in a regular section. Thus, differential predictions are of two somewhat different kinds, one referring to a difference between areas and the other to a difference between treatments. Differential predictions are at the heart of most educational decisions, because most decisions represent choices between different actions. Thus, they are based on predictions of differences associated with the different possible choices that the individual or school faces.

Why are differential predictions relatively undependable? Primarily, it is because many of the predictive factors bear a similar relationship to both alternatives. A high level of general abstract ability, a supportive and culturally rich home environment, motivation to achieve in academic pursuits, a conscientious disposition, patterns of organizing one's time and doing one's work systematically are all predictive of good achievement, be it in English or in mathematics, and account in considerable measure for our ability to predict in either direction. Thus, the remaining components that are different—*specific* talent in numerical thinking *vs specific* fluency with words, or preference for devoting time to reading or writing *vs* preference for working on quantitative problems—account for only a modest fraction of final performance.

In the same way, the facts about an individual that determine whether he will do well or poorly in freshman English are in large part the same without regard to the treatment he receives. If he comes to us with a large vocabulary, effective skills in expressing himself, and the ability to read rapidly and with understanding, he is likely to show good achievement at the end of the year no matter what kind of an instructor or curriculum he is exposed to; and if he falls at the other end of the scale on these predictive measures, he can be expected to do relatively poorly. This is not to say that differential treatments for different kinds of individuals are of no importance, or that we are completely blind in our estimations of who will benefit most from which treatment. But it is to say that judgments of these matters are far from precise and much more difficult to make than a simple judgment of who will do well or poorly.

## SALVATION VIA HUMILITY

Recognizing the difficulty and fallibility of differential predictions, what are the practical implications of this state of affairs for administrators, counselors, and individual pupils? One implication is to reinforce even more strongly the humility and tentativeness with which we make choices and plans for and with students. When we have a low level of certainty that occupation A or course A or section A or method A will work out better for Roger than will occupation or course or section or method B, we can ill afford to be dogmatic and rigid in our effort to bring about or enforce the choice of A. And we need, so far as possible, to maintain the doorways open for shifting to B or C or D if further developments suggest that A is not working out well.

Secondly, we need to recognize that there are many roads to salvation for each individual and that a number of them may be almost equally satisfactory. That is, there is no *one* best job, no *one* best curriculum for each pupil. In many of the choices that must be made, where the basis for differential prediction is inadequate, the choice may actually not make much real difference in the long run. Whether to take French or Latin, whether to be in the advanced math section or the regular section, whether to enter college X or college Y, the important thing may be less which choice is made than that some choice is made and is followed up wholeheartedly once a commitment has been made to it.

Thirdly, when we lack any clear indication from the objective evidence as to which choice is likely to be more successful, as may often be the case, we may find it wise to be guided by the subjective preferences of the individual. Where we have little basis for affirming a difference from without, it may be wise to be guided from within.

Let me try to recapitulate the points I have tried to make, first about the facts of the case and then about the strategy for using measurement in educational decision-making. As basic facts or principles, I would affirm these points:

> Decisions are based jointly on judgments of fact as to what would occur and judgments of value as to what should occur.
>
> Educational and psychological measurements have their function in making more accurate our judgments of what would occur if a certain action were taken.
>
> The information most likely to permit accurate judgments is information on past behavior most similar to that which we are trying to predict in the future.
>
> The information most likely to permit accurate judgments is recent information, especially when the function being studied is undergoing rapid change.
>
> Joint prediction from several measures can be more accurate than prediction from any one taken singly.
>
> The gain from adding on additional measures, however, is sharply limited by overlapping of the measures and by our difficulty in weighting them properly.
>
> It is much more difficult to make sound judgments about growth and change than about status.
>
> It is more difficult to make sound judgments about differences—of area or of treatment—than about status in a single role or dimension.

The elements of decision-making strategy that seem to me to flow from these considerations are as follows:

> So far as possible, think of decisions as hypotheses to be made tentatively, subject to review and revision in the light of further data and events.

Do not force decisions in advance of the time that they need to be made, but take each decisive step as the time for it arrives.

Since there are many differential decisions for which measurement data provide meager evidence on which to make a choice, be relaxed about the whole affair and at the same time give scope for subjective evaluations.

Finally, clarify the values involved first; only as you know what you are seeking can measurement be of any help to you in finding it.

ROBERT L. EBEL

# 40. MEASUREMENT AND THE TEACHER

The principles of measurement of educational achievement presented in this article are based on the experience and research of a great many people who have been working to improve classroom testing. The particular principles discussed here were selected on the basis of their relevance to the questions and problems which arise most often when tests of educational achievement are being considered, prepared and used. While some of the principles may seem open to question, we believe a case can be made in support of each one.

1. *The Measurement of Educational Achievement Is Essential to Effective Education.* Learning is a natural inevitable result of human living. Some learning would occur even if no special provision were made for it in schools, or no special effort were taken to facilitate it. Yet efficient learning of complex achievements, such as reading, understanding of science, or literary appreciation, requires special motivation, guidance and assistance. Efforts must be directed toward the attainment of specific goals. Students, teachers and others involved in the process of education must know to what degree the goals have been achieved. The measurement of educational achievement can contribute to these activities.

It is occasionally suggested that schools could get along without tests, or indeed that they might even do a better job if testing were prohibited. It is seldom if ever suggested, though, that education can be carried on effectively by teachers and students who have no particular goals in view,

Reprinted from *Educational Leadership* (October 1962), pp. 20–24, by permission of the author and publisher.

or who do not care what or how much is being learned. If tests are outlawed, some other means of assessing educational achievement would have to be used in their place.

2. *An Educational Test Is No More or Less Than a Device for Facilitating, Extending and Refining a Teacher's Observations of Student Achievement.* In spite of the Biblical injunction, most of us find ourselves quite often passing judgments on our fellow men. Is candidate A more deserving of our vote than candidate B? Is C a better physician than D? Is employee E entitled to a raise or a promotion on his merits? Should student F be given a failing mark? Should student L be selected in preference to student M for the leading role in the class play?

Those charged with making such judgments often feel they must do so on the basis of quite inadequate evidence. The characteristics on which the decision should be based may not have been clearly defined. The performances of the various candidates may not have been observed extensively, or under comparable conditions. Instead of recorded data, the judge may have to trust his fallible memory, supplemented with hearsay evidence.

Somewhat similar problems are faced by teachers, as they attempt to assess the achievements of their students. In an effort to solve these problems, tests have been developed. Oral examinations and objective examinations are means for making it easier for the teacher to observe a more extensive sample of student behavior under more carefully controlled conditions.

The price that must be paid for a test's advantages of efficiency and control in the observation of student achievements is some loss in the naturalness of the behavior involved. In tests which attempt to measure the student's typical behavior, especially those aspects of behavior which depend heavily on his interests, attitudes, values or emotional reactions, the artificiality of the test situation may seriously distort the measurements obtained. But this problem is much less serious in tests intended to measure how much the student knows, and what he can do with his knowledge. What is gained in efficiency and precision of measurement usually far outweighs what may be lost due to artificiality of the situation in which the student's behavior is observed.

3. *Every Important Outcome of Education Can Be Measured.* In order for an outcome of education to be important, it must make a difference. The behavior of a person who has more of a particular outcome must be observably different from that of a person who has less. Perhaps one can imagine some result of education which is so deeply personal that it does not ever affect in any way what he says or does, or how he spends his time. But it is difficult to find any grounds for arguing that such a well concealed achievement is important.

If the achievement does make a difference in what a person can do or does do, then it is measurable. For the most elementary type of measurement requires nothing more than the possibility of making a verifiable observation that person or object X has more of some defined characteristic than person or object Y.

To say that any important educational outcome is measurable is not to say that satisfactory methods of measurement now exist. Certainly it is not to say that every important educational outcome can be measured by means of a paper and pencil test. But it is to reject the claim that some important educational outcomes are too complex or too intangible to be measured. Importance and measurability are logically inseparable.

4. *The Most Important Educational Achievement Is Command of Useful Knowledge.* If the importance of an educational outcome may be judged on the basis of what teachers and students spend most of their time doing, it is obvious that acquisition of a command of useful knowledge is a highly important outcome. Or if one asks how the other objectives are to be attained—objectives of self-realization, of human relationship, of economic efficiency, of civic responsibility—it is obvious again that command of useful knowledge is the principal means.

How effectively a person can think about a problem depends largely on how effectively he can command the knowledge that is relevant to the problem. Command of knowledge does not guarantee success, or happiness, or righteousness, but it is difficult to think of anything else a school can attempt to develop which is half as likely to lead to these objectives.

If we give students command of knowledge, if we develop their ability to think, we make them intellectually free and independent. This does not assure us that they will work hard to maintain the status quo, that they will adopt all of our beliefs and accept all of our values. Yet it can make them free men and women in the area in which freedom is most important. We should be wary of an educational program which seeks to change or control student behavior on any other basis than rational self-determination, the basis that command of knowledge provides.

5. *Written Tests Are Well Suited to Measure the Student's Command of Useful Knowledge.* All knowledge can be expressed in propositions. Propositions are statements that can be judged to be true or false. Scholars, scientists, research workers—all those concerned with adding to our store of knowledge, spend most of their time formulating and verifying propositions.

Implicit in every true-false or multiple-choice test item is a proposition, or several propositions. Essay tests also require a student to demonstrate his command of knowledge.

Some elements of novelty are essential in any question intended to test a student's command of knowledge. He should not be allowed to respond successfully on the basis of rote learning or verbal association. He should not be asked a stereotyped question to which a pat answer probably has been committed to memory.

6. *The Classroom Teacher Should Prepare Most of the Tests Used to Measure Educational Achievement in the Classroom.* Many published tests are

available for classroom use in measuring educational aptitude or achievement in broad areas of knowledge. But there are very few which are specifically appropriate for measuring the achievement of the objectives of a particular unit of work or of a particular period of instruction. Publishers of textbooks sometimes supply booklets of test questions to accompany their texts. These can be useful, although all too often the test questions supplied are of inferior quality—hastily written, unreviewed, untested, and subject to correct response on the basis of rote learning as well as on the basis of understanding.

Even if good ready-made tests were generally available, a case could still be made for teacher-prepared tests; the chief reason being that the process of test development can help the teacher define his objectives. This process can result in tests that are more highly relevant than any external tests are likely to be. It can make the process of measuring educational achievement an integral part of the whole process of instruction, as it should be.

7. *To Measure Achievement Effectively the Classroom Teacher Must Be (a) a Master of the Knowledge or Skill to Be Tested, and (b) a Master of the Practical Arts of Testing.* No courses in educational measurement, no books or articles on the improvement of classroom tests, are likely to enable a poor teacher to make good tests. A teacher's command of the knowledge he is trying to teach, his understanding of common misconceptions regarding this content, his ability to invent novel questions and problems, and his ability to express these clearly and concisely; all these are crucial to his success in test construction. It is unfortunately true that some people who have certificates to teach lack one or more of these prerequisites to good teaching and good testing.

However, there are also some tricks of the trade of test construction. A course in educational measurement, or a book or article on classroom testing can teach these things. Such a course may also serve to shake a teacher's faith—constructively and wholesomely—in some of the popular misconceptions about the processes of testing educational achievement. Among these misconceptions are the belief that only essay tests are useful for measuring the development of a student's higher mental processes; that a test score should indicate what proportion a student does know of what he ought to know; that mistakes in scoring are the main source of error in test scores.

8. *The Quality of a Classroom Test Depends on the Relevance of the Tasks Included in It, on the Representativeness of Its Sampling of All Aspects of Instruction, and on the Reliability of the Scores It Yields.* If a test question presents a problem like those the student may expect to encounter in his later life outside the classroom, and if the course in which his achievement is being tested did in fact try to teach him how to deal with such problems, then the question is relevant. If the test questions involve, in proportion to their importance, all aspects of achievement the course undertakes to develop, it samples representatively. If the scores students receive on a test

agree closely with those they would receive on an independent, equivalent test, then the test yields reliable scores.

Relevance, representativeness and reliability are all matters of degree. Procedures and formulas for calculating estimates of test reliability are well developed, and are described in most books on educational measurement. Estimates of representativeness and relevance are more subjective, less quantitative. Yet this does not mean that relevance and representativeness are any less important than reliability. The more a test has of each the better. While it is possible to have an irrelevant and unrepresentative but highly reliable test, it is seldom necessary and never desirable, to sacrifice any one of the three for the others.

Either essay or objective test forms can be used to present relevant tasks to the examinees. Ordinarily, the greater the novelty of a test question, that is, the smaller the probability that the student has encountered the same question before, or been taught a pat answer to it, the greater its relevance. Because of the greater number of questions involved, it is sometimes easier to include a representative sample of tasks in an objective than in an essay test. For the same reason, and also because of greater uniformity in scoring, objective tests are likely to yield somewhat more reliable scores than are essay tests.

9. *The More Variable the Scores from a Test Designed to Have a Certain Maximum Possible Score, the Higher the Expected Reliability of Those Scores.* Reliability is sometimes defined as the proportion of the total variability among the test scores which is not attributable to errors of measurement. The size of the errors of measurement depends on the nature of the test— the kind and the number of items in it. Hence for a particular test, any increase in the total variability of the scores is likely to increase the proportion which is not due to errors of measurement, and hence to increase the reliability of the test.

Figure 1 shows some hypothetical score distributions for three tests. The essay test consists of 10 questions worth 10 points each, scored by a teacher who regards 75 as a passing score on such a test. The true-false test consists of 100 items, each of which is worth one point if correctly answered, with no subtraction for wrong answers. The multiple-choice test also includes 100 items, each of which offers four alternative answer options. It, too, is scored only for the number of correct answers given, with no "correction for guessing."

Note, in the data at the bottom of Figure 1, the differences among the tests in average score (mean), in variability (standard deviation), in effective range and in estimated reliability. While these are hypothetical data, derived from calculations based on certain assumptions, they are probably reasonably representative of the results most teachers achieve in using tests of these types.

It is possible to obtain scores whose reliability is above .90 using 100

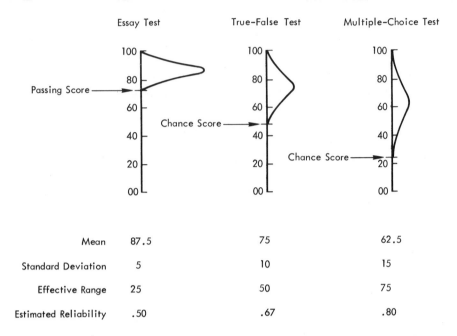

FIG. 1. HYPOTHETICAL SCORE DISTRIBUTIONS FOR THREE TESTS.

multiple-choice items, but it is not easy to do, and classroom teachers seldom do it in the tests they construct. It is also possible to handle 100-point essay tests and 100-item true-false tests so that their reliability will equal that of a 100-item multiple-choice test. But again, it is not easy to do and classroom teachers seldom succeed in doing it.

10. *The Reliability of a Test Can Be Increased by Increasing the Number of Questions (or Independent Points to Be Scored) and by Sharpening the Power of Individual Questions to Discriminate Between Students of High and Low Achievement.* Figure 2 illustrates the increases of test reliability which can be expected as a result of increasing the number of items (or independent points to be scored) in a test. Doubling the length of a 10-item test whose reliability coefficient is .33 increases the reliability to .50. Doubling again brings it up to .67, and so on. These estimates are based on the Spearman-Brown formula for predicting the reliability of a lengthened test. While the formula requires assumptions which may not be justified in all cases, its predictions are usually quite accurate.

Figure 3 shows how the maximum discriminating power of an item is related to its level of difficulty. These discrimination indices are simply differences between the proportions of correct response from good and poor students. Good students are those whose total test scores fall among the top 27 percent of the students tested. Poor students are those whose scores make up the bottom 27 percent. An item of 50 percent difficulty does not

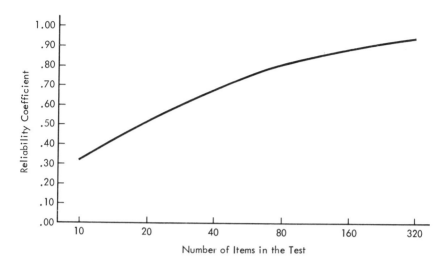

FIG. 2. RELATION OF TEST RELIABILITY TO TEST LENGTH.

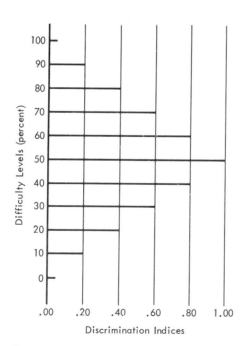

FIG. 3. MAXIMUM DISCRIMINATION ATTAINABLE WITH
ITEMS AT DIFFERENT LEVELS OF DIFFICULTY.

necessarily have (and usually will not have) an index of discrimination of 1.00. Its discriminating power may be zero, or even negative. But items of middle difficulty have higher ceilings on their discriminating power. What is more important, they not only can have, but usually do have, greater discriminating power than very easy or very difficult items. An item that no one answers correctly, or that everyone answers correctly, cannot discriminate at all. Such an item adds nothing to the reliability of a test.

In summary, the 10 principles stated and discussed in this article represent only a sample of the important things classroom teachers need to know about educational measurement. These principles, and the brief discussion of each presented here, may serve to call into question some common practices in classroom testing, or to suggest some ways in which classroom tests might be improved. They are not likely, and are not intended, to say all that needs to be said or do all that needs to be done to improve educational measurement in the classroom. It is our sincere belief, however, that a teacher whose classroom testing reflects an understanding of these principles will do a better than average job of measuring student achievement.

JAMES H. RICKS

# 41. ON TELLING PARENTS ABOUT TEST RESULTS

Like any other organization dealing with people, a school has many confidences to keep. School administrators, teachers, and especially guidance workers inevitably come to know items of private information. A gossip who carelessly passes such information around abuses his position and his relationship with his students. It is both right and important that some kinds of information be kept in confidence.

What about test results? Do they belong in the category of secrets, to be seen only by professional eyes and mentioned only in whispers? Or is their proper function best served when they become common knowledge in the

Reprinted from *Test Service Bulletin No. 54* (December 1959) by permission of The Psychological Corporation, New York City.

school and its community? (In some towns, names and scores have been listed in the local newspaper, much like the results of an athletic contest.)

We think neither extreme is a good rule. Sometimes there is reason to make group data—figures such as the average and the range from high to low—generally public. Seldom should individual results be published except for the happy announcement of a prize won, a scholarship awarded, and the like. But short of general publication, school guidance workers face a particularly important question: Should parents be told their children's test results?

Hard questions, often, are hard because they deal with genuinely complicated problems. Simple "solutions" to such questions are likely to be a trap rather than an aid if their effect is to divert our attention from the difficulties we truly face. Simple rules or principles, on the other hand, can be of real help as one tackles complex problems and situations. This article will present some rules that we have found useful in facing questions such as:

"What should I say when a mother wants to know her son's IQ?" "Should we send aptitude test profiles home with the children?" "We feel that parents in our school ought to know the results of the achievement tests we give, but then it's hard to explain the discrepancies between these and the teachers' grades."

No single procedure, obviously, can be appropriate for every kind of test. Nor for every kind of parent. To Mr. Jones, a well-adjusted and well-educated father, a report of his daughter's test scores may enhance his understanding of her capacities and of what the school has been giving her. To Mr. Green, a somewhat insecure and less knowledgeable man, the identical information may spark an explosion damaging to both child and school. And the counselor or teacher often has no sure way of knowing which kind of person he will be reporting to.

Two principles and one verbal technique seem to us to provide a sound basis for communicating the information obtained from testing. The two "commandments" are absolutely interdependent—without the second the first is empty, and without the first the second is pointless.

The first: *Parents have the right to know whatever the school knows about the abilities, the performance, and the problems of their children.*

The second: *The school has the obligation to see that it communicates understandable and usable knowledge.* Whether by written report or by individual conference, the school must make sure it is giving *real* information —not just the illusion of information that bare numbers or canned interpretations often afford. And the information must be in terms that parents can absorb and use.

Few educators will dispute the first principle. It is in parents that the final responsibility for the upbringing and education of the children must lie. This responsibility requires access to all available information bearing on educational and vocational decisions to be made for and by the child. The school is the agent to which parents have delegated part of the educational process—but the responsibility has been delegated, not abdicated. Thoughtful parents do not take these responsibilities and rights lightly.

The parents' right to know, then, we regard as indisputable. But, to know what?

Suppose that, as a result of judicious testings, the school knows that Sally has mastered social studies and general science better than many in her ninth grade class, but that few do as poorly as she in math. In English usage she stands about in the middle, but her reading level is barely up to the lower border of the students who successfully complete college preparatory work in her high school. The best prediction that can be made of her probable scores on the College Boards three years hence is that they will fall in the range which makes her eligible for the two-year community college, but not for the university. She grasps mechanical concepts better than most boys, far better than most girls. Looking over the test results and her records, her experienced teacher recognizes that good habits and neatness of work have earned Sally grades somewhat better than would be expected from her test scores.

All of these are things Sally's parents should know. Will they know them if they are given the numbers—Sally's IQ score, percentiles for two reading scores, percentiles on another set of norms for several aptitude tests, and grade-placement figures on an achievement battery?[1]

Telling someone something he does not understand does not increase his knowledge—at least not his correct and usable knowledge. We are reminded of the guide's observation about the tenderfoot. "It ain't so much what he don't know, it's what he knows that ain't so that gits him in trouble." Transmitting genuine knowledge requires attention to content, language, and audience. We have already referred to some of the characteristics of parents as an audience. Let's look at the other two elements.

Content means that to begin with *we* must ourselves know what we are trying to get across.

We need to know just what evidence there is to show that the test results deserve any consideration at all. We need equally to know the margins and probabilities of error in predictions based on tests. If we don't know *both* what the scores mean *and* how much confidence may properly be placed in them, we are in trouble at the start—neither our own use of the information nor our transmission of it to others will be very good.

*Content*—what we are going to say—and *language*—how we are going to put it—are inseparable when we undertake to tell somebody something. In giving information about test results, we need to think about the general

---

[1] The implied "No" answer to this question does not, of course, refer to those few parents trained in psychometrics—perhaps even to a point beyond the training of the school staff. Parents include all kinds of people.

content and language we shall use and also about the specific terms we shall use.

To illustrate the general content-and-language planning: a guidance director may decide that he wants first to get across a sense of both the values and the weaknesses of test scores. One excellent device for his purpose would be an expectancy table or chart. Such a chart can make it clear to persons without training in statistics that test results are useful predictors *and* that the predictions will not always be precise. Local studies in one's own school or community are of greatest interest. But the guidance director who lacks local data may still find illustrative tables from other places helpful in preparing parents and students to use the results in a sensible way. (An example is given in Table 1, with references to others that may be found elsewhere.)

Specific terms used in expressing test results vary considerably in the problems they pose. Consider, for example, the different kinds of numbers in which test results may be reported.

IQ's are regarded as numbers that should rarely if ever be reported as such to students or to their parents. The reason is that an IQ is likely to be seen as a fixed characteristic of the person tested, as somehow something more than the test score it really represents. The effect, too often, is that of a final conclusion about the individual rather than that of a piece of information useful in further thinking and planning. Few things interfere more effectively with real understanding than indiscriminate reporting of IQ scores to parents.

Grade placement scores or standard scores of various kinds are less likely

Table 1   THE CHART FOR THE BOYS' CEEB VERBAL RESULTS*

| Of Each Ten Boys in the Tenth Grade Whose VR + NA Scores Are in the | On the CEEB SAT-V When They Are Seniors, How Many Will Score | | | | And How Many Will Score 500 or Above |
|---|---|---|---|---|---|
| | 399 and lower | 400– 499 | 500– 599 | 600 and over | |
| Top quarter of the class | ½ | 2 | 4 | 4 | 4 out of 5 |
| Second quarter | 2 | 4 | 5½ | ½ | 3 out of 5 |
| Third quarter | 6 | 4½ | 3 | 1 | 2 out of 5 |
| Lowest quarter of the class | 4 | | | | Very few |

* The guidance director found, in the classes of 1953 and 1954, 101 boys and 85 girls who had taken the *Differential Aptitude Tests* (including Verbal Reasoning and Numerical Ability) in their Tenth Grade years and the *Scholastic Aptitude Test* of the College Entrance Examination Board as Seniors. Since the CEEB reports two scores—Verbal and Math—there were four sets of data: Boys—Verbal, Boys—Math, Girls—Verbal and Girls—Math. (For more data from this school, see the *Journal of Counseling Psychology,* 1954, I, 106–15, and 1955, II, 229–30). The other three charts were similar in appearance. For additional illustrations of expectancy charts and tables, see Test Service Bulletins 38 and 53; the *Differential Aptitude Tests* Manual, third edition, pp. 62–64; and the *Modern Language Aptitude Test* Manual, 1959 edition, pp. 15 and 16.

to cause trouble than IQ scores are. Still, they may substitute an illusion of communication for real communication. Standard scores have no more meaning to most parents than raw scores unless there is opportunity for extensive explanations. Grade placements *seem* so simple and straightforward that serious misunderstandings may result from their use. As noted in a very helpful pamphlet,[2] a sixth-grade pupil with grade-placement scores of 10.0 for reading and 8.5 for arithmetic does not necessarily rank higher in reading than he does in arithmetic when compared to the other sixth graders. (Both scores may be at the 95th percentile for his class—arithmetic progress much more than reading progress tends to be dependent on what has been taught, and thus to spread over a narrower range at any one grade.)

Percentiles probably are the safest and most informative numbers to use *provided* their two essential characteristics are made clear: (1) that they refer not to percent of questions answered correctly but to percent of people whose performance the student has equalled or surpassed, and (2) who, specifically, are the people with whom the student is being compared. The second point—a definite description of the comparison or "norm" group—is especially important in making the meaning of test results clear.

Much more can be said about the kinds of numbers used to convey test score information. Good discussions can be found in a number of textbooks.[3] But a more fundamental question remains: *Are any numbers necessary?*

We intend nothing so foolish as suggesting a ban on the use of numbers in reporting test results. But we have been struck repeatedly by the fact that some of the very best counselors and many of the best written reports present numerical data only incidentally or not at all.

Along with the two "commandments" at the beginning of this article, we mentioned a verbal technique. Generally, we dislike formulas for writing or speaking. This one, however, seems to have advantages that outweigh the risks attending its suggestion. It's just a few words:

> "You score like people who. . . ." Or, to a parent, "Your son (or daughter) scores like students who. . . ."

The sentence, of course, requires completion. The completion depends on the test or other instrument, the reason for testing, and the person to whom the report is being given. Some sample completions:

> . . .people who are pretty good at office work, fast and accurate enough to hold a job and do it well.
> . . .people who don't find selling insurance a very satisfactory choice. Three

---

[2] M. R. Katz, *Selecting an Achievement Test.* E. and A. Series No. 3, 1958, page 26. Available free from Educational Testing Service, Princeton, New Jersey.

[3] See, for example, Chapters 17 and 18 in *Measurement and Evaluation in Psychology and Education,* by Thorndike and Hagen (New York: Wiley, 1955), or pages 556–63 and 584–88 in *Appraising Vocational Fitness,* by Super (New York: Harper, 1949).

out of four who score as you do and become insurance salesmen leave the job for something else in less than a year.

...students who find getting into liberal arts college and getting a B.A. degree something they can attain only with extra hard work. On the other hand, they find a year or two of technical school interesting and they probably do well in the jobs to which that leads.

...students who are disappointed later if they don't begin a language in the ninth grade and plan take some more math and science. It's easier to head toward business later if you still want to than to go from the commercial course into a good college.

...students who don't often—only about one out of four—manage to earn a C average their freshman year at State.

...students who have more than average difficulty passing in arithmetic—you [*or, to a parent,* he] may need some extra help on this in the next few years.

Many more samples will come readily to mind. The most important thing to note is that a satisfactory report combines two kinds of information:

1. the test results of the individual person, and
2. something known about the test or battery and its relationship to the subsequent performance of others who have taken it.

Also, a satisfactory completion puts the school or the counselor out on a limb, at least a little. Some variant of "That's not so!" or, more politely, "How do you know?" will be the reaction in some cases, probably less frequently voiced than it is felt.

Well, let's face it. The decision to use a test at all is a step out on a limb. Some limbs are broad and solid and the climber need feel little or no anxiety. Some are so frail that they offer only hazard, with the bait of an improbable reward. We climb out on some limbs of medium safety because there is evidence of a real chance that they will help us, and those whom we test, toward a worthwhile goal.

The words of the formula need not actually be used in each case. Sometimes percentiles, grade placement scores, or a profile may be what the parents should receive. But it is well to try first mentally stating the meaning of the results in the language suggested above. If this proves difficult or discomforting, a warning signal is on—reporting the numbers is likely not to be constructive in the case at hand!

The audience of parents to which our test-based information is to be transmitted includes an enormous range and variety of minds and emotions. Some are ready and able to absorb what we have to say. Reaching others may be as hopeless as reaching TV watchers with an AM radio broadcast. Still others may hear what we say, but clothe the message with their own special needs, ideas, and predilections.

The habit of using the formula, and of thinking a bit about what answer to give if the response is a challenging or doubtful one, puts the interpreter of test scores in the strongest position he can occupy. In the case of achievement tests, it requires him to understand why and how the particular test or battery was chosen as appropriate for his school and his purpose. In the case of aptitude (including scholastic aptitude or intelligence) tests, it requires him to examine the evidence offered in the test manual and research studies to back up the test's claim to usefulness. And it reminds him always that it is in the end *his* thinking, *his* weighing of the evidence, *his* soundness and helpfulness as an educator or counselor that are exposed for judgment—not the sometimes wistful ideas of the test author or publisher.

The school—or the counselor—*is* exposed for judgment when telling parents about the abilities and performances of their children. The parents have the right to know. And knowledge in terms they can understand and absorb is what the school must give.

KAORU YAMAMOTO

# 42.   EVALUATION IN TEACHING

We, as active teachers, have wondered about many matters in teaching and raised numerous questions about education and our role in it. Most of these queries have been private in nature, while some remained even subconscious. For the purposes of the present discussion, however, let us make the basic questions explicit.

### TEACHING AND ITS QUESTIONS

Just as all roads lead to Rome, so do all our questions point to one central inquiry: "What is teaching?" The latter can be answered in myriad ways, but I am submitting here (Table 1) a convenient scheme to systematize most of these questions and answers. As you see in Table 1, the questions are classified by interrogative pronouns and further divided into normative and descriptive forms.

For example, one of the fundamental questions takes the form, "Why should we teach?" This asks for the rationale of teaching, probably in terms of cultural values, goals, intentions, and motives, and the answer is

Reprinted from *Texas Journal of Secondary Education,* Vol. 21, No. 3 (Spring 1968), 4–11, by permission of the author and publisher.

Table 1 "WHAT IS TEACHING?"—SCHEMATIZATION OF QUESTIONS

| Question | | Area of Concern |
| --- | --- | --- |
| *Normative* | *Descriptive* | |
| Why should we teach? | Why are we teaching? | Values, goals, intentions, and motives |
| Who should teach? | Who is teaching? | Teacher qualification (recruitment, selection, and preparation) |
| Whom should we teach? | Whom are we teaching? | Student characteristics (recruitment, selection, and distribution) |
| When should we teach? | When are we teaching? | Readiness and logistics (physical, cognitive, and social development, timing, duration and continuity) |
| What should we teach? | What are we teaching? | Curriculum (types and quantity of material, structure, and sequence) |
| How should we teach? | How are we teaching? | Instruction (methods, media, climate, and control) |
| Where should we teach? | Where are we teaching? | Ecology and logistics (context, physical facilities, and geo-cultural administration) |

expressed as an *ought,* or normative, statement (e.g., "we ought to teach our children to convert them from animals to humans"). Our concept of the nature of universe and of *Homo sapiens* determines the specific form of our answer here.[1]

A variant of the above question is, "Why are we teaching?" This version asks for a description of our present practice and the answer must therefore clarify the immediate and real reasons for teaching, instead of some ideals. We may insist, in response to the normative form of the question, that our aim is to induce insight and innovation in the face of an unknown world into which students are destined to grow, while the actual goal of our teaching may be mere conservation and perpetuation of the past. The two answers, therefore, may or may not agree with each other.

Similarly, when the question, "Whom should we teach?," is raised, we may answer that we should teach every child, regardless of his race, color, sex, creed, social status, and aptitude. If, however, the question is in the descriptive form, "Whom are we teaching?," our answer will be radically different from the above, due to a gap between our dream and practice.[2]

Now, my thesis is that we are engaged in "evaluation" whenever we compare our answer to the normative question with that to the descriptive question. In other words, we are evaluating our current activities against what we know or believe we should be doing. Accordingly, if we are conscientious, we will be continuously and forever involved in evaluation. Quite often, such evaluation is expressed as feelings of dissatisfaction, insecurity, and anxiety.

In this sense, we cannot escape evaluating various aspects of education, including ourselves as a teacher. It is nothing mysterious or threatening. Whether such action is carried out consciously or unconsciously, publicly or privately, constructively or destructively, and systematically or randomly—that is, however, another matter. In any case, evaluation is here to stay as an essential component of teaching activities.

### PROCESS OF EVALUATION

We said that evaluation is fundamentally the comparison between our answer to the normative question and that to the descriptive question. No matter what specific aspects of teaching we are concerned with, therefore, evaluation follows the same basic pattern shown in Table 2.

[1] See, for example: Lee, Gordon C., *Education and Democratic Ideals* (New York: Harcourt, Brace & World, 1965); Scheffler, Israel, "Philosophical Models of Teaching," *Harvard Educational Review* 35: 131–43 (Spring 1965); Yamamoto, Kaoru, "The Rewards and Results of Teaching," *Education* 87: 67–72 (October 1966).

[2] See, for example: Myrdal, Gunnar, *An American Dilemma* (New York: Harper & Brothers, 1944); Passow, Harry, ed., *Education in Depressed Areas* (New York: Teachers College Press, Teachers College, Columbia University, 1963); Warner W. Lloyd, *American Life: Dream and Reality* (revised edition) (Chicago: University of Chicago Press, 1962).

## Table 2   AN EVALUATIVE LOOP

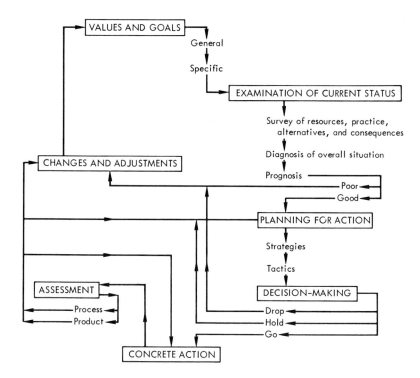

Let us take an example of the curriculum question, "What should we teach?" The general goal here may be to teach students the use of American language, while a more specific goal could be to teach certain children of the poor[3] how to understand a formal version of this language used by teachers, other children, and textbook writers.[4]

We next answer the descriptive question, "What are we teaching?," by an examination of the current status of curriculum. To arrive at a diagnosis of the situation, we survey our resources (what different curricula are available to be taught?), practice (what is actually being taught?), alternatives (what other choices are possible as for curriculum material, structure, and sequence?), and consequences (what are the possible results of the current practice and of the alternatives?). On the basis of such diagnosis,

---

[3] This presumes our treatment of another set of questions, namely, "Whom should we teach?" and, "Whom are we teaching?" It seems that we usually do well to think of more than one aspect of teaching.

[4] We may further wish to define what is meant by such concepts as "to understand," or "a formal version." The more specific our goals and intentions are, the easier it is to plan for an action, to carry it out, and to assess the results. Often, however, too specific efforts are rendered ineffective because of the absence of consideration of broader factors.

we derive a prognosis for the original goal, forecasting the probability of reaching it.

Specifically, we may find that no attention has been paid to the possibility of communication difficulty between students of the poor who use a particular vernacular and teachers who use another.[5] No teaching material has been prepared in such informal dialects and a wholesale shifting to the informal language may entail confusion on the part of both teachers and students. It may be advisable for the teacher to find out the kind and extent of such communication gaps on both sides, that is, what he does not understand in children and what they do not understand in him.[6] If the gap is too large, the prognosis for the original intention to teach students to understand teachers' formal vernacular would be poor and, hence, would demand either reformation of the values and goals or re-examination of the current status, or both.

If, on the other hand, the prognosis is good, we start planning for action, first the overall strategy and next the specific tactics. A gradual transition may be preferred to an outright showdown, while a frank and open comparison of the different languages (we call them "police"—you call them "fuzz," etc.) may be included as one of the tactics.[7] We must use our imagination in making up plans since there is no safe and sure way which is applicable to any and every teaching situation.

When a plan is ready, we must make a final decision before plunging into action. A reanalysis of the plan and of the overall situation may reveal that we have to drop the particular blueprint at this point. If so, we have to go back to several earlier points and re-loop. Administrative, interpersonal, financial, health, and other reasons may prevent the action plan from being executed. It may have to be held up, temporarily, pending further revisions and elaboration.

On the other hand, the decision may be a "go" and the plan can be put into concrete action. Then, both the process and product (results) must

5 Incidentally, this kind of information comes from activities labeled "research." Research can take many forms but here, in contrast with evaluation, we can ask various questions singly and in their own right. Thus, we ask, "Who should teach?" or, "Who do you think should teach?," without coupling it with another question, "Who is teaching?" For this reason, it is sometimes said that evaluation needs criteria (the normative question), while research does not. Naturally, we can conduct research on evaluation or research on research operations themselves.

6 As for the specific form such a gap takes, see, for example: Bernstein, Basil, "Language and Social Class," *British Journal of Sociology* 11: 271–76 (September 1960); Deutsch, Martin, "The Role of Social Class in Language Development and Cognition," *American Journal of Orthopsychiatry* 35: 78–88 (January 1965); Riessman, Frank, and Alberts, Frank, "Digging 'The Man's' Language," *Saturday Review* 49: 80–81 & 98 (September 17, 1966); Peisach, Estelle Cherry, "Children's Comprehension of Teacher and Peer Speech," *Child Development* 36: 467–80 (June 1965).

7 Here again we see the closs relationships among different sets of questions. The matter of what-to-teach is actually intermeshed with that of how-to-teach and also with the question of whom-to-teach.

be carefully observed and assessed. If things go well, keep the action up; if not, changes and adjustment are necessary to the operation, or its plan, or its goals. In this manner, the entire loop is closed and the self-corrective feature becomes clear. This is why we say evaluation is a crucial component in teaching. Without this closed loop, teaching will be reduced to random, haphazard activities.

## IN A LOOP

As mentioned above, the closed nature of the evaluative loop is important because this is the only way we can get any feedback from our action. The word, "feedback," should be a familiar one to us, since most of our physiological functions, mediated by central nervous systems, work on this principle. For example, it is important to be able to hear what we are saying in order for us to adjust our speech continuously to the temporal and situational requirements. As another example, most of us can remember the feelings of powerlessness and panic when we have had to drive on solid ice at night with the minimum of information fed back through either our tactile or visual sense organs.

Not only humans but other animals also depend upon the information feedback to guide their behavior. It is well known that bats and porpoises, among others, emit high frequency signals, and navigate themselves by receiving the feedback reflected by other objects standing in their way. Needless to say, this is exactly the mechanism used in our sonars, radars, and guided missile systems. Without such feedback, neither animals nor scientific apparatuses would operate successfully.

Another familiar word is "reward" or "reinforcement" in learning. Something is reinforcing precisely because it gives the learner some information concerning his performance, namely, whether he is operating on a right level or plane, whether he is moving to the proper direction, and whether he is traveling at a satisfactory speed. Even though many of us disliked certain aspects of the grade system, we depended heavily upon our teachers' grading (A, B, C, etc.) to steer our course and we used to complain bitterly when no information was made available because we could not know what was expected of us and how we were doing. Under the circumstances, our efforts were something like blasting a shotgun in the dark.

So, students need some information from teachers to set up their own goals, to examine their current status, to map out a plan for action, to assess their action, and to make necessary changes and revisions. It is certainly one of our duties to provide whatever feedback is relevant to students' progress and development.

Do not, however, forget that the closed evaluative loop is indispensable, first and foremost, to teachers themselves in their teaching activities. It is not primarily for the sake of students that we ask the normative and descriptive questions. We evaluate teaching, not out of any immediately altruistic motives, but because we will be unable to function as teachers without it. If we think we can teach without engaging at the same time in evaluation, we are deceiving ourselves and we will soon be lost and useless.

Now, it was earlier mentioned that many evaluative efforts are executed informally and even subconsciously. In fact, if we can make evaluation as an automatic habit in teaching and if we can forget about it just as we ordinarily do the presence and role of our automatic or involuntary nervous system, this will be wonderful. Unfortunately, we tend to forget about evaluation long *before* we have established it as a habit. We must therefore make some conscious efforts to build such activities where there has been little and to recognize the loop clearly where such has implicitly existed.

By now it must have been surmised that the familiar appraisal activity of test administration and score-reporting is but a fraction of the entire evaluative function performed by teachers. More fundamental questions have to be asked first and any such part operations should be interpreted in the total context of an evaluative loop. What specific methods of assessment are to be used is obviously determined by the full sequence and not by whims and fads.

For example, when we answer the normative question on instruction, "How should we teach?," our response may be phrased in terms of some rules (logical, evidential, or social), of certain criteria, or of personal preferences and desires.[8] In each case, a different loop will be planned and executed and different assessment techniques will be employed. If, therefore, we decide that we should teach according to the rules of deductive logic or discovery method, our assessment will be different from when we answered in terms of the distribution of time among various subactivities (such as lecture, discussion, prompting, disciplining, etc.). Likewise, if our normative definition is made in reference to the proportion of students surpassing national norms on a standardized achievement test battery, the techniques used will be quite dissimilar to those adopted when the definition is couched in personal feeling terms.

Actually, most of these forms of answers are intermixed and, hence, evaluation is seldom complete with a single loop. Both quantitative and qualitative approaches are adopted and judgments are made on both (so-called) objective and subjective bases. Teacher and peer nominations,

---

[8] The readers may be interested in consulting such references as the following for further discussion of this point: Meux, Milton, "The Evaluating Operation in the Classroom," pp. 11–24 in *Theory and Research in Teaching*, edited by Arno A. Bellack (New York: Bureau of Publications, Teachers College, Columbia University, 1963); Taba, Hilda, *Curriculum Development* (New York: Harcourt, Brace & World, 1962); Wilhelms, Fred T., ed., *Evaluation as Feedback and Guide* (1967 ASCD Yearbook); (Washington: Association for Supervision and Curriculum Development, 1967).

students' writings and oral reports, observation, anecdotal records, interview results, and projective techniques are as useful as standardized and non-standardized tests, inventories, course examinations, and grades. A close working relationship with other teachers and parents, as well as with specialists, including remedial teachers, doctors, school nurses, social workers, school counselors, and school psychologists, is obviously desirable. Here, it can easily be seen that public and communicable evaluative efforts are necessary to facilitate each other's work for the ultimate benefit of our students.[9]

By all means, therefore, let us ask the basic questions on teaching and continue to ask them time and again to keep the evaluative loop working well. What, in your mind, is teaching?

[9] Skillful integration of all the information is a skill to be developed through practice. See, for example: Brackenbury, Robert L., *Getting Down to Cases* (New York: G. P. Putnam's Sons, 1959); Hymes, James L., Jr., *Behavior and Misbehavior* (Englewood Cliffs, New Jersey, 1955); Kaufman, Bel, *Up the Down Staircase* (New York: Avon Books, 1966, N-130); Marshall, Sybil, *An Experiment in Education* (New York: Cambridge, University Press, 1963); Sears, Pauline, and Sherman, Vivian, *In Pursuit of Self-Esteem* (Belmont, Calif.: Wadsworth Publishing, 1964); White, Robert W., *Lives in Progress,* second edition (New York: Holt, Rinehart and Winston, 1966).

# CHAPTER 7

# MENTAL HEALTH

# AND

# PERSONALITY

# DEVELOPMENT

BETTYE M. CALDWELL

# 43.  WHAT IS THE OPTIMAL LEARNING ENVIRONMENT FOR THE YOUNG CHILD?

A truism in the field of child development is that the milieu in which development occurs influences that development. As a means of validating the principle, considerable scientific effort has gone into the Linnaean task of describing and classifying milieus and examining developmental consequences associated with different types. Thus we know something about what it is like to come of age in New Guinea,[29] in a small Midwestern town,[4] in villages and cities in Mexico,[25] in families of different social-class level in Chicago[12] or Boston,[27, 31] in a New York slum,[46] in Russian collectives,[9] in Israeli Kibbutzim,[23, 34, 41] in the eastern part of the United States,[33] and in a Republican community in Central New York.[10] Most of these milieu descriptions have placed great stress on the fact that they were just that and nothing more, i.e., they have expressed the customary scientific viewpoint that to describe is not to judge or criticize. However, in some of the more recent milieu descriptions which have contrasted middle- and lower-class family environments or highlighted conditions in extreme lower-class settings,[31, 46] often more than a slight suggestion has crept in that things could be better for the young child from the deprived segment of the culture. Even so, there remains a justifiable wariness about recommending or arranging any environment for the very young child other than the type regarded as its natural habitat, viz., within its own familiy.

Of course, optimizing environments are arranged all the time under one guise or another. For example, for disturbed children whose family environments seem effectively to reinforce rather than extinguish psychopathology, drastic alterations of milieu often are attempted. This may take the form of psychotherapy for one or both parents as well as the disturbed child, or it

Reprinted from the *American Journal of Orthopsychiatry*, Vol. 37, No. 1 (January 1967), 8–21, by permission of the author and publisher. Copyright, the American Orthopsychiatric Association, Inc.

may involve total removal of the child from the offending environment with temporary or prolonged placement of the child in a milieu presumably more conducive to normal development. Then there is the massive milieu arrangement formalized and legalized as "education" which profoundly affects the lives of all children once they reach the age of five or six. This type of arrangement is not only tolerated but fervently endorsed by our culture as a whole. In fact, any subculture (such as the Amish) which resists the universalization of this pattern of milieu arrangement is regarded as unacceptably deviant and as justifying legal action to enforce conformity.

For very young children, however, there has been a great deal of timidity about conscious and planned arrangement of the developmental milieu, as though the implicit assumption has been made that any environment which sustains life is adequate during this period. This is analogous to suggesting that the intrauterine environment during the period of maximal cellular proliferation is less important than it is later, a suggestion that patently disregards evidence from epidemiology and experimental embryology. The rate of proliferation of new behavioral skills during the first three years of life and the increasing accumulation of data pointing to the relative permanence of deficit acquired when the environment is inadequate during this period make it mandatory that careful attention be given to the preparation of the developmental environment during the first three years of life.

## CONCLUSIONS FROM INADEQUATE ENVIRONMENTS

It is, of course, an exaggeration to imply that no one has given attention to the type of environment which can nourish early and sustained growth and development. For a good three decades now infants who are developing in different milieus have been observed and examined, and data relating to their development have made it possible to identify certain strengths and deficiencies of the different types of environments. Of all types described, the one most consistently indicted by the data is the institution. A number of years ago Goldfarb[19] published an excellent series of studies contrasting patterns of intellectual functioning shown by a group of adopted adolescents who had been reared in institutions up to age three and then transferred to foster homes or else placed shortly after birth in foster homes. The development of the group that had spent time in the institution was deficient in many ways compared to the group that had gone directly into foster homes. Provence and Lipton[33] recently published a revealing description of the early social and intellectual development of infants in institutions, contrasting their development with that of home-reared children. On almost every measured variable the institutional infants were found wanting—less socially alert and outgoing, less curious, less responsive, less interested in objects, and generally

less advanced. The findings of this study are almost prototypic of the literature in the field, as pointed out in excellent reviews by Yarrow[47] and
Ainsworth.[1]

Although there are many attributes in combination that comprise the
institutional environment, the two most obvious elements are (1) absence of
a mother and (2) the presence of a group. These basic characteristics have
thus been identified as the major carriers of the institutional influence and
have been generalized into an explicit principle guiding our recommendations for optimal environments—learning or otherwise—for young children
whenever any type of milieu arrangement is necessary. This principle may
be stated simply as: the optimal environment for the young child is one
in which the child is cared for in his own home in the context of a warm,
continuous emotional relationship with his own mother under conditions of
varied sensory input. Implicit in this principle is the conviction that the
child's mother is the person best qualified to provide a stable and warm
interpersonal relationship as well as the necessary pattern of sensory stimulation. Implicit also is the assumption that socio-emotional development has
priority during the first three years and that if this occurs normally, cognitive
development, which is of minor importance during this period anyway, will
take care of itself. At a still deeper level lurks the assumption that attempts
to foster cognitive development will interfere with socio-emotional development. Advocacy of the principle also implies endorsement of the idea that
most homes are adequate during this early period and that no formal training (other than possibly some occasional supervisory support) for mothering
is necessary. Such an operating principle places quite an onus on mothers
and assumes that they will possess or quickly acquire all the talents necessary
to create an optimal learning environment. And this author, at least, is
convinced that a majority of mothers have such talents or proclivities and
that they are willing to try to do all they can to create for their children the
proper developmental milieu.

But there are always large numbers of children for whom family resources
are not available and for whom some type of substitute milieu arrangement
must be made. On the whole, such attempts have followed the entirely
logical and perhaps evolutionary approach to milieu development—they
have sought to create substitute families. The same is usually true when
parents themselves seek to work out an alternate child-care arrangement
because of less drastic conditions, such as maternal employment. The most
typical maneuver is to try to obtain a motherly person who will "substitute"
for her (not supplement her) during her hours away from her young child.

Our nation has become self-consciously concerned with social evolution,
and in the past decade a serious attempt has been made to assimilate valid
data from the behavioral and social sciences into planning for social action.
In this context it would be meaningful to examine and question some of

the hidden assumptions upon which our operating principle about the optimal environment for the young child rests.

## EXAMINING THE HIDDEN ASSUMPTIONS

1. *Do Intermittent, Short-term Separations of the Child from the Mother Impair the Mother-Child Relationship or the Development of the Child?* Once having become sensitized to the consequences of institutionalization, and suspicious that the chief missing ingredient was the continued presence of the mother, the scientific and professional community went on the *qui vive* to the possibly deleterious consequences of any type of separation of an infant from its mother. Accordingly, a number of studies[10, 18, 21, 35, 39] investigated the consequences of short-term intermittent separation and were unable to demonstrate in the children the classical syndrome of the "institutional child." In reviewing the literature, Yarrow[47] stressed the point that available data do not support the tendency to assume that maternal deprivation, such as exists in the institutional environment, and maternal separation are the same thing. Apparently short cyclic interruptions culminated by reunions do not have the same effect as prolonged interruptions, even though quantitatively at the end of a designated period the amount of time spent in a mother-absent situation might be equal for the two experiences. Also in this context it is well to be reminded that in the institutional situation there is likely to be no stable mother-child relationship to interrupt. These are often never-mothered rather than ever-mothered children, a fact which must be kept in mind in generalizing from data on institutional groups. Thus until we have data to indicate that such intermittent separation-reunion cycles have similar effects on young children as prolonged separations, we are probably unjustified in assuming that an "uninterrupted" relationship is an essential ingredient of the optimal environment.

2. *Is Group Upbringing Invariably Damaging?* In studies done in West European and American settings, social and cognitive deficits associated with continuous group care during infancy have been frequently demonstrated. Enough exceptions have been reported, however, to warrant an intensification of the search for the "true" ingredient in the group situation associated with the observed deficits. For example, Freud and Dann[17] described the adjustment of a group of six children reared in a concentration camp orphanage for approximately three years, where they were cared for by overworked and impersonal inmates of the camp, and then transported to a residence for children in England. The children, who had never known their own mothers but who had been together as a group for approximately three years, were intensely attached to one another. Although their adjustment to their new environment was slow and differed from the pattern one would expect from home-reared children, it was significant that they eventually did make a reasonably good adjustment. That the children were able

to learn a new language while making this emotional transition was offered as evidence that many of the basic cognitive and personality attributes remained unimpaired in spite of the pattern of group upbringing. The accumulation of data showing that Kibbutz-reared children[34] do not have cognitive deficits also reinforces the premise that it is not necessarily group care *per se* that produces the frequently reported deficit and that it is possible to retain the advantages of group care while systematically eliminating its negative features. Grounds for reasonable optimism also have been found in retrospective studies by Maas[26] and Beres and Obers,[6] although in both cases the authors found evidence of pathology in some members of the follow-up sample. Similarly Dennis and Najarian[14] concluded from their data that the magnitude of the deficit varied as a function of the type of instrument used to measure deficit, and Dennis[13] showed that in institutions featuring better adult-child ratios and a conscious effort to meet the psychological needs of the infants the development of the children was much less retarded than was the case in a group of children residing in institutions with limited and unsophisticated staff. It is not appropriate to go into details of limitations of methodology in any of these studies; however, from the standpoint of an examination of the validity of a principle, it is important to take note of any exceptions to the generality of that principle.

In this context it is worth considering a point made by Gula.[20] He recently has suggested that some of the apparent consistency in studies comparing institutionalized infants with those cared for in their own homes and in foster homes might disappear if it were possible to equate the comparison groups on the variable of environmental adequacy. That is, one could classify all three types of environments as good, marginal, or inadequate on a number of dimensions. Most of the studies have compared children from palpably "inadequate" institutions with children from "good" foster and own homes. He suggests that, merely because most institutions studied have been inadequate in terms of such variables as adult-child ratio, staff turnover, and personal characteristics of some of the caretakers, etc., one is not justified in concluding *ipso facto* that group care is invariably inferior or damaging.

3. *Is Healthy Socio-emotional Development the Most Important Task of the First Three Years? Do Attempts to Foster Cognitive Growth Interfere with Social and Emotional Development?* These paired assumptions, which one finds stated in one variety or another in many pamphlets and books dealing with early child development, represent acceptance of a closed system model of human development. They seem to conceptualize development as compartmentalized and with a finite limit. If the child progresses too much in one area he automatically restricts the amount of development that can occur in another area. Thus one often encounters such expressions as "cognitive development at the *expense* of socio-emotional development." It is perhaps of interest to reflect that, until our children reach somewhere around high school age, we seldom seem to worry that the reverse might occur. But, of

course, life is an open system, and on the whole it is accurate to suggest that development feeds upon development. Cognitive and socio-emotional advances tend on the whole to be positively, not negatively correlated.

The definition of intelligence as *adaptivity* has not been adequately stressed by modern authors. It is, of course, the essence of Piaget's definition[32] as it was earlier of Binet.[7] Unfortunately, however, for the last generation or so in America we have been more concerned with how to measure intelligent behavior than how to interpret and understand it. Acceptance of the premise that intelligent behavior is adaptive behavior should help to break the set of many persons in the field of early child development that to encourage cognitive advance is to discourage healthy socio-emotional development. Ample data are available to suggest that quite the reverse is true either for intellectually advanced persons[42, 43] or an unselected sample. In a large sample of young adults from an urban area in Minnesota, Anderson[3] and associates found that the best single predictor of post-high school adjustment contained in a large assessment battery was a humble little group intelligence test. Prediction based on intelligence plus teacher's ratings did somewhat better, but nothing exceeded the intelligence test for single measure efficiency.

It is relevant here to mention White's[45] concept of competence or effectance as a major stabilizing force in personality development. The emotional reinforcement accompanying the old "I can do it myself" declaration should not be undervalued. In Murphy's report[30] of the coping behavior of preschool children one sees evidence of the adjustive supports gained through cognitive advances. In his excellent review of cognitive stimulation in infancy and early childhood, Fowler[16] raises the question of whether there is any justification for the modern anxiety (and, to be sure, it is a modern phenomenon) over whether cognitive stimulation may damage personality development. He suggests that in the past severe and harmful methods may have been the culprits whenever there was damage and that the generalizations have confused methods of stimulation with the process of stimulation *per se*.

4. *Do Cognitive Experiences of the First Few Months and Years Leave No Significant Residual?* Any assumption that the learnings of infancy are evanescent appears to be a fairly modern idea. In his *Emile,* first published in 1762, Rousseau[38] stressed the point that education should begin while the child is still in the cradle. Perhaps any generalization to the contrary received its major modern impetus from a rather unlikely place—from longitudinal studies of development covering the span from infancy to adulthood. From findings of poor prediction of subsequent intellectual status[5] one can legitimately infer that the infant tests measure behavior that is somewhat irrelevant to later intellectual performance. Even though these behaviors predictive of later cognitive behavior elude most investigators, one cannot infer that the early months and years are unimportant for cognitive development.

Some support for this assumption has come from experimental studies in which an attempt has been made to produce a durable effect in human subjects by one or another type of intervention offered during infancy. One cogent example is the work of Rheingold,[36] in which she provided additional social and personal stimulation to a small group of approximately six-month-old, institutionalized infants for a total of eight weeks. At the end of the experimental period, differences in social responsiveness between her stimulated group and a control group composed of other babies in the institution could be observed. There were also slight but nonsignificant advances in postural and motor behavior on a test of infant development. However, when the babies were followed up approximately a year later, by which time all but one were in either adoptive or boarding homes or in their own natural homes, the increased social responsiveness formerly shown by the stimulated babies was no longer observed. Nor were there differences in level of intellectual functioning. Rheingold and Bayley[37] concluded that the extra mothering provided during the experimental period was enough to produce an effect at the time but not enough to sustain this effect after such a time as the two groups were no longer differentially stimulated. However, in spite of their conservative conclusion, it is worth noting that the experimentally stimulated babies were found to vocalize more during the follow-up assessments than the control babies. Thus there may have been enough of an effect to sustain a developmental advance in at least this one extremely important area.

Some very impressive recent unpublished data obtained by Skeels, offer a profound challenge to the assumption of the unimportance of the first three years for cognitive growth. This investigator has followed up after approximately 25 years most of the subjects described in a paper by Skeels and Dye.[40] Thirteen infants had been transferred from an orphanage because of evidence of mental retardation and placed in an institution for the retarded under the care of adolescent retardates who gave them a great deal of loving care and as much cognitive stimulation as they could. The 13 subjects showed a marked acceleration in development after this transfer. In contrast a group of reasonably well matched infants left on the wards of the orphanage continued to develop poorly. In a recent follow-up of these cases, Skeels discovered that the gains made by the transferred infants were sustained into their adult years, whereas all but one of the control subjects developed the classic syndrome of mental retardation.

The fact that development and experience are cumulative makes it difficult ever to isolate any one antecedent period and assert that its influence was or was not influential in a subsequent developmental period. Thus even though it might be difficult to demonstrate an effect of some experience in an adjacent time period, delayed effects may well be of even greater developmental consequence. In a recent review of data from a number of longitudinal studies, Bloom[8] has concluded that during the first three to four years (the noncognitive years, if you will) approximately 50 per cent of the development of intelligence that is ever to occur in the life cycle takes place. During this period a particular environment may be either abundant or deprived in terms of the ingredients essential for providing opportunities for the development of intelligence and problem solving. Bloom[8] states:

> The effects of the environments, especially of the extreme environments, appear to be greatest in the early (and more rapid) periods of intelligence development and least in the later (and less rapid) periods of development. Although there is relatively little evidence of the effects of changing the environment on the changes in intelligence, the evidence so far available suggests that marked changes in the environment in the early years can produce greater changes in intelligence than will equally marked changes in the environment at later periods of development. (pp. 88–89)

5. *Can One Expect That, Without Formal Planning, All the Necessary Learning Experiences Will Occur?* There is an old legend that if you put six chimpanzees in front of six typewriters and leave them there long enough they eventually will produce all the works in the British Museum. One could paraphrase this for early childhood by suggesting that six children with good eyes and ears and hands and brains would, if left alone in nature, arrive at a number system, discover the laws of conservation of matter and energy, comprehend gravity and the motions of the planets, and perhaps arrive at the theory of relativity. All the "facts" necessary to discern these relationships are readily available. Perhaps a more realistic example would be to suggest that, if we surround a group of young children with a carefully selected set of play materials, they would eventually discover for themselves the laws of color mixture, of form and contour, of perspective, of formal rhythm and tonal relationships, and biological growth. And, to be sure, all this *could* occur. But whether this will necessarily occur with any frequency is quite another matter. We also assume that at a still earlier period a child will learn body control, eye-hand coordination, the rudiments of language, and styles of problem solving in an entirely incidental and unplanned way. In an article in a recent issue of a popular woman's magazine, an author[22] fervently urges parents to stop trying to teach their young children in order that the children may learn. And, to be sure, there is always something to be said for this caution; it is all too easy to have planned learning experiences become didactic and regimented rather than subtle and opportunistic.

As more people gain experience in operating nursery school programs for children with an early history deficient in many categories of experience, the conviction appears to be gaining momentum that such children often are not able to avail themselves of the educational opportunities and must be guided into meaningful learning encounters. In a recent paper dealing with the preschool behavior of a group of 21 children from multiproblem families, Malone[28] describes the inability of the children to carry out self-directed exploratory maneuvers with the toys and equipment as follows:

When the children first came to nursery school they lacked interest in learning the names and properties of objects. Colors, numbers, sizes, shapes, locations, all seemed interchangeable. Nothing in the room seemed to have meaning for a child apart from the fact that another child had approached or handled it or that the teacher's attention was turned toward it. Even brief play depended on the teacher's involvement and support. (p. 5)

When one reflects on the number of carefully arranged reinforcement contingencies necessary to help a young child learn to decode the simple message, "No," it is difficult to support the position that in early learning, as in anything else, nature should just take its course.

6. *Is Formal Training for Child-Care During the First Three Years Unnecessary?* This assumption is obviously quite ridiculous, and yet it is one logical derivative of the hypothesis that the only adequate place for a young child is with his mother or a permanent mother substitute. There is, perhaps unfortunately, no literacy test for motherhood. This again is one of our interesting scientific paradoxes. That is, proclaiming in one breath that mothering is essential for the healthy development of a child, we have in the very next breath implied that just any mothering will do. It is interesting in this connection that from the elementary school level forward we have rigid certification statutes in most states that regulate the training requirements for persons who would qualify as teachers of our children. (The same degree of control over the qualifications and training of a nursery school teacher has not prevailed in the past, but we are moving into an era when it will.) So again, our pattern of social action appears to support the implicit belief in the lack of importance of the first three years of life.

In 1928, John B. Watson[44] wrote a controversial little trade book called *The Psychological Care of Infant and Child.* He included one chapter heretically entitled, "The Dangers of Too Much Mother Love." In this chapter he suggested that child training was too important to be left in the hands of mothers, apparently not because he felt them intellectually inadequate but because of their sentimentality. In his typical "nondirective" style Watson[44] wrote:

Six months' training in the actual handling of children from two to six under the eye of competent instructors should make a fairly satisfactory child's nurse. To keep them we should let the position of nurse or governess in the home be a respected one. Where the mother herself must be the nurse—which is the case in the vast majority of American homes—she must look upon herself while performing the functions of a nurse as a professional woman and not as a sentimentalist masquerading under the name of "Mother." (p. 149)

At present in this country a number of training programs are currently being formulated which would attempt to give this kind of professional training called for by Watson and many others. It is perhaps not possible to advance on all fronts at the same time, and the pressing health needs of the young child demanded and received top priority in earlier decades. Perhaps it will now be possible to extend our efforts at social intervention to encompass a broader range of health, education, and welfare activities.

7. *Are Most Homes and Most Parents Adequate for at Least the First Three Years?* Enough has been presented in discussing other implicit assumptions to make it unnecessary to amplify this point at length. The clinical literature, and much of the research literature of the last decade dealing with social-class differences, has made abundantly clear that all parents are not qualified to provide even the basic essentials of physical and psychological care to their children. Such reports as those describing the incidence of battered children[15, 24] capture our attention, but reports concerned with subtler and yet perhaps more long-standing patterns of parental deficit also fill the literature. In her description of the child-rearing environments provided by low lower-class families, Pavenstedt[31] has described them as impulse determined with very little evidence of clear planfulness for activities that would benefit either parent or child. Similarly, Wortis and associates[46] have described the extent to which the problems of the low-income mother so overwhelm her with reactions of depression and inadequacy that behavior toward the child is largely determined by the needs of the moment rather than by any clear plan about how to bring up children and how to train them to engage in the kind of behavior that the parents regard as acceptable or desirable. No social class and no cultural or ethnic group have exclusive rights to the domain of inadequate parentage; all conscientious parents must strive constantly for improvement on this score. However, relatively little attention has been paid to the possibly deleterious consequences of inadequacies during the first three years of life. Parents have been blamed for so many problems of their children in later age periods that a moderate reaction formation appears to have set in. But again, judging by the type of social action taken by the responsible professional community, parental inadequacy during the first three years is seldom considered as a major menace. Perhaps, when the various alternatives are weighed, it appears by comparison to be the least of multiple evils; but parental behavior of the first three years should not be regarded as any more sacrosanct or beyond the domain of social concern than that of the later years.

## PLANNING ALTERNATIVES

At this point the exposition of this paper must come to an abrupt halt, for insufficient data about possible alternative models are available to warrant recommendation of any major pattern of change. At present there are no completed research projects that have developed and evaluated alternative approximations of optimal learning environments for young children in our culture. One apparent limitation on ideas for alternative models appears to be the tendency to think in terms of binary choices. That is, we speak of individual care *versus* group care, foster home *versus* institution, foster home *versus* own home, and so on. But environments for the very young child do not need to be any more mutually exclusive than they are for the older children. After all, what is our public education system but a coordination of the efforts of home plus an institution? Most of us probably would agree that the optimal learning environment for the older child is neither of these alone but rather a combination of both. Some of this same pattern of combined effort also may represent the optimal arrangement for the very young child.

A number of programs suggesting alternatives possibly worth considering are currently in the early field trial stage. One such program is the one described by Caldwell and Richmond.[11] This program offers educationally oriented day care for culturally deprived children between six months and three years of age. The children spend the better part of five days a week in a group care setting (with an adult-child ratio never lower than 1:4) but return home each evening and maintain primary emotional relationships with their own families. Well child care, social and psychological services, and parent education activities are available for participating families. The educational program is carefully planned to try to help the child develop the personal-social and cognitive attributes conducive to learning and to provide experiences which can partially compensate for inadequacies which may have existed in the home environment. The strategy involved in offering the enrichment experience to children in this very young age group is to maximize their potential and hopefully prevent the deceleration in rate of development which seems to occur in many deprived children around the age of two to three years. It is thus an exercise in circumvention rather than remediation. Effectiveness of the endeavor is being determined by a comparison of the participating children with a control group of children from similar backgrounds who are not enrolled in the enrichment program. Unfortunately at this juncture it is too early for such projects to do more than suggest alternatives. The degree of confidence which comes only from research evidence plus replicated experience will have to wait a little longer.

Effective social action, however, can seldom await definitive data. And in the area of child care the most clamorous demand for innovative action appears to be coming from a rather unlikely source—not from any of the professional groups, not particularly from social planners who try to incorporate research data into plans for social action, but from *mothers*. From mothers themselves is coming the demand that professionals in the field look at some of the alternatives. We need not be reminded here that in America at the present time there are more than three million working mothers with children under six years of age.[2] And these mothers are looking for professional leadership to design and provide child-care facilities that help prepare their children for today's achievement-oriented culture. The challenge which has been offered is inevitable. After almost two decades of bombarding women with the importance of their mothering role, we might have predicted the weakening of their defenses and their waving the flag of truce as though to say, "I am not good enough to do all that you are saying I must do."

It is a characteristic of social evolution that an increased recognition of the importance of any role leads to the professionalization of that role, and there can be no doubt but that we are currently witnessing the early stages of professionalization of the mother-substitute role—or, as I would prefer to say, the mother-supplement. It is interesting to note that no one has as yet provided a satisfactory label for this role. The term "baby-sitter" is odious, reminding us of just about all some of the "less well trained" professionals do—sit with babies. If English were a masculine-feminine language, there is little doubt that the word would be used in the feminine gender, for we always speak of this person as a "she" (while emphasizing that young children need more contact with males). We cannot borrow any of the terms from already professionalized roles, such as "nurse" or "teacher," although such persons must be to a great extent both nurse and teacher. Awkward designations such as "child-care worker," or hybridized terms such as "nurse-teacher" do not quite seem to fill the bill; and there appears to be some reluctance to accept an untranslated foreign word like the Hebrew "metapelet" or the Russian "Nyanya." When such a word does appear, let us hope that it rhymes well and has a strong trochaic rhythm, for it will have to sustain a whole new era of poetry and song. (This author is convinced that the proper verb is *nurture*. It carries the desired connotations, but even to one who is not averse to neologisms such nominative forms as "nurturist," "nurturer," and "nurturizer" sound alien and inadequate.) [a]

Another basis for planning alternatives is becoming available from a less direct but potentially more persuasive source—from increasing knowledge about the process of development. The accumulation of data suggesting that the first few years of life are crucial for the priming of cognitive development call for vigorous and imaginative action programs for those early years. To say that it is premature to try to plan optimal environments because we do not fully understand how learning occurs is unacceptable. Perhaps only by the development of carefully arranged environments will we attain a complete understanding of the learning process. Already a great deal is known which enables us to specify some of the essential ingredients of a growth-fostering milieu. Such an environment must contain warm and responsive people who by their own interests invest objects with value. It must be supportive and as free of disease and pathogenic agents as possibly can be arranged. It also must trace a clear path from where the child is to where he is to go developmentally; objects and events must be similar enough to what the child has experienced to be assimilated by the child and yet novel

[a] In a letter to the author written shortly after the meeting at which this paper was presented, Miss Rena Corman of New York City suggested that the proper term should be "nurcher," a compound of the words, "nurse" and "teacher." To be sure, a "nurcher" sounds nurturant.

enough to stimulate and attract. Such an environment must be exquisitely responsive, as a more consistent pattern of response is required to foster the acquisition of new forms of behavior than is required to maintain such behavior once it appears in the child's repertoire. The timing of experiences also must be carefully programmed. The time table for the scheduling of early postnatal events may well be every bit as demanding as that which obtains during the embryological period. For children whose early experiences are known to be deficient and depriving, attempts to program such environments seem mandatory if subsequent learning difficulties are to be circumvented.

## SUMMARY

Interpretations of research data and accumulated clinical experience have led over the years to a consensual approximation of an answer to the question: what is the optimal learning environment for the young child? As judged from our scientific and lay literature and from practices in health and welfare agencies, one might infer that the optimal learning environment for the young child is that which exists when (a) a young child is cared for in his own home (b) in the context of a warm and nurturant emotional relationship (c) with his mother (or a reasonable facsimile thereof) under conditions of (d) varied sensory and cognitive input. Undoubtedly until a better hypothesis comes along, this is the best one available. This paper has attempted to generate constructive thinking about whether we are justified in overly vigorous support of (a) when (b), (c) or (d), or any combination thereof, might not obtain. Support for the main hypothesis comes primarily from other hypotheses (implicit assumptions) rather than from research or experimental data. When these assumptions are carefully examined they are found to be difficult if not impossible to verify with existing data.

The conservatism inherent in our present avoidance of carefully designed social action programs for the very young child needs to be re-examined. Such a re-examination conducted in the light of research evidence available about the effects of different patterns of care forces consideration of whether formalized intervention programs should not receive more attention than they have in the past and whether attention should be given to a professional training sequence for child-care workers. The careful preparation of the learning environment calls for a degree of training and commitment and personal control not always to be found in natural caretakers and a degree of richness of experience by no means always available in natural environments.

## REFERENCES

1. AINSWORTH, MARY. 1962. Reversible and irreversible effects of maternal deprivation on intellectual development. Child Welfare League of America, 42–62.

2. American Women. 1963. Report of the President's Commission on the Status of Women. (Order from Supt. of Documents, Washington, D.C.)

3. ANDERSON, J. E., ET AL. 1959. A survey of children's adjustment over time. Minneapolis, Minn. University of Minnesota.

4. BARKER, R. G., AND H. F. WRIGHT. 1955. *Midwest and its children: the psychological ecology of an American town.* Row, Peterson, New York.

5. BAYLEY, NANCY. 1949. Consistency and variability in the growth of intelligence from birth to eighteen years. *J. Genet. Psychol.* 75: 165–96.

6. BERES, D., AND S. OBERS. 1950. The effects of extreme deprivation in infancy on psychic structure in adolescence. *Psychoanal. Stud. of the Child.* 5: 121–40.

7. BINET, A., AND T. SIMON. 1916. *The development of intelligence in children.* Elizabeth S. Kite, trans. Williams and Wilkins, Baltimore.

8. BLOOM, B. S. 1964. *Stability and change in human characteristics.* John Wiley and Sons, New York.

9. BRONFENBRENNER, URIE. 1962. Soviet studies of personality development and socialization. In *Some views on Soviet psychology.* Amer. Psychol. Assoc., Inc. pp. 63–85.

10. CALDWELL, BETTYE M., ET AL. 1963. Mother-infant interaction in monomatric and polymatric families. *Amer. J. Orthopsychiat.* 33: 653–64.

11. CALDWELL, BETTYE M., AND J. B. RICHMOND. 1964. Programmed day care for the very young child—a preliminary report. *J. Marriage and the Family.* 26: 481–88.

12. DAVIS, A., AND R. J. HAVIGHURST. 1946. Social class and color differences in child-rearing. *Amer. Sociol. Rev.* 11: 698–710.

13. DENNIS, W. 1960. Cause of retardation among institutional children. *J. Genet. Psychol.* 96: 47–59.

14. DENNIS, W., AND P. NAJARIAN. 1957. Infant development under environmental handicap. *Psychol. Monogr.* 71: (7 Whole No. 536).

15. ELMER, ELIZABETH. 1963. Identification of abused children. *Children.* 10: 180–84.

16. FOWLER, W. 1962. Cognitive learning in infancy and early childhood. *Psychol. Bull.* 59: 116–52.

17. FREUD, ANNA, AND SOPHIE DANN. 1951. An experiment in group upbringing. *Psychoanal. Study of the Child.* 6: 127–68.

18. GARDNER, D. B., G. R. HAWKES, AND L. G. BURCHINAL. 1961. Noncontinuous mothering in infancy and development in later childhood. *Child Developm.* 32: 225–34.

19. GOLDFARB, W. 1949. Rorschach test differences between family-reared, institution-reared and schizophrenic children. *Amer. J. Orthopsychiat.* 19: 624–33.

20. GULA, H. January, 1965. Paper given at Conference on Group Care for Children. Children's Bureau.

21. HOFFMAN, LOIS WLADIS. 1961. Effects of maternal employment on the child. *Child Developm.* 32: 187–97.

22. HOLT, J. 1965. How to help babies learn—without teaching them. *Redbook.* 126(1): 54–55, 134–37.

23. IRVINE, ELIZABETH E. 1952. Observations on the aims and methods of child-rearing in communal settlements in Israel. *Human Relations.* 5: 247–75.

24. KEMPE, C. H. ET AL. 1962. The battered-child syndrome. *J. Amer. Med. Asso.* 181: 17–24.

25. LEWIS, O. 1959. *Five families.* New York: Basic Books.

26. MAAS, H. 1963. Long-term effects of early childhood separation and group care. *Vita Humana.* 6: 34–56.

27. MACCOBY, ELEANOR, AND PATRICIA K. GIBBS. 1954. Methods of child-rearing in two social classes. In *Readings in Child Developm.* W. E. Martin and Celia B. Stendler, eds. Harcourt, Brace & Co., New York. Pp. 380–96.
28. MALONE, C. A. 1966. Safety first: comments on the influence of external danger in the lives of children of disorganized families. *Amer. J. Orthopsychiat.* 36: 3–12.
29. MEAD, MARGARET. 1953. *Growing up in New Guinea.* The New American Library, New York.
30. MURPHY, LOIS B., ET AL. 1962. *The widening world of childhood.* Basic Books, Inc., New York.
31. PAVENSTEDT, E. 1965. A comparison of the child-rearing environment of upper-lower and very low-lower class families. *Amer. J. Orthopsychiat.* 35: 89–98.
32. PIAGET, J. 1952. *The origins of intelligence in children.* Margaret Cook, trans. International Universities Press, New York.
33. PROVENCE, SALLY, AND ROSE C. LIPTON. 1962. *Infants in institutions.* International Universities Press, New York.
34. RABIN, A. I. 1957. Personality maturity of Kibbutz and non-Kibbutz children as reflected in Rorschach findings. *J. Prof. Tech.* Pp. 148–53.
35. RADKE YARROW, MARIAN. 1961. Maternal employment and child rearing. *Children.* 8: 223–28.
36. RHEINGOLD, HARRIET. 1956. The modification of social responsiveness in institutional babies. Monogr. Soc. Res. *Child Developm.* 21: (63).
37. RHEINGOLD, HARRIET L., AND NANCY BAYLEY. 1959. The later effects of an experimental modification of mothering. *Child Develpm.* 30: 363–72.
38. ROUSSEAU, J. J. 1950. *Emile* (1762). Barron's Educational Series, Great Neck, N. Y.
39. SIEGEL, ALBERTA E., AND MIRIAM B. HASS. 1963. The working mother: a review of research. *Child Developm.* 34: 513–42.
40. SKEELS, H. AND H. DYE. 1939. A study of the effects of differential stimulation on mentally retarded children. *Proc. Amer. Assoc. on Ment. Def.* 44: 114–36.
41. SPIRO, M. 1958. *Children of the Kibbutz.* Cambridge, Mass.: Harvard U. Press.
42. TERMAN, L. M., ET AL. 1925. *Genetic studies of genius:* Vol. 1. Mental and physical traits of a thousand gifted children. Stanford University, Calif.: Stanford University Press.
43. TERMAN, L. M., AND MELITA H. ODEN. 1947. *The gifted child grows up: twenty-five years' follow-up of a superior group.* Stanford University, Calif.: Stanford University Press.
44. WATSON, J. B. 1928. *Psychological care of infant and child.* Allen and Unwin, London.
45. WHITE, R. W. 1959. Motivation reconsidered: the concept of competence. *Psychol. Rev.* 66: 297–333.
46. WORTIS, H., ET AL. 1963. Child-rearing practices in a low socio-economic group. *Pediatrics.* 32: 298–307.
47. YARROW, L. J. 1961. Maternal deprivation: toward an empirical and conceptual re-evaluation. *Psychol. Bull.* 58: 459–90.

JOHN L. SCHIMEL

# 44. PARENTS VS. CHILDREN: FRUSTRATING GAMES FAMILIES PLAY

I once had occasion to ask a little girl what she did when someone gave her a gift.

"I wait," she answered.
"Wait for what?" I asked.
"I wait until Mommy says, 'Say thank you.' Then I say, 'Thank you.'"

The incident shows how literally a child may learn and repeat a sequence of actions or words. Mother is teaching Good Manners—a commendable subject, but too abstract for Daughter to grasp. Daughter, in order to get what she wants, is learning lines of dialogue and demonstrating her ability to imitate. At this point, of course, she has not learned Good Manners. She has learned that in order to get her gift, she must at the proper moment say, "Thank you."

Children live in a world of magic words, a world in which "please" produces playthings, "excuse me" exonerates, "I'm sorry" expiates and "I love you" placates. They learn to combine these with tears, threats, entreaties, hugs, smiles and occasional silences to produce even greater magic in their dealings with others. The child is learning the combinations of words and actions that "work," that produce the effects he wants in dealing with his family and later with the world. This is very much to be desired, for to function well we must use patterns that "work" in relating to other people.

And as he adopts the actions and words that his parents tell him are appropriate to each situation the child learns to play roles in life. The little "thank-you" girl is working on Giver and Receiver, for example, and the behavior expected of each. When both roles are played properly—when she finally says "thank you"—everyone feels good. We psychiatrists call it "role complementarity"; that is, two roles that fit together—in this instance, those of a proper Giver and a proper Receiver.

But sometimes the happy balance is upset. Suppose the child decides that the gift is something less than she wants; instead of playing the role of Receiver, she seizes the initiative.

"But I wanted Batman cards like Charlie's," she whines.

Consider how radically she has changed the situation with this maneuver. Instead of playing Grateful Little Girl, she is playing Helpless Deprived Waif. She has managed to cast the giver in the role of Depriver of Small Children instead of Generous Benefactor, and most important, she has taken the upper hand and upset a situation in which she ought to be the passive (but grateful) Receiver. She has refused to play her part in a common and desirable social exchange, and instead has initiated an uncomfortable and undesirable situation. If she does this habitually, if she forces a recasting of roles and a redistribution of the power that underlies them, she is involved in a "game" of the sort that psychiatrist Eric Berne brought to the attention of the millions of readers of his book *Games People Play.*

The word "game" seems frivolous, but it is accurate. Like pastime games, interpersonal games have a purpose; they are always played according to the same rules; they are played to win; the roles can be interchanged. But unlike pastime games, interpersonal games are often played without our knowing it unless they are called to our attention. And we don't realize how wasteful and even destructive they can be.

Viewing these struggles as games makes them easier to recognize and classify. Although this approach does not take the place of psychotherapy or offer any new theories of human behavior, it is useful because the game concept provides a relatively simple way of analyzing behavior. Once alerted to games, most people quickly grasp their meaning and effect, and can make an effort to stop them. Game playing in families is inevitable and not necessarily dangerous, but it brings recurring unpleasantness into relationships that should be warm and productive. Furthermore, if these games get out of hand, they can lead to lifelong difficulties.

A good relationship between parent and child can exist only when the two understand that the parent is the more powerful. The parent's natural position is that of benevolent dictator. If a child is allowed to challenge that position successfully, the battle for supremacy will become constant. Games occur at the points of conflict; they are recurring dramatizations of the underlying power struggle. Although each scene, at mealtime or bedtime, may seem different, on study they all turn out to be more or less stereotyped. In effect, they follow the same script.

Usually the players are so immersed in the sea of emotion surrounding the conflict that they cannot notice very much of what is really going on. Before the game player can change the pattern, therefore, he must learn to recognize the roles, the players, the sequence of remarks and actions. To do this, he must develop a degree of detachment. With parent-child games this responsibility falls largely on the parent.

A game is a pattern of repetitive and abrasive behavior that requires at least two participants and may involve many more in its unfolding. It is the wise mother who is prepared to recognize and reverse an inclination to play these unfunny games with her children.

We will look at some of the common ones, starting with the earliest and simplest. We will see that as the child becomes capable of more and more complex behavior, the game playing will become more complicated.

I must warn the reader that if she is to understand the notion of games, she must be prepared to set aside her normal sympathetic feelings, because at times they distort the facts. Try not to take sides. I will not be describing villains or true victims in this essay, but the little people—our children—and the bigger if somewhat more harassed people—their parents—all caught in the sticky flypaper of games.

"I don't know what to do about their quarreling," the mother says. "David is always hitting little Josh and making him cry. He seems to enjoy doing it. I've punished him. I've told him to apologize." A not-uncommon situation: two brothers quarreling, the older getting the upper hand and the younger weeping, the mother trying to correct and teach—and wondering, endlessly wondering, whether she did the right thing.

The quarreling brothers are playing the game of Bully and Victim, a venerable human institution. Note that the crying of the Victim tends to produce an ally, in this case the mother, or Rescuer (this is a three-role game). The Bully, now apprehended, may be corrected, instructed or punished by the Rescuer. He may in his turn be reduced to tears. At this point the Bully resembles the Victim. Let us take the next logical step and say that the Bully *is* now the Victim. And the erstwhile Victim, whose eyes are beginning to shine through his tears as he contemplates his now-tearful older brother—what role does he have?

Josh now fits all the criteria by which we earlier classified David as the Bully. But we are softened in our judgment by the memory of what he has suffered at his older brother's hands. True, he does seem to take delight in his brother's sobs, just like a Bully. But isn't it simply that he appreciates seeing justice done, that he is a Good Citizen Vindicated? Don't you believe it!

David won't stop bedeviling Josh until Mother intervenes or until he tires of the sport. In fact, the cries of his Victim may actually stimulate him, and forestall the boredom that tends to terminate most childhood games quickly. The young child has a very short attention span. If the Victim does not resist, the sport palls and soon ends.

The roles of Bully and Victim, when they are interchangeable, together constitute a "game." It is essentially a primitive game, even when played (as it sometimes is) by grown and sophisticated players. We classify it as a Pantomime or Preverbal Game, because it can be observed in the child before speech is mastered and because it can be played at any age without words.

A second pantomime game, this one with only two basic roles, is Sick Call. Usually it originates with a child's genuine physical or emotional distress, which stimulates his mother's sympathy and desire to relieve him.

In a word, Sick Call brings forth the role of Comforter in the mother. Since such distress signals will recur naturally and frequently, the mother's responses are of crucial importance for her child's further development.

In the child's earliest years the parents, in most cases, can alleviate his physical ailments. And his fears, apprehensions and other manifestations of mental distress often yield to simple fondling and cuddling. With the advent of speech and out-of-the-home activities for the child, life becomes more complex. A child's apprehensions about nursery school or day camp cannot always be so simply relieved. He may balk, but he must attend school! The parent is torn between the roles of Comforter and Coercer. The mother's distress may be very great when she is unable or justifiably unwilling to be the Comforter.

It is very common for children and adolescents to refuse to go to school. When this resistance is severe, it is referred to as a "school phobia." In case after case, the mother's (and often the father's) actions as Comforter seem to reinforce the child's determination to stay out, unwittingly sabotaging the efforts of the physician, the teacher and the school counselor to get the child back to school. The child is pained at the prospect of going to school. The mother is pained at the prospect of insisting. So she relieves the pain for both of them; she lets him stay home.

Though it seems cruel to interpret such a situation in terms of power, we must acknowledge the fact that the child is exerting a not-so-subtle power over his mother in a protracted game of Sick Call, whether it takes the form of school phobia or any other condition that puts her sympathies to the test. This not-so-subtle power is evident in the poignant words of a mother who was consulting me: "When he turns those big brown eyes on me and they fill with tears, I begin to feel smaller and smaller. I begin to feel mean and despicable. I feel like Simon Legree."

When a mother feels like Simon Legree, she is hardly in a position to refuse even a wildly unreasonable request. If she does refuse, as she often must, she is incapable of doing it firmly and dispassionately. Being rattled or uncertain in her refusal can undermine her self-confidence still further, softening her up for the next stage of the game.

I have known some wily child game players who, like chess champions, plan many moves ahead, counting on the process of attrition. A seemingly demure young game player told me her plan for getting a new and, to her, expensive leather pencil case that was the rage among her classmates.

"First I'm going to fuss some more over not getting a new winter coat," she said. "I don't really care about that any more. Then I'll cry about the pencil case."

An adolescent told me that he expected it would take about ten days of harassment before his parents broke down and let him get a car. He was right—to the day.

Parents, particularly with a first child, usually do everything possible to avoid the discomfort of being cast in the role of Simon Legree. They overlook the fact that the child's actions are purposeful and that his coercive lever is precisely the stimulation of that feeling in them.

A simple form of Sick Call is the I Need game. This ploy is particularly popular with small children. A child who is refused ice cream may switch from "I want it" to "I *need* it!" in the wink of an eye. The child has realized that the word "need" has greater leverage than the word "want"; only a Simon Legree would deprive a child of something the poor kid *needed*. What are parents for if not to meet their children's needs? Later the child will learn that further dissimulation may be required. "I *need* a new pencil case because everyone in the class has one—my old one is too small—I can't find my other one—you bought one for Willie. . ." and so on.

Mothers who feel the mantle of Simon Legree settling about their shoulders are tempted to act in either of two ways. On the one hand a mother can go on Sick Call herself. Retreating from her natural position of authority, she becomes apprehensive, inept and incompetent. The mother who does this habitually often finds her child emerging as the real Simon Legree, sometimes called the Child Tyrant. This happens, for example, to the mother who comes to pick up her Joey at his friend Alex's house. Her child (Tyrant) doesn't want to leave—he howls, he runs away to the back of the house, he cajoles, he distracts her. It may take her an hour to get him out. Alex's mother can easily guess what must go on at Joey's house at bedtime.

Other mothers, challenged by their children, embrace all too wholeheartedly the role of Simon Legree. "I'm wise to you," they say, in effect. "You're just trying to get out of going to school. Well, you're going, whether you like it or not, and you'll be punished as well." After a time such parents can become remarkably calloused to the suffering of their children. An eight-year-old patient of mine, a veteran Sick Call player, once turned up at my office, looking pale and dejected. On questioning, he finally burst out: "I told Mommy I feel terrible. She didn't listen. She never does. She said I just didn't want to come to see you." When I took his temperature, it was 104.

The boy had originally been brought for treatment because he was a Child Tyrant. Mother and he played interchangeable roles. Either way—Sick Call or Simon Legree—game playing between children and parents is fostered.

Parents are constantly in the same position as the executives who must make a decision when all the facts are not yet in. The good executive has been defined as a person who makes right decisions when there isn't enough information at hand to make them obvious. Mothers and fathers, dealing with their rambunctious children, have to make decisions based on partial information, withheld information and misinformation. But unless the right decision is obvious, many parents compromise, double-talk, negotiate, threaten and permit themselves to be manipulated and hoodwinked.

Every executive feels inadequate sometimes, but he must do his job. So must the parent. But when a child can make his mother feel that in fulfilling her natural executive role she is behaving like Simon Legree, she invites him to bid for power. Parents and children both must know who has the final authority in the family. When there is uncertainty about who possesses that power, game playing is stimulated among mothers, fathers and children.

Children recognize the use of power at a remarkably early age. At two or three the child has already begun to discover the stunning effect of words like "no" and "why." These words represent man's right to dissent, his right to question and explore. But on the tongue of a little game player "no" and "why" can create frustration, despair, anarchy and tyranny.

The child's first "no" often comes as a shock to adult and child alike. The pliant baby has suddenly become formidable, someone to be reckoned with. The relative potency of a "no" in comparison with an acquiescent "yes" is very great indeed. However, the sensitive child soon learns that the naked "no" carries with it confrontation and the risk of defeat. So he learns to mask it in a variety of ways. The most important way is the manipulation of language. The temper tantrum, although not necessarily abandoned, gives way to the "no" games, like I Can't Because, Deaf-Mute and Later, Mom.

The I Can't Because game develops early. The child (like his parents) becomes skilled in following the word "because" with plausible statements. "I can't take the garbage out *because* the pail is too heavy—it's raining— I can't find my shoes—I can't get my dress dirty." A mother who knows her child well and listens and observes carefully could continue this list indefinitely.

Parents frequently describe the phrases following the "because" as excuses. This indicates their realization that "I can't because..." is a masquerade for "no." The sensible response to "I can't because" is usually: "Do it anyhow." But many parents feel compelled to take all excuses or explanations seriously. They attempt to explain away the child's explanations. This can be fun and a challenge to the bright child, but eventually it exasperates even the most long-suffering parent. The keen youngster soon learns which of his explanations Mother cannot easily explain away. The mother will win some of these engagements, since she must. But she and her child are continually pretending that coercion plays no real role in their relationship.

In effect, the child is saying, "You can't make me." He is deluded, and so are his parents, who created the delusion. The fact is that adults *do* "make" children do things they would not do otherwise. "Making" a child do something may take many forms, including insistent explanations of why the hoped-for behavior is necessary. Game-playing parents all seem to agree that explanations are *always* required. I hardly think so. I am more sympathetic to Ring Lardner's approach: " Shut up,' he explained."

With explaining parents, the child learns to become an explainer. He also learns the art of challenging explanations; he learns the Why? game. In that one the child tests the parent's ingenuity in offering explanations or excuses (the line between them is often a thin one). This is a sucker's game, since parents are often ill-informed in certain areas—and the child wouldn't understand the true explanation even if the parents knew it. In any case, the child is not interested in the answer. Why eat vegetables? "They are good for you," the parent "explains." Why? "People need a balanced diet." Why doesn't Daddy eat vegetables? "It's more important for children to eat vegetables than for grownups." Why? "Children are growing and they need vitamins." Why? Why? Why?

Parents who are victims of the Why? game often look at me plaintively and say, "*Yes, but* don't psychiatrists advise explaining things to children? Don't children have a right to know?" (One may note that the Yes, But game is a variation of the Why? game.) Children *do* have a right to know. But parents must learn to differentiate the use of "Why?" as an expression of curiosity from the challenging and coercive use that can and often is made of it.

In the variation of the "no" game called Deaf-Mute, a mother says to the Deaf-Mute player, "You're not listening to a word I say," and she may be quite right. Or, explaining away some sin of omission, he may innocently say, "I didn't hear you, Mom." "After all, if he didn't hear me," the mother explains to herself, "I can't get angry about it." And the child notes that this is a stratagem that works.

Later, Mom is another variant of the basic "no" game. Most mothers know in their bones that "Later, Mom," means "No," but Mother may be defeated or confused by the reasonableness of the requested postponement or by the fact that occasionally the player may actually perform later. This game will be fostered or discouraged according to whether or not Mother recognizes the announced postponement for what it really is.

The mother who says, "No" to the child is—let us take courage and say it—a Dictator. She dictates, for well or ill, what is to be done and what is not to be done. She can apply sanctions. She can approve with a caress or a cookie. She can disapprove with a spanking or a frown. Or she can initiate the child into the next level of game playing.

She does this by introducing moral concepts. On the simplest level, this shift consists of substituting the word "bad" for the word "no." Seemingly this substitution is a trifle, but really it is a giant step—in the wrong direction. The effect is that the one-to-one encounter between mother and child is put on an abstract level.

The advantage for Mother is that she gets off the hook of feeling she is Bully or Simon Legree. By using the word "bad" she is no longer one individual coercing another, but instead has become the agent of a noble tradition.

Morality games offer an opportunity to dissociate oneself from one's own behavior, to deny or dilute personal responsibility. Mother is, in effect, no longer a big person who is frustrating a small person; she is now the agent of an ideal, grappling not with the child but with an aspect of his behavior.

These days, parents often substitute concepts like "fairness" and "selfishness" for "good" and "bad." Our young game players, their keen eyes on the goal of winning, then attempt to turn these words to their own purposes. "It's not *fair!*" soon stands high on the roster of magic phrases.

The youngster's first effort to dissociate himself from his own behavior will probably be in the context of the game called Innocence. The classic example is the child who, when caught raiding the cookie jar, says, "I didn't do it. My hand did it." This early attempt at Innocence will resemble lying because the child is not yet skilled in manipulating words and concepts. But soon enough he will master the dissociating element that his Mother employs when, in hauling him over her knee, she comments, "This hurts me more than it does you."

The reliance the child places on Innocence will depend upon how heavily his mother and father are engaged in this game, both with each other and with him. With children it is played interminably in some homes in relation to dressing for school, getting to meals on time and going to bed. Often a game of Innocence will follow a round or two of Later, Mom. Mother says, "It's bedtime." Johnny says, "In a minute, Mother." "Go to bed now, John." "In a minute." More minutes pass. After all, it is reasonable for Johnny to be allowed to finish his chapter or his game or to see that fascinating new TV commercial that will be coming on shortly. But Mother notices an irritability, an unreasoning anger, rising in herself. She reviews her virtues and his provocations. Then she explodes. Her words may be brutal, but "under the circumstances" (which she helped bring about) her words are "justified." She is innocent!

Courtroom is an advanced version of Innocence. Charges are made and denied; countercharges are made and denied—ad infinitum. I have talked with some husbands and wives who have played this game with each other for years. As I listen to them, I note that the one who is talking is clearly innocent of all charges, full of good intentions and in possession of some really damning evidence against the other. But the spouse also has a persuasive case. What the husband calls an attack by the wife, the wife defines as simply a counterattack that was certainly provoked by the husband's behavior. You are left with a playlet in which a man and wife may be saying horrible, hurtful and damning things to each other and yet each, with the utmost sincerity, presents himself as occupying a superior moral position. It is as though being morally wronged (like the mother who plays Innocence at bedtime with Johnny) frees the affronted one of restraints and issues a kind of hunting license. A spouse (more often the wife than the husband, in my experience) or a parent may sum up this basically immoral position succinctly by stating, "After what he's done, he doesn't deserve any better treatment from me."

Children learn Courtroom quite easily, since like all games it is basically simple. At bedtime Johnny may charge unfairness: "But Willie is still up— you promised I could finish my book [maybe you did, but that was this morning and he picked the book up after bedtime]—all the other kids are allowed to stay up later than I am." Mother explains, defends or counterattacks instead of establishing and enforcing a reasonable routine. The game is on.

Democracy is the culmination of this series of games. It requires an added ingredient. The parent must feel obligated at least to pay lip service to the notion of the actual equality of persons, a kind of "one man, one vote" doctrine. It has been my observation that middle-class, well-educated Americans are especially likely to carry their deeply held feelings about social equality into parent-child relations, and feel real guilt when the situation forces them to use their raw power. But the fact is that except in very disturbed families, the power to decide does and should lie in the hands of the parents. I believe in family discussions to explore ideas, plans or decisions; I am often impressed with the ingenious and novel ideas and solutions my own children come up with in such discussions. Sometimes they have helped me greatly in working out problems. But it is possible to respect children's thoughts without pretending that they are decisive.

Parents, and all of us, ought to take a franker and more unabashed view of the actual power relationships that exist within the family if they are to avoid unpleasantness and possibly serious problems. The rational exercise of power depends upon acknowledging its existence, upon understanding its nature and upon then applying it appropriately, firmly, flexibly and compassionately.

A great deal of game playing in a family is evidence that power is not being rationally exercised. Fortunately, game playing can be avoided to the extent that it can be recognized. Parents are often amazed when they learn that they have been playing the same game repeatedly with their child. Their sincerity, their good intentions and the strength of their emotions—in a word, their intense involvement—have obscured (for them) the fact that it is essentially the same script in each instance.

"How amazing," a mother said to me recently, "that I would use the same approach over and over again, even though it has never worked!"

The key to the socialization of the child lies not in outside coercion but within the child himself—in his curiosity, playfulness, his imitativeness and his remarkable zeal to become able to do the things he sees his parents and brothers and sisters do. Games are like weeds, stifling the valuable and tender growths whose soil they usurp.

HELEN HEFFERNAN

# 45. THE ORGANIZATION OF THE ELEMENTARY SCHOOL AND THE DEVELOPMENT OF PERSONALITY

"For every child a healthy personality," the theme of the Mid-Century White House Conference on Children and Youth, emphasized an important goal of education. One session of the California Conference of Elementary School Principals and District Superintendents of Schools was devoted to evaluating elementary school practices in relation to this goal. The practices evaluated were presented by the elementary education staff of the State Department of Education. The staff, basing its judgment on research and experience, chose for presentation the elementary school practices indicated by the following questions:

1. Does the practice of grade placement assure pupils opportunities to develop healthy personalities?
2. Does the departmental teaching in the elementary school offer opportunities for pupils to develop healthy personalities?
3. Do current practices in reporting pupil progress to parents tend to give pupils good opportunities to develop healthy personalities?

Reprinted from *California Journal of Elementary Education* (February 1962), pp. 129–53, by permission of the author and publisher.

4. Does the maintenance of grade standards assure opportunities for pupils to develop healthy personalities?
5. Does an articulated program of instruction provide superior opportunities for pupils to develop healthy personalities?

No brief was held for the selection of these questions in preference to others, but the staff believed that the questions cover areas that are of concern to every principal and teacher who sees in healthy personality development the major purpose of modern child-rearing.

## A HEALTHY PERSONALITY

Before approaching the problems set by the questions, common ground was sought for the meaning of the term "healthy personality." The concept of personality that was expressed during the White House Conference gave significant emphasis to the qualitative aspects of human relations and indicated that everyone who works in the service of children must take *children's feelings* into account. This way of looking at children leads inevitably to the conclusion that demeaning poverty, inadequate school and health services, and racial or ethnical discrimination not only are in and of themselves handicapping to children but also constitute a denial of the democratic ideal that every person is of precious and equal worth. As Allison Davis pointed out, these are serious considerations in a country which at this moment urgently needs all the skilled people it can get. More than 60 out of every 100 children in the United States live in families of low socioeconomic status. The ability represented in this large group of children is largely undiscovered and unused.

To be sure, emotional ill health may have many causes. Inadequate food and housing, racial discrimination, physiological malfunctioning, lack of guidance toward sound life values, and lack of love and affection of parents are all part of the pattern which may disturb or obstruct well-balanced development in children. The problem in the elementary school is to determine ways to be sure that none of its practices constitute hazards to sound development.

The origin of the word "personality" is interesting. The word comes from the Greek *persona* or "mask," something which an actor puts on to conceal his true identity. Many advertisers seem to use the word in somewhat the same sense—the "man of distinction" becomes associated with a commodity available in bottles; an irresistible epidermis can be attained by liberal applications of a gooey substance in a tube or jar; social acceptability is somehow connected with the advertiser's toothpaste or deodorant.

But these were not the meanings of "personality" basic to the White House Conference. Rather, the philosopher, the psychologist, the physiologist, the sociologist, the psychiatrist pooled their ideas and came out with another meaning of personality. They said, "By personality we mean the thinking, feeling, acting human being, who conceives of himself as an individual separate from other individuals. The human being does not have a personality; he is a personality."

What then are the components of a healthy personality? These components, said Erikson, are the sense of trust, the sense of autonomy, the sense of initiative, the sense of accomplishment, the sense of identity, the sense of intimacy, the parental sense, and the sense of integrity. These components will bear elaboration as bases for consideration of the organization of the elementary school.

## THE SENSE OF TRUST

The first component of the healthy personality is the sense of trust. Trust can exist only in relation to something. The baby begins at an early age to develop the sense of trust as he learns that there are adults in this world who will relieve his hunger, provide for his physical comfort, and give him the affection he needs. Infants that are brought up in institutions in which the environments are unfavorable to their emotional stability show by listlessness, emaciation, pallor, immobility, unresponsiveness, poor appetite, poor digestion, and a wide variety of evidences of unhappiness that their experiences have not led them to develop a sense of trust. Fortunately most infants in our society find the comfort and affection that are essential to a developing sense of trust. Both nature and culture are conducive toward making mothers motherly at the very time the child's personality is in need of the nurture which develops this basic component of the healthy personality.

## THE SENSE OF AUTONOMY

Next in chronological order of development is the sense of independence or autonomy. The second and third years of life are roughly the beginning of the individual's struggle to establish himself as a human being with a mind and will of his own. The young child must experience over and over that he is a person who is permitted to make choices. Personal autonomy is an outstanding feature of the American way of life. Every red-blooded American resents being bossed, being pushed around; he maintains vigorously that everyone has a right to express himself, has a right to control his own affairs. The American people want each child to grow up to be the upstanding, look-you-in-the-eye kind of individual. That is the type of person Americans admire.

Although the beginnings of this sense of autonomy are important in the early years of life, independence is not established once and for all time any more than is the sense of trust. The period during which these components of personality first emerge is crucial, but if we want youngsters to emerge into adulthood with healthy personalities, we must continue to nurture their sense of trust, respect their desire to assert themselves, help them learn to hold their desire for independence within bounds, and avoid treating them in ways to arouse any doubts in themselves or feelings of shame in connection with their accomplishments.

## A SENSE OF INITIATIVE

At four or five years of age, the young child wants to find out what kind of a person he can be. He watches the activities of adults about him; he recreates their activities in his play and yearns to share in their activities. It is important for the child's developing personality that much encouragement be given to the enterprise and imagination which characterize these years. The child is ready and avid to learn. This sense of initiative must be constantly fostered. If it is restricted, resentment and bitterness and a vindictive attitude toward the world may develop as a functioning part of the child's personality.

## A SENSE OF ACCOMPLISHMENT

If during the early years of life a child has developed the sense of trust, the sense of autonomy, and the sense of initiative, we may expect when he is about six years of age to see the beginning of great development of the sense of accomplishment. While this sense is developing, a child wants to engage in real tasks that he can carry through to completion. After a period of time characterized by exuberant imagination, a child then wants to settle down to learning exactly how to do things and how to do them well. Much of this period of a child's life is spent in the elementary school. Under reasonably favorable circumstances, this is a period of calm, steady growth, especially if the problems of the previous stages have been well worked out. Although this is a rather unspectacular period in human growth, it is an important period, for during it there is laid the basis for responsible citizenship. And during this period children acquire knowledge and skills that make for good workmanship, the ability to cooperate and to play fair, and otherwise to follow the rules of the larger social game.

The chief danger a child may encounter during this period is the presence of conditions which may lead to a sense of inadequacy and inferiority. If in the home or school too much is expected of a child, or if a child is made to feel that achievement is beyond his ability, he may lapse into discouragement and lack of interest. It is important, therefore, that children have a feeling of successful accomplishment in connection with their school work. Studies of delinquent children frequently show that they hated school—hated it because they were marked as stupid, awkward, and not able to do so well as other children. Children who accept their inferiority passively are perhaps more damaged psychologically than those who react aggressively to frustrating experience.

## A SENSE OF IDENTITY

At the onset of adolescence an individual begins to seek clarification of his concept of who he is and what his role in society is to be. During this period a youth is preoccupied with his appearance in the eyes of others—particularly his peers. If the course of personality development has been healthy up to this period, the young person will have acquired a reasonable feeling of self-esteem which will carry him through the tensions and strains that are biologically or culturally imposed on adolescents.

## A SENSE OF INTIMACY

Only if the young person has acquired a sense of identity can he achieve the next component of a healthy personality in his relation to others—a sense of intimacy. The surer the young person is of himself, the more successfully can he enter into relations of friendship, love, and inspiration.

## THE PARENTAL SENSE

In its broadest meaning, the parental sense involves the qualities of creativity and productivity. As the individual advances into adulthood, this sense develops normally if the preceding steps have been achieved with reasonable success.

## THE SENSE OF INTEGRITY

The final component of a healthy personality is the sense of integrity. Throughout the child's development, his home and school have been helping him to accept the dominant ideals of the culture—honor, courage, purity, grace, fairness, self-discipline. These are the core of integration of the healthy personality. The acquisition of these values and ideals is the ultimate goal of American culture.

With this abbreviation of the background concepts that the White House Conference used as a guide, present practices in elementary education may be examined to determine whether or not they contribute to healthy personality development.

## THE EFFECT OF GRADE STANDARDS

Do grade standards contribute to the development of a healthy personality? Is the development of a healthy personality extended by a classification of pupils based on rigid grade standards? For those who accept the findings of research regarding individual differences, the answer is "No." Would healthy personality growth be furthered if the organization of the school provided a program of continuous learning and advancement in accordance with the growth patterns of individuals?

Research clearly indicates that the personality development of a child may be greatly affected by the maintenance of formal grade standards. Successful accomplishment gives the child confidence in himself, while retardation or assignment to slower groups tends to destroy the child's sense of personal worth and to cause him to have feelings of frustration. Rigid grade standards cannot be met by all members of any class. To the child with strong academic interest and ability, who succeeds almost effortlessly in school, the grade standard has no threatening consequences. To the child whose limitations are greater than average, the grade standard constantly threatens defeat and thereby prevents wholesome personality growth.

Grade standards originated as an administrative device and not as an answer to the question, What is best for the child? Can we justify the continuance of rigid grade standards as a basis for classifying pupils? Fixed grade standards are untenable in the light of what is now known about the best ways to meet the needs of children. A plan for continuous growth is widely recognized as more desirable than the experience of annual evaluation followed by promotion or nonpromotion. Learning is continuous and must progress according to individual rate and ability. Schools cannot, therefore, justify the continuance of annual promotion or retardation as sound practice.

An adult can never fully know how a child feels about failure unless the adult has experienced such failure. Were you ever failed? Who knew that you failed? Did you lose status with your mother or your father, with big brother or sister? Children have feelings about failure even though some teachers say that children do not mind failure. How would you cover it up if you failed in your job? The hurt is deep, it must be hidden. To carry on, one must appear indifferent. Children are courageous. They are helpless in the face of adult decisions—decisions which so irrevocably affect their personality growth.

Can each of thirty-five children, all nine years old, make the third-grade standard on May 26? Can each of the thirty-five youths, fourteen years old, be expected to pass the *same test* in United States history for graduation from the eighth grade? Can thirty-five children, six years old, each read all the same pre-primers, primers, and first readers? Roma Gans in her book, *Reading Is Fun,* says that "perhaps no subject has been taught with greater disregard for child development than has reading." The eyes of all six-year-old children do not focus well; the children may not speak in complete sentences; their family may speak Spanish at home; Dad may have gone to war and Mother may be working. Are children in each of these circumstances equally ready to read?

Statistics show that teachers fail over one-seventh of the children in their classes. Are teachers aware that under such circumstances it is the school that has failed? Grade standards for subject and skill mastery do not promote the development of healthy personalities. Yet there appears to be something compulsive about the desire of teachers and school authorities to make all children alike even though they know that each child differs from all other children.

A basic democratic principle is violated when the school fails to recognize the worth of the individual. The educational principle of individual differences is widely accepted. Equally widely accepted is the knowledge that learning is an individual, not a mass, accomplishment. More than twenty-five years ago psychologists publicized information about individual rates of development, abilities, interests, and needs. For many years William Heard Kilpatrick has directed our attention to the fact that a child learns what he lives. If the child is to learn democracy, teachers and principals must make the school environment such that he lives democratically and successfully in accordance with his potentialities. Success motivates, failure frustrates children.

The child as a whole must be accepted. Intelligence, which is measurable to a degree, is but one of the factors which the child brings to the learning situation. To a high degree, ability to learn is conditioned by emotions, health, and past experiences as well as by native mental ability. Teachers must help children to grow, not attempt to force them nor to drive them down standardized roads to learning through slavish attention to the same book. Children must be helped to know themselves, and to build their destinies in terms of their strengths. No one ever had his personality developed by constant emphasis on his weaknesses. Since individuals are different, fixed standards are not conducive to healthy growth. In a flexible program, differentiated materials and opportunities permit each child to explore and experiment, to figure, to discuss, to share and collect, and to find answers at a rate that is commensurate with his ability and interest.

When individuals have purpose they can master arithmetic combinations, learn to write a business letter, and read for information material adapted to their level of achievement. They will move steadily ahead, even though they may move slowly. When the child knows his needs, knows the next steps to be undertaken, and has had a part in planning how to attain his objectives, he is ready to learn. Interest motivates the child to put forth effort. Opportunities for continuous growth are challenging and stimulating to him. Attempts to force learning are not only unnecessary, but they are also futile unless the child is responding to inner drives of interest which encourage him to put forth effort.

Education to meet the needs of all children includes education to help parents understand their children and their children's problems. Parents must be helped to understand that there are some things that the school cannot do for children. Leaders in education to whom parents rightfully turn for information and guidance must help parents to understand individual differences and to accept their child and to love him as he is, even if he is a slow learner. Parents must know that the school cannot teach the child to read before he is ready and that no amount of effort to do so will produce the results desired. And parents must know that attempting to force a child toward mastery of a skill, before he is capable, produces frustration and delays learning. Schools must prevent frustrations, emphasize prevention, and do away with the need for remedying problems that they have created. Parents must realize that each child is unique; that his rate of learning, his ability, experiential background, health, and emotions strongly influence his learning. The individual's ability to learn differs from that of others as does his personal appearance or physical strength. Teachers must be honest and straightforward but kindly and understanding as they seek the help of parents. Parents and school people must become a team that believes in and supports each child.

Expediency should never be the basis for determining the treatment that a child shall be accorded. Democratic philosophy emphasizes the sanctity of individual personality. Change requires effort. When principals and teachers become dissatisfied with present practices in education they will willingly put forth the effort necessary to find improved ways of helping children. If inflexible grade standards do not meet individual differences or provide for continuous learning, schools must find better ways to do these things. The task of schools is to build, not to destroy, personalities. Each child must be accepted as he is, where he is, and provided with opportunities for continuous growth. Democracy needs confident, healthy personalities. Schools must modify practices so that during each day each child has satisfying opportunities for growth toward the realization of his individual potentialities.

## DEPARTMENTALIZATION AND PERSONALITY DEVELOPMENT

As part of the major topic—"Does the organization of the elementary school contribute to the development of a healthy personality?"—one subtopic to be considered is the following: "Does departmentalization of the elementary school or departmental teaching in the elementary school contribute to the development of a healthy personality?"

By departmentalization or departmental teaching we mean the type of organization in which a group of children has a different teacher for instruction in each subject or in a combination of subjects.

We will agree that any type of organization has advantages and disadvantages. Before a principal and a faculty adopt a program of departmentalization, they should weigh the advantages and disadvantages of such an organization in terms of the wholesome personality development of children.

Departmentalization has its roots in tradition. In the development of schools in our country there came into prominence, particularly in New England toward the close of the eighteenth century, the type of school organization known as the "departmental school." The chief characteristic of the departmental school was the vertical division of the course into a reading school and a writing school. Although the two departments were housed in the same buildings, each of them had its own master, its own room, its own set of studies. The pupils attended each department in turn, changing from one to the other at the end of each half-day session. This type of organization appeared to further the purposes for which schools were maintained at that time.

Another quick look at the organization of elementary schools in our country reveals that departmentalization passed out of the picture during the nineteenth century but was reintroduced in the New York City schools, particularly in the upper grades, in 1900. Various types of departmentalization were introduced into elementary schools during the next twenty years. During this period the "platoon school" reached full development.

The various types of organization in existence in the twenties and thirties gave rise to extensive research relative to the values of different types of organization. The chief claim of the advocates of departmentalization was in terms of better achievement in understanding subject matter. The advocates of the platoon school were the most ardent supporters of departmentalization. The studies which were made to evaluate the platoon school and various types of departmentalization failed to show unquestioned superiority of that form of organization in teaching subject matter. The research of such men as Stewart, Gerberich, Prall, Spain, Shepard, Courtis, and Bonser supports this statement.

It would appear from the research evidence this group made available that by the early thirties departmentalization had ceased to grow. But the tendency at the present time for certain elementary schools to reintroduce departmentalization, especially in the seventh and eighth grades, makes it appear that the facts pertaining to departmentalization have to be rediscovered by each generation of educators.

Let us look, then, at the advantages and disadvantages of departmentalization. As we consider the purposes of schools in a democratic society, the objectives of education, the needs of boys and girls, and the ways of learning that are psychologically sound and conducive to wholesome personality development as the basis for analyzing departmental organization, there appear the following disadvantages in departmental organization:

1. It organizes learning experiences in terms of areas of subject matter.
2. It disintegrates rather than integrates learning experiences.
3. It separates the tool subjects from the activities in which the tools are used.

4. It fails to utilize ways of learning that are psychologically sound.
5. It interrupts continuity and destroys the relatedness of learning experiences.
6. It requires a teacher to meet an exceedingly large number of children each day; thus no teacher knows each child well enough to perform important guidance functions.
7. It results in the situation where a number of teachers make demands upon one pupil.
8. It requires a rigid schedule, which interrupts activities and thus prevents purposes from being realized and interests satisfied.

The scales are heavily weighted against departmentalization. Except in a few instances, departmentalization appears to be unjustified in the first six grades of the elementary schools. Departmentalization might be justified in those rare instances in which certain teachers are unable to instruct pupils in such specialized areas as music and art.

In the seventh and eighth grades some departmentalization may be justified in the organization of learning experiences for young adolescents only if it permits these youth to satisfy their special interests and develop their abilities in such areas as art, music, physical education, and science. If a departmental organization making these provisions is used, it should permit the child to spend at least half his school time with one teacher. The social studies should constitute the core of his learning experiences. The social studies, language arts, science, and mathematics should be integrated in his learning experiences.

## REPORTING PUPIL PROGRESS TO PARENTS

The answer to the question: "Do current practices in reporting pupil progress to parents contribute to the development of a healthy personality?" is "No," if the practice involves sending home at regular intervals one of several varieties of what have been called "nasty little status cards" as the sole means of acquainting parents with the social and academic progress of their children.

Analyze a few of the cards used to report pupil progress. The fairly innocuous one sometimes given to children in the kindergarten asks the teacher to respond to two items: (1) "He does his best," and (2) "He could do better." Perhaps the child is marked: "Does his best." Why? Does the teacher like the child? Does the family see that his physical and emotional needs are being adequately met? Do the school and the home work well together? He may be marked: "Could do better." Why he could do better is left out. Could he do better if his tonsils were out, if his mother prepared more nourishing meals, if he felt better about the new baby, if his mother and father got along without quarreling, if his father were home from the army, if the teacher gave him more chances to succeed, if the experiences of the school were closer to his out-of-school experiences and made sense to him?

The unanswered questions that arise in the minds of many parents as they read such a report cause them to lose confidence in the school program and to develop a feeling of separation from activities of the classroom. Such reports make it difficult for attitudes of confidence to develop between home and school.

In discussing another type of report card, one that is marked S and U, a mother remarked that these report cards were "U" to her. In one case a child received a U in physical education although both the parents and the teacher knew that the child's flat feet prevented him from running and playing games as well as the other children. On being questioned about this mark, the teacher said: "I couldn't give Tommy an S because it is apparent that he can't play the same games other children play. It wouldn't be fair to the others or keep up the standards. Besides, the children know that he doesn't play as well as they do. You can't fool them." And so a child is marked down for having a physical defect and is made to feel even more inadequate.

Another type of marking employs a series of numbers or letters—1, 2, 3, 4, or A, B, C, D, and F. One of the arguments for this kind of marks on a report card is that they are "so definite." Great importance is often given to the value of retaining the "F." The argument for it is that failure occurs in life and, therefore, children must be habituated early to experiences of failure. People holding this position are saying in effect that lessons in failure must begin when one is young and must be continuous; otherwise—to carry out this thought—the strength of the human spirit might triumph and a nonreader might grow up to think he amounts to something.

"A" marks may be bad for a child, too. They may cause him to have feelings of smugness or an exaggerated sense of intellectual power when he is only being rewarded for natural ability, docility, or skill in pleasing the teacher.

Marks are meaningless and unreliable. Try a little experiment to prove this fact to yourself. Mark a set of papers as efficiently as you know how. Put them away for three months. Mark them again. Compare the two sets of marks. The testimony in your own handwriting will be convincing.

Unreliable measures of achievement encourage destructive competition. Yet the evidence is clear that competitive systems are not effective in stimulating effort toward the attainment of desirable goals. A child who has done well feels that he has failed because someone else has surpassed him. Another child may be proud of mediocre achievement if he is ahead of others, and thus the levels of aspiration are lowered for both children.

Report cards on which a marking system is used do not contribute to the development of healthy personality. Their evil effect may be minimized by many factors; teachers who realize the harm which competitive and comparative marks do may mark accordingly, or strong feelings of friendliness and confidence between home and school may exist in spite of report cards only because both discount the importance of the report card.

Reporting to parents can be a positive factor in building mental health if parents are informed of their child's growth through frequent conferences with the child's teacher. In order to make these conferences successful, teachers should be given time within the school day for conducting them.

The yearbook of the Association for Supervision and Curriculum Development, *Fostering Mental Health in Our Schools,* will prove helpful to teachers conducting conferences with parents. The section on developmental tasks is especially useful. Clerical assistance in the typing of anecdotal records, in the preparation of cumulative records, and in preparing reports of conferences should also be available to teachers.

An important part of any parent-teacher conference should be the development of a plan of action outlining the next step in learning. A parent and teacher sit down together to consider the total development of the child, his strength, his weaknesses, and how home and school can best help him. A record should be made of the simple steps which parents and teacher plan to take to help the child. A part of such a record might read as follows:

### THE PARENT'S PLAN

Mr. Jones will play ball with Jerry after school so that he will learn to catch better and will be willing to play with the other children. Mrs. Jones will invite small groups of children to play with Jerry after school so that he will not be alone so much. Billy was suggested as a good child to be included in this group.

Now that Mrs. Jones is busy with the new baby, she realizes that Jerry may be feeling rejected and left out; so she is planning to have her mother give him some special attention by taking him on trips and entertaining him. She also realizes that he needs to have some responsibility for the care of his little brother.

### THE TEACHER'S PLAN

I will see that Jerry gets some playground success. I will also give him some special attention in the room. He might have charge of the hall exhibit box for the rest of the term.

What does this tell a teacher who may have the child the following year? This program for action indicates to the discerning teacher that Jerry has been feeling insecure because of a new baby brother in the family, that he needs more attention from adults, that he should develop playground skill, and that home and school share responsibility for helping him.

This child might have had a report card that would have read: "Deportment, U, Physical Education, U." What would either the child, the parent, or a new teacher have known about the child under these circumstances? It is possible that the new teacher would have pushed Jerry further from the attention he needed, that the mother would have felt that his bad behavior in school added one more burden to her problems at the time that she was much concerned with the new baby. Jerry's father may have looked at the U in physical education and wondered how in the world he could have a son who couldn't catch a ball. Jerry's new teacher would take a look at the report card and say with a sigh: "Another child who doesn't know how to behave and who can't do anything on the playground!" Clues to the underlying causes of behavior do not appear in the traditional report card, and no provision is made for suggestions as to remedial action.

Parent-teacher conferences can be supplemented by having the children prepare and take home statements of their own progress, by frequent classroom evaluations, by informal notes or phone calls, and by planned programs which acquaint parents with the purposes of education in a democracy and the specific ways in which the school is working to fulfill those purposes.

Parents have a right to know the facts about the progress of their children in school. The cumulative record tells more than any report card. The major purpose of reporting to parents is to provide the information necessary for a sound working relation between them and school, and many avenues of communication should be opened to make this relation operate successfully.

## GRADE PLACEMENT OF PUPILS

Does the grade placement of pupils contribute to healthy personalities? In answering this question regarding the effect of grade placement on personality, children who have been retained in a grade should be considered. Should judgment regarding the placement of a child be left to a teacher who may not be familiar with the research in the field or who may be operating on the basis of personal opinion and limited experience? To answer these questions let us consider the problem of Larry.

Larry, a 13-year-old, is in the sixth grade. Larry is of average size for his age, which means he is one of the larger boys in the class. He was retained in the first grade because he seemed immature and did not learn to read. He was retained again in the third grade because of poor progress and because he was not ready for fourth-grade work.

Larry's ability is low average as measured by standardized tests. His achievement is about two years below the norm for the class he is in and three years below his potential. Larry wastes his time, fools around, and shows little interest in school activities.

Larry's father is a sheet-metal worker in the railroads yards. He is disgusted with Larry. "What that kid needs," he says, "is a job and the sooner the better. He is wasting his time in school." His father is disgusted with the school, too. "It's this modern education," he says, "it's too soft. They don't make the boy work. The discipline is poor. Too much time is spent on frills and not enough on the three R's."

Larry says, "I don't like school. It's not much fun. I'd like to learn a trade if I ever get to high school, but I doubt if I'll ever make it."

The teacher asks the following questions: "Should I promote Larry this year? Promotion would reward lack of effort. Would that destroy the morale of the others who worked hard? Would Larry believe that he could always get by without working? Wouldn't promotion for Larry mean lowering standards—a soft education?"

The teacher says, "Larry is not ready for seventh-grade work. To promote him would mean too wide a range of achievement for the seventh-grade teacher to handle. He would surely fail in the seventh grade. Shouldn't Larry understand that he has to work if he is going to get anywhere in this tough world?"

What does educational research show about Larry? Research shows that to dislike school, to waste time, to make little effort, to achieve below capacity is the behavior expected of a child who has experienced nonpromotion. Larry is running true to form.

The threat of nonpromotion, or nonpromotion itself, does not increase motivation but lowers the level of aspiration for most children. So it is with Larry. Larry has no fun in school because he is not well accepted by the others. The findings of research show that this is what usually happens to children who have experienced nonpromotion. The other children in Larry's grade either overtly state or tacitly think that he is stupid, which colors all their attitudes toward him.

Has Larry's nonpromotion reduced the range of achievement in Larry's class and thus provided a more homogeneous group? No, Larry is still at the tag end in achievement but he is the most mature boy in interests and physiological development. This heterogeneity in development and interests of the pupils is more of a problem to the teacher than the wide range of materials she must provide.

Will Larry straighten out when he gets to high school and learns a trade? The probability is that he will not get through high school. One research study showed that of 643 pupils who dropped out of high school, 638 had repeated the first grade. Research also shows that the most common characteristic of "drop outs" from high school is overageness.

How will Larry get along socially and emotionally as an adolescent? This is problematical. The correlation of school failure to delinquency is high. The effect of failure on personality is to develop either withdrawing behavior or compensating mechanisms which are usually unwholesome in their effect on social adjustment. Grade retardation has not been profitable for Larry nor has it eased the instructional problem in school.

Larry's problems have not all arisen from nonpromotion in school. A meager home background, limited ability, lack of understanding and encouragement by parents, and too little home guidance have been the roots of his problem. When it allowed Larry to fail in school work, the school relinquished its opportunity to guide, inspire, and help him, and to compensate for the inadequacies in his hom⊙ He has lost his trust in the school and in himself. His initiative, if he has any left, will never be directed toward improving himself through education. . . .

Would Larry have had a better chance of promotion had his name been Loretta? Yes, the facts show that among girls and boys of equal ability and achievement, girls are promoted more frequently. Why is this true? Research regarding the causes has not been completed but a good guess is that a Loretta would have been more submissive and less annoying to her teachers than Larry was and thus her failure to meet standards might have been overlooked.

How many children in California schools raise similar questions in the minds of teachers? The age-grade status of 234,000 children in 28 counties was studied in 1950. In this study it was found that 51 per cent of the boys and 37 per cent of the girls were over the expected age by the time they had reached the eighth grade. No doubt some of these children had entered school late, but it can be presumed that most of them had been retarded one or more years in grade placement. The range in age in each grade was from five to ten years, and 19,528 of the children were more than one year over-age. Many youths 15, 16, 17, and 18 years old were found in the eighth grade. Eighth-grade enrollment was significantly lower than other grades even when differences in birth rate were considered, showing that drop-outs occur in elementary as well as in high school.

Certainly individual cases exist in which nonpromotion is desirable. No truth is universal; there are exceptions to every rule. There may even be individuals for whom grade failure could be a salvation. But the mountains of research evidence against nonpromotion are so high that the burden of proof that a child should be failed rests with the school that fails him. Only a psychologist qualified to evaluate the physical development of a child, to measure his maturity, to diagnose his personality needs, and to understand his home should say, "*This* child should not be promoted." The psychologists should be able to say with certainty: "All the bad effects of nonpromotion which we know happen to most children will not happen to this child because he is so different." Only then is a school justified in running counter to well-established research evidence by insisting upon nonpromotion of any pupil. And even in these circumstances, careful follow-up studies should be made to detect the onset of possible bad effects and to prevent permanent harm to any pupil through nonpromotion.

## ARTICULATION OF UNITS OF THE SCHOOL SYSTEM

Does an articulated program of education contribute to the development of a healthy personality? Recently an elementary school teacher who is unusually adept in establishing friendly rapport with her pupils and who is teaching

children in a large elementary school from which pupils enter a depart-
mentalized junior high school was reviewing certain of her observations
during the past three years. She said:

> I have been teaching children in the sixth grade in this school for the past
> three years. The children who were with me during my first year in this posi-
> tion are now in the eighth grade of a highly departmentalized junior high
> school. Last year when they were in the seventh grade, and this year, too, they
> have invited me to their social gatherings which are usually held in a home
> of one of the group. Sometime before each evening is over they discuss their
> school activities. They tell one another and me, too, what they like about
> school. They also tell the things in elementary school that they miss, and one
> thing comes up over and over. It seems that in their junior high school the
> pupils not only have different teachers every hour on the hour but find them-
> selves with different members of their group in the different classes. They miss
> most the opportunity to become acquainted with one another and with their
> teachers. They speak of one teacher as a home-room teacher but discern little
> difference between their home-room teacher and other teachers except that she
> appears to have more records to keep. They miss particularly a close association
> with one another. They enjoy and keep alive the social gatherings that were
> begun three years ago because they can meet with boys and girls they know
> well and with people who know them. They seek a sense of intimacy, friend-
> ship, love, and inspiration.

An eighth-grade teacher was talking about a boy who completed the eighth
grade last June. She said:

> I teach in a rural school. After students finish the eighth grade, they are picked
> up by a school bus provided by the high school district and ride many miles
> to the high school. I don't see them often after they start to high school because
> they leave early and get home late. Last week, however, one of the boys who
> finished the eighth grade last June came to talk with me. He was a good pupil
> in my class. I thought he was an unusually promising boy. While in the eighth
> grade, he had talked about taking courses in high school that would prepare
> him to work with the 'business part of getting fruit ready for the market,' to
> use his words. But now, after we had talked for a while, he said he was thinking
> about quitting school and getting a job. When I asked him why he was thinking
> about quitting he said, 'My grades aren't very good. We have a lot more
> homework to do now than we had last year and I don't get mine done. Last
> year we didn't have much homework and I got along fine. Whenever we did
> have homework last year, I didn't get mine done at home. You know there
> are three of us kids at home and we still live in the trailer. When I try to do
> my homework I'm in everybody's way and I don't get it done. I've thought
> about it for a long time now and believe the thing for me to do is to earn some
> money. Maybe after I have earned some money to help at home I will be able
> to go to school again. Then, too, I'll have enough money to buy clothes and
> go places like the others do.' I felt depressed after he left and began to wonder
> what I could do to familiarize his high school teacher with the problems con-
> fronting him.

This statement by the eighth-grade teacher raises several questions. If feelings of discouragement persist in this once promising boy, can he have a healthy personality? Will such feelings give him the help he needs to develop a sense of accomplishment, a willingness to settle down to learning how to do things and to them well? Will they permit him to select desirable social goals and to feel reasonable security with his peers?

The two incidents mentioned are not isolated. They are typical of statements by teachers regarding young adolescents in many elementary schools.

A program of education contributes to the development of a healthy personality if each administrative unit is articulated in a total, continuous program. More specifically, schools which contribute to the development of a healthy personality are those in which the following statements describe school goals, planning, and procedures:

1. Twelve years of education are regarded as minimum preparation for citizenship in today's complex society.
2. School activities are guided by a unified philosophy of education which combines the guidance concept with intellectual education.
3. The objectives or goals for each administrative unit are arrived at with joint representation and mutual understanding of all administrative units which constitute the school system.
4. The curriculum is planned jointly by elementary and secondary teachers, particularly for grades 6-7 and 9-10 in the 6-3-3 systems and for grades 8 and 9 in the 8-4 systems.

Educators today are accepting the idea of separate elementary and secondary schools only as convenient administrative units in a continuous, total program of public education. Educators today recognize that problems peculiar to elementary or secondary schools derive from the maturity levels of young people, not from any special institutional function or purpose. The elementary, junior high, and senior high schools joined end-to-end should provide an articulated program for the child from the time he enters school until he is prepared for adult citizenship in our modern society.

A principal in an elementary school enrolling young adolescents in grades seven and eight reported the following incident which led to improved articulation in his school system.

One boy in the school was frequently referred to the principal because he did not always conform to the pattern of conduct expected of pupils. The principal said that he had long ago become convinced of the value of looking at the cumulative record of individuals before talking about their personal problems. He recalled that this youth was nearing his seventeenth birthday, was in the eighth grade, and was rated as average in ability by most of his teachers but below average by certain teachers. The boy was tall, well-developed physically, and would pass for a youth older than his actual age. The principal judged that the youth had a wide background of experience, responsibility, and association with older people. He had come to school by transfer from another state and seemed to get along satisfactorily most of the time.

The principal listened with interest whenever he succeeded in getting the boy to talk about himself, for then his hostility would diminish and before the end of the conversation he could analyze his present situation and his problems.

During one of these meetings, the boy said, "I like my home-room teacher very much. If it weren't for my home-room teacher I would quit school. It is lucky for me that I am in her room a half day every day and longer on some days. I could quit school, you know. I am old enough to quit."

The principal said, "Yes, you are old enough to stop coming to this school and go to continuation school, providing it is necessary for you to work and providing you find a job. But you haven't done that and there are reasons why. Would you mind telling me what they are?"

This is a part of the boy's reply: "No one in our family [and the principal remembered that there were two brothers and a sister] has finished the eighth grade. Where we lived before coming to California we did not have to stay in school until we were sixteen, so my brothers and sisters dropped out to work as soon as they could. My parents wish they had gone to school longer. They are getting along, but I see the need to get more schooling. I want to graduate. The thing that bothers me most is getting mixed up with the rules around the school. I'm careful about some things. I know that I shouldn't smoke around the school so I don't. All my afterschool friends are in high school or out of high school. We are mostly interested in cars and ways to earn money. I'd sure like to be in that auto mechanics shop in the high school."

The principal concluded the discussion with this statement: "This boy and others like him caused us to examine our promotion policy in kindergarten through grade twelve. As a result we now have provision for steady progression through the twelve grades. The high school accepts children from the elementary school after they have gone through our school. They pass from grade eight to grade nine on the same basis as they go from grade three to four or five or six.

"Our high school recognizes the principles of human growth and development. The faculty knows that we have done our best to help each child achieve his fullest potentiality as he moved through our school. The high school teachers accept their guidance function and think of their great task as that of meeting the physical, social, and emotional needs of young people as well as their intellectual needs. We are working to provide educational experiences that will keep all or nearly all of the young people of our community in school for twelve years. We want children and youth to stay in their normal social group and not acquire feelings of inferiority by being classified with younger and smaller children. The problem of adjusting instruction to the needs of individuals must be met in every group. We are gradually getting away from artificial grade standards as we understand children better."

Healthy personality will be promoted as the elementary and secondary schools of a community put themselves through the process of developing and employing an educational philosophy that will make education a continuous, developmental experience for boys and girls.

MARGARET MEAD

# 46. EARLY ADOLESCENCE IN THE UNITED STATES

When the behavior of young American adolescents is compared with the known behavior of adolescents in other modern industrialized societies and in developing countries, and with their own behavior in past decades, several things stand out.

American adolescents are expected to mimic the ways of adults, long before they are emotionally ready for them. The category *teenager,* inclusive from 13 through 19, has resulted in a public image which expects great precocity from the *young* teenager and irresponsibility from the *old* teenager. This category inappropriately lumps together immature children whose growth spurts have hardly begun and mature young people who are permitted to marry and produce children and expected to support themselves. By making "the teens" a category, within which a nineteen-year-old hoodlum's vicious destructiveness and a thirteen-year-old's mischief are bracketed together, we have endowed the younger teenager with a whole series of real and potential precocities that are not only inappropriate but also burdensome.

One of the striking features of the last two decades has been the steady spread downwards in age level of dating; going steady; pairing-off (rather than one-sex friendship); and in emphasis on vocational choice, criminal behavior, competitive athletics, religious affiliation, and permission to spend money on an increasingly lavish scale. The recent book, *Teen Age Tyranny,* which reifies the teenager into a kind of mass menace, documents this money-spending phase heavily, perhaps too heavily, relying on quantity amount spent in the United States—to overwhelm the listener with numbers.[1]

---

Reprinted from *Bulletin of the National Association of Secondary School Principals* (April 1965), pp. 5–10, by permission of the National Association of Secondary School Principals. Copyright © 1965.

---

[1] Hechinger, Grace and Fred M., *Teen Age Tyranny.* New York: William Morrow and Company, 1963.

This precocity, which exists in all fields of life, may be partly exaggerated by other trends in the society—the enormous dependence upon the automobile for transport; the dependence of this age-group on their parents' driving them wherever they go; the increased importance of the mass media, especially television (which means that individual homes and even individual schools have a hard struggle against a commercially supported and propagated national style); the expectation of many more years of schooling which is complemented by a demand for some real life now. The student, who has entered school in kindergarten or nursery school, and who has traveled laboriously through every grade of elementary school, with high school and post-high school education all to come, feels as if school would last forever. The fact that the schools have been geared to help the more poorly prepared students, have insisted on children staying within their age group, and have discouraged the participation of parents in their young children's education, all adds to the thirteen-year-old's feeling that school is an endless and wearisome process. It might as well be enlivened by as much simulation of adult life—which seems impossibly far off—as can be arranged.

This early reaching for the signs of adulthood, such as clothes, dates, spending money, alcohol—all the things to which age and work were once the tickets of admission—is undoubtedly accentuated by the orientation of older brothers and sisters. They, at sixteen and eighteen, are being forced to reach for adult status parenthood for which they are neither economically nor emotionally ready. The attempt of the older adolescent to become a parent before his time reflects the general uncertainty in American society today about the future of the world. Our apprehension that any change may be a change for the worse leading to economic depression, if not to nuclear catastrophe, makes for a restless drawing upon the possibilities of the present and a decline in the willingness to save, to postpone spending, or to defer marrying, buying a house, having children, or taking a trip. The pervasive fear that the future can only be worse than the present, is accompanied by this clinging to and exploitation of the present, which parents in turn express in letting their children do everything earlier rather than later. The American tendency of noting what other people are doing and attempting to do it a little bit better means, now that national mass media are so important, that every time some precocity is reported, other towns, other high schools, other junior high schools, other clubs will try to emulate it. And the direction of emulation since World War II has been toward precocity, marrying younger—and among juvenile delinquents, sensitive to the world stage on which the mass media place them, committing crimes younger.

This emphasis on earlier and earlier participation in adult activities is superficially incongruent with the junior high school movement designed as it was to protect the young adolescent by a separate pace of slower induction into the complexities of high school life. The whole movement began when thinking in chronological age group terms had not been amplified by our knowledge of the great extremes of variation in the ages that boys and girls enter their growth spurt and enter puberty. Junior high schools were designed for children in three "grades" of school: 7th, 8th, and 9th. The grades were postulated on age and not on size, strength, or stage of puberty. They have resulted inadvertently in classifying together boys and girls at the age when they vary most, within each sex, and between the sexes, and are least suited to a segregated social existence. Also, they have divorced them from the reassurances of association with the children like their own recent past selves and older adolescents like whom they will someday become. When a type of school that was designed to cushion the shock of change in scholastic demands has become the focus of the social pressures which were once exerted in senior high school, problems have been multiplied.

## KILLING THE ABILITY TO EXPERIENCE

Young adolescents today are bored. They have received too many slight and superficial communications about almost everything. They have "had" something about almost everything, and the tendency to give predigested easy previews of what will come later acts as a kind of deadening of the ability to experience. Bright children are bored with this repetition, and other children are not stimulated to more effort. During the early adolescent years children are now developing one strong definite purpose, to get it over with—school, or college, or living at home—and get the real autonomy and independence that is now only spuriously theirs, as mother drives a 14 year old boy and his "date" to the movies.

The appropriate experiences of the early teens are pair friendship with members of their own sex, a just-emerging recognition that the other sex can after all be interesting, admiration and emulation of adult models, heroes, and ideals (who reincarnate the early childhood sense that the parents and teachers were all-knowing and wise), and an enormous curiosity about the outside world, about their own changing bodily responses and shifting sense of identity. At present all of these are inhibited by the present cultural style of aping of a later stage.

Another set of pressures on this age comes from the present styles of education and social life of smaller children. The dull routine of schools, in which children learn a tenth of what they could, results in blunting the curiosity that might carry them through junior high school. More ambitious kindergarten and elementary school programs, entrance to school based on readiness and not on birthday date, might produce a group of early teenagers with more capacity to be interested in what the junior high school could offer them.

The delimitation of the teens has also produced a decrease in the sense of individual growth; where the onset of puberty for a boy or girl once marked a stage in the individual life cycle, emphasis is placed on grade and age alone. Just as we keep children born a day too late out of school for a year, doing an injustice comparable to some of our worst forms of ethnic discrimination, so the fine nuances of individual growth and change are obscured by the magic of the 13th birthday. Assurance that one will be a "teenager" for seven whole years is like being handed life on a silver platter at 13. It is an intolerable tyranny at 19 when—grown, subject to the draft, married, and a parent—the drinking laws and car insurance rules treat one as a child.

The crying out against conformity which has been such a prominent feature of post World War II years is partly a response to this kind of stylization of a whole decade of life in which the most dramatic changes occur as if it were in fact, one single decade, the sections separated by junior high school, senior high school, and college, with the overall style still that of a teenager. "She's a typical teenager," says the older sister. "She might have come right out of television." And indeed she did.

There are further complications. The children of today mature earlier and grow taller than their parents. These coupled with clothes which thirteen year-olds share with nineteen-year-olds, make them seem bigger, older, more able to handle adult activities. The parent compares his son with his own image of himself as a boy. His junior high school son looks like a college student to him; often without consciously recognizing his own feeling, he treats him as older than he is.

Furthermore, through the mass media, adolescents who know about adolescence, consider themselves as *teenagers* and include in their self picture the research that is done on their age group. Just as adult educators have tended to take behavior that was found to be average, and transform the average into the norm, and therefore the desirable, so every bit of uproar over teenage characteristics helps form their self-image. By locating most of the behavior which is appropriate to the late teens in the early teens, we have increased this quality of acting out a kind of behavior which has no emotional or intellectual basis.

It is true that the greatest tragedy of our present day adolescents are the millions that are condemned by social circumstances to learn very little at school, and to live a life in which their potentialities are practically unrealized. This great wasting of youth is due to the present inability to manage cities, deploy resources, and deal with economic and ethnic minorities. The specific smaller tragedies of our present cultural style for the junior high school age are dropouts in high school, after high school and college, too early marriage, too early parenthood, under-achievement for a third of our young people.

## WHAT ABOUT THE FUTURE?

Corrective measures are on the horizon: far better early childhood education, including the permission to parents to teach their own children what they know; school admissions as a result of readiness not birthday month: more differentiation by special interests within junior high schools; more association of junior high school students with younger and older students; consciously diversified summer experiences; and not least important but with possibilities for great good and great harm, the increasing strength of the organizations for junior high school teachers, principals, and curriculum specialists. If this increasing organizational strength of a field that has always been treated as somehow transitional and with very little sense of special status and identity is used to increase sensitivity to the problems of the junior high school students, great changes for good may be expected. But it might work the other way. We have imprisoned our adolescents within a category, teenager, and our early adolescents with all the striking differences and discrepancies within a category—junior high school student. To date the junior high school teacher has been less categorized, more transitional, just out of elementary school or just moving in to senior high school styles of teaching. If the organizing of junior high school administrators, teachers, curricular specialists, is spelled with a capital, and results in their being frozen in a single style, this may intensify the way in which all junior high school students are treated alike, regardless of their levels of physical, emotional, and intellectual maturity. This would be a loss rather than a gain. Junior high school students are more unlike each other than they have ever been before or ever will be again in the course of their lives. If a lively sum of these differences can be maintained and strengthened among those who plan for them and teach them—the whole school system, and the adolescents of the coming generation will be the gainers.

GORDON W. ALLPORT

# 47. CRISES IN NORMAL PERSONALITY DEVELOPMENT

There is one trick every teacher knows. When trapped in a state of ignorance, throw the question back to the class. Without suspecting the teacher's predicament, bright students will often rescue you.

This is the strategy I employed to learn something about "crises in normal

Reprinted from *Teachers College Record,* Vol. 66, No. 3 (December 1964), 235–41. by permission of the publisher.

personality development." I passed along the assignment to my class of 100 captive undergraduates, and they obligingly provided me, through their own autobiographical writing, with insights that I shall share with you. (Parenthetically, let me say that in my opinion no teacher or counselor has the right to require intimate autobiographical documents from students. Yet when given a completely free choice, the large majority will choose to write in the autobiographical vein. For the few who would find the experience too threatening, it should not be prescribed.)

I asked the hundred students, mostly sophomores and juniors, four questions, and found the results here indicated:

### The Influence of Teachers

1. Approximately how many different teachers at school and college have you had up to the present stage of your education?

4632

*Percentage reported as having various degrees of influence*

2. How many had a very strong or powerful influence on your development (intellectual or personal)?

8.50

3. How many others would you say had a reasonably strong, well-remembered influence?

14.80

4. How many do you remember only vaguely, or who seem to have had no substantial influence on your development?

76.70

—————

100.00

We are immediately struck by the fact that more than three-quarters of the teachers are remembered only vaguely, and are credited with no appreciable influence, whether intellectual or personal. As teachers we all know the shock of discovering how little impact we have had. A former student of mine brightened my day by remarking, "Years ago I took a course with you, but all I can remember about it is that the textbook had a blue cover." He grinned pleasantly while I shuddered inwardly.

Only about 8 percent of teachers are reported as having a very strong influence, and about 15 percent are credited with a less strong but well-remembered influence.

Another way of stating this finding is to say that the average teacher (assuming all teachers are equally effective) "gets through" to less than a quarter of the class, and exerts a really strong influence on not more than one student in ten.

Asked to tell when and in what way they were influenced the students give us three facts of special interest.

1. About half all their examples deal with experiences of intellectual awakening. For example,

She encouraged me to read poetry and drama beyond the class assignment.

In chemistry the instructor asked us why bubbles appeared overnight in a water glass. When we said we had never wondered about that, he told us that everyone must question even the most common and seemingly trivial things.

And about half of the examples deal with personal development:

She made me see that others did not judge me as harshly as I was judging myself.

He had so much warmth and humanity that I wanted to be like him.

She seemed tough and disagreeable, but was so kind and helpful to me that I realized I must think twice before passing judgment on anyone.

2. A second insight based on the large array of illustrative incidents reveals the remarkably casual nature of the influence. In hardly any case could the teacher or counselor have known that what he was saying at a given moment would make a lasting impression on the growing mind and character of the student. Elsewhere I have argued that in teaching values and attitudes it is not the deliberately adopted curriculum that is effective. It is rather the *obiter dicta,* the parenthetical remark, the "little true things," and above all the example of the teacher that count (Allport, 1961). And what holds for teachers no doubt holds for the counselor too.

3. Finally, and most relevant to our topic, is the finding that in elementary school there are few remembered influences of special strength. Apparently development is gradual at this time, and the teacher does not often bring a sudden and traumatic experience of "dawn" to the pupil. Only 12 percent report any strong or even appreciable teacher-influence in elementary school. Fully 88 percent of the reports date the occurrences in high school (58 percent) or in college (30 percent, with the college years still incomplete).

And so it is in middle and late adolescence where the role of the teacher is most vivid to the student. It is in this period, according to Erikson (1950), that the identity crisis is in the ascendance. The young person seems to be moving from past childhood into present adulthood in a jerky manner. Development is not continuous like a hill; rather it is episodic like a flight of stairs. It is this episodic or crisis character of development that brings both challenge and opportunity to the guidance officer.

### DEFINING "CRISIS"

What precisely is a "crisis"? It is a situation of emotional and mental stress requiring significant alterations of outlook within a short period of time. These alterations of outlook frequently involve changes in the structure of personality. The resulting changes may be progressive in the life or they may be regressive. By definition a person in crisis cannot stand still; that is, he cannot redact his present traumatic experience into familiar and routine categories, or employ simple habitual modes of adjustment. He must either separate himself further from childhood and move toward adulthood; or else move backward to earlier levels of adjustment which may mean becoming disorganized, dropping out of school, escaping from the field, developing hostilities and defenses, and in general becoming a thorn in the flesh of the teacher, the parent, the counselor, the dean, and occasionally the police.

Sometimes following a crisis the adolescent will become stabilized anew after four or five weeks of severe disorganization; but in many cases the trauma retards development for a year or more, and may even leave a life-long scar.

### THE PHENOMENOLOGY OF CRISIS

Turning now to my data, drawn from college undergraduates, we ask first about the phenomenology of crisis. What does it "feel" like to the student? Common is a sense of numbness and apathy. Upon entering college the youth finds fewer strict role prescriptions than at home. He is no longer tied to his domestic filial role, to the highly structured routine of high school, to his siblings, to his church connections, to his teenage subcultures. He has left his possessions behind: his stamp collection, his television, his girlfriends, his boy friends. All his familiar roles are in suspension. As one student writes,

> The complete freedom of college is itself a crisis. For the first time I live in close contact with people who are not members of my family. They don't even resemble people I have known before. They have different opinions, different origins, and different emotions. I feel numbed by it all.

Interestingly enough, this sense of hollowness does not necessarily have its maximum effect during the freshman year. The excitement of new scenes, and especially frequent correspondence with, and visits back to, the home-town, keep the silver cord intact. The student feels that he should prove to his parents, teachers, and friends that he can master the college environment and thus please them and win their approval as he has done in the past. The impending crisis has not yet overwhelmed him (or her—for what I am saying is as true for college girls as for boys).

It is the sophomore year that seems (from my data) to be the year of crisis *par excellence*. Suddenly it becomes no longer tolerable to live one's life for the edification of people "back home." The time has come for the child of the past to be separated once and for all from the adult of the present. Here are typical phenomenological statements of this stage of the crisis:

> I feel I have been dragged into something against my will.
> I feel like a rat in a maze.
> I want to be a law unto myself, but cannot.
> It seems suddenly that the decisions I make must be valid for the rest of my life.

To shake off parental norms and values seems to me the most important thing I must do.

The life of the past and the life of the future seem suddenly to be at cross purposes. There is often an intolerable feeling of suspended animation. Recrystallization is not yet possible. The youth is waiting still to make a choice of careers, a suitable marriage, and to find an integrative philosophy of life which his diverse college courses are too discordant to supply.

It is small wonder that apathy and a paralysis of will often occur. But apathy is only a mask for anxiety. The whole framework of life is disturbed. Whereas the majority of students contrive gradually to build a new framework in spite of, or perhaps because of, the goads of anxiety, yet a large minority cannot cope with the situation unaided.

From my data I would estimate that three-quarters are able to take the progressive road in creating their new frame of existence. About one-quarter cannot immediately do so. Proof of this point is that the dropout rate during undergraduate years is surprisingly high—over 20 percent at Harvard, about three-quarters of the cases representing voluntary withdrawals (Blaine and McArthur, 1962).

The dropouts present a special problem of guidance. Blaine and McArthur (1962) write:

> The drop-outs as a group ultimately do quite well if properly handled. We attempt to establish a relationship, however brief or tenuous, with these students, not so much to prevent their leaving school, but rather in the hope of giving them some insight into the determinants of their difficulties so that their dropping out can be ultimately converted into a meaningful constructive experience instead of mere failure.

After a year or two of constructive work elsewhere the majority of voluntary dropouts return to college and graduate. But they could not have met their crisis by remaining in the environment that was the context of their conflict.

The regressive road is surprisingly common. Among eventual dropouts, but also among other students, we find such self-destroying behavior as quitting classes, a compulsion to do trivial things, playing bridge until 4 A.M., drinking bouts, feelings of unreality, fugues, and general debauchery. The candid documents received startle me a bit by the extent of plain juvenile delinquency among my innocent-appearing students.

> One student, finding himself unable to handle his conflicts over choice of career and over friction with his roommate, indulged in plagiarism on a term paper in such a way that he would be caught and forcibly separated from college. In this case a wise instructor, catching him in the transgression, turned the occasion into constructive counseling, forgave the deed, and put the lad onto the progressive rather than regressive road.

Here I venture a theoretical digression. The problem, as I see it, is one of interiorizing motivation. To put it in a student's words,

I am fed up with having everybody else cheer me on. I want to work to please myself rather than others, but I don't know how to do it.

This plaintive statement points to a serious dilemma in our educational process. In school the child is rewarded and punished by good grades and bad grades. Even in college A's and B's are pats on the back, D's and E's are punishments. To gain love the student must read books and toe the academic line. Finally he obtains his degree (which is a symbol of academic love) and is freed from this external form of motivation. What then happens? Well, we know that a shockingly high percentage of college graduates rarely or never read another book after receiving their bachelor's degree. Why should they? Their love now comes from their employer, their wife, their children, not from the approval of parents and teachers. For them intellectual curiosity never became a motive in its own right. External rewards are appropriate props in early childhood. But we educators, being limited by current inadequate theories of learning, do not know how to help the student free himself from the props of reward and develop a functionally autonomous zeal for learning. With our slavish dependence on "reinforcement theory" I think it surprising that we arouse as much internal motivation as we do. In any event we cannot be proud of the many educational cripples who, lacking the routine incentive of college, sink into intellectual apathy.

### CRISIS AREAS

The counselor, of course, cannot wait for better theories of learning. He is confronted here and now with crises in the concrete. Four areas of conflict, judging from my data, are especially common.

*Intellectual Crises.* First there are students whose problem is one of intellectual malplacement. Among my cases a large number report that in primary and secondary school they were too bright for their class. The penalty is one of boredom lasting into college work which they still do not find challenging enough for their abilities. At the same time, double promotions in elementary and high school are not a solution. To be placed with older children often creates social difficulties far more serious than boredom. In fact the evil consequences reported from double promotion are so numerous that we should challenge this particular solution of the bright child's dilemma.

The opposite type of intellectual crises is also common. It is the deep disturbance that often results in college from intensified competition. It is statistically impossible for most students to maintain the same relative superiority in college that they enjoyed in high school. Although this fact does not trouble the majority, it is a critical experience for those who depend on scholarship aid or who frame their self-image almost entirely in terms of scholarly preeminence. They are suffering a severe narcissistic wound.

*Specific Inferiorities.* A second area of crisis is the old familiar "inferiority complex." Besides the sense of intellectual inferiority just described, we encounter deep disturbance due to physical handicaps or to plain physical appearance, with resulting shyness, loneliness, and misery. To be poor at athletics creates a crisis for males, probably more acute in high school than in college. To be a member of a minority group likewise creates an inevitable crisis somewhere along the line. Here again I suspect the major adjustments and defenses are prepared before the college age. Occasionally the inferiority concerns guilt due to moral lapses. One student is still haunted by her dishonesty which enabled her to pass a certain course three years ago. She has felt miserable ever since about this critical experience, and badly needs a means of expiation.

In this connection we may speak of religious crises. Although they are uncommon in my sample, Havens (1963) estimates that at any given time 12 percent of college students have a critical concern, and sometimes acute crises, due to their religious conflicts. I suspect the concern is even more widespread, but since it pertains to one's whole ground of being it is seldom configurated as a specific crisis at a given moment of time.

Another area, seldom mentioned but surely important, is the ideological crisis of modern society as a whole. Youth is inevitably worried, as are adults, by our uncertain future. Elsewhere I (Gillespie and Allport, 1955) have discussed the withdrawal of American youth from the social and political context of their lives. Both the earlier and present data show an almost exclusive concern among American youth with their own lives. Compared with autobiographies of youth in other cultures, the American documents are far more self-centered, more privatistic. They are too baffled to articulate their distress, and so take refuge in their private concerns.

*Sex Conflicts.* Needless to say our candid discussions of crises frequently, in fact usually, report acute sex conflicts. Extremely common are breakups in boy-girl relationships which are usually taken as a disaster only slightly less fatal than the end of the world. Such breakups are so recently experienced that college students do not realize that they will, in spite of their present feelings, eventually make a good recovery.

We should face the fact that at least in the early years of college life crises in the sexual sphere are for the most part frankly genital in their reference. The biological drive is so powerful that the youth is concerned with it almost by itself. Its integration into mature love, into marriage, into career plans, into an embracing philosophy of life, exceeds his present capacity. He is likely to think that genitality by itself is maturity. Sexual gratification is frankly the aim, often with devastating consequences. At this stage of development the students have much to say about sex, and little to say about mature love.

*Family Conflicts.* I have left until last the most pervasive area of conflict and crisis. I am referring of course to the situation that exists between every adolescent and his parents. It is not enough to say that adolescent rebellion against the parents is the rule. Of course it is, but my documents show that the whole history of the relationships from the time of earliest memories is important. Almost any irregularity in normal family life is felt bitterly, and may trouble a student even into adulthood. A mother who is neglectful or self-centered, or perhaps overpossessive and neurotic, leaves traumatic traces in the child's life. A father who is ineffectual and weak, or cruel, or absent (if only for wartime service), leaves the child with a lasting feeling of protest. Broken homes are, of course, a major dislocation for the child. The documents have convinced me that every child needs two parents. (A student points out to me that God had reached the same conclusion at an earlier date.)

One document of unusual maturity notes that many college students seem to need their parents as scapegoats. They find it comfortable to blame parents for their own shortcomings. Perceiving that their parents are not all-powerful, all-wise, and all-perfect, they can say, "Well, no wonder I am having a hard time growing up; they didn't raise me right." Thus the adolescent can soak himself in self-pity, not yet mature enough to relate his restricted image of his parents to the totality of human nature; not yet ready to appreciate the fact that his parents, considering human limitations, may have done a good job. Even if the job was not especially good, the adolescent seems not yet able to appreciate the parents' good intentions as an important value in its own right. From talking with many parents I hazard the hypothesis that normally it is not until the age of 23 that a child encounters his parents on a mature, adult-to-adult basis.

## A THEORETICAL OBSERVATION

This brief account of crises emanating from the parent-child relationship leads me to a final point. My students were required to discuss their crises from the point of view of personality theory. They were free to employ any of the theories they were studying in my course. Most of them took Freud. (I may add that the reason was not because Freud was their instructor's favorite author.)

Now my observation is this: their Freudian interpretations seemed to fit well if and when the family situation in early life was disturbed. When the father was absent or ineffectual, when the mother was notably aggressive, when there was deliberate sex stimulation within the family—in such cases it seems that the Oedipal formula is a good fit, together with all its theoretical accouterments of identification, superego conflict, defense mechanisms, castration threats, and all the rest.

When, on the other hand, the family life is reasonably normal and secure, a Freudian conceptualization seems forced and artificial. If we say, by way of rough estimate, that 60 percent of the students try a Freudian conceptualization of their own cases, about 10 percent turn out to be wholly convincing and theoretically appropriate. The remaining 50 percent appear to be somehow contrived and badly strained.

I am wondering whether the same ratio might be applicable to cases that come to counselors. If a counselor or a therapist approaches every client or patient with the preconceived belief that his life must fit a Freudian frame of conceptualization, he may win in a minority of the cases, but lose in the majority.

Even where a Freudian approach is clearly justified, exclusive adherence to it may distract the counselor from many significant developments within the life—for example, from the present functional significance of religious and esthetic values, from the competence and interests that extend beyond the neurotic core, from the client's conscious plans for the future, and from his "will to meaning," and existential concern with life as a whole.

Every person concerned with guidance, or for that matter with teaching, needs as background some general theory of the nature of human personality (Allport, 1962). Our tendency, I fear, is to draw our theories from the realm of illness and deviance. It is somehow tempting to apply psychiatric rubrics to all personalities, for psychiatric rubrics are vivid, incisive, dramatic, and easy. Our conceptual banners bear such sloganized concepts as Oedipal complex, character disorder, identity diffusion, schizoid, acting out, and maybe an array of dimensions drawn from the Minnesota Multiphasic Personality Inventory. All such concepts, of course, have their proper place. But personality theory for guidance and teaching needs also to be woven of less lurid fabrics.

Youth, whatever neurotic threads may lie in his nature, is busy with his realistic perceptions, with his gradual learning and quiet coping, with the slow extension of selfhood, with noncritical failures and successes, with developing a generic conscience and a personal style of life. Even in the throes of crisis he seeks in undramatic ways to consolidate his gains and continue on the path of becoming. A theory of personality adequate to undergird the art of guidance will keep such nondramatic facts in mind. Crises in normal personality development are important, but so too is the slow growth of each youth's unique style of life.

## REFERENCES

ALLPORT, GORDON W., Psychological models for guidance, *Harvard Educational Review*, 1962:32, 373–81.

——, *Patterns and growth in personality.* New York: Holt, Rinehart and Winston, 1961.

BLAINE, G. B., and C. C. MCARTHUR, *Emotional problems of the student*. New York: Appleton-Century-Crofts, 1961.

ERIKSON, E. H., *Childhood and society*. New York: Norton, 1950.

GILLESPIE, J. M., and G. W. ALLPORT, *Youth's outlook on the future*. Garden City, N.Y.: Doubleday, 1955.

HAVENS, J., A study of the religious conflict in college students, *Journal for the Scientific Study of Religion*, 1963:3, 52–69.

THOMAS J. FLEMING

# 48.   THE SUPERIOR PERSON

At the turn of the century when Horatio Alger was in bloom, a man succeeded with pluck and luck, hard work and brains. But over the decades,
this image of the adventurous entrepreneur got smeared and pommeled.
Horatio Alger became the robber baron, the sweatshop Simon Legree.
Today, instead of the rugged individualist, the successful man is the affable,
democratic member of an executive team. The same democratic leveling has
been at work in the family and in politics. The Father of the past has been
replaced by the companionable Dad. The political leader today takes polls
and strives to tell the people what they are already thinking.

Progress? In many ways, yes. But a number of scientists have become
concerned that our passion for democracy and equality may be destroying
one of our invisible but most valuable resources: our superior persons. The
word *superior* is explosive. In an era when debunking has become a mass
art, the universal instinct is to dismiss superiority and get to work with
suitable invective and democratic fervor to destroy it. But these scientists
have proved that superior people exist. They even suggest that the way a
nation uses—or fails to use—its superior persons can be the difference
between its survival and annihilation. There is also evidence that superior
persons lead different lives on every level—socially, personally, sexually—
lives we would all live if we could overcome our limitations.

Psychiatrists have been among the leaders in this remarkable exploration.
Intrigued by the fact that people are different, they ask themselves why one

Reprinted from *Cosmopolitan* (November 1964), pp. 60–64, by permission of
the author.

person does a job in a literal, unimaginative way—grudging every hour of work—and another brims with energy and new ideas. Other psychologists, reacting from a Freudian overemphasis on disease—attempting to define all human behavior in terms of neurosis—have taken an interest in attempting to find out what is normal and healthy. One of the leaders in this field is Dr. Abraham H. Maslow of Brandeis University. Dr. Maslow has spent over two decades studying what he sometimes calls "self-actualizing" or "socially dominant" people. As a result of his research, he throws down a challenge which has awesome psychological and social implications. "None of the writers that I have been reading dare to lock horns with the problem which is so unpopular in any democracy: that some people are superior to others in any specific skill or, what is more provocative to the democrat, in general capacity. There is evidence that some people tend to be generally superior, that there are simply superior biological organisms born into this world."

## ARE GENIUSES WEIRDOS?

A confirmation of Dr. Maslow's startling thesis comes from one of the classic experiments of modern psychology, Dr. Louis M. Terman's thirty-five-year study of gifted children. One of the creators of the IQ test, Dr. Terman was among the first to recognize the phenomenon of the gifted child. In 1921, he chose 1,528 of these children (857 males and 671 females) and decided to study them over the entire course of their lives. Even today, the prejudice persists that very intelligent people are weirdos who wind up as Bowery bums or department store clerks. In 1921, the opinion was even more widespread. Terman tested it against scientific reality. The average IQ in his group was 151 (Stanford-Binet) and the range was from 135 to 200. This put them within the highest 1 percent of the school population. Terman examined his group from all points of view and, to his amazement, found they were not only intellectually superior but exceeded the average American in emotional balance and even in physique. Their birth weight was three quarters of a pound above the norm. They learned to walk a month earlier and learned to talk about three-and-a-half months earlier than average children. Puberty and menstruation came earlier. They were healthier in almost every respect. "The combined results," writes Dr. Terman, "provide a striking contrast to the popular stereotype of a child prodigy commonly depicted as a pathetic creature, overserious and undersized, sickly, hollow-chested, stoop-shouldered, clumsy, nervous, bespectacled. There are gifted children who bear some resemblance to this stereotype but the truth is that almost every element in the picture, except the last (the gifted tend to wear eyeglasses more often than the average), is less characteristic of the gifted child than of the mentally average."

Tested for character and emotional stability, the gifted group scored better than average groups at every age from ten to fourteen. Thus, is 1921 when most were only age eleven, the gifted group's researchers concluded "the deviation of gifted children from the generality is in the upward direction for nearly all traits. There is no law of compensation whereby the intellectual superiority of the gifted is offset by inferiorities along nonintellectual lines." They were, in other words, generally superior.

Even more impressive have been the follow-up studies which have tracked these gifted children into middle age. Some 86 percent were in the professions, the semiprofessions or higher positions in business. Their average income was some two thousand dollars ahead of the rest of the country. They had lower divorce rates, showed better general adjustment on psychological tests and their health continued to be superior. Eighty-three percent of the men and 86 percent of the women rated their marriages as happier than average. Seventy-seven of them are listed in *American Men of Science* and thirty-three in *Who's Who in America*. All this in their mid-forties when the majority of them had not yet reached the peaks of their careers.

### LIFE IS ACHIEVEMENT

Perhaps the most revealing item in the report, *The Gifted Group at Mid-Life,* is their answer to this question: "From your point of view, what constitutes success in life?" At the top of the list, they put "realization of goals, vocational satisfaction, a sense of achievement." This is what Dr. Maslow has found again and again in his studies of self-actualizing people. It also corresponds rather closely with the findings of David C. McClelland, professor of psychology and chairman of the staff of the Center for Research in Personality at Harvard University. In his book, *The Achieving Society,* Dr. McClelland isolates a factor which he calls "*n* achievement." This, in McClelland's opinion, is what makes not merely individuals, but whole societies, move forward.

Because these people are so important, we must answer the question of how best to deal with them in our society so that they can make maximum contributions. Maslow likes to insist that these people are also guideposts, symbols, toward which we should all strive. They are basically healthy. Their needs for safety, a sense of belonging, love, respect and self-esteem have been satisfied so that they are motivated primarily by a desire to fulfill their potentials, to use their capacities and talents. With this often comes a sense of mission, a feeling of almost mystical unity with their fellows and a desire to serve them. Here is a list of what Dr. Maslow calls "their clinically observed characteristics."

1. Superior perception of reality.
2. Increased acceptance of self, of others and of nature.
3. Increased spontaneity.
4. Increase in problem centering.

5. Increased detachment and desire for privacy.
6. Increased autonomy and resistance to enculturation.
7. Greater freshness and richness of emotional reaction.
8. More frequent peak experiences.
9. Increased identification with the human species.
10. Changed (the clinician would say improved) interpersonal relations.
11. More democratic character structure.
12. Greatly increased creativeness.
13. Own highly individual system of values.

A New York writer named Charles Sopkin recently published a book called *Money Talks* in which eleven new self-made millionaires discuss themselves, their money and their rise in the business world. The number of ways in which these people correspond to Maslow's self-actualizing persons is amazing. Increased acceptance of self? Here is Wallace Johnson, one of the founders of Holiday Inns: "One of the great reasons that people fail to succeed is because they do not know themselves and they are not honest with themselves." Superior physical ability? Here is J. J. Mascuch, founder and president of Breeze Corporations and an inventor with one hundred and fifty patents: "I'm approaching seventy years of age and I still can do things that I did when I was thirty. Calisthenics; I actually can walk a tightrope today at my age. Ice skate; ski; I am a good horseman." Creativeness? Here is William P. Lear, Sr., who at age sixty sold his electronics company to begin a new career manufacturing jet planes. "One time when I was busted flat I became frantic. But then I said to myself, 'Wait a minute. Calm down. All you have to do is figure out something that the world needs and make it.' I figured that the world needed an all-wave radio set that could be manufactured at a low price. Applying myself day and night for two weeks resulted in perfecting an idea that I sold for a substantial amount."

Detachment? "If I had to select one trait which would explain how these men became successful," Sopkin says, "I would select their fantastic ability to concentrate on the problem in front of them. Phones can be ringing, the office can be going crazy all around them, but every bit of their conscious attention will be focused on the business deal they are discussing."

All of these people have incredible energy. They work a seven-day week and, Sopkin says, "Ten hours a day is minimum." Two other traits stand out, a fantastic love of their work down to the smallest detail, and a terrific drive for achievement which usually began early in life. Philip J. Sagona, the young president of Lancôme, Inc., says, "I was always a bad loser. Even now I hate to lose. I like to think I'm always a winner which was why I did many things with greater practice than the average person. Success—and money—were not the important things to me. I wanted an achievement. I wanted to be the outstanding athlete, to have the highest marks."

But from another point of view, the most important thing about Sopkin's millionaires is the way they have made their money. Most did it by going into business for themselves. Here we return to one of Dr. Maslow's major concerns: In our democratic society we do not really know how to utilize these superior people. The bigger the company, the less room it tends to give to individuality, creativity, self-actualization. This experience runs like a lament through all the personal stories in *Money Talks*. And these are superior people who have made it. Too often, if they lack social opportunities, superior people can spend their lives as unhappy clerks. Their very superiority can cause them to become victims instead of leaders.

Victor B. Serebriakoff, international secretary of Mensa, a society for high IQs, is an example. Serebriakoff grew up in a poor, working-class family in England and became a machine operator in a woodworking factory. "I was neither better nor worse than the run of the workers, but I had ideas on better ways to do the job," he says. But fellow workers laughed at his ideas and the foreman told him to do the job the way it had always been done.

### SCORE BROKE THE SCALE

World War II rescued Serebriakoff. The British Army gave him an IQ test and, when his score went right off the scale, they made him the head of a school in Yorkshire. Mensa, which he joined in 1948, was founded in 1945 out of the conviction that many persons of exceptional intellect "feel cut off, frustrated and isolated," as Serebriakoff did in his young manhood. To judge from the eagerness with which high IQs have been joining Mensa in the United States, Serebriakoff is right.

Unfortunately Mensa has as yet no plans or programs to better utilize our superior people. This is what Maslow and his associates feel we must find. "No society can be really efficient unless its superior persons are preferred and elected by the other people," Dr. Maslow says. "This whole delicate problem is ducked by democrats. Our society has never squarely faced the question of the objective superiority of some people and the inferiority of others. In fact, people who are superior at anything tend to feel guilty about it and apologetic. In our democratic society, superiority is generally masked. Nobody runs around saying how superior he is; democrats are a tribe in which there are no chiefs, only Indians. This can make it very difficult for the superior person to function."

With his better perception of reality, greater energy and creativity, the superior person knows the answer to problems long before his average associates. If he is working in a company run by an authoritarian boss who simply gives orders and wants them obeyed with no questions asked, he will be desperately unhappy. But the superior person will be almost equally frustrated under so-called enlightened management because here he is expected to function as part of a team and is supposed to arrive at decisions group-wise. Even when he is the boss, he is not supposed to give orders in the old-fashioned sense. He is supposed to "work together" with his subordinates toward a good solution to a problem. But as Maslow points out, the superior boss "is apt to get restless and irritated. Keeping his mouth shut can be physical torture. The less intelligent subordinates are also affected adversely. Why should they sweat for days on a particular problem when they know that the superior can see the solution in three minutes? Their tendency is to become passive and resentful."

Maslow recommends a less dogmatic approach to management. "The best way to handle the problem of the very superior boss might be to try to analyze what makes the boss superior and how he functions best without any obeisance at all to democratic dogma. A functional boss is a person who is more efficient, capable, more talented than the follower. The optimum arrangement of an industrial organization would be one that provided this functional boss with an environment best suited to the advancement of the organization's aims. The situation should be synergic. *Synergy* refers to a situation so arranged that each person involved, by pursuing his own selfish aims, aids the other people involved and the institution itself. For an industrial situation to be synergic, the special qualities of the superior boss must be actually encouraged."

## CHURCHILLIAN SOPORIFIC

The superior person is happiest, Maslow points out, when he has maximum control of his situation. He cites Winston Churchill who, during the early days of World War II, was First Lord of the Admiralty and had only limited control over British military policy. As a result, he was in a constant state of anxiety. When he became Prime Minister, with Britain facing imminent annihilation from Germany, he paradoxically wrote, "I was conscious of a profound sense of relief. At last I had authority to give directions over the whole scene. . . . I slept soundly and had no need for cheering dreams. Facts are better than dreams."

## "PEOPLE NEED TO BE PUNISHED"

Maslow admits that in certain industrial situations the participative I'm-just-one-of-the-boys type boss may be the best choice. But in many other areas—commanding a ship at sea, running an Army, or the U.S. Presidency—we should actively seek out and encourage the decisive, superior boss. "The superior, self-actualizing leader may at certain points clash with democratic dogma," Dr. Maslow says, "but in another sense he has a democratic character structure. Because his ego has few, if any, deficiency needs, he is able to take positive pleasure in the achievement of others around him and he goes out of his way to give his associates as much autonomy as he can within the arena of his own functioning."

The superior person who has achieved self-actualization is thus more likely to form and lead a Theory Y, rather than a Theory X organization. These terms are derived from a book, *The Human Side of Enterprise,* by Douglas McGregor, professor of industrial management at MIT. Published in 1960, the book has created a tremendous stir throughout American business. McGregor's Theory X is the conventional management approach which, he says, springs from certain assumptions about human beings in the work situation—assumptions that are frozen in our culture. According to McGregor these assumptions are: (1) Human beings are inherently lazy and will shun work if they can. (2) People must be directed, controlled and motivated by fear of punishment or deprivation to impel them to work as the company requires. (3) The average person prefers to be directed, wishes to avoid responsibility, has little ambition and wants security above all.

McGregor claims these assumptions have been completely disproved by objective research in the psychological and social sciences. From the scientific facts, he assembles the following assumptions which he calls Theory Y: (1) The expenditure of physical and mental effort in work is as natural as play or rest. (2) External control and the threat of punishment are not the only means of inducing people to work toward organizational goals. Man will exercise self-direction and self-control in the service of objectives to which he is committed. (3) Commitment to objectives is a function of the rewards associated with their achievement. (4) The average human being learns, under proper conditions, not only to accept but also to seek responsibility. (5) The capacity for exercising a relatively high degree of imagination, ingenuity and creativity in solving organizational problems is widely, not narrowly, distributed in the population. (6) Under conditions of modern industrial life, the intellectual potentialities of the average human being are only partially utilized.

More than a little of Theory Y rests upon the formulation of human needs developed by Dr. Maslow. For him, man is a creature of ever-expanding wants. Once his basic needs have been satisfied, others take their place, starting with basic biological requirements and proceeding through a series of levels, each more intangible than the preceding one. In this hierarchy of needs, Maslow has identified five levels: (1) Physiological needs—food, water, air, shelter, rest, exercise. (2) Safety needs—freedom from fear of deprivation, danger and threat. (3) Social needs—men like to group together for many purposes both on the job and off. They need to associate, to belong, to accept, to be accepted. (4) Ego needs—reputation, self-respect, self-esteem. Men need respect, recognition, status. (5) Self-actualization needs—the realization of individual potential, the liberation of creative talents, the widest possible use of abilities and aptitudes. In short, personal fulfillment.

## PLAY UP HUMAN DIGNITY

Maslow estimates that in American society the average citizen satisfies about 85 percent of his physiological needs, 70 percent of his safety needs, 50 percent of his social needs, 40 percent of his ego needs, but only 10 percent of his self-actualization needs. If this record could be improved, vast numbers of us, even if we are not endowed with extraordinarily high IQs, could at least move toward the ideal model of the self-actualizing superior person.

Is such a move possible? Electronics manufacturer Andrew Kay and his fellow executives at Non-Linear Systems Inc., Del Mar, California, decided to find out. They went to Maslow and asked him what percentage of the population were, in his estimate, incapable of operating according to Theory Y. As a rough guess, Maslow estimated that about 30 percent were not mature enough to handle the freedom and responsibility.

"This seemed like pretty good odds to us," says Arthur H. Kuriloff, vice president for management performance and development. "So we went ahead and turned Non-Linear into a Theory Y operation." To guarantee fulfillment of physiological needs, they established a minimum wage of one hundred dollars a week. Simultaneously they did away with time clocks because they were "an offense to human dignity and imply mistrust of people." They also abandoned the practice of docking employees for illness.

To provide satisfaction of safety needs, they aimed at achieving a calm, unharried atmosphere. "We try, as a company, to maintain steady employment," Kuriloff says. "When sales are low, we stockpile finished products. When orders come pouring in we do not hire at an accelerated pace. We prefer to ask our customers to bear with us for a little longer delivery than usual. In this way we avoid those cyclical hiring and firing peaks that cause employees to feel insecure and uncertain about their jobs." For satisfaction of social needs, they used the small group approach wherever possible. They discarded assembly lines and reorganized their workers into seven-man teams, each headed by a competent technician whom they called an assistant assembly manager. Under his tutelage the groups were asked to build complete instruments.

"The group method," Kuriloff says, "is an ideal way to provide for the ego needs. Within the group a man is recognized for his excellences. He attains status by virtue of his demonstrated abilities. Since everyone has skills of one kind or another, each member of the group is deferred to in the area of his special competence. Each man can speak up and be listened to. He develops pride both in his product and in the company as he perfects his skills."

The approach also pays off on the level of self-actualization. Workers are constantly stimulated to improve old skills and develop new ones. "Almost all our training courses are voluntary," Mr. Kuriloff says. "Sometimes we have a senior engineer teaching a class of young engineers logic circuitry theory at night, an electronics technician teaching basic electricity to a group of men and women assemblers during the lunch period, and another group learning the elements of selling from an outside consultant in the morning."

How are they doing? When Non-Linear began the experiment three years ago, they had two hundred and twenty-five employees. Today they have three hundred and fifty. Their absentee rate is less than half the prevailing rate in similar businesses in their community. Complaints about the quality of their products have decreased by 70 percent. Their man-hour productivity has risen 30 percent. They have multiplied their product line fourfold. "We think," Mr. Kuriloff says, "that this approach is a return to the rugged, inner-directed qualities that drove our forefathers to hew civilization out of the wilderness. We have made mistakes along the way, of course, but we have corrected them. The calculated democratization of our enterprise represents, we think, an organic situation in which individual growth is encouraged and stimulated and, in turn, contributes to the continued growth of the enterprise as a whole."

The Non-Linear experiment is important not only because it suggests the possibility of a new era in American business. It also demonstrates in living, human terms how gifted, self-actualizing persons, such as president Andrew Kay, relate to those less gifted. We have pointed out that the superior person has an ability to reach conclusions and make decisions at a much faster rate than the average person. This decisiveness can be very attractive to insecure people and, if it is the only trait by which we judge the presence of superior talents, we can easily go astray. "Pseudo-superior, paranoid leaders like Hitler or Stalin or McCarthy often exhibit a decisiveness which relieves their followers of all anxiety," Dr. Maslow says. "But the good boss is psychologically healthy. He is healthy enough to make and impose unpopular decisions if that is what the situation demands. He is also healthy enough to relinquish control and develop the capacities of his subordinates if the situation permits such an approach."

Another pseudo-superior man has been delineated by psychologist Dr. Sidney Blau of New York. He is the so-called superman, the brainy, poised, overhandsome character who dominates our movies, television and sports. The superman, in Blau's experience, is all facade. He lives a haunted inner life. "He may be able to love five women in one night, but he never achieves genuine satisfaction with any of them. Conquering them is just one more prop to his ego. He can't develop a deep relationship. The same psychology dominates his relationships with men. He must *always* win."

## DISINTEGRATING SUPERMEN

And if he loses? "Then you see the little boy inside the superman. The superman is magnificent as long as he wins," Dr. Blau says. "But when things go wrong and his front no longer works, he often disintegrates." To find out if you are dealing with a phony superman or a truly superior person, then, you must see him both as a winner and as a loser.

The personal life of a self-actualizing individual is also significant. In friendships, games, in his life at home with his family, he is a giver, not a taker. In sexual relationships he delights in giving his partner pleasure and at the same time does not hesitate to admit his own wholehearted enjoyment. "These people," Dr. Maslow says, "have a far greater ability to know what they want. There seems to be better communication between their inner, biological selves and their egos. They almost always have specific likes and dislikes in food, clothes, women."

Because most people are much less precise in these areas, Dr. Maslow has, in another context, called these people "socially dominant" types.

A socially dominant role comes naturally to a man. But what happens if the superior, socially dominant person happens to be a woman? The answer is one word: trouble.

In his study of dominance, Dr. Maslow makes a very sharp distinction between feeling and behavior. There are, it would seem, a great number of people who have high dominance *feelings,* but if their social situation does not permit them to *express* these feelings, they may act like low dominance persons, meanwhile seething and writhing internally.

Maslow has noted many contrasting high and low dominance characteristics. The high dominance person tends to be self-confident, socially poised, extroverted, unconventional, relaxed, independent, adventurous. The low dominance person, on the other hand, tends to be shy, neat, self-conscious, more inhibited, introverted, conventional, reliable, modest.

It does not take more than a glance to see that the low dominance traits are the ones commonly held up as an example to women in our culture. Thus even though there are about an equal number of high dominance men and high dominance women, high dominance or superior women are more out of step with our culture than are superior men. "Unless these women can find a man who at least equals or, better, surpasses them in dominance feeling," Dr. Maslow says, "they may have very unhappy sex lives. A rather high percentage of them give up on men and become homosexuals."

The isolation of the superior or high dominance woman has too often been ignored by sexual researchers. Kinsey, for instance, did not take into account the existence of such women. Dr. Maslow once performed a survey with the famous sexual explorer in which he suggested that they select women according to their social dominance ratings. To Kinsey's distress, the resulting figures on virginity, sexual experience, etc., were much different from his published findings. "Low dominance women have much higher rates of virginity than high dominance types. They are also much less likely to cooperate with sexual surveys," Dr. Maslow says. "Kinsey did not take into account that the women who were willing to talk to him included too many high dominance types. These, of course, lead more adventurous sex lives."

Surprisingly, Maslow does not feel that the ideal marriage needs a high dominance man and a low dominance woman. *"Somewhat* higher dominance feeling in the husband is probably better, but ideal lovemaking occurs when you have a really high dominance woman and a high dominance man, genuinely in love. The average high dominance woman prefers straightforward, unsentimental, sometimes even brutal, lovemaking. It must come quickly rather than after a long period of wooing. She wishes to be suddenly swept off her feet, not courted. She wants her favors taken, not asked for. In other words, she must be dominated, forced into subordinate experience."

These superior men and women, Dr. Maslow is convinced, "are an evolutionary breakthrough." They are forerunners, espousing in their personal lives the real meaning of equality between the sexes. "In fifty or a hundred years they will be the majority," Dr. Maslow says. Since there seems to be about the same number of superior men as there are superior women, there are reasonable grounds for expecting them to multiply at about equal rates. "What we are moving toward," Maslow says, "is a genuinely healthy society. These people are the pioneers leading the way. There is no reason why we cannot achieve a world where everyone can satisfy 70, 80, 90 percent of his self-actualizing needs. That's why I think it's so important for us all to accept these superior people, to encourage them to develop their creative potentiality to the utmost. We, or our children, will be the richer for it."

CARL R. ROGERS

# 49. TOWARD A MODERN APPROACH TO VALUES: THE VALUING PROCESS IN THE MATURE PERSON

There is a great deal of concern today with the problem of values. Youth, in almost every country, is deeply uncertain of its value orientation; the values associated with various religions have lost much of their influence; sophisticated individuals in every culture seem unsure and troubled as to the goals they hold in esteem. The reasons are not far to seek. The world culture, in all its aspects, seems increasingly scientific and relativistic, and the rigid, absolute views on values which come to us from the past appear anachronistic. Even more important, perhaps, is the fact that the modern individual is assailed from every angle by divergent and contradictory value claims. It is no longer possible, as it was in the not too distant historical

Reprinted from *Journal of Abnormal and Social Psychology,* 68, No. 2 (1964), 160–67, by permission of the American Psychological Association and the author.

past, to settle comfortably into the value system of one's forebears or one's community and live out one's life without ever examining the nature and the assumptions of that system.

In this situation it is not surprising that value orientations from the past appear to be in a state of disintegration or collapse. Men question whether there are, or can be, any universal values. It is often felt that we may have lost, in our modern world, all possibility of any general or cross-cultural basis for values. One natural result of this uncertainty and confusion is that there is an increasing concern about, interest in, and a searching for, a sound or meaningful value approach which can hold its own in today's world.

I share this general concern. As with other issues the general problem faced by the culture is painfully and specifically evident in the cultural microcosm which is called the therapeutic relationship, which is my sphere of experience.

As a consequence of this experience I should like to attempt a modest theoretical approach to this whole problem. I have observed changes in the approach to values as the individual grows from infancy to adulthood. I observe further changes when, if he is fortunate, he continues to grow toward true psychological maturity. Many of these observations grow out of my experience as therapist, where I have had the mind-stretching opportunity of seeing the ways in which individuals move toward a richer life. From these observations I believe I see some directional threads emerging which might offer a new concept of the valuing process, more tenable in the modern world. I have made a beginning by presenting some of these ideas partially in previous writings (5, 6); I would like now to voice them more clearly and more fully.

## SOME DEFINITIONS

Charles Morris (4) has made some useful distinctions in regard to values. There are "operative values," which are the behaviors of organisms in which they show preference for one object or objective rather than another. The lowly earthworm, selecting the smooth arm of a Y maze rather than the arm which is paved with sandpaper, is giving an indication of an operative value.

There are also "conceived values," the preference of an individual for a symbolized object. "Honesty is the best policy" is such a conceived value.

There is also the term "objective value," to refer to what is objectively preferable, whether or not it is sensed or conceived of as desirable. I will be concerned primarily with operative or conceptualized values.

## INFANT'S WAY OF VALUING

Let me first speak about the infant. The living human being has, at the outset, a clear approach to values. We can infer from studying his behavior that he prefers those experiences which maintain, enhance, or actualize his organism, and rejects those which do not serve this end. Watch him for a bit:

> Hunger is negatively valued. His expression of this often comes through loud and clear.
>
> Food is positively valued. But when he is satisfied, food is negatively valued, and the same milk he responded to so eagerly is now spit out, or the breast which seemed so satisfying is now rejected as he turns his head away from the nipple with an amusing facial expression of disgust and revulsion.
>
> He values security, and the holding and caressing which seem to communicate security.
>
> He values new experience for its own sake, and we observe this in his obvious pleasure in discovering his toes, in his searching movements, in his endless curiosity.
>
> He shows a clear negative valuing of pain, bitter tastes, sudden loud sounds.

All of this is commonplace, but let us look at these facts in terms of what they tell us about the infant's approach to values. It is first of all a flexible, changing, valuing *process*, not a fixed system. He likes food and dislikes the same food. He values security and rest, and rejects it for new experience. What is going on seems best described as an organismic valuing process, in which each element, each moment of what he is experiencing is somehow weighed, and selected or rejected, depending on whether, at that moment, it tends to actualize the organism or not. This complicated weighing of experience is clearly an organismic, not a conscious or symbolic function. These are operative, not conceived values. But this process can nonetheless deal with complex value problems. I would remind you of the experiment in which young infants had spread in front of them a score or more of dishes of natural (that is, unflavored) foods. Over a period of time they clearly tended to value the foods which enhanced their own survival, growth, and development. If for a time a child gorged himself on starches, this would soon be balanced by a protein "binge." If at times he chose a diet deficient in some vitamin, he would later seek out foods rich in this very vitamin. The physiological wisdom of his body guided his behavioral movements, resulting in what we might think of as objectively sound value choices.

Another aspect of the infant's approach to values is that the source or locus of the evaluating process is clearly within himself. Unlike many of us, he *knows* what he likes and dislikes, and the origin of these value choices lies strictly within himself. He is the center of the valuing process, the evidence for his choices being supplied by his own senses. He is not at this point influenced by what his parents think he should prefer, or by what the church says, or by the opinion of the latest "expert" in the field, or by the persuasive talents of an advertising firm. It is from within his own experiencing that his organism is saying in nonverbal terms, "This is good for me." "That is bad for me." "I like this." "I strongly dislike that." He would laugh at our concern over values, if he could understand it.

## CHANGE IN THE VALUING PROCESS

What happens to this efficient, soundly based valuing process? By what sequence of events do we exchange it for the more rigid, uncertain, inefficient approach to values which characterizes most of us as adults? Let me try to state briefly one of the major ways in which I think this happens.

The infant needs love, wants it, tends to behave in ways which will bring a repetition of this wanted experience. But this brings complications. He pulls baby sister's hair, and finds it satisfying to hear her wails and protests. He then hears that he is "a naughty, bad boy," and this may be reinforced by a slap on the hand. He is cut off from affection. As this experience is repeated, and many, many others like it, he gradually learns that what "feels good" is often "bad" in the eyes of significant others. Then the next step occurs, in which he comes to take the same attitude toward himself which these others have taken. Now, as he pulls his sister's hair, he solemnly intones, "Bad, bad boy." He is introjecting the value judgment of another, taking it in as his own. To that degree he loses touch with his own organismic valuing process. He has deserted the wisdom of his organism, giving up the locus of evaluation, and is trying to behave in terms of values set by another, in order to hold love.

Or take another example at an older level. A boy senses, though perhaps not consciously, that he is more loved and prized by his parents when he thinks of being a doctor than when he thinks of being an artist. Gradually he introjects the values attached to being a doctor. He comes to want, above all, to be a doctor. Then in college he is baffled by the fact that he repeatedly fails in chemistry, which is absolutely necessary to becoming a physician, in spite of the fact that the guidance counselor assures him he has the ability to pass the course. Only in counseling interviews does he begin to realize how completely he has lost touch with his organismic reactions, how out of touch he is with his own valuing process.

Perhaps these illustrations will indicate that in an attempt to gain or hold love, approval, esteem, the individual relinquishes the locus of evaluation which was his in infancy, and places it in others. He learns to have a basic *dis*trust for his own experiencing as a guide to his behavior. He learns from others a large number of conceived values, and adopts them as his own, even though they may be widely discrepant from what he is experiencing.

## SOME INTROJECTED PATTERNS

It is in this fashion, I believe, that most of us accumulate the introjected value patterns by which we live. In the fantastically complex culture of today, the patterns we introject as desirable or undesirable come from a variety of sources and are often highly contradictory. Let me list a few of the introjections which are commonly held.

Sexual desires and behaviors are mostly bad. The sources of this construct are many—parents, church, teachers.

Disobedience is bad. Here parents and teachers combine with the military to emphasize this concept. To obey is good. To obey without question is even better.

Making money is the highest good. The sources of this conceived value are too numerous to mention.

Learning an accumulation of scholarly facts is highly desirable. Education is the source.

Communism is utterly bad. Here the government is a major source.

To love thy neighbor is the highest good. This concept comes from the church, perhaps from the parents.

Cooperation and teamwork are preferable to acting alone. Here companions are an important source.

Cheating is clever and desirable. The peer group again is the origin.

Coca-Colas, chewing gum, electric refrigerators, and automobiles are all utterly desirable. From Jamaica to Japan, from Copenhagen to Kowloon, the "Coca-Cola culture" has come to be regarded as the acme of desirability.

This is a small and diversified sample of the myriads of conceived values which individuals often introject, and hold as their own, without ever having considered their inner organismic reactions to these patterns and objects.

## COMMON CHARACTERISTICS OF
## ADULT VALUING

I believe it will be clear from the foregoing that the usual adult—I feel I am speaking for most of us—has an approach to values which has these characteristics:

The majority of his values are introjected from other individuals or groups significant to him, but are regarded by him as his own.

The source or locus of evaluation on most matters lies outside of himself.

The criterion by which his values are set is the degree to which they will cause him to be loved, accepted, or esteemed.

These conceived preferences are either not related at all, or not clearly related, to his own process of experiencing.

Often there is a wide and unrecognized discrepancy between the evidence supplied by his own experience, and these conceived values.

Because these conceptions are not open to testing in experience, he must hold them in a rigid and unchanging fashion. The alternative would be a collapse of his values. Hence his values are "right."

Because they are untestable, there is no ready way of solving contradictions. If he has taken in from the community the conception that money is the *summum bonum* and from the church the conception that love of one's neighbor is the highest value, he has no way of discovering which has more value for *him*. Hence a common aspect of modern life is living with absolutely contradictory values. We calmly discuss the possibility of dropping a hydrogen bomb on Russia, but find tears in our eyes when we see headlines about the suffering of one small child.

Because he has relinquished the locus of evaluation to others, and has lost touch with his own valuing process, he feels profoundly insecure and easily threatened in his values. If some of these conceptions were destroyed, what would take their place? This threatening possibility makes him hold his value conceptions more rigidly or more confusedly, or both.

## FUNDAMENTAL DISCREPANCY

I believe that this picture of the individual, with values mostly introjected, held as fixed concepts, rarely examined or tested, is the picture of most of us. By taking over the conceptions of others as our own, we lose contact with the potential wisdom of our own functioning, and lose confidence in ourselves. Since these value constructs are often sharply at variance with what is going on in our own experiencing, we have in a very basic way divorced ourselves from ourselves, and this accounts for much of modern strain and insecurity. This fundamental discrepancy between the individual's concept and what he is actually experiencing, between the intellectual structure of his values and the valuing process going on unrecognized within—this is a part of the fundamental estrangement of modern man from himself.

## RESTORING CONTACT WITH EXPERIENCE

Some individuals are fortunate in going beyond the picture I have just given, developing further in the direction of psychological maturity. We see this happen in psychotherapy where we endeavor to provide a climate favorable to the growth of the person. We also see it happen in life, whenever life provides a therapeutic climate for the individual. Let me concentrate on this further maturing of a value approach as I have seen it in therapy.

As the client senses and realizes that he is prized as a person[1] he can slowly begin to value the different aspects of himself. Most importantly, he can begin, with much difficulty at first, to sense and to feel what is going on within him, what he is feeling, what he is experiencing, how he is reacting. He uses his experiencing as a direct referent to which he can turn in forming accurate conceptualizations and as a guide to his behavior. Gendlin (2, 3) has elaborated the way in which this occurs. As his experiencing becomes more and more open to him, as he is able to live more freely in the

---

[1] The therapeutic relationship is not devoid of values. When it is most effective it is, I believe, marked by one primary value, namely, that this person (the client) has *worth*.

process of his feelings, then significant changes begin to occur in his approach to values. It begins to assume many of the characteristics it had in infancy.

### INTROJECTED VALUES IN RELATION TO EXPERIENCING

Perhaps I can indicate this by reviewing a few of the brief examples of introjected values which I have given, and suggesting what happens to them as the individual comes closer to what is going on within him.

> The individual in therapy looks back and realizes, "But I *enjoyed* pulling my sister's hair—and that doesn't make me a bad person."
> The student failing chemistry realizes, as he gets close to his own experiencing, "I don't like chemistry; I don't value being a doctor, even though my parents do; and I am not a failure for having these feelings."
> The adult recognizes that sexual desires and behavior may be richly satisfying and permanently enriching in their consequences, or shallow and temporary and less than satisfying. He goes by his own experiencing, which does not always coincide with social norms.
> He recognizes freely that this communist book or person expresses attitudes and goals which he shares as well as ideas and values which he does not share.
> He realizes that at times he experiences cooperation as meaningful and valuable to him, and that at other times he wishes to be alone and act alone.

### VALUING IN THE MATURE PERSON

The valuing process which seems to develop in this more mature person is in some ways very much like that in the infant, and in some ways quite different. It is fluid, flexible, based on this particular moment, and the degree to which this moment is experienced as enhancing and actualizing. Values are not held rigidly, but are continually changing. The painting which last year seemed meaningful now appears uninteresting, the way of working with individuals which was formerly experienced as good now seems inadequate, the belief which then seemed true is now experienced as only partly true, or perhaps false.

Another characteristic of the way this person values experience is that it is highly differentiated, or as the semanticists would say, extensional. The examples in the preceding section indicate that what were previously rather solid monolithic introjected values now become differentiated, tied to a particular time and experience.

Another characteristic of the mature individual's approach is that the locus of evaluation is again established firmly within the person. It is his own experience which provides the value information or feedback. This does not mean that he is not open to all the evidence he can obtain from other sources. But it means that this is taken for what it is—outside evidence—and is not as significant as his own reactions. Thus he may be told by a friend that a new book is very disappointing. He reads two unfavorable reviews of the book. Thus his tentative hypothesis is that he will not value the book. Yet if he reads the book his valuing will be based upon the reactions it stirs in *him,* not on what he has been told by others.

There is also involved in this valuing process a letting oneself down into the immediacy of what one is experiencing, endeavoring to sense and to clarify all its complex meanings. I think of a client who, toward the close of therapy, when puzzled about an issue, would put his head in his hands and say, "Now what *is* it that I'm feeling? I want to get next to it. I want to learn what it is." Then he would wait, quietly and patiently, trying to listen to himself, until he could discern the exact flavor of the feelings he was experiencing. He, like others, was trying to get close to himself.

In getting close to what is going on within himself, the process is much more complex than it is in the infant. In the mature person it has much more scope and sweep. For there is involved in the present moment of experiencing the memory traces of all the relevant learnings from the past. This moment has not only its immediate sensory impact, but it has meaning growing out of similar experiences in the past (3). It has both the new and the old in it. So when I experience a painting or a person, my experiencing contains within it the learnings I have accumulated from past meetings with paintings or persons, as well as the new impact of this particular encounter. Likewise the moment of experiencing contains, for the mature adult, hypotheses about consequences. "It is not pleasant to express forthrightly my negative feelings to this person, but past experience indicates that in a continuing relationship it will be helpful in the long run." Past and future are both in this moment and enter into the valuing.

I find that in the person I am speaking of (and here again we see a similarity to the infant), the criterion of the valuing process is the degree to which the object of the experience actualizes the individual himself. Does it make him a richer, more complete, more fully developed person? This may sound as though it were a selfish or unsocial criterion, but it does not prove to be so, since deep and helpful relationships with others are experienced as actualizing.

Like the infant, too, the psychologically mature adult trusts and uses the wisdom of his organism, with the difference that he is able to do so knowingly. He realizes that if he can trust all of himself, his feelings and his intuitions may be wiser than his mind, that as a total person he can be more sensitive and accurate than his thoughts alone. Hence he is not afraid to say, "I feel that this experience [or this thing, or this direction] is good. Later I will probably know *why* I feel it is good." He trusts the totality of himself, having moved toward becoming what Lancelot Whyte (7) regards as "the unitary man."

It should be evident from what I have been saying that this valuing process in the mature individual is not an easy or simple thing. The process is complex, the choices often very perplexing and difficult, and there is no guarantee that the choice which is made will in fact prove to be self-actualizing. But because whatever evidence exists is available to the individual, and because he is open to his experiencing, errors are correctable. If this chosen course of action is not self-enhancing this will be sensed and he can make an adjustment or revision. He thrives on a maximum feedback interchange, and thus, like the gyroscopic compass on a ship, can continually correct his course toward his true goal of self-fulfillment.

## SOME PROPOSITIONS REGARDING THE VALUING PROCESS

Let me sharpen the meaning of what I have been saying by stating two propositions which contain the essential elements of this viewpoint. While it may not be possible to devise empirical tests of each proposition in its entirety, yet each is to some degree capable of being tested through the methods of psychological science. I would also state that though the following propositions are stated firmly in order to give them clarity, I am actually advancing them as decidedly tentative hypotheses.

*Hypothesis I.* There is an organismic base for an organized valuing process within the human individual.

It is hypothesized that this base is something the human being shares with the rest of the animate world. It is part of the functioning life process of any healthy organism. It is the capacity for receiving feedback information which enables the organism continually to adjust its behavior and reactions so as to achieve the maxmium possible self-enhancement.

*Hypothesis II.* This valuing process in the human being is effective in achieving self-enhancement to the degree that the individual is open to the experiencing which is going on within himself.

I have tried to give two examples of individuals who are close to their own experiencing: the tiny infant who has not yet learned to deny in his awareness the processes going on within, and the psychologically mature person who has relearned the advantages of this open state.

There is a corollary to this second proposition which might be put in the following terms. One way of assisting the individual to move toward openness to experience is through a relationship in which he is prized as a separate person, in which the experiencing going on within him is emphatically understood and valued, and in which he is given the freedom to experience his own feelings and those of others without being threatened in doing so.

This corollary obviously grows out of therapeutic experience. It is a brief statement of the essential qualities in the therapeutic relationship. There are already some empirical studies, of which the one by Barrett-Lennard (1) is a good example, which give support to such a statement.

## PROPOSITIONS REGARDING THE OUTCOMES
## OF THE VALUING PROCESS

I come now to the nub of any theory of values or valuing. What are its consequences? I should like to move into this new ground by stating bluntly two propositions as to the qualities of behavior which emerge from this valuing process. I shall then give some of the evidence from my experience as a therapist in support of these propositions.

*Hypothesis III.* In persons who are moving toward greater openness to their experiencing, there is an organismic commonality of value directions.

*Hypothesis IV.* These common value directions are of such kinds as to enhance the development of the individual himself, of others in his community, and to make for the survival and evolution of his species.

It has been a striking fact of my experience that in therapy, where individuals are valued, where there is greater freedom to feel and to be, certain value directions seem to emerge. These are not chaotic directions but instead exhibit a surprising commonality. This commonality is not dependent on the personality of the therapist, for I have seen these trends emerge in the clients of therapists sharply different in personality. This commonality does not seem to be due to the influences of any one culture, for I have found evidence of these directions in cultures as divergent as those of the United States, Holland, France, and Japan. I like to think that this commonality of value directions is due to the fact that we all belong to the same species —that just as a human infant tends, individually, to select a diet similar to that selected by other human infants, so a client in therapy tends, individually, to choose value directions similar to those chosen by other clients. As a species there may be certain elements of experience which tend to make for inner development and which would be chosen by all individuals if they were genuinely free to choose.

Let me indicate a few of these value directions as I see them in my clients as they move in the direction of personal growth and maturity.

They tend to move away from façades. Pretense, defensiveness, putting up a front, tend to be negatively valued.

They tend to move away from "oughts." The compelling feeling of "I ought to do or be thus and so" is negatively valued. The client moves away from being what he "ought to be," no matter who has set that imperative.

They tend to move away from meeting the expectations of others. Pleasing others, as a goal in itself, is negatively valued.

Being real is positively valued. The client tends to move toward being himself, being his real feelings, being what he is. This seems to be a very deep preference.

Self-direction is positively valued. The client discovers an increasing pride and confidence in making his own choices, guiding his own life.

One's self, one's own feelings come to be positively valued. From a point where he looks upon himself with contempt and despair, the client comes to value himself and his reactions as being of worth.

Being a process is positively valued. From desiring some fixed goal, clients come to prefer the excitement of being a process of potentialities being born.

Sensitivity to others and acceptance of others is positively valued. The client comes to appreciate others for what they are, just as he has come to appreciate himself for what he is.

Deep relationships are positively valued. To achieve a close, intimate, real, fully communicative relationship with another person seems to meet a deep need in every individual, and is very highly valued.

Perhaps more than all else, the client comes to value an openness to all of his inner and outer experience. To be open to and sensitive to his own *inner* reactions and feelings, the reactions and feelings of others, and the realities of the objective world—this is a direction which he clearly prefers. This openness becomes the client's most valued resource.

These then are some of the preferred directions which I have observed in individuals moving toward personal maturity. Though I am sure that the list I have given is inadequate and perhaps to some degree inaccurate, it holds for me exciting possibilities. Let me try to explain why.

I find it significant that when individuals are prized as persons, the values they select do not run the full gamut of possibilities. I do not find, in such a climate of freedom, that one person comes to value fraud and murder and thievery, while another values a life of self-sacrifice, and another values only money. Instead there seems to be a deep and underlying thread of commonality. I believe that when the human being is inwardly free to choose whatever he deeply values, he tends to value those objects, experiences, and goals which make for his own survival, growth, and development, and for the survival and development of others. I hypothesize that it is *characteristic* of the human organism to prefer such actualizing and socialized goals when he is exposed to a growth promoting climate.

A corollary of what I have been saying is that in *any* culture, given a climate of respect and freedom in which he is valued as a person, the mature individual would tend to choose and prefer these same value directions. This is a significant hypothesis which could be tested. It means that though the individual of whom I am speaking would not have a consistent or even a stable system of conceived values, the valuing process within him would lead to emerging value directions which would be constant across cultures and across time.

Another implication I see is that individuals who exhibit the fluid valuing process I have tried to describe, whose value directions are generally those I have listed, would be highly effective in the ongoing process of human evolution. If the human species is to survive at all on this globe, the human being must become more readily adaptive to new problems and situations, must be able to select that which is valuable for development and survival out of new and complex situations, must be accurate in his appreciation of reality if he is to make such selections. The psychologically mature person as I have described him has, I believe, the qualities which would cause him to value those experiences which would make for the survival and enhancement of the human race. He would be a worthy participant and guide in the process of human evolution.

Finally, it appears that we have returned to the issue of universality of values, but by a different route. Instead of universal values "out there," or a universal value system imposed by some group—philosophers, rulers, priests, or psychologists—we have the possibility of universal human value directions *emerging* from the experiencing of the human organism. Evidence from therapy indicates that both personal and social values emerge as natural, and experienced, when the individual is close to his own organismic valuing process. The suggestion is that though modern man no longer trusts religion or science or philosophy nor any system of beliefs to *give* him values, he may find an organismic valuing base within himself which, if he can learn again to be in touch with it, will prove to be an organized, adaptive, and social approach to the perplexing value issues which face all of us.

## SUMMARY

A description is given of the change in the value orientation of the individual from infancy to average adulthood, and from this adult status to a greater degree of psychological maturity attained through psychotherapy or fortunate life circumstances. On the basis of these observations, the theory is advanced that there is an organismic basis for the valuing process within the human individual; that this valuing process is effective to the degree that the individual is open to his experiencing; that in persons relatively open to their experiencing there is an important commonality or universality of value directions; that these directions make for the constructive enhancement of the individual and his community, and for the survival and evolution of his species.

## REFERENCES

1. BARRETT-LENNARD, G. T. Dimensions of therapist response as causal factors in therapeutic change. *Psychol. Monogr.*, 1962, 76 (43, Whole No. 562).
2. GENDLIN, E. T. Experiencing: a variable in the process of therapeutic change. *Amer. J. Psychother.*, 1961, 15, 233–45.
3. GENDLIN, E. T. *Experiencing and the creation of meaning.* Glencoe, Ill.: Free Press, 1962.
4. MORRIS, C. W. *Varieties of human value.* Chicago: Univer. Chicago Press, 1956, pp. 9–12.
5. ROGERS, C. R. *Client-centered therapy.* Boston: Houghton Mifflin, 1951.
6. ROGERS, C. R. A theory of therapy, personality and interpersonal relationships. In S. Koch (ed.), *Psychology: A study of a science.* Vol. 3. *Formulations of the person and the social context.* New York: McGraw-Hill, 1959, pp. 185–256.
7. WHYTE, L. L. *The next development in man.* New York: Mentor Books, 1950.

# NAME INDEX

# SUBJECT INDEX